WITHDRAWN

The French Fifth Republic

Hoover Institution Bibliographical Series: XLIV

The French Fifth Republic
Establishment and Consolidation (1958–1965)

An annotated bibliography of the holdings at the Hoover Institution

By

Grete Heinz and Agnes F. Peterson

Hoover Institution Press
Stanford University • Stanford, California

The Hoover Institution on War, Revolution and Peace, founded at Stanford University in 1919 by the late President Herbert Hoover, is a center for advanced study and research on public and international affairs in the twentieth century. The views expressed in its publications are entirely those of the authors and do not necessarily reflect the views of the Hoover Institution.

DC
412
.Z99
H45

Standard Book Number 8179-2441-8
Library of Congress Card Number 70-92497
Printed in the United States of America
© 1970 by the Board of Trustees of the Leland Stanford Junior University
All rights reserved

Contents

Introduction	vii
Abbreviations	xiii
Part I: Non-serial publications	3
Part II: Serial publications	131
Subject index	143
Author index	155
Title index	166

Introduction

The crises and dilemmas confronting the French political system during the years 1958-1965 exemplify in heightened form those that have beset all the leading Western democracies over the past two decades. Because the French crises were compressed into a relatively short time span by a dramatic sequence of events and because they were relentlessly debated and scrutinized by a highly analytical and self-critical people, they can be examined more readily in retrospect, and their interconnections more easily unraveled, than is true of most historical periods. Thus, in keeping with the Hoover Institution's traditional interests, collecting efforts have been concentrated on this significant period and on the concomitant changes in French political life and institutions.

The works identified in the pages that follow encompass all the books, pamphlets, individually catalogued leaflets, broadsides, etc.—as well as government publications, serials, and newspapers—at the Hoover Institution pertaining to the origins, establishment, and consolidation of the Fifth Republic. A few pertinent works in the Stanford Main Library and Law Library are also listed. Although the materials listed here do not constitute an exhaustive bibliography of the works relating to the Fifth Republic published in France and elsewhere, it is hoped that no serious omissions will be discovered as far as scholarly studies, reference works, memoirs, biographies, government documents, and periodicals are concerned. It was of course out of the question to obtain more than a representative sample from among the thousands of ephemeral publications distributed halfway across the globe, but with the enthusiastic support of volunteer on-the-spot collectors and the collaboration of French organizations, some of these important source materials were preserved. Military affairs, which played such a crucial role during these years, are extensively represented in their less technical and more political aspects. Economic affairs, social questions, and education, which were more peripheral to the political arena during the period, are not systematically covered aside from the basic documentary sources, except where individual issues became embroiled in political controversy. Coverage in the fields of philosophy and literature may appear even more capricious, inasmuch as works were included not in terms of their intrinsic merit but as reflections of political attitudes and opinions in the intellectual community.

The chronological limits of this bibliography are somewhat flexible. Generally speaking, works published before 1956 are not included, and for the final two years of the Fourth Republic only those works which bear on the collapse of its political institutions or shed light on subsequent events are listed. These works constitute only a small fraction of the holdings of the Hoover Institution on the Fourth Republic's last years. December 1965 is the terminal date—again with minor exceptions—but books published since that time dealing wholly or principally with pre-1966 events have been included whenever technically possible.

Geographical limitations deserve special mention. During the period in question France was to relinquish all its African possessions and, but for a few far-flung outposts, to shrink to a relatively modest European hexagon. All material on the final stages of the French Union, which was dismantled in the wake of the Fourth Republic's collapse, and on the elaboration and later dissolution of the French Community is found in the bibliography.

In general, material at the Hoover Institution relating specifically to individual African members of the French Community is not itemized here, since this task was assumed by the Institution's African collection. However, a number of French-language serials published in France and dealing with Africa (usually ex-French Africa) are included because they served as vehicles for the debate over the proper relations between France and its former colonies. In addition, all material on Algeria prior to its independence (July 1962) has been included because it is so intimately linked with developments in metropolitan France. After that date, only selected publications, primarily those reflecting French relations with or attitudes toward the newly independent country, have been listed.

The main section of the survey consists of 2,234 entries (plus last-minute additions) arranged in strictly alphabetical order under their formal catalogue headings. This section is divided into two separately alphabetized but consecutively numbered parts. Part I covers all non-serial publications, whether by individual authors, organizations, or government agencies; Part II covers all serials (newspapers, periodicals, regularly issued governmental and organizational publications). Many entries are amplified by brief annotations concerning the author, as well as the nature, scope, and special contribution of the work. Appended are three indexes: a subject index, an author index, and a title index. The detailed subject index serves as a guide to the vast amount of material presented in unclassified form in the main part of the survey and is tailored to the anticipated needs and interests of researchers. The author and title indexes facilitate the location of works whose formal heading might be problematic or at variance with that used in other bibliographies (for more complete explanations see introductory note to author and title indexes).

To acquaint the user of this survey with the principal topics and themes that yield a sizable amount of documentation, the major subject index categories will be discussed here. In the interest of clarity, main headings in this explication are in italics; sub-headings appear in quotation marks.

Before exploring the substantive categories, the reader is advised to check all entries under the index categories *Bibliographies, Reference works, Year books, Special collections*. It should be mentioned that only primarily bibliographical works are listed under *Bibliographies,* but useful bibliographies contained in scholarly works can be found under specific topics (e.g., *Algerian war*—"bibliographies"). The only extensive special collection is the one described under no. 811. One non-substantive category that might prove helpful in locating elusive publications is *Conferences, congresses, colloquia, meetings, etc.,* which is subdivided, somewhat arbitrarily, into "academic" and "political." Others are *Organizations* and its many subdivisions; *Press,* whose subdivisions identify the major types of newspapers and periodicals at the Hoover Institution; and *Russian and Polish works,* which enumerates all works on the Fifth Republic by Russian and Polish authors.

Works that treat the Fifth Republic as an entity have been grouped under *Fifth Republic. Fifth Republic (General)* is divided into surveys and appraisals published during the first year of the new regime and those written in subsequent years. Publications which review individual developments during the period will be found under such headings as "Algerian conflict," "economic developments," and "foreign affairs," and those documenting governmental policy as a whole will be under "Gaullist policy." On the other hand, "political history" and "political chronicles and diaries" (mainly memoirs and collections of journalistic pieces) emphasize the chronological element. Works focused on the new political institutions, many of them scholarly and a number by foreign observers, are under "political institutions," with a subdivision reserved for those of a polemical rather than analytic nature. Documentation on the founding of the Fifth Republic is concentrated under the heading "inception" and shows the role of various factors and groups in bringing it about or resisting it. Since the topics covered in this bibliography generally refer to the Fifth Republic, the subject category *Fourth Republic* contains materials that emphasize the background and continuity of certain issues such as "European policy" and "colonial policy." Indirect documentation on the origins of the Fifth Republic is contained in the numerous indictments of the Fourth Republic's political weaknesses under "political institutions" and more detailed accounts of its "collapse," published either before or after 1958.

Many of the topics around which publications have been organized clearly reflect the preoccupations of the Fifth Republic's first seven years.

The first major area is *Algeria,* a subject to which perhaps a third of all the publications listed in this survey are devoted either in part or in full. (The next most prolific category is *de Gaulle.*) In view of the complexity of the subject and the multiplicity of approaches it elicited, it was felt that divisions into *Algeria; Algeria, post-independence; Algerian nationalism; Algerian question; Algerian revolution;* and *Algerian war* would do the greatest justice to the material. A separate category applies to the *Sahara.*

Under *Algeria* are grouped the main descriptive and scholarly works "economic conditions," "history," "sociological studies." Government publications as well as other works describing and evaluating government policy are listed under "Gaullist policy" and "economic development." The works on Algeria's European population are found under "European settlers." Another important sub-topic is "political developments," bringing together the numerous works on Algerian politics before and during the Fifth Republic, with special subdivisions for the three most critical episodes: May/June 1958, the crisis culminating in the collapse of the Fourth Republic; January 1960, the rebellion dramatizing the European settlers' rejection of de Gaulle's self-determination policy for Algeria; and April 1961, the final test of strength between de Gaulle and his recalcitrant generals. The sub-heading "independence" covers the brief transitional period between the end of French control and Algerian statehood in July 1962 and includes the works describing the hasty departure of many European settlers under "exodus of European settlers."

Algeria, post-independence contains all works listed in the bibliography dealing with Algeria after the granting of statehood. As mentioned above, however, the bibliography does not encompass all the Hoover Institution's holdings on independent Algeria. Sub-topics of special interest are "economic reform" and "political developments," which give French and Algerian interpretations of how the bold promises of the Algerian revolution were actually implemented after independence. "French aid and cooperation" documents the new mold into which Franco-Algerian relations were cast after the severing of political bonds.

Algerian nationalism groups those works dealing with nationalist aspirations of the Moslem population and its leaders before and during the period of revolutionary activity. *Algerian revolution* focuses on the numerous publications directly concerning the overthrow of French domination. Most of the works are either by writers sympathetic to the revolutionary cause (this is not true of the sub-section "Communist support and influence") or by Algerian revolutionary leaders and political agencies, and a number of them trace the history of the revolution. An interesting sub-topic is "French support," which contains material on French individuals and groups actively aiding the revolutionary movement. Specific aspects of the revolution are treated under "leadership," "military aspects," and "political institutions." Important source material is listed under "documents." International recognition for the Algerian provisional government is dealt with under "international aspects." Official organs expressing the views of pro-revolutionary organizations are grouped under "press."

Neither *Algerian question* nor *Algerian war* lists topics that can be considered distinct from those just enumerated, but each of them introduces new treatments and perspectives. Under *Algerian question* are all the books and pamphlets concerned with the problem of how an underdeveloped country with 10 million inhabitants, 90 percent of whom are Moslems, can keep its ties with a highly centralized modern European nation. Particular approaches include "economic aspects," "integration," "minority problem," and "political solutions." Works of a purely polemical nature (in the other subdivisions the approach is at least predominantly rational) are designated as "pro-French Algeria polemics" and "pro-independence polemics." Major studies and less scholarly contributions that shed light on the total impact of the Algerian question on French political life are to be found under *Algerian question—*"and French political life," and in less concentration under *Algerian question—*"and French political parties." The main international repercussions of the Algerian problem were best subsumed under *Algerian question—*"and the United Nations," since the UN was the principal international forum for debate on Algerian independence. However, appeals to international opinion against atrocities committed by the French in the course of the fighting are found under *Algerian war—*"international aspects."

Algerian war covers almost all the material at the Hoover Institution on this crucial revolutionary conflict, since almost all the publications which sprang from it were issued between 1956 and 1967. Directly under the heading *Algerian war* will be found the few comprehensive studies of the war, three of them in English (nos. 337, 1041, 1333), only two (nos. 176a and 1333) written after the conclusion of the conflict. However, *Algeria—*"history" and *Algerian revolution—*"history" cover some of the same ground in less detail. All other material bears on specific aspects of the struggle or expresses a special point of view on the war. Important topics are "atrocities," describing or inveighing against horrors of the war for which mainly the French but also the F.L.N. are blamed. A different aspect of this tragedy is brought out under "final months of violence," which concentrates on the last six months of the war when civilians, both Moslem and European, became victims of an orgy of mutual hatred. The purely military component of the war is treated under "military operations" and, more broadly, under "military strategy." Under "pacification program," the euphemistic term applied by the French government to the Algerian war, are numerous laudatory or derogatory descriptions of French efforts to improve the lot of the Moslem civilian population simultaneously with crushing rebel elements. Of special interest here are the sub-topics "psychological action" and the related "resettlement centers," involving the relocation of a quarter of the Moslem population.

Two other types of publications were generated by the Algerian war. "Personal narratives" of the participants in the military operations provide much valuable documentation on individual phases of the war. To these must be added the fourteen novels, "fictional works" centering on the fighting and the psychological problems connected with the conflict. Under "opposition" are collected the many French voices raised against the war. For an overall view of this opposition, the partisan but well-informed study no. 266 should be consulted. Significantly, few publications can be categorized under "support" of the war, but denunciations of the consequences of French withdrawal abound (see below).

Repercussions of the Algerian conflict dominated five of the seven years under consideration. War-generated tensions between political and military elements can be studied under the topics *Army in Algeria, Civilian-military relations, Military doctrine—*"counter-insurgency," and *Revolutionary warfare.* The consequences of opposition to official Algerian policy can be traced under *Prisoners, political,* and *Trials, political.* The trial documents in particular contain highly eloquent statements by those who condemned the war and favored Algerian independence at a time when the government was vigorously pursuing the war. Then, as the government's determination to achieve peace at any price became apparent, defenders of French Algeria were brought to court for seditious activites: "barricades," "generals' putsch" are the headings under which these trials will be found. The impact on French life of chaotic conditions in Algeria immediately before and after the peace agreement can be followed under several categories. The activities of the most determined opponents of current Algerian policy can be traced under *Organisation de l'armée secrète* (OAS) and in the political trials of opposition leaders, including the would-be de Gaulle assassins. *Nationalist opposition to de Gaulle* brings together the opinions of those disillusioned by de Gaulle's "betrayal" of nationalist interests in Algeria. Finally, the fate of French settlers after Algerian independence can be seen under *Repatriation.*

The dilemmas surrounding the Algerian question are often reflected in the more general problem of *Decolonization* and the manner in which it was handled by the Gaullist regime. Under *French Community* the process of decolonization can be studied more specifically. Ways in which an advanced European country can help guide the development of areas formerly under its political control are documented under *Assistance, technical and economic.* Specific aspects of economic relations are further treated under *Common Market*—"and African states" and *International economic relations*—"franc zone." Material concerning the few remaining outposts of the French Empire will be found under *Overseas departments and territories.*

The Algerian problem and decolonization contributed more than other factors to the establishment of the Fifth Republic and were also the prime sources of conflicts that repeatedly threatened the republic's survival over the first four years. But two other issues have had more enduring consequences, since they go to the very roots of the Gaullist regime. One is the reform of political institutions in the direction of greater political stability, the other the reorientation of France's international position following the dissolution of the French Empire. Under *Gaullism* will be found the political doctrine elaborated by de Gaulle and his followers in the post-World War II years. In addition, innumerable works on de Gaulle *(de Gaulle*—"personality," "political methods," "political philosophy") attempt to clarify the doctrines, motivations, and methods characterizing the founder and pivotal political figure of the Fifth Republic. Gaullist aspirations to national greatness and independence are most clearly reflected in *European integration, Atlantic Alliance, International relations*—"Gaullist views." Their concrete, practical implications can be seen in *European integration, economic*—"Gaullist policy," *Foreign policy, Foreign relations*—"Germany," "Soviet Union," "United States," and *North Atlantic Treaty Organization,* as well as in *Military policy*—"nuclear."

The nature of the political changes set in motion in 1958 and their successes and failures can be studied under *Constitution, 1958* and *Political institutions*—"executive-legislative balance," "parliamentary function," "personalization of power," "presidential elections," and "presidential regime," all of which were subjects of passionate debate in the more tranquil years following the end of the Algerian war. The parliamentary bodies are examined under *National Assembly,* and the more elusive executive agencies are grouped under *Administration, governmental.* Legislative innovation is documented under *Laws and statutes.*

Some of the fundamental implications of current political innovations are elaborated and analyzed under *Democracy, Depolitization,* and *Technocracy.* The impact of the Fifth Republic's political institutions on French political parties can be traced under *Political parties*—"regrouping" and *Political institutions*—"bi-party system," which analyze the prospects for a consolidated opposition to the dominant Gaullist forces. The works under *Sociology, political* convey the interpretations by leading French political scientists of the new regime and the alterations in French political styles. *Political attitudes* gives some insight into changing public sentiment on many of these issues.

The pulse of political life during the Fifth Republic's first seven years is recorded under *Elections* and *Referenda,* which contain much unpublished campaign literature from political parties in addition to the standard documentary sources issued by the French Ministry of the Interior. Materials listed here relate to the 1958, 1962, and 1967 elections to the National Assembly and to the first presidential election open to universal suffrage, a key Gaullist reform whose successful implementation marked the consolidation of the Fifth Republic. Special attention is given to the use of radio and television, two media that acquired considerable importance on the political scene during the Fifth Republic. For scholarly studies on elections, *Electoral systems* and *Electoral sociology* should also be consulted.

The paucity of works on economic and social

reform reflects the fact that such reforms were not among the major preoccupations of the period. Public concern with economic problems found its main expression in the field of planning. Although the mechanisms for central economic planning antedate the Fifth Republic, these institutions were identified with Gaullist efforts to adapt the French economy (and French society as a whole) to the demands of an increasingly complex industrial and technological civilization and to enable France to catch up with its more highly modernized neighbor, Germany. Under *Planning* will be found both theoretical discussions on French planning methods and the official government documentation on the Third, Fourth, and Fifth plans. A new area of interest in the so-called "aménagement du territoire," whose most urgent objectives are the decongestion of the Paris region and the revival of decaying provinces, is documented under *Planning, regional.* In addition to the categories under *Economic conditions* and *Economic policy,* topics of current economic interest will be found under *Democracy, economic; Industrial relations; Economic growth;* and *Technology, industrial.* Broader concerns as to the quality of life in modern society are reflected in *Civilization, modern.* The growing recognition that increasing investment in human beings must go hand-in-hand with greater technical sophistication finds its expression in works on *Education,* particularly in the debates about the extent to which education has been "democratized." Information on various population sectors is to be found under the different subdivisions of *Social groups.*

Although Gaullism was the major ideological force shaping political events between 1958 and 1965, other political movements have not been neglected. Publications by and about the major political parties are listed under the individual party names (see Author Index and final entry under *Political parties* in Subject Index). Documentation is most extensive for the *Parti communiste français,* whose views on most issues are represented. There is considerable documentation on other parties antedating the Fifth Republic *(Parti socialiste, Parti républicain radical et radical socialiste, Mouvement républicain populaire)* and on the new Gaullist and opposition parties founded after 1958 *(Union pour la nouvelle république, Union démocratique du travail* on the one hand, *Parti socialiste unifié* and *Fédération de la gauche démocrate et socialiste* on the other). The many splinter groups challenging the ideological purity or political wisdom of the heavyhanded French Communist Party leadership are grouped under *Communist opposition.* Views of organizations or individuals tied to the Catholic hierarchy have been brought together under *Catholic Church.* Under *Socialism* and *Marxism* are grouped political and scholarly discussions attempting to adjust Communist and Socialist thought to the exigencies of contemporary reality, while efforts to extricate the Communist party from its ideological rigidity and political isolation are documented under *Political parties*—"unification of the Left" and *Parti communiste français*—"relations with non-Communist groups." Developments in the Communist world that affect internal French political trends are found under *International Communism.* More traditional problems of the French Left are discussed under *Labor movement* and *Trade unions.* A phenomenon peculiar to the Fifth Republic is the new type of political organization which attempts to provide a less clearly ideological and more pragmatic approach to political and economic problems. Such organizations have sprung up all over France, and their activities are described under *Clubs, political.*

Though most of the energies of the French political Right were either directly absorbed by Gaullism or galvanized into violent opposition by Algerian developments *(Nationalist opposition to de Gaulle),* two other strands of anti-democratic political philosophy can be followed under *Nationalism,* which represents the views of the traditional Right, and *Nationalism, European,* a new movement combining an elitist philosophy with a supranational, European orientation.

The topics described above indicate the range of the works listed in the pages that follow. Inevitably, many works contribute to more than one topic and will therefore be found as entries in several subject categories. Wherever periodicals and serials published by the government or other organizations contribute to specific topics they too will be listed in the appropriate subject category, but the less specifically oriented newspapers and periodicals are treated only under *Press.*

In conclusion, it should be kept in mind that the publications collected, while they faithfully reflect the intense public concentration on problems linked with current crises, are but a careful sampling of the literature actually generated. As the crises themselves subside, the problems, though perhaps as far from solution as ever, have been shelved and replaced by a new set of concerns. And while historians are still plowing their way through the wealth of publications that record the troubled years covered by this bibliography, a new French student generation is rushing to the barricades as ignorant of and as unconcerned by threats of military dictatorship or O.A.S.-fomented civil war as if these problems belonged not to the last decade but to a dim and unrecorded past.

Abbreviations

C.F.T.C.	Confédération française des travailleurs chrétiens
C.G.T.	Confédération générale du travail
F.L.N.	Front de libération nationale
M.R.P.	Mouvement républicain populaire
O.A.S.	Organisation de l'armée secrète
P.C.F.	Parti communiste français
P.S.U.	Parti socialiste unifié
R.P.F.	Rassemblement du peuple français
S.A.S.	Sections administratives spécialisées
S.F.I.O.	Section française de l'internationale ouvrière
U.D.T.	Union démocratique du travail
U.N.E.F.	Union nationale des étudiants français
U.N.R.	Union pour la nouvelle république

The French Fifth Republic

Part I: Non-serial Publications

Unless preceded by an asterisk or designated ML (Main Library, Stanford) or LL (Law Library, Stanford) items can be located in the Main Catalog of the Hoover Institution. Items preceded by an asterisk can be located in one of the following Collections: Society Publications, Government Documents, Special Collections, or Vault.

1 ABBAS, FERHAT. Full text of the policy declaration made on September 26, 1958, by Mr. Ferhat Abbas, prime minister in the name of the Provisional Government of the Algerian Republic. Cairo, 1958. 6 l (Front de libération nationale, Cairo)

2 ABBAS, FERHAT. Guerre et révolution d'Algérie: Vol. 1, La nuit coloniale. Paris, R. Julliard, 1962. Bibliographical footnotes.

Nationalist leader reviews colonial rule in Algeria, describes own efforts to reform this rule and later to overthrow it. This volume stops in 1956, and nothing further has been published. Also published in Italian as "Guerra e revoluzione in Algeria" (1963).

3 ABBAS, FERHAT. Memorandum on the denunciation of the North Atlantic Treaty by the Provisional Government of the Algerian Republic. New York, 1960. 11 l. (Delegation of the Provisional Government of the Algerian Republic, N.Y.)

4 ABBAS, FERHAT. On the eve of the Franco-Algerian negotiations at Evian; text of the appeal addressed to the Algerian people by Premier Ferhat Abbas, Tunis, May 19, 1961. New York, 1961. 2 l. (Delegation of the Provisional Government of the Algerian Republic, N.Y.) Doc. 61-16-E

5 ABBAS, FERHAT. "The Provisional Government of the Algerian Republic is ready to meet with the French Government to determine the conditions for a cease-fire"; declaration of Prime Minister Ferhat Abbas to "El Moudjahid," the official organ of the Algerian Front of National Liberation. (October 10, 1958) Issued by: Ministry of Information, Provisional Government of the Algerian Republic. Cairo, 1958.

6 ABBAS, FERHAT. Text of the appeal addressed to the Algerian people by Premier Ferhat Abbas, Tunis, June 20, 1960. New York, 1960. 2 l (Delegation of the Provisional Government of the Algerian Republic, N.Y.)

7 ABBAS, FERHAT. Text of the appeal addressed to the Algerian people by Premier Ferhat Abbas, Tunis, March 23, 1961 2 l. (Delegation of the Provisional Government of the Algerian Republic, N.Y.)

8 ABBAS, FERHAT. Text of the declaration of Mr. Ferhat Abbas, Premier of the Provisional Government of the Algerian Republic, Tunis, February 29, 1960. New York, 1960. 3 l. (Delegation of the Provisional Government of the Algerian Republic, New York)

9 ABBAS, FERHAT. Text of the speech...on the occasion of November 1, 1960, sixth anniversary of the Algerian revolution. New York, 1960. 5 l (Delegation of the Provisional Government of the Algerian Republic, N.Y.)

FOR ADDITIONAL WORKS BY AND ABOUT FERHAT ABBAS, SEE AUTHOR INDEX.

10 ACTION SOCIALE DE SEINE-ET-OISE. Réforme de l'entreprise; un débat avec Fr. Bloch-Lainé, G. Levard et al. Compte rendu des deux tables rondes. Paris, 1964. 32 p. "Nos équipes d'action sociale, mars 1964, no. 157, numéro spécial."

Text of discussion between Bloch-Lainé, Catholic trade unionists, industrialists, and economists, organized by Catholic Action sociale de Seine-et-Oise. Oct. 1063. Starting point is Bloch-Lainé's controversial book "La réforme de l'entreprise" and whole subject of industrial relations and worker participation in management.

11 L'activiste. [Écrit en prison.] [Paris?] Éditions Jeanne d'Arc, 1961. 124 p. illus.

Extreme nationalist credo expressed in the form of replies to questions by Mr. Middle-of-the-Road combined with cartoons. This clandestine publication (its authors were imprisoned for O.A.S. activity) was distributed December 1961 and reprinted by Editions Saint-Just in 1963. Appendix lists French Communist-front organizations, such as Communist-dominated publishing houses.

12 ADAM, GERARD. Atlas des élections sociales en France. Paris, A. Colin, 1964. 173 p. diagrs. (Cahiers de la Fondation nationales des sciences politiques, partis et élections, 137)

Social elections are held for representatives to Social Security administration, with voters drawn from all Social Security contributors. Contest is mainly between these three trade union organizations: Confédération générale du travail, Confédération française des travailleurs chrétiens, and Force ouvrière. Results for the April 1947, June 1950, November 1955, and December 1962 elections are presented and compared with standing of political parties closest to each faction.

13 ADAM, GERARD. La C.F.T.C., 1940-1958; histoire politique et idéologie. Paris, A. Colin, 1964. 302 p. (Cahiers de la Fondation nationale des sciences politiques, 134) Bibliographical footnotes.

Epilogue covers 1958-1964: international reorganization and new political conceptions of C.F.T.C.

14 ADAM, GERARD. La C.G.T.-F.O. Paris, 1965. 74 p. tables. (Fondation nationale des sciences politiques. Centre d'étude de la vie politique française. Série: Etudes syndicales, no. 3)

Organization, statutes, finances of Force ouvrière, which split off from Confédération générale du travail in 1948. Appendix includes list of national, federal, and local publications, as well as names and addresses of industrial federations and secretariat in each department.

14a AHMED, HOCINE AIT. La guerre et l'après-guerre. Paris, Editions de Minuit, 1964. 204 p. (Grands documents, 11)

First half of volume by Algerian nationalist leader contains reports from prison (April 1957, December 1959, July 1959) to Conseil national de la révolution algérienne and Gouvernement provisoire de la république algérienne on urgency to establish an official Algerian government, best strategy for getting international support and negotiating with de Gaulle after break-off of Melun negotiations. Second part of volume reproduces speeches before the Algerian National Assembly showing growing concern about Ben Bella's leadership.

15   AILHAUD, RENE.   La gauche française à la sorti du tunnel? Paris, Gedalge, 1967. 256 p. Bibliography: p. 253-254.

Joint program of the Left, as formulated in the wake of the 1965 presidential elections, weaknesses of this program, and incapacity of Fédération de la gauche démocrate et socialiste to galvanize Socialist and Radical parties or work fruitfully with Communists. Author sees need to form a new modern socialist party of which political clubs could be nucleus, and which would prepare the passage to a socialist state.

16   AIX-MARSEILLE, UNIVERSITE D'. INSTITUT D'ETUDES JURIDIQUES DE NICE. CENTRE DE SCIENCES POLITIQUES. Les affaires étrangères. By J. Basdevant et al. Paris, Presses universitaires de France, 1959. 459 p. (Bibliothèque des Centres d'études supérieures spécialisés, 5)

Based on summer 1958 lecture series on international law, diplomacy, and international relations. Among dozen participants are Maurice Schumann discussing parliamentary control over foreign affairs in France, Robert Schuman outlining France's European policy. A career diplomat describes the organization of the French Ministry of Foreign Affairs.

17   AIX-MARSEILLE, UNIVERSITE D'. INSTITUT D'ETUDES JURIDIQUES DE NICE. CENTRE DE SCIENCES POLITIQUES. La défense nationale. By General Albord et al. Paris, Presses universitaires de France, 1958. 1662 p. (Bibliothèque des Centres d'études supérieures spécialisés, 4)

Lectures by professors of law, economics, political science and a few military men, among them Colonel Lacheroy, held summer 1957 at Nice. The topic: relation of civil and military authorities in the face of revolutionary and nuclear warfare. Colonel Lacheroy spoke on "La guerre révolutionnaire."

18   AKADEMIIA NAUK SSSR. INSTITUT MIROVOI EKONOMIKI I MEZHDUNARODNYKH OTNOSHENII. Problemy ekonomiki i politiki Frantsii posle Vtoroi Mirovoi voiny. Edited by A. V. Kirsanov, E. A. Menzhinskii, and A. I. Pokrovskii. Moskva, Izd-vo Akademii nauk SSSR, 1962. 603 p. tables. Bibliographical footnotes.

Systematic survey of French economic and political questions 1945-1962. Among economic questions discussed are investment policy, agriculture, labor, public finances. Political problems covered are decolonization, foreign policy, political party struggles.

19   AKADEMIIA NAUK SSSR. INSTITUT NARODOV ASII. Politika Frantsii v Azii i Afrike, 1945-1964 gg. Edited by Boris Moiseevich Dantsig. Moskva, Nauka; Glav. red. vostochnoi lit-ry, 1965. 406 p. Bibliographical footnotes.

French economic domination in its African colonies before independence and transformation, but not elimination of hegemony after political independence had been granted. In addition, the evolution since 1945 and current status of each part of the French Empire (Near East, Indochina, North Africa, and tropical Africa) is described separately. Final chapter follows French position at U.N. on colonial questions.

20   ALBERTINI, JEAN MARIE. Les rouages de l'économie nationale. Avec le concours de A. Kérével, L. Turin, et F. Lerouge. Paris, Économie et humanisme, Éditions ouvrières, 1960. 215 p. illus. (Initiation économique) Includes bibliography.

Elementary economics textbook for worker education, with examples and statistics drawn from the French economy (data revised and brought up to date for 1966 edition). Good bibliography on individual aspects of economy.

21   ALDEBARAN, pseud. De Gaulle et les patries ... Paris, Sedimo, 1965. 168 p. (Collection "Mise au point")

Despite title, book does not deal directly with de Gaulle's opinions, except for 20 page appendix with de Gaulle's declarations on nationhood, 1944-Sept. 1965. Rather, it is exposition of the Gaullist tenets of international relations, starting from such basic concepts as open and closed communities. In this framework, author shows what are genuine French communal bonds (e.g., French Canada), and to what extent the "nation patrie" is the best institution for fostering them. He denies the Free World/Communist dichotomy as fundamental in the coming years and rejects the principle of an Atlantic Alliance, since it would lead to American hegemony, while the instability of the Socialist world makes fear of communism out of date in Europe. Europe as a community makes sense only as an entity independent of and destructive to the existing blocks. Book gives one of most coherent statements of future-oriented version of Gaullist nationalism; author, under pen name, is a Gaullist politician.

22   ALEXANDRE, PHILIPPE. L'adversaire du Général: Gaston Defferre. Paris, R. Solar, 1964. 174 p. illus., ports.

Political and personal biography of Gaston Defferre written in summer of 1964 after his designation as presidential candidate. Includes description of how political clubs agreed on his opposition candidacy in fall of 1963. Appendices with Defferre speeches and statements.

23   ALGERIA. Algérie; quelques aspects des problémes économiques et sociaux. Alger, Impr. officielle, 1956. 118 p. illus.

Government General's views of economic and social problems in Algeria and activities of the French government to solve them. Useful statistics on economy, population. Handsome photographs of new constructions.

24   ALGERIA. Budget des services civils en Algérie pour 1962. Annexes I-II au projet de loi portant fixation des crédits ouverts aux services civils en Algérie pour 1962 et des voies et moyens qui leur sont applicables. Alger, Impr. officielle, 1961. 2 v.

Series of tables breaking down entire French government expenditures in Algeria planned for 1962, totalling three billion new francs. First volume covers total appropriations for Algeria; second volume gives newly approved authorizations.

25   ALGERIA. L'industrie algérienne. [Paris, Desfossesneogravure, 1957?] 33 p. illus.

1956 survey of different Algerian industries and obstacles to industrialization. This is probably Government General's publication.

26   ALGERIA. Notions essentielles sur l'Algérie. [Edited by the Gouvernement Général de l'Algérie.] Paris, Impr. G. Lang, 1956. 31 p. illus., map.

Propaganda pamphlet describing French contributions to Algerian economy, education. Brief survey of status of Algerian pacification and political and social reforms as of 1956. English edition published simultaneously as "Essential Notions about Algeria."

27   Algeria, a synthesis of civilizations. Paris, 1961. 141 p. illus. fold. map.

Pictorial work consisting of aerial photographs of cities and countryside, showing contrast between modern and traditional Algeria. Text is limited to captions underlining French achievements in industrialization, housing, medicine, schooling.

28   ALGERIA. CABINET DU GOUVERNEUR GENERAL. Programme et action du Gouvernement en Algérie; mesures de pacification et réformes. Alger, Service de l'information du Cabinet du Ministre résidant en Algérie, 1956. 181 p.

Statement of Mollet government's Algerian policy, as presented to French National Assembly March 1956 and implementation by pacification and political and social reform measures in following months. Laws, decrees, decisions related to this program February-July 1956 are quoted in annexes.

29   ALGERIA. DELEGATION GENERALE DU GOUVERNEMENT EN ALGERIE. Rapport sur l'activité de l'administration en Algérie au cours de l'année 1960, présenté par Jean Morin, délégué général en Algérie, sur la proposition de Max Moulins, secrétaire général de l'administration. Alger, 1961. 260 p. diagrs.

Covers administrative reforms, education, housing, implementation of Constantine Plan.

30   ALGERIA. DELEGATION GENERALE DU GOUVERNEMENT EN ALGERIE. DIRECTION DU PLAN ET DES ÉTUDES ÉCONOMIQUES. Plan de Constantine, 1959-1963. Rapport général. Alger, Impr. officielle, 1960. xiv, 526 p. fold. col. map, tables (part fold.) diagrs. (part fold.)

This is the basic report, drawn up June 1960, on the 5-year plan for Algerian economic and social development, 1959-1963, including law on which it is based and the names of members of special council. Report contains description of Algerian economy and anticipated investments in different sectors. Many maps.

31*   ALGERIA. OFFICE ALGERIEN D'ACTION ECONOMIQUE ET TOURISTIQUE. Algeria (French North Africa) Alger [1961?] 1 folder.

32*   ALGERIA. OFFICE ALGERIEN D'ACTION ECONOMIQUE ET TOURISTIQUE. Algeria (French North Africa) in twelve pictures, Algiers, n.d. 1 env.

33*   ALGERIA. OFFICE ALGERIEN D'ACTION ÉCONOMIQUE ET TOURISTIQUE. Tourisme au Sahara. Alger, 1961. 1 folder.

34*   ALGERIA. SERVICE D'INFORMATION ET DE DOCUMENTATION. Sahara algérien. Paris, Imp. G. Lang, 1957. 39 p. illus., double map.

Pamphlet giving facts on Saharan resources and economy with emphasis on oil.

35   ALGERIA. SERVICE DE LA STATISTIQUE GENERALE. Résultats statistiques du dénombrement de la population effectué le 31 octobre 1954. Données statistiques sur les immeubles et les logements. Alger, Service de statistique générale, 1958. 272 p. tables, diagrs.

1954 statistics on housing for different segments of the population; publication was delayed until 1958.

36   ALGERIA. SERVICE DE LA STATISTIQUE GENERALE. Tableaux de l'économie algérienne. Alger, 1958. 189 p. fold. maps. diagrs. (part col.) tables.

Statistics for economy and finances, facts on climate, education, through 1957. Includes administrative organization as of October 1, 1958.

37*   ALGERIAN FRONT OF NATIONAL LIBERATION DELEGATION. The Algerian army of national liberation; progress toward the total liberation of the national territory. New York [1958?] (2) p.

The Algerian Front of National Liberation Delegation served as F.L.N. spokesman at the at the United Nations General Assembly and in the U.S. between 1957 and Sept. 1958, when the Provisional Government of the Algerian Republic was created and the New York office's name was changed to Delegation of the Provisional Government of the Algerian Republic, New York (see nos. 466-486).

38*   ALGERIAN FRONT OF NATIONAL LIBERATION DELEGATION. The Algerian question; background document; a private report of high French officials. New York, 1958. 10 l. (Algerian Front of National Liberation Delegation. Publications, Series C, no. 1)

Report dated Jan. 1958.

39*   ALGERIAN FRONT OF NATIONAL LIBERATION DELEGATION. The Algerian question; background document; Oil in the Sahara. New York, 1958. 6 l. (Algerian Front of National Liberation Delegation. Publications, Series C, no. 2)

40*   [ALGERIAN FRONT OF NATIONAL LIBERATION DELEGATION.] Aspects of the Algerian revolution. [New York], 1957. 91 p. illus.

Focuses on Army of National Liberation.

41*   ALGERIAN FRONT OF NATIONAL LIBERATION DELEGATION. Fighters for freedom. New York, Free Algeria Front of National Liberation Delegation, n.d. 1 v. of photos.

42*   ALGERIAN FRONT OF NATIONAL LIBERATION DELEGATION. Memorandum on the declarations of the French government concerning a cease-fire in Algeria. New York, 1957. 4 l.

Addressed to the members of the United Nations.

43*   ALGERIAN FRONT OF NATIONAL LIBERATION DELEGATION. Memorandum submitted... to the Secretary General of the United Nations on the situation in Algeria following the debate and the adoption of a resolution on the "Algerian question" by the Eleventh Session of the General Assembly of the United Nations. New York, 1957. 9 l.

44*   ALGERIAN FRONT OF NATIONAL LIBERATION DELEGATION. The question of Algeria; background documents: An army and a people. New York, 1957 7 l. (Algerian Front of National Liberation Delegation. Publication Series B, no. 1)

45*   ALGERIAN FRONT OF NATIONAL LIBERATION DELEGATION. The question of Algeria; background document: The European minority. New York, 1957. 7 l (Algerian Front of National Liberation Delegation. Publications, Series B, no. 2)

46*   ALGERIAN FRONT OF NATIONAL LIBERATION DELEGATION. The "referendum" in Algeria. New York, 1958. 5 l.

On Sept. 1958 referendum.

47*   ALGERIAN FRONT OF NATIONAL LIBERATION DELEGATION. Report on the forcible enrolment of Hungarian refugees in the French Foreign Legion for service in the war against Algeria. New York, 1957. 4 l.

48*   ALGERIAN FRONT OF NATIONAL LIBERATION DELEGATION. War in Algeria: The "massacre" of Melouza. New York, 1957. 4 l.

49   L'Algérie de demain; voici tout ce que vous devez savoir après le cessez-le-feu. [n.p.] Impr. Speciale de la S.N.E.P., 1962. 24 p.

Official summary of provisions of Evian agreement regarding future status of Algeria and rights of European minority, distributed March 1962.

50 L'Algérie nouvelle et la presse française. Paris, Editions Galic, 1962. 158 p. (L'Histoire au jour le jour, no. 9)

Excerpts from Parisian and provincial press, June 19-September 21, 1962, on Algerian independence, ensuing power struggle, Ben Bella triumph.

51 Die algerische Revolution, von einem Mitglied des Politischen Büros der Obersten Heeresleitung der Algerischen Nationalen Befreiungsarmee (ALN) Stuttgart, Deutsche Verlags-Anstalt, 1962. 90 l. p. facsim.

Anonymous military leader, member of the Armée de la Libération Nationale (ALN) political bureau, summarizes history of Algerian revolution from 1954 to Algerian independence, August 1962, describing final negotiations and internal leadership crisis, as well as basic F.L.N. program for Algeria. Included are statutes of F.L.N., provisional institutions of Algerian state, and minutes of meeting of Conseil National de la Révolution Algérienne of June 7, 1962, with signatures of members.

52 ALLAIS, MAURICE. Les accords d'Évian, le réferendum et la résistance algérienne, l'autorité, la majorité, le droit. Paris, L'Esprit nouveau, 1962. 379 p.

Book based on articles written before April 1962 referendum approving Evian agreements. Author opposes approval by analyzing errors of Gaullist Algerian policy and flaws in agreement from legal and constitutional point of view. Author had not been proponent of French Algeria, but had urged as early as 1956 a plan for dividing country into separate or partitioned communities under a federal Algerian government. Book printed May 1962, adds suggestions for amending agreements to protect French minority by international guarantees and describes conditions under which Algeria awaits peace settlement, assessing O.A.S. responsibilities. Appendices contain text of agreement, good chronology of Algerian war.

53 ALLAIS, MAURICE. L'Europe unie; route de la prospérité. Paris, Calmann-Lévy, 1960. 368 p. (Collection Liberté de l'Esprit) "Bibliographie": p. 343-358.

Study based on course given Spring 1959 at University of Virginia, reviews economic advantages of free market economy as exemplified by highly productive U.S. economy and points out real gains and obstacles to realization of European Common Market. Incompatibility of Common Market with national centralized planning, though not ultimate socialist objectives, is emphasized. Final section analyzes 1959 prospects of European Communities and Common Market, European Free Trade Association, larger Atlantic economic community, as well as French government's position on these issues. Author is partisan of political and economic Atlantic community and spokesman for Mouvement pour une Société Libre.

54 ALLEG, HENRI. Prisonniers de guerre. Paris, Éditions de Minuit, 1961. 250 p. (Documents)

Prison diary Aug. 1957- June 1960, continuing "La question," narrating author's experiences in Barberousse prison in Algiers until his transfer to French prison for testifying in the so-called "Affaire Audin."

55 ALLEG, HENRI. La question. Paris, Éditions de Minuit, 1958. 111 p. (Documents)

Author, former editor of outlawed pro-independence newspaper "Alger Républicain" and Algerian Communist Party member, went underground and was captured June 1957 by parachute troops near Alger. This account (written in prison and smuggled out) of torture to which he was subjected. As one of the first personal accounts of torture by French troops, it aroused strong public indignation. See also no. 54.

56 ALQUIER, JEAN YVES. Nous avons pacifié Tazalt; journal de marche d'un officer parachutiste rappelé en Algérie. Avec une lettre-préf. du Général Sauvagnac. Paris, R. Laffont, 1957. 272 p. map.

Diary notes of reserve officer in 25th parachute division, serving in Algeria Aug. 1956-June 1957 as head of his S.A.S. unit and giving enthusiastic description of French army's paification program.

56a ALTHUSSER, LOUIS. Pour Marx. Paris, F. Maspero, 1966, c1965. 258 p. (Théorie, 1) Bibliographical footnotes.

1965 introduction explaining the threadbareness of French Marxist thought in terms of the history of the French Communist Party (author is recognized Communist Party theoretician) and articles published 1960-1963 seeking a deeper understanding of Marxist dialects, which would help to provide a theory for the fate of the different revolutionary movements, personality cult in Russia, and the obstacles to "humanizing" socialism in socialist states.

57 ALWAN, MOHAMED. Algeria before the United Nations. [Cairo] Middle East Publications [1960?] 175 p. Includes bibliography.

Iraqian diplomat and U.N. representative gives factual account of U.N.'s handling of Algerian question in its 10th-13th Assembly, 1955-1958. Appendices give voting records, resolutions 1957-1958, chronology of Algerian conflict. This work was originally written as M.A. thesis at American University, Washington, D.C.

58 AMBLER, JOHN STEWARD. The French Army in politics, 1945-1962. Columbus, Ohio State University Press, 1966. x, 427 p. Bibliography: p. 377-406.

Well-documented study on the impact of the war in Indochina and Algeria on the a-politically-minded French army, both in terms of the development of the doctrines of revolutionary warfare, with its political overtones and the civilian-military clashes accompanying the birth of the Fifth Republic and the final years of the Algerian war. The book is based on research and interviews in France 1961-1962 and does not shed any light on ulterior military developments. Extensive bibliography.

59 AMERICAN COMMITTEE FOR FRANCE AND ALGERIA. Special report on the communist background of the Algerian rebellion. New York, 1962. 13 l.

Drawn up Jan. 1962 by American committee backing French Algeria (among sponsors are chairman Clifford Forster, James Burnham) to warn about close ties between F.L.N. and communism through direct international communist support of the rebellion, diplomatic agreements with Communist bloc, and communists among F.L.N. leaders. See also Committee's newsletters under nos. 1975, 2114, 2119.

60 AMERICAN UNIVERSITY, WASHINGTON, D.C., FOREIGN AREAS STUDIES DIVISION. Area handbook for Algeria. Washington, For sale by the Superintendent of Documents, U.S. Govt. Print. Off., 1965. xii, 520 p. illus., maps. Includes bibliographies.

Reference work on pre- and post-independence Algeria compiled for the U.S. Army with general information about the country's geography, sociology, history, and political evolution, followed by a survey of its current political, economic and military situations (September 1964). Good bibliographies after each section.

61 AMERICAN UNIVERSITY, WASHINGTON, D.C. SPECIAL OPERATIONS RESEARCH OFFICE. Case studies in insurgency and revolutionary warfare: Algeria, 1954-1962. Primary research responsibility: Paul A. Jureidini. Washington, 1963. 151 p. illus. Bibliography: p. 125-127.

Study sponsored by U.S. Department of Army and done under Special Operations Research Office as part of research program on modern revolutionary movements. Framework that might be applicable elsewhere is formulated respecting economic, social, and political factors inducing revolution and the dynamics of revolution (political and military leadership, ideology, techniques of guerilla warfare and terrorism, nature of international intervention.).

62 AMICALE DES ANCIENS MEMBRES DU P.C.F. Histoire du Parti communiste français. Paris, 1960-64? 3 v.

Critical history of French Communist Party by left-wing communist opposition group founded in 1952 as "Unir" and later working in conjunction with the Amicale des anciens membres du P.C.F., whose organ, "Débat communiste," was initiated in 1962 (see no. 1906). Third volume covers 1945-June 1964 and for Fifth Republic brings to light internal leadership crises, reactions to changes in Soviet directives, co-operation with other left-wing organizations working for Algerian peace. Party congresses are described in detail. Appendix reproduces in full Feb. 1956 secret Khrushchev report on Stalinist crimes.

63 AMICALE DES ELEVES DE L'INSTITUT D'ETUDES POLITIQUES. Avant le troisième tour [ouvrage réalisé à l'initiative de l'Amicale des élèves de l'Institut d'études politiques par Didier Millet et al.] Avec la collaboration d'une équipe de journalistes de Combat. Paris, Table ronde, 1966. 206 p. Includes bibliography.

Joint study, by group of students of Institut d'Etudes Politiques, Paris, and journalists of "Combat," on 1965 presidential election and its aftermath, as of spring 1966. The "troisième tour" refers to 1967 legislative elections. It gives analysis of results and tables for first and second rounds by departments, role of mass media, European unification as election theme, and prospects for political regrouping and bi-party system. Statements from scores of political leaders on these topics were collected by students in wake of election.

64 AMRANI, DJAMAL. Le témoin. Paris, Éditions de Minuit, 1960. 83 p. (Documents)

Author is brother-in-law in Ahmed Boumendjel, the defense lawyer who disappeared mysteriously Feb. 1957. This is account of events as they affected him, a postal service employee, when he was caught in web of interrogations, though not personally a nationalist.

65 AMROUCHE, MARCEL. Terres et hommes d'Algérie; enquêtes documentaires de la Radiodiffusion-télévision française en Algérie. Alger, Société algérienne de publication 1957? 315 p. illus., maps (1 fold. col.) Bibliography: p. 307-312.

Broadcast originally over Algerian radio 1955-1956, these talks by specialists on Algerian history barely touch contemporary period.

66 AMSELEK, PAUL. Le budget de l'état sous la Ve république. Préf. de Pierre Lavigne. Paris, Librairie générale de droit et de jurisprudence, R. Pichon et R. Durand-Auzias, 1966. 657 p. (Bibliothèque de science financière, t. 5) Includes bibliography.

Changes in fiscal institutions introduced by 1958 Constitution and very detailed description of elaboration of budget and its approval by parliament. Budget is seen as link in economic planning mechanism rather than central focus of parliamentary control.

67 ANDREU, PIERRE. Histoire des prêtres-ouvriers. Paris, Nouvelles éditions latines, 1960. 255 p. (Collection Itinéraires)

After banning of "prêtres ouvriers" movement proper in 1954, French episcopate approved the Mission ouvrière, whose evolution author follows through 1960.

68 ANDREWS, WILLIAM GEORGE. French politics and Algeria; the process of policy formation, 1954-1962. New York, Appleton-Century-Crofts, 1962. 217 p. (Current political problems)

American political scientist summarizes popular opinion, stands of press and political parties, actions of parties, government, parliament toward Algerian problem 1954-1962. Gives figures for public opinion polls, results of elections, referenda, specific government policies and laws dealing with Algeria, excerpts from parliamentary debates. Shows efficacy of institutions of 4th and 5th Republic in solving problem. Role of army is not considered. Nov. 1954-July 1962 chronology and index.

69 L'Année politique; revue chronologique des principaux faits politiques, économiques et sociaux de la France. 1 - 23 1944-45-1967. Paris, Éditions du grand siècle. 23 v.

The most comprehensive annual reference source for French political life. Month by month review of developments is given for four areas: internal political affairs, economic policy, social policy, foreign affairs (separate section up to 1963 for Algeria) and complemented by exact chronology at end of volume. Other information includes texts of important speeches, letters by members of government, resolutions of party congresses, election results. Comprehensive name, organization and subject index. Up to 1963, each volume has introductory survey by prominent political scientist of major political issues of year. This feature is replaced thereafter by a documentary, statistical section on state of economy.

70 Annuaire de la presse et de la publicité, 63-81 année; 1945-50, 1951-1968. Paris. 19 v. illus., ports., facsims.

Annal classified listing of current French newspapers, weeklies, and periodicals, with information on editors, political orientation. Index of publications, journalists. Title changed from "Annuaire de la presse française et étrangère et du monde politique" in 1965, from "Annuaire de la presse française et étrangère" in 1966 to its current form.

71 Annuaire statistique de la ville de Paris et des communes suburbaines de la Seine. 82.année. Paris, 1961. 1 v. illus.

Prefecture de la Seine's tabulations for 1961 and sometimes cumulative figures covering population movement, medical care, education, economic conditions, election results (January 1961 referendum) for Paris area.

72 ARAB STATES DELEGATIONS OFFICE, NEW YORK. Algeria speaks; the case for Algeria at the 12th U.N. General Assembly. New York, The Arab States Delegations Office, the United Nations Section, 1958. 19 p. map.

Excerpts from speeches by Arab delegations (Syria, Iraq, Jordan, Saudi Arabia, Morocco, Tunisia, Egypt, etc.) in favor of Algerian self-determination.

73 ARCY, FRANCOIS D', ANNIE KRIEGER, and ALAIN MARILL. Essais sur l'economie de l'Algérie nouvelle. Préf. de Gaston Leduc. Paris, Presses universitaires de France, 1965. 254 p. (Travaux et recherches de la Faculté de droit et des sciences économiques de Paris. Série "Afrique," no. 1) Includes bibliography.

Three essays on reforms initiated in independent Algeria: communal administration (François d'Arcy) land redistribution and self-administration in agriculture (Annie Krieger) self-administration in industry (Alain Marill). Programs and results are evaluated through 1964 and compared with efforts in other socialist countries. Extensive bibliography for each topic.

74 ARGOUD, ANTOINE, (defendant). L'affaire Argoud; préf. de Michel Dacier. Paris, Éditions du Fuseau, 1964. 221 p. (Collection "Les Chemins du réel," 5)

Introductory biography, personal account of friendship by Jean Brune. Documents on kidnaping and trial of Col. Antoine Argoud before Cour de Sureté de l'Etat, Dec. 26-30, 1963 for his participation in 1961 General's Putsch and leading rôle in O.A.S. Main document is text of trial, partly summarized, in full where it deals with defense's contention that the extradition procedure from Germany was illegal. Supporting documents relating to extradition and kidnaping.

FOR ADDITIONAL WORKS BY AND ABOUT ANTOINE ARGOUD, SEE AUTHOR INDEX

75 L'Armée et la nation. By René Rémond et al. Paris, A. Fayard, 1960. 214 p. (Recherches et débats du Centre catholique des intellectuels français. Nouv. sér., no. 30) Bibliographical footnotes.

Only first 97 pages of this issue of "Recherches et débats" are devoted to problems of army. Articles were completed before January 1960 revolt. Military are represented by unsigned appeal for renewed patriotism (from 1958 issue of "Message des Forces Armées") and Col. G. de Villiers de l'Isle Adam's article on counter-faith to Communist 'religion.' Civilians, among whom Maurice Mégret, Etienne Borne, Jean Planchais, Pierre Henri Simon, Jean-Pierre Prévost, all are concerned with questions raised by new reliance on psychological warfare in a democratic state.

76 ARON, RAYMOND. L'Algérie et la République. Paris, Plon, 1958. 146 p. (Tribune libre, 33)

Writing in June 1958, author recapitulates his dispassionate dissection of Algerian alternatives and assesses prospects of new regime for transcending the impasse.

77 ARON, RAYMOND. Démocratie et totalitarianisme. Paris, Gallimard, 1965. 378 p. (Collection Idées)

Reprint in its original form of "Sociologie des sociétés industrielles," with introduction by author reviewing, with 8 years' perspective, the validity of his diagnosis for both French and Soviet society. (See no. 82.)

78 ARON, RAYMOND. Immuable et changeante; de la IVe à Ve République. Paris, Calmann-Lévy, 1959. 265 p. (Collection Liberté de l'esprit)

Based on a lecture series at Harvard October 1957 explaining the functioning of French political and economic system and French efforts to adapt to modern world. Aron shows basic trends common to 4th and 5th Republic and factors (mainly decolonization) which led to collapse of 4th Republic. Only one chapter is specifically devoted to history of first half year of Fifth Republic, but much of diagnosis remains applicable.

79 ARON, RAYMOND. Espoir et peur du siècle; essais non partisans. Paris, Calmann-Lévy, 1957. 367 p. (Liberté de l'esprit)

Reflections on conservatism, French and European decadence. While generally optimistic about French revival, author views Algerian impasse as potential powder keg for its democratic institutions.

80 ARON, RAYMOND. The great debate; theories of nuclear strategy. Translated from the French by Ernst Pawel. Garden City, N.Y., Doubleday, 1965. ix, 265 p. Bibliographical footnotes.

Based on 1962-63 lectures at Sorbonne and revised 1963-64. The great debate refers to world nuclear strategy. Includes study of French nuclear deterrent.

81 ARON, RAYMOND. Paix et guerre entre les nations. Paris, Calmann-Lévy, 1962. 794 p.

Sweeping study of international relations, with some references to French foreign policy and military strategy.

82 ARON, RAYMOND. Sociologie des sociétés industrielles; esquisse d'une théorie des régimes politiques. Paris, Centre de documentation universitaire, 1958. 241 p. ("Les Cours de Sorbonne." Sociologie)

1957-58 course at Sorbonne on different types of regimes in modern societies centered on dichotomy: constitutional multiparty vs. single-party states. The degradation of French version of multiparty state is explained by the lack of loyalty to it of large political segments. Last lecture, given in late May 1958, illuminates current upheavals in this framework.

83 ARON, RAYMOND. La tragédie algérienne. Paris, Plon, 1957. 76 p. (Tribune libre, 2)

One of first politically moderate voices raised publicly to urge Algerian independence as a lesser evil to continuing war and pointing out what would be material costs of integration compared to withdrawal from Algeria. Philosophy and sociology professor is also columnist for "Figaro." First section written April 1956, second May 1957. Direct replies to Aron's arguments are given by Soustelle and Beau de Loménie (see nos. 152 and 1649).

FOR ADDITIONAL WORKS BY AND ABOUT RAYMOND ARON, SEE AUTHOR INDEX

84 ARON, ROBERT. Charles de Gaulle. Paris, Librairie adadémique Perrin, 1964. 262 p. illus., ports.

Historian specializing in Vichy and liberation period gives critical but sympathetic interpretation drawing on both pre- and post-1958 years of de Gaulle's character, political strategy, philosophy, via series of anecdotes, some not found elsewhere. Good photographs, including snapshots of all Fourth Republic prime ministers. In second part of book author analyzes place of Gaullism in French history, particularly its impact on political parties, French nationalism. Most of book was written originally for a Paris newspaper, and the introduction cites readers' letters to Aron. English translation: "An Explanation of De Gaulle" (New York, 1966).

85 ARON, ROBERT, FRANÇOIS LAVAGNE, et al. Les Origines de la guerre d'Algérie; textes et documents contemporains. Paris, Fayard, 1962. 332 p. map. Includes bibliography.

Documentation only goes up to 1954.

86 ARRIGHI, PASCAL. La Corse atout décisif. Paris, Plon 1958. 182 p.

Account of events in Algeria, Corsica, and Paris between May 13 and June 2, 1958 and concluded a month after events described by deputy from Corsica who personally participated in Algerian and Corsican uprising in support of de Gaulle.

87 ASHCROFT, EDWARD. De Gaulle. London, Odhams Press, 1962. 272 p. ports. Bibliography: p. 267-268.

British journalist's balanced work on all phases of de Gaulle's life, drawing on main published works of de Gaulle. Though no unfamiliar facts are presented, it contains good summary of de Gaulle's career and actions during Fifth Republic up to summer 1962.

88 Aspects de la sociologie française. [By] G. Le Bras, P. H. Chombart de Lauwe, R. Aron, J. Berque, et al. Paris. Éditions ouvrières, 1966. 221 p. (Collection "L'Évolution de la vie sociale") Includes bibliographical references.

Areas of research in French sociology, as described briefly by respective specialists (note Raymond Aron's chapter on political sociology and Jacques Berque's on the sociology of decolonization), as well as university curriculum in sociology and research methods at the Centre National de la Recherche Scientifique.

89 ASSAC, JACQUES PLONCARD D'. Critique nationaliste. Paris, Libraire Française [1966?] 255 p. (Voix de l'Occident, Publications, 13)

Radio broadcasts from Lisbon station explaining nationalist position on Right and Left, individual and state, Freemasonry, war and politics, European nationalism, the influence of the Left within the Catholic Church. (See also "La Voix de l'Occident" no. 2134)

90 ASSAC, JACQUES PLONCARD D'. La nation, l'Europe et la Chrétienté. Paris, La Voix de l'Occident [1963?] 114 p. Bibliographical footnotes.

Disciple of Maurras and admirer of Salazar repudiates doctrines of men of the new Right like Jean Thiriart and Philippe Heduy who wish to drown their national disappointments in a Nation-Europe. Author believes that only nations are vital forces, unless a resurgent Christianity can once more bind together European peoples. He finds support for his stand in position of popes on European unification.

91 Assises de la démocratie, Vichy, 1964. Compte-rendu des débats. 85 l.

Participating in this April 1964 gathering are representatives from 11 political clubs: 1. Club Jean Moulin, 2. Citoyens 60, 3. Groupes Rencontres, 4. Centre de réflexion et d'études politiques, 5. Centre d'information politique, économique et sociale, 6. Positions, 7. Association des jeunes cadres, 8. Association pour la Démocratie, 9. Cercle Tocqueville, 10. Après-demain, 11. Démocratie nouvelle. This is their first joint meeting. These clubs were later in the year to endorse Defferre as presidential candidate, but the candidacy was not discussed in Vichy.

92* ASSOCIATION CHRETIENNE DES ETUDIANTS DE PARIS. [Appeal to students to demand the abrogation of discriminatory measures against Algerian workers in France.] Paris, 1961. 1 p.

93* ASSOCIATION D'ETUDES ET D'INFORMATIONS POLITIQUES INTERNATIONALES. Le parti communiste devant les élections. Paris, 1958. 29 p. (Est et ouest. Supplement)

Communist Party's unsuccessful "no" campaign on Sept. 1958 referendum and tactics for Nov. 1958 legislative elections.

94* ASSOCIATION D'ETUDES ET D'INFORMATIONS POLITIQUES INTERNATIONALES. Les syndicalistes face à Khruchtchev. Paris, 1959. 46 p. (Est et Ouest. Supplement)

Reviews Khrushchev's relations with French and foreign labor leaders.

95 ASSOCIATION FRANÇAISE DE SCIENCE POLITIQUE. Le bipartisme est-il possible en France? Débat introduit par Maurice Duverger et Jacques Fauvet. Paris, 1965. 31 l. (Its Entretiens du samedi, no. 3)

Discussion on prospects of a bi-party system after de Gaulle through consolidation of a right wing and left wing block. Main speakers are political scientists Maurice Duverger, Jacques Fauvet, François Goguel, and Léo Hamon (the only Gaullist participant). Although bi-partism as such is considered desirable by most speakers, Duverger alone sees trends in that direction, while others predict a four-way split in French political parties as the greatest simplification to be expected.

96 ASSOCIATION FRANÇAISE DE SCIENCE POLITIQUE. La dépolitisation, mythe ou réalité? Sous la direction de Georges Vedel. Paris, A. Colin, 1962. 285 p. (Cahiers de la Fondation nationale des sciences politiques, 120. Partis et elections) Includes bibliography.

Bases on round-table discussion held by Association Nov. 1960 and complemented by fuller studies made subsequently. In first part, Jean Touchard, Jean-Yves Calvez and Marcel Merle discuss methodological problems of measuring depolitization; in second part, René Rémond, Georges Dupeaux and Léon Hamon describe its manifestations in current French politics, with statistical studies on electoral participation and effect on political parties. A third part by Georges Lavau gives sociocultural aspects and a final section studies worker and farmer depolitization (Marcel David, Henri Mendras).

97 ASSOCIATION FRANÇAISE DE SCIENCE POLITIQUE. Les élections du 2 janvier 1956, sous la direction de Maurice Duverger, François Goguel et Jean Touchard. Paris, A. Colin, 1957. xv, 504 p. maps, tables, diagrs. (Cahiers de la Fondation nationale des sciences politiques, 82) Bibliographical footnotes.

Individual studies on election campaign as seen in party programs, mass media, case studies of different geographic areas, and analysis of results.

98 ASSOCIATION FRANÇAISE DE SCIENCE POLITIQUE. L'établissement de la Cinquième république: le référendum de septembre et les élections de novembre 1958. Préf. de Jean Touchard. Paris, A. Colin, 1960. xxiii, 390 p. and atlas of 11 fold. maps. (Cahiers de la Fondation nationale des sciences politiques, 109. Partis et élections) Bibliographical footnotes.

15 political scientists of the Fondation Nationale des Sciences politiques, among them Maurice Duverger, Jacques Fauvet, François Goguel, and René Rémond describe campaigns for the referendum and general elections, study public opinion on the basis of questionnaires, analyze results, with numerous statistical breakdowns.

99 ASSOCIATION FRANÇAISE DE SCIENCE POLITIQUE. Les institutions politiques de la France. Débat introduit par Georges Vedel et François Goguel. Paris, 1964. 35 l. (Its Entretiens du samedi, no. 1, février 1964)

Round-table initiated by Francois Goguel's article in Feb. 1964 issue of "Revue française de science politique," Main speakers are Goguel, George Vedel, Maurice Duverger, René Capitant, Léo Hamon, Emile Giraud. Debate deals with desirability of constitutional reform involved in direct election of president and the prospects of this innovation after de Gaulle. Vedel and Duverger are mildly critical of new institutions, while other speakers take their defense.

100 ASSOCIATION FRANÇAISE DE SCIENCE POLITIQUE. Le parlementarisme peut-il être limité sans être annihilé? Débat introduit par Marcel Prélot. Paris, 1965. 37 l. (Its Entretiens du samedi, no. 4)

Discussion on Senate and National Assembly's declining influence under Fifth Republic. Main speakers are Marcel Prélot, senator and jurist, and René Capitant, Gaullist deputy and jurist, each of whom draws on his own experiences.

101 ASSOCIATION FRANÇAISE DE SCIENCE POLITIQUE. Partis politiques et classes sociales en France. Sous la direction de Maurice Duverger. Paris, Librairie A. Colin, 1955. 331, 1 p. (Cahiers de la Fondation nationale des sciences politiques, 74. Partis et élections) Bibliography: p. 329-332.

Based on June 1955 round-table, this study gives detailed breakdown of political affiliations of different sectors of French society and social structure of main political parties as of 1955.

102 ASSOCIATION FRANÇAISE DE SCIENCE POLITIQUE. Les paysans et la politique dans la France contemporaine. Sous la direction de Jacques Fauvet et Henri Mendras. Paris, A. Colin, 1958. xxv, 531 p. maps. (Cahiers de la Fondation nationale des sciences politiques, 94) Bibliography: p. 519-527.

Based on a 1956 round-table on political representation of peasantry, information goes up to 1957.

103 ASSOCIATION INTERNATIONALE DES SOCIOLOGUES DE LANGUE FRANÇAISE. COLLOQUE. 5th, QUEBEC, 1964. Les classes sociales dans le monde d'aujourd'hui. Paris, Presses universitaires de France, 1965. 2 v. (Cahiers internationaux de sociologie, v. 38-39, 1965) Includes bibliography.

First volume has series of articles on France (working class, rural communities, feelings of class and national identity).

104* ASSOCIATION NATIONALE POUR LE SOUTIEN DE L'ACTION DU GENERAL DE GAULLE. [Appeal to support de Gaulle after January 24, 1960 uprising in Algeria] Paris, 1960.

105* ASSOCIATION NATIONALE POUR LE SOUTIEN DE L'ACTION DU GENERAL DE GAULLE. Poster 1958, on microfilm.

For "yes" vote on Sept. 1958 referendum. For additional referendum material, see no. 811(b). See also Association's Bulletin under no. 1841.

106 ASSOCIATION POUR L'ETUDE DE LA REFORME DES STRUCTURES DE L'ETAT. Nécessité d'un parti du peuple. Paris, 1961. 23 p. port.

Political organization founded Nov. 1961 and headed by parachutist colonel Roger Trinquier who resigned from army some months earlier. This is Party program, stating its aims to replace the U.N.R. in the coming election and carry out the renovation of France which did not materialize in May 1958. It is strongly anti-Gaullist, anti-Communist, but also anti-capitalist, favoring French Algeria and European federation. See also nos. 1717, 1930.

107 ASSOCIATION POUR LE RESPECT DES FRONTIÈRES SUR L'ODER ET LA NEISSE. La Frontière Oder-Neisse et l'opinion publique en France. Préf. de Paul Bastid. Paris, Éditions Odene, 1963. 87 p.

83 brief declarations, 1960-1963, by prominent political and academic figures supporting the Oder-Neisse frontier, followed by appeal for recognition of the new frontier and names of signers.

108 ASTIER DE LA VIGERIE, EMMANUEL D'. Les Grands. Paris, Gallimard, 1961. 213 p. (L'Air du temps)

Includes an 80-page portrait of de Gaulle, part biography, part character analysis, which makes use of personal recollections during the Resistance and interviews up to 1960. The tone is critical, sometimes biting.

FOR ADDITIONAL WORKS BY AND ABOUT EMMANUEL D'ASTIER DE LA VIGERIE, SEE AUTHOR INDEX.

109 Atlas de l'élection présidentielle de décembre 1965, établi par Alain Lancelot et al. Paris, 1966. 83 p. diagrs. (Fondation nationale des sciences politiques. Centre d'étude de la vie politique française. Série Documents, no. 3)

Results of presidential election visualized in the form of maps with dots for each voting district. Comparative maps are drawn up for 1962 elections and 1962 referenda.

110 AUBURTIN, JEAN. Le Colonel de Gaulle. Paris, Plon, 1965. 176 p.

Memoirs of encounters with de Gaulle in immediate pre-war period and at time of French defeat.

111 AUMERAN, ADOLPHE. Paix en Algérie. Paris, the Author, 1959. 509 p.

Author was deputy from Algeria in National Assembly 1946-1955. Book is based on editorials appearing in "Africain" Ja 1956 - Sept. 1959 and expressing his opposition to various proposals to change status quo in Algeria. Even integration and social improvements are seen as threat to French Algeria.

112 AUVADE, ROBERT. Bibliographic critique des oeuvres parues sur l'Indochine française; un siècle d'histoire et d'enseignement. Paris, G.-P. Maisonneuve and Larose, 1965. 153 p.

Annotated topically arranged bibliography, with some works on Vietnam after French defeat.

113 L'Avenir de l'Alliance atlantique. By Claude Delmas et al. Préf. de Jules Romains. Paris, Berger-Levrault, 1961. 350 p. maps, diagrs. (Institutions politiques d'aujourd hui) Bibliography: p. 342-246.

Generals Pierre Gallois and Marcel Carpentier, and politician Maurice Faure expose principles of Atlantic strategy for the nuclear age.

114 AVENIRS (periodical). Possibilités actuelles et perspectives d'emploi. Les plans d'action régionale et l'orientation de la jeunesse. Paris, 1960. 120 p. illus., maps. "Numéro hors série, mars-avril, 1960."

This vocational guide was drawn up in collaboration with Ministère du Travail and gives up-to-date figures for employment in different industries.

115 AVRIL, PIERRE. Un président pour quoi faire? Préf. de Georges Vedel. Paris, Éditions du seuil, 1965. 156 p. (Collection Jean Moulin)

Political scientist's case for a genuine presidential regime differing from that introduced by de Gaulle, with the aim to achieve stability and effectiveness in a free society by granting president full executive powers and parliament strong controls.

116 AVRIL, PIERRE. Le régime politique de la Ve République. Préf. de Roger Pinto. Ouvrage honoré d'une subvention du Ministère de l'éducation nationale. Paris, R. Pichon et R. Durand-Auzias, 1964. 398 p. (Bibliothèque constitutionnelle et de science politique, t. 8) Bibliography: p. 379-386.

The political institutions of the Fifth Republic (parliament, executive, judiciary) are subjected to a minutely documented, detailed, and impartial study. The letter and spirit of the 1958 constitution are viewed against the evolution between January 1959 and January 1961, in which the regime assumed its definitive shape, which the author defines as a plebiscitary principate, with all power resting in hands of chief of state. The only political issue covered in detail is Algerian policy. Only the U.N.R., as the government party, is discussed. Extensive bibliography of books, articles, documents.

117 AVRIL, PIERRE. Le régime politique de la Ve république. Préf. de Roger Pinto. 2. éd. mise à jour. Paris, Librairie générale de droit et de jurisprudence, R. Pichon et R. Durand-Auzias, 1967. 439 p. (Bibliothèque constitutionelle et de science politique, 8) Includes bibliography.

Final section of revised edition examines developments between 1962 general election and presidential election further corroborating tendency toward presidential regime and degradation of parliament. Presidential election campaign exemplifies logic of political system as a whole and proposals are made to make it more coherent and workable. Bibliography not brought up to date.

118 AYACHE, ALAIN. Monsieur Y, Pierre Marcilhacy. Paris, Nouvelles éditions latines, 1965. 171 p. illus., ports.

Journalist, writing two months before presidential election and before announcement of Lecanuet candidacy, tries to prove that Senator Marcilhacy, the dark horse candidate without major party backing, has all the personal qualities voters admire in de Gaulle. Book gives short biography, candidate's earlier political declarations, his campaign program, and his stand on European unification, relations with United States.

119 AYMARD, CAMILLE. Tragédie française en Afrique du Nord. Les responsables - Témoignages et documents - À quand, la Haute-cour? Paris, Éditions des Quatre fils Aymon, 1958. 253 p.

French journalist's attack on his country's decadence as expressed in Mendès-France's granting independence to Tunisia and eyewitness account of events leading up to this "tragedy."

120 AZAR, ANTOINE. Genèse de la Constitution du 4 octobre 1958; solution gaulliste à la crise du pouvoir. Préf. de Philippe Ardant. Paris, Librairie générale de droit et de jurisprudence, R. Pichon et R. Durand-Auzias, 1961. xi, 284 p. (Bibliothèque de droit public, t. 36) "Bibliographie": p. 169-279.

Work of Lybian jurist, based on Ph.D. thesis, first examines failure of the Fourth Republic to combine imperial rule with parliamentary sovereignty, then shows in last third of book how Gaullism has solved the crisis of state power, parliamentary control, and ties with overseas territories. The author is very favorable to Gaullist concepts and emphasizes longterm rationality of African policy, with the hopeful interpretation (as of mid-1961) that independence and association can be reconciled in Algeria. Extensive bibliography of books and articles.

121 AZEAU, HENRI. Révolte militaire, Alger, 22 Avril 1961. Paris, Plon, 1961. 274 p.

French journalist uses extensive published sources and private information to write a comprehensive history of the Generals' Putsch in Algeria: antecedents of Army's role in Algeria, doctrines of psychological warfare and counter-revolution, political-military alliance in Algeria and its collapse, leading to formation of O.A.S. (it does not cover any of the treason trials), confrontation of contingent, reserve officer corps, colonels and generals, CIA and NATO entanglements. One of the best surveys of the Army-Algeria-de Gaulle complex, and of the myths and rationalizations inspiring military and civilian proponents of French Algeria.

122 BABINI, VENIERO. L'Africa francese dalla Terza Repubblica alla Communità rinnovata. Padova, CEDAM, 1961. 319 p. (Pubblicazioni della Società italiana per l'organizzazione internazionale) Bibliographical footnotes.

History of French Union and brief description of its 1958 successor, the French Community. Appendices reproduce 1958 Constitution and that of 12 African and Malagasy members of Community as of 1961 (in French).

123 BABY, JEAN. Critique de base; le Parti communiste français entre le passé et l'avenir. Paris, F. Maspero, 1960. 256 p. (Cahiers libres, no. 5-6)

Attacks on various phases of P.C.F. policy, 1956-1959, such as economic policy and stand on Algeria, relation with other leftist parties. Baby is himself a member of the P.C.F.

124 BABY, JEAN. Un monde meilleur; recherche marxiste. Paris, F. Maspero, 1964. 91 p. (Cahiers libres, no. 63-64)

Projection, in line with Marxist doctrine, of how French society, especially family and education, would be transformed under a socialist regime. There is no reference to stand of French Communist Party on these issues.

125 BACCOUCHE, HACHEMI. Décolonisation; grandeurs et servitudes de l'anti-colonialisme. Paris, Nouvelles éditions latines, 1962. 124 p.

For author, Tunisian living in exile, decolonization is not necessarily equivalent to repudiating all contributions of former colonial power and insisting on the departure of all European settlers. He makes the case that the people of North Africa are mature enough politically to avoid a one-party dictatorship, which the French Left is willing to condone. The book written March 1961, makes frequent references to Algerian evolution and shows understanding for the violence of European settlers' reactions to French withdrawal.

126 BACRI, ROLAND. Le guide de Colombey; écrit par Roland Bacri, filmé par Alain Ayache, dessiné par Jacques Lap: préf. d'André Ribaud. Paris, Jeune Parque, 1965. 154 p. illus.

De Gaulle's life from birth to presidential election narrated in coarse verse and illustrated with photographs of Colombey on which cartoons have been superimposed.

127 BAGGIO, JEAN. Un faux problème: après de Gaulle ... qui? Bordeaux, The Author, 1964. 148 p.

The real problem, as analyzed in this essay, is to find a viable republican form of government which incorporates Gaullist innovations accepted by the people but which is operable without de Gaulle. Author examines potential of Defferre, the candidate of the opposition, to bind together republican forces and win Gaullist succession.

128 BAILLOU, JEAN and PIERRE PELLETIER. Les affaires étrangères. Introd. de Jacques de Bourbon-Busset. Paris, Presses universitaires de France, 1962. 378 p. ("L'Administration française")

Guide to organization of Ministère des Affaires Etrangères and mechanics of foreign policy making, with information on Ministry for 1961.

129 BANKWITZ, PHILIP CHARLES FARWELL. Maxime Weygand and civil-military relations in modern France. Cambridge, Harvard University Press, 1967. xiii, 445 p. (Harvard historical studies, v. 81) Bibliography: p. 383-437.

Weygand's role in politization of French army in Third Republic. Epilogue covers general's attitude in May 1958 and during trials of seditious generals, 1961-62. Extensive bibliography of books and articles on civilian-military relations.

130 BANNAN, JOHN F. The philosophy of Merleau-Ponty. New York, Harcourt, Brace and World, 1967. xii, 273 p. Bibliographical footnotes.

Analysis of existentialist philosopher's works, including sections on his stand on Marxism and his critique of communism.

131 BARALE, JEAN. La IVème République et la guerre. Aix-en-Provence, "La Pensée universitaire," 1961. 539 p. Bibliography: p. 515-531.

Study analyzing in detail the breakdown of parliamentary mechanisms in the wake of intra-party dissensions caused by colonial wars in Indochina and Algeria and the progressive loss of control over military policy culminating in regime's collapse. Good bibliography for Algeria, problems of military-civilian relations.

132 BARBEROT, ROGER. Malaventure en Algérie avec le général Paris de Bollardière. Paris, Plon, 1957. 241 p. (Tribune libre, 4)

Personal experiences of reserve officer serving in Algeria under general de Bollardière July 1956- March 1957 and describing general's efforts to overcome the political and military sclerosis preventing effective pacification program, one that would win over Algerians to French side by welfare measures rather than counter-terrorism. Author with contacts in military establishment gives interesting sketches of military and political figures like general Salan, Robert Lacoste, Max Lejeune. Jean-Jacques Servan-Schreiber based his "Lieutenant en Algérie" on service under same general, who resigned rather than disavow Servan-Schreiber's account.

133 BARDECHE, MAURICE. Qu'est-ce que le fascisme? Paris, Sept couleurs, 1961. 195 p.

Self-styled "fascist" explores different forms of fascism from Hitler and Mussolini through Nasser and Fidel Castro, isolating historically conditioned features like antisemitism and police state methods from pure fascist ideology, in contrast to democratic ideology, which might find different modes of expression and new labels in modern world. He finds much that is basically congenial in the program of "Patrie et Progrès" with its authoritarian and technocratic socialist program, despite the organization's loyalty to de Gaulle.

134 BARDONNET, DANIEL. Évolution de la structure du Parti radical. Paris, Editions Montchrestien, 1960. 293 p. "Bibliographie": p. 281-287; bibliographical footnotes.

Contains some information on the party's organization for the 1955-1959 period when one wing of the party split off, but stops with the withdrawal of Mendès-France to join Parti socialiste unifié in Sept. 1959.

135 BARETS, JEAN. La fin des politiques. Paris, Calmann-Lévy, 1962. 276 p. illus. (Questions d'actualité)

Young engineer's technocratic program for France's and world's political and economic problems in the face of the decline of ideologically-oriented political parties. Author is president of political club, Technique et Démocratie.

136 BARING, ARNULF and CHRISTIAN TAUTIL. Charles de Gaulle; Grösse und Grenzen. Übersetzung der französischen Teile des Manuskripts Heidi Baring. Köln, Kiepenheuer and Witsch, 1963. 154 p. (Information 3) Includes bibliography.

Essays by a Frenchman and a German journalist critically evaluating Gaullism and interrelation between de Gaulle's philosophy, personality, political conduct and style as expressed in his whole career.

137 BARRACHIN, EDMOND. Les indépendants et les paysans face à l'élection présidentielle. Paris, L'Indépendant, 1965.

13 p. port. "Indépendant numéro spécial."

Appeal to Independants to support Lecanuet for presidency.

138 BARRON, RICHARD WILLIAM. Parties and politics in modern France. Introd. by Charles Micaud. Washington, Public Affairs Press, 1959. xi, 213 p. Includes bibliographical references.

Detailed study on organization and programs of Communist Party, M.R.P., Socialist Party, R.P.F. and its successor groups through end of Fourth Republic, with interpretation of Gaullist support after his return to power.

139 BARS, HENRY. La politique selon Jacques Maritain. Préf. de Jacques Maritain. Paris, Éditions ouvrières, 1962. 247 p. (Collection "Points d'appui")

Analysis of Maritain's writings to disengage his political philosophy (democracy, Catholic action).

140 BARSALOU, JOSEPH. La mal-aimée; histoire de la IVe République. Paris, Plon, 1964. 333 p. Bibliographical footnotes.

Editor of "Dépêche de Toulouse" gives chronological account of Fourth Republic, organized around its major crises and achievements, giving special attention to the rôle played by de Gaulle and the Gaullists in bringing about its collapse.

141 BASTIEN-THIRY, GABRIEL. Plaidoyer pour un frère fusillé. Paris, Table ronde, 1966. 216 p.

Arrest, August 1962, trial, and execution half a year later of Jean Bastien-Thiry as witnessed by his brother Gabriel, who only became aware of Jean's involvement in the assassination plot after the arrest was made. In addition to rounding off the portrait of this young officer as it emerges from trial record, book recreates atmosphere in family of accused and shows reactions to issue of Algeria, O.A.S., de Gaulle, on the part of the various people with whom he had to deal in trying to save Jean. Interesting view of political trial as seen from the defense side.

142 BASTIEN-THIRY, JEAN MARIE. Déclaration du colonel Bastien-Thiry, 2 février 1963. Paris, Éditions du Fuseau, 1963. 54 p.

Complete text of plea by accused, before military tribunal, motivating his attempt to kidnap (rather than assassinate, as claimed by prosecution) de Gaulle as response to Algerian betrayal and threat of internal dictatorship. He even draws parallel with plot to assassinate Hitler. Accused speaks as one of leaders of the Conseil National de la Résistance, at whose instigation the plot was carried out.

143 BASTIEN-THIRY, JEAN MARIE (defendant). Le procès de l'attentat du Petit-Clamart; compte rendu sténographique. Paris, A. Michel, 1963. 2 v.

1000-page transcript of the trial before the Cour militaire de justice, Jan. 28 - Mar. 4, 1963 of Col. Bastien-Thiry and 14 others for the attempted assassination of de Gaulle August 22, 1962 at Petit-Clamart. Bastien-Thiry, a former air force technician, personally defends his actions (see his "Déclaration") with the help of defense attorneys Tixier-Vignancour and Isorni, the latter being disqualified from the bar during the trial. The procession of military witnesses and victims of exodus of French settlers reinforce accused's attack on betrayal of French Algeria and the catastrophes ensuing from Evian agreement. The prosecution argues the necessity of de Gaulle's Algerian policy and the disasters flowing from O.A.S. intervention. One of the points highlighted at trial is the shooting on March 26, 1962 in Algiers, rue d'Isly between French troops and French settlers. Only Bastien-Thiry was condemned to death and shot at once. (For another trial record see no. 999.)

FOR ADDITIONAL WORKS BY AND ABOUT JEAN MARIE BASTIEN-THIRY SEE AUTHOR INDEX

144 BATAILLER, FRANCINE, ALAIN SCHIFRES, and CLAUDE TANNERY. Analyses de presse. Préf. de Georges Vedel. Paris, Presses universitaires de France, 1963. 236 p. diagrs., tables. (Travaux et recherches de la Faculté de droit et des sciences économiques de Paris; Série "Science politique," 1)

Monographs by three young scholars: 1) comparison of the way two illustrated weeklies, the pro-Gaullist "Paris-Match" and the a-political "Jours de France" presented the first year of the Fifth Republic, the Algerian question, international affairs; 2) ideology of the satirical weekly "Canard enchainé," including its critique through mid-1961 of the Fourth and Fifth Republic; 3) study of the financial press as of 1961.

145 BAUCHARD, PHILIPPE. L'économie au service du pouvoir. Paris, Calmann-Lévy, 1967. 295 p. (Questions d'actualité)

Stages in Fifth Republic's economic policy, analysis of de Gaulle's neutralization of business and labor's economic power and shift thereof to the administration, methods deployed to stabilize economy, and evaluation of regime's success in dealing with specific economic problems (housing, social security, unemployment, regional planning, etc.) Chronology of significant economic measures and incidents.

146 BAUCHARD, PHILIPPE. La mystique du plan; les menaces de la prospérité. Paris, Arthaud, 1963. 266 p. (Collection Notre temps, 7) Includes bibliography.

History and critical evaluation of planning in Fifth Republic, and emergence of 4th and 5th Plan as one of central pieces of Gaullist policy, tying together wage, housing, regional development and foreign aid programs. Author also describes the background of technocrats who hold position of power and the role of Michel Debré and Georges Pompidou in promoting planning.

147 BAUCHARD, PHILIPPE. Les technocrates et le pouvoir, X-crise, synarchie, C.G.T., clubs. Paris, Arthaud, 1966. 320 p. (Collection Notre temps, 12) Bibliography: p. 317-318.

History of technocratically oriented groups in France from 1930's to 1965, with emphasis on their direct political failures and indirect influence on long-range economic and social policy. Last chapter deals with political clubs, particularly the Club Jean Moulin and its unsuccessful promotion of Defferre's presidential candidacy.

148 BAUCHET, PIERRE. L'expérience française de planification. Paris, Éditions du Seuil, 1958. 237 p. (Collections "Esprit." La cité prochaine) "Bibliographie": p. 201-205.

First major study on French planning, completed in 1957 and covering first two plans.

149 BAUCHET, PIERRE. La planification française; quinze ans d'expérience. Paris, Éditions du Seuil, 1962. 347 p. (Collections Esprit. "La cité prochaine") Includes bibliography.

Author is professor of economic planning at Ecole Nationale d'Administration. This is the most comprehensive study of French planning, with numerous tables on French economy. It examines the philosophy, historical experience of the four plans, the administrative procedures and technical contents, as well as their impact on society as a whole. Extensive bibliography and list of government decrees related to planning.

150 BAUCHET, PIERRE. Propriété publique et planification. (Entreprises publiques non-financières.) Paris, Editions Cujas, 1962. 347 p. diagr., tables. Bibliography: p. 317-321. ML

Reference work on nationalized industries, describing price, wage, investment policies, and worker participation in management, with lists of all industrial and commercial fully or majority-state-owned enterprises as of December 1959 and statistics on major nationalized industries.

151 BAUM, WARREN C. The French economy and the state. Princeton, N.J., Princeton University Press, 1958. xvi, 391 p. tables. "Bibliographical notes": p. 359-373. Bibliography: p. 375-384.

Systematic study sponsored by Rand Corporation presenting full range of state intervention in economy, but giving no data beyond 1956.

152 BEAU DE LOMENIE, EMMANUEL. L'Algerie trahie par l'argent - réponse à M. Raymond Aron. Paris, Éditions Etheel, 1957. 109 p.

Answers arguments in Aron's "La tragédie algérienne" (see no. 831), by predicting catastrophic consequences to all of Europe if France is pushed out of Africa. Aron, says author, speaks for large capitalists in Algeria who would be compensated in any case and could place money more profitably elsewhere.

153 BEAU DE LOMENIE, EMMANUEL. Le référendum des affairistes; votez non à la finance internationale. Paris, Ecrits de Paris 1961. 31 p.

Attack on supporters of January 1961 referendum on Algerian self-determination as tools of "affairistes" (French financiers with international ties) who have risen to power in de Gaulle's cabinet.

154 BEAUFRÉ, ANDRE. Dissuasion et stratégie. Paris, A. Colin, 1964. 207 p.

Analysis of bilateral and multilateral nuclear deterrence methods, based on general's research at Institut Français d'études stratégiques 1963-64, followed by author's conclusions on proper military strategy for France and Atlantic Alliance. Beaufré is editor of periodical "Stratégie" (see no. 2104).

155 BEAUFRE, ANDRE. L'expédition de Suez, Paris, B. Brasset, 1967. 246 p. plates, ports, plans.

Eye-witness account of undertaking by one of its principal military leaders, with conclusion that it failed because military action remained isolated from political context.

156 BEAUFRE, ANDRE. L'O.T.A.N. et l'Europe. Paris, Calmann-Lévy, 1966. 236 p. (Questions d'actualité)

NATO crisis serves as point of departure for examining organization's present frailties and making proposals for renovating the Atlantic Alliance by giving equal weight to U.S. and political-strategic directorate of Western European governments, joined together in a sort of "military common market." General Beaufré a former top NATO official, tries to make French stand plausible to U.S.

157 BEAUMONT, PIERRE DE. La IVe République; politique intérieure et européenne. Préf. de René Pleven. Bruxelles, Librairie Encyclopédique, 1960. 99 p. tables. "Bibliographie": 99-100.

Evolution of main political parties during Fourth Republic and first year of Fifth Republic in terms of their programs and participation in successive governments, as well as policies actually adopted, particularly on European integration.

158 BEAUVOIR, SIMONE DE, and GISELE HALIMI. Djamila Boupacha; the story of the torture of a young Algerian girl which shocked liberal French opinion. Translated from the French by Peter Green. New York, Macmillan 1962. 250 p. ports.

French lawyer Gisèle Halimi's account of her own struggle during 1960 to establish the fact that Djamila Boupacha was tortured and move the case from Algeria to a French court. Simone de Beauvoir, who introduces this account, headed her defense committee. Included are testimonies by Henri Alleg, Madame Maurice Audin, General de Bollardière, R. P. Chenu, Daniel Mayer, Jean-François Revel, Jules Roy, and Françoise Sagan.

158a BEAUVOIR, SIMONE DE. La force des choses. Paris, Gallimard, 1963. 686 p. Bibliographical footnotes. ML

Final third of this autobiography concentrates on author's personal involvement in supporting the F.L.N. 1959-1961 and in the political trials against opponents of the Algerian war. English translation published as "Force of Circumstance" (New York, 1965).

159 BEDJAOUI, MOHAMMED. La révolution algérienne et le droit; préf. de Pierre Cot. Bruxelles, Editions de l'Association internationale des juristes démocrates, 1961. 262 p. fold. map. Bibliographical footnotes.

Algerian nationalist, who is a French-trained jurist, systematically explains political institutions of Algerian revolution: F.L.N., Army of National Liberation (A.L.N.) the Algerian Provisional Government. Their stand on political questions (e.g., the Sahara) at beginning of 1961 Evian conference is defined. A long section treats the international recognition of the provisional government and the F.L.N.'s respect of conventions of international law. Final section deals with organization of a self-determination referendum acceptable to Algerian negotiators.

160 BEHR, EDWARD. The Algerian problem. London, Hodder and Stoughton, 1961. 256 p. illus. Includes bibliography.: 255-256.

Journalist, on "Time" staff in North Africa since 1951, tries to give impartial picture of Algerian problem, going back to history of French conquest and covering systematically, from its inception, the Algerian nationalist struggle as well as the reactions of successive French governments, European settlers, Army. Particular stress is given to de Gaulle's steps for ending war, although book was concluded before completion of negotiations. Good discussions of Algeria's economy and the controversy on the use of torture. Photographs of French and nationalist leaders.

161 BELLEVILLE, PIERRE. Une nouvelle classe ouvrière. Paris, R. Julliard, 1963. 316 p. (Collection "Les temps modernes")

Author analyses changes in structure of French working class in terms of specific industrial situations (steel production in Lorraine, textile industry in Roubaix, railroads, hydroelectric industry in Grenoble, the strike action in mines in early 1963) and describes the role of the major trade union organizations. His contention is that the tendency is toward greater participation in enterprises for all types of employees, rather than class struggle or integration into neo-capitalism.

162 BELOFF, NORA. The General says no; Britain's exclusion from Europe. London, Penguin Books, 1963. 180 p. (A Penguin special. S201)

"Observer" correspondent personally acquainted with many officials involved in Franco-British Common Market negotiations, examines de Gaulle's personality and attitudes toward Great Britain, U.S., European unification and gives history of Great Britain's vacillating position on European ties.

163 BELORGEY, GERARD. Le gouvernement et l'administration de la France; préf. de François Gazier. Paris, A. Colin, 1967. 447 p. diagrs. (Collection U; Série "Société politique") Includes bibliography.

Experienced civil servant's informative, up-to-date, and unconventional survey of the Fifth Republic's administrative structure. One section examines its foundation in the 1958 constitutional provisions, another the different governmental organs and their functions, the parliamentary control through the vote on the budget, a third section describes legal, material and human instruments of administration on a national, departmental, and local plane. A final section describes administrative means of fostering regional economic development, including that of the Paris area. Annexed readings, documents, bibliography for each chapter.

164 BENEBDALLAH, ABDESSAMAD, MOURAD OUSSEDIK and JACQUES VERGES. Nuremberg pour l'Algérie! Paris, F. Maspero, 1961. 2 v. illus. ("Libertés," 2, 4)

Algerian lawyers' evidence of crimes against humanity by French army in Algerian war, produced January 1961. First volume cites international convention on genocide. Second volume is text of legal defense of publisher and two of the authors for their part in publication of pamphlet.

165 BEN BARKA, ABDELKADER. El Mehdi Ben Barka, mon frère. Paris, R. Laffont, 1966. 251 p. illus., ports.

Political biography, with chronology, of assassinated Moroccan nationalist, written by his younger brother who demanded the reopening of the case by French authorities in 1966. For other works on al-Mehdi Ben Barka, see Author Index under Bin Barakah.

166 BEN KHEDDA, BEN YOUSSEF. Statement by Mr. Benyoussef Benkhedda, Premier of the Provisional Government of the Algerian Republic, Tunis, May 9, 1962. New York, 1962. 4 l. (Delegation of the Provisional Government of the Algerian Republic, N.Y.) Doc. 62-10-E

167 BEN KHEDDA, BEN YOUSSEF. Statement by Mr. Benyoussef Benkhedda, Premier of the Provisional Government of the Algerian Republic on the occasion of the French-Algerian agreement and the proclamation of the cease-fire in Algeria, Tunis, March 18, 1962. New York, 1962. 6 l. (Delegation of the Provisional Government of the Algerian Republic, N.Y.) Doc. 62-6-E

168 BEN KHEDDA, BEN YOUSSEF. Text of the declaration made by Premier Benyoussef Benkhedda on behalf of the Provisional Government of the Algerian Republic, Tunis, October 24, 1961. New York, 1961. 3 l. (Delegation of the Provisional Government of the Algerian Republic, N.Y., distr.) Doc. 61-35-E

169 BENZINE, ABDELHAMID. Le camp. Préf. d'Henri Alleg. Paris, Éditions sociales, 1962. 94 p.

Author, collaborator on "Alger Républicain" and Algerian Communist Party member, writes of his experiences in special detention camp for A.L.N. prisoners at Boghari, where he was imprisoned in 1961.

170 BERARD, ARMAND. U.N. Security Council votes to recommend the admission of the Malagasy Republic to the United Nations; address, New York, 1960. 4 p. (France. Ambassade. U.S. Service de presse et d'information.)

171 BERARD, ARMAND. U.N. Security Council votes to recommend the admission of the Mali Federation to the United Nations; address... June 28, 1960. New York, 1960. 5 p. (France. Ambassade. U.S. Service de presse et d'information.)

172 BERGASSE, HENRY. Histoire de l'Assemblée, des élections de 1789 aux élections de 1967. Paris, Payot, 1967. 365 p. (Bibliothèque historique)

Short but informative final chapter on National Assembly in the Fifth Republic, summarizing its year-by-year evolution (changing composition, relations with government, stand on main issues) 1958-1967.

173 BERQUE, JACQUES. Dépossession du monde. Paris, Editions du Seuil, 1964. 214 p.

Essays on sociological and psychological forces set in motion in process of decolonization, with specific examples drawn from French North Africa. See also Berque's contribution under no. 439.

174 BERTIN, GILLES Y. L'investissement des firmes étrangères en France, 1945-1962. Paris, Presses universitaires de France, 1963. 323 p. illus. (Études économiques internationales) Bibliography: p. 313-318.

Economist's carefully documented study on foreign investments in France: theoretical motivation of foreign investors, the form investment has taken in France particularly since the initiation of the Common Market (size of total investment, distribution by country of origin, industrial sector), and its impact on French economy (regional development, competition, technical progress). Appendix summarizes figures on foreign investment, 1955-61 and lists major French firms with substantial foreign participation.

175 BEUCHARD, GEORGES. L'équivoque algérienne. Paris, Debresse, 1959. 94 p.

After examining all the misapprehensions concealed under terms "integration" and "Algerian personality," author appeals to de Gaulle to trace a clear path rather than continue past ambiguities.

176 BEUVE-MÉRY, HUBERT. Le suicide de la IVe République, by Sirius (pseud.) Paris, Éditions du Cerf, 1958. 116 p. (Tout le monde en parle)

"Le Monde" editor's collected articles on the weaknesses of the Fourth Republic, written for his newspaper between 1945 and June 3, 1958, with over half of this autopsy devoted to the weeks between April 25 and June 3, 1958.

176a BEYSSADE, PIERRE. La guerre d'Algérie, 1954-1962. Paris, Editions Planète, 1968. 269 p. Bibliographical footnotes.

Rather than a military history of the Algerian war, this equitable work by a French administrator in Algeria uses a chronological approach to synthesize and clarify all the elements which contributed to the course of the conflict, basing himself on the vast literature that has accumulated. The first half of the book reviews events during the Fourth Republic: political origins of the revolution, responses of the successive French governments, both military and political, the chain of events leading to the collapse of the Fourth Republic. The second half shows the phases of Gaullist disengagement and civilian and military countermoves in Algeria, with a final chapter on the genesis, deployment, and disbandment of O.A.S. No bibliography or index.

176b BIBLIOGRAPHIE DE LA FRANCE (periodical). L'édition française, numéro du cent-cinquantenaire. Paris, Cercle de la librairie, 1961. xxxvi, 207 p. illus., ports., facsims.

Main part of this special issue is devoted to alphabetically arranged publicity for over 160 leading French publishers (as of 1961) with information on their founding, staff, current publications and collections. Many small, politically oriented publishing houses are not represented.

177 BIDAULT, GEORGES. Algérie, l'oiseau aux ailes coupées. Paris, Table ronde, 1958. 226 p.

Collection of articles published in "Carrefour" on political events in North Africa 1955 - Spring 1958, with pleas for French Algeria.

178 BIDAULT, GEORGES. D'une résistance à l'autre. Paris, Presses du Siècle, 1965. 382 p. Includes bibliography.

About half of this volume of political memoirs deals with years leading up to and including the Fifth Republic. Emphasis is on foreign policy (Indochina, North Africa, Algerian policy before and after peace treaty). The final section covers Bidault's role in the Conseil National de la Résistance in 1962, the kidnaping of Col. Argoud, one of his collaborators in Germany, and his years in exile. A postscript gives a 1965 evaluation of Gaullist institutions. Includes name index. German translation: "Noch einmal Rebell; von einer Resistance in die andere." (Berlin, Propyläen Verlag, 1966), and English translation "Resistance, the Political Autobiography of Georges Bidault" (New York, Praeger, 1967)

FOR ADDITIONAL WORKS BY AND ABOUT GEORGES BIDAULT, SEE AUTHOR INDEX

179 BIENAYME, ALAIN. Politique de l'innovation et répartition des revenus; essai sur les relations intersectorielles dans l'économie française contemporaine. Avant-propos de J. Dehaussu. Préf. de B. Ducros. Paris, Cujas, 1966. 179 p. (Travaux et recherches de la Faculté de droit et des sciences économiques de Dijon 1) Bibliographical footnotes.

Sector by sector analysis of productivity gains in different industries and repercussion thereof on wages, prices, and output. Author's thesis is that inflation has gone hand in hand with productivity gains because most technologically advanced industries have increased their share of national product through product differentiation, while only in textiles and agriculture higher productivity has meant less resources devoted to these sectors and a relative decline in wages.

180 BILLOTTE, PIERRE. Du pain sur la planche. Paris, Plon, 1965. 189 p.

Text of speeches before National Assembly and elsewhere, 1964 - June 1965 and summer 1965 comments. Author is founding member of Union Démocratique du Travail and Gaullist deputy after 1962. Texts collected shortly before presidential campaign justify Gaullist institutions as the optimum combination of freedom and authority and Gaullist foreign policy as a rational interpretation of Atlantic Alliance (of which author was one of instigators).

181 BILLY, JACQUES. Les techniciens et le pouvoir. 2. ed. Paris, Presses universitaires de France, 1963. 126 p. (Que sais-je? no. 881) Includes bibliography and bibliographical footnotes.

First half of book surveys rise to position of influence in France of technocrats, second half describes this group and the nature of their power in France of early 1960's, with statistics on composition and income. Good up-to-date bibliographical footnotes.

182 BIN BARAKAH, AL MAHDI. Option révolutionnaire au Maroc. Suivi de Écrits politiques 1960-1965. Paris, F. Maspero, 1966. 167 p. (Cahiers libres, 84-85)

"Option révolutionnaire" was presented as a report to Moroccan Union nationale des forces populaires at its 1962 congress. Here and in other political studies Moroccan socialist leader shows failure of political independence to lead to economic growth and greater social equality. Book does not shed light on author's violent death.

183 BISHOP, DONALD GORDON. The future of the new political system in France. Santa Barbara, Calif., Technical Military Planning Operation, General Electric Co., 1959. 27 l. (TEMPO report; research memorandum, RM 59TMP-90) Includes bibliography.

American political scientist's assessment of Fifth Republic's promise of political and economic stability and prospects for French Community, Algeria, NATO under new regime. Author is sceptical about the impact of the new institutions as such and looks only to de Gaulle for decisive changes.

184 BJØL, ERLING. La France devant l'Europe; la politique européenne de la IVe République. Copenhague, Munksgaard, 1966. 456 p. Bibliographical references included in "Notes" (p. 307-350)

Aarhus University (Denmark) doctoral dissertation analyzing the decision-making process in foreign affairs, as exemplified by French European policy, 1950-1957. Attitudes and actions of the main parties (M.R.P., Socialists, Radicals, Independents, Gaullists, Communists, and Poujadists) are individually studied, as are those of business and labor groups. Appendix gives text of 18 interviews held in 1964 with representatives from these parties and groups, as well as individuals active in European unification in which past and present attitudes on European unification are clarified.

185 BLAMONT, EMILE. Le Parlement dans la Constitution de 1958. Paris, Librairies techniques, 1960. 35 p.

Legal framework established by 1958 Constitution for Assembly and Senate organization and operating procedures.

186 BLANC, DANIEL. Après les armes, citoyens. Paris, UDAA 1962? 153 p.

Reconstruction of typical attitudes to Algerian war among contingent (non-officer draftees): degree of political commitment to French Algeria, on the one hand, responsiveness to communist indoctrination on the other (both were nearly nil), feelings toward professional officers, European and Moslem inhabitants and in the end toward the repatriated "pieds-noirs" in France. Author stresses the political education war experience brought to the nearly 3 million draftees that took part in it, giving basic figures for social background and career perspectives of these young veterans.

187 BLANC, EMMANUEL. Les institutions françaises, racontées aux Français. Paris, Éditions de Minuit, 1959. 457 p.

Civics manual presenting institutions governing private and public life of French citizens, with only minor references to those introduced since beginning of Fifth Republic.

188 BLAUDIN DE THE, BERNARD MARIE SAMUEL. Essai de bibliographie du Sahara français et des régions avoisinantes. 2. éd. Édité avec le concours de l'Organisation commune des Régions sahariennes. Paris, Arts et métiers graphiques, 1960. 258 p.

First section reprints 1923, 1930 bibliographies, but second 200-page section by Blaudin de Thé covers different aspects of Sahara (natural and human sciences) with lists of books, articles, and documents through 1958, totalling 9300 items. Author index and list (with addresses) of main periodicals cited.

189 BLETON, PIERRE. Le capitalisme français... Paris, Éditions Économie et humanisme, Éditions ouvrières, 1966. 263 p. illus. (Initiation économique, 6) Bibliography: p. 253-255.

Descriptive analysis of French capitalism: major industrial firms and their interconnections, major investment institutions. Author claims that privately owned companies and wealthy individuals no longer play a leading role in the dynamic French economy, and that technical experts are taking over decision-making.

190 BLOCH-LAINE, FRANÇOIS. A la recherche d'une "économie concertée." 3. éd. Paris, Éditions de l'Épargne, 1964. 23 p. (De quoi s'agit-il?)

1959 speech and 1960 addenda on trends in France toward a system of permanent voluntary planning in which state acts as information collector and harmonizer of investment plans between firms.

191 BLOCH-LAINE, FRANÇOIS. Pour une réforme de l'entreprise. Paris, Editions du Seuil, 1963, 158 p. (Collection Histoire immédiate) ML

Author is head of "Caisse de dépots," which funds major French investments. This work is the outcome of his consultation with Club Jean Moulin and representatives of management, trade unions, and civil servants on needed changes and specific proposals for a new legal apparatus to foster economic democracy within enterprises and to take account of France's thoroughly "mixed" economy by the creation of special arbitration courts for conflicts between economic groups, changing property laws.

FOR ADDITIONAL WORKS BY AND ABOUT FRANÇOIS BLOCH-LAINE, SEE AUTHOR INDEX

192 BLOCH-MORHANGE, JACQUES. Fonder l'avenir; une dynamique sociale pour les Français. Paris, A. Fayard, 1962. 186 p. (Les idées et la vie)

A French road for economic growth and achievement of high-priority welfare objectives by member of Conseil économique et social.

193 BLOCH-MORHANGE, JACQUES. Le gaullisme. Paris, Plon, 1963. 238 p. ML

Gaullist journalist reviews pillars of Gaullist regime: favorable attitudes of women, good relations with "notables," - that is, politicians, military, civil servants, industrialists, labor leaders, agricultural organizations. He examines underlying principles of foreign policy and Gaullist philosophy of civism and education, gauging prospects of maintaining Gaullist majority in power after de Gaulle and reiterating his own 10-year plan (drawn up in 1958) for a program of social justice. (See no. 192.)

194 BLOCH-MORHANGE, JACQUES. Les politiciens. Paris, A. Fayard, 1961. 251 p.

Editor of "Informations et conjoncture" gives behind-the-scene anecdotal account of foreign affairs developments from Fourth to Fifth Republic. There are portraits of dozens of leading parliamentarians and other prominent politicians such as Bidault, Monnet, Edgar Faure, Lacoste, Mendès-France, coupled with unkind judgments by the author. The central episode concerns efforts by a group of anti-American and anti-Monnet politicians, the author among them, to defeat the European Defense Community. The book concludes with a description, as seen from Paris, of de Gaulle's return to power, in which author played a part. Includes memorandum given author by Pierre Poujade in autumn 1956 on his position toward de Gaulle. No index.

195 BLOCH-MORHANGE, JACQUES. Réponse à de Gaulle. Paris, Plon, 1966. 160 p. facsim.

Criticism of Fifth Republic's insufficient success in revitalizing economy and attracting support of new elites for regime, but approval of de Gaulle's international and military options. Includes exchange of letters with de Gaulle respecting author's previous works.

196 BLOCH-MORHANGE, JACQUES. La stratégie des fusées; postface de Paul Gérardot. Paris, Plon, 1958. 190 p. maps. (part fold. in pocket) (Les Documents de Tribune libre, 2)

On the basis of study of vulnerabilities of different countries, main industrial and military centers to Russian nuclear guided missiles, journalist urges reassessment of French reliance on U.S. nuclear deterrent. He predicts nuclear stalemate and advocates gradual downgrading of Atlantic Alliance as cornerstone of French relations, in favor of a more independent European and colonial policy. This study was drawn up December 1957.

197 BLOCQ-MASCART, MAXIME. La prochaine république sera-t-elle républicaine? Préf. de Michel Debré. Paris, Plon, 1958. xx, 90 p. (Tribune libre, 23)

Journalist's prophetic vision, November 1957, of a new regime brought into being by the Algerian crisis and headed by de Gaulle. He proposes a federal constitution in which Algeria and other overseas territories would have a fitting place. Debré's preface, written in early 1958, expresses faith that de Gaulle would tide France over to more stable political institutions.

198 BLOND, GEORGES. La Légion étrangère. Paris, Stock, 1964. 427 p. maps.

Last 50 pages of this sympathetic history of Foreign Legion relate its military contributions in Algerian war and role in 1961 Generals' Putsch.

199 BOCCA, GEOFFREY. La légion! The French Foreign Legion and the men who made it glorious. New York, Cromwell, 1964. viii, 307 p. illus., ports. Bibliography: p. 295-300.

Final 100 pages of this popular work on Foreign Legion concern its involvement in Algerian war, part in 1961 Generals' Putsch and departure from Algeria.

200 BOCCA, GIORGIO. Les jeunes lions de l'économie européenne. I giovani leoni del neocapitalismo. Traduit de l'italien par Jacqueline Rémillet. Paris, R. Laffont, 1964. 204 p.

Italian journalist's investigation of young French industrialists' careers, their professional organizations, changes in business structure and changes in ideology. The study also briefly presents examples of Italian, German, and Swiss businessmen.

201 BODIN, LOUIS. Les intellectuels. Paris, Presses universitaires de France, 1962. 124 p. tables. (Que sais-je?) "Bibliographie sommaire": p. 123-124.

Broad definition of term "intellectuals" in contemporary society, with few figures going beyond 1956, although some of bibliographical references deal with current French situation.

202 BÖKENKAMP, WERNER. Frankreich, Maske und Gesicht. Karlsruhe, Stahlberg, 1964. 253 p.

Comments on French daily life, literature, political events, education, by cultural correspondent for "Frankfurter Allgemeine Zeitung" in Paris, 1952-1964.

203 BOGANDA, BARTHELEMY. Pres. Central African Republic. Enfin, on décolonise. 2. éd., Bangui, Impr. centrale d'Afrique, 1962. 38 p. port.

Speeches by President Boganda, October 5, 1957 - September 7, 1958, as well as de Gaulle's brief Brazzaville address outlining his conception of new French Community shortly before referendum on 1958 Constitution.

204 BOISDE, RAYMOND. Technocratie et démocratie. Paris, Plon, 1964. 251 p.

Deputy belonging to Independent Republican Party describes increasing sway of technical experts in governmental decisions, as illustrated by governmental planning, which he contrasts with weaknesses of political forces (labor and business groups, political parties, parliament). Author suggests methods for giving people and elected politicians better understanding of and greater participation in major technical decisions. Views reflect preoccupations of managerial groups in private industry.

205 BOISSEL, PIERRE. Les Hussards perdus ... Paris Éditions Saint-Just, 1966. 255 p. (Collection "Action," 17)

Combat experiences of career officer in parachutist regiment (formed from hussar or light cavalry elements) in Algeria, 1959-1961, giving combat troops' view of January 1960 and April 1961 uprisings in Algers.

206 BOISSON, JEAN. Essai sur le problème algérien. Paris, Éditions du Scorpion, 1960. 286 p. (Collection Alternance)

Background of Algerian problem - political, economic, and social in 130 years of Algerian colonization. Author refutes charges of exploitation and racism against France and French settlers, but quotes pro- and anti-French views.

207 BOISSON, O. and MONTEIL. Législation, administration et comptabilité militaires. Paris, O. Lavauzelle, 1959. 460 p.

Textbook for military personnel on Fifth Republic's political institutions and organization of national defense, as well as on all laws and statutes affecting military service, rights and duties of members of armed forces.

208 BOISSONNAT, JEAN. La politique des revenus. Paris, Éditions du seuil, 1966. 128 p. (Société, 10.) Bibliographical footnotes.

French income distribution and Fifth Republic's measures related to wage policy and income redistribution.

209 BOKANOWSKI, MICHEL MAURICE. Contre le Parti communiste et ses organisations satellites; étude présentée au nom de la Fédération du 5e Secteur de la Seine. Paris, 1957. 10 p. (Républicains sociaux. 2nd Congress, Bordeaux, 1957)

Foreign anti-communist legislation and Républicains sociaux's own proposals for purging communists from administration, army and outlawing French Communist Party.

210 BONHEUR, GASTON. Charles de Gaulle; biographie, éd. 14. Paris, Gallimard, 1958. 302 p.

Nothing beyond 1956 and only a few pages on years at Colombey.

211 BONIFACE, JEAN. Arts de masse et grand public (La consommation culturelle en France) Préf. d'Alfred Sauvy. Paris, Les Éditions ouvrières, 1961, 1962. 160 p. (Collection "Vivre son temps"). Includes bibliography.

Pattern of consumption of cultural products: books, press, movies, radio, and television.

212 BONNAUD, JEAN JACQUES. Le Ve plan; une stratégie de l'expansion. Paris, Éditions de l'Epargne, 1967. 310 p. (De quoi s'agit-il?)

Evolution of planning techniques, achievements of Fourth's Plan, elaboration and contents of Fifth Plan.

213 BONNAUD, ROBERT. Itinéraire. Préf. de Pierre Vidal-Naquet. Paris, Éditions de Minuit, 1962. 155 p. (Documents)

Collection of letters and articles, 1956-1961, by active opponent of Algerian war imprisoned 1961 for tie-up with Réseau Jeanson. Writings reflect his military experiences in Algeria and subsequent vain efforts to encourage a more militant stand on part of French left, and promote desertions in French army.

214 BONNEFOUS, EDOUARD. Les milliards qui s'envolent; l'aide française aux pays sous-développés. Paris, Fayard, 1963. 293 p. Includes bibliography.

History of French colonial expenditures and the nature of economic and technical aid after decolonization. Author decries incoherence of programs and extent of burden on French economy, advocating more multilateral or at least Common Market aid. The case of Algeria is described to prove the futility of aid as a means of keeping a country from communist path. Appendix gives tabulations of aspects of French and other nations' aid to underdeveloped countries.

215 BONNET, GABRIEL GEORGES MARCEL. Les guerres insurrectionnelles et révolutionnaires de l'antiquité à nos jours. Paris, Payot, 1958. 287 p. (Bibliothèque historique) Includes bibliography.

Colonel and professor at Ecole supérieure de guerre gives historical antecedents of revolutionary warfare, with last section on Algerian experience.

216 BONNET, GEORGES ETIENNE. Le Quai d'Orsay sous trois Républiques, 1870-1961. Paris, A. Fayard, 1961. 519 p.

Short final chapter on diplomacy under Fifth Republic.

217 BONTE, FLORIMOND. Le militarisme allemand et la France. Préf. de Jeannette Vermeersch. Paris, Éditions sociales, 1961. 242 p.

Member of French Communist Party's Central Committee and deputy for Paris marshals traditional arguments about German militarism and Soviet peaceloving policy, condemning de Gaulle for reversing his own pro-Soviet policy by his military alliance with Adenauer. The French Communist Party's encouragements of peace movements in France and Germany in 1960 are detailed. Documents include 1960 interview with Maurice Thorez in "Neues Deutschland."

218 BORELLA, FRANÇOIS. Le gouvernement des Français; éléments d'initiation civique. Paris, Éditions de l'Epi, 1960. 334 p. ills. Includes bibliography. 38 p.

Civics textbook by law professor describing the functioning of public power in France and the French Community and the ties binding France to international organizations, as of 1959. July 1963 supplement summarizes changes in political institutions and dissolution of French Community.

219 BORIS, GEORGES. Servir la République; textes et témoignages. Présentation de Pierre Mendès France. Paris, R. Julliard, c1963. 493 p. ports.

Only concluding pages record reactions to early months of Fifth Republic.

220 BORNECQUE-WINANDYE, EDOUARD. Droit et contentieux des élections législatives et sénatoriales. Paris, les Éditions sociales françaises, 1967. 126 p.

Exposition of electoral code for local and national legislative elections currently in force (1958 code and 1966 amendments) accompanied by decisions of Conseil Constitutionnel, 1958-1966 on contested elections. Appendix includes 1966 electoral districts and newly created departments in Paris region.

221 BORTOLI, GILBERT. Sociologie du référendum dans la France moderne. Préf. de Robert Charlier. Paris, Librairie générale de droit et de jurisprudence, R. Pichon et R. Durand-Auzias, 1965. 412 p. maps. (Bibliothèque constitutionnelle et de science politique, t. 13) Includes bibliography.

Volume deals mainly with referenda under Fifth Republic: September 1958, January 1961, April and October 1962. After description of individual referenda, position taken by parties, sociological and geographic distribution of opinions in Guallist France, final section reproduces poll of political leaders after 1961 referendum on value of this method of popular consultation and compares results to de Gaulle's own position.

222 BOSWORTH, WILLIAM. Catholicism and crisis in modern France; French Catholic groups at the threshold of the Fifth Republic. Princeton, N.J., Princeton University Press, 1962. xv, 407 p. maps, diagrs, tables. "Bibliographical essay": p. 361-395.

Much material on political aspects of Catholicism: Catholic social action groups, press, Catholic-inspired political parties and organizations relations to state, stand on school question, with a number of statistical breakdowns. Extensive annotated bibliography. American scholar based study in part on interviews with Catholic figures between 1958 and 1960 (names given).

222a BOUALAM, SAÏD BENAISSA. L'Algérie sans la France. By Bachaga Boualam. Paris, Éditions France-Empire, 1964. 352 p.

History of final months before independence, documents on violation of Evian agreements, massacres of pro-French Moslems after independence, failures of French cooperation and critical views on Algerian version of a popular democracy, with emphasis on the drift toward Communist world.

223 BOUALAM, SAÏD BENAISSA. Les Harkis au service de la France. By Bachage Boualam. Paris, Éditions France-Empire, 1963. 269 p. illus.

Author, Algerian tribal chief as well as deputy in National Assembly, of which he was vice-president at one time, served as one of commanders of Harkis, the auxiliary troops made up of non-European Algerians, first organized in 1957 and disbanded at close of Algerian war. This is a combat history of the individual units and an account of their eventual fate after independence and relocation in French camps.

224 BOUALAM, SAÏD BENAISSA. Mon pays ... la France! Paris, Editions France-Empire, 1962. 265 p. plates, ports.

Author's personal and family ties to France, his own experiences in National Assembly, and his relocation in France together with his large family, May 1962, are reviewed after Algerian independence. He gives his own interpretation of France's achievements in Algeria and of the internal political factors which led to abandonment: the pressure of the French Left (he gives some details on Algerian Communist Henri Maillot, who tried to form a "Red maquis") and describes his gradual disillusionment with de Gaulle.

225 BOUDIAF, MOHAMED, 1919. Où va l'Algérie? Paris, Éditions Librairie de l'Étoile, 1964. 208 p. (Notre révolution, 1)

Algerian nationalist who subsequently became an opponent of Ben Bella's government describes his 1963 imprisonment, his ideological quarrel with Ben Bella, and his own down-to-earth program for introducing democratic socialism in Algeria.

226 BOUDOT, PIERRE. L'Algérie mal enchaînée. Paris, Gallimard, 1961. 292 p.

December 1958 - February 1960 diary of sensitive, liberal French officer serving in "psychological action" unit in Orania and his frustrated attempts to engage dialogue with F. L. N.

227 BOUHALI, LARBI. La guerre de libération et la lutte pour la paix. [n. p., 1961?] 19 p.

18

Pamphlet by Secretary of Algerian Communist Party situating Algerian war of liberation in framework of "anti-imperialist" struggle.

227a BOUISSOU, MICHEL. La Reconnaissance de la République populaire de Chine devant l'opinion ... Paris, Presses universitaires de France, 1967. viii, 96 p. (Travaux et recherches de la Faculté de droit et de sciences économiques de Paris. Série Sciences politiques, 9) Bibliography: p. 94-95.

Case study of how Gaullist government makes use of mass media to guide public opinion on foreign policy questions, the effectiveness of government action, and the response of the press. The example chosen is the government's decision to recognize Communist China, January 1964.

228 BOURDET, CLAUDE. Les chemins de l'unité. Paris, F. Maspero, 1964. 94 p. (Cahiers libres, no. 57)

The unity which left-wing journalist and P.S.U. leader has in mind is that between Communist and non-Communist Left. Book analyzes realistically aspects of French Communist Party standing in way of unity and what guarantees it could give to overcome genuine "anti-communism" on Left. His method of transcending split is axed on labor movement rather than ephemeral political alliances.

229 BOURDIER, JEAN. Le Comte de Paris; un cas politique. Paris, Table Ronde, 1965. 229 p. (L'Histoire contemporaine revue et corrigée)

Political career of Count of Paris, emphasizing his role in February 1934 and Darlan murder and his increasing dependence on de Gaulle's support for his last chance of attaining power - as his successor. Only final chapter deals with Fifth Republic.

230 BOURDIER, JEAN. La dictature qui vient; la technocratie. Paris, Presses continentales, 1959. 73 p. (Les Documents français, 4)

Violent indictment of Gaullist regime for strengthening the "technocrats'" control over France. Technocrats are accused of denying all traditional national values (including maintenance of French Algeria) and supporting international finance by favoring European integration.

231 BOURDIEU, PIERRE. The Algerians. Translated by Alan C. M. Ross. With a pref. by Raymond Aron. Boston, Beacon Press, 1962. xiv, 208 p. illus., maps. Bibliography: p. 202-203.

Translation of revised 1961 edition of "Sociologie de l'Algérie" with an extensive final section describing the breakdown of traditional culture produced by the consequences of the Algerian war (resettlement policy, creation of national consciousness). Author sees no hope for reforming colonial system or integration in the face of sociological factors, but only for a new, indigenous, collective modern society. Good maps, graphic presentations of social and economic structure as of 1960. Glossary of Arab terms.

231a BOURDIEU, PIERRE and ADBELMALEK SAYAD. Le déracinement; la crise de l'agriculture traditionnelle en Algérie. Paris, Éditions de Minuit, 1964. 225 p. tables, diagrs. (Grands documents, 14)

Presentation of resettlement policy incorporated in pacification program and which affected over two million Algerians by 1960 as a culminating point in the destruction of traditional Algerian agriculture and society. Operation of several resettlement centers is described to explain effect of salaried work and urbanization in breaking down traditional values. Authors emphasize that contradictions between peasant mentality and economic rationality will not automatically disappear in an independent socialist Algeria.

232 BOURDIEU, PIERRE and JEAN-CLAUDE PASSERON. Les étudiants et leurs études. Avec la collaboration de Michel Eliard. Paris, Mouton, 1964. 149 p. forms., diagrs. (Ecole pratique des hautes études. VIe section: Sciences économiques et sociales. Centre de sociologie de l'éducation, 1)

Results of questionnaires given to students preparing degrees in sociology and philosophy at Sorbonne and 6 provincial universities 1961-1963, in which variables such as age, sex, social origins were correlated with political attitudes, professional orientation, cultural level.

233 BOURDIEU, PIERRE and JEAN-CLAUDE PASSERON. Les héritiers; les étudiants et la culture. Paris, Éditions de Minuit, 1966. 191 p. illus. (Le Sens commun)

Conclusions based on several sociological investigations of student attitudes toward their studies: their self-image as students, representation of age, sex, and social groups in university as a whole and in different academic branches. Authors demonstrate not only the systematic underrepresentation of students of worker and farmer origin but the way in which the existing system of education works to the disadvantage of students whose families are not culture-oriented, so that democratization of higher education cannot be achieved merely by financial support but must be reinforced by a pedagogic revolution. Appendices reproduce figures from Bourdieu's "Les étudiants et leurs études" and from government statistical services giving historic evolution of university attendance, 1900-1963 and social breakdown for 1961-62 academic year for all of France.

234 BOURDIEU, PIERRE. Sociologie de l'Algérie. Paris, Presses universitaires de France, 1958. 126, 1 p. ("Que sais-je?" no. 802) "Bibliographie sommaire": p. 127.

French sociologist describes traditional social structure of four main segments of non-European Algerian population: Kabyles, Chaoui, Arabs, Mozabites, their common heritage, and the impact of French colonialism thereon.

FOR ADDITIONAL WORKS BY PIERRE BOURDIEU, SEE AUTHOR INDEX

234a BOURGES, HERVE. L'Algérie à l'épreuve du pouvoir (1962-1967). Préface de Jacques Berque. Paris, B. Grasset, 1967. 247 p.

Well-informed political history of independent Algeria and evaluation of how close Algeria has come to implementing its revolutionary objectives. Author was only Frenchman who played an important advisory role in Algerian government from 1962 to 1966.

235 BOUSCAT, RENE. De Gaulle Giraud, dossier d'une mission. Paris, Flammarion, 1967. 237 p. (Argos)

Personal account by French air force general of his role in bringing de Gaulle to North Africa, May 1943. Bouscat, who had remained aloof from all political commitments, was sent to London April 1943 as Giraud's personal representative to arrange for de Gaulle's acceptance of Giraud's position. Documents include London diary and correspondence.

236 BOUTANG, PIERRE. La terreur en question: lettre à Gabriel Marcel. Paris, Fasquelle, 1958. 113 p. (Collection "Libelles")

Editor of "Nation francaise" replies to Gabriel Marcel's appeal against torture in Algeria, in which Boutang puts blame on F.L.N. for inciting it by its own terrorism. He attacks French intellectuals who support F.L.N. and encourage defeatism.

237 BOUVIER-AJAM, MAURICE and GILBERT MURY. Les classes sociales en France. Paris, Éditions sociales, 1963, 2 v. Bibliographical footnotes.

First volume is historical survey of social classes from Marxist viewpoint, second volume summarizes current sociological and statistical knowledge on French classes (business and managerial groups, technical personnel, salaried employees, industrial and agricultural workers) with interesting information on social mobility and consumption patterns. Validity of class struggle even under technologically advanced society is reaffirmed in conclusion and in postscript by Maurice Thorez.

238 BOYER DE LATOUR, PIERRE. Demain ... la France. Paris, Librairie française, 1965. 63 p.

Polemic against de Gaulle and failure of his Algerian and foreign policy, written in anticipation of presidential election, with program for reform of judicary institution and Senate, new economic and foreign policies, as well as appeal for a convention selecting a single opposition candidate to de Gaulle.

239 BOYER DE LATOUR, PIERRE. Le drame français. Paris, Au fil d'Ariane, 1963. 269 p.

French general's laments on the consequences of de Gaulle's Algerian policy: O.A.S., exodus of European settlers and criticism of de Gaulle's military policy: NATO, nuclear weapons, destruction of army "with a soul."

240 BOYER DE LATOUR, PIERRE. Le martyre de l'armée française; de l'Indochine à l'Algérie. Paris, Presses du Mail, 1962. 380 p. plates, ports., maps, facsims.

Concluded just before April 1961 Generals' putsch, general's work on French army's colonial defeats retraces at length the military and political evolution in Algeria since 1958, with a violently critical stand on de Gaulle's current Algerian policy.

241 BRACE, RICHARD MUNTHE, and JOAN BRACE. Algerian voices. Princeton, N.J., Van Nostrand, 1965. xi, 233 p. illus., group port.

Sympathetic personal impressions of FLN leaders and French sympathizers in Tunisia, April 20 - May 15, 1961, Feb. 1962. Description of conditions under which Algerian refugees subsist.

242 BRACE, RICHARD and JOAN BRACE. Ordeal in Algeria. New York, D. Van Nostrand, 1960. xi, 453 p. Bibliography included in "Notes" (p. 403-431)

American historian's popular work on the Algerian revolution, 1954-1960, with an effort to do justice to both French and nationalist point of view. There is a good deal of material on May 1958, de Gaulle's Algerian policy, the January 1960 uprising.

243 BRIGNEAU, EMMANUEL ALLOT, called FRANÇOIS. Mon après-guerre. Paris, Éditions du Clan, 1966. 363 p.

Memoirs (1944-1963) of reporter for "Paris-Presse-l'Intransigeant" (1958-1962) and "Aurore" (1962), as well as contributor to nationalist press. Last 100 pages deal with Fifth Republic and give glimpses of episodes such as Khrushchev's visit of state, political trials.

244 BROIZAT, JEAN. La fureur de mieux vivre; croissance économique et bien-être des Français. Illus. de Cavory. Paris, Editions de l'Entreprise modern, 1962. 207 p. illus. Includes bibliography.

26 charts and explanatory text surveying French economy (consumption patterns, price levels, income distribution, etc.) and demography of the 1960's and highlighting mechanisms of economic expansion.

245 BROMBERGER, MERRY, SERGE BROMBERGER, GEORGETTE ELGEY, and J.-F. CHAUVEL. Barricades et colonels, 24 janvier 1960. Paris, A. Fayard, 1960. 444 p.

Journalists' day-by-day inside account of January 1960 uprising in Algeria up to the fall of the barricades, moving back and forth between Algiers and Paris, with background material on earlier military and civilian plots against de Gaulle's Algerian policy. Good sketches of many military and civilian figures involved in plot, but no index.

246 BROMBERGER, MERRY. Le destin secret de Georges Pompidou. Paris, Fayard, 1965. 349 p.

Sympathetic political biography of French Prime Minister, with considerable information on his close collaboration with de Gaulle since 1944. The book covers critical issues during the Fifth Republic in which Pompidou had a share, such as the writing of the 1958 constitution, the 1962 referendum on the election of the president, economic and education policy 1962-1965.

247 BROMBERGER, MERRY, and SERGE BROMBERGER. Les 13 complots du 13 mai, ou La délivrance de Gulliver. Paris, A. Fayard, 1959. 443 p.

Journalists' detailed reconstruction of manipulations by military and political figures in Paris, Algeria, and Southern France leading to de Gaulle's return to power, May 5 - June 3, 1958. No index, but short sketches of dozens of participants.

248 BROMGERGER, SERGE. Les rebelles algériens. Paris, Plon, 1958. 278 p. maps.

Military and political history of Algerian revolution, 1954 - April 1958, inside Algeria and beyond its borders, by "Figaro" reporter with personal contacts among F.L.N. leaders.

249 BROUSSE, HENRI. Le niveau de vie en France. 2e éd. Paris, Presses universitaires de France, 1962. 127 p. maps, tables, diagrs. ("Que sais-je?" Le point des connaissances actuelles, no. 371). Bibliographical footnotes.

Statistical analysis by social groups and regions, of economic conditions (consumption statistics, employment, etc.) for 1949-1960.

250 BRUCLAIN, CLAUDE, Pseud. Le socialisme et l'Europe. Paris, Éditions du seuil, 1965. 141 p. (Collection Jean Moulin)

Club Jean Moulin study group under pen name of Claude Bruclain sifts socialist ideology to retain only those elements applicable to modern society (Sweden comes closest to ideal) and concludes that only European unification allows socialist values to be reconciled with the rapidly rising standard of living on which Western European masses now insist.

251 BRUHAT, JEAN, and MARC PIOLOT. Esquisse d'une histoire de la C.G.T., 1895-1965. 2e éd. Paris, Confédération générale du travail, 1967. 384 p. Bibliographical footnotes.

Last 100 pages concern C.G.T.'s opposition to Algerian war and to de Gaulle's return to power and its disapproval of social and economic policies of Fifth Republic, as expressed at recent congresses (work stops with C.G.T.'s 35th congress, May 1965).

252 BRUNE, JEAN. Cette haine qui ressemble à l'amour. Paris, Table ronde, 1961. 705 p.

Central figure in this novel dealing with the operations of the French Army in Kabylia at an unspecified date is a colonel who sees his duty in turning violence and hate into love, but is surrounded by the passions of European settlers, pro- and anti-French Algerians, Westernized and Islamic rebels, whose clashing views are sympathetically presented. For author's personal views, see nos. 74, 1311.

253 BRUNHOFF, SUZANNE DE. Capitalisme financier public; inluence économique de l'état en France, 1948-1958. Paris, Société d'édition d'enseignement supérieur, 1965. 212 p. (Paris, École pratique des hautes études. Observation économique, 22) Includes bibliography.

Covers whole range of state intervention in economy - public investment, fiscal and monetary policy, role of treasury, with some of data continued through 1958 and 1959. Good up-to-date bibliography on French economy.

254 BRUSSELS. UNIVERSITE LIBRE. INSTITUT DE SOCIOLOGIE. Les problèmes de la planification; colloque de janvier 1962. Publié avec l'appui de Ministère de l'education nationale et de la culture. Bruxelles, 1962. 264 p. (Its Etudes d'économie politique)

Speakers representing France and discussing French approach are Bernard Cazes "Démocratie et plan," Susini "Les techniques de planification," and François Perroux "Le IVe Plan français 1962-1965."

255 BUCHARD, ROBERT. Organisation armée secrète. Paris, A. Michel, 1963. 2 v illus. (Aujourd'hui)

Journalist for "Paris-Presse" writes inside history of O. A. S. from its founding in Madrid February 1961 to exodus of leaders July 1962. Volume 1 covers February - 14 December 1961, volume 2 covers December 15, 1961 - July 10, 1962.

256 BUFFELAN, JEAN PAUL. Le complot du 13 mai 1958 dans le sudouest. Préf. de Louis Périllier. Postface de Roger Miquel et de Joseph Cathala. Paris, Librairie générale de droit et de jurisprudence, R. Pichon et R. Durand-Auzias, 1966. 226 p. ports. (Bibliothèque constitutionnelle et de science politique, t. 17)

A close-up study of the confrontation of political forces in Toulouse region between May 13 and May 27, 1958: political parties, "Dépêche du Midi," military, Prefecture, Committee of Public Safety. Author was himself garrisoned in Toulouse at the time and has personally interviewed principal actors in drama: Prefect Louis Perillier, General Roger Miquel, the pivotal military figure, and Prof. Joseph Cathala, the leading plotter. In Appendix unpublished official communications and texts of leaflets. Good bibliography.

257 BUIS, GEORGES. La Grotte. Paris, P. Julliard, 1961. 317 p.

An episode in the pacification operations in an isolated mountain area serving as F. L. N. stronghold in 1958-1959 period. This forceful novel in which the liquidation of the rebels in a mysterious cave symbolizes the elusive struggle for the loyalty of the Algerian people gives insight into the relations between French Army and villagers and the meaning of "liberation" from rebel control as seen from French and native side.

258 BURDEAU, GEORGES. La démocratie. nouvelle éd. Paris, Éditions du Seuil, 1966. 185 p. (Politique) Includes bibliography.

Political theorist's reflections on evolving conceptions of democracy from purely political democracy to the current aspiration for social democracy, leading to strong governmental power. The nature of political institutions in Fifth Republic is defined as plebiscitary democracy with strong tendencies toward closed power.

258a BURDEAU, GEORGES. Droit constitutionnel et institutions politiques, conforme au programme des facultés de droit et écoles d'enseignement supérieur. 11 ed. Paris, Librairie générale de droit et de jurisprudence, 1965. 610 p.

Final third of work discusses 1958 constitution and the conceptions it embodies: electoral system, executive, legislative, and judiciary institutions, their functioning and evolution (French Community, presidential election, political tribunals.)

259 BUREAU D'INVESTISSEMENT EN AFRIQUE. Rapport annuel 1959, 1961. Paris, 2 vols.

Report on research and development work done by participating companies of Bureau in Algeria and Sahara (mining, oil, transportation, communications).

260 BURGARD, MARC. L'économie des mandarins; essai sur les problèmes économiques de notre temps. Paris, Sept couleurs, 1963. 239 p.

Business economist, keeping away from doctrinal quarrels, stresses problems of administration, decentralization, fiscal policy, and suggests ways of transcending rigidities of present structures and elites (the Mandarins of the title).

260a BURNIER, MICHEL ANTOINE. Les Existentialistes et la politique. Paris, Gallimard, 1966. 192 p. (Collection Idées, 116) Bibliographical footnotes.

Sympathetic presentation of political views and activities of group of intellectuals connected with "Temps modernes," 1945-1965, prominent among whom are Sartre, Merleau-Ponty, Jeanson, and in later years André Gorz. First part retraces abortive attempt to create a political "third force," second part shows fluctuating relations with Communist party and active opposition to Algerian war, final part concentrates on recent efforts to support revolutions in underdeveloped countries while revitalizing Marxist thought for modern industrial societies. Good bibliographic notes.

261 BURON, ROBERT. Carnets politiques de la guerre d'Algérie; par un signataire des Accords d'Évian. Paris, Plon, 1965. 267 p.

Political diary November 1954 - May 1962 of M. R. P. leader and consistent advocate of decolonization who was member of Mendès-France's government and Minister of Public Works under de Gaulle. He records discussions on Algerian policy at cabinet meetings, personal impressions on trips to Algeria, eye-witness accounts of Generals' Putsch April 1961 as prisoner with Delegate General in Algiers, stages of negotiations with F. L. N. at Evian Spring 1962 as one of principal negotiators, "inside" information on de Gaulle's vacillations on Algeria. For Soustelle's views on this diary, see no. 1655.

262 BURON, ROBERT. Le plus beau des métiers. Paris, Plon, 1963. 252 p.

Practical sides of politician's career - glorified as the most important profession for humanizing modern life - are illustrated by M. R. P. parliamentarian and member of Gaullist cabinet: how one becomes deputy and operates in National Assembly, what is the sphere of activity of cabinet members, etc. On the basis of his personal experiences, author examines institutional reforms under de Gaulle.

263 BUSINESS EUROPE (periodical). France's Fifth Republic and the business world [Business International French Roundtable] Paris, May 27-31, 1963. Geneva, 1963. 72 p. tables.

Memorandum drawn up by Business International on current state of French economy, with statistics on wages, prices, consumer spending, taxes, balance of payments, etc., and trends in government economic policy (budgetary, social, planning, investment, foreign trade and aid). Written with the cooperation of French government agencies, compendium is intended for the information of American investors in France.

264 BUY, FRANÇOIS. La République algérienne démocratique et populaire. Préface de Pierre André. Paris, Librairie française, 1965. 257 p. tables.

Political history of independent Algeria through Spring 1965, survey of its political institutions and its economic, defense, education, religious, and information policy, relations with Arab, Western, and Communist countries, and continuing ties with France. Author shows degradation of country's institutions and economy, as well as its drift into Communist orbit, notwithstanding French cooperation.

265 CACERES, BENIGNO. Histoire de l'éducation populaire. Paris, Éditions du Seuil, 1964. 253 p. illus., ports. Includes bibliography.

Final chapter and selected documents on current institutions of adult education, with list of private and governmental organizations concerned with adult education.

266 CAHEN, JANINE and MICHELINE POUTEAU. Una resistenza incompiuta; la guerra d'Algeria e gli anticolonialisti francesi 1954-1962. Traduzzione di Bruno Maffi. Milano, Casa Editrice Il Saggiatore, 1964. 2 v. illus. Includes bibliography.

History of French anti-colonial efforts, specifically resistance to the Algerian war, as told by two participants, who were themselves arrested and wrote this work in Italian exile. History is told in the form of an anthology, composed of excerpts from newspapers, periodicals, fiction and non-fiction, and private archives, assembled chronologically. First volume covers 1954-May 1958, second volume goes from June 1958 to Algerian independence. Themes are public controversy over Algerian conflict, manifestations and other forms of opposition to the war, encouragement of desertions, and financial aid for F.L.N. Excellent bibliography on Algerian question and revolution arranged year by year, 1954-1963, giving books as well as influential articles and special issues, pamphlets, appeals, etc. Many illustrations.

267 CAHIERS PEDAGOGIQUES (periodical). Manifeste pour l'éducation nationale. Lyon, Comité universitaire d'information pédagogique, 1963. 32 p. "Numéro spécial, avril 1963."

Appeal for modernization of French education covering wide range of reforms.

268 CAIRNS, JOHN CAMPBELL. France. Englewood Cliffs, N.J., Prentice-Hall 1965. x, 180 p. maps. (The Modern nations in Historical perspective) "Suggested readings": p. 166-171.

Gaullist political institutions, major political issues (decolonization, civilian-military relations, ties with Atlantic Alliance) current status of economy and cultural life are presented in their historical setting. Good topically arranged bibliography of recent books in English.

269 CALBRETTE, JEAN. El catolicismo de izquierda. Buenos Aires, Editorial Nuevo Orden, 1964. 64 p.

Translation of French work written around 1960 and describing press organs of Catholic Left, notably "Témoignage chrétion," with special reference to its stand on Algeria, alliance with non-Catholic Left. Author is sympathetic to integrist Catholic groups.

270 CALVERT, HENRI. La presse contemporaine. Paris, F. Nathan, 1958. 366 p. (L'Activité contemporaine) "Aperçu bibliographique": p. 353-354.

One chapter on French press since Liberation, with 1955-1966 figures for circulation of dailies and weeklies.

271 CAMPBELL, PETER. French electoral systems and elections, 1989-1957. London, Faber and Faber, 1958. 144 p. Includes bibliography: p. 139-140.

History of French electoral systems through 1956.

272 CAMUS, ALBERT. Actuelles, III. Chronique algérienne, 1939-1958. 10 éd. Paris, Gallimard, 1958. 312 p.

Articles, speeches, essays on Algeria appealing for a more conciliatory attitude on all sides. Book concluded before May 1958.

FOR ADDITIONAL WORKS ABOUT ALBERT CAMUS, SEE AUTHOR INDEX

273 LE CANARD ENCHAINE (periodical). Le Canard de poche vous présente 50 ans de Canard; anthologie du Canard enchaîné. Paris, 1966. 2 v. illus.

Volume 2 (1944-1965) concentrates on Fifth Republic, lampooning de Gaulle but not systematically hostile to regime. Selections include weekly's political satire and cartoons.

274 CANDAS, MAURICE. Plaidoyer pour l'Algérie. Paris, Éditions des Quatre fils Aymon, 1957. 107 p.

Lawyer from Oran speaks for French settlers' rights and opposes either granting equal voting privileges to Moslems or negotiating with F.L.N.

275 CANTRIL, HADLEY. The politics of despair. New York, Basic Books, 1958. xv, 289 p. diagrs.

Book based on 1956 interviews and questionnaires of French and Italian citizens who regularly vote Communist. These case studies in political alienation are part of the Institute for International Social Research's investigation on the dynamics of social change. Author gives valuable insights into French political sociology.

276 CAPELLE, JEAN. L'école de demain reste à faire. Préf. de Louis Armand. Paris, Presses universitaires de France, 1966. 266 p. (A la pensée, 4)

University administrator, former member of official commission on educational reform, makes realistic assement of future needs and steps already taken under Fifth Republic to expand educational opportunities in terms of reorganization of school system, teacher recruitment, higher education.

277 CAPELLE, RUSSELL BECKET. The MRP and French foreign policy. New York, Praeger, 1963. 196 p. Includes bibliography.

Epilogue covers M.R.P. foreign policy during Fifth Republic.

278 CAPOCCI, ARMAND. L'avenir du syndicalisme. Paris, Hachette, 1967. 267 p. (Collection Les Grands problèmes)

Organizational, doctrinal, and political divisions in the French trade union movement both in its most current form (up to 1967) and in historical and international perspectives. Trade unionist author discusses controversies respecting trade union participation in economic planning, plant management, relations with political parties, horizontal as against vertical integration, as exemplified by the issue of the place of the Confédération générale des cadres. Author gives pessimistic estimate as to unification of French trade unions.

279 CARIO, ROBERT. Vanuxem acquitté. Qui est Verdun? Paris, Presses du Mail, 1963. 201 p.

Journalist's report on imprisonment and trial of General Paul Vanuxem, September 1963, in which general was acquitted of charges of plotting de Gaulle's assassination September 1961 as head of an O.A.S. network in France under cover name of "Verdun." For trial, see no. 1749.

280 CARMOY, GUY DE. L'adaptation de l'économie française au Marché commun. Sirey, 1958. 17 p. "Extrait de la Revue d'économie politique no. 1, janvier-février 1958. Numéro spécial."

Proposals for combatting French economy's structural rigidities.

281 CARMOY, GUY DE. L'Alliance atlantique disloquée ... Paris, Éditions S. P. E. P. H. E., 1966. 49 p. col. maps.

Facts on NATO (with maps of NATO bases) and Gaullist policy of disengagement, whose consequences author deplores.

282 CARMOY, GUY DE. L'économie française devant le Marché commun. Paris, Édité par l'Organisation française du Mouvement européen, 1957. 44 p.

Position of industry and agriculture in the face of Common Market adoption.

283 CARMOY, GUY DE. Professions et régions devant le Marché commun. Paris, Édité par l'Organisation française du Mouvement européen, 1959. 95 p.

Competitive position of French economy in Common Market at the end of 1958 and steps taken by professional and industrial associations to meet the challenge of a wider market.

284 CAROUS, PIERRE. Rapport sur les élus locaux. [Paris, Secrétariat général du Conseil national des Assises nationales de l'UNR.-U.D.T., 1963].

Speech at May 1963 Conseil National de l'U.N.R.-U.D.T. urging better party representation in local government than in 1959 elections.

285 CARRERAS, FERNAND. L'Accord F.L.N.-O.A.S., des négociations secrètes au cessez-le-feu. Paris, R. Laffont, 1967. 253 p. plates. (L'Histoire que nous vivons)

Inside story of negotiations between O.A.S. leaders, notably Jacques Susini, and F.L.N. representatives, with European liberal Jacques Chevallier acting as mediator, between conclusion of Evian agreement and declaration of Algerian independence. As editor of moderate "Journal d'Alger," author had contacts with all participants and reconstructs motivation of O.A.S. negotiators trying to exchange cessation of destruction for a guaranteed share in the new Algeria. Texts of propositions and final agreement of June 17, 1962 are reproduced. Photographs of negotiators.

286 CARRIAS, EUGENE. La pensée militaire française. Paris, Presses universitaires de France, 1960. 378 p. "Bibliographie, références et notes": p. 361-367.

History of French military doctrines from Middle Ages to end of 4th Republic.

287 CASTA, FRANÇOIS. Le drame spirituel de l'Armée. Paris, Éditions France-Empire, 1962. 252 p. diagr. Includes bibliography.

Army chaplain with 25th Parachute Division in North Africa discusses spiritual conflicts of military in Algeria between realities of counter-revolutionary warfare and Christian principles. Bibliography of military and pastoral statements.

288 CASTEL, ROBERT and PIERRE HORAY. L'inoubliable Algérie. Paris, 1965. 251 p. illus.

Photographs and captions provide nostalgic evocation of daily life in pre-independence Algeria.

289 CATALOGNE, GERARD DE. Haïti à l'heure du tiers-monde, précédé d'une "Lettre ouverte au général de Gaulle." Port-au-Prince, Éditions du Nouveau Monde, 1964. 226 p.

Appeal to de Gaulle as the symbol of new French greatness, of independence both from the U.S. and the Communist bloc, and of a generous policy of aid to underdeveloped nations to save Haiti from reckless U.S. intervention as much as from the danger of a Communist thrust from Cuba. Author as a Haiti writer emphasizes his country's cultural ties with France. Failures of American assistance program in Latin America and Haiti in particular are described in detail.

290 CATHOLIC CHURCH. Document "Pax" [lettre de la Secrétairerie d'état du Vatican concernant "Pax" au Secrétariat de l'Episcopat français, Paris le 6 juin 1963. Paris, 1963] 25 p.

Vatican's proscription of Polish organization Pax, claiming to be a progressive pacifist Catholic movement and appealing to Western, and in particular French Catholics by advocating peaceful co-existence. Pax is accused of being in reality a propaganda arm of Polish Ministry of Interior. See also no. 986.

291 CATHOLIC CHURCH IN ALGERIA. BISHOPS. Les évêques face à la guerre d'Algérie. Paris, 1960. 79 p. (Cahiers du Témoignage chrétien, 40)

Topically organized excerpts from statements by members of Catholic hierarchy, 1954-1960, on Algerian war and related issues of racism, social justice, violence, conflicts of conscience, national independence.

292 CATTAUI, GEORGES. Charles de Gaulle. Paris, Éditions universitaires, 1956. 120 p. illus., ports. (Témoins du XXe siècle 4) "Bibliographie": p. 117-120.

Ends with liberation period.

293 CATTAUI, GEORGES. Charles de Gaulle; l'homme et son destin. Paris, A. Fayard, 1960. 359 p. "Bibliographie": p. 351-359.

"Official" biography, including detailed genealogy and brought up to date to cover return to power and first months of Fifth Republic. Author emphasizes de Gaulle's democratic, pro-European views and progress toward new forms of French Community and peace in Algeria, high-lighting personality traits of integrity and self-control.

294 CAUTE, DAVID. Communism and the French intellectuals, 1914-1960. London, A. Deutsch, 1964. 412 p. Includes bibliography.

Study of contributions of Communist intellectuals in different fields, their movement in and out of Communist party, and party's changing relations with them. Sartre's case receives special attention. Author attacks theory that intellectuals' affinity for communism is a purely irrational phenomenon. Although Gaullist period is not singled out, conclusions apply also to Fifth Republic. Excellent bibliography of publications by French Communists.

295 CAVIGLIOLI, FRANÇOIS. Ben Barka chez les juges. Paris, Table ronde, 1967. 217 p. (La Table ronde de Combat. Les Brûlots, 8)

Originally published in daily "Le Combat," this is a session by session description of the trial held Sept.-Oct. 1966 to determine the guilt of the police and secret service men involved in the kidnaping and killing of Ben Barka a year earlier. Defense was assumed by Tixier-Vignancour, prosecution by some of lawyers active in F.L.N. cases.

296 CAZES, BERNARD. La planification en France et le IVe plan. Paris, Éditions de l'Épargne, 1962. 282 p. tables. (De quoi s'agit-il?)

Philosophy and history of French planning, with detailed outline of channels for elaborating plan and instruments for executing it. The impending Fourth Plan's objectives and specific programs with costs for each sector (such as urban development) are given, together with current statistics on consumption, investment, employment.

297 CENTRE D'ARCHIVES ET DE DOCUMENTATION POLITIQUE ET SOCIALE, PARIS. Documentation sur la politique communiste. Paris, 1958. 31 bound leaflets. "Supplément aux 'Informations politiques et sociales' no. 350."

Anti-Communist leaflets for use by different parties and groups in November 1958 general elections. Each leaflet concentrates on a special target, such as Communist Party against socialism, against army, against religion, Communist Party and Algeria, Communist Party and education.

298 CENTRE D'ARCHIVES ET DE DOCUMENTATION POLITIQUE ET SOCIALE, PARIS. Le Parti communiste et les collectivités locales; élections municipales 1959. Paris 1960? 10 pts. in 1 v. (40 p.) "Supplément à Observateur municipal no. 28"

Attack on French Communist Party's municipal mismanagement in communities where it is in control, to serve as anti-communist propaganda for March 1959 municipal elections.

298a CENTRE D'ETUDES SOCIALISTES, PARIS. L'Intégration européenne et le mouvement ouvrier; colloque international, 4-5-6 octobre, 1963, Paris. Paris, 1964. 314 p. (Its Cahiers, no. 45-51)

Reports and discussions by André Gorz, Ernest Mandel, Pierre Naville and French and Italian trade unionists on Common Market and national planning, prospects for capitalists growth, agricultural and regional disequilibria, and proper role toward these questions of European labor movement. See also no. 1870.

299 CENTRE DE DOCUMENTATION CONTEMPORAINE. Plan de classification. 6 éd. Paris, 1964. 56 l.

Fondation Nationale des Sciences Politique's classification for its library, as of 1964, with detailed breakdown of its sections on political, economic, social, and educational questions. The actual holdings are not indicated.

300 CENTRE DE RECHERCHES ECONOMIQUES ET SOCIALES. La politique économique et sociale de la Ve république. Paris, 1959. 66 p. (Its Etudes et documents. Nouv. Sér. VII no. 5)

Economic, fiscal, and agricultural measures passed up to December 1958.

301 CENTRE DE RECHERCHES ECONOMIQUES ET SOCIALES. La politique sociale de la Ve république. Paris, 1959. 1 v. (various paging) (Its Etudes et documents. Nouv. Sér. Vii, no. 8)

Reforms in Social Security and text of Rueff report on this topic.

302 CENTRE DEMOCRATE, PARIS. Publications. Paris, 1964. 15 l.

Mimeographed notes of Comité d'études et de liaison des démocrates français, later Comité des démocrates, finally Centre démocrate, founded 1963 as a centrist opposition group to de Gaulle. Notes discuss committee's origins, aims, as of early 1964, list membership. For other publications of Centre démocrate, see nos. 811(l), 1903, 1908a.

303 CENTRE DEMOCRATE, PARIS. 30 minutes avec le Comité des démocrates. Paris, 1965. 61 p. illus.

Program of Centre démocrate, also known as Comité des démocrates, some months before the official candidacy of Lecanuet, one of its executive committee members. Includes list of executive committee members.

304 CENTRE MARXISTE-LENINISTE DE FRANCE. Le marxisme-léninisme triomphera! [Paris, Edité par le Bulletin d'information marxiste-léniniste] 1965. 132 p.

Attack on both the Soviet and the French Communist parties for revisionism and degeneration and role of Marxist-Leninist organization as nucleus of a revolutionary labor movement. Statutes of Centre marxiste-léniniste.

305 CERCLE D'ETUDES SOCIALES ET JURIDIQUES, PARIS. Populations et nationalités dans l'Algérie future. Paris [1962?] 16 p.

Study concurrent with Evian negotiations and presenting legal possibilities for protection of Algerian minority that might want to retain French nationality as residents in an independent Algeria.

305a CERCLE D'ETUDES SOCIALES ET JURIDIQUES, PARIS. Unité et diversité des communautés dans l'Algérie future. Paris, 1961. 36 p.

June 1961 discussion presided by jurist René Thorp, organizer of Colloque de Grenoble, on methods of providing legal guarantees for French minority in Algeria after independence. Some participants in debate emphasize currently inflamed state of mind of French settlers and their indifference to legal accommodations, as well as their lack of interest in anything but retaining French citizenship.

306 CERCLE "LES VOIX DU SOCIALISME." Pour un front des travailleurs. Paris, R. Julliard, 1963. 155 p.

Group composed of Marxists and trade unionists concludes from defeat of "Cartel des non" in November 1962 elections that rejection of Gaullist political institutions is unrealistic because they are natural outgrowth of country's present economic structure. Opposition should come from alliance of labor movement rather than tactical agreement of Socialists and Communists, axed on concrete economic alternatives leading to democratic socialism.

307 CERCLE TALEB-MOUMIE. Fidel Castro ou Tshombé? La voie algérienne vers le socialisme. Paris, F. Maspero, 1962. 84 p. (Cahiers libres, no. 36)

Review of several proposals for independent Algeria's economic policy (Club Jean Moulin, Francois Perroux, Francis Jeanson) which all have elements of Franco-Algerian cooperation and are rejected in favor of a program of austerity, large-scale nationalization and autonomous growth coordinated with rest of Maghreb.

308 CESAIRE, AIME. Letter to Maurice Thorez. Paris, Présence Africaine, 1957. 15 p.

Communist deputy from Martinique motivates his October 1956 resignation from Communist Party by attacking party's chauvinism and insincere anti-colonialism.

309 CEUX D'ALGERIE. Lettres de rappelés, précédées d'un débat entre Jean Yves Alquier, Roger Barberot et al. Paris, Plon, 1957. vi, 173 p. (Les débats de "Tribune libre" 1)

Results of inquiry by Association "Ceux d'Algérie," (founded March 1957) on reaction of soldiers having served in Algeria to their war experiences. The nearly 3,000 replies are largely favorable to pacification measures. Preliminary round-table discussion of former reserve officers representing different services include Jean-Yves Alquier, Roger Barberot, civilians Michel Massenet and Thierry Maulnier.

310 CHAFFARD, GEORGES. Les carnets secrets de la décolonisation. Paris, Calmann-Lévy [1965-1967] 2 v.

First volume deals with pre-1958 instances of colonial troubles, and second volume traces dissolution of French Union and French Community: Algerian war - outbreak and repercussions in French politics, negotiations between F. L. N. and O. A. S., May-June 1962; Guinea's break with French Community and subsequent relations with France; political developments in Niger and Cameroon before and after dissolution of French Community.

311 CHALIAND, GERARD. L'Algérie est-elle socialiste? Paris, F. Maspero, 1964. 168 p. (Cahiers libres, no 56)

Brief political history of Algerian nationalism and struggle for leadership in independent Algeria, followed by critical description of socialization and self-administration in agriculture and industry to demonstrate that these measures and expropriation of French settlers mainly benefited Algerian bourgeoisie and state bureaucracy. Appendices reproduce Jan. 1963 report of Union générale des travailleurs algérien and text of March 1963 decrees on "vacant" European property. Author was editor of left-wing Algerian weekly "Révolution africaine" during 1963. (See no. 2069.)

312 CHALLE, MAURICE (defendant). Les procès des généraux Challe et Zeller; textes complets des débats, réquisitoires, plaidoiries, annexes. Paris, Nouvelles éditions latines, 1961. 318 p. ports.

Trial of Generals Challe and Zeller May 29-31, 1961 before Haut Tribunal Militaire in Paris. Report on April 1961 military revolt precedes trial, in which Challe gives lengthy explanation of his conduct. Witnesses are mainly military commanders on duty in Algeria at time of revolt.

312a CHALLE, MAURICE. Notre révolte. Paris, Presses de la Cité, 1968. 448 p. illus., maps, plates. (Collection "Coup d'oeil.)

Notes written in prison, the first half in 1961-62 recapitulating his rôle in military operations in Algeria, (including text of directives and Oct. 1959 speech explaining strategy) January 1960 and April 1961 and own trial. General's purpose here is to rectify official version of Algerian war and to defend the French Army. In remainder of volume, author records his reactions, 1963-1967, to changing international situation (European unification, Atlantic Alliance, developments in former colonies and growing U. S. involvement in Vietnam, which he judges in the light of French experiences. In all these areas he condemns de Gaulle's options on foreign and military policy.

313 CHALUMEAU, JEAN LUC. Les relations publiques de l'état; avantpropos de Pierre Dumas. [Paris, Sedes, 1965]. 199 p., tables. (Bibliothèque des attachés de presse, 2)

Effort of government agencies under Fifth Republic to dispel the negative attitude of the public toward governmental machinery (e. g., police, armed forces) by public relations and information services.

314 CHANDERNAGOR, ANDRE. Un Parlement, pour quoi faire? Paris, Gallimard, 1967. 192 p. (Collection Idées, 122) Bibliography: p. 185-186.

Socialist deputy's analysis of institutional and practical weaknesses of National Assembly under Fifth Republic and concrete suggestions for giving it greater rights and instituting working methods more in keeping with parliamentary functions in a complex modern democracy.

315 CHANDESSAIS, CHARLES. La psychologie dans l'armée. Paris, Presses universitaires de France, 1959. 195 p. (Le Psychologue, 7) "Bibliographie": p. 189-191.

Concrete psychological problems of adaptation to military life and administrative measures to handle them within armed services.

316 CHANRION, FERNAND. La Moselle, une victoire européenne. Paris, Berger-Levrault, 1964. 179 p. illus., map.

A case history of European co-operation, the canalization of the Moselle as a shipping link to the Rhine. Author, one of promoters and executors of the scheme, gives personal account of struggles from initiation of project in 1950 to its completion in 1964. Interesting sidelights on European and French economic policy of successive French governments and autonomous operations of administrative machinery.

317 CHANTEBOUT, BERNARD. L'organisation générale de la défense nationale en France depuis la fin de la seconde guerre mondiale ... Paris, Librairie générale de droit et de jurisprudence, 1967. xii, 500 p. (Bibliothèque constitutionnelle et de science politique, t. 26)

Doctoral dissertation which offers first major study of national defense in the Fourth and Fifth Republic. For both republics, author analyzes evolution of military policy of the government and National Assembly, the changes in location of civilian control over military in terms of constitutional provisions and actual administrative practice. The final third of the volume examines the military establishment as such: army, navy, air force, and such important but often neglected components as civil defense, intelligence services, psychological warfare and military research divisions. Extensive bibliography and chronological table for 1945-1966 summarizing military events and the corresponding civilian and military leaders in charge of national defense.

317a CHAPSAL, JACQUES. La vie politique et les partis en France depuis 1940. Paris, Cours de droit [1961] 3 v. in 1. Includes bibliography.

1960-61 political science course at Sorbonne's Institut d'Etudes Politiques covering political developments from 1940 through spring of 1961, closer study of individual political parties, political institutions of Fourth and Fifth Republic, in particular electoral systems and election results. Most of v. 3 is devoted to Fifth Republic: its establishment and the first two years of political life of the new regime.

318 CHARBONNEL, JEAN. Les problèmes actuels de la recherche scientifique et technique [rapport. Paris, Secrétariat général du Conseil national et des Assises nationales, 1963] 18 p.

Speech at U. N. R. -U. D. T. 's 3rd Assises Nationales, Nice, Nov. 1963 reporting on Fifth Republic's support of scientific research and remaining bottlenecks.

319 CHARBY, JACQUES. L'Algérie en prison; préf. d'André Mandouze. Paris, Éditions de Minuit, 1961. 106 p. (Documents)

Experiences in Fresnes prison February - June 1960, in which author met group of Algerian political prisoners.

320 CHARDONNET, JEAN. Algérie et métropole; la rançon d'une sécession. Étude économique du coût de la sécession pour la France métropolitaine et l'Algérie. Paris, Centre d'études politiques et civiques,1961. 30 p. (Cahiers du CEPEC, 16)

Feb. 1961 estimate made for Centre d'études politiques et civiques of costs to France of Algerian independence in terms of lost trade, support of repatriates, lost Saharan oil.

321 CHARDONNET, JEAN. L'économie française; étude géographique d'une décadence et des possibilités de redressement. Paris, Dalloz, 1958. maps. (Études politiques, économiques, et sociales, 13) "Bibliographie": p. 431-443.

Late 1958 survey of strengths and weaknesses of French economy and individual industrial sectors.

322 CHARLOT, JEAN and MONICA CHARLOT. Les partis politiques en France depuis 1941. Paris, 1960. 48 l. (Fondation nationale des sciences politiques. Cycle supérieur d'études politiques. Guide de recherches, no. 3) Bibliography: l. 37-48

Survey of research on and source material for major political parties. Guide gives listing of Fondation nationale's library cards of periodical and other publications for: 1) Communist party and Communist dissidents; 2) independent Left; 3) S. F. I. O.; 4) Radical party, with its splinters and U. D. S. R.; 5) M. R. P.; 6) R. P. F. and U. N. R., U. D. T.; 7) Independents; 8) Poujadists; 9) Extreme Right. The listing for the Communist party is nearly complete, preliminary for other parties.

323 CHARLOT, JEAN. L'Union pour la nouvelle République; étude du pouvoir au sein d'un parti politique. Préf. de René Rémond. Paris, A. Colin, 1967. 361 p. diagrs, (Cahiers de la Fondation nationale des sciences politiques, 153) Includes bibliography.

First major scholarly work on U. N. R., covering party's genesis and formative years during ideological split over Algerian question, 1958-1962, its internal power structure, background and qualifications of parliamentary and local leaders, inner circle of Gaullists, and the party's conception of its function. Documentation rests on party archival material and interviews and questionnaires of 21 Gaullist cabinet members and 20 other party leaders. Good bibliography.

324 CHARNAY, JEAN PAUL. Les scrutins politiques en France de 1815 à 1962; contestations et invalidations. Paris, A. Colin, 1964. 281 p. maps, tables. (Cahiers de la Fondation nationale des sciences politiques. Partis et élections, 132)

Section on Fifth Republic describes contested election results in 1958 and 1962 parliamentary elections and protests about 1961 and 1962 referenda.

325 CHARNAY, JEAN PAUL. Le suffrage politique en France; élections parlementaires, élection présidentielle, référendums. Préf. de Marcel Prélot. Paris, Mouton, 1965. 832 p. (École pratique des hautes études, Sorbonne. 6. section: Sciences économiques et sociales. Etudes européennes, 3) Includes bibliography.

Basic, comprehensive study of the institution of political suffrage in the Fifth Republic. Aside from a detailed description of the laws regulating elections to all political bodies (electoral system, eligibility rules of candidates, campaign regulations, voting procedure, invalidation) work gives insight into philosophy of representative vs direct democracy, rationale of different voting systems, mechanisms of voter and candidate psychology. For each section relevant legal texts are cited. Excellent subject index makes this vast compendium useful for quick reference. Good bibliography.

326 CHATAGNER, JACQUES. [Editorial correspondence and criticism by Catholic hierarchy. A sequel to the periodical: Le Bulletin... after its publication has been discontinued.] Paris, 1958. 13 p. (Le Bulletin. Documents et recherches) For periodical, see no. 1849.

326a CHATELAIN, ABEL. Le Monde et ses lecteurs sous la IVe République. Paris, A. Colin, 1962. 279 p. illus., facsims., diagrs. (Kiosque: les faits, la presse, l'opinion 18) Bibliography: p. 273-276.

Covers years from 1944-1960 and presents results of studies on geographic distribution and social status of Le Monde readers, as well as stand taken over these years by the newspaper and some information about its editorial staff.

327 CHATELAIN, JEAN. La nouvelle constitution et le régime politique de la France. Paris, Berger-Levrault, 1959. 461 p. (Institutions politiques d'aujourd'hui)

Law professor's systematic presentation of September 1958 Constitution and political organization of the Fifth Republic in comparison with earlier French constitutions and regimes. There are separate sections on governmental organs in metropolis and overseas. Annexes give articles of Constitution and complete texts of ordinances complementing Constitution, such as election of president, legislature.

327a CHATELET, F. Logos et praxis; recherches sur la signification théorique du marxisme. Paris, Société d'édition d'enseignement supérieur, 1962. 205 p. Includes bibliography.

Marxist critique of dialectic materialism as expounded by French Communist thinkers such as Garaudy and Kanapa. In this revised doctoral dissertation author attempts to take into account the more sophisticated arguments of existentialist philosophy and do justice to both existentialism and dialectic Marxism by synthesizing the contributions of each.

328 CHERDEVON, MAURICE. Les causes morales de l'affaissement de la France en 1940 et du gâchis actuel. Paris, Éditions du Scorpion, 1960. 94 p. (Collection Alternance)

Indictment of main social groups for their lacking sense of social responsibility, but without reference to current political regime.

329 CHESNE, GUY. L'établissement des étrangers en France et la Communauté économique européenne. Préf. de Y. Loussouarn. Paris, Librairie générale de droit et de jurisprudence, 1962. ix, 364 p. (Bibliothèque de droit privd, t. 34) Bibliography: p. 331-350.

French law and administrative regulations are studied to determine in what areas the Rome Treaty's provision that persons and corporations from European Community countries have free access to French economy is effective and where it is not fully recognized. Extensive bibliography of books, articles, theses, colloquia.

330 CHEVALLIER, JACQUES. Nous, Algériens... Paris, Calmann-Lévy, 1958. 187 p. (Questions d'actualité)

Former Algiers mayor reviews sabotaging of political and social reforms by European settlers in Algeria and consequent outbreak of nationalist rebellion, applauding de Gaulle's October 1958 speech at Constantine. For Chevallier's later conciliatory attempts, see no. 285.

331 CHOMBART DE LAUWE, JACQUES LOUIS (FELIX). Anniversaire de la révolution du 13 mai; ou La situation politique de la France en 1959. Guérande, Éditions de la Presqu'île guérandaise 1959. 34 p.

Former parliamentarian delineates forces and circumstances leading to the collapse of the Fourth Republic, divergences between motivation for revolt in Algeria and supporters of new regime in France, de Gaulle's personal stand on Algerian integration, which author finds reasonable, although he attacks Gaullist nationalism as being a poorer bulwark against communism than European nationalism.

332 CHOMBART DE LAUWE, JACQUES LOUIS (FELIX). L'évolution de la situation en Algérie: le référendum et les élections. Guérande, Impr. Presqu'île guérandaise, 1962. 31 p.

As background to April 1962 referendum on Algerian independence author retraces de Gaulle's hypocritical Algerian policy from 1958 onward. O.A.S. reaction is justified and seen as potentially effective.

333* CHRONIQUE SOCIALE DE FRANCE (periodical). Les aspects moraux du drame algérien; note théologique. Lyon 1960. 12 p.

Stand of Catholic Church as of October 1960 on warfare (torture, etc.) in Algeria, conscientious objectors, collaboration with F.L.N., and methods of restoring peace.

334 CHRONIQUE SOCIALE DE FRANCE (periodical). L'avenir du communisme après Togliatti. Lyon, 1965. 96 p. illus. Second issue for 1965.

Articles on evolution of international communism, as symbolized by Togliatti's 1964 testament, and on significance of increasingly autonomous communist parties for Christian dialogue with communist parties.

335 Chronologie internationale. Jan. 1956-Dec. 1963. Paris, Direction de la documentation. 8 v.

Semi-monthly supplement to "Notes et études documentaires" (see no. 2016) compiled jointly by Direction de la documentation and Centre d'études de politique étrangère. Each issue gives chronology of internal and foreign affairs for two-week period for major countries of world, in alphabetical order, followed by chronology for major supra-national organizations such as U.N., NATO, and European Economic Community. Subject index for each issue but no index for entire volume. Each issue contains detailed chronology for France and overseas departments and territories (Algeria through June 1962, then separately under Algeria) of governmental and parliamentary activity, other important domestic and foreign developments. Publication ceased 1963.

336 CIVICUS (pseud). Monsieur Mendès-France et les communistes. Paris, P. Amiot, 1957. 116 p.

Indictment of Mendès-France for supporting Communist stand on Algeria, Hungary, economic questions and for leading Radical Party into progressive camp.

337 CLARK, MICHAEL K. Algeria in turmoil: a history of the rebellion. New York, Praeger, 1959. xvi, 466 p. maps. (Books that matter) "Selected bibliography": p. 455-456.

American journalist's detailed history of political and military evolution of Algerian nationalism and French and French-Algerian response to its onslaught. Author is sympathetic to Soustelle's thesis that no compromise "liberal" solution could satisfy this Arab-nationalist orientation short of independence, and that integration based on strength of French army is only hope. He is therefore skeptical of de Gaulle's moderate policy. Author gives eye-witness, day-by-day account of May 13 - June 4 in Algeria, analysis of referendum, elections, Fall 1958.

338 CLARK, STANLEY FREDERICK. The man who is France; the story of Charles de Gaulle. London, G. Harrap, 1960. 202 p. port.

British brigadier's biography, with emphasis on military career, up to de Gaulle's return to power.

339 CLARTÉ, ABEL. Le vrai drame de l'école de France. Paris, Table ronde, 1965. 225 p.

Personal memories and reflections on life as a secondary school history teacher, with interesting inside information on such controversial aspects of French education as the baccalaureate examinations, politics in education, and school discipline. Author describes his clashes with Communist-dominated teacher organizations as a result of his Catholic, pro-European, anti-Gaullist views.

340 CLAUDE, HENRI. La concentration capitaliste, pouvoir économique et pouvoir gaulliste. Paris, Éditions sociales, 1965. 304 p.

Description of interpenetration of large capital and industries with state regulatory agencies, trends toward concentration in major industries. Gaullist political institutions are presented as natural outgrowth of this economic concentration of power, a transposition of economic power to the political arena, where leaders are all recruited from financial oligarchy (many cases cited). Author concludes with Communist Party's program for restoring political democracy and alliance of workers and middle classes opposed to financial oligarchy, along lines proposed by Mitterand.

341 CLAUDE, HENRI. Gaullisme et grand capital. Paris, Éditions sociales, 1960. 224 p. Bibliographical footnotes.

Communist interpretation of institutions, ruling elite, and policies of Gaullist regime, 1958-1960, in which de Gaulle is seen as defender of interests of technologically advanced sector of big business and monopoly capitalism.

342 CLEMENCEAU, JEAN (ed.) Le guide administratif, juridique et social du rapatrié. Paris, Études et éditions juridiques et sociales "EJUS," 1964. 165 p. (L'actualité juridique et sociale)

Current (1963) laws, decrees, administrative procedures applicable to French repatriates from Algeria settling down in metropolis.

343 CLOSTERMANN, PIERRE. Blutende Wüste. [Übertragung aus dem Französischen von Leopold Voelker.] Bern, A. Scherz, 1961. 215 p.

Translation of "Appui-feu sur l'oued Hallaïl" (1960) the fictionized account of a pilot's combat experiences in Algeria 1956-57.

344 CLUB DE GRENELLE. Siècle de Damoclès; la force nucléaire stratégique. Paris, P. Couderc, 1964. 120 p.

Documentation assembled by study group composed of technical experts on French nuclear capacity as of 1964 and 1968, cost of total military program and nuclear components, effects on economy and technology, as well as official justification for independent nuclear deterrent strategy.

345 CLUB DEMOCRATIE NOUVELLE. CENTRE D'ETUDES ET DE RECHERCHES POLITIQUES ET ÉCONOMIQUES. L'avenir des partis politiques français. Marseille [1962] 8 p.

December 1962 criticism of political parties as constituted at that time and proposal for strong Leftist party axed around S.F.I.O. and Radicals.

346 CLUB DEMOCRATIE NOUVELLE. CENTRE D'ETUDES ET DE RECHERCHES POLITIQUES ET ÉCONOMIQUES. Réflexions sur l'aide aux pays sous-développés. Marseille, 1963. 13 p.

Guidelines for action of individual citizens and professional groups.

347 CLUB DEMOCRATIE NOUVELLE. CENTRE D'ETUDES ET DE RECHERCHES POLITIQUES ET ÉCONOMIQUES. La réforme de la Constitution: l'élection du président de la République au suffrage universel. Marseille [1962] 9 p.

Impartial presentation of pros and cons on constitutional referendum of October 28, 1962 regarding direct election of French president.

348 CLUB DEMOCRATIE NOUVELLE. CENTRE D'ETUDES ET DE RECHERCHES POLITIQUES ET ÉCONOMIQUES. Une solution au problème de la circulation à Marseille; l'utilisation du réseau ferré urbain. Marseille [1963] 17 l. map.

Study of special Marseille traffic problems and proposal for rapid transit combining existing railroad with new subway.

349 CLUB JEAN MOULIN. Deux pièces du dossier Algérie. Pour une politique du rapatriement. La solidarité économique franco-algérienne. Paris, Éditions du Seuil, 1962. 186 p.

Two studies made Spring 1962, before mass exodus of Europeans. The first analyses prospects of settlers' reintegration into French economy and concrete proposals for improving procedures, the second examines continued economic interdependence between France and an independent Algeria.

350 CLUB JEAN MOULIN. L'état et le citoyen. Paris, Éditions du Seuil, 1961. 409 p.

First major study of Club Jean Moulin, founded 1958, on relation of state and citizen in modern French society and ways of bringing democracy up to date while preserving traditions of liberty. Specific proposals are made for improving citizen education and democratic participation in existing organizations. Among institutional reforms proposed is the introduction of elected presidents.

351 CLUB JEAN MOULIN. La force de frappe et le citoyen. Éditions du Seuil, 1963. 127 p. tables.

Exposition of technical and political issues connected with nuclear strategy. Having shown drawback of independent small French nuclear deterrent in terms of costs, effectiveness, unfavorable impact on economy, foreign policy, Club Jean Moulin also rejects independent European nuclear deterrent and reluctantly favors joint European and U.S. nuclear force under Atlantic Alliance.

352 CLUB JEAN MOULIN. Un parti pour la gauche. Paris, Éditions du Seuil, 1965. 90 p. (Collection Jean Moulin)

Discussion of preconditions for left-oriented party becoming a majority party in the France of 1965. Pivotal party is found to be S.F.I.O., which is to serve as rallying point for other moderate groups such as M.R.P. and Radicals, becoming an "action" rather than a "doctrinaire" party in the process. Collaboration with Communists is rejected.

353 CLUB JEAN MOULIN. Les perspectives d'emploi des Européens en Algérie. Paris, 1960? 26 p.

Pessimistic 1959 estimate of long-run prospects of cohabitation of Moslems and large fraction of European population, which competes for jobs with Moslems under existing economic conditions. Constantine Plan is criticized for aggravating tensions, and alternative plan for gradual repatriation is offered.

354 CLUB JEAN MOULIN. Peut-on fixer des objectifs sociaux au progrès économique? Paris, 1962. 14 p. "Extrait du numéro de février 1962, Esprit."

Report on Royaumont meeting November 1961 of Club Jean Moulin on broad goals of French planning.

355 CLUB JEAN MOULIN. Pour une politique étrangère de l'Europe. Paris, Éditions du Seuil, 1966. 67 p. (Collection Jean Moulin)

Discussion at the eve of the presidential election of alternatives for French policy as a choice between an Atlantic Alliance, national independence, and a policy of European unification, a European Europe, which, without being anti-American, can serve peace and international economic development. The Atlantic Alliance is viewed as out-dated and Gaullist policy is approved only to the extent that it calls attention to this fact, but support of U.S. is still essential. Special problems of Germany and Great Britain are examined.

FOR ADDITIONAL WORKS BY AND ABOUT THE CLUB JEAN MOULIN, SEE AUTHOR INDEX

356 CLUB JEAN-LOUIS RICHARD. La technocratie et les libertés. [Paris, Diffusion assurée par le Centre du livre civique, 1963] Bibliography: p. 77-79.

Attack on organizations that promote modernization, worker participation in management such as the Club Jean Moulin, Centre National des Jeunes Patrons as being fundamentally Marxist and opposed to the teachings of the Catholic Church, whose social philosophy the club propagates. Bloch-Lainé's proposal for industrial reform is singled out as undermining property. For a similar criticism of Bloch-Lainé, see no. 1571.

357 COCATRE-ZILGIEN, ANDRE. L'affaire Argoud; considérations sur les arrestations internationalement irrégulières. Paris, A. Pedone, 1965. 71 p.

Legal and international implications of 'l'Affaire Argoud,' the kidnaping of one of O.A.S. leaders in Germany and bringing him to trial before the Cour de Sûreté de l'Etat Dec. 1963. Law professor, after presenting particulars of case, points to dangerous nature of this precedent for principles of political asylum.

358 COFFY, ROBERT. Dieu des athées, Marx, Sartre, Camus. 2e éd. Lyon, Chronique sociale de France, 1966. 176 p. (Le Fond du problème, no. 8) Bibliographical footnotes.

Contemporary atheism as represented by communism, the philosophies of Sartre and Albert Camus, and the Catholic Church's answer to these challenges as well as to that posed by rapidly expanding scientific knowledge.

359 COGNIOT, GEORGES. Laïcité et réforme démocratique de l'enseignement. Paris, Éditions sociales, 1963. 287 p.

Author is Senator and Communist Party's specialist on education. The book is not only a clear statement of Communist views but a serious examination of education in a modern society. The first part gives history of non-confessional education and relevant legislation during 4th and 5th Republic, the second and major part describes Gaullist education reforms, which are shown to result in a lowering of the quality (Americanization) of education without lessening of social inequities; the final portion presents Communist program for extending highest quality of French education to entire population.

360 COGNIOT, GEORGES. Pour l'union dans la bataille laïque; conférence présenté le 3 juin 1959 à La Roche-sur-Yon. [Paris, Parti communiste français, 1959] 30 p. (Problèmes actuels)

Arguments against state support of Catholic schools, attack on Gaullist education policy strengthening Church schools and neglecting public schools, a policy tacitly supported by Socialist party, and Communist party's own education program.

361 COGNIOT, GEORGES. Les problèmes de l'enseignement et de la recherche dans le IV. plan. Deux discours prononcés devant le Sénat le 6 juillet 1962. Paris, 1962. 15 p. "Supplément aux 'Cahiers du communisme' no. 9, septembre 1962."

Attack on Fourth Plan for its insufficient provisions for education, in particular teacher salaries, and university research.

362 COGNIOT, GEORGES. Qu'est-ce le communisme? 2. éd., rév. et mise à jour. Paris, Éditions sociales, 1964. 246 p. (Notre temps) Bibliographical footnotes.

Post-1961 ideology and achievements of Soviet Communism illustrate meaning of Communism and serve to refute claims of Chinese Communists as well as to rebut current sociological "revisionist" findings about changes in French society in the direction of socialism. Despite attacks on non-Marxist Left, union of all anti-Gaullist forces is urged.

363* COLLOQUE DE ROYAUMONT (SEINE ET OISE), 1960. Schéma d'un rapport de Messieurs Ancel et Rolland: Le problème des libertés individuelles et la guerre d'Algérie. Royaumont, 1960. 8 p.

364 COLLOQUE DE STRASBOURG, 1963. Forces religieuses et attitudes politiques dans la France comtemporaine, sous la direction de René Rémond. Colloque de Strasbourg, 23-25 mai 1963. Paris, A. Colin, 1965. 397 p. (Cahiers de la Fondation nationale des sciences politiques, 130) Includes bibliography.

Reports and discussions from conference organized jointly by Strasbourg University and Fondation nationale des sciences politiques, covering such topics as the political attitudes and behavior of Catholic, Protestant, and Jewish groups, Catholic press, religious groups and the school question, the position of the Catholic hierarchy on various issues of foreign policy. Good bibliographies on each of these topics.

365 COLLOQUE DE VINCENNES. 1st, 1960. Colloque de Vincennes sur l'Algérie française. Comité du 20 juin 1960. 1er Colloque, Salle d'honneur de l'Hôtel de ville de Vincennes. [Paris, Comité de Vincennes, 1960] 77 p.

Gathering of political leaders in support of French Algeria. Speakers include: George Bidault, Maurice Bourges-Maunoury, Jacques Soustelle, André Morice, François Valentin, André Malterre, Robert Lacoste and Algerian deputy Marc Lauriol. For an account of this meeting, see Soustelle, no. 1863.

366 COLLOQUE "FRANCE-FORUM," ST.-GERMAIN-EN-LAYE, 1962. La démocratie à refaire; rapports de René Rémond et al. et débats. Préf de Maurice Duverger. Paris, Éditions ouvrières, 1963. 288 p.

Meeting organized by "France-Forum" January 27-28, 1962 and attended by political figures from M.R.P. and S.F.I.O., labor leaders and political scientists to discuss crisis of French democracy, i.e., depolitization and weakness of political parties, and propose new political institutions and renovation of political organizations. Among speakers are René Remond, George Vedel, Jacques Fauvet; politicians participate in debate.

367 COLLOQUE FRANCO-POLONAIS, PARIS, 1960. Choix et efficience des investissements; Colloque franco-polonais; Paris, 17-20 mai 1960. Textes réunis par Charles Bettelheim avec la collaboration de Maurice Godelier. Paris, Mouton, 1963. 124 p. illus. (Congrès et colloques, 5)

Polish and French economists compare methods and results of planning investments in their respective economies. Prof. C. Gruson reports on evolution of French investments 1954-1959.

368 COLLOQUE INTERNATIONAL SUR "L'EVALUATION ET LE ROLE DES BESOINS DE BIENS DE CONSOMMATION DANS LES DIVERS REGIMES ECONOMIQUES," GRENOBLE, 1961. L'évaluation et le role des besoins de biens de consommation dans les divers régimes économiques, Grenoble, 11-15 septembre 1961. Paris, Éditions du Centre national de la recherche scientifique, 1963. 225 p. diagrs. (Colloques internationaux du Centre national de la recherche scientifique. Sciences humaines) Includes bibliographies.

Centralized planning schemes and methodological problems of measuring and predicting consumption needs. Among French economists speaking at colloquium are Maurice Allais, Fourgeaud, Georges Rottier.

369 COLLOQUE INTERNATIONAL SUR LES ALGERIENS ET LE DROIT DES GENS, BRUSSELS, 1961. Les Algériens et le droit des gens; Colloque international, Bruxelles, 18-19 mars 1961. [Bruxelles, 1961] 93 p. ports.

Congress of over 50 lawyers from France, Algeria, Belgium, Italy, Morocco, Netherlands, Switzerland devoted to rights of asylum of Algerian nationalists, status of Algerian emigrés and refugees, recognition of Algerian Provisional Government. For second colloquium on Algerian nationalism, see no. 1753.

370 COLLOQUE SUR L'ENSEIGNEMENT EN AFRIQUE DU NORD, PARIS, 1961. L'enseignement en Afrique du nord; colloque organisé par l'Union nationale des étudiants de France, l'Union nationale des étudiants du Maroc; l'Union nationale des étudiants de Tunisie et l'Association des étudiants musulmans nord-africains. Paris, 13-14 mai 1961. Le gérant: B. Giraudy. Paris, 1961. 133 p. (UNEF informations)

Complete text of speeches and discussions. In addition to information on current educational practices and proposed reforms in Morocco, Tunisia, and Algeria (there are statistics for school and university attendance in Algeria for 1958-59) discussion revolves around possibilities of French-North African technical cooperation. One of reports is by sociologist Pierre Bourdieu on cultural mutations induced by Algerian war.

371 COLLOQUES DE BERLIN: La démocratie à l'épreuve du XXe siècle, par Raymond Aron et al. Paris, Calmann-Levy, 1960. 262 p. (Collection "Liberté de l'esprit")

Some of addresses at this 10th anniversary meeting of Congress for Cultural Freedom appraise French Fifth Republic in terms of its democratic potential.

372 COLLOQUES SOCIALISTES, 1964. La pensée socialiste contemporaine; actes des Colloques socialistes de 1964. Paris, Presses universitaires de France, 1965. 345 p.

Purpose of colloquia was to find common ground among groups sympathetic to social democracy and opposed to de Gaulle. 5 meetings were held between December 1962 and June 1964 and participants included François Mitterand, P.S.U. leaders (Gilles Martinet, Robert Verdier) S.F.I.O. (Christian Pineau) political clubs (Alain Savary, Georges Suffert, Roger Quilliot, Charles Hernu) trade unions (Serge Mallet, Pierre Lebrun.) Topics discussed were: 1) ideological problems; 2) foreign and European policy; 3) planning and agriculture; 4) political institutions of Fifth Republic; 5) education and information policy; 6) cooperation with trade unions, co-operatives.

373 COMBE, PAUL. Le drame français; du libre-échange au marché commun. Préf. d'André Siegfried. Paris, Plon, 1959. 230 p. (Tribune libre, 49)

Analysis of French economic decline and list of remedies (such as freer market economy, reduced government expenses) to permit integration in Common Market. Economic measures of Fifth Republic are welcomed.

374* COMITE ANTICOLONIALISTE. [Protest against Algerian war by student organization grouping 18 student associations opposed to war, 1961]

375* COMITE ANTICOLONIALISTE ETUDIANT. [Protest against mistreatment of Algerians in France and list of member student organizations in Comité, 1961] 2 p.

376* COMITE ANTICOLONIALISTE ETUDIANT. [Protest against police reprisals taken against Algerians in France, October 23rd, Paris 1961] 2 p.

377 COMITE DE COORDINATION SCIENTIFIQUE DU SAHARA. Les Mekhadma; étude sur l'évolution d'un groupe humain dans le Sahara moderne. Effectuée par le Centre d'études et d'informations des problèmes humains dans les zones arides (Prohuza) Paris, Arts et métiers graphiques, 1960. 223 p. illus., ports., 3 double maps, tables, diagrs. "Ouvrages cités": p. 221-224.

This nomadic Saharan tribe was subjected to battery of psychological and medical tests to study the impact of introduction of oil industry on demography, economy, culture within this microcosm. The committee itself was established by Soustelle in 1958.

378 COMITE FRANC-DOLLAR. Business operations in France; a guide for American investors. Washington, D.C. 1959, 1961. 2 v. diagrs.

Information on French economy, investment credit, taxation policy, list of U.S. companies in France, members of Comité franc-dollar.

379 COMITE FRANÇAIS DES SCIENCES HISTORIQUES. La recherche historique en France de 1940 à 1965. Paris, Centre national de la recherche scientifique, 1965. lxiv, 518 p. Bibliography: p. 207-477.

Essay on recent achievements of French historiography, followed by description of centers for historical research and teaching, publishing organs for historical studies. Appendix lists, by topic, over 6000 historical works by French authors, 1940-65, with author index.

380* COMITE MAURICE AUDIN. L'Affaire Audin. Paris, 1958. 4 p.

Short statement on Maurice Audin's arrest and death, June 1957.

381 COMITE MAURICE AUDIN. Sans commentaire. Paris, Éditions de Minuit, 1961. 111 p. (Collection documents)

Testimony reprinted by Comité Maurice Audin, which was given by Colonel Argoud at closed session of Barricades trial, December 21, 1960, stating army's and civilian government's views on use of torture in Algerian war. Appendix reproduces reforms suggested by Argoud November 1959 for military justice against F.L.N.

381a COMITE MAURICE AUDIN. The "Comité Maurice Audin" and "Vérité-Liberté" present "October in Paris," Paris, 1962. 8 p.

Short description of two sponsoring organizations and summary of film, as well as problems of production and distribution. Film deals with events of Oct. 17, 1961, when a mass demonstration of Algerians in Paris was harshly repressed by police. Film also shows background of living conditions of Algerians and gives as sequel the Feb. 8, 1962 demonstration for peace, in which Frenchmen suffered equally harsh treatment by police. Film was seized by police when first shown Oct. 1962.

382 COMITE POUR LA PAIX EN ALGERIE. La Belgique devant le problème algérien. [Chênée, 1960?] 68 p.

Arguments against Belgian support of French position at U.N. citing documents on use of torture and Algerian majority's backing of F.L.N.

383 COMITE POUR LA VERITE SUR L'AFFAIRE BEN BARKA. L'affaire Ben Barka; suivi d'une lettre-postface de Maurice Clavel. Paris, 1966. 88 p. (Cahiers du Témoignage chrétiens, no. 45)

Biography of Ben Barkha, summary of the assassination, statements by Committee and its members, November 1965 - March 1966.

384 COMITE POUR LA VERITE SUR L'AFFAIRE BEN BARKA. Enseignements et lacunes du premier procès; complément au Cahier no. 45, september 1966. Paris, 1967. 88 p. (Cahiers du Témoignage chrétien, no. 46)

Further details on assassination and police responsibilities revealed during trial, and testimonies before court of friends of victim. Committee activities are recorded through March 1967.

385 COMITE RESISTANCE SPIRITUELLE. Des rappelés témoignent... Paris, Imp. Chaffiotte-Ruaud, 1957. 95 p.

Testimonies by former soldiers and officers in Algeria on use of torture, violence against civilians, as part of pacification program. These are preceded by Comité des Intellectuels' appeal against war crimes in Algeria with signatures including those of François Mauriac and André Philip.

386* COMMUNAUTE CATHOLIQUE DE SCIENCES POLITIQUES. [A leaflet, 1961.]

Invitation to lecture by Jacques Fauvet.

387 CONFEDERATION GENERAL DU TRAVAIL. C.G.T.: 70 années de luttes ouvrières. Paris, 1965. 96 p. illus. (part mounted) facsims.

Pictorial history of C.G.T. with final pages illustrating clashes with Gaullist government 1958-1964.

388 CONFÉDÉRATION GÉNÉRALE DU TRAVAIL. CONGRES NATIONAL, 35th, IVRY, 1965. Compte rendu in extenso des débats, Gymnase A.-Delaune, Rue Robespierre, Ivry-sur-Seine, 16-21 mai, 1965. Paris, 1965. 535 p.

No specific discussion of union's role in coming presidential election, but only of union's economic demands.

389 CONGAR, YVES and JOSEPH FOLLIET. Armée et vie nationale. Lyon, Chronique sociale de France, 1962. 139 p. ("Le Fond du problème" 1) Bibliography: p. 53-55.

Exposition of Christian point of view on patriotism and conscientious objection in new roles of army by Catholic theologian (Congar) and social scientist's survey of army's place in a democratic society (Folliet).

390 CONGO (BRAZZAVILLE) MINISTERE DE L'INFORMATION. Le voyage official du Président de la République en France, 18-23 décembre 1961. [Brazzaville, Impr. Officielle, 1961] 23 p.

Speeches by President Youlou of Congo Republic during his official visit to France.

391 CONSCIENCES MAGHRIBINES (periodical). Documents algériens. [Alger] Éditions Résistance algérienne [1956] 62 p.

Documentation on Algerian revolution edited by André Mandouze. It consists of texts of F.L.N. appeals, directives, leaflets since outbreak of revolution, together with documents on administration of justice and medicine. Collection includes Soustelle's reply to appeal of "Comité d'action contre la guerre en Afrique du Nord" signed by 300 French intellectuals.

392 CONSEIL COLMARIEN DE LA JEUNESSE. Que lisent les jeunes d'aujourd'hui? Résultats d'une enquête du Conseil colmarien de la jeunesse, 1958-59. By A. Ostertag. Colmar, 1959? 10 l.

Study of 5,000 children and adolescents in Colmar schools giving results for quantity and types of books and periodicals read.

393 CONSEIL NATIONAL DU PATRONAT FRANCAIS. ASSEMBLEE GENERALE. 30th, 1961. Assemblée générale 17 janvier, 1961. Paris, 1961. 159 p.

Reports of committees on French economy, international economic situation, social questions, and activities of C.N.P.F. in these spheres during 1960. For C.N.P.F.'s regular publication, see no. 2041.

394 CONSEIL NATIONAL DU PATRONAT FRANÇAIS. COMMISSION DE TOURISME TECHNIQUE. France; its industries. Paris, 1962. 44 p. illus., fold. map (in pocket)

Industry by industry survey of output, 1961.

395 CONTE, ARTHUR. La succession; pour "la France neuve" une charte des temps nouveaux. Paris, R. Julliard, 1963. 229 p.

Non-partisan survey of transformations in French political, social, economic scene after liquidation of the Algerian problem and on heels of November 1962 general elections, on the basis of which possible successors to de Gaulle (individuals and parties) for 1965 or 1972 are examined. Constitutional reforms for a more viable presidential regime are formulated and the prospects for European unification reviewed.

396 CONTENS, PIERRE. Gaullisme et prolétariat. Paris, Éditions du Scorpion, 1960. 94 p. (Collection Alternance)

French worker's confused indictment of government and society.

397 Contre-révolution; stratégie et tactique. By *** Liège, P. Joly, [1957?] 133 p. tables. Half-title: De la "guerre révolutionnaire" à la "guerre de libération nationale." "Editeur responsable: P. Joly."

1943 study on strategy of Communist revolutionary warfare is brought up to date for 1956-57 by schematically alligning French political forces either in revolutionary or counter-revolutionary camp. Thus the government of the Fourth Republic, with its policy of European integration and Algerian liberalization becomes a revolutionary element while nationalist groups, Army, French Algerians are presented as counter-revolutionary groups, and Algeria is foreseen as likeliest battleground. (Editor Pierre Joly later played part on Algerian scene.) May 1958 Paris edition by Editions francaises et internationales. (150 p., "Revolution et contre-révolution," 2) offers no new material. See also no. 630.

398 CONVENTION DES INSTITUTIONS REPUBLICAINES. Bilan économique de la Ve République. [Paris, 1967] 61 p. (Its Cahiers, 7) "Supplément à 'Combat républicain,' no. 25, mars, 1967."

Area by area criticism of Fifth Republic's economic policy and achievements.

399 CONVENTION DES INSTITUTIONS REPUBLICAINES. L'esprit de décembre. Paris, 1966. 30 p. (Its Cahiers, 5) "Supplément à 'Combat républicain,' no. 20, octobre 1966."

Excerpts from and comments on correspondence received at Mitterand's headquarters after Dec. 1965 presidential elections.

400 CONVENTION DES INSTITUTIONS REPUBLICAINES. Le programme de la Fédération de la gauche démocrate et socialiste. Paris, 1966. 57 p. (Cahiers, 4) "Supplément à 'Combat républicain,' no. 19, septembre 1966."

Official July 1966 program of Fédération de la gauche démocrate et socialiste, covering political institutions, foreign affairs, social and economic policy.

401* THE COOLEY (JOHN K.) COLLECTION. Documents concerning the Algiers military putsch, April 19-27, 1961. 4 envelopes in pam box. Table of contents in Envelope 1.

Christian Science Monitor North African correspondent's collection of news dispatches and texts of news broadcasts emanating from Algiers, April 18-27, 1961 and memoranda on his personal conversations with officers at that time. Other items of interest are typescripts of interviews by Cooley with Ferhat Abbas and Belkacem Krim and political bulletins of Algerian Provisional Government's mission in Morocco, December 1961 and January 1962.

402 COPFERMANN, EMILE. La génération des blousons noirs; problèmes de la jeunesse française. Préf. de Claude Bourdet. Paris, F. Maspero, 1962. 223 p. (Cahiers libres, no. 30)

Study of factors influencing French youth: family, school, work, organization of leisure, military service, youth movements and Gaullist youth policy, which author finds inadequate.

403 COPFERMANN, EMILE. Le théâtre populaire, pourquoi? Paris, F. Maspero, 1965. 165 p. (Cahiers libres, 69) Includes bibliography.

Theatrical productions for popular (mainly working class) audiences, their cultural and political objectives and criticisms of this art form. The work of the Théatre National Populaire is described in detail.

404 COSSE-BRISSAC, PIERRE, DUC DE. Longitudes. Paris, O. Perrin, 1964. 286 p.

Personal travel diary of French economist in 1950's and 1960's.

405 COSTON, HENRY, éd. Dictionnaire de la politique française. Paris, H. Coston, La Librairie française, 1967. 1088 p. illus., ports.

Revised edition of author's "Partis, journaux et hommes politiques d'hier et d'aujourd'hui" (no. 407) brought up to date through March 1967. This reference work is a mine of information on all aspects of French political life in the 20th century. Entries from a paragraph to several pages and arranged alphabetically identify political figures and political writers, political parties and other organizations, political newspapers and journals. For organizations and journals, political evolution is traced and current address, leading members listed.

406 COSTON, HENRY. Dictionnaire des pseudonymes. Paris, 1961. 260 p. "Lectures françaises. Numéro spécial."

Pen names, alphabetically arranged, of contemporary journalists, writers, artists. Pen names are followed by profession and real name.

407 COSTON, HENRI, éd. Partis, journaux et hommes politiques d'hier et d'aujourd'hui. Paris, 1960. 620 p. "Lectures françaises. Numéro spécial, Décembre 1960."

Repertory of major and minor French political parties and organizations, political figures, political press for Fourth and Fifth Republic divided by principal ideological orientation. A 60-page name index and good table of contents facilitate use. See no. 405 for an up dated and revised edition.

408 COSTON, HENRY. Le retour des "100 familles." Paris, Librairie française, 1960. 190 p. col. diagrs. (part fold.)

Interpenetration of business and political life during Fourth and Fifth Republic. On Fifth Republic, author highlights support of big business for de Gaulle May 1958, big business representatives in Gaullist "brain trust" and in National Assembly. There is considerable information on growth of U.S. investment in France, trade with Communist states, impact of industrial and commercial concentration, with lists of 200 leading French companies and commercial establishments. The basic thesis is that international capitalist interests dictate policies even under de Gaulle.

409 COTTA, MICHELE. La presse française. Paris, 1960. 9, 14, 24 p. (Fondation des sciences politiques. Cycle supérieur d'études politiques. Guide de recherches, no. 2) Includes bibliography.

History of French press since 1944, including political classification and general statistical information on dailies and weeklies. Detailed identification is provided for 13 Paris dailies and 11 French weeklies (Aspects de la France, Canard Enchaîné, Carrefour, Express, France Catholique, France Nouvelle, France-Observateur, Nation Française, Paris-Match, Rivarol, Témoignage Chrétien.)

410 COTTAZ, MAURICE. Les procès du Putsch d'Alger et du complot de Paris. Paris, Nouvelles éditions latines, 1962. 250 p. ports.

Excerpts from trials of 130 military figures, mainly high-ranking officers such as Commandant Denoix de Saint-Marc, Generals Bigot, Petit, Gouraud, as well as captains and colonels, implicated in April 1961 Generals' Putsch in Algeria. The trials took place June 1961 and January 1962 before the Tribunal militaire permanent de Paris. Seven officers (among them General Jacques Faure) and fifteen civilians were tried for "complot de Paris" in connection with Algerian putsch. Name index of defendents.

411 COTTERET, JEAN MARIE, CLAUDE EMERI and PIERRE LALUMIÈRE. Lois électorales et inégalités de représentation en France, 1936-1960, by Jean Marie Cotteret. Introd. de Maurice Duverger. Paris, A. Colin, 1960. xxii, 409 p. diagrs. (Cahiers de la Fondation nationale des sciences poliques. Partis et élections, 107) "Bibliographie": p. 395-403.

Detailed study of laws and parliamentary controversy on electoral system during Third and Fourth Republic, with analysis of inequalities of representation due to geographic malapportionment and distortions due to method of suffrage (proportional representation vs majority suffrage). The elections studied in detail are those of 1936, 1945, 1946, 1951, and 1956. A concluding chapter describes electoral system and reapportionment introduced Sept. 1958 and results of Nov. 1958 elections in terms of new inequalities of representation. Book stops with this election. Of particular interest is explanation of success of U.N.R. Extensive bibliography of documentary sources, books and articles.

412 COTTERET, JEAN MARIE. Le pouvoir législatif en France. Ouvrage honoré d'une subvention du Ministère de l'éducation nationale. Paris, Librairie générale de droit et de jurisprudence, R. Pichon et R. Durand-Auzias, 1962. 191 p. (Bibliothèque de droit public, t. 46) Bibliography: p. 185-188.

First part gives history of parliamentary role from French revolution to 1958, second part studies shift of power to executive by analyzing relevant provisions (and their genesis) of the 1958 Constitution restricting legislative prerogatives and follows up consequences in terms of legislative activity 1959-1962.

413 COULMAS, PETER, éd. Frankreich deutet sich selbst; 12 prominente Franzosen über Politik, Wirtschaft, Gesellschaft und Kultur. Übersetzung der französischen Texte von H. G. Brenner. Hamburg, Hoffman und Campe, 1961. 227 p.

Collection of talks given over Norddeutscher Rundfunk to interpret current French politics, economy, culture to German audience. Speakers were: George Vedel (French constitution) Jean-François Gravier (centralization) Emile Roche (economy) Raymond Aron (Franco-German relations) Pierre Emanuel (Franco-American relations) André Philip (French Left) Pierre-Henri Simon (Church-state problems in education) Gabriel d'Arboussier (French Community in Africa) François Bondy (French intellectuals) Jean Bloch-Michel (post-war literature) Jean Duvignaud (French youth) Romain Gary (de Gaulle.)

414 COURRIER DE LA COLERE (periodical). Le "Courrier de la colère;" contribution à une anthologie du gaullisme: préf. de Georges Guille. Paris, Parti socialiste, 1958? 31 p.

Chronologically arranged short excerpts from weekly "Courrier de la Colère" edited by Michel Debré between Nov. 1957 and July 1958. This republication of Debré's violent indictment of Fourth Republic and its Algerian policy implicitly condemns new regime for having done no better.

415 COURTIN, RENE. L'Europe de l'Atlantique à l'Oural. Paris, Esprit nouveau, 1963. 142 p.

Critical analysis of de Gaulle's "grand design" for a Europe from the Atlantic to the Urals and reconciliation with Russia. Author shows tortuous Gaullist strategy in light of recent Franco-German Treaty and rejection of British Common Market application, drawing parallels with Algerian disengagement. Excerpts from de Gaulle's writings and speeches on European policy 1945-June 1963.

416 COUTANT, PIERRE. La fonction publique militaire; le statut des officiers et des sous-officiers de carrière des armées. De la situation dans l'État des officiers, des fonctionnaires militaires assimilés et des sous-officiers des armées actives de terre, de mer et de l'air. Paris, Charles-Lavauzelle, 1961. 285 p. Includes bibliography.

Guide with specific references to applicable statutes, decrees, court decisions, on duties and rights of commissioned and non-commissioned career officers in all branches of armed forces (pay scales, advancements, pensions, civil rights, special limitations on marriage, etc.).

417 COUTROT, ALINE. Les forces religieuses en France depuis 1945. Paris, 1960. 14, vii l. (Fondation nationale des sciences politiques. Cycle supérieur d'études politiques. Guide de recherches, no. 6) Bibliography: p. i-vii.

Bibliography of books and articles on 1) Catholic press; 2) Catholic Church and political issues; 3) Catholics and politics; 4) Catholic organizations. Most of publications refer to pre-1958 period, but some of articles deal with Fifth Republic.

418 CRAIPEAU, YVAN. La révolution qui vient; les voies nouvelles du socialisme. Paris, Éditions de Minuit, 1957. 311 p. (Documents)

This program for a united democratic socialist left was originally presented as a report to the congress of the Nouvelle gauche, a small leftist group that, together with other leftist splinter groups, formed the Union de la gauche socialiste some months later. Among the writers of the program are Louis Alvergnat, Claude Bourdet, Gilles Martinet.

419 LE CRAPOUILLOT (periodical). Les élections présidentielles de 1965; numéro spécial dirigé par Jean-François Revel. Historique de la campagne électorale et des élections présidentielles, par Michèle Cotta. Paris, 1966. 86 p. illus., ports. "No. 68: mars 1966."

History of presidential election campaign, sketches of candidates by Michele Cotta, evaluation of election outcome and attack on contradictions between Gaullist promises and actual policies by François Revel.

420 LE CRAPOUILLOT (periodical). Histoire du Parti communiste, par Roger Hagnauer et al. Paris, 1962. 79 p. illus., ports. "Numéro spécial."

Last pages review party's stand on Algerian war and internal leadership conflicts during Fifth Republic.

421 LE CRAPOUILLOT (periodical). Le petit de Gaulle illustré. Paris, 1967. 87 p. illus., ports. facsims. "Nouvelle série, no. 1. Hiver 1967-68."

Satirical biography going from childhood through 1967 with numerous illustrations and cartoons.

422 CREMIEUX, FRANCIS. Entretiens avec Emmanuel d'Astier. Paris, P. Belfond, 1966. 191 p.

April-May 1966 television interviews confronting Communist journalist with Emmanuel d'Astier de la Vigerie, political journalist, writer, and former deputy of Union progressiste (extreme left party allied with Communists). Interviews retrace Astier's childhood and youth, participation in Resistance, editorship of pro-Communist newspaper "Libération," parliamentary experience, break with Communists and recent support for de Gaulle in presidential campaign, abandonment of "Libération" in favor of a new monthly, "L'événement."

423 CREMIEUX-BRILHAC, JEAN LOUIS, éd. L'éducation nationale, le Ministère, l'administration centrale, les services. Préf. de Francis-Louis Closon. Paris, Presses universitaires de France, 1965. 760 p. (L'Administration française)

Collective work by 60 contributors from different branches of educational establishment, teachers, administrators, and researchers. Work summarizes current problems and state of primary, secondary, and university education, presenting all recent reforms and up-to-date figures on enrollment, supply, salaries, mentality of educators, etc., with separate sections on administrative and teaching corps subdivisions.

424 CROZIER, BRIAN. The rebels: a study of post-war insurrections. London, Chatto and Windus, 1960. 256 p.

Motivations and techniques of insurrection against colonial rule, with Algeria used as prime example for techniques of terrorism and official repression and for typical leadership conflicts among rebels.

425 CROZIER, MICHEL. Le Phénomène bureaucratique; essai sur les tendances bureaucratiques des systèmes d'organisation modernes et sur leurs relations en France avec le système social et culturel. Paris, Éditions du Seuil, 1964, c1963. 413 p. illus.

Concrete illustration of the effects of bureaucratic organization through investigation of two typical bureaucratic establishments, a large government accounting agency in Paris and a nationalized industry. Social scientist, on the basis of these examples, analyzes specific features of French bureaucracy, its manifestations in education, colonization, labor movement, political organization, relations between bourgeoisie and bureaucracy, factors favoring bureaucracy's effectiveness and adaptation to change through alternation of routine and crisis, with interesting reflections on the current challenges to the system. Author does not share obsession about dangers of technocratic evolution.

426 CRUBELLIER, MAURICE. Un civisme pour notre temps. Tournai, Casterman, 1964. 161 p.

Lycée history teacher's experiences in teaching civics and reflections on the proper contents for contemporary French education.

427 CRUGER, DORIS M. A list of American doctoral dissertations on Africa, covering 1961-62 through 1964-65; France, covering 1933-34 through 1964-65; Italy, covering 1933-34 through 1964-65. Compiled by Doris M. Cruger. Ann Arbor, Mich., Xerox, University Microfilms Library Services, 1967. 36 p.

Within each section, dissertations are alphabetically arranged by author. A few of theses deal with Fifth Republic.

428 CY, CLAUDE, éd. Paroles de chefs [1940-1962] Nogent-sur-Marne, Éditions Inter-France-monde, 1963. 412 p.

Excerpts from press conferences, speeches by de Gaulle retracing chronologically his changing views on Algeria. Biting comments underline his reversals and contradictions and de Gaulle's personal responsibility for the loss of Algeria. Michel Debré and whole spectrum of French political parties (Gaullists, M.R.P., Communists, Radicals, Socialists, Independents) have their statements and programs recorded and analyzed similarly to prove that they too repudiated their original position favoring French Algeria and welcomed Evian agreements.

429 DALMA, ALFONS, éd. De Gaulle, die Deutschen, Europa; im Spiegel der kommentierten Texte, Dokumente und Zitate. Karlsruhe, 1962. 136 p. plates, ports. (Der aktuelle Punkt)

De Gaulle's state visit in Germany, September 1962, with excerpts from speeches, commentaries explaining de Gaulle's gradual acceptance of German friendship and European unification.

430 DARBOIS, DOMINIQUE and PHILIPPE VIGNEAU. Les Algériens en guerre. Milano, G. Feltrinelli, 1961. 1 v. (unpaged) illus.

Pictorial work on Algerian nationalists engaged in combat and as refugees in Tunisia.

431 DARBOISE, JEAN MARIE, MAURICE HEYNAUD and JACQUES MARTEL. Officiers en Algérie. Postface de R. Barrat. Paris, F. Maspero, 1960. 113 p. (Cahiers libres, no. 11)

Authors served as reserve officers in Algeria Summer 1958-1959 and describe different aspects of war: failure of pacification program, effects of fighting on French soldiers, Algerian reactions. Gaullist "self-determination" policy is viewed sceptically in the light of actual situation.

432 DARBOY, MARCEL. Jeunesse de France en Algérie. [Paris] R. Lacoste [1959]. 137 p.

Law student having served as officer in Algeria June 1956-Dec. 1958 traces impact of experience on his attitude toward Algerian war, from cynicism to identification with French cause.

433 DAUDET, YVES. La Présidence des assemblées parlementaires françaises. Préf. de Georges Berlia. Paris, Presses universitaires de France, 1965. 146 p. (Travaux et recherches de la Faculté de droit et des sciences économiques de Paris. Série "Droit public," no. 2) Includes bibliography.

Presidency of National Assembly and Senate prior to and during Fifth Republic. Special attention is paid to the current holders of the office, Jacques Chaban-Delmas, an unconditional Gaullist, who is president of the Assembly, and Gaston Monnerville, an equally unconditional anti-Gaullist, who is president of the Senate.

434 DAUER, JACQUES and MICHEL RODET. Les orphelins du gaullisme. Paris, R. Julliard, 1962. 251 p.

Authors broke away from U.N.R. to found "Mouvement pour la Communauté" in May 1959. Movement has militant stand on Franco-African cooperation and social reforms, accepts Fifth Republic but does not expect it to survive de Gaulle. Included is detailed account of movement's clash with pro-French Algeria forces inside and outside U.N.R., particularly in Algeria, 1959-1962. See also "Le Télegramme de Paris" (no. 2109) of which Dauer was editor.

435 DAUER, JACQUES and MICHEL RODET. Le 13 mai sans complots. Paris, Pensée moderne, 1959. 192 p.

Militants of R.P.F. youth movement until de Gaulle's withdrawal from politics, editors from January 1956 of "Télégramme de Paris" (no. 2109) authors describe their efforts

436 DAVEY, ELIZABETH, éd. France in Crisis. New York, Wilson, 1957. 208 p. (The Reference shelf, v. 19, no. 2) Bibliography: p. 197-208.

Short articles by American journalists on problem areas of French politics, domestic, colonial, and international.

437 DAVEZIES, ROBERT. Le front. Paris, Éditions de Minuit, 1960. 233 p. (Documents)

French priest's interviews in Tunisia and Morocco Spring 1959 with Algerian refugees, militants of Union générale du travail algérien, members of F.L.N. and combatants. The conclusion is that F.L.N. is real spokesman of ordinary Algerians.

438 DAVID, JEAN. La gauche coupable. Paris, Éditions du Seuil, 1960. 105 p.

Attack on non-Communist French Left as exemplified by "L'Express" for failing to support de Gaulle in his Algerian policy, aiding F.L.N., and confining their efforts to futile verbal opposition instead of advancing condition of working class, whose culture and ideals they, as academic and professional men, do not genuinely share.

438a DAVID, RENE. Bibliographie du droit français, 1945-1960, établie pour le Comité international pour la documentation des sciences sociales, sous le patronage de l'Association internationale des sciences juridiques. Paris, Mouton, 1964. 252 p. (Maison des sciences de l'homme, Service d'échange d'informations scientifiques. Publications. Série A: Bibliographies, I.) LL

Annotated and topically arranged bibliography giving general and specialized works on French jurisprudence and collections of laws, publications of individual government agencies. Law Library has current French administrative, civil, commercial, family, labor, military, penal, press, rural, and tax codes.

439 De l'impérialisme à la décolonisation. By Gabriel Ardant, Kostas Axelos, Jacques Berque, Charles Bellelheim etc. Edited by Jean-Paul Charnay. Paris, Éditions de Minuit, 1965. 505 p. (Grands documents, 23)

First half of essays by individual contributors (mainly French economists and sociologists) gives glimpses of impact of colonization in North Africa and other parts of French empire on colonial economies and cultures, second half shows problems of continuing economic progress after political independence in a manner compatible with a genuine integration of native culture and society. The concept of neo-colonialism is defined in this context, and the attempt is made to determine the proper role of economic and technical assistance. Jacques Berque's introduction and conclusion tie together the individual essays.

440 DEADLINE DATA ON WORLD AFFAIRS. "Algerian Algeria." New York, Keynote Publications, 1963. 72 p. map. (Its On record, v. 1, no. 8)

Synopsis of events leading to independence, followed by chronology and comments by U.S., British, and French statesmen, on events June 1962 to December 1963.

441 DEADLINE DATA ON WORLD AFFAIRS. France; "grandeur" vs Atlantic unity. New York, 1965. 68 p. (Its On record, v. 2, no. 7)

Nov. 1963 - Nov. 1964 chronology of French foreign policy, highlighting withdrawal from the Atlantic Alliance (recognition of Communist China, pro-Soviet statements, lack of cooperation with NATO, reluctance to accept tariff reductions in favor of U.S.)

442 DEBATISSE, MICHEL. La révolution silencieuse; le combat des paysans. Préf. de Fr. Bloch-Lainé. Paris, Calmann-Lévy, 1963. 275 p. (Questions d'actualité)

Secretary of Centre National des Jeunes Agriculteurs describes rebellion of young French farmers against former conditions of life and organizations set up to adapt to needs of modern agriculture. Agricultural programs of Fifth Republic are summarized and found basically acceptable.

443 DEBATTY, ANDRE. Le 13 mai et la presse. Paris, A. Colin, 1960. 327 p. illus., ports., tables, facsims. (Kiosque; les faits, la presse, l'opinion. 8) "Bibliographie sommaire": p. 315-322.

Excerpts from French, Algerian, and foreign press on events in Algeria May 13 - June 6, 1958, with facsimiles of individual pages and illustrations. Good chronology and extensive bibliography on Algerian crisis and origins of Fifth Republic. The series is edited by Jean Prinet of the Bibliothèque Nationale's periodical division.

444 DEBESSE, M. L. et al. La vie économique du monde et place de la France dans l'économie mondiale; 3e année collèges techniques. Paris, J.-B. Ballière, 1965. 163 p. illus., maps, diagrs. (Cours de géographie, Collèges d'enseignement)

Survey of major agricultural products and output of basic industrial commodities for world as a whole and for France.

445 DEBRE, MICHEL. Au service de la nation; essai d'un programme politique. Paris, Stock, 1963. 279 p.

Guidelines of government policies and programs in fields of economic expansion, social welfare, demography, military security, European unification, foreign relations, constitutional reform.

446 DEBRE, MICHEL. Ces princes qui nous gouvernent; lettre aux dirigeants de la Nation. Paris, Plon, 1957. 206 p. (Tribune libre, 7)

Condemnation of divisive parliamentary system, with specific attack on policies of European economic and military integration.

447 DEBRE, MICHEL. Déclaration de M. le Premier ministre sur la politique économique et sociale à l'Assemblée nationale, séance du mardi 3 octobre 1961. Paris, Documentation française, 1961. 24 p.

448 DEBRE, MICHEL and PIERRE MENDES-FRANCE. Le grand débat. Préf. de Georges Altschuler. Paris, Gonthier, 1966. 204 p.

Stenographic text of three debates on Radio Europe No. 1, November 22 - December 1, 1965 covering: social and economic problems; France's position in the world; political institutions. This passionate clash of opinions at the eve of presidential election gives voice to opposing evaluations of Fifth Republic's achievements.

449 DEBRE, MICHEL. Jeunesse, quelle France te faut-il?; Essai pour une politique nationale. Meaux (S.-et-M.) Plon, 1965. 215 p.

Defense of Gaullist principles of strong executive power and national solidarity as the best safeguards for individual liberty and most realistic path toward eventual European solidarity. Other points of Gaullist program of national defense, demographic and economic expansion, promotion of social welfare and mobility are briefly outlined.

450 DEBRE, MICHEL. La mort de l'état républicain. Paris, Gallimard, 1947. 238 p. fold. map (Problèmes et documents)

Attack on parliamentary system established by 1946 Constitution, with detailed criticism and counterproposals regarding proportional parliamentary representation.

451 DEBRE, MICHEL. Pour l'Algérie; deux discours prononcés le 15 mars et le 29 mai 1956 à la tribune du Conseil de la République. Le Mans, 1956. 31 p.

Plea for strong military action in Algeria and statements on international repercussions of struggle. As editor of "Courrier de la Colère," Debré stated his stand even more forcefully (see no. 414).

452 DEBRE, MICHEL. Refaire une démocratie, un état, un pouvoir. Paris, Plon, 1958. 79 p. (Tribune libre, 35)

Four campaign speeches July-August 1958 held at local gatherings in Loire region and covering case for French Algeria, discussion of proposed constitution, plans for African Community, plea in favor of September 1958 referendum.

453 DEBRE, MICHEL. La république et son pouvoir. Paris, Nagel, 1950. 204 p. (Écrits politiques)

Principles for a strong and free republic with stable governmental authority and how to achieve it in the face of existing institutions.

454 DEBRE, MICHEL. Sur le gaullisme. Paris, Plon, 1967. 24 p. (Tribune libre 67)

Campaign speech before March 1967 legislative elections on what Gaullism has done for France and what is its interpretation of nationalism.

455 DEFENSE DE L'OCCIDENT (periodical). L'armée française. Paris, 1958. 159 p.

One group of articles covers technical status and needs of French Army and its role within NATO. A second group of articles centers on army's relation with nation (intellectuals' view of army, myth of the "paras," army's stand on military European integration, political intervention of army) with only scattered references to Algeria and changes brought by Fifth Republic. There are special studies on officer corps, reserve corps, and veterans.

456 DEFENSE DE L'OCCIDENT (periodical). Le drame algérien commence maintenant. By Frédéric-Dupont et al. Paris, Sept couleurs, 1961. 126 p. "Numéro spécial, no. 10-11 - janvier-février 1961."

Short contributions by deputies Frédéric-Dupont, J. B. Biaggi, on Algerian war, study by Jules Monnerot on nature of subversive warfare and Communist influence in France and Algeria. Personal testimonies on Barricades trial, correspondence between Algerian and French workers, May-June 1958 Algerian diary.

457 DEFENSE DE L'OCCIDENT (periodical). La jeunesse. By Maurice Bardèche et al. Paris, 1964. 112 p. "Numéro spécial, avril-mai 1964."

Short articles on different segments of French youth (delinquents, society youth, students, political activists, Communist students, farm youth), questions of worker education and military service. Some of contributors are active in nationalist youth organizations, one is functionary of Parti national syndicaliste français.

458 DEFENSE DE L'OCCIDENT (periodical). Où mène le gaullisme? Paris, Sept couleurs, 1967. 120 p. "No. spécial, février 1967."

Pierre Fontaine's demonstration of contradictory monarchist and collectivist tendencies latent in Gaullism, which provide ideal setting for international business interests.

459 DEFENSE DE L'OCCIDENT (periodical). Le Poujadisme. Paris, Sept couleurs, 1956. 133 p. "Numéro spécial, no. 33, mai, 1956."

Sympathetic history of Poujade movement, its program, statutes, organization, and prospect in 1956 National Assembly.

460 Défense politique. By A. Benabdallah, M. Courrégé, M. Oussedik et al. Paris, F. Maspero, 1961. 114 p. (Cahiers libres, no. 15)

Five lawyers (Abdessamad Benabdallah, Maurice Courrégé, Mourad Oussedik Jacques Vergès, and Michel Zavrian) report collectively their experiences as defense attorneys in trials of Algerian nationalists before French courts, showing how defendants used trials as political tool to prove that they were revolutionary militants rather than criminal terrorists. Lawyers develop new technical procedures for this type of political defense. Annexes summarize main trials involving Algerian nationalists.

461 DEFFERRE, GASTON. Un nouvel horizon; le travail d'une équipe. Paris, Gallimard, 1965. 183 p. (Collection idées)

Collective work by members of Association Horizon 80, formed to support Defferre's presidential candidacy, summarizing his economic, educational, and European platform.

462 DELBECQUE, LEON. Speeches, interpellations, reports, 1961. 1 env.

Delbecque's activities as member of the National Assembly until his eviction as U.N.R. dissident.

463 DEGRANGE, ERNEST. Un soldat de vraie France: Charles de Gaulle. [Marcinelle, J. Dupuis, 1958?] 91, [1] p. ports. "Bibliographie": p. [92]

Biography essentially based on de Gaulle's own writings and going up to 1945.

464 DEGUILLAUME, JACQUES. Hippolyte le Grand; préf. de Pierre Labracherie. Illus. de Paul Astruc et Lydia. Rodez, Editions Subervie, 1965. 179 p. illus.

Benignly satirical political biography of de Gaulle in the guise of a small-town Caesar.

465 DELARUE, LOUIS. Avec les paras du 1er R. E. P. et du 2e R. P. I. Ma. Paris, Nouvelles éditions latines, 1961. 250 p. illus., ports., map.

Diary entries by chaplain of parachutist regiment stationed in Algeria from 1955 until his recall in January 1961, describing the regiment's combat experiences and attempting to counteract notion that parachutists were enemies of Algerian people.

466 DELEGATION OF THE PROVISIONAL GOVERNMENT OF THE ALGERIAN REPUBLIC, NEW YORK.

Note: Propaganda and information organ of the Algerian Provisional Government, taking over the function of the Algerian Front of National Liberation Delegation in New York. (See no. 37.) Between September 1958 and May 1959, its official name is uncertain. The organization is also known as the Algerian Office. In addition to the items listed in subsequent entries, the Delegation's documents at the Hoover Institution include: 1) Reports on situation at United Nations, memoranda, declarations for U.N. sessions 13-16. 2) Reports on current Franco-Algerian negotiations (Melun, Evian). 3) Communiqués of the Provisional Government (see also Ferhat Abbas, Ben Khedda for statements by these political leaders). 4) Review of events in Algeria. The Delegation also published the statements of various French politicians and scholars favorable to the cause of Algerian nationalism; these will only be found under the authors (e.g., Tillion, no. 1703).

467* DELEGATION OF THE PROVISIONAL GOVERNMENT OF THE ALGERIAN REPUBLIC, N.Y. Algeria; questions and answers. New York, 1960. 26 p.

468* DELEGATION OF THE PROVISIONAL GOVERNMENT OF THE ALGERIAN REPUBLIC, N.Y. The Algerian problem and the question of the European minority... New York, 1961. 8 l. Doc. 61-5-E

469* DELEGATION OF THE PROVISIONAL GOVERNMENT OF THE ALGERIAN REPUBLIC, N.Y. The Algerian question; war in Algeria; the FLN carries the war to France. New York, 1958. 3 l. (Delegation of the Provisional Government of the Algerian Republic. Publications, series D, no. 1)

470* DELEGATION OF THE PROVISIONAL GOVERNMENT OF THE ALGERIAN REPUBLIC, N.Y. Background document on the situation of the thousands of Algerian prisoners in France and Algeria. New York, 1961. 3 l. Doc. 61-39-E

471* DELEGATION OF THE PROVISIONAL GOVERNMENT OF THE ALGERIAN REPUBLIC, N.Y. Bibliography of Algeria. New York, 1962. 7 l. Doc. no. 62-3

Good general bibliography on Algerian question and war, as of Jan. 1962.

472* DELEGATION OF THE PROVISIONAL GOVERNMENT OF THE ALGERIAN REPUBLIC, N.Y. The charter of self-determination. New York, 1961. 4 l. Doc. 61-6-E

Report on Colloque de Grenoble, 1961, favorable to Algerian independence.

473* DELEGATION OF THE PROVISIONAL GOVERNMENT OF THE ALGERIAN REPUBLIC, N.Y. Documents: The Franco-Algerian negotiations, Evian. I - 5, May 20, 1961-. New York, 1961. 5 docs. Doc. 61-17-E, 61-18-E, 61-21-E, 61-22-E, 61-26-E

473* DELEGATION OF THE PROVISIONAL GOVERNMENT OF THE ALGERIAN REPUBLIC, N.Y. The European minority in Algeria. New York, 1960. 7, 2 p.

475* DELEGATION OF THE PROVISIONAL GOVERNMENT OF THE ALGERIAN REPUBLIC, N.Y. France on trial. New York, 1960. 7 l.

Report on trial against signers of "Manifeste des 121," September 1960.

476* DELEGATION OF THE PROVISIONAL GOVERNMENT OF THE ALGERIAN REPUBLIC, N.Y. The French cantonal elections in Algeria. New York, 1960. 3 p.

477* DELEGATION OF THE PROVISIONAL GOVERNMENT OF THE ALGERIAN REPUBLIC, N.Y. French church leaders denounce army's excesses and use of torture in Algeria. New York, 1959. 3 l.

478* DELEGATION OF THE PROVISIONAL GOVERNMENT OF THE ALGERIAN REPUBLIC, N.Y. French elections in Algeria. New York, 1958. 4 l.

Report on Nov. 1958 elections.

479* DELEGATION OF THE PROVISIONAL GOVERNMENT OF THE ALGERIAN REPUBLIC, N.Y. French justice in Algeria. For Djamila Boupacha by Simone de Beauvoir. New York, 1960. 4 l.

480* DELEGATION OF THE PROVISIONAL GOVERNMENT OF THE ALGERIAN REPUBLIC, N.Y. The meeting of the National Council of the Algerian revolution at Tripoli (Libya) August 9 - August 27, 1961. New York, 1961. 3 l. 61-27-E

481* DELEGATION OF THE PROVISIONAL GOVERNMENT OF THE ALGERIAN REPUBLIC, N.Y. The meeting of the National Council of the Algerian Revolution at Tripoli (Libya) December 16, 1959 - January 18, 1960. New York, 1960. 5 l.

482* DELEGATION OF THE PROVISIONAL GOVERNMENT OF THE ALGERIAN REPUBLIC, N.Y. Partition. New York, 1961. 3 l. Doc. no. 61-23.

483* DELEGATION OF THE PROVISIONAL GOVERNMENT OF THE ALGERIAN REPUBLIC, N.Y. Policy declaration made by Mr. Ferhat Abbas, Prime Minister of the Provisional Government of the Algerian Republic, on September 26, 1958. New York, 1958. 3 l.

484* DELEGATION OF THE PROVISIONAL GOVERNMENT OF THE ALGERIAN REPUBLIC, N.Y. The pressing need for cooperation; editorial published in "Algérie Presse Service" no. 153, May 3, 1962. New York, 1962. 2 l. Doc. 62-11-E

485* DELEGATION OF THE PROVISIONAL GOVERNMENT OF THE ALGERIAN REPUBLIC, N.Y. The report of the International Committee of the Red Cross on torture and inhuman treatment of Algerians held in French prisons and camps. New York, 1960. 14 l.

486* DELEGATION OF THE PROVISIONAL GOVERNMENT OF THE ALGERIAN REPUBLIC, N.Y. The territorial integrity of Algeria; text of an editorial published in "El-Moujahid," the official organ of the Algerian Front of National Liberation, June 4, 1961. New York, 1961. 1 l. Doc. 61-19-E

487 DELIGNY, HENRI. H-S hors service. Lausanne, La Cité, 1961. 206 p. Novel of army life in Algeria, illustrating carry-over of political ideas from civilian life and a case of desertion by anti-militarist.

488 DELMAS, CLAUDE. L'alliance atlantique; essai de phénomenologie politique. Préf. du général Valluy. Paris, Payot, 1962. 278 p. (Bibliothèque historique) Bibliography: p. 265-268.

History and prospects of Atlantic Alliance by member of NATO International Secretariat.

489 DELMAS, CLAUDE. La guerre révolutionnaire. Paris, Presses universitaires de France, 1959. 127 p.

Study of ideological and psychological motivation underlying revolutionary wars, with special attention to role of terrorism, commissioned by Defense Minister Bourges-Maunoury, on whose staff author was serving. Algeria serves as a prime example of 20th century pattern imposed by communism and as a warning that simple "counterrevolutionary tactics" will not work in hands of western democracies.

490 DELMASURE, ADOLPHE. Les catholiques et la politique. Préf. de Pierre Tiberghien. Paris, La Colombe, 1960. 379 p.

Papal and other pronouncements of Catholic hierarchy on political questions, but only discussion of secular education is pertinent to Fifth Republic. Subject index, list of documents going back to 19th century.

491 DELON, PIERRE. Le syndicalisme chrétien en France. Préf. de Georges Cogniot. Paris, Éditions sociales, 1961. 90, 1, p. (Politique et religion) "Bibliographie": p. 91

Last chapters deal with Confédération Française des Travailleurs Chrétiens' political stand and collaboration with Confédération Générale du Travail.

492 DEON, MICHEL. L'armée d'Algérie et la pacification. Paris, Plon, 1959. 252 p. (Tribune libre, 47)

French army's response to communist-inspired revolutionary strategy in the work of the S. A. S. (Sections administratives specialisées) units, regroupment camps, education programs, psychological warfare, in which author sees only hope of saving Algeria. Appendices on communist assistance to F. L. N., Colonel Godard's report on dismantling terrorist organizations in Algiers in 1957, Minister Resident Robert Lacoste's general directives to officers in Algeria, nos. 1-5, May 1956-August 1957.

493 DEPREUX, EDOUARD. Renouvellement du socialisme. Préf. de Pierre Mendès-France. Paris, Calmann-Lévy, 1960. 212 p. (Questions d'actualité)

National Secretary of newly formed Parti Socialist Unifié gives party's position not only on potentialities of socialism in a prosperous industrial society but stand on strictly political questions like Algerian war, secular education, role of political parties. Socialist Party is criticized and new relations with P. C. F. envisaged. For Depreux speeches and statements, see Author Index.

494 DEROGY, JACQUES and JEAN-FRANÇOIS KAHN. Les secrets du ballottage; le récit, heure par heure, de la course à L'Elysée. Paris, Fayard, 1966. 279 p. illus., maps, ports.

The complete story of the 1965 presidential election, from the failure of Defferre's candidacy to the analysis of election results. All candidacies are analyzed, details of television and radio debates, campaign techniques before first and second round are presented, with good photographs of participants. Although there is little "secret" information and sources are primarily newspapers and public opinion surveys, journalist authors are well-informed on de Gaulle's own considerations and strategies of Gaullist leaders. There is an interesting chapter on support of de Gaulle by French intellectuals.

495 DESCLOITRES, ROBERT, JEAN-CLAUDE REVERDY, and CLAUDINE DESCLOÎTRES. L'Algérie des Bidonvilles; le tiers monde dans la cité. Paris, Mouton, 1961. 127 p. diagrs. (Le Monde d'outremer passé et présent, 2. sér.: Documents, 6) Bibliographical footnotes.

Urban sociology of Algeria studied on basis of pre-1954 statistics.

496 DESCLOITRES, ROBERT, JEAN-CLAUDE REVERDY, and CLAUDINE DESCLOÎTRES. Organisation urbaine et structures sociales en Algérie. [Aix-en-Provence, 1963] 31 p. "Extrait de la Revue 'Civilisations' vol. XII, 1962, no. 2."

Social structure of Algerian "bidonvilles" and their special coherence through ties with communities of origin, published by Centre africain des sciences humaines appliquées.

497 DESCLOITRES, ROBERT and LAID DEBZI. Système de parenté et structures familiales en Algérie. [Aix-en-Provence, 1963] 63 p. Includes bibliography

Analysis of traditional Agerian family structure, published by Centre Africain des sciences humaines appliquées.

498 DESSAIGNE, FRANCINE. Déracinés! ... Paris, Éditions du Fuseau, 1964. 222 p. (Collection Les Chemins du réel)

Not an autobiographical work like the author's earlier publication (see no 499), but a series of chronologically arranged vignettes on the lives of French Algerians from the last weeks of the war to April 1964. Most of the episodes reflect the repatriates' feelings of grief, hurt pride, experiences of rejection and incomprehension in the process of repatriation, although there are cases of successful adaptation. The author also describes reactions to a visit to Algeria in mid-1963.

499 DESSAIGNE, FRANCINE. Journal d'une mère de famille pied-noir. Avant-propos de Louis Rougier. Lagny-sur-Marne, L'Esprit nouveau, 1962. 239 p.

Diary of wife of French electrical engineer stationed in Algeria recording last 18 months of her stay before June 1962 exodus. These purportedly non-political reactions to the height of F. L. N. and O. A. S. violence bring out Europeans' anguish at atrocities and French disengagement, involvement with O. A. S. and decision to leave newly independent nation.

500 DES VALLIERES, JEAN. Et voici la Légion étrangère. Paris, Éditions André Bonne, 1963. 249 p. illus., ports., maps. (Les grands documentaires illustrés)

History of Foreign Legion, with third part describing its participation in campaigns of Algerian war.

501 DE TARR, FRANCIS. The French Radical Party. With a foreword by Pierre Mendès-France. London, Oxford University Press, 1961. 264 p. port. Bibliography: p. 251-253.

Factions within Radical Party up to end of Fourth Republic, with Sept. 1958 foreword by Mendès-France.

502 DEUTSCH, EMERIC, DENIS LINDON, and PIERRE WEILL. Les familles politiques aujourd'hui en France. Paris, Éditions de Minuit, 1966. 128 p. illus. (Grands documents, 27) Bibliography: p. 93-95.

Study interpreting results of 1964-1966 public opinion statistics to show division of French voters into 6 political families (extreme left, moderate left, center, moderate right, extreme right, floating electorate) and describing social background, political attitudes, voting behavior of each group in first and second round of 1965 presidential elections in order to determine what two-party configuration could have stability (authors see no hope, because of shifting, a-political 30% of voters who hold balance).

502a DEUTSCH, KARL WOLFGANG et al. French and German elite responses, 1964: code book and data. New Haven, Yale University, Political Science Research Library, 1966. 267 l.

Questionnaires and complete results of questionnaires used in a study of French and German politicians, military, business, union, and professional elite to determine attitudes on domestic and international political issues, notably disarmament, the Atlantic Alliance, and European unification. Results of this study were incorporated in "France, Germany, and the Western alliance" (no. 803).

502b DICTIONNAIRE DE DROIT. 2. éd. Paris, Dalloz, 1966 2 v. LL

Well-informed up-to-date encyclopedic dictionary defining not only legal concepts but giving accurate definitions of political and administrative terms and their current legal meaning. Dictionary is based on voluminous Dalloz law compendium.

503 DIDIER, RENE and ANDRE VOISIN. Économie et vie quotidienne; du budget familial aux comptes de la nation. Préf. d'Alain Barrère. Paris, Institut culture et promotion, Éditions du Centurion, 1964. 173 p. illus. (Faits sociaux, faits humains)

Text on basic economics using household budget as model and designed for use at Institut Culture et Promotion for adult education.

504   EL-DJEZAIRI. Où va l'économie algérienne? Économie intégrée ou économie associée? [Paris, 1960?] 55 p. (Problèmes de l'Algérie et du Sahara, no. 4)

Pamphlet published by Centre d'Information pour les problèmes de l'Algérie et du Sahara, under Soustelle, emphasizing economic interdependence between France and Algeria and need for further economic integration.

505   DOCUMENTATION FRANÇAISE ILLUSTREE (periodical). L'Afrique d'expression française [Rédigée avec le concours du Ministère de la coopération.] Paris, 1962. 60 p. illus., maps.

Brief history of road to independence and survey of each of African Republics, indicating joint technical and economic programs and ties with Common Market.

506   DOLLFUS, DANIEL F. La force de frappe. Paris, R. Julliard, 1960. 112 p.

Military and economic arguments against independent French or even European nuclear weapons as of late 1960. In place of Gaullist policy, author advocates coordination of military, including nuclear, efforts inside NATO, although U.S. missiles are judged inferior to Russian ones. Report was endorsed by Comite d'études pour la République.

507   DOLLOT, LOUIS. La France dans le monde actuel. Paris, Presses universitaires de France, 1960. 124 p.

France's position in world in terms of Frenchmen living outside country, diffusion of language and culture, achievements of its economy, science, technology, with list of "firsts" of French technology as of early 1959.

508   DOMENACH, JEAN-MARIE and ROBERT DE MONTVALON (comps). The Catholic avant-garde; French Catholicism since World War II. Translated from the French by Brigid Elson and others. New York, Holt, Rinehart and Winston, 1967. x 245 p. Bibliographical references included in "Notes" (p. 241-245)

Contributions of leading Catholic thinkers, writers, men of action to basic issues of post-war years, loosely arranged by topics such as involvement in political and social action, worker priests, trade unions, school question, anti-colonialism and world peace. Editors selected key passages from these men, with extensive explanatory sections of their own.

509   DOMENACH, JEAN-MARIE. La propagande politique. 5. éd. rév. Paris, Presses universitaires de France, 1965. 127 p. ("Que sais-je?" no. 448)

No significant revision from original 1950 edition, with examples of political propaganda drawn from communist and fascist states. Function of political propaganda in democracies is analyzed.

510   DOUENCE, JEAN-CLAUDE. La mise en place des institutions algériennes. Paris, 1964. 68 p. (Fondation nationale des sciences politiques. Centre d'étude des relations internationales. Ser. G: Études maghrebines, no. 2) Includes bibliography.

1962 dissertation, Univ. of Bordeaux, tracing series of political and legal crises, March 18 - Sept. 19, 1962 by which transfer of power took place from France to F.L.N. Evian agreements are analyzed, as are the violent confrontations within Algerian nationalist leadership leading to Ben Bella's consolidation as head of a one-party state after having eliminated all other political forces. Chronology for 1962 developments in Algeria.

511   Le Dossier politique de l'électeur français. Preface de Louis Armand ... 40 questions, 40 documents, 40 réponses des partis. Vous voterez pour qui? pour quoi? Paris, Editions Planète, 1967. 519 p. illus.

Non-partisan summary of facts and figures on controversial areas of political life (trends among political parties, political clubs and other politically influential groups) social and economic development, education and information media, European policy and international relations. For each area, there are comments by the major political parties, either through individual spokesmen (notably Jean Lecanuet, Pierre Mendès-France) or through party programs, given shortly before the March 1967 National Assembly elections.

512   DRACHKOVITCH, MILORAD M., ed. French Fifth Republic; constitutional developments, African prospects, European integration. Report of a conference held at the University of California, Berkeley, March 28-30, 1960. [Berkeley, Calif., University of California, Dept. of Political Science, 1961] vii, 127 p.

Papers and discussions between 44 French academic and political figures, including economist Jacques Rueff, U.N.R. spokesman Lucien Neuwirth, General Pierre Gallois, and American and British social scientists, with excerpts of public addresses given by André Philip and Jacques Soustelle at the University of California October 1959. List of conference participants.

513   DRANCOURT, MICHEL. Bilan économique de la Ve République. Paris, Éditions de l'enterprise moderne, 1961. 158 p.

Report drawn up by business journalist for "Groupe Rencontres" a political club made up of civil servants, managerial personnel, and unionists, summarizing economic achievements at eve of 4th Plan, with statistics for principal economic data. Author also examines contradictory Gaullist conceptions of favoring free market trends at the same time as seeking planned economic expansion and national power. List of program laws, 1958-61.

514   DRANCOURT, MICHEL. Les clés du pouvoir, avec une conclusion de Louis Armand. Paris, Fayard, 1964. 238 p. (Les grandes études contemporaines) Bibliographical footnotes.

Non-partisan essays on the men holding the keys of power in modern France - the managers of large industries and technocrats (civil servants) who by-pass political processes, and whose motivations are analyzed. Study contains up-to-date figures on different sectors of economy, leading industrialists, companies, nature of state intervention in economy, names of leading civil servants. Alternatives of American or integrated European lines of development are weighed.

515   DRESCH, JEAN et al. La question algérienne. Paris, Éditions de Minuit, 1958. 120 p. double map. (Documents)

Essays written winter 1957-58 on historical, political, economic, and demographic perspectives of Algerian question, all leading to conclusion that Algeria must become independent. Other four contributors are Charles-André Julien, Henri Marrou, Alfred Sauvy, and Pierre Stibbe.

516   DRESCH, JOSEPH EMILE. L'agriculture en Afrique du Nord. Paris, Centre de documentation universitaire, 1957. 2 v. in 1. (220 p.) ("Les Cours de Sorbonne")

Lectures on physical, economic, and ethnic aspects of agriculture in Morocco, Tunisia, and Algeria, contrasting traditional and modern types of agriculture and giving changes in output of main crops. After reviewing French agricultural legislation and European contributions to the development of Algerian agriculture in particular, author shows failure of colonial agriculture to feed growing population.

517   DREVET, PAUL. La procédure de révision de la Constitution du 27 octobre, 1946; ses applications, sa modification par la loi du 3 juin, 1958. Paris, Librairie générale de droit et de

jurisprudence, R. Pichon et R. Durand-Auzias, 1959. 191 p. (Bibliothèque de droit public, t. 16) "Bibliographie": p. 185-188.

Final chapter retraces steps whereby 1946 constitution was abrogated.

518 DRIF, ZOHRA. La mort de mes frères. Paris, F. Maspero, 1960. 17 p.

Testimony of Algerian law student arrested for her participation in terrorist F.L.N. network.

519 DROGAT, NOËL. Pays sous-développés et coopération technique. Paris, Spes, 1959. 193 p. illus., maps. (Collection Action populaire) "Bibliographie sommaire": p. 185-187.

Description of international technical assistance, with special sections on French responsibilities. Appendix lists French organizations active in the field. Study was sponsored by Institut Catholique de Paris.

520 Le Droit à indemnisation des Français d'Algérie atteints par des mesures de dépossession. By G. Vedel et al. Paris, Editions Montchrestien, 1965. 195 p.

French jurists' interpretation of legal rights to compensation and legal means of redress against expropriations in Algeria, in the light of the Evian agreement, subsequent Algerian legislation annulling its guarantees, 1962-63, and decisions on specific suits before Algerian courts. Jurists also analyze repatriates' rights as French citizens on the basis of the Evian agreement and the Dec. 1961 law on compensation to repatriates. Annexed documents give text of Evian agreement, Algerian decrees and court decisions, 1962-64., and 1965 amendment to French 1961 law.

521 DROIT ET LIBERTE (periodical). Les racistes contre la république. Paris, 1965. 55 p. illus. "Supplément au no. 247." Bibliographical footnotes.

Mouvement contre le racisme, l'antisemitisme et pour la paix (M.R.A.P.), documentation that Tixier-Vignancour resorts to racism in his campaign for presidency. Pamphlet gives useful information on extreme-nationalist groups and press.

522 DROIT SOCIAL (periodical). Problèmes actuels du syndicalisme. Pithiviers (Loiret), 1965. 208 p. Special issue of March 1965.

First part reprints reports presented before a "Journée d'études" Jan. 1965 in Lille, attended by social scientists, trade unionists, and employers, on current status of trade unionism: scope, relations with state organs and planning, Common Market. The second part reprints report of Conseil économique et social on legal rights of trade unions within the firm. Final part describes transformation of Confédération française des travailleurs chrétiens into non-denominational Confédération française démocratique du travail, as resolved at its 1964 congress.

523 DRONNE, RAYMOND. La révolution d'Alger. Paris, Éditions France - Empire, 1958. 238 p.

Eyewitness account of events leading to de Gaulle's return to power, by deputy who flew to Algeria May 18 in order to channel revolution in Algiers in de Gaulle's interest. Activities of politicians and military are recorded May 13 - June 13 and origins of Algerian revolt retraced. After presenting own version of de Gaulle's solution for Algeria, author foresees possible disparities between Algerian and French interpretation of Algerian integration.

524 DROUIN, PIERRE. L'Europe du Marché commun. Paris, R. Julliard, 1963. 350 p.

Based on articles originally published in "Le Monde" and giving history of first five years of Common Market, with emphasis on French interventions and effects on French economy and society.

525 DRU, JEAN (pseud.) Le pari démocratique. Paris, R. Julliard, 1962. 179 p.

Closely reasoned and cliché-free examination of prospects of Communist and non-Communist left in France by group of communist dissidents writing under pen name. Current status of P.C.F., P.S.U., their membership and methods, are well described, as are strength and genuineness of anti-communism in French left and changes that would have to take place within Communist Party to permit long-term collaboration of left for a democratic socialist society.

526 DUBERGE, JEAN. La psychologie sociale de l'impôt dans la France d'aujourd'hui. Préf. de Jean Stoetzel. Paris, Presses universitaires de France, 1961. 230 p. illus. Includes bibliography.

Doctoral thesis, Univ. of Paris, on the attitude of French tax payers toward tax collection, income tax declaration, possibilities of new types of taxes. This ground-breaking study of "fiscal psychology" is based on public opinion survey.

527 DUBOS, JEAN. L'intégration et l'agriculture française. Avant-propos de G. Buchet. Montpellier, I.N.R.A., 1964. 95 p.

Professor of agronomy identifies pressures toward concentration in French agriculture and urges formation of agricultural cooperatives, a form of "horizontal" integration as a countervailing pressure to avoid agriculture's being swallowed up by "vertical" integration.

528 DUCHEMIN, JACQUES C. Histoire du F.L.N. Paris, Table ronde, 1962. 330 p. illus., ports. map, facsims. (L'Ordre du jour)

Written shortly after Algerian independence, book aims for historical rather than partisan perspective. Documents (letters, photographs) are drawn from secret French and F.L.N. archives. Details on military leaders, internal liquidations, description of fighting in the individual wilayas, clandestine tactics in France and other countries are to be found.

529 DUCHET, ROGER. Pour le salut public; les Indépendants devant les grands problèmes nationaux. Paris, Plon, 1958. 176 p. (Tribune libre, 32)

Founder and secretary general of Centre national des indépendants et paysans reproduces his weekly editorials in "France indépendante," Jan. 1956 - June 9, 1958. The dominant theme is the defense of French Algeria.

530 DUCLOS, JACQUES. L'avenir de la démocratie. Paris, Éditions sociales, 1962. 249 p.

Communist Party Secretary's work on democratic institutions in France of the past, present, and future, written March 1962 and addressed to a wider audience. The Fifth Republic is attacked for its undemocratic features such as personal power and technocracy, as is proposal for election of presidents. Devotion to parliamentary democracy of French and international communism is underlined both by quotations from C.P.S.U. XXII. Congress and P.C.F. XVI. Congress and by French Communists' militant resistance to O.A.S.

531 DUCLOS, JACQUES. De Napoléon III à De Gaulle. Paris, Editions sociales, 1964. 286 p. illus.

Parallels are drawn between Napoleon III's and de Gaulle's assumption of power, the manipulations of financiers under both governments, conceptions of both rulers on conduct of state and personal power. Quotations from speeches of both men are set side by side to illustrate similarities.

532 DUCLOS, JACQUES. "Le dernier mot restera au peuple"; discours prononcé à l'Assemblée nationale... le 1er juin 1958 (séance d'investiture du gouvernement de Gaulle) Paris, 1958. 2 p. (Parti communiste français. Comité central)

533 DUCLOS, JACQUES. Gaullisme, technocratie, corporatisme. Paris, Éditions sociales, 1963. 198 p.

Attack on Gaullist plan to reform political institutions by eliminating Senate and existing municipal governments and substituting corporate organs (representatives of economic and social groups) instead. Senate and municipalities are represented as remaining bulwarks against personal power and technocracy. P. C. F.'s stand on these and related issues is stated and unity with socialists advocated.

534 DUCLOS, JACQUES. Paix en Algérie! Intervention à l'Assemblée nationale le 25 septembre 1957 et réponses aux ministres. Paris, 1957. 31 p. (Parti communiste français)

535 DUCROCQ, MARCEL. Une oeuvre fraternelle: notre Algérie. Lettre du marchéchal Juin. Préf. de Robert Abdesselam. Paris, Nouvelles éditions latines, 1962. 124 p.

Forlorn appeal to French conscience by fifth generation French settler in Algeria not to abandon people in Algeria tied to French civilization. Written Spring 1962, this is a defense of French Algerians as human beings who have succeeded in bringing the Moslem and European communities together.

536 DUFRESNOY, CLAUDE. Des officiers parlent; présentation de Jules Roy. Paris, R. Julliard, 1961. 197 p.

Texts of Dufresnoy's interviews with 70 officers in Algeria, ranging from lieutenant to general, in all the different branches of the army, administrative and combat. Spaced between April 1959 and November 1960, interviews elicited straight-forward responses on officers' attitude toward de Gaulle, the Algerian war, possibilities of army mutiny and showed trend toward accepting peace with F. L. N. and an independent Algeria.

537 DUMAS, ANDRE. Der Krieg in Algerien. Zollikon, Evangelischer Verlag, 1958. 148 p. (Polis; evangelische Zeitbuchreihe, 2) "Literaturverzeichnis": p. 140-143.

Attempts to make complexities of Algerian war comprehensible to Christians outside France, with special sections on position of Christian churches in Algeria and chronology of pronouncements by Protestant and Catholic Churches in France toward the war.

538 DUMON, FREDERIC. La communauté franco-afro-malgache; ses origines, ses institutions, son évolution, octobre 1958—juin 1960. Bruxelles, Institut de sociologie Solvay, 1960. 294 p. (Études d'histoire et d'ethnologie juridiques, 2)

Genesis of the French Community in 1958 Constitution and response of African leaders during its elaboration and after its establishment. Belgian professor traces evolution of the community through granting of sovereignty to its members. Appendices give December 1958 statutes of French Community's Executive Council, Senate, and Court, and decisions of Executive Council during 1959.

539 DUMOULIN, ROGER. La structure asymétrique de l'économie algérienne, d'après une analyse de la région de Bône. Paris, M.-Th. Génin, 1959. xiii, 375 p. illus., maps, tables, diagrs. (1 fold.) (Collection d'économie moderne) "Bibliographie": p. 363-365.

Case study of Bône region, showing contrasting income level between traditional (majority) and modern (minority) sectors of economy. Author sees remedy in careful selection of local investment and integration in a complementary Eurafrican economy.

540 DUPUY, AIME. L'Algérie dans les lettres d'expression française. Paris, Éditions universitaires, 1956. 167 p. plates, fold. map. Bibliographical footnotes.

Very little on Algerian literature since outbreak of Algerian war.

541 DUPONT-DURANT, JACQUES. Réflexions d'un Français moyen; essai. Paris, La Nef de Paris éditions [1957?] 79 p.

Critical thoughts on French political divisions and colonialism, representative of average citizen's dissatisfaction in last year of Fourth Republic.

542 DUPOUY, BERNARD. Essai sur le problème electoral. Alger, Maison des livres, 1958. 35 p.

May 1958 proposal for Algerian electoral reform in line with policy of integration.

543 DUQUESNE, JACQUES. L'Algérie, ou La guerre des mythes. Paris, Desclée De Brouwer, 1958. 200 p. (Questions actuelles) Bibliographical footnotes.

In spirit of "justice and charity" author attempts to dispel the myths surrounding the most controversial issues of the Algerian war: effectiveness of pacification, use of torture, terrorism, changing role of French army, representativeness and ideology of F. L. N., loyalties of Moslems and Europeans, various political solutions proposed by France. Written April 1958, book contains afterword on May uprising and de Gaulle's first steps in solving Algerian problem.

544 DURAND, PIERRE. Vingt ans; chronique 1945-1965. Paris, Éditions sociales, 1965. 445 p.

Communist journalist's political chronicle, May 1945 - April 1965, uncritically based on party reports and "L'Humanité" with emphasis on elections and strike movements. Useful name, place, citation, and subject index.

545 DURAND-REVILLE, LUC. L'assistance de la France aux pays insuffisamment développés; linéaments d'une doctrine. Paris, M. Th. Génin, 1961. 126 p. Bibliographical footnotes.

French aid as of 1960 and its efficacy in terms of raising countries' standard of living and gaining political influence among elites.

546 DUROSELLE, JEAN-BAPTISTE and JEAN MEYRIAT, eds. Politiques nationales envers les jeunes états. Paris, A. Colin, 1964. 347 p. (Cahiers de la Fondation nationale des sciences politiques. Relations internationales, 131) Bibliographical footnotes.

Comparative studies on economic, technical and diplomatic ties with newly independent countries of U. S., U. S. S. R., Great Britain, France and other European states. Duroselle's chapter on France deals with its economic and cultural cooperation with former colonies.

547 DUVAL, LEON ETIENNE, Abp. Messages de paix, 1955-1962. Paris, Desclée De Brouwer, 1962. 230 p. (Questions actuelles)

Algiers Archbishop's sermons, pastoral letters, and radio addresses preaching papal and his own message of peace and Christian brotherly love between the two Algerian communities to European settlers. Final sermons, Easter 1962, deplore O.A.S. violence. Archbishop remained in Algeria after independence.

548 DUVERGER, MAURICE. La Cinquième République. Paris, Presses universitaires de France, 1959. 323 p. diagrs.

Leading French political sociologist's preliminary synthesis of the political institutions of the Fifth Republic, offered as part of the curriculum on constitutional law. The first part analyzes the constitutional framework, the second the operation of political forces within it. Annotated bibliography incorporated in chapters.

549 DUVERGER, MAURICE, ed. Constitutions et documents politiques. Paris, Presses universitaires de France, 1960. 535-633 p. tables. ("Thémis"; textes et documents)

Includes the following documents: 1) Draft of 1958 constitution 2) final version of constitution and related ordinances, Nov. 1958 - Feb. 1959 3) U.N.R. statutes and oath of U.N.R. deputies, and 4) election results in first year of Fifth Republic. 2nd ed. (1960) also has currently valid statutes of Parti Communiste Français, Parti Socialiste, Mouvement Républicain Populaire, and Parti Républicain Radical et Radical Socialiste, as well as preliminary version of Parti Socialiste Unifié statutes. At Law Library.

550 DUVERGER, MAURICE. Cours de sociologie politique, rédigé d'après les notes et avec l'autorisation de Maurice Duverger. D.E.S., science politique, 1959-1960. Paris, Cours de droit, 1960. 94 p.

Course on political sociology of Fifth Republic delving into causes of Fourth Republic's collapse, nature of new institutions, old and new parties, predictions as to success of Fifth Republic in dealing with old problems after its first year of existence.

551 DUVERGER, MAURICE. De la dictature. Paris, R. Julliard 1961. 211 p. "Indications bibliographiques": p. 205-206.

Historical models of dictatorships and possible forms military (praetorian) dictatorship might take in France if dissatisfied officers led a successful coup d'état against de Gaulle in the wake of the Algerian conflict.

552 DUVERGER, MAURICE. Demain, la République. Paris, R. Julliard, 1958. 151 p.

July 1958 considerations on drawing up a new constitution, assessing dangers from right and left and effectiveness of different types of regimes.

553 DUVERGER, MAURICE. La démocratie sans le peuple. Paris, Éditions du Seuil, 1967. 251 p. (L'Histoire immédiate)

Trends in French political families (conservative-liberal, Catholic, socialist, communist) as seen in the context of other European parties. Author describes the French system as inherently centrist: the moderate left and right alone have held power through parliamentary democracy, the "democracy without the people." Evolution in consequence of Gaullist reforms, notably presidential election, and greater possibility for unification of socialists and communists on one hand, U.N.R. and other conservatives on the other, leads author to see long run hope for bi-party democracy.

553a DUVERGER, MAURICE. Droit public. 2. ed., entièrement refondue. Paris, Presses universitaires de France 1961. 406 p. ("Thémis" manuels de capacité) Includes bibliography. LL

Almost entire work deals with Fifth Republic and describes provisions for elections, presidency, Cabinet, parliament, consultative bodies, regulations of civil liberties, central and local administration, civil service, fiscal organs.

553b DUVERGER, MAURICE. Institutions politiques et droit constitutionnel. 5. ed. Paris, Presses universitaires de France, 1960. viii, 818 p. ("Thémis": manuels juridiques, économiques et politiques) LL

Political institutions of Fifth Republic (to which about half of volume is devoted) in framework of those of other countries. The rôle of political parties and pressure groups is analyzed.

554 DUVERGER, MAURICE. Introduction à la politique. Paris, Gallimard, 1964. 382 p. (Collection Idées, 44)

Popular introduction to basic concepts of political science: political institutions as a form of organized struggle on the one hand and as forces of integration on the other. It is attempted to use sufficiently comprehensive categories for integrating communist and non-communist theories of government, class struggle, etc., and bringing out the convergence between all highly industrialized societies.

555 DUVERGER, MAURICE. La VIe République et le régime présidentiel. Paris, A. Fayard, 1961. 140 p. (Les Idées et la vie)

Proposals for direct popular election of head of government for de Gaulle's successor, in the light of current electoral sociology. De Gaulle's own proposal of electing the President of the Republic while retaining a non-elected prime minister is rejected for resemblance to Weimar Republic's ill-fated regime.

556 DUVERGER, MAURICE. Sociologie politique. Paris, Presses universitaires de France, 1966. 506 p. (Manuels juridiques, économiques et politiques)

Course for law students at Sorbonne divided into four main sections: 1) framework in which political life functions; 2) factors generating political conflict and integration; 3) political parties; 4) pressure groups. Examples in these sections drawn from various regimes, countries, periods, not only French contemporary institutions, with consistent effort to present Marxist views on all points and weigh them dispassionately. Each section has a good bibliography with subsection on France.

FOR ADDITIONAL WORKS BY AND ABOUT MAURICE DUVERGER, SEE AUTHOR INDEX

557 ECHANGES FRANCO-ALLEMANDS. Le problème de Berlin; colloque organisé à Paris les 25 et 26 novembre 1961 sur le thème: La question de Berlin-Ouest dans le cadre d'un réglement négocié du problème allemand. Paris, Presses universitaires de France, 1962. 86 p.

Gathering of French parliamentarians, professors, journalists, trade-unionists to clarify opinion on crisis connected with Berlin wall. Main speakers are Georges Castellan on the history of the Berlin crisis and André Hauriou on its legal aspects. U.N.R. position on German question is summarized by U.N.R. parliamentarian and conforms with final resolution of meeting favoring recognition of DDR and internationalization of West Berlin. Includes roster of 400 participants.

558 ECHEVERRIA, RAFAEL. La V República Francesa. Madrid, Ediciones Rialp, 1962. 182 p. (Publicaciones de la Facultad de Derecho del Estudio General de Navarra, 15) Bibliography: p. 175-182.

Scholarly study of political institutions, strengths and weaknesses of Fifth Republic after three years of operation. Extensive bibliography of books and articles.

559 EDITIONS DE MINUIT (defendant). Provocations à la désobéissance; le procès du déserteur[compte rendu sténographique de débats devant la XVIIe Chambre correctionnelle.] Paris, Editions de Minuit, 1962. 167 p.

Text of trial against Jerome Lindon, publisher of Editions de Minuit, December 1961, before the Tribunal de première instance de la Seine, for having published "Le Déserteur" by Maurienne (see no. 970). The book, considered non-fiction, is held to be an incitement to military disobedience. Among witnesses are officers having served in Algeria, who had vainly protested against torture. Lindon was found guilty.

560 EFFEL, JEAN. De la Debré à la Pompidour. Paris, Denoël, 1964. 141 p. illus.

Witty cartoons of which de Gaulle is the principal target chronicling political events November 1960 - January 1964.

561 EGLISE REFORMEE DE FRANCE. CONSEIL NATIONAL. L'église chrétienne et les problèmes posés par l'action psychologique et la guerre subversive; plan d'étude. Paris, 1962. 31 p. Includes bibliography.

Conclusions of a Sept. 1962 colloquium on subversive warfare organized by the national council of French protestant churches, in which methods of psychological warfare and propaganda deployed by French army in Algeria are condemned as a perversion of Christian conscience.

562 EGRETAUD, MARCEL. Réalité de la nation algérienne; nouv. 2. éd., rev. et augm. Paris, Editions sociales, 1961. 313 p.

History of Algeria, facts on Algerian economy and social structure under colonial regime, history of Algerian revolution up to Melun negotiations, and steps taken under various French governments 1945-1960 to settle Algerian problem. The 1957 edition of this work became standard text on Algeria in Communist countries, reflecting as it does the French Communist Party's official version of the question.

563 EHRHARD, JEAN. Communauté ou sécession? Paris, Calmann-Lévy, 1959. 176 p.

Political and economic forces involved in keeping intact the newly established framework for the French Community in French Equatorial Africa and French West Africa, with particular reference to Guinea's decision to withdraw from community.

564 EHRHARD, JEAN. Le destin du colonialisme. Paris, Éditions Eyrolles, 1957. 236 p. map.

Survey of France's past and current contributions to economic development in Africa and methods most likely to succeed in the future.

565 EHRMANN, HENRY WALTER. Organized business in France. Princeton, Princeton University Press, 1957. xx, 514 p. diagrs.

Business organizations (Conseil National du Patronat Français is examined most extensively) in Third and Fourth Republic, their political influence and stand on economic issues.

566 ELBE, MARIE. Et à l'heure de notre mort. Paris, Presses de la Cité, 1963. 280 p.

Fictional account of year of violence in Algeria from Generals' Putsch to exodus of Europeans in June 1962. Events are seen through the eyes of French settlers, officers participating in O.A.S., and uncommitted French journalist and reconstruct sympathetically the climate of mounting violence, madness, and despair on part of Europeans.

567 ELGOZY, GEORGES. La France devant le Marché commun. Paris, Flammarion, 1958. 300 p.

Economist's analysis of country's economic situation at time of establishment of Common Market (January 1, 1958) and measures taken during that year to adapt French economy to it.

568 ELY, PAUL HENRI RONUALD. L'armée dans la nation. Paris, A. Fayard, 1961. 191 p. (Les Idées et la vie)

General's essays on 1) international relations, current form of conflict with communist world and appropriate defense mechanism of Atlantic Alliance; 2) qualities needed in military leadership. Appendix reproduces articles on Indochina, Algeria, 1954, 1958, 1959 from "Revue de défense nationale."

569 ENCYCLOPEDIE PERIODIQUE ECONOMIQUE, POLITIQUE ET ADMINISTRATIVE. SERVICE DE DOCUMENTATION ELECTORAL. Les élections en France; lois, réglementation, jurisprudence. Elections municipales, cantonales, législatives, sénatoriales, présidentielles. Paris, Société générale de presse [1964?] 300 p.

Sections for each type of election, giving historical background, general procedures, and text of relevant electoral codes through 1964.

570 ENSEMBLE, JULIEN (pseud.). Le contre-plan. Paris, Éditions du Seuil, 1965. 125 p. (Société, 3)

Collective work presenting alternative proposals to government's Fifth Plan primarily in terms of what could be achieved with higher growth rates. This counterplan is not backed by any specific opposition group, but expresses a reformist socialist perspective and has backing of trade union leaders.

571 ENTIN, L. Le néo-colonialisme et l'indépendance sont incompatibles. [By L. Entine] Moscou, Ed. de l'Agence de presse Novosti [1965?] 27 p.

Translation of Russian pamphlet attacking French government for continuing domination of African countries after political independence through economic assistance and military presence.

572 ENTRETIENS DE DIJON. La personnalisation du pouvoir; Entretiens de Dijon, organisés avec le concours de l'Association française de science politique et publiés sous la direction de Léo Hamon et Albert Mabileau. Paris, Presses universitaires de France, 1964. 499 p. (Publications du Centre d'études des relations politiques, Université de Dijon)

After preliminary sessions on concept of personal power and contemporary experiences in U.S.S.R., U.S., Germany, Italy, Great Britain, Near East, French experience is analyzed, with special reports on: 1) Legitimacy in de Gaulle's thinking; 2) Public opinion on personalization of power; 3) Propaganda, mass media; 5) Institutional channels of personalized power. Among speakers are François Goguel, Maurice Duverger, Alfred Grosser, Marcel Prélot. French experience is summed up by Léo Hamon.

573 ESCARPIT, ROBERT. École laïque, école du peuple. Paris, Calmann-Lévy, 1961. 238 p. (Questions d'actualité) Bibliography: p. 235-238.

Educational and social philosophies underlying the conflict between non-religious and Catholic education and status of controversy in laws and institutions of the Fifth Republic. The admittedly atheist but politically uncommitted author makes an eloquent plea for "public education" in the light of currently relevant values. Good bibliography.

574 ESTIER, CLAUDE. Ce qu'est la Convention. Préf. de Louis Mermaz. Paris, 1967. 61 p. (Cahiers de la Convention des institutions républicaines, 8) "Supplément à 'Combat républicain,' no. 30. septembre 1967."

Updated history (see no. 577) of Convention des institutions républicaines, with statutes, documents from 1966 and 1967 meetings, and Jan. 1967 membership of executive committee.

575 ESTIER, CLAUDE. La gauche hebdomadaire, 1914-1962. Paris, A. Colin, 1962. 287 p. illus., ports., facsims. (Kiosque: les faits, la presse, l'opinion, 21) Bibliography: p. 281-282.

Final chapters summarize position of leftist weeklies (Express, France-Observateur, Témoignage chrétien, France nouvelle) toward Algerian war and give audience of leading leftist weeklies. Appendix lists leftist weeklies, 1914-1962, of which only 17 are currently appearing, with basic information about publications and their principal contributors.

576 ESTIER, CLAUDE. Pour l'Algérie. Paris, F. Maspero, 1964. 192 p. (Cahiers libres, no. 52)

"Nouvel Observateur" correspondent's favorable report on Algeria and its leaders since independence, drawing special attention to position of remaining European settlers and response to newly arrived French technical experts.

577 ESTIER, CLAUDE. Qu'est-ce que la Convention? Préf. de Louis Mermaz. Paris, 1966. 38 p. (Cahiers de la Convention des institutions républicaines, 3)

Includes Jan. 1966 statutes, 1964 charter, current executive committee and list of participating clubs.

578 ETUDES SOCIALES NORD-AFRICAINES. Africains noirs en France. Paris, 1961. 63 p. (Its Cahiers nord-africains, 86)

Statistics on sub-Saharan African workers and students in France.

579 ETUDES SOCIALES NORD-AFRICAINES. L'économie algérienne de demain: suggestions. Paris, 1960. 47 p. (Cahiers Nord-africains, 79) Includes bibliography.

Extracts from proposals of Secrétariat Social d'Alger published under title "Au service de l'industrialisation de l'Algérie: la micro-industrie," preceded by a more general lecture by Maurice Bye on different approaches to economic development in underdeveloped countries, with illustrations based on Algeria's assymetric economic growth.

580 ETUDES SOCIALES NORD-AFRICAINES. Essai de bibliographie algérienne, 1er janvier 1954 - 30 juin 1962; lectures d'une guerre. Paris, 1962. 115 p. (Its Cahiers nord-africains, 92)

The only comprehensive bibliographical survey of the Algerian revolution, covering about 1,000 books and pamphlets (but no articles) written between 1954 and June 1962. Works are divided by subject area (Maghreb, general works on Algeria, Algerian history and history of Algerian war, political, socio-economic, and psycho-sociological problems, literature and art). Within each of these topics, finer breakdowns take into account approach and point of view of authors. Rapid characterization and evaluation of more important works accompanies each sub-section. Publications are identified in index by name of author, and title. Addresses of periodicals with special issues on Algeria are listed in appendix.

581 ETUDES SOCIALES NORD-AFRICAINES. Les familles nord africaines en France: essai de mise au point. Paris, 1961. 39 p. illus. (Cahiers nord-africains, 83)

Statistical summary of evolution and current status (through 1960) of North African workers in France by region and occupation, as well as of the number of women and children. The 1960 figure for workers is around 200,000, as against commonly assumed 400,000, which exceeds the total number of North Africans in France at the time. Figures for immigrations from other countries for the same period (1950-1960) are recapitulated.

582 ETUDES SOCIALES NORD-AFRICAINES. Intégration? Citoyenneté? Part entière? Paris, 1958. 47 p. (Its Cahiers nord-africains, no. 65) Bibliographical footnotes.

Legal, economic, social, and psychological implications of Algerian integration, as of July 1958.

583 ETUDES SOCIALES NORD-AFRICAINES. Notes de lecture. Paris, 1958. 56 p. (Cahiers nord-africains, no. 63)

Book reviews of most controversial 1957 works on Algeria (Aron, Soustelle, Beau de Loménie, Tillion, Massenet, Simon) and annotated bibliography of books on economic and military aspects of Algerian question.

584 ETUDES SOCIALES NORD-AFRICAINES. Pour un développement normal de l'Algérie. Paris, 1959. 64 p. (Cahiers nord-africains, 75)

Extracts from Secrétariat Social d'Alger's "Sous-développement en Algérie" and summary of René Gendarme's "L'Economie de l'Algérie," which show the special social and economic conditions hindering Algeria's progress.

585 EULOGE, ANDRE and ANTOINE MOULINIER. L'envers des barricades; vingt mois d'insurrection à Alger. Paris, Plon, 1960. 176 p.

French journalists' eye-witness report of January 1960 uprising, with background information on political situation among European settlers in Algeria since May 1958 and sketches of rebel leaders Lagaillarde, Ortiz, Lefèvre and their relations with military leaders.

586 L'Europe au défi. By Jeanne Hersch et al. Paris, Plon, 1959. 240 p. (Tribune libre, 42)

Political, economic, and military case for European unification by Jeanne Hersch, Henri Frenay, Henri Rieben, François Bondy, Pierre M. Gallois, and André Philip.

587 L'Europe gaulliste et la presse française. Paris, Éditions Galic, 1962. 158 p. (L'Histoire au jour le jour no. 5)

Comments in Parisian and provincial dailies, February - August 1962, on de Gaulle's stand on European unification, Franco-German relations, the Atlantic Alliance.

588 EUROPEAN PARLIAMENT. Hommage à Robert Schuman, président d'honneur du Parlement européen. [Discours par] G. Martino et al. 16 septembre 1963. Luxembourg, 1963. 23 p. port.

4 speeches before European Parliament honoring Schuman's contributions to European unification two weeks after his death.

589 EUROPEUS (pseud.). La crise de la zone de libre échange; document E.P.I. Paris, Plon, 1959. 111 p. tables (Tribune libre, 43).

Études politiques impartiales' (EPI) study of impasse between Common Market and European Free Trade Association and necessary coordination of trade policies in Western Europe.

590 Les extraditions d'Algériens; ou, Le Chemin de la guillotine. By Marc de Kock, Serge Moureaux et al. Bruxelles, 1961. 96 p.

November 1960 appeal to Belgian public opinion and Minister of Justice to stop extradition of Algerian refugees by defense lawyers for Algerian nationalists Serge Moureaux, Marc de Kock, and Mourad Oussedik. Text of court appeal by these lawyers at October 1960 extradition trial in Brussels.

591 FABRA, PAUL, et al. French industry and the Common Market. A survey under the direction of Pierre Drouin. London, 1962. 55 p. (European Communities. Information Service. Community topics, no. 5)

Impact of Common Market on French industry as a whole and its effect on specific branches and changes in attitude toward Common Market on part of Conseil National du Patronat Français.

592 FABRA, PAUL. Y a-t-il un marché commun? Paris, Éditions du Seuil, 1965. 127 p.

Common Market impact on French economy as of mid-1965 in terms of foreign trade, agricultural policy, free movement of persons and corporations.

593 FABRE-LUCE, ALFRED. Le couronnement du prince. Paris, Table ronde, 1964. 270 p. Includes bibliographical references.

Critical discussion of recent books on de Gaulle: to wit, those by François Mauriac, Louis Terrenoire, Paul Marie de la Gorce, Eugène Mannoni, George Izard, with special attention to de Gaulle's real rôle in Resistance, Liberation, Algeria, decolonization, foreign affairs, nuclear policy. Although author is highly critical of many aspects of Gaullist policy and de Gaulle's personality, he is no unconditional opponent. Author also describes his own experiences with seizure of book "Haute-Cour." (See no. 596.)

594 FABRE-LUCE, ALFRED. Demain en Algérie. Paris, Plon, 1958. 114 p. (Tribune libre, 19)

After weighing economic arguments in favor of Algerian independence given by Raymond Aron, author still fears it would be too divisive internally and proposes transitional solutions along lines of November 1957 "loi cadre" (text in appendix) leading to federation or partition as more realistic and conciliatory for feuding Frenchmen. Author, writing February 1958, does not suspect imminent political crisis.

595 FABRE-LUCE, ALFRED. Gaulle deux. Paris, R. Julliard, 1958. 171 p. Bibliography included in "Notes" (p. 169-171)

At eve of constitutional referendum for 5th Republic, author who has opposed de Gaulle since World War II, gives critical but not hostile appraisal of de Gaulle's assumption of power, past and current policies for Algeria and European integration, attitude toward French greatness, and prospects for the new regime.

596 FABRE-LUCE, ALFRED. Haute cour. Lausanne, J. F. G., 1962. 285 p. Bibliographical references included in "Appendice A": p. 257-262.

Fictitious impeachment of de Gaulle by French Senate constituted as "Haute-Cour" on the ground that he has violated the constitution by abandoning French territory and mismanaging his office. Author cleverly parodies arguments and procedures of recent political trials, incorporates testimonies of real adversaries and admirers of de Gaulle as well as a number of imaginary figures, among them a psychoanalyst who portrays de Gaulle as a paranoiac. De Gaulle himself does not appear. Entire range of Gaullist policies from 1958-1962 - Algeria, diplomacy, methods of administration and finances, etc., is scrutinized. Seizure of book described in no. 593. An English translation has been published as "The Trial of Charles De Gaulle" (1963).

597 FABRE-LUCE, ALFRED. Le plus illustre des Français. Paris, R. Julliard, 1960. 262 p. Includes bibliography.

Critical de Gaulle biography, concentrating on war years, with detailed chronology of de Gaulle's career. Author uses recently concluded de Gaulle memoirs as a frequent target of his attacks.

598 FAGERBERG, ELLIOTT PENNELL. The "Anciens Combattants" and French foreign policy. Ambilly-Annemasse, Impr. "Les Presses de Savoie," 1966. 338 p. (Université de Genève. Institut universitaire des hautes études internationales. Thèse no. 175) Bibliography: p. 273-310.

Primarily concerned with the influence of veterans' organizations in the inter-war years, with some reference to the organizations' more recent stand on colonial issues, participation in fight for French Algeria, and support for O. A. S.

599 FAJON, ETIENNE. En feuilletant l'Humanité, 1904-1964. Paris, 1964. 190 p. illus., ports., facsims. "Supplément de l'Humanité no. 6.070 du 2 mars 1964."

Includes chapters on "Humanité's" stand during Fifth Republic and newspaper's current collaborators. Fajon is current editor-in-chief.

600 FAJON, ETIENNE. La lutte pour la paix en Algérie; discours prononcé le 13 avril 1956 à l'Assemblée des communistes de la région parisienne, Salle des métallurgistes, à Paris. Paris, S. G. P., Imp. Poissonière, 1956. 15 p. (Parti communiste français)

601 FAJON, ETIENNE. Les mesures financières du gouvernement et la lutte pour les revendications et la paix en Algérie; rapport à l'Assemblée d'information des communistes parisiens le 28 août 1957 à la Maison des métallurgistes. Paris, 1957. 29 p. (Parti communiste français)

602 FANON, FRANTZ. L'an V de la révolution algérienne. Paris, F. Maspero, 1959. 181 p. (Cahiers libres, v. 3)

First-hand observation by Martinique-born psychiatrist on psychological transformation of colonized people as a result of nationalist revolution. Author, who personally supported Algerian nationalists, describes impact of revolution on role of women, family structure, attitudes toward medicine and technology and concludes that only independence can eliminate cultural sclerosis by means of which colonized resisted colonizer. Special chapter on European settlers favorable to independence. English translations "Studies in a Dying Colonialism" (New York, Monthly Review Press, 1965) and "A Dying Colonialism" (New York, Grove Press, 1967.)

603 FANON, FRANTZ. Les damnés de la terre; préf. de Jean-Paul Sartre. Paris, F. Maspero, 1961. 242 p. (Cahiers libres, nos. 27-28)

Study of psychological mechanisms to which colonized peoples, including native bourgeoisie and intellectuals, are subjected and those set in motion with decolonization, particularly violence and counterviolence. Author examines different possibilities of political, economic, and social restructuring in the wake of national independence and rejects Western values because leadership must come not from a westernized elite but through a collective and popularly accepted effort. Although not specifically on Algerian revolution, examples are drawn largely from that experience, and book strongly influenced French left-wing intellectuals' stand on independent Algeria, as indicated by Sartre's preface. English translation (at Main Library) is entitled "The Wretched of the Earth" (New York, 1963)

604 FAUCHER, JEAN ANDRE. L'Algérie rebelle. Paris, Editions du Grand Damier, 1957. 253 p. illus.

Journalist's history of Algerian resistance to French colonization and very detailed account of revolution after 1954; sketches leaders, political rivalries, methods of guerilla warfare and organization of F. L. N. in Algeria and networks in France, sources of weapons and money, role of Communist party and Algerian Communists. Author is convinced that extremists in F. L. N. and French army are preventing real negotiations and that both sides will emerge defeated.

605 FAUCHER, JEAN ANDRE. L'agonie d'un régime (1952-1958) Paris, Éditions Atlantic, 1959. 248 p.

Journalist's unaltered diary notes on successive political crises, 1952 - September 1958. There is no inside information on period preceding de Gaulle's return to power.

606 FAUCHER, JEAN ANDRE. Alger, la maudite. Paris, Édition Galic, 1962. 485 p. (Collection Vérité)

Thinly veiled fictional reconstruction of Algerian conflict both in Algeria and in France 1956 - 1961, covering all the main political episodes and including protagonists from entire political spectrum - politicians, intellectuals, military - all of them treated with some degree of sympathy, although French Left is given most of blame.

607 FAUCHER, JEAN ANDRE. Les barricades d'Alger, janvier, 1960. Paris, Éditions Atlantic, 1960. 429 p.

Inside account of January 1960 uprising in Algeria beginning with maneuvers preceding actual conflict and ending with arrest of participants. As journalist for the pro-French Algerian weekly "Juvenal" author had close contact with right-wing leaders and gives minute descriptions of Joseph Ortiz, Robert Martel Pierre Lagaillarde, Jean-Jacques Susini and their relations with French Army and right-wing.

608 FAUCHER, JEAN ANDRE. La Cinquième République. Paris, Éditions Galic, 1962. 325 p. (Collection Vérité)

Political history of Fifth Republic told as a month-by-month chronicle, May 1958-June 1962, with emphasis on banking interests behind technocrats in de Gaulle's government and groups, parties, individuals hostile to de Gaulle in both right and left. Name index.

609 FAUCHER, JEAN ANDRE. Les clubs politiques en France. Paris, J. Didier, 1965. 301 p. (Forum)

Author is himself secretary of political club, l'Atelier Républicain, which was connected with Radical Party at one time. In 1965 this club joined the Convention des Institutions Républicaines, the nucleus of the Fédération de la gauche démocrate et socialiste. Book describes individual clubs under Fourth and Fifth Republic, their ideas of modern democratic socialism, clubs' relations with leftist parties, and prospects of renovating French Left as of August 1965. Short biographies of 250 leading clubists in appendix.

610 FAUCHER, MAURICE (ed.). Les réformes de la Ve République; essai de classement systématique. Préf. de Maurice Vidal. Paris, 1960. 3 v.

Annual compilation of laws, ordinances, and decrees, with references to full texts in Journal Officiel, legal digests, etc. and divided into such topics as judicial procedure, civil, criminal, and commercial law, and social welfare legislation. Vol. 1 covers Nov. 1958-Oct. 1959, vol. 2 covers Oct. 1959-Oct. 1960, and vol. 3 covers Oct. 1960-Oct. 1962.

611 FAUCIER, NICOLAS. La presse quotidienne; ceux qui la font, ceux qui l'inspirent. 2. éd. Paris, Éditions syndicalistes, 1965. 343 p. Includes bibliography.

Detailed technical description of composition, printing, and distribution of newspapers and condition of workers in the industry, government regulation of press and television, influence of business interests, with comprehensive list of financial groups controlling major dailies and associated magazines. Author is professional newspaper proof-reader.

612 FAURE, EDGAR. Prévoir le présent. Paris, Gallimard, 1966. 255 p. (Idées actuelles, 118) Bibliographical footnotes.

Analysis of the current status of Russian and international communism and of the revolutionary, though not necessarily communist trends in underdeveloped countries leads to a justification of French foreign policy of independence from the Atlantic Alliance, permitting France to become the standard-bearer of peaceful international relations and promoter of economic growth at home and in the underdeveloped world. Author sees no contradiction in Gaullist nuclear policy and promotion of peace, since, as a second-rate power, France does not present an imperialist threat. A cautious progress in European economic integration is favored for economic expansion, political unification seen as premature. Gaullist economic policy and new political institutions are upheld. At time of publication author became Minister of agriculture.

613 FAUVET, JACQUES. La France déchirée. Paris, A. Fayard, 1957. 152 p. (Les idées et la vie)

Divisive forces in French civilization (individualism, intellectualism, and conservatism) as expressed in French political parties, their role in parliament, relation with voters.

614 FAUVET, JACQUES and JEAN PLANCHAIS. La Fronde des généraux. Paris, Arthaud, 1961. 273 p. ports., maps. (Collection Notre temps, 1)

Antecedents and day-to-day account of putsch, April 20-25, 1961, seen from both Algeria and Paris, with biographies of main participants. Emphasis is on civilian-military relations and Algerian policy. Subsequent trials are not covered.

615 FAUVET, JACQUES. Histoire du Parti communiste français. Paris, Fayard, 1964. 2 v. (Les Grandes études contemporaines) Includes bibliography.

Vol. 1 covers 1917-1939, v. 2 1939-1965. Final 50 pages of vol. 2 deal briefly with leadership crisis within Communist party since 1958, current organization, sociology of supporters, relations with intellectuals. In appendices are tables on party congresses, voter statistics, revised 1964 statutes, list of opposition communist periodicals. Short bibliographical notes after each chapter. First volume was written in collaboration with Alain Duhamel.

FOR ADDITIONAL WORKS BY JACQUES FAUVET, SEE AUTHOR INDEX

616 FAVREL, CHARLES. Ci-devant légionnaire. Paris, Presses de la Cité, 1963. 275 p. illus.

Frenchman's adventures in Foreign Legion, 1938-1944, serving to illustrate mentality and conditioning of Legionnaires, which led to their participation in 1961 military revolt in Algeria and in O.A.S.

617 FAVRELIERE, NOEL. Le désert à l'aube. Paris, Éditions de Minuit, 1960. 225 p. (Collection "Documents")

French paratrooper's autobiographical account of desertion in Algeria and experiences with F.L.N.

618 FAVROD, CHARLES HENRI. Le F.L.N. et l'Algérie. Nouv. éd. rev. et mise à jour. Paris, Plon, 1962. 349 p. map.

Swiss journalist's political, economic, and social history of French colonization presented through documents and facts, as is the political and military history of the revolution through independence, with documents giving texts of F.L.N. appeals, negotiations and interviews with F.L.N. leaders. Very detailed chronology of Algerian revolution, Oct. 1954 - July 1962. Originally published as "La révolution algérienne."

619 FAVROD, CHARLES HENRI. La révolution algérienne. Paris, Plon, 1959. 233 p. (Les Documents de "Tribune libre," 5)

Original version of above, with each of sections including material only up to June 1958.

620   FAYARD, JEAN. Un isolé dans l'isoloir, les Français devant leur destin. Paris, Genève, La Palatine, 1967. 176 p.

Moderate assessment of de Gaulle's political personality and Gaullism in terms of achievements in internal affairs and international relations. In weighing his vote for the March 1967 elections, author gives vote of confidence domestically but condemns de Gaulle's policy of French political and military independence.

621* LA FEDERATION. CONGRES NATIONAL, 10e, BEAUNE, 1959. Les congrès de Beaune 3, 4,et 5 juillet 1959. [Paris, 1959] [11] p.

Organization devoted to questions of municipal government.

622* FEDERATION DES GROUPES D'ÉTUDES DE LETTRES. [Appeal to students to join a march of protest against the mistreatment by O.A.S. of certain professors, November, 27, 1961] 1 p.

Handbill issued conjointly with the U.N.E.F.

623* FEDERATION NATIONALE DES ETUDIANTS DE FRANCE [F.N.E.F.] [Appeal to students, 1961] 2 p.

Dissident student organization which broke away from U.N.E.F. in 1961.

624   FEJTO, FRANÇOIS. The French Communist Party and the crisis of international communism. Cambridge, Mass., M.I.T. Press 1967. xi, 225 p. (Massachusetts Institute of Technology. Center for International Studies. Studies in international communism, 9) Biographical footnotes.

Expanded version of article in "Arguments" by Hungarian-born French journalist and expert on international communism tracing internal developments of P.C.F. as a reflection of shifts in international communism. The major part of work deals with decade from 1956-1966, drawing on party literature and author's private information. For Fifth Republic, focus is on internal leadership conflicts, party congresses, stand on Algerian war, split with Chinese Communists, aftermath of Thorez' death and Khrushchev's fall, collaboration with other parties during presidential election.

625   FELLER, JEAN. Le dossier de l'armée française, la guerre de "cinquante ans," 1914-1962. Préface de Robert Aron. Paris, Perrin, 1966. 525 p. Bibliography: p. 499-510.

Last 40 pages of this sympathetic history of French Army summarize army's role in Algerian war and its vain groping for a response to revolutionary warfare in the absence of national support. Good bibliography.

626   FERAOUN, MOULOUD. Journal, 1955-1962. Paris, Éditions du Seuil, 1962. 347 p. (Collection Méditerranée)

Posthumously published diary by Kabylian teacher and novelist (see no. 1471) assassinated by O.A.S. March 1962. Diary relates his personal observation of terror, counter-terror, torture, and different stages of pacification program in Kabylia, where he was teaching until July 1957 and records his growing horror at the senseless violence on both sides. Despite nationalist sympathies, he kept his ties with French administration and with many French intellectuals, notably his friend Albert Camus. The years from 1957 till his death were spent in Algiers, but there is little information on political events.

627   FERAOUN, MOULOUD. Textes sur l'Algérie. Paris, 1962. 32 p. facsim. "Supplément à Preuves no. 139, septembre, 1962."

Collection of short texts gathered by "Preuves" after author's assassination: an article Sept. 1958 on Algerian problem, another on the death of his friend Camus, diary notes Dec. 1961-Feb. 1962 reflecting his own work at Centres Sociaux for Franco-Algerian cultural cooperation and havoc wreaked by O.A.S. violence.

628   FERNIOT, JEAN. De Gaulle et le 13 mai. Paris, Plon, 1965. 492 p. Includes bibliography.

Most comprehensive account of events leading to de Gaulle's return to power. It is based on memoirs, eyewitness accounts of dozens of participants published since 1958, as well as author's private interviews. Going back to 1956 to retrace groupings and plots in France and Algeria he unravels the interweaving strands which converged to produce the May 13 uprising in Algeria, the appeal to de Gaulle and the final maneuvering between de Gaulle and parliament. Although de Gaulle himself remains in the background, this is likely to be the last word on the extent of de Gaulle's personal responsibility for the fall of the Fourth Republic and his return to power. Extensive bibliography but no index.

629   FERNIOT, JEAN. Les ides de mai. Paris, Plon, 1958. 185 p.

Writing in summer of 1958, "Express" journalist reconstructs political maneuvers in parliament and Algeria beginning with May 13 and leading up to de Gaulle's confirmation as head of the government.

630   FERTAL, ROBERT. Le manifeste de la contre-révolution française. Paris, Éditions françaises et internationales, 1958. 63 p. (Révolution et contre-révolution, 1)

Printed version of 1957 manifesto distributed by the group "Action nationale contre-révolutionnaire" (A.C.N.R.) giving its Christian-social credo and program for political, social, and economic change, Algerian integration serving as answer to revolutionary tactics. It is not only anti-Communist but hostile to European integration and Atlantic Alliance. May 1958 uprising is described in introduction as an example of counter-revolution. See also no. 397.

631   FIGUERAS, ANDRE. Algérie française. Paris, Éditions A.F. [1958?] 158 p.

Acrimonious criticism of Gaullist Algerian policy as too lax to keep Algeria French, as well as counterproposals for removing the main obstacle to integration, namely Algerian overpopulation.

632   FIGUERAS, ANDRE. Charles le Dérisoire (Pièce en V actes) Paris, Au fil d'Ariane, 1964. 213 p. (Collection politique)

Crude satire on de Gaulle (roi Charles) and his ministers, centering on autocracy, decolonization, trials of rebel generals, succession.

633   FIGUERAS,ANDRE. Les gaullistes vont en enfer. Paris, Librairie française, 1965. 159 p.

Diatrabe written from Portuguese asylum summer 1965 in which Gaullists as a group are made responsible for loss of Algeria and Communist successes. Leading U.N.R. and government figures are singled out for near-libelous attack.

634   FIGUERAS, ANDRE. Guide d'anti-cinquième. Paris, Au fil d'Ariane, 1963. 171 p.

Polemic against betrayals of Fifth Republic (particularly Algeria) and rallying cry to all nationalist groups to join in overthrowing Gaullist regime.

635   FIGUERAS, ANDRE. Paris, Diffusion française, 1966. 191 p. plate.

Author describes his struggles with the government over his most recent books, "Le général mourra," "Figueras contre de Gaulle," and "Les Gaullistes vont en enfer" all of which were seized because they constituted offenses against the chief of state and provocation to murder. Author takes issue with the whole concept of political censorship and reviews the specific accusations against "Le général mourra." Work contains list of all books and periodicals seized and authors condemned, 1959-1965.

636 FIGUERAS, ANDRE. Nous sommes Frey! La vérité sur l'U.N.R. Paris, Éditions A. F., 1958. 125 p.

Indictment of de Gaulle, Soustelle, Chaban-Delmas, and victorious U.N.R. for failing to end abuses of political system and for neglecting France's real problems. Author was Gaullist supporter until 1958 elections.

637 FIGUERAS, ANDRE. Les pieds noirs dans le plat. Paris, Presses du Mail, 1962. 218 p. illus.

Fate of European settlers and pro-French Moslems in Algeria, their exodus, unkind reception by French population and harsh treatment by government. A good part of book reports on author's personal inspection of relocation centers in South and Southwest of France, including special centers for harkis.

638 FIGUERAS, ANDRE. Salan, Raoul, ex-général. Paris, Table ronde, 1965. 272 p. (L'Ordre du jour)

Account of Salan's military and political career, based largely on documents produced at 1962 trial and complemented by private communications and interview with author July 1957 about Algerian prospects at that time. This relatively unpolemical work fails to bring new material on Salan's role May 1958, April 1961, or as O.A.S. leader. At the time of writing, Salan was in prison.

639 FIGUERAS, ANDRE. Les origines étranges de la Ve République. Paris, Les Presses du Mail, 1962. 250 p. facsims.

Journalist's and pamphleteer's account of political intrigues leading to collapse of Fourth Republic and de Gaulle's recall to power, as well as early months of new regime. As an insider (author at one time was a Gaullist supporter) he was able to collect malicious anecdotes and personal information on leading political figures within Gaullist circle. One interesting story is his interview with Malraux, who in Spring of 1958 predicted exact manner of de Gaulle's return to power; another concerns the possibility of de Gaulle's connivance with F.L.N. in 1955 to bring about collapse of Fourth Republic. Name index.

640 FIGUÈRES, LÉO, (ed.). Le Parti communiste français, la culture et les intellectuels; textes de Maurice Thorez, Waldeck Rochet et al. Témoignages de A. France, R. Lefebvre et al. Hors-texte de Picasso, Marquet, Léger et Lurçat. Paris, Éditions sociales, 1962. 315 p.

Articles and speeches, 1959-1962, by leading P.C.F. members Maurice Thorez, Jacques Duclos, Waldeck Rochet, Georges Cogniot, Roger Garaudy, and Louis Aragon on communism and intellectuals, cultural questions, science and research on the French scene.

641 FIGUÈRES, LÉO, (ed.). La jeunesse et le communisme; choix de textes marxistes. 2. éd. rev. et augm. Paris, Éditions sociales, 1963. 198 p.

Mainly excerpts from texts of Marxist classics, with a few speeches by French Communist leaders at youth rallies.

642 FISHER, SYDNEY NETTLETON, (ed.). France and the European community. Columbus, Ohio State University Press, 1965, 1964. viii, 176 p. (Graduate Institute for World Affairs. Publication no. 4)

Based on papers presented by 8 American scholars at Ohio State University's Graduate Institute of World Affairs, Oct. 1963 on a variety of topics including French culture within the European community, French policy toward NATO and the Soviet bloc, French agriculture and natural resources within the Common Market.

642a FLAMENT, MARC. Aucune bête au monde... Texte du colonel Marcel Bigeard, photos du sergent-chef Marc Flament. Paris, Pensée moderne, 1959. 1 v. (unpaged, chiefly illus.)

Pictorial work on military operations in Algerian mountains glorifying heroism of French soldiers. Colonel Bigeard was in charge of all operational sectors of the French army in Algeria 1958-59.

643 FLANNER, JANET (Genêt). Paris journal, 1944-1965. Edited by William Shawn. New York, Atheneum, 1965. 615 p.

Collection of monthly or bi-weekly reports, published originally in "The New Yorker," by American correspondent residing in Paris. About half of book deals with Fifth Republic and aims to keep a sophisticated American audience up-to-date on current political and cultural events. Information is based on Paris press rather than personal contacts of author. Good index.

644 FOLLIET, JOSEPH. Guerre et paix en Algérie; réflexions d'un homme libre. Lyon, Chronique sociale, 1958. 186 p.

Algerian problem and conflicting myths around it as seen by French Catholic seeking non-partisan judgment and solution acceptable to men of good will. Work was concluded March 1958.

645 FONDATION NATIONALE DES SCIENCES POLITIQUES. L'administration française; bibliographie commentée établie par Bernard Gournay. Paris, 1961. (Bibliographies françaises de sciences sociales, 2) 153 p.

This first volume of projected series on French administration is limited to central administration. Bibliography covers 1944-1958 publications (books and articles) about public administration in France and documents issued by administrative agencies. First part deals with general problems of administration, second part is devoted to individual organs: parliamentary assemblies, Presidence du Conseil, Conseil d'état, Cour des Comptes, and ministries, as organized under Fifth Republic. Within each subsection, the arrangement is chronological, so that works on Fifth Republic are easily located. Author index.

646 FONDATION NATIONALE DES SCIENCES POLITIQUES. Parti républicain radical et radical-socialiste; compte-rendu sténographique des congrès nationaux 36-59, 1944-1962. Reproduction de documents appartenant aux archives du Parti républicain, et radical-socialiste, Paris. Table des matières. Paris, 1962. 1 v. (Its Documentation sur les partis politiques français)

This volume contains only table of contents, which indicates speakers for sessions at each of congresses. There are 300-400 frames per congress, but table of contents does not give microfilm reel for each congress. For microfilms themselves, see no 1407.

647 FONDATION NATIONALE DES SCIENCES POLITIQUES. La planification comme processus de décision [colloque, Grenoble, 2 au 4 mai 1963] Paris, A. Colin, 1965. 224 p. (Its Cahiers, 140)

Political scientists, economists, and jurists discuss ideology of French planning, process of drawing up plan, its legal and administrative aspects, and its impact on the country's economic structure. Among participants at the conference are officials connected with planning, trade unionists, businessmen, and technical experts. Conference was jointly sponsored by Fondation and Grenoble University's Institut d'études politiques.

648 FONDATION NATIONALE DES SCIENCES POLITIQUES. Travaux inédits de science politiques; liste de thèses, mémoires et diplômes soutenus en France. Paris, 1963, 1964. 2 v.

Complete list of theses (diplôme and doctoral) from French universities and Institutes of Political Science, divided into these 11 topics: political ideas, French institutions, administration, press and public opinion, political forces, elections, local studies (French), international relations, attitudes toward international affairs, foreign countries, French Africa, complemented by subject index. A number of studies deal with Fifth Republic. For each item author, title, pages, date and place of presentation, type of thesis, research professor, are given. 1963 volume covers 1959-1962 (477 entries), and 1964 volume covers 1962-63. From 1964 - lists appear annually in 2. issue of "Revue française de sciences politiques." Fondation nationale has up-to-date card file on theses, but not actual theses.

649 FONDATION NATIONALE DES SCIENCES POLITIQUES. CENTRE D'ETUDE DE LA VIE POLITIQUE FRANÇAISE. La campagne électorale, octobre-novembre 1962; discours et débats réunis par Monica Charlot, Michèle Cotta, Nicole Racine. Avec le concours de la Radiotélevision française, d'Europe no. 1 et de Radio Luxembourg. Paris, 1963, 2 v. (Its Série "Documents," no. 1)

First volume reproduces text of official campaign speeches by spokesmen for major political parties; second volume gives text of debates, round table discussions, and interviews during the campaign period on non-governmental radio and television stations between governmental and opposition candidates, including Debrè, Capitant, Chaban-Delmas, Frey, Vallon on government side, and Depreux, M. Faure, Isorni, Mollet, Mitterand, and Waldeck-Rochet for opposition. Main topic of discussion is reform of political institutions. Index of speakers, chronology of radio and TV appearances.

650 FONDATION NATIONALE DES SCIENCES POLITIQUES. CENTRE D'ETUDE DE LA VIE POLITIQUE FRANÇAISE. Le référendum du 8 janvier 1961, sous la direction de François Goguel. Préf. de Jean Touchard. Paris, A. Colin, 1962. 237 p. diagrs., facsims, and atlas of 10 maps. (Cahiers de la Fondation nationale des sciences politiques. Partis et élections, 119)

Chronology and analysis of referendum campaign and over-all results plus special studies on Paris, Lyon, Lille, Ain and Ardennes departments. Maps show results graphically by canton for both 1958 and 1961 referenda, with separate map for Paris and vicinity.

651 FONDATION NATIONALE DES SCIENCES POLITIQUES. CENTRE D'ETUDE DE LA VIE POLITIQUE FRANÇAISE. Le référendum du 8 avril 1962, sous la direction de François Goguel. Préf. de Jean Touchard. Paris, A. Colin, 1963. 221 p. diagrs., facsims, and atlas of 7 maps. (Cahiers de la Fondation nationale des sciences politiques. Partis et élections, 124)

Chronology and description of referendum campaign by political parties, press, radio, television, with texts of each party's speeches on both media. Short analysis of results and tables for all departments and maps comparing 1962 and 1961 results graphically. One map for Paris and vicinity.

652 FONDATION NATIONALE DES SCIENCES POLITIQUES. SERVICE DE DOCUMENTATION. Guide sommaire des instruments de documentation en science politique. Paris, 1960. 38 l. (Fondation nationale des sciences politiques. Cycle supérieur d'études politiques. Guide de recherches, no. 5)

Classified bibliography of French and international reference works on political science held by Fondation Nationale's library.

FOR OTHER WORKS BY FONDATION NATIONALE DES SCIENCES POLITIQUES, SEE AUTHOR INDEX

653 FONSECA, OSMAR SANTOS. Confrontation de la presse brésilienne et de la presse française pendant le voyage du général de Gaulle au Brésil. Nancy, 1966. 46 p. (Université de Nancy. Publications du Centre européen universitaire. Collection des mémoires, no. 20) Includes bibliography.

Breakdown of six French and six Brazilian dailies' presentation of de Gaulle's official visit to see how far official views on foreign policy are reflected in press, including opposition press.

654 FONTAINE, ANDRE. L'alliance atlantique à l'heure du dégel. Paris, Calmann-Lévy, 1960, 1959. 221 p. (Questions d'actualité)

Assessment of Atlantic Alliance at end of Eisenhower era, with comments on de Gaulle's proposals for change and his initiation of an independent nuclear policy.

655 FONTAINE, FRANÇOIS. La démocratie en vacances; préf. de Jacques Fauvet. Paris, R. Juillard, 1959. 214 p.

Prospects of democratic institutions under de Gaulle in terms of France's total psychological and social predispositions. Author discusses likely effects of greater governmental stability on political institutions and on possibilities for Algerian settlement.

656 FONTAINE, MARCEL. La République populaire roumaine contre la culture française; 15 ans de guerre, 1948-1962. Paris, Fundatia regala universitara Carol I, 1962. 253 p. illus.

Recent French efforts toward improved cultural relations with Rumania are set against background of Rumania's unremitting hostility toward the French government and French civilization, 1948-1962. Author, a former French teacher in Rumania, condemns the non-reciprocal nature of this rapprochement with a communist country.

657 FONTAINE, PIERRE. Alerte au pétrole franco-saharien. Paris, Sept couleurs, 1961. 267 p.

History of Saharan oil discovery and exploitation and attack on Gaullist government's oil policies as benefiting private French and international business at the expense of French control over Sahara.

658 FONTAINE, PIERRE. L'aventure algérienne continue. Paris, Sept couleurs, 1967. 188 p. (Collection "Escales nouvelles," 2)

Algerian revolution viewed as convergence of plots by foreign petroleum interests (British, U.S.) to evict France from North Africa, and of Communist and American aim to replace European colonial power by their own domination. Evolution in Fourth and Fifth Republic of French Algerian policy is reviewed in this light, as is growth of Algerian nationalism and current attempts of foreign powers to penetrate Algeria.

659 FONTAINE, PIERRE. Le dossier secret de l'Afrique du Nord. Paris, Sept couleurs, 1957. 217 p. Bibliographical footnotes.

Inside story of plots by English, American, German, Spanish interests and Russian agents as well as pan-Arab groups to undermine French control in North Africa by fomenting Moslem rebellion and keeping rebels supplied with arms in Algeria. Any concession to Arab nationalism is therefore viewed as step toward loss of Algeria.

660 FONTAINE, PIERRE and PIERRE LEBLANC-PENAUD. L'heure des paysans; révolte ou révolution paysanne? Paris, 1963. 148 p. "Défense de l'Occident. Numero spécial, juillet-août, 1963."

Analysis of declining share of farmer in French economy by means of figures on agricultural prices, size of farms, extent of government credit, effects of Common Market on agriculture, description of agricultural organizations representing farmers' interests and possibilities for stronger political action. The newly founded anti-collectivist and anti-cooperative Union nationale des paysans de France is described by Leblanc-Penaud.

661 FONTAINE, PIERRE (ed.). Histoire mondiale de l'après-guerre 1945-1965. Paris, Sphinx, 1965-66. 2 v. illus.

Handsome collective work on world evolution in the two postwar decades, arranged topically and geographically rather than chronologically. First volume covers: 1) history of cold war; 2) economic and social developments, including European integration; 3) international organizations; 4) religious evolution. Second volume is divided by areas: 1) Western world (a long chapter on France); 2) Communist world; 3) decolonization and Third World (long chapter on Algeria); 4) Latin America; 5) technical revolution. Author's strong anti-Communist views are in evidence.

662 FONTANET, JOSEPH; LECANUET, JEAN. Pour construire ensemble la démocratie de demain, by Joseph Fontanet. Une voie nouvelle pour la démocratie, le progrès de l'Europe, by Jean Lecanuet. Paris, 1963. 2 v. in 1. (55 p.) (Action civique et politique, no. 8)

Speakers at Mouvement Républicain Populaire's 20th congress (La Baule, 1963) report on proposals for democratization of political institutions.

663 FONVIELLE-ALQUIER, FRANÇOIS. Réapprendre l'irrespect, bréviaire pour l'après-gaullisme. Paris, Table ronde, 1966. 171 p. (La Table ronde de Combat. Collection "Le Brûlot," 2)

Journalist's polemic against de Gaulle's personalization of power through astute use of father-image and other myths, deployment of clever public relations techniques, all aiming at citizens' abdication of responsibility. Presidential election's result is seen as reawakening of "disrespect" through democratic opposition.

664 FOUGEYROLLAS, PIERRE. La conscience politique dans la France contemporaine; essai. Paris, Denoël, 1963. 337 p. diagrs., tables. Includes bibliography.

Underlying trends of political life in Fifth Republic are brought to light by author's novel approach of breaking down French political mentality into a partisan and a national component and showing what institutional crises have resulted from incompatibility between these two elements. The partisan element is isolated by study of election results including Nov. 1962 election, findings of public opinion polls and electoral sociology as to mentality of Communist, Socialist, Radical, Gaullist, M.R.P., Independent voters, and militants of extreme Left and Right. National consensus is reflected in response to certain events, as well as by anti-parliamentarian, anti-partisan, and anti-ideological reactions. Communists are seen as outside the national consensus, while Gaullism is limited to goal of national leadership. Prospects of presidential regime are analyzed. Many tables, good bibliography.

665 FOUGEYROLLAS, PIERRE. Le marxisme en question. Paris, Éditions du Seuil, 1959. 172 p. (Collections "Esprit." La cité prochaine) Bibliographical footnotes.

Critique of Marxist philosophy (class struggle, alienation, historical determinism) and Soviet society by former French Communist. Author attempts to separate viable Marxist contributions from myths disproved by 20th century history. There are no direct references to French political scene.

666 FOURASTIE, JEAN. Le grand espoir du XXe siècle. éd. définitive. Paris, Gallimard, 1963. 372 p. (Collection Idées)

Differential effects of technical progress on standard of living and contemporary civilization, with numerous comparisons of French and U.S. prices, wages, production costs, productivity, employment in different sectors of economy for 1959-1962, although core of this influential book was written a decade earlier. Author's main thesis is that U.S. has already reached and France is coming closer to what he calls a "tertiary civilization" in which food and manufactured products are superabundant but services scarce, because not susceptible to technical progress for the time being.

667 FOURASTIE, JEAN. La grande métamorphose du XXe siècle; essais sur quelques problèmes de l'humanité d'aujourd'hui. Paris, Presses universitaires de France, 1961. 223 p. plates. "Note bibliographique": p. 216.

Reflections on effects of technical progress on human capacities, motivations, thinking process.

668 FOURASTIE, JEAN and JEAN-PAUL COURTHÉOUX. La planification économique en France. Paris, Presses universitaires de France, 1963. 208 p. ("L'Organisateur") ML

Philosophy and concepts underlying French planning and Jean Monnet's contribution to first plans. Elaboration, execution, and anticipated results of Fourth Plan are given in detail. As specialist on economic forecasting and technical progress, author was involved with French planning from its inception.

669 FOURASTIE, JEAN. Les 40,000 heures. Paris, R. Laffont, 1965. 246 p. (Inventaire de l'avenir, 1) Bibliographical footnotes.

Title refers to the 40,000 hours of work per lifetime presently enjoyed by the most privileged, and which it is socialist aim to grant all wage earners. First section shows lack of realism of this goal for French economy in coming generation. Second part projects 1985 society, concentrating on problems of education, urbanism, income distribution, collective vs. individual consumption. The final projection is that of the abundant society of 2050, in which 40,000 hours will have become the norm, and for which author gives penetrating insights in terms of the human implications of abundance. Fourastié's conceptions are reflected in the collective work "Reflexions pour 1985" (no. 768).

670 FOURNIER, CHRISTIANE. Des gosses à amnistier; enquêtes et témoignages. Préf. du général Valluy. Paris, Maisonneuve, 1965. 122 p.

Visits to several typical families among the 700 political prisoners jailed for O.A.S. activities and report of effects political stigma has on children.

671 FOX, EDWARD W. The position of France in world affairs; [a lecture delivered on March 8th, 1960] Washington, D.C., Industrial College of the Armed Forces [1961] 18 p.

Cornell professor's explanation before U.S. military group of de Gaulle's and French attitudes toward European unification, NATO, and Algeria, and likely developments in these areas. He is convinced that ultimately Algerian conflict will culminate in evacuation of European settlers.

672* FRANCE. General declaration drawn up in common agreement at Evian, March 18, 1962 by the delegations of the Government of the French Republic and The Algerian National Liberation

Front. New York, 1962. 7 p. French affairs, No. 130.

673*   FRANCE. AMBASSADE. U.S. SERVICE DE PRESSE ET D'INFORMATION. Algeria. New York, 1957. 8 p.

674*   FRANCE. AMBASSADE. U.S. SERVICE DE PRESSE ET D'INFORMATION. Algeria at work. New York, 1957. 48 p.

Description of Algerian economy, French assistance in housing, health, and education, and recent political reforms.

675*   FRANCE. AMBASSADE. U.S. SERVICE DE PRESSE ET D'INFORMATION. Balance sheet of the De Gaulle administration, June 3, 1958-February 5, 1959. New York, 1959. 44 p. French affairs, no. 84, May 1959.

676*   FRANCE. AMBASSADE. U.S. SERVICE DE PRESSE ET D'INFORMATION. The Central African Republic. New York, 1960. 28 p.

677*   FRANCE. AMBASSADE. U.S. SERVICE DE PRESSE ET D'INFORMATION. The Comoro Islands. New York, 1962. 14 p.

678   FRANCE. AMBASSADE. U.S. SERVICE DE PRESSE ET D'INFORMATION. The Constantine Plan for Algeria; opening new frontiers in development. [New York, 1961?] 40 p. illus., double map.

Survey of plan's achievements through 1960.

679*   FRANCE. AMBASSADE. U.S. SERVICE DE PRESSE ET D'INFORMATION. Constructive action of the French government in Algeria. New York, 1957. 31 p. French Affairs no. 40.

680   FRANCE. AMBASSADE. U.S. SERVICE DE PRESSE ET D'INFORMATION. The Fifth plan, 1966-1970; twenty years of planning in France. New York, 1967. 32 p. tables.

Projection of aggregate figures for economy in 1970 and specific targets of Fifth Plan, with brief summary of previous four plans.

681*   FRANCE. AMBASSADE. U.S. SERVICE DE PRESSE ET D'INFORMATION. First draft of the constitutional law prepared by the government in accordance with the law of June 3, 1958. New York, 1958. 24 p.

French and English versions.

682   FRANCE. AMBASSADE. U.S. SERVICE DE PRESSE ET D'INFORMATION. The first five years of the Fifth Republic of France, January 1959-January 1964. New York, 1964. 66 p.

Gaullist policy discussed under such headings as foreign policy, defense, economic policy.

683   FRANCE. AMBASSADE. U.S. SERVICE DE PRESSE ET D'INFORMATION. France; aid and cooperation. New York, 1962. 56 p. illus., diagrs.

Organization and financing, as of 1961, of French economic and technical assistance to Africa and other parts of the world.

684   FRANCE. AMBASSADE. U.S. SERVICE DE PRESSE ET D'INFORMATION. France; air and space. New York, 1963. 56 p. illus., ports., maps, diagrs.

Developments in military and commercial aviation, research in guided missiles.

685   FRANCE. AMBASSADE. U.S. SERVICE DE PRESSE ET D'INFORMATION. France; town and country environment planning. New York, 1965. 55 p. illus., diagrs.

Definition of concept of "aménagement du territoire," history of regional planning since 1944, agencies presently administering program, large-scale regional projects now under way, problems and guidelines for 1985 (transport, industrial and educational decentralization) and a special section on new Paris master plan.

686   FRANCE. AMBASSADE. U.S. SERVICE DE PRESSE ET D'INFORMATION. France and agriculture. New York, 1963. 56 p. illus.

Survey of agricultural production and government aid to agriculture.

687   FRANCE. AMBASSADE. U.S. SERVICE DE PRESSE ET D'INFORMATION. France and economic planning. New York, 1962. 48 p. illus., diagrs.

History of French planning and detailed figures for objectives of Fourth Plan.

688   FRANCE. AMBASSADE. U.S. SERVICE DE PRESSE ET D'INFORMATION. France and Europe. New York, 1962. 47 p. illus.

French economy in context of Common Market.

689   FRANCE. AMBASSADE. U.S. SERVICE DE PRESSE ET D'INFORMATION. France and its armed forces. New York, 1964. 56 p. illus.

Current military organization, after 1962 reforms, weapons research, military budget, 1965-1970 weapons system program.

690*   FRANCE. AMBASSADE. U.S. SERVICE DE PRESSE ET D'INFORMATION. France and petroleum. New York, 1961. 40 p.

Survey of French oil refining industry.

691   FRANCE. AMBASSADE. U.S. SERVICE DE PRESSE ET D'INFORMATION. France and the merchant marine. New York, 1962. 47 p. illus.

Survey of shipbuilding industry, passenger and freight capacity, share in world shipping trade.

692*   FRANCE. AMBASSADE. U.S. SERVICE DE PRESSE ET D'INFORMATION. France and the Sahara. New York, 1961. 15 p.

693   FRANCE. AMBASSADE. U.S. SERVICE DE PRESSE ET D'INFORMATION. France and the southern and Antarctic lands. New York, 1962. 32 p. illus.

694   FRANCE. AMBASSADE. U.S. SERVICE DE PRESSE ET D'INFORMATION. French economic and financial aid to the developing countries. New York, 1966. 8 p. (Its French affairs, no. 197)

Selected summary figures for world-wide French bilateral and multilateral aid 1962-1965.

695*   FRANCE. AMBASSADE. U.S. SERVICE DE PRESSE ET D'INFORMATION. Michel Debré, premier of France. New York, 1959. 2 p.

696*   FRANCE. AMBASSADE. U.S. SERVICE DE PRESSE ET D'INFORMATION. Pierre Pflimlin, premier of France. New York, 1958. 1 p.

697* FRANCE. AMBASSADE. U.S. SERVICE DE PRESSE ET D'INFORMATION. Regulations concerning the election of deputies from metropolitan France and the overseas departments; ordinance no. 58-945 of October 13, 1958. New York, 1958. 4 p.

698* FRANCE. AMBASSADE. U.S. SERVICE DE PRESSE ET D'INFORMATION. René Coty, president of the Republic of France. New York, 1957. 3 l.

699* FRANCE. AMBASSADE. U.S. SERVICE DE PRESSE ET D'INFORMATION. The Republic of Chad. New York, 1961. 32 p.

700* FRANCE. AMBASSADE. U.S. SERVICE DE PRESSE ET D'INFORMATION. The Republic of Congo (Brazzaville). New York, 1961. 32 p.

701* FRANCE. AMBASSADE. U.S. SERVICE DE PRESSE ET D'INFORMATION. The Republic of Dahomey. New York, 1960. 32 p.

702* FRANCE. AMBASSADE. U.S. SERVICE DE PRESSE ET D'INFORMATION. The Republic of the Ivory Coast. New York, 1960. 32 p.

703* FRANCE. AMBASSADE. U.S. SERVICE DE PRESSE ET D'INFORMATION. The Republic of the Niger. New York, 1960. 32 p.

704* FRANCE. AMBASSADE. U.S. SERVICE DE PRESSE ET D'INFORMATION. The Republic of Senegal. New York, 1960. 32 p.

705* FRANCE. AMBASSADE. U.S. SERVICE DE PRESSE ET D'INFORMATION. The Republic of the Upper Volta. New York, 1960. 31 p.

706* FRANCE. AMBASSADE. U.S. SERVICE DE PRESSE ET D'INFORMATION. Reunion, the perfume island. New York, 1961. 22 p.

707* FRANCE. AMBASSADE. U.S. SERVICE DE PRESSE ET D'INFORMATION. State visit to the United States of General Charles de Gaulle, President of the French Republic and of the Community, April 22-29, 1960. New York, 1960. 1 portfolio.

708 FRANCE. AMBASSADE. U.S. SERVICE DE PRESSE ET D'INFORMATION. Texts of declarations drawn up in common agreement at Evian, March 18, 1962, by the Delegations of the Government of the French Republic and the Algerian National Liberation Front. English translation. New York, 1962. 60 p.

FOR ADDITIONAL WORKS BY FRANCE. AMBASSADE, SEE AUTHOR INDEX

709 FRANCE. ARMEE. CORPS MEDICAL. Alger 26 mars 1962; temoignages recueillis par les médecins ayant assisté à la fusillade ou ayant soigné les blessés. n.p., 1962. 32 p. fold plans.

Eye-witness accounts of shooting of European settlers in Algiers, rue d'Isly, on March 26, 1962, with list of 50 dead. Shooting was done by French Army and C.S.R. (Compagnie de Sécurité Républicaine) Title on cover is: "Le massacre d'Alger, 26 mars 1962."

710 FRANCE. ASSEMBLEE NATIONALE, 1958- Notices et portraits. Paris, Impr. de l'Assemblée nationale, 1959. xxii, 565 p. ports.

Photographs, brief biographical data, and party and parliamentary group affiliation for each member of National Assembly from France, Algeria, Sahara, overseas departments and territories.

711 FRANCE. ASSEMBLEE NATIONALE, 1958- Règlement de l'Assemblée nationale. Instruction générale du Bureau de l'Assemblée. Assemblées européennes. Constitution et textes intéressant l'Assemblée nationale. Paris, 1959. 532 p.

Rules and procedures for Assembly and its committees, Senate, Senate of French Community, European Assembly, with text of 1958 constitution and subsequent organic laws, decrees, Constitutional Council decisions affecting these organs. Subject index. For 1965 version, consult Law Library.

712 FRANCE. ASSEMBLEE NATIONALE, 1958- SECRETARIAT GENERAL. Recueil des textes authentiques des programmes et engagements électoraux des députés proclamés élus à la suite des élections générales. 1958, v. 1-2; 1962, v. 1-2. Paris, Impr. de l'Assemblée nationale. 4 v.

This compendium, informally known as the "Barodet" reproduces each elected deputy's official campaign statement (his "profession de foi"). It is arranged by departments with statements of each department's deputies. Also included are programs of each of parliamentary groups.

713 FRANCE. ASSEMBLEE NATIONALE, 1958- Sénat. SECRETARIAT GENERAL DE LA QUESTURE. Liste alphabétique et par circonscriptions électorales de mesdames et messieurs les sénateurs avec l'indication de leurs adresses. Groupes et commissions, Octobre 1961. Paris, Impr. des Journaux Officiels, 1961. 85 p.

Includes list of Senate members appointed to Assembly of European Communities, Council of Europe, Constitutional Council, and Haute Court de Justice.

714* FRANCE. CENTRE DE DIFFUSION FRANÇAISE. The young face of France. Paris, 1959. 63 p.

Pictorial work on French youth and educational facilities, compiled by Direction de la Documentation.

715 FRANCE. CENTRE NATIONAL DE LA RECHERCHE SCIENTIFIQUE. Centre de recherches sahariennes. Paris, 1960. 40 p. illus., maps.

This center, which is part of C.N.R.S., has headquarters in Sahara, where it studies seismographic, geological, and biological aspects of Saharan desert.

716 FRANCE. CENTRE NATIONAL DE LA RECHERCHE SCIENTIFIQUE. Rapport d'activité. 1963-1966. Paris.

Survey of research projects in physical sciences, anthropology, contemporary history, and sociology in progress under the C.N.R.S.'s "Recherches coopératives sur programme," 1963-66.

717 FRANCE. CENTRE NATIONAL DE LA RECHERCHE SCIENTIFIQUE. GROUPE D'ÉTHNOLOGIE SOCIALE. La femme dans la société; son image dans différents milieux sociaux. By Marie-José et Paul-Henry Chombart de Lauwe et al. 2 annexes by Philippe Robert et al. Paris, 1963. 439 p. (Its Travaux)

Results of collective study, 1960-1962, based on 360 carefully sampled families in working, middle, upper-class districts of Paris and suburbs, plus small sample of students. Information on style of life for these different social levels serves as background to conception of role of women in society. Focus is on the professional role of women, but their function in household is also examined. Appendices on legal status of French married women and statistics on female employment. Good bibliography on woman's professional status.

718 FRANCE. COMITE CONSULTATIF D'ETUDE DES AIDES A LA PROMOTION SOCIALE. Rapport du Comité consultatif

d'étude des aides à la promotion sociale, institué par décision du Premier ministre du 14 juin 1962. Paris, Documentation française, 1963. 79 p. (Recueils et monographies, no. 44)

June 1963 proposals of Comité consultatif on reform of social security and vocational training.

719* FRANCE. COMITE D'HISTOIRE DE LA DEUXIÈME GUERRE MONDIALE. Réunion plénière du 20 mars 1959; rapport de M. H. Michel, secrétaire général. Paris, 1959. 6 l.

720 FRANCE. COMITE MONETAIRE DE LA ZONE FRANC. Rapport. 5, 7-8 1957, 1959-60. Paris, Impr. nationale. 3 v.

Statistics for agricultural and raw material production, trade, movement of capital, investment within Franc Zone (Metropolitan France, Algeria, French Community) for 1957, 1959, 1960, with introductory description of changes in political framework.

721 FRANCE. COMITE RUEFF. Rapport sur la situation financière présenté à monsieur le ministre des finances et des affaires économiques en exécution de sa décision du 30 septembre 1958. Paris, Impr. nationale, 1958. 55 p.

December 1958 report of committee headed by Jacques Rueff and appointed by Finance Minister Pinay to propose measures for franc devaluation, internal monetary stabilization and 1959 budget. For English translation, see no. 723.

722 FRANCE. COMITE RUEFF. Rapport sur les obstacles à l'expansion économique, présenté par le Comité chargé d'examiner les situations de fait ou de droit qui constituent d'une manière injustifiée un obstacle à l'expansion de l'économie institué par le décret no 59-1284 du 13 novembre 1959. Paris, Impr. nationale, 1960. 98 p.

The committee headed by Jacques Rueff and Louis Armand reported July 1960 on structural rigidities of French economy and made specific recommendations for liberalizing economy.

723 FRANCE. COMITE RUEFF. Report on the financial situation of France, submitted to the Minister of Finance and Economic Affairs, pursuant to instruction of September 30, 1958. With an introd. by Jacques Rueff, specially written for the English ed. Translated April 6, 1959. New York, Distributed by United States Council of the International Chamber of Commerce, 1959. 36 p. tables.

Introduction summarizes effect of stabilization plan on French participation in Common Market and free convertibility of French currency.

724* FRANCE. COMMISSARIAT A L'ENERGIE ATOMIQUE. C.E.N. Saclay, nuclear research center. Paris, S.N.A.P. edition, 1959. 62 p.

725* FRANCE. COMMISSARIAT GENERAL AU PLAN. SERVICE DES ETUDES ECONOMIQUES ET FINANCIÈRES. Perspectives de l'économie française en 1965. Paris, 1956. 43 p.

Prepared as background for Third Plan, 1957-1961, document gives 1965 projections for gross national product, composition of output, and distribution of expenditures.

726 FRANCE. COMMISSARIAT GENERAL DU PLAN D'ÉQUIPEMENT ET DE LA PRODUCTIVITE. Rapport annuel sur l'exécution du plan de modernisation et d'équipement. 1959. Paris, Impr. nationale. illus., maps, diagrs.

Objectives and achievements in different sectors of economy during first year of Third Plan. This is only part 1 of report: "Vue d'ensemble et réalisations par secteurs."

726a FRANCE. COMMISSARIAT GENERAL DU PLAN DE MODERNISATION ET D'EQUIPEMENT. COMITÉ D'ETUDES DE L'INTÉGRATION ECONOMIQUE DE LA METROPOLE ET DES PAYS D'OUTRE-MER. Rapport général. 2. éd. Paris, 1957. iv, 57. 1.

Report presented to Mollet government May 1956 and coinciding with the preliminary stages of the European Economic Community in which subcommittees' conclusions on agricultural production, the promotion of industrialization, harmonization of trade in the franc zone while keeping it open to world markets, and on prospective population increase in individual countries (Algeria, Tunisia, Guadelupe, etc.) are brought together to show limits of possible integration policy within French Union, notwithstanding political appeals for "assimilation-integration."

727 FRANCE. COMMISSION D'ETUDE DE LA POLITIQUE DE COOPERATION AVEC LES PAYS EN VOIE DE DEVELOPPEMENT. French aid; the Jeanneney report. An Abridged translation of La politique de coopération avec les pays en voie de développement. London, Overseas Development Institute, 1964. 50 p.

Commission headed by Jean-Marcel Jeanneney was set up by government March 1963 to orient its technical aid policy. For full report, see no. 728.

728 FRANCE. COMMISSION D'ETUDE DE LA POLITIQUE DE COOPERATION AVEC LES PAYS EN VOIE DE DEVELOPPEMENT. La politique de coopération avec les pays en voie de développement. Rapport de la Commission d'étude instituée par le décret du 12 mars 1963, remis au Gouvernement le 18 juillet 1963. Paris, La Documentation française, 1963. 133 p.

_____. Annexes. Paris, La Documentation française, 1963. 287 p.

Principles underlying French assistance to former colonies and other underdeveloped countries and specific guidelines for quantity and kind of assistance. This is the so-called "Jeanneney report" - after the Commission's chairman. Annex consists of 23 individual reports by outside experts.

729 FRANCE. COMMISSION DE COORDINATION POUR LA REINSTALLATION DES FRANÇAIS D'OUTRE-MER. Avis définitif sur le rapport général du 5 décembre 1962. Paris, Documentation française, 1963. 11 p. "Supplément aux Notes et études documentaires."

Commission's approval of proposals contained in "Rapport général" (see no. 730).

730 FRANCE. COMMISSION DE COORDINATION POUR LA REINSTALLATION DES FRANÇAIS D'OUTRE-MER. Rapport général. Paris, Documentation française, 1963. 119 p. "Supplément aux 'Notes et études documentaires.'"

Report on situation of Algerian repatriates, Fall 1962, with statistics on their ethnic and social composition and temporary resettlement in France, as well as proposals for national and regional aid. By Jan. 1963, repatriates numbered 750,000.

731 FRANCE. COMMISSION DE L'ECONOMIE GENERALE ET DU FINANCEMENT. Ve plan 1966-1970; rapport général. Paris, Documentation française [1966?] 2 v. tables.

Projections of production, savings, state financing and incentives for projected investment. Volume 2, entitled "Annexes" contains individual reports of commission members and comments of labor union representatives.

732 FRANCE. COMMISSION DE L'EQUIPEMENT SCOLAIRE, UNIVERSITAIRE ET SPORTIF. Ve Plan 1966-1970; rapport général. Paris, Documentation française [1966?] 251 p. tables.

Projections of student enrollments on all levels through 1972 and predicted needs for new buildings and teachers, with special section on equipment for athletics outside the schools.

733 FRANCE. COMMISSION DE L'HABITATION Ve Plan 1966-1970. Rapport général et rapports spéciaux annexés. Paris, Editions du Moniteur des travaux publics, 1966. 192 p. tables.

Commission report on housing proposals for Fifth Plan, components of construction programs (demographic and consumption needs, price and cost structure, geographic distribution) with detailed tables on each point. Rural housing, rent subsidies, credit mechanisms for home purchase and construction are subjects of separate reports.

734 FRANCE. COMMISSION DE LA MAIN-D'OEUVRE. Ve plan 1966-1970; rapport général. Paris, Documentation Française, 1966. 423 p. tables. "Extrait de la Revue française du travail, no. 1, janvier-mars 1966."

Employment projections by sectors, professions, regions, needs for vocational training, with special section on immigration, demands for foreign workers and their specific training requirements.

735 FRANCE. COMMISSION DE LA PRODUCTIVITE. Facteurs et réserves de productivité de l'entreprise; étude réalisée par un groupe de travail de la Commission de la productivité lors de l'élaboration des travaux préparatoires du Ve plan. Paris, 1966. 246 p. fold. tables.

Systematic outline of factors affecting productivity within firms, how productivity has been increased, what are common obstacles, and how government policy can help in each area. Committee composed of administration and efficiency experts from private industry and government give no figures for existing productivity or possible gains but reflect informed thinking on industrial management. Standardization, specialization, proper use of human resources of management and personnel are emphasized over investment in machinery and large-scale use of computers.

736 FRANCE. COMMISSION DES PRESTATIONS SOCIALES. Ve plan 1966-1970; rapport général. Paris, Documentation française [1966?] 173 p. tables.

1966-1970 statistical projection of social security payments, payments for old age pensions, family and housing allowances and proposals for financing of social welfare program.

737 FRANCE. COMMISSION DU SECTEUR DES METIERS ET DE L'ARTISANAT. Ve plan de développement économique et social 1966-1970; rapport général. [Paris, Documentation française 1966?] 120 p. tables.

Projected needs for apprenticeship centers and other forms of vocational training.

738 FRANCE. COMMISSION NATIONALE DE L'AMENAGEMENT DU TERRITOIRE. Rapport. Paris, 1964.

August 1964 report to Commissariat général du plan on objectives of regional planning, basic alternatives and specific proposals to be incorporated in Fifth Plan as well as major reorientations after 1985.

739 FRANCE. CONSEIL CONSTITUTIONNEL. Recueil des décisions, 1961, 1964. Publié sous le haut patronage du Conseil Constitutionnel. Paris.

Decisions on constitutionality of government's organic laws, parliamentary jurisdiction, etc. For 1961, the decisions include approval of de Gaulle's proclamation of a state of emergency April 23, 1961 and his subsequent decrees purging the military and police forces and establishing the Haut Tribunal Militaire to try the officers involved in the Generals' putsch. For 1964, decisions approve procedure for presidential election, quoting text in full.

739a FRANCE. CONSEIL D'ETAT. Études et documents. fasc. 4-12, 14-20. 1950-1958, 1960-1967, Paris. LL

Studies on current administrative, political, and judicial questions and review of activities of different sections of Conseil d'État during the year.

739b FRANCE. CONSEIL D'ETAT. Recueil des décisions du Conseil d'État et des jugements des tribunaux administratifs. Paris, Librairie Sirey, 1918-1967. LL

Conseil d'Etat's decisions on administrative and judicial appeals during each year's sessions, followed by analytical summaries for each area of activities and index of persons involved in each case. Among claimants are those deprived of civil rights in connection with political trials.

740* FRANCE. CONSTITUTION, 1958. Constitution; project présenté par le Gouvernement de la République. Discours prononcé par le Général de Gaulle...le 4 septembre 1958,...à Paris, Impr. nationale, 1958. 8 p.

741 FRANCE. CONSTITUTION, 1958. Constitution; les lois organiques et ordonnances relatives aux pouvoirs publics. Paris, Journaux officiels, 1968. 153 p. "No. 119."

Text of Constitution and supplementary ordinances and organic laws, 1958-1967, concerning presidency and government, parliament, Conseil constitutionnel, judiciary, and Conseil économique et social.

742 FRANCE. CONSTITUTION, 1958. Constitution du 4 octobre 1958; revisée en 1960, 1962 et 1963. Paris, Librairie générale de droit et de jurisprudence, R. Pichon et R. Durand-Auzias, 1964. 23 p.

Amended sections inserted in main text.

743 FRANCE. CONSTITUTION, 1958. The French Constitution adopted by the referendum of September 28, 1958 and promulgated on October 4, 1958. French text and English translation. New York, French Embassy, Press and Information Division, 1958. 75 p.

743a* FRANCE. DELEGATION EN ALGERIE. Algeria's development 1959. [Paris, Information Service of the Delegation General of the French Government in Algeria, 1960] 120 p.

Graphic survey of Algerian economy, educational system, civil service.

743b* FRANCE. DELEGATION EN ALGERIE. Algérie 1961. [Alger, Direction de l'information de la délégation générale, 1961] 47 p.

No current information, just general description of country.

744 FRANCE. DELEGATION GENERALE A LA RECHERCHE SCIENTIFIQUE ET TECHNIQUE. Recherche et développement dans l'industrie française en 1962; résultats de l'enquête menée en 1963 dans le secteur industriel. Paris, 1964. 63 p. (Its Études statistiques sur la recherche et le développement) Includes bibliography.

Results of questionnaires sent to private and nationalized aeronautics, chemical, electronics, steel, oil, automobile, food, construction, electrical companies concerning research personnel, type of research, costs, financing.

744a FRANCE. DIRECTION DE LA COOPERATION CULTURELLE ET TECHNIQUE. Rapport d'activité, 1964-1966. Paris. 215 p. tables, diagrs.

Review of Direction de la cooperation's activities in Africa (technical assistance and educational aid) and training for African students in France, 1964-1966 with detailed tables and charts for different types of aid and by country. For earlier years, see no. 789.

745 FRANCE. DIRECTION DE LA DOCUMENTATION. Accords passés entre la France et l'Algérie de juillet 1962 au 31 décembre 1963. Paris, Documentation française, 1964. 127 p. (Its Recueils et monographies, no. 49)

Texts of agreements between France and independent Algeria.

746 FRANCE. DIRECTION DE LA DOCUMENTATION. L'aménagement du territoire. Paris, 1964. 77 p. (Its Recueils et monographies, no. 46)

February 1963 decrees and ministerial speeches on regional planning as well as other administrative measures for regional coordination.

747 FRANCE. DIRECTION DE LA DOCUMENTATION. Le Vème plan édité par la Documentation française en collaboration avec le Commissariat général du plan d'équipement et de la productivité. Paris, Documentation française illustrée, 1966. 94 p. illus. (part col.) diagrs. "La Documentation française illustrée, no. spécial (220-221) octobre-novembre 1966."

Vivid, simplified presentation of general objectives of new plan and goals of economy for 1970.

748 FRANCE. DIRECTION DE LA DOCUMENTATION. La Direction de la documentation, 1943-1963. Paris, 1963. 150 p. illus., ports., facsims. Includes bibliography.

History of Direction de la documentation, its structure (it is attached to Secrétariat général du gouvernement) services, operation, publications and research, with selective 40-page bibliography by topics of items published through 1963 and devoted to France, such as de Gaulle speeches and press conferences, political, social, economic questions, foreign affairs, and European Community issues.

749 FRANCE. DIRECTION DE LA DOCUMENTATION. Documents relatifs à la politique agricole, avril 1960-avril 1962. Paris, Documentation française, 1962. 180 p. (Its Recueils et monographies no. 41)

Speeches of prime minister and ministers of agriculture on government farm policy, followed by texts of laws, decrees etc. on new agricultural legislation, 1960-1962.

750 FRANCE. DIRECTION DE LA DOCUMENTATION. Documents relatifs à la promotion sociale et se rapportant aux lois nos. 59-960 du 31 juillet 1959 et 50-1481 du 28 décembre 1959. Paris, Documentation française, 1961. 76 p. (Its Recueils et monographies, no. 38)

Laws and ministerial speeches on government measures for improving professional training of workers, farmers, and technicians.

751* FRANCE. DIRECTION DE LA DOCUMENTATION. The economic and social development of French West Africa. Paris, 1958. 14 p.

752 FRANCE. DIRECTION DE LA DOCUMENTATION. L'économie française; texte établi sous la direction de Jacques Dumontier et Jean Teissedre. Paris, 1959. 255 p. illus. "Supplément à La documentation française illustrée." Includes bibliography.

National output, wages, commerce, budget through 1957, with supplementary statistics through 1959.

753 FRANCE. DIRECTION DE LA DOCUMENTATION. France. Paris, 1962. 142 p. illus., ports., map, diagrs. "Supplément à La documentation française illustrée."

Illustrated synthesis of political, industrial, social, and cultural features of France.

754 FRANCE. DIRECTION DE LA DOCUMENTATION. France. Paris, 1965. 147 p. illus., ports., maps, diagrs. "Supplément à La documentation française illustrée."

1962 edition (no. 753) brought up to date.

755 FRANCE. DIRECTION DE LA DOCUMENTATION. La France à travers les publications de la Documentation française. Catalogue spécial. 4. éd. Paris, 1965. 63 p.

Topically arranged books and monographs currently in print, published by the Direction de la Documentation.

756 FRANCE. DIRECTION DE LA DOCUMENTATION. L'harmonisation des circonscriptions administratives françaises. Paris, Documentation française, 1962. 71 p. maps. (Its Recueils et monographies, 42)

Alignment of regional planning districts with other governmental administrative units, with relevant decrees, maps, and lists of areas for each of 50 administrative agencies.

757 FRANCE. DIRECTION DE LA DOCUMENTATION. Les institutions politiques de la France. Paris, La Documentation Française, 1959-1960. 2 v. (Its le Monde contemporain)

French political, judicial, and administrative institutions at the end of the Fourth Republic, surveyed by members of Conseil d'Etat and compiled by Marcel Martin. No attempt was made to bring this erudite and carefully documented work up-to-date for Fifth Republic's reformed institutions. Vol. 1 deals with political institutions, vol. 2 with administrative and judicial institutions.

758 FRANCE. DIRECTION DE LA DOCUMENTATION. Les institutions sociales de la France. [2. éd. Rédigé sous la direction de Pierre Laroque] Paris, Documentation française, 1963. 1022 p. diagrs., tables. (Its Le Monde contemporain)

Detailed 1962 survey of social service administrations, legislation, conditions, policy with respect to: social assistance, social security, health, housing, urbanism, family welfare, worker protection, popular education. The survey is preceded by an up-to-date statistical summary of French population.

759 FRANCE. DIRECTION DE LA DOCUMENTATION. La politique étrangère de la France. Textes et documents, 1966-. Paris.

Chronology of French foreign relations and chronologically arranged texts of speeches, statements, decrees, agreements, press conferences on foreign affairs. Much of material deals with NATO crisis. Final section reproduces statements made to press after each of the sessions of the Conseil des Ministres.

760 FRANCE. DIRECTION DE LA DOCUMENTATION. La politique sociale de la France. Texte établi sous la direction d'André Philbert, chargé de mission au cabinet du Ministre du travail. Paris, Documentation française, 1960. 223 p. illus., ports. "Supplément à La documentation française illustrée."

Description of public and private social welfare agencies currently in operation.

762 FRANCE. DIRECTION DE LA DOCUMENTATION. Rapport sur la politique des revenus établi à la suite de la Conférence des revenus, octobre, 1963 - Janvier, 1964, présenté par Pierre Massé, 13 février, 1964. Paris, 1964. 29 p. (Its Recueils et monographies, 47)

Report by Pierre Massé, head of Commissariat général du plan, on wage and profit policy as part of planning economic expansion. The conference itself brought together labor, farmer, and business representatives.

763 FRANCE. DIRECTION DE LA DOCUMENTATION. Répertoire permanent de l'administration française. Années 1964, 1966. Paris. 2 v.

Directories for 1964, 1966 of 21 ministries and Secrétariats d'Etat with names of staff of main and subsections, office addresses, index of names. Under Ministry of the Interior, directory lists Prefecture de la Seine with all its subsections, prefects only for other departments.

764 FRANCE. DIRECTION DE LA DOCUMENTATION. Trois années de gouvernement, juin 1958 - juin 1961. Paris, Documentation française, 1961. 63 p.

Official review of Fifth Republic's accomplishments in political, economic, social, educational, and cultural realms.

FOR ADDITIONAL WORKS BY FRANCE. DIRECTION DE LA DOCUMENTATION, SEE AUTHOR INDEX

765 FRANCE. DIRECTION DES BIBLIOTHEQUES DE FRANCE. Répertoire des bibliothèques d'étude et organismes de documentation. Paris, Bibliothèque nationale, 1963. 3 v. in 1 (XV, 1233 p.)

Completely revised edition, undertaken by staff of the Bibliothèque Nationale of 1950-1951 "Répertoire des bibliothèques de France" listing over 2300 libraries and documentation centers in all fields. V. 1 covers 959 institutions in Paris, Seine and Seine-et-Oise departments; v. 2 1401 in rest of France. Within each volume, entries are listed alphabetically and give information obtained through 1961-62 questionnaires on specialties, size of holdings, publications, name of sponsoring organization, date of founding. V. 3 is devoted to extensive index of areas of specialization and cross-references. Thus one can get the names of institutions specializing in political science, 20th century history, education, French legal documents, economics, etc.

766 FRANCE. DIRECTION GENERALE DE LA SECURITE SOCIALE. Social security in France. Paris, Documentation française [1965?] 112 p. illus.

1965 information booklet on French social security.

767 FRANCE. GROUPE D'ETUDES [CHARGE] DE DEFINIR LES CONDITIONS DE DEVELOPPEMENT, DE RECRUTEMENT, DE FONCTIONNEMENT ET DE LOCALISATIONS DES GRANDES ECOLES. Les conditions de développement, de recrutement, de fonctionnement et de localisation des grandes écoles en France. Rapport du Groupe d'études au Premier Ministre 26 Septembre 1963. Paris, Documentation française, 1964. 98 p. illus., map. (France. Direction de la documentation. Recueils et monographies, 45)

Current needs for specialists (technical, scientific, commercial, administrative) of French economy, on basis of questionnaires to prospective employers and current flow of students into higher education and institutions available for receiving them. Study group's proposals call for reorganization and relocation of existing institutions and see basic bottleneck in shortage of 'bacheliers' in mathematics, the pool from which future scientists are recruited and which is limited to 20,000 a year currently.

768 FRANCE. GROUPE 1985. Réflexion pour 1985. Paris, Documentation française, 1964. 155 p. illus.

Groupe 1985 was appointed to give a general orientation to Fifth Plan and met Jan. 1963 - Feb. 1964. Members are: Guillaumat, Mme Krier, J. Bernard, E. Claudius-Petit, Demonque, L. Estrangin, J. Fourastié, C. Gruson, B. de Jouvenel, P. Lamour and G. Levard. This is summary of group's projections and recommendations, covering changes in consumption patterns and family structure.

769 FRANCE. HAUT COMITE CONSULTATIF DE LA POPULATION ET DE LA FAMILLE. Information de l'opinion sur les problèmes démographiques. Rapporteurs: M. de Chambure, M. Puissochet. Paris, Documentation française, 1965. 42 p. diagrs. Includes bibliography.

Report on public ignorance of true demographic situation in France and proposals for better demographic education.

770 FRANCE. INSTITUT NATIONAL DE LA STATISTIQUE ET DES ETUDES ECONOMIQUES. Mouvement économique en France de 1944 à 1957. Paris, Impr. nationale, 1958. 325, 14 p. diagrs., tables.

Survey of economic development of metropolitan France from liberation to establishment of Common Market, economic measures by government, demographic evolution, as well as production, wage, price, fiscal, and monetary developments. All statistics are up-dated through 1957.

771 FRANCE. INSTITUT NATIONAL DE LA STATISTIQUE ET DES ETUDES ECONOMIQUES. Population de la France: départements, arrondissements, cantons et communes. Paris, Direction des journaux officiels, Documentation française, 1962. 1141 p.

March-April 1962 census for metropolitan France giving number of inhabitants for departments and smaller administrative units, as well as for communes and cities over 9,000. Comparative figures review 1936, 1954 census, with 1962 total population given as 46.5 millions. Additional title is "Recensement de 1962."

772 FRANCE. INSTITUT NATIONAL DE LA STATISTIQUE ET DES ETUDES ECONOMIQUES. Tableaux de l'économie française. 5th ed. 1966. Paris. 1 vol. tables.

Comparative international statistics and evolution since 1900, results of 1962 population census, and principal economic data for 1963-1965 for the whole country as well as for individual departments.

773 FRANCE. INSTITUT NATIONAL DES TECHNIQUES DE LA DOCUMENTATION. OFFICE DES ETUDIANTS D'OUTREMER. Documentation administrative et bibliographique des problèmes propres aux étudiants des états, républiques d'Afrique noire, de Madagascar et des territoires d'outre-mer faisant leurs études en France; mémoire déposé à l'Institut national des techniques de la documentation, Office des étudiants d'outre-mer, par S.C. Morel. Paris, 1960. 200 l. tables. Loose-leaf.

Compendium made by Office des étudiants d'outremer listing available government assistance and special laws relating to students from French Community, statistical information on students from individual areas, including list of dissertations presented by them 1950-1959. Register of student and administrative centers, with addresses, at leading French institutions of higher learning.

774 FRANCE. LAWS, STATUTES, ETC. Cinquième plan de développement économique et social, 1966-1970 [loi no. 65-1001 du 30 novembre 1965 portant approbation du Plan de développement économique et social. Paris, Imprimerie des journaux

officiels, 1966?] 2 v.

Outline and rationale of plan adopted Nov. 1965 (vol. 1) with complementary explanations on certain aspects of plan (employment, housing, educations, etc.) by Commissariat général du plan (vol. 2.).

775 FRANCE. LAWS, STATUTES, ETC. Code électoral; décrets nos. 64-1086 et 64-1087 du 27 octobre 1964. Paris, Berger-Levrault, 1964. 261 p.

Election laws for National Assembly and municipal councils.

776 FRANCE. LAWS, STATUTES, ETC. Code électoral; décrets nos. 64-1086 et 64-1087 du 27 octobre 1964 et textes ultérieurs; nouvelle éd. refondue regroupant la partie législative et les règlements d'administration publique et décrets en Conseil d'état. Mise à jour au 1er février 1967. Paris, Berger-Levrault, 1967. 239 p.

Articles of October 1964 electoral code regulating election of National Assembly, Senate, general and municipal councils, with list of changes from earlier to present code and exact references to relevant laws and decrees.

777 FRANCE. LAWS, STATUTES, ETC. Manuel général des élections; édition refondue selon le Code électoral, 27 octobre 1964, et mise à jour selon la jurisprudence en vigueur au 1er janvier 1965, par André Jabin, en collaboration avec Janine Vacherand. Paris, Berger-Levrault, 1965. 474 p.

Follows scheme of Charles Rabany's "Guide général des élections" but is based on 1964 decrees, regulations, and court decisions on contested elections. Code covers National Assembly and all municipal offices.

778 FRANCE. LAWS, STATUTES, ETC. Organisation générale de la défense; ordonnance no. 59-147 du 7 janvier 1959 modifiée et textes d'application. Paris, Journaux officiels, 1965. 132 p. (Journal officiel de la République française, no. 1022 bis)

Includes laws and decrees through February 1965.

779 FRANCE. LAWS, STATUTES, ETC. Préparation du Ve plan; rapport sur les principales options [rapport annexé à la loi no. 64-1265 du 22 décembre 1964] Paris, Journaux officiels, 1964. 245 p. diagrs. (Journal officiel de la République française, no. 1251)

Government statement of guiding principles of Fifth Plan and options in terms of expenditure of increasing gross product, growth rates, and reduction of working hours (whose effect on economic growth is studied here in detail).

779a FRANCE. LAWS, STATUTES, ETC. Recueil des lois, décisions, résolutions et ordres du jour adoptées par l'Assemblée nationale. Préparé par les soins du secrétaire général de la Présidence de l'Assemblée nationale. 1945-46 - 1967. Paris, Impr. de l'Assemblée nationale. LL

Exact title varies. From 1963 on it is "Recueil des lois. Motions et résolutions." Recueil gives text of laws promulgated by National Assembly, its motions and resolutions, and a chronological table of Ministers' answers to oral questions.

780 FRANCE. MINISTERE D'ÉTAT CHARGE DES AFFAIRES ALGÉRIENNES. L'Algérie à l'heure de la paix. [Paris, 1962]. 14 p.

Official statement of provisions for period between cease-fire and self-determination vote.

781 FRANCE. MINISTERE DE L'ALGERIE. Aspects véritables de la rébellion algérienne. [n.p., 1957?] 155 p. (chiefly illus., facsims.)

Pictures of F.L.N. atrocities and figures for terrorist incidents.

782 FRANCE. MINISTERE DE L'INTERIEUR. Les élections législative du 2 janvier 1956. Paris, Documentation française, 1957. 504 p. Microfilm copy (negative)

Introductory section on electoral code, 1951-1955, and National Assembly debates on electoral reform prior to Dec. 1955 dissolution, electoral alliances ("apparentements") and contested elections. Election results are presented in atlas form for major parties, with various statistics such as age, sex, professions of candidates. The major portion of volume is devoted to final, complete tally for election results to National Assembly arranged by departments, including overseas territories and overseas departments with the exception of Algeria, where no elections were held. Comparative figures are given for 1951 National Assembly election. Alphabetical list of deputies as of Oct. 1957.

783 FRANCE. MINISTERE DE L'INTÉRIEUR. Les élections législatives. Métropole, départements d'outre-mer: 23 et 30 novembre 1958; Algérie: 30 novembre 1958; départements des Oasis et de la Saoura: 30 novembre 1958; territoires d'outre-mer: 19 avril-10, 24 et 31 mai 1959. Paris, Documentation française, 1960. 1103 p.

New electoral code, statistical breakdown by major parties both for first and second round of election to National Assembly, statistics on profession of candidates and age and sex of elected deputies. The major part of the volume gives complete, final election results arranged by departments, overseas departments and territories, Algeria and the Sahara. For each election district ("circonscription") results are given for each candidate in first and second round of election, with comparative figures for Jan. 1956. Candidates' party affiliation and profession are indicated.

784 FRANCE. MINISTERE DE L'INTERIEUR. Les élections législatives. Métropole, départements d'outre-mer: 18 et 25 novembre 1962. Territoires d'outre-mer: 18 novembre, 2 décembre 1962. Paris, Impr. nationale, 1963. 1131 p.

Changes in electoral code 1958-1962, statistical and graphic analysis of election results by parties, and results by circonscriptions of Oct. 1962 referendum. The major part of the volume gives complete, final election results for the National Assembly arranged by departments, overseas departments and territories as for 1958 election.

785 FRANCE. MINISTERE DE L'INTERIEUR. Les élections sénatoriales. Métropole - Départements d'outre-mer: 26 avril 1959. Départements des Oasis et de la Saoura: 24 mai 1959. Territoires d'outre-mer: 26 avril 1959. Français établis hors de France: 5 mai 1959. Paris, Documentation française, 1961. 361 p.

New electoral code for senatorial election, statistical breakdown of elected senators' age, profession, party affiliation. For departments with four or less senators, voting is for individual candidates, with majority-type suffrage; in five largest departments, proportional representation for parties is retained. Comparative figures for June 1955 election are given.

786 FRANCE. MINISTÈRE DE L'INTERIEUR. Les élections sénatoriales du 26 septembre 1965, série B, métropole, départements d'outre-mer, territoires d'outre-mer, Français établis hors de France. Annexe: élections partielles. Paris, Impr. nationale, 1965. 163 p.

Text of electoral code relating to Senate, statistics on Senate as of Sept. 1965, and election results for departments Indre-et-Loire through Pyrénees Occidentales, with recall of April 1959 results.

786a   FRANCE. MINISTERE DE LA CONSTRUCTION. Plan d'aménagement et d'organisation générale de la région parisienne. Paris, 1960. 151 p. illus., maps (in pocket) LL

Paris region's physical, economic, and demographic factors underlying plan, agencies to supervise city's transformation, anticipated public investments and financing. Plan was signed into law August 1960.

787   FRANCE. MINISTERE DE LA COOPERATION. Un bilan culturel; France, Afrique, Madagascar. Paris, 1963. 60 p. illus., maps, diagrs.

Survey of current (1962) French contributions to education and culture in French-speaking Sub-Saharan Africa, with list of French-language African periodicals.

788   FRANCE. MINISTERE DE LA COOPERATION. Coopération: France, Afrique, Madagascar. Paris, 1963. [32] p. illus., ports., diagrs.

Survey and statistics of French technical assistance in Sub-Saharan Africa.

789   FRANCE. MINISTERE DE LA COOPERATION. 1959-1964: cinq ans de fonds d'aide et de coopération. [Présenté par Raymond Triboulet.] Paris, 1964. 71 p.

Report by Minister in charge of French aid on Fifth Republic principles of technical and economic assistance, nature of current aid, and future needs, followed by statistics on aid to individual countries, African students currently enrolled in France, number and type of technical assistance personnel, and current distribution of foreign trade. Additional title is "Rapport sur la coopération franco-africaine." (For later years, see no. 744a.)

790   FRANCE. MINISTERE DES AFFAIRES ETRANGERES. Full text of the speech delivered by French Foreign Minister Maurice Couve de Murville before the French National Assembly on April 14, 1966. New York, Ambassade de France, Service de presse et d'information 1966. 8 p. (France. Ambassade. U.S. Service de presse et d'information, New York. Speeches and press conferences no. 244a)

Justification of French withdrawal from NATO.

791   FRANCE. MINISTERE DES POSTES, TELEGRAPHES ET TELEPHONES. Annuaire officiel des abonnés au téléphone. Circonscription de Paris. 1959. Paris, Impr. nationale. v. 1-2.

Paris arrondissements in vol. 1, surrounding communities in vol. 2. No classified section.

792*   FRANCE. MINISTERES DU SAHARA, DES DEPARTEMENTS D'OUTRE-MER, ET DES TERRITOIRES D'OUTRE MER. Sahara. [Paris, Ministry of State in Charge of the Sahara and the Overseas Departments and Territories, 1961] 1 folder containing 9 leaflets (42 p.)

793   FRANCE. PREMIER MINISTRE. Bilan, 8 janvier 1959 - 14 avril 1962. Paris, 1962. 45 p.

Prime Minister Debré's progress report at the conclusion of the Algerian peace treaty on political, economic, and social achievements under his government.

794   FRANCE. PREMIER MINISTRE. Discours sur la coopération prononcé par M. Pompidou, Premier ministre, devant l'Assemblée nationale, le 10 juin, 1964. Paris, Documentation française, 1964. 27 p.

Review and spirited defense of Fifth Republic's methods of "cooperation," i.e., assistance to underdeveloped countries.

795*   FRANCE. PRESIDENCE DU CONSEIL. DELEGATION GENERALE EN ALGERIE. Documents algériens. General progress report. Printed in France, 1958. 117 p.

Handsome pictorial work illustrating French contributions to Algerian well-being.

796   FRANCE. PRESIDENCE DU CONSEIL. DELEGATION GENERALE EN ALGERIE. Documents algériens; Algerian documents, 1960. [Paris?] 1960. 127 p.

Same text and pictures as 1958 edition.

797*   FRANCE. PRESIDENCE DU CONSEIL. SECRETARIAT GENERAL DU GOUVERNEMENT. DOCUMENTATION FRANÇAISE. La République de Côte d'Ivoire. Paris, 1961. 29 p. La Documentation française illustrée, no. 164, février 1961.

798   FRANCE. SERVICE DE DOCUMENTATION SCIENTIFIQUE ET TECHNIQUE DE L'ARMEMENT. Lexique mots-clés de l'armement. Paris, Service de documentation scientifique et technique de l'armement, 1965. xii, 539 p.

Alphabetically arranged key words for use in machine retrieval of information to be found in military scientific and technical literature.

799   FRANCE. TREATIES, ETC., 1958- (DE GAULLE). Les accords d'Evian; textes et commentaires. Paris, Documentation française, 1962. 76 p. (Recueils et monographies, no. 40)

Official texts of March 1962 agreements on cease-fire, political amnesty, self-determination vote, guarantees for European population, and principles of economic, cultural, and military cooperation. The texts were issued by Ministère d'Etat chargé des affaires algériennes. For agreements concluded between France and independent Algeria, see no. 745.

800   FRANCE. TREATIES, ETC., 1958- (DE GAULLE). Algérie: accord de cessez-le-feu; déclarations gouvernementales du 19 mars 1962. Paris, Journaux officiels, 1962. 44 p. (Journal officiel de la République française. Textes d'intérêt général, no. 63-43, mars 1962)

French official statement of Evian agreement.

801   La France d'aujourd'hui; son visage, sa civilisation. Avant-propos de Marc Blancpain, préface de Pierre Clarac. 4th ed. London, Toronto, etc. Harrap, 1966. 448 p. tables. Includes bibliographies.

Revised edition of manual written for Alliance Francaise institutes all over the world, in which government officials and specialists contribute brief chapters surveying contemporary French cultural, social, economic, and political conditions as of 1964-65. Short bibliographies follow each chapter.

802   La France économique. 1965, 1966. Paris, Recueil Sirey, 2 vols.

Statistics and interpretive essays by individual contributors on main aspects of the economy for 1965 and 1966: population trends, agriculture, construction, commodity and stock prices, wages and strikes, monetary, fiscal, and social policy, foreign trade. For 1966, achievements of Fourth Plan, 1962-65, are assessed. This economic survey is published annually as an issue of "Revue d'économie politique" (no. 2072) and can be found there for prior years.

803   France, Germany, and the Western alliance; a study of elite attitudes on European integration and world politics. By Karl W. Deutsch and others. New York, Scribner, 1967. xi. 324 p. illus.

Study of French elites carried out by Roy C. Macridis, on the basis of interviews, July 1964, of 147 leading politicians from major parties (with the exception of the Communist Party), military figures, intellectuals, civil servants, businessmen and trade unionists. Content analysis of mass media, public opinion polls, and a variety of statistics on actual population behavior patterns supplied background information. From attitudes on internal party politics, foreign policy, European integration, military policy and disarmament, French elites reveal acceptance of main tenets of Gaullist foreign policy, growing skepticism toward European integration, disinterest in disarmament and distrust of Germany. Analogous study of German elite permits comparative results. (For questionnaires and results, see 502a; for another study whose results are incorporated here, see no. 1220a.)

804* FRANCE NOUVELLE (periodical). Négociez en Algérie: Paris, 1956. 11 p. "Supplément au No. 540, 21 avril 1956."

805   FRANCE NOUVELLE (periodical). La vérité sur la sanglante répression du 8 février 1962. Des faits irréfutables...des témoignages. Paris, 1962. 37 p. illus., ports. "Supplément à France nouvelle, no. 857 du 21 mars au 27 mars 1962."

Indictment of police brutality, which resulted in the death of eight demonstrators during an anti-O.A.S. demonstration, and evidence of connivance between O.A.S. and government forces.

806   FRANÇOIS-PONCET, ANDRE. Au fil des jours; propos d'un libéral, 1942-1962. Paris, Flammarion, 1962. 372 p.

Short articles written for "Le Figaro" Oct. 1955-Oct. 1962 by retired French ambassador to Germany and dealing with European unification, Franco-German relations, dangers of Communist expansion. Internal political developments and resolution of Algerian conflict are viewed dispassionately.

807   FRANGEOT, MAURICE. La presse française. Paris, Centre d'études et de documentation, 1963. 40 p. (Études et documents de la Nouvelle revue politique). Les Cahiers de la Nouvelle revue politique, n.s. Sér. A, nos. 3-4.

1962 survey of French dailies and weeklies, with information on their circulation, political orientation, press cartels, relations with government.

808   FRANZA, ANGELO (ed.). La rivoluzione algerina; problemi, aspetti e testimonianze della lotta per l'independenza. Milano, Feltrinelli editore, 1959. 159 p. (Documenti e discussioni, 11)

F.L.N. documents, 1956-1958, drawn primarily from F.L.N. publications, on objectives and program of revolution. Includes interviews with Ferhat Abbas (July 1957), Belkassem Krim, and Sherif Mahmud (May 1958).

808a FRASER, W.R. Education and society in modern France. London, Routledge and Kegan Paul, 1963. 140 p. (International Library of Sociology and Social Reconstruction, Sociology of Education). "Selected bibliography": p. 135-7. ML

Attempts at reforming French educational system (expansion, democratization, increased scientific and technical training) as expressed in government planning, the 1957 Billières bill and Fifth Republic's Jan. 1959 ordinance and Dec. 1959 law extending schooling to 16 years and introducing two-year observation cycle for 11-13-year olds. Author describes forces arrayed against change (strongly centralized administration, skeptical lycée teachers, defenders of humanist education) and complications involved in by-passing unresolved Church-State controversy, whose manifestations in political debates around support of Catholic schools author follows in detail. Good bibliography of manifestos and documents through 1959 and current educational literature. List of education journals with addresses.

809   FRATERNITE FRANÇAISE. Pierre Poujade vous l'avait dit. Paris, 1958. 92 p. illus., ports., facsims. "Numéro spécial, supplément au no 167."

August 1958 pamphlet commemorating Fraternité française's fifth anniversary by reproducing documents and photographs of the movement's history and stand on Algeria, political institutions, economic questions. For other publications, see Mouvement Poujade in Author Index.

810   FREEDEMAN, CHARLES ELDON. The Conseil d'État in modern France. New York, Columbia University Press, 1961. ix, 205 p. (Columbia studies in the social sciences, no. 603). Bibliography: p. 195-198.

Very little material on Conseil d'Etat in Fifth Republic.

811* French Fifth Republic Collection.

This special collection focuses on the founding of the Fifth Republic and the series of popular consultations confirming and shaping its institutions. Books and government documents, newspapers, periodicals, society publications regularly received by the library have not been incorporated, even when they bear directly on the subject. The main part of the material stems from political parties and other political groups. The collection includes inportant source material on the legislative elections of 1958, 1962, and 1967 in the form of complete sets of official programs, the so-called "professions de foi" submitted by each of the candidates for the Department of the Seine and analogous sets for nearly forty other departments for the 1958 and 1967 elections, presented by the "prefectures" of the respective departments.

Two microfilm newspaper collections fill in the background for the turbulent weeks between the collapse of the Fourth Republic and de Gaulle's return to power, with day-by-day coverage of 15 French and 10 Algerian newspapers. A third microfilm newspaper collection covers the French provincial press for the days preceding the two rounds of the November 1958 legislative elections.

811 (a) Box 1: Material from various groups on May 1958 uprising in France and Algeria.
        Pt. 1: Leftist publications on Algeria, May 1958.
        Pt. 2: Algerian official information service (temporarily merged with Conité de Salut Public) May 1958.
        Pt. 3: Circulars and leaflets from groups (mostly student and faculty) opposing de Gaulle's return to power.
        Pt. 4: Leaflets of Mouvement d'action civique non-violente advocating cessation of French atomic bomb tests, June 1958.

811 (b) Box 2: Material on September 1958 Referendum.
        Pt. 1: Informational literature on new constitution.
        Pt. 2: Material distributed by Association nationale pour le soutien de l'action du Général de Gaulle.
        Pt. 3: Material distributed by Comité d'action commune pour le référendum (posters).
        Pt. 4: Misc. posters and leaflets supporting referendum.

811 (c) Box 3-5: Material from political parties. The material included herein (leaflets, posters, special election issues, pamphlets, etc.) reflects the parties' stand on de Gaulle's return to power, the referendum, and the November 1958 election, with some material on the March 1959 municipal elections.

    Box 3: Pt. 1: Centre national des indépendants et des paysans.
        Pt. 2: Convention républicaine.
        Pt. 3: Démocratie chrétienne.

    Box 4: Pt. 1: Mouvement républicain populaire.
        Pt. 2: Parti communiste français.
        Pt. 3: Parti républicain radical et radical socialiste.
        Pt. 4: Parti socialiste S.F.I.O.

Box 5: Pt. 1: Républicain sociaux.
Pt. 2: Union de la gauche socialiste.
Pt. 3: Union démocratique et socialiste de la résistance.
Pt. 4: Union pour la nouvelle république.

811 (d) Box 6-8: Periodicals and newspapers on collapse of Fourth Republic, referendum, and November 1958 elections.

Box 6: Pt. 1: Periodical literature from leftist groups.
Pt. 2: Periodical literature from rightist groups including Gen. Chassin's manifesto for Mouvement populaire 13 mai.
Pt. 3: Periodical literature from Catholic groups.
Pt. 4: Misc. weekly and monthly publications.
Pt. 5: "Notes d'actualités" (Catholic information bulletin) June-July 1958.
Pt. 6: "Les Informations françaises" (pro-Gaullist weekly press releases) September 1958 - January 1959.
Pt. 7: "Le Bled; hebdomadaire militaire d'information" May-June 1958.

Box 7: Pt. 1: French daily and Sunday editions.
Pt. 2: Algerian daily and Sunday editions, including "Dimanche matin," Ag 1958.
Pt. 3: U.S. Army newspapers.

Box 8: Pt. 1: "Paris Match" May - October 1958, scattered issues.
Pt. 2: "Jours de France," "Radar," "Entreprise."

811 (e) Box 9-10: Newspaper collection on microfilm of 50 days in French history (so-called Journal Synchronique) Microfilm compiled by Bibliothèque nationale reproducing in full the day's issue of the following French papers for Ap. 10 - June 2, 1958: L'Aurore, Le Combat, Les Echos, Le Figaro, L'Humanité, Libération, New York Herald Tribune (Paris edition) Paris Journal, Le Parisien libéré, Le Populaire, La Croix, France-Soir, L'Information, Le Monde, Paris-Presse-l'Intransigeant. (11 reels).

811 (f) Box 11: Newspaper collection on microfilm of the Algerian press, May 1958 (Journal Synchronique) Microfilm similarly compiled by Bibliothèque nationale, May 2 - June 6, 1958 for: Journal officiel de l'Algérie, La Dépêche quotidienne d'Algérie, l'Echo d'Alger, Le Journal d'Alger, Dernière heure, Dépêche de l'Est, Dépêche de Constantine et de l'Est algérien, L'Echo d'Oran, Oran républicain, Echo soir. (4 reels).

811 (g) Newspaper collection on microfilm of the provincial press for November 22-25, December 1-2, 1958 (Journal synchronique). Microfilm similarly compiled by Bibliothèque nationale as background for Fifth Republic's first legislative elections. Each reel contains the day's issue from 89 non-Parisian dailies arranged alphabetically according to the department where published (last eight papers are additions), with 50 different departments represented. Name of department is given in brackets. (6 reels).

1) Le Courrier de Bourg-en-Bresse et des pays de l'Ain [Ain]; 2) La République nouvelle [Ain]; 3) Centre-Matin [Allier]; 4) L'Espoir de Nice et du Sud-Est. [Alpes-Maritimes]; 5) Nice Matin [Alpes-Maritimes]; 6) Le patriote de Nice et du Sud-Est. [Alpes-Maritimes]; 7) L'Ardennais [Ardenne]; 8) L'Est-Eclair [Aube]; 9) Indépendant de l'Aube [Aube]; 10) Libération Champagne [Aube]; 11) Le Rouergue [Aveyron]; 12) La Marseillaise [Bouches-du-Rhône]; 13) Le Méridional - La France [Bouches-du-Rhône]; 14) Le Provençal [Bouches-du-Rhône]; 15) Liberté de Normandie [Calvados]; 16) Le Cantal [Cantal]; 17) La Charente Libre [Charente]; 18) Le Berry [Cher]; 19) Brive-Information [Corrèze]; 20) L'Echo de la Corrèze [Corrèze]; 21) Le Comtois [Doubs]; 22) Les Nouvelles de Franche Comté et du territoire [Doubs]; 23) La République quotidien régional de Franche Comté et du territoire de Belfort [Doubs]; 24) L'Echo républicain de la Beauce et du Perche [Eure-et-Loir]; 25) Le Télégramme de Brest et de l'Ouest [Finistère]; 26) La Dépêche du Midi [Haute-Garonne]; 27) La France, la nouvelle République [Gironde]; 28) Sud-Ouest [Gironde]; 29) Ouest-France [Illes-et-Vilaine]; 30) La nouvelle République du Centre-Ouest [Indre-et-Loire] ; 31) Les Allobroges [Isère]; 32) Le Dauphiné libéré [Isère]; 33) La Dépêche - La Liberté [Loire]; 34) L'Espoir. Le journal des hommes libres fondé en 1941 [Loire]; 35) Le patriote (Lyon) [Loire]; 36) L'Eveil de la Haute Loire [Haute-Loire]; 37) L'Eclair (Nantes)[Loire-Atlantique]; 38) La Résistance de l'Ouest [Loire-Atlantique]; 39) La République du Centre [Loiret]; 40) L'Union (Reims) [Marne]; 41) Le Haut Marnais Républicain [Haute Marne]; 42) La Haute Marne libérée [Haute-Marne]; 43) L'Est-Républicain [Meurthe et Moselle]; 44) Le Républicain-Lorrain [Moselle]; 45) Le Nouveau Nord [Nord]; 46) Liberté (Lille) [Nord]; 47) Nord-Eclair (Lille) [Nord]; 48) Nord-Matin [Nord]; 49) La Voix du Nord [Nord]; 50) L'Oise-Matin [Oise]; 51) L'Oise libérée [Oise]; 52) Journal du Pas-de-Calais et de la Somme [Pas-de-Calais]; 53) Nord-Littoral [Pas-de-Calais]; 54) La Liberté (Clermont-Ferrand) [Puy-de-Dôme]; 55) La Montagne [Puy-de-Dôme]; 56) Le Républicain du Sud-Ouest [Basses Pyrénées]; 57) Journal de Biarritz [Basses Pyrénées]; 58) La nouvelle Gazette de Biarritz [Basses Pyrénées]; 59) Eclair-Pyrénées [Basses Pyrénées]; 60) La République des Pyrénées (Toulouse) [Basses Pyrénées]; 61) La nouvelle République des Pyrénées [Hautes Pyrénées]; 62) Indépendant (Perpignan) [Pyrénées Orientales]; 63) Les Dernières nouvelles d'Alsace [Bas Rhin]; 64) L'Alsace [Haut Rhin]; 65) L'Echo-Liberté (Lyon) [Rhône]; 66) Le progrès (Lyon) [Rhône]; 67) Le Courrier de Saône-et-Loire [Saône-et-Loire]; 68) Le Maine libre [Sarthe]; 69) Le Havre [Seine-Maritime]; 70) Havre libre [Seine-Maritime]; 71) Le progrès (Fécamp) [Seine-Maritime]; 72) Paris-Normandie [Seine-Maritime]; 73) Le Courrier Picard [Somme]; 74) Le Petit Varois - La Marseillaise [Var]; 75) La République (Var) [Var]; 76) La Gazette Provençale [Vaucluse]; 77) Centre-Presse (Limoges) [Haute-Vienne]; 78) L'Echo du Centre [Haute-Vienne]; 79) Le populaire du Centre [Haute-Vienne]; 80) La Liberté de l'Est [Vosges]; 81) L'Yonne Républicaine [Yonne]; 82) Le Soir (Marseille) [Bouches-du-Rhône] 83) Le Gaillard [Corrèze]; 84) La Dordogne libre [Dordogne]; 85) La Liberté du Morbihan [Morbihan]; 86) Libre Artois [Pas-de-Calais]; 87) Côte Basque-Soir [Basses Pyrénées]; 88) Le Soir de Bayonne [Basses Pyrénées]; 89) Le Soir (Lyon) [Rhône]

811 (h) Box 12-17: November 1958 legislative elections: candidates' "professions de foi" and election results arranged by departments. In some electoral districts, as many as ten candidates may be vying for one seat. Typically these leaflets, distributed as election propaganda by the candidates before the first and second round of the election, contain: 1) Identification of candidate and his substitute: age, profession, political experience, photograph; 2) Sponsoring political organization; 3) Electoral program. Material was supplied by Préfecture of respective departments.

Box 12-13: Département de la Seine.
Box 14: Département de l'Ain, Allier, Basses-Alpes, Hautes-Alpes, Aude, Bouches du Rhône, Calvados, Cher, Côtes-du-Nord, Deux-Sèvres, Doubs, Drôme, Eure.

Box 15: Gironde, Jura, Loir-et-Cher, Loire, Loire-Atlantique, Marne, Haute-Marne, Mayenne, Meurthe-et-Moselle, Morbihan, Nord.

Box 16: Oise, Pas-de-Calais, Puys-de-Dôme, Pyrénées—Orientales, Bas-Rhin, Haut-Rhin, Rhône, Saône, Saône-et-Loire.

Box 17: Seine-Maritime, Seine-et-Marne, Vaucluse, Yonne.

811 (i) Box 18: Election returns, correspondence, Nov. 1958 elections; March 1959 municipal elections, and January 1961 referendum.

Pt. 1: Photocopy of election results by department and party.
Pt. 2: Correspondence with departments.
Pt. 3: List of departments replying negatively.
Pt. 4: Map of France.
Pt. 5: French Embassy compilation of election results.
Pt. 6: Municipal elections, March 1959.

811 (j)   Box 19: October 1962 referendum and November 1962 legislative election.
- Pt. 1: Miscellaneous material on referendum and elections.
- Pt. 2: Parti communiste français.
- Pt. 3: Mouvement républicain populaire.
- Pt. 4: Parti socialiste S. F. I. O.

811 (k)   Box 20: November 1962 legislative elections: candidates' "professions de foi" and election results arranged by departments.
- Pt. 1: Département de la Seine.
- Pt. 2: Bouches-du-Rhône.
- Pt. 3: Seine-et-Marne.
- Pt. 4: List of new parliamentary groups in Assemblée nationale and their programs, December 1962.

811 (l)   Box 21-23: December 1965 presidential election.

Box 21:
- Pt. 1: Preliminary studies on presidential campaign by Club Jean Moulin, Centre d'Etude pour la démocratie.
- Pt. 2: Campaign material issued by Parti socialiste unifié, Parti communiste français, Parti socialiste S. F. I. O.
- Pt. 3: Campaign material issued by Tixier Vignancour.

Box 22:
- Pt. 1: De Gaulle-Mitterand radio and television addresses.
- Pt. 2: Campaign documents and election results, Department de la Seine (official).
- Pt. 3: Campaign material distributed by U. N. R. - U. D. T.
- Pt. 4: Campaign material issued by Féderation de la gauche démocrate et socialiste for Mitterand.
- Pt. 5: Campaign material issued by Centre démocrate for Lecanuet.
- Pt. 6: Documentation française: "Textes et documents relatifs à l'élection présidentielle" April 1966.

Box 23: Newspapers, November, December 1965.
- Pt. 1: Dailies: Le Monde, Figaro, Humanité, Combat (Nov. 20-Dec. 20).
- Pt. 2: Weeklies: Témoignage chrétien, Aux écoutes (Nov. 18-Dec. 16).
- Pt. 3: Monthlies: Esprit public (Nov., December 1965).

811 (m)   Box 24-28: March 1967 legislative elections: candidates' "Professions de foi" and election results.

Box 24: Départment de la Seine.

Box 25-28: Département de L'Allier, Basses Alpes, Hautes Alpes, Alpes-Maritimes, Aube, Bouches-du-Rhône, Calvados, Cantal, Charente, Charente, Charente-Maritime, Corrèze, Corse, Côte-d'Or, Côtes-du-Nord, Creuse, Dordogne, Doubs, Drôme, Eure, Eure-et-Loir, Gard, Jura, Loire-Atlantique, Loir-et-Cher, Loire, Loiret, Lôt, Lôt-et-Garonne, Lozère, Maine-et-Loire, Manche, Marne, Mayenne, Meurthe-et-Moselle, Morbihan, Moselle, Pas-de-Calais, Puy-de-Dôme, Hautes Pyrénées, Pyrénées Orientales, Bas-Rhin, Haut-Rhin, Haute-Saône, Saône-et-Loire, Sarthe, Haute-Savoie, Seine-Maritime, Deux-Sèvres, Somme, Tarn-et-Garonne, Vienne, Yonne. Départements d'outremer: Guyane, Île de la Réunion.

811 (n)   Box 29: March 1967 campaign material from U. N. R. /U. D. T., Parti communiste français, Centre républicain, Républicains indépendants, Convention gauche de la Ve République.

811 (o)   Box 30: Official television campaign by majority and opposition spokesmen and television debate between Mendès-France and Georges Pompidou, Feb. 27, 1967 (texts of broadcasts).

811a   FRENCH UNION. ASSEMBLÉE. Débats; compte rendu in extenso des séances. Session de 1948-1958, Paris. 11 v. (In France: Journal officiel, Dec. 11, 1947-1958).

Documents end with May 29, 1958, after which French Union Assembly did not reconvene. Debates of the Senate and Executive Council of the French Community are not available, but for selected documents, see no. 538. French Union Assembly drew its members both from overseas departments and territories, including Algeria, and from metropolitan France. May 1958 debates do not reflect Algerian crisis, and preoccupations of Assembly remain focused on economic, financial, and cultural questions till its unceremonious dissolution.

811b   FRENCH UNION. ASSEMBLÉE. Documents. Annexes aux procès-verbaux des séances. Propositions et propositions de résolution, demandes d'avis, rapports. Sessions de 1947-48 - 1958. Paris. 11 v. annual.

Vols. 1947-48 - 1950 are at Hoover, remaining volumes are on microfilm at Main Library. Documents consist of texts of delegates' motions, including a lengthy March 1958 proposal to reorient French military strategy permanently on an Euro-African basis.

812   [FRESSOZ, ROGER]. La cour; chronique du royaume. [By] André Ribaud [pseud.] Illus. de Moisan. Paris, R. Julliard, 1961. 211 p. illus.

Satirical chronology of de Gaulle's political rounds between Sept. 1960 and July 1961, with witty characterizations of "monarch" and his "court" thinly disguised as that of Louis XIV's. Text and cartoons based on author's weekly column in "Canard enchaîné."

813   [FRESSOZ, ROGER]. Le règne, chronique de la Cour. [By] André Ribaud [pseud.] Dessins de Moisan. Paris, R. Julliard, 1967. 224 p. illus.

Continues author's "La Cour" and "Le Roi" by following political events, in reverse chronological order for Oct. 1962-June 1966. Final section of sketches of Gaullist and opposition leaders.

814   [FRESSOZ, ROGER]. Le Roi; chronique de la Cour. [By] André Ribaud [pseud.] Dessins de Moisan. Paris, R. Julliard, 1962. 222 p. illus.

Continuation of "La cour" for August 1961 through July 1962.

815*   FRONT DE LIBERATION NATIONALE. L'Afrique en marche vers l'unité. [n.p., 1960]. 61 p. (Front de libération nationale. Éditions "El Moudjahid," 3)

Excerpts from "El Moudjahid" 1958-1960 on North African unity and future of Sahara.

816*   FRONT DE LIBERATION NATIONALE. L'Afrique se libère. [n.p., 1960]. 79 p. (Front de libération nationale. Éditions "El Moudjahid," 2)

Excerpts from "El Moudjahid," 1957-1960 on dissolution of French Community.

817*   FRONT DE LIBERATION NATIONALE. The Algerian people and their revolution. [n.p., 1957]. 73 p. (Résistance algérienne)

818*   FRONT DE LIBERATION NATIONALE. The Freedom Fighter. Special issue. [Excerpts from proceedings of the congress held on August 20, 1956 and excerpts from the political platform of the Front, n.p., 1956]. 30 p. (Résistance algérienne)

See also no. 822.

819* FRONT DE LIBERATION NATIONALE. La lutte du peuple algerien s'inscrit dans la lutte des peuples d'Afrique et d'Asie. [n. p., 1958?] 16 p. (El Moudjahid)

820* FRONT DE LIBERATION NATIONALE. Le peuple slgérien et sa révolution. [n. p., 1956] 84 p. (Résistance algérienne)

821* FRONT DE LIBERATION NATIONALE. La révolution algérienne et la libération de l'Afrique. [n. p., 1960] 45 p. (Front de libération nationale. Edition "El Moujahid," v. 1)

822* FRONT DE LIBERATION NATIONALE. [Special number of "El Moudjahid" giving extracts from the procès-verbal of the congress of August 20, 1956.] [n. p., clandestine] 1957.

French and Spanish editions. See also no. 818.

823* FRONT DE LIBERATION NATIONALE. What is Algeria? [n. p.] 1956. 24 p. (Résistance algérienne)

FOR ADDITIONAL WORKS BY AND ABOUT FRONT DE LIBERATION NATIONALE, SEE AUTHOR AND SUBJECT INDEX

824* FRONT DE LIBERATION NATIONALE, CAIRO. Statement of of the Provisional Government of the Algerian Republic in answer to General de Gaulle's press conference, Cairo, October 25, 1958. Issued by: Provisional Government of the Algerian Republic, Minstry of Information. Cairo, 1958. 3 l.

825* FRONT DE LIBERATION NATIONALE. FEDERATION DE FRANCE. Appeal sux Européens d'Algérie, Paris 25 janvier 1961. 2 p.

826* FRONT DE LIBERATION NATIONALE. FEDERATION DE FRANCE. F. L. N. documents. [Paris, 1961]. 20 p. [Publication no. 7, janvier 1961]

Algerian war in international perspective and trends toward decolonization.

827* FRONT ET ARMEE DE LIBERATION NATIONALE, ALGERIE. L'Algérie en guerre. [n. p.,] 1958. [21] p. (El Moudjahid)

828* FRONT UNIVERSITAIRE FRANÇAIS. [Appeal to students at Institut d'études politiques to break away from leftist U. N. E. F.] [Paris, 1960?]

829 FUNK, ARTHUR LAYTON. Charles de Gaulle: the crucial years, 1943-1944. Norman, University of Oklahoma Press, 1959. iv, 336 p. illus. Includes bibliography.

De Gaulle's relations with American and British governments from Casablanca Conference to Yalta Conference. The study is based on interviews with French and American military and political figures and French and American archival material.

830 FURNISS, EDGAR STEPHENSON. De Gaulle and the French Army; a crisis in civil-military relations. New York, Twentieth Century Fund, 1964. x, 311 p. "Bibliographical note": p. 313-318.

Scholarly analysis of de Gaulle-French Army clash during and immediately after Algerian war, with emphasis on trials of generals Salan, Challe, etc., and O. A. S. leaders. After end of Algerian war, disagreements revolve around nuclear strategy, ties to NATO, European unification. Author describes modernization efforts after 1962.

831 FURNISS, EDGAR STEPHENSON. France under de Gaulle. New York, Foreign Policy Association, 1960. 62 p. illus. (Headline series, no. 139)

Brief summary of de Gaulle's economic, internal and foreign policy achievements in his first 18 months of power.

832 GAGLIARDI, JACQUES; PASCAL, JEAN. La décolonisation de l'Europe, by Jacques Gagliardi. Querelle des continents, by Jean Pascal. Paris, Plon, 1964. 156 p.

Two essays on Europe's relations with the U. S. and ways in which France under de Gaulle has and should continue to oppose U. S. hegemony and eventually create a genuinely independent unified socialist Europe. Gagliardi describes approvingly de Gualle's program for French nuclear weapons, Common Market and NATO policy, aid to underdeveloped countries. Government economist Pascal concentrates on U. S. investments in Europe and attempts to attain political leadership in Europe through control of Common Market.

833 GAGLIARDI, JACQUES. Les hexagonaux; ou, La liberté consommée. Paris, Plon, 1962. 314 p. (Tribune libre, 64)

Often penetrating analysis of manner in which Western Europe and France in particular are drifting toward American-style capitalism and purposeless affluent society. De Gaulle's impact and that of other political forces is critically assessed by former Gaullist militant who is dissatisfied with conservative nature of Fifth Republic, while simultaneously condemning cowardice of Algerian solution. Author, while critical of de Gaulle, upholds his anti-Atlantic, not dogmatically anti-communist views.

834 GAGLIARDI, JACQUES and PHILIPPE ROSSILLON. Survive à De Gaulle. Paris, Plon, 1959. iii, 174 p. (Tribune libre, 46)

Program of group of young R. P. F. and socialist Gaullists, who founded "Patrie et Progrès" in summer of 1958 to militate for a French nationalism based on a modern socialist economy, of which this work gives an outline. Authors favor French Algeria and seek ways to bring together army and worker goals. For "Patrie et Progrès" see nos. 1422, 1885, 2040.

835 GALLAGHER, CHARLES F. The United States and North Africa: Morocco, Algeria, and Tunisia. Cambridge, Harvard University Press, 1963. xii, 275 p. maps (1 col.) (The American foreign policy library) Bibliography: p. 257-263.

Colonial history of the three North African states, their transition to independence, with summary of Algerian revolution, the state of their economy, political and social structure after independence, and relations with France as well as other nations, including the U. S. It is a book for American readers rather than a book about American policy in the area.

836 GALLISSOT, RENE. L'économie de l'Afrique du nord. Paris, Presses universitaires de France, 1961. 126, [2] p. ("Que sais-je?" Le point des connaissances actuelles, 965) "Bibliographie": p. 127.

Brief survey of economic underdevelopment in Morocco, Tunisia, and Algeria and impact of colonial status on economies, tracing effect of political autonomy in Moroccan and Tunisian economies.

837 GALLOIS, PIERRE. Paradoxes de la paix. Paris, Presses du temps présent, 1967. 369 p. (Présence du siècle)

Contradictions and vagaries of U. S. views on Atlantic Alliance, 1949-1966, are presented and used as justification of de Gaulle's countermeasures: retreat from NATO, independent nuclear force. General Gallois is one of leading Gaullist military strategists.

FOR ADDITIONAL WORKS BY PIERRE GALLOIS, SEE AUTHOR INDEX

838 GANGL, HANS. Verfassungsfragen der Fünften Republik. Graz, Leykam, 1964. 264 p. (Grazer Rechts- und Staatswissenschaftliche Studien, Bd. 13) Includes bibliography.

After an introductory summary on genesis and main provision of 1958 constitution, including 1962 amendment on presidential election, author concentrates on two problems of constitutional law which are traced back to 1789 constitution, with relatively brief sections on 1958 constitution, namely the regulation of political parties and the compatibility of parliamentary and ministerial functions. Subject and person index.

839 GALTIER-BOISSIERE, JEAN. Mémoires d'un Parisien. v. 3 Paris, La Table ronde, 1963. 406 p.

1939-1963 memoirs of editor of "Le Crapouillot" including brief jottings on de Gaulle's return to power and author's views on Algeria (favorable to decolonization and anti-militarist).

840 GALTIER-BOISSIERE, JEAN, (ed.). Nouveau dictionnaire des contemporains; publié sous la direction de Jean Galtier-Boissière, avec la collaboration de Georges Allary et al. Paris, 1958/9. 2 v. in one. illus., ports. Special numbers of Le Crapouillot: nos. 42/3, Oct. 1958, Jan. 1959.

Alphabetically arranged selected biographies, with illustrations, of politicians (e.g., Edgar Faure, Mendès-France, Mollet, Pflimlin, Pinay) journalists, literary and artistic figures, some of them quite extensive, and mixing concise factual information based on questionnaires with editors' political interpretations. Only currently prominent figures are included and those covered in an earlier biographical selection are not repeated.

841 La gangrène. Paris, Editions de Minuit, 1959. 107 p. (Documents)

Testimony of seven Algerians living in Paris on torture of prisoners by Direction de la Sûreté du Territoire (D.S.T.) in December 1958. Book was seized by government June 1959. Defense of publisher Jerome Lindon's position at trial is reproduced in postscript. English translation is entitled "Gangrene" (London, 1959) and German translations appeared as "Folter in Paris; Berichte algerischer Haeftlinge," and "Krebsuebel" (1959).

842 GANNE, GILBERT. Interviews impubliables; nouv. éd. rév. et augm. Paris, Plon, 1965. 262 p.

Interviews with French literary figures.

843 GARAS, FELIX. Charles de Gaulle, seul contre les pouvoirs. Préf. du général Catroux. Paris, R. Julliard, 1957. 303 p.

De Gaulle's political career during World War II, his brief experience as head of French government, the R.P.F. experiment, and author's predictions about de Gaulle's eventual return to power.

844 GARAUDY, ROGER. Le Centre d'études et de recherches marxistes, C.E.R.M. Paris, Siège du Secrétariat, 1963. 31 p.

Statement by Center's director on research center's general purpose in terms of post-Stalinist liberalization: dialogue with non-communists, research taking into account work of non-communists, etc. Center was established by French Communist Party in 1960 and since 1962 has organized annual Semaine de la Pensée Marxiste (see nos. 1612-1614). Lists Center's publications, staff members.

845 GARAUDY, ROGER. Perspectives de l'homme: existentialisme, pensée catholique, marxisme. 2. éd., rev. et corr. Paris, Presses universitaires de France, 1960. 359 p. (Bibliothèque de philosophie contemporaine. Histoire de la philosophie et philosophie générale)

Exposition of main tendencies of contemporary French philosophy aiming to show the convergence of both existentialism and Catholic thought with Marxism, making dialogue possible. Sartre comments on the existentialist chapter. Author is Marxist philosopher and leading member of French Communist Party.

846 GARAUDY, ROGER. Questions à Jean-Paul Sartre, prédédées d'une lettre ouverte. Paris, Revue Clarté, 1960. 111 p. (Collection Clarté, 1)

Letter dated Oct. 15, 1960 reaffirming author's confidence in French Communist Party and opposing Sartre's negativism, which makes him espouse F.L.N. cause rather than support a French united front in favor of negotiation. Main part of work is a rebuttal to Sartre's "Critique de la raison dialectique" in which Sartre claims to complement Marx but actually rejects main tenets of Marxism.

847 GARCIA LUPO, ROGELIO. A qué viene de Gaulle? Buenos Aires, J. Alvarez Editor, 1964. 132 p. Bibliographical footnotes.

Argentinian journalist analyzes French internal and foreign economic policy as manifestation of independence from and competition with American imperialism. Gaullism is welcomed in Latin America as a counterweight to U.S. and as channel for capital-rich European Common Market, so that pro-Gaullist stand, contrary to internal French views, is compatible with Latin American revolutionary hopes.

848 GARÇON, MAURICE. Plaidoyer contre la censure. Paris, J.J. Pauvert, 1963. 41 p.

Jurist's opposition to government censorship of juvenile literature on the basis of a December 1958 ordinance giving control over it to the Ministry of the Interior. The immediate provocation of Garçon's plea is a May 1963 trial against a bookdealer displaying obscene juvenile books.

849 GARDT, JEAN and CLAUDE ROQUE. Service militaire, pourquoi? Du conscrit de 1813 à l'appelé d'Algérie. Paris, EPI, 1960. 137 p. diagr.

History of conscription since French Revolution, leading up to situation since beginning of Algerian war, when 28-month conscripts were not only trained but actually engaged in battle. Authors emphasize relations between conscripts and regular army, which wants to make them accept its own closed authoritarian universe and its ideological conception of revolutionary war. Stages of military training and warfare experiences are described, as well as psychological transformation of civilians. Authors give own reform proposals for training of conscripts in keeping with democratic values but in line with military realities and discuss other recent plans for reforming military service. In appendix, Jan. 1959 ordinance on organization of defense and summaries of provisions for military service in other countries.

850 GASCUEL, ALAIN. Aspects du quatrième plan. Préf. de Pierre Massé. Paris, Berger-Levrault, 1962. 176 p.

Popular version of "plan de développement économique et social" enacted August 1962, with simplified statistics and emphasis on underlying principles.

851 GAULLE, CHARLES DE, PRES. FRANCE. Allocutions prononcées par le général de Gaulle et entretiens avec Michel Droit à l'occasion de l'élection du Président de la République; textes et notes. Paris, 1965. 43 p.

Verbatim texts of radio and television addresses before presidential election, Nov. 4, 30, Dec. 3, 11, 17, 1965, and Dec. 13, 14, and 15 television interviews (the only de Gaulle television interviews) with Michel Droit, one on domestic problems, one on foreign and military affairs, and one on political institutions. Mimeographed.

852 GAULLE, CHARLES DE, PRES. FRANCE. The complete war memoirs. New York, Simon and Schuster, 1964. 3 v. in 1 (vi, 1048 p.) maps.

Translation of "Mémoires de guerre" (see no. 860) but not of documents. Vol. 1, entitled "The call to honour, 1940-1942" was translated by J. Griffin, v. 2-3 "Unity, 1942-1944" and "Salvation, 1944-1946" were translated by R. Howard. This edition does not include the appended documents. They must be consulted in the earlier translation "The war memoirs of Charles de Gaulle" (New York, Simon and Schuster, 1959-1960) in which the main text is identical, but the documents have been translated by Joyce Murchie and Hamish Erskine. Both English editions, but not the French original, are indexed.

853 GAULLE, CHARLES DE, PRES. FRANCE. De Gaulle hat gesagt... Eine Dokumentation seiner Politik. Ed. by Hans Stercken. Stuttgart, Seewald Verlag, 1967. 366 p.

Excerpts (in German) from de Gaulle's speeches, 1958-1967, arranged by topic and subtopic and chronological within each subtopic. Main divisions are: Political institutions, French history (including Algerian question) French greatness, domestic problems, foreign relations (by country) problems of international politics (including European unification and Atlantic Alliance). Excerpts speak for themselves.

854 GAULLE, CHARLES DE, PRES. FRANCE. De Gaulle parle des institutions, de l'Algérie, de l'Armée, des affaires étrangères, de la Communauté, de l'économie et des questions sociales. By André Passeron, Préf. de J.-R. Tournoux. Paris, Plon, 1962. 592 p.

De Gaulle's official declarations May 1958 - April 1962 speeches, press, radio, and television conferences and interviews, etc. - organized chronologically within major themes of Fifth Republic (as enumerated in title) and reflecting his evolving views and policies, situated in the context in which they were delivered. Texts are often incomplete, but always authentic. Editor André Passeron, as "Le Monde" parliamentary reporter, followed de Gaulle on his trips through provinces and reproduces some characteristic personally witnessed anecdotes. Appendix gives complete list of speeches, press conferences, trips.

855 GAULLE, CHARLES DE, PRES. FRANCE. De Gaulle parle, 1962-1966 Anthologie analytique par André Passeron. Paris, Fayard, 1966. 450 p. (Les Grandes études contemporaines)

Official declarations for May 1962 - Jan. 1966, following same pattern as for earlier period. Themes are: 1) political institutions and elections; 2) East-West relations; 3) defense and NATO; 4) Europe; 5) Germany; 6) relations with 'tiers monde'; and 7) Algeria (nothing beyond 1963). Editor accompanied de Gaulle on all French and foreign trips. Appendix gives governments of Fifth Republic after April 1962, results of elections and referenda, chronology of events and attempted assassinations, lists of speeches, etc. Index to key Gaullist expressions. Good general bibliography on Fifth Republic. The two volumes together constitute the most important compendium on Gaullist politics during the Fifth Republic.

856 GAULLE, CHARLES DE, PRES. FRANCE. La France et son armée. Paris, Union générale d'éditions, 1965. 312 p. (Le monde en 10/18. La collection des grands textes, 257/258)

Reprint of 1938 work on French military history originally published by Plon.

857 GAULLE, CHARLES DE, PRES. FRANCE. La France sera la France; ce que veut Charles de Gaulle. Paris, 1951. 358 p.

Excerpts from over 120 speeches, press conferences, published declarations made by de Gaulle 1940-1950. The anthology put together by the R. P. F. is arranged by major themes: political institutions, French ideological divisions, social and political reforms, the French Union, foreign policy, with short comments linking excerpts and pointing out continuity in de Gaulle's views. Appendix gives chronological list of speeches.

858 GAULLE, CHARLES DE, PRES. FRANCE. Full text of the fourteenth press conference held by French President Charles de Gaulle in Paris at the Elysée Palace on Friday, October 28, 1966. New York, Ambassade de France, Service de presse et d'information 1966. 13 p. (Speeches and press conferences no. 253a)

All of de Gaulle's press conferences are reproduced in translation in the Ambassade de France, New York, Service de presse et d'information's regular series "Speeches and press conferences," as are selected speeches by other leading French statesmen (see no. 1954). For original French texts, consult "Articles et documents" (see fuller explanation in no. 859).

859 GAULLE, CHARLES DE, PRES. FRANCE. Major addresses, statements and press conferences of General Charles de Gaulle, May 19, 1958-January 31, 1964. New York, Ambassade de France, Service de presse et d'information, 1964. 258 p.

Complete text of over 50 statements, speeches, and press conferences in English translation. Original French texts can be found in the Direction de la Documentation's "Articles et Documents" (see no. 1839) and located in the Direction de la Documentation's annual "Index Général" under: France-personnalités-de Gaulle. (See no. 1913.)

860 GAULLE, CHARLES DE, PRES. FRANCE. Mémoires de guerre. Paris, Plon, 1954-59. 3 v. fold. col. maps.

Half of each volume is devoted to documents either emanating from or received by de Gaulle for the relevant period. For English translation, see "The complete war memoirs," (no. 852). Volumes are: 1) L'appel, 1940-1942; 2) L'unité, 1942-1944; 3) Le Salut, 1944-1946.

861 GAULLE, CHARLES DE, PRES. FRANCE. President de Gaulle holds tenth press conference; full text of General de Gaulle's press conference held as President of the French Republic, in Paris at the Elysée Palace, on July 23, 1964. New York, Ambassade de France, Service de presse et d'information, 1964. 12 p. (Speeches and press conferences no. 208)

See no. 858 for comments.

FOR ADDITIONAL WORKS BY AND ABOUT CHARLES DE GAULLE, SEE AUTHOR AND SUBJECT INDEX. SEVERAL OTHER PRE-1956 PUBLICATIONS BY DE GAULLE ARE ALSO AT THE HOOVER INSTITUTION.

862 GAUTHIER, PAUL (ed.) Lettres d'ouvriers aux évêques. Préface de Ch. M. Himmer... Paris, Éditions ouvrières, 1966. 200 p. (Collection " Eglise et monde ouvrier")

Letters in response to inquiry in France and Belgium among Catholic workers reflecting their feelings about their working conditions and about the Catholic Church in terms of its effectiveness within the industrial environment, its social doctrine, and the outcome of the Vatican Council. Letters were to be transmitted to bishops at Vatican Council.

863 GENDARME, RENE. L'économie de l'Algérie; sous-développement et politique de croissance. Paris, A. Colin, 1959. 234 p. maps, diagrs. (Cahiers de la Fondation nationale des sciences politiques, 101) "Bibliographie": p. 375-379.

Basic work on Algerian economy by professor at Université d'Alger, highlighting French contributions to Algerian economy and obstacles to growth. Author presents optimum 10-year program to end underdevelopment - investment, population control,

864　Le général de Gaulle et la presse française. Paris, Éditions Galic, 1962. 158 p. (L'Histoire au jour le jour, no. 4)

June 1961-June 1962 press excerpts on de Gaulle's personality, political ideas, his style, his methods of governing and institutions of the Fifth Republic.

865*　GENERAL UNION OF ALGERIAN MOSLEM STUDENTS. Memorandum...to the Twelfth General Assembly of the United Nations. New York, 1957. 11 l. (Algerian Front of National Liberation Delegation. Publication series B, no. 3)

Indictment against France for suppressing Arabic culture in Algeria.

866　La génération du twist et la presse française. Paris, Éditions Galic, 1962. 159 p. (L'Histoire au jour le jour no. 6)

1961-1962 press excerpts (interviews, results of questionnaires, etc.) revealing situation of French youth: education, political attitudes, involvement in O.A.S., rebellious youth and generational conflicts, special portraits of juvenile delinquents, rural youth.

867　GEORGE, PIERRE and PIERRE RANDET. La région parisienne. Avec la collaboration de Jean Bastié. Paris, Presses universitaires de France, 1959. 159 p. plates, maps, diagrs. (France de demain, 1)

One of 8 regional studies, this volume covers North-West-Central France. Demographic status, transportation system, industry, and agriculture, possibilities for regional planning are surveyed. Excellent maps and illustrations.

868　GEORGEL, JACQUES. Critiques et réforme des Constitutions de la République. De la Quatrième à la Sixième? Préf. de Pierre-Henri Teitgen. Paris, CELSE, 1959-60. 2 v. Includes bibliography.

First volume of this doctoral thesis was written before May 1958 and is a vigorous criticism of Fourth Republic's parliamentary institutions, making proposals for constitutional reforms for a stabler and more effective government based on a two-party system and a strong executive. Second volume describes transition to Fifth Republic (collapse of Fourth, drawing up of new constitution) from point of view of parliament, analyzes provisions and actual functioning of new constitution, and assesses prospects of parliamentary as against presidential evolution of regime on basis of first year's experiences. Separate index for each volume, good bibliography, extensive footnotes giving contemporary comments of politicologists and politicians.

869　GERARD, JO. Où va la France! Bruxelles, Éditions du Ponant, 1962. 116 p. (Questions brûlantes)

Belgian's comments on Algerian decolonization and O.A.S. repeating anti-Gaullist nationalist arguments, particularly de Gaulle's weakness before communism.

870　GERIN, PAUL. L'Algérie du 13 mai. 10e éd. Paris, Gallimard, 1958. 236 p. (L'Air du temps)

French journalist's eyewitness account of events in Algeria and discussion of factors leading to overthrow of Fourth Republic. Despite apprehensions about future rôle of politicized army and Algerian illusions about integration, author is optimistic about prospects of new strong regime and improved relations between Moslems and Europeans. Appendix with Algerian chronology, 1942-1958 and texts of appeals of public vigilance and public safety committees May 13-15, speeches of Salan, Massu, Soustelle May 15-17.

871　GERVAIS, MICHEL, CLAUDE SERVOLIN ET JEAN WEIL. Une France sans paysans. Paris, Éditions du Seuil, 1965. 127 p. diagrs. Includes bibliography.

History of French agriculture highlighting the changes in rural population through 1962 census reflecting the rapid mechanization of post-1945 years. Authors give a good summary of government's farm policy and main organs for its implementation as well as political and social philosophy of Centre National des Jeunes Agriculteurs and Nouvelle Entreprise Agricole, new farm organizations accepting the implications of modern agricultural technology. Prospects of different types of agriculture and adaptation to a "France without peasants" (as a distinct social group) are analyzed.

872　GICQUEL, JEAN and LUCIEN SFEZ. Problèmes de la réforme de l'état en France depuis 1934. Préf. de Maurice Duverger. Paris, Presses universitaires de France, 1965. 286 p. (Travaux et recherches de la Faculté de droit et des sciences économiques de Paris. Série "Science politique," no. 3) Includes bibliography.

The monograph by Gicquel deals with controversy of constitutional reform in 1934. The Sfez study traces the evolution of Socialist ideas from 1944 to 1964, as expressed in S.F.I.O. and P.S.U. statements, as well as interviews with Edouard Depreux, Francis Leenhardt, Gilles Martinet, Mendès-France, Mollet, André Philip, Alain Savary, on constitutional issues such as strong vs. weak executive. The ideas of the Club Jean Moulin are also examined.

873　GILLESPIE, JOAN. Algeria, rebellion and revolution. New York, F.A. Praeger, 1960. xiv, 208 p. maps (1 fold.) (Nations of the modern world) "Selected bibliography": p. 193-198.

American journalist specializing in African affairs describes relations between settlers and natives, early forms of Algerian nationalism and violent stage of conflict through Jan. 1959, with postscript going up to Jan. 1960. Algerian nationalists' military and political strategy is presented sympathetically.

874　GIOVANA, MARIO. Algeria anno sette; con la collaborazione di Sergio Liberovici et al. Milano, Edizioni Avanti! 1961. 209 p. (Il Gallo; collana omnibus, 62)

Brief history of Algerian revolution, followed by interviews, Spring 1960, with various Algerian writers and politicians in Tunisia. Italian translation of nationalist poems.

875　GIRARD, ALAIN. La réussite sociale en France; ses caractères, ses lois, ses effects. Avec deux études par Henri Laugier et al. Présentation par Alfred Sauvy. Paris, Presses universitaires de France, 1961. 355 p. maps, diagrs. (Institut national d'études démographiques. Travaux et documents. Cahier no. 38)

Statistical and sociological results of three studies by Institut national d'études démographiques of successful men in France, one based on 1957-58 questionnaires to 3,000 outstanding men in 1955 Dictionnaire biographique contemporain, one based on 1958 questionnaires to alumni of Ecole normale supérieure, Ecole centrale des arts et manufactures, Institut national agronomique, Ecole polytechnique, Ecole nationale d'administration (the last intensively studied), and one based on a historical study of famous men. Results were analyzed to find social, psychological, family, and regional factors determining membership in French elite.

876　GIRARD, HENRI GEORGES CHARLES ACHILLE. Mon procès. By Georges Arnaud, pseud. Illustré par Siné. Paris, Éditions de Minuit, 1961. 200 p. illus. (Documents)

trade policies, etc., relying on continued French presence. For review of this work, see no. 926.

April 1960 trial of "Paris-Presse" journalist for publishing interview with Francis Jeanson (in which latter described his methods for collecting funds for F. L. N. and organizing desertion of French soldiers) and for refusing to denounce other participants at interview. At stake is journalist's privilege to keep his sources secret. Text of trial proceedings, at which prominent intellectuals favorable to Algerian independence appeared for defense.

877 GIRARD, HENRI GEORGES CHARLES ACHILLE and JACQUES VERGES. Pour Djamila Bouhired [Plaidoirie pour une condamnée à mort.] By Georges Arnoud, pseud. and Jacques Vergès. Paris, Editions de Minuit, 1957. 108 p. (Documents)

Description of June 1957 trial of woman liaison agent of F. L. N. leader Saadi Yacef in Algiers court. French journalist protests against use of torture and gross miscarriage of justice during trial and reproduces text of defense plea by Jacques Vergès, which was not allowed to be read in court.

878 GIRARDET, RAOUL, (ed.). La crise militaire française, 1945-1962; aspects sociologiques et idéologiques. Paris, A. Colin, 1964. 235 p. diagrs., tables. (Cahiers de la Fondation nationale des sciences politiques, 123)

Main part of volume is result of collective study by "commission de sociologie militaire" consisting of scholars from Ecole Supérieure de Guerre and the Fondation nationale des sciences politiques, on the structure, recruitment, social background of officer corps of French ground forces, as well as living conditions and pay of officers as compared to civilian professionals. Concluding section by Raoul Girardet gives history of moral and ideological crisis in army from 1940 defeat to disengagement from Algeria, synthesizing current literature on concept of revolutionary warfare, the Algerian struggle, civilian-military conflict.

879 GIRARDET, RAOUL. Pour le tombeau d'un capitaine. Paris, Esprit nouveau, 1962. 54 p. illus.

Based on articles in "Combat" written at time of Evian agreements and indicting the government, French bourgeoisie and intellectuals for sanctioning disengagement under the pretense of granting Algerian self-determination. Pamphlet is dedicated to friend of author, a professional soldier, killed in action in Algeria in the course of working to improve the lot of Kabylians; author views Evian agreement as turning point on road to French moral decadence.

880 GISCARD D'ESTAING, VALERY. La stabilté, chance de la France, conférence faite le mardi 26 mai 1964. Paris, 1964. 19 p. (Grands discours français et internationaux, n. s. 9a)

Plea by Finance Minister for monetary stability as a precondition for rather than an alternative to economic expansion and as a necessity under free trade conditions.

881 GLUKHAREV, LEONID IVANOVICH. Alzhirskaia problema. Moskva, Znanie, 1961. 30, 1 p. (Vsesoiuznoe obshchestvo po rasprostranenniu politicheskikh i nauchnykh znanii. Seriia 7: Mezhdunarodnaia, no. 3)

Summary of Algerian history through 1961.

882 GODFREY, EDWIN DREXEL, JR. The government of France, 2nd ed. New York, Thomas Y. Crowell Co., 1963. 197 p. (Crowell Comparative Government Series) Bibliography. ML

Good survey of political life of Fifth Republic, its constitution and institutions, political parties, administration, economic and foreign policy, French Community and Algeria.

883 GODFRIN, JACQUELINE and PHILIPPE GODFRIN. Une centrale de presse catholique: la Maison de la bonne presse et ses publications. Préf. de Jean Rivero. Paris, Presses universitaires de France, 1965. 238 p. (Travaux et recherches de la Faculté de droit et des sciences économiques de Paris. Série "Science politique," no. 4) Includes bibliography.

One monograph describes the operation of the Catholic publishing house, the second concentrates on "La Croix" the Paris Catholic daily issued by the Maison de la bonne presse.

884 GOEAU-BRISSONNIERE, YVES. Par delà l'Union française. Arras, Société d'éditions du Pas-de-Calais, 1958. 92 p. diagrs., fold. tables.

Political evolution in Sub-Saharan Africa - the new federal and semi-autonomous institutions accepted by parliament October 1957 - is contrasted with the Algerian impasse. Author proposes British-Commonwealth type of organization for entire French Union and steps toward peace in Algeria. The book was concluded in 1957.

885 GOETZ-GIREY, ROBERT. Le mouvement des grèves en France 1919-1962. Collaboration de: Guy Triolaire et al. Concours du Centre national de la recherche scientifique. Paris, Éditions Sirey, 1965. 220 p. tables, diagrs. (L'Économique, 3) Includes bibliography.

Professor of industrial relation's study on changes in motivation, structure, duration, and outcome of strikes in France compared with other countries. Many of statistical tables span entire period and give principal data on strikes for 1958-1962.

886 GOGUEL-NYEGAARD, FRANÇOIS and ALFRED GROSSER. La politique en France. Paris, A. Colin, 1963. 298 p. (Collection U/Série "Société politique")

Main topics are methods of local and national political representation, elections, political parties, pressure groups, public information, parliament and government. Though some historical background is given, most of information is current, with up-to-date bibliography for each of sections. Each of co-authors contributed separate chapters on his specialties.

887 GOGUEL-NYEGAARD, FRANÇOIS, (ed.). Le référendum d'octobre et les élections de novembre 1962. Paris, A. Colin, 1965. xii, 437 p. tables, (1 fold.,) facsims. (Cahiers de la Fondation nationale des sciences politiques, 142)

Collective work of Fondation nationale's Centre d'étude de la vie politique française, first part of which deals with October 1962 referendum (on presidential election) and Nov. 1962 general elections (political parties, press, television) while second part analyses results and political attitudes of voters as measured by public opinion survey, with comparisons to 1958 referendum and elections. The study was completed at the eve of the December 1965 election.

FOR ADDITIONAL WORKS BY FRANCOIS GOGUEL-NYEGAARD, SEE AUTHOR INDEX

888 GOHIER, JACQUES. Instructeur en Algérie. Rodez, Éditions Subérvie, 1966. 160 p.

Personal account of year spent in a Saharan oasis as a member of a team of 70 young special instructors recruited in France and Algeria to improve primary education in Saharan schools. Only weak echoes of the fighting reach this desert outpost during Sept. 1958-1959. Author describes the local culture and progress in imparting French education.

889 GOLDEMANN, GOTLIND. Die Sprache Charles de Gaulles. Gedanken und Sprachstil seiner Schriften und Reden. Inauguraldissertation zur Erlangung des Doktorgrades einer Hohen Philosophischen Fakultät der Eberhard-Karls Universität zu Tübingen. Fischbach-Druck, Reutlingen, 1964. 140 p. Bibliography. ML

Linguistic dissection of de Gaulle's style based primarily on de Gaulle's pre-war writings, memoirs, and war-time speeches followed by a short evaluation of stylistic peculiarities of political speeches 1958-1962. Complete bibliography of de Gaulle's writings and critical literature on these works.

890 GOLDMANN, LUCIEN. Recherches dialectiques. Paris, Gallimard, 1959. 356 p. (Bibliothèque des idées) "Bibliographie": p. 355-356.

Collection of articles by Marxist philosopher, 1947-1958 illustrating the relevance, vitality, and also the inadequacies of Marxist thought and the dialectic method in political, social, and literary areas.

891 GONIDEC, P. F., (ed.). Constitutions des états de la Communauté; textes recueillis et présentés par P.-F. Gonidec. Paris, Sirey, 1959. 185 p.

Short introduction on common elements between French constitution and those of the 14 Republics making up the French Community: (9 in former French West Africa, 4 in former French Equatorial Africa plus Madagascar) followed by texts of individual constitutions adopted between January and April 1959.

891a GONIDEC, P. F. Droit d'outre-mer. Paris, Éditions Montchrestien, 1959-60. 2 v. Includes bibliographies. LL

Survey, intended for law students, on political and judicial evolution of non-metropolitan France, outlining political, administrative, and judiciary institutions of French Community as a whole and those of its individual members, as well as for overseas departments and territories, among them Algeria and the Sahara. V. 1: "De l'empire colonial de la France à la Communauté" was concluded in the early months of the Fifth Republic, but v. 2: "Les rapports actuels de la France métropolitaine et des pays d'outre-mer" goes to the end of 1959.

892 GORDON, DAVID C. North Africa's French legacy, 1954-1962. Cambridge, Distributed for the Center for Middle Eastern Studies of Harvard University by Harvard University Press, 1962. 121 p. (Harvard Middle Eastern monographs, 9) Includes bibliography: p. 85-93.

Study by American historian of French cultural legacy in Morocco, Tunisia, and Algeria. Author's sources are novels, newspapers, periodicals, interviews with Moslem intellectuals. Changes in educational system in independent Morocco and Tunisia and attitudes on education reforms of Algerian nationalists at the verge of the country's independence are reviewed. There is no attempt made to assess impact of economic and administrative legacy. Selective annotated bibliography and informative notes.

893 GORDON, DAVID C. The passing of French Algeria. London, New York, Oxford University Press, 1966. 265 p. Bibliography: p. 247-256.

Carefully documented study on independent Algeria up to June 1965. A short section on the pre-1962 history of France in Algeria (attempted assimilation and the period of the active revolution) is followed by a sympathetic description of how independent Algeria is coping with the task of evolving a national identity. Book includes chapters on the end of the European community in Algeria, Franco-Algerian cooperation, and the reactions of different sectors of French society to developments in independent Algeria. Good bibliography on Algerian history and culture, current periodicals and government documents.

894 GORZ, ANDRE. Le Socialisme difficile. Paris, Éditions du Seuil, 1967. 249 p. (Collection L'Histoire immédiate) Bibliographical footnotes.

Collection of lectures held in Mexico, Italy, and Sweden and articles published in Marxist journals by close collaborator of Sartre. Ideas on modern revolutionary socialism presented in his earlier "Stratégie ouvrière et néocapitalisme" are expanded here. Specific topics are: political strategies for the labor movement, relations between students and workers, the meaning of reform and revolution in the contemporary context, the limitations of the Soviet experience as a socialist model, the significance of the Sino-Soviet conflict for European socialism, and Sartre's contributions to Marxist thought.

895 GORZ, ANDRE. Stratégie ouvrière et néocapitalisme. Paris, Editions du Seuil, 1964. 174 p. (Collection "L'Histoire immédiate")

Proposed strategy for labor movement in affluent society, whereby such partial objectives as the extension of worker participation in the economy and expansion of the collective sector of consumption, including demands for higher educational and cultural achievements are integrated in a revolutionary rather than a reformist program. Author, emphasizing that genuine socialist democratic models do not yet exist anywhere, insists that labor movement must gradually build up a positive alternative model for affluent capitalist society, showing what neo-capitalism fails to achieve. Implications for labor movement's Common Market stand are spelled out. See also no. 260a for a discussion of Gorz' views.

896 GOURDON, ALAIN. Le carnaval des régents; essai sur le désordre césarien. By Julien Cheverny, pseud. Paris, R. Julliard, 1963. 245 p.

Essays written in the wake of O.A.S. violence, attempts on de Gaulle's life, and the controversy on 1962 constitutional reform, draw attention to dangers of a military coup d'état by making historical parallels (Germany, Italy) and comparisons with Caesarism in underdeveloped countries. Weaknesses of Gaullist regime are analyzed, especially vulnerability to extra-legality, for which de Gaulle himself set precedent. Left is encouraged to accept concept of strong executive and as most effective countermeasure at once select a common presidential candidate.

897 GOURDON, ALAIN. Ces princes que l'on gouverne; essai sur l'anarchie autoritaire. By Jules Cheverny, pseud. Paris, R. Julliard, 1960. 209 p.

Political history of French democracy from Third through Fifth Republic centered on shortcomings of both parliamentary and Gaullist system in facing problems of decolonization and needs of a modern democracy. Author is not systematically hostile to de Gaulle, drawing parallels with Mendès-France's efforts to modernize government.

898 GOURDON, ALAIN. Eloge du colonialisme; essai sur les révolutions d'Asie. By Julien Cheverny, pseud. Paris, R. Julliard, 1961. 370 p. illus.

Observations (based on four years' experience as economic adviser in South East Asia) on political and economic failures in that part of the world, with U.S. leadership judged ineffective and Chinese Communist potential rated high. Author urges French and West European Left to adopt a policy of "social-neutralism" as best way to promote peace and economic growth in underdeveloped countries, in contrast to French Left's unsuccessful Algerian stand.

899 Le gouvernement Pompidou et la presse française. Paris, Éditions Galic, 1962. 157 p. (L'histoire au jour le jour no. 10)

June-Oct. 1962 press excerpts on Prime Minister Pompidou and seven Cabinet members: Maurice Couve de Murville, Valéry Giscard d'Estaing, Jean Foyer, Louis Jacquinot, Louis Joxe, Pierre Sudreau, and Roger Frey.

900 GRALL, XAVIER. La génération du djebel. Paris, Éditions du Cerf, 1962. 125 p. (Tout le monde en parle)

Survey of attitudes of young Frenchmen who had fought in Algeria undertaken by Catholic periodical "Vie catholique." Work gives numerical results of 607 questionnaires returned November 1960 concentrating on moral and political evaluation of Algerian war and personal role in the conflict. Statistics are supplemented by individual military experiences.

901 GRANDMOUGIN, JEAN. Lettre ouverte au ministre de l'information. Paris, A. Michel, 1967. 160 p. (Collection Lettre ouverte)

Personal narrative by former political commentator on privately-owned Radio-Luxembourg describing his "temporary" retirement (he was never reinstated) from that position in March 1962 because of trumped-up charges of O.A.S. ties during a police round-up of potential O.A.S. sympathizers. According to author, now journalist for "Aurore," the real reason for dismissal was government pressure against a scrupulously impartial news program, which failed to obey the government's current information approach. Author stresses lack of support from usual opponents of censorship in left-wing press, with the exception of "Témoignage chrétien" and "Canard Enchaîné."

902 GRANDVAL, GILBERT. Discours prononcé...à la grande réunion d'information de l'Union démocratique du travail le 2 juin 1959. [n.p., 1959] 9 l.

Gaullist views on international relations.

903 GREER, HERB. A scattering of dust based upon the experience of two winters reporting the Algerian war from the rebel side. London, Hutchinson, 1962. 224 p. plates.

Notes by American making documentary movie behind F.L.N. lines during winter of 1956 and 1958, dealing with human rather than political side of war.

904 GREGOIRE, ROGER. The French civil service; a revised edition, translated from French, for the United Nations, of La Fonction publique. Brussels, International Institute of Administrative Sciences, 1964. 363 p. Bibliographical footnotes.

History, comparison with other nations, and current status of French civil servants (through 1962) with all relevant statistics and ordinances of the Fifth Republic.

905 GREINDL, E. Les fatômes accusent. By Cincinnatus, pseud. Bruxelles, 1961. 204 p.

Attack on de Gaulle's repression of army and press to reinforce his personal power and carry through abandonment of Algeria. Author explains motives of officers leading to formation of O.A.S., analyzes stages of negotiations with Algerian nationalists July-Sept. 1961. Appendices reproduce excerpts from trials of Alain de Sérigny March 1961 and of rebellious generals.

906 GRENIER, RENE. L'Union française sera fédérale ou ne sera pas! Paris, J. d'Halluin, 1956. 310 p. (Collection Alternance) Bibliographical footnotes.

Plea for making French Union a reality by granting greater autonomy and greater economic rights to components of French Empire.

907 GRENOBLE. UNIVERSITE. CENTRE D'ETUDES ET DE RECHERCHES SUR L'ADMINISTRATION REGIONALE ET LOCALE. Administration traditionnelle et planification régionale. Paris, A. Colin, 1964. 306 p. maps. (Cahiers de la Fondation nationale des sciences politiques, 135) Includes bibliographies.

Studies made at University of Grenoble on disarray of traditional administrative structures in the face of regional planning, as exemplified by Fourth Plan. March 1964 decrees reorganizing departmental administration are cited and examined in detail, and previous decrees listed chronologically. Extensive classified bibliography of books and articles on regional planning (aménagement du territoire) with list of periodicals concerned with problem and author index.

908 GRIMAL, HENRI. La décolonisation, 1919-1963. Paris, A. Colin, 1965. 407 p. maps. (Collection U. Sér. "Histoire contemporaine") Includes bibliography.

Includes chapters on decolonization of French Sub-Saharan Africa and North Africa during Fifth Republic, giving good summary of steps leading French Community and Algeria toward independence.

909 GRINNELL-MILNE, DUNCAN WILLIAM. The triumph of integrity; a portrait of Charles de Gaulle. London, The Bodley Head, 1961. 320 p. illus., ports. Includes bibliography.

Liaison officer of British Air Ministry with de Gaulle from French collapse to Oct. 1940 and personally acquainted with many French officers, centers his portrait of de Gaulle on wartime years and struggles against French and Allied political and military figures, notably Rossevelt. Author is highly partial to de Gaulle in all controversies. Photos of wartime leaders.

910 GROS, SIMONE. La politique de Carthage; abandon ou sauvegarde de l'union franco-tunisienne. Suivi d'une lettre postface de Pierre Mendès-France. Paris, Plon, 1958. 109 p. (Tribune libre, 34)

Plea for negotiated independence as illustrated by the successful negotiations at Carthage in July 1954 under Mendès-France, leading to Tunisia's bloodless separation from France. June 1958 letter by Mendès-France explains his colonial policies and their applicability to Algeria.

911 GROSSER, ALFRED. French foreign policy under de Gaulle. Translated by Lois Ames Pattison. Boston, Little, Brown, 1967. xiv, 175 p. "Uncorrected page proof." Bibliographical footnotes.

English edition of no.912 has preface by Stanley Hoffmann on political science in present-day France, as well as final chapter bringing book up to date for 1965-67, particularly regarding controversies with U.S. over Vietnam and NATO.

912 GROSSER, ALFRED. La politique extérieure de la Ve République. Paris, Éditions du Seuil, 1965. 189 p. (Collection Jean Moulin)

Lectures held at Institut des Sciences Politiques, Paris, in early 1964 and revised Dec. 1964 for Club Jean Moulin. Main topics covered are Algeria, relations with underdeveloped countries, Franco-German relations, European integration, defense within Atlantic Alliance, relations with Communist countries. Author shows underlying aims and conflicting objectives taken over from Fourth Republic, de Gaulle's personal conception of international affairs, his style of handling them and consistency in carrying out his vision. Successes and failures are judged in line with de Gaulle's own aims and those shared by French opinion. Criticism of de Gaulle's policies is tempered by pointing out difficulties of genuine alternatives to a policy of nationalism, prestige, and independence from U.S.

913 GROSSER, ALFRED. La IVe République et sa politique extérieure. Paris, A. Colin, 1961. 438 p. tables. (Collection "Sciences politiques")

Study made at Fondation nationale des sciences politiques' Centre d'étude des relations internationales on the forces determining foreign policy under the Fourth Republic (governmental, parliamentary, pressure groups, public opinion) and the main areas of controversy (Franco-German relations,

European unification, decolonization.) Legacy of Fifth Republic in all these areas is clarified.

FOR ADDITIONAL WORKS BY ALFRED GROSSER, SEE AUTHOR INDEX

914* GROUPE D'ACTION SYNDICALE. [Appeals of U.N.E.F. internal opposition group.] Paris, 1961.

915 GROUPE DE RECHERCHES OUVRIERES ET PAYSANNES. Pour une démocratie économique; objectifs, moyens et choix. Préf. de A. Jeanson et M. Debâtisse. Paris, Editions du Seuil, 1964. 237 p. (Collection Jean Moulin)

Study group composed of agricultural and industrial trade unionists as well as members of Club Jean Moulin and Citoyens 60 discuss paths to economic democracy and problems presented by economic growth, state planning and centralization of decisions, reforms of existing structures, and income redistribution.

916 GROUPE FRANÇAIS D'EDUCATION NOUVELLE. Le plan Langevin-Wallon de réforme de l'enseignement; compte rendu du colloque organisé par le Groupe français d'éducation nouvelle et de la Société française de pédagogie. Paris, Presses universitaires de France, 1964. 298 p.

Text of plan elaborated by Commission Langevin-Wallon in immediate post-war years, but never adopted, drawing up program for compulsory unified education up to 18. Text is preceded by proceedings of 1963 colloquium organized by pedagogic society and teachers' unions. Reports cover such topics as number and quality of teachers, curriculum for unified schools, democratization of university education, equal opportunities in all schools for working class children, adult education, with sharp criticisms of Gaullist educational reforms. Langevin and Wallon, both deceased, were Communist Party functionaries, as are many of teachers' union spokesmen.

917 GROUPEMENT NATIONAL POUR L'INDEMNISATION DES BIENS SPOLIES OU PERDUS OUTRE-MER. L'indemnisation des spoliations d'outre-mer. Paris, Éditions du Scorpion, 1964. 252 p.

Results of 1963-64 study by ad hoc study committee drawn from main repatriate organizations reviewing over-all compensation policy and legislation, total volume of reparations due, and methods of disbursement. Appendices reproduce subcommittee reports regarding different types of property (agricultural, industrial, small businesses, etc.) to be compensated.

918 GUENA, YVES. Historique de la Communauté. Paris, A. Fayard, 1962. 188 p. (Les Idées et la vie)

Origins of French Community, stages of its establishment and dissolution, current (1962) status of relations between its former members and France.

919 GUERANDE, PAUL. O.A.S. métro; ou, Les enfants perdus; récit. Paris, Éditions du Fuseau, 1964. 184 p.

Fictional account of operation of an O.A.S. network in Paris, seen through the eyes of a young officer who has just deserted from French army. Author shows unheroic, human, and practical side of this confused conspiracy.

920 GUERIN, DANIEL. L'Algérie caporalisée? Suite de L'Algérie qui se cherche. Paris, 1965. 96 p.

Based on articles in "Combat" Jan. 1964-65, with introductory explanation (and condemnation) of Ben Bella's overthrow by Boumedienne June 1965. Articles illuminate deterioration leading to coup: army's growing strength, corruption and confusion in self-administration programs, sterility of F.L.N.

921 GUERIN, DANIEL. L'Algérie qui se cherche. Paris, Présence Africaine, 1964. 105 p.

Based on articles in "Combat" written during trip through Algeria Nov. 1963 and examining successes and failures (such as self-administration of farms and industries) on the road to a modern socialist democracy. Includes March decree on self-administration.

922 GUERIN, PAUL. Un péril pour la France; le marché commun à six. Il existe de meilleures solutions. Publié sous l'egide du Comité d'entente des anciens combattants pour la défense de la France, de l'Union française et de son Armée et du Comité de la défense pour l'unité française. Paris, S.E.I.M.R.H.A., 1957. 64 p.

Economic and political considerations militating against Common Market and in favor of a European free trade zone including Great Britain and all overseas territories of European members.

923 GUERRY, EMILE MAURICE, Abp. La doctrine sociale de l'Église; son actualité, ses dimensions, son rayonnement. Édition mise à jour après l'encyclique "Mater et magistra." Paris, Éditions du Centurion, 1962. 212 p.

Systematic presentation of papal and other official Catholic pronouncements on Christian conceptions of human nature and the social order, applied to such specific questions as planning, nationalization, worker participation in management, wages.

924 GUERY, LOUIS. Les maîtres de l'U.N.R. Avec la collaboration de Manuel Bridier, Claude Estier et Louis Houdeville. Préf. de Claude Bourdet. Paris, Éditions du Monde ouvrier, 1959. 175 p. illus., ports., facsims.

Origins of U.N.R. (R.P.F., Républicain Sociaux, Union pour le Salut et le Renouveau de l'Algérie, the Soustelle-led semi-clandestine group) the party's current organization and financing and composition of parliamentary group. Sketches and photos identify members of its central committee. In this guide for left-wing opposition, U.N.R. is presented as a traditional rightist party with fascist potential.

925 GUICHARD-AYOUB, ELAINE, and CHARLES ROIG ET JEAN GRANGE. Etudes sur le Parlement de la Ve République. Préf. de Marcel Prélot. Paris, Presses universitaires de France, 1965. 294 p. fold. diagrs. (Travaux et recherches de la Faculté de droit et des sciences économiques de Paris; série "Science politique," no. 2) Includes bibliography.

Three monographs, one on the representativeness of the Senate elected in 1959, one on the control mechanisms of the National Assembly in the first year of the Fifth Republic, and one on the Assembly's legislative function in its first legislature. Each monograph contains a great deal of statistical information and short bibliographies.

926 GUILLOT, J. Le développement économique de l'Algérie. Paris, I.S.E.A., 1960. 219 p. (Institut de science économique appliquée. Cahiers no. 108, sér. F., Développement, croissance, progrès, no. 15) Bibliographical footnotes.

Five studies on Algerian economy written Oct. 1959-1960, giving history of Algerian industrialization before 1958, a review of the work by René Gendarme (see no. 863), and a summary of plans for Algerian industrialization, including Constantine Plan.

927 GUITARD, LOUIS. Lettre sans malice à François Mauriac sur la mort du général Weygand et quelques autres sujets. Avignon, Aubanel, 1966. 317 p.

Open letter to Mauriac, in which author, a journalist sympathetic to Vichyist writers uses incident of General Weygand's funeral which Mauriac failed to attend as an occasion for attacking Mauriac's hero-worship of de Gaulle, de Gaulle's past and current errors and specifically his relations with Weygand,

and certain aspects of French cultural life during the Fifth Republic.

928 GUKASIAN-GANDZAKETSI, LEVON GURGENOVICH. Frantsuzskii imperializm i Afrika. Moskva, Izd-vo vostochnoi litry, 1962. 398 p. Includes bibliography.

African colonial policy under Fourth and Fifth Republic, through 1962, with detailed examination of French economic efforts, Algerian developments up to independence, and independence movement in Sub-Saharan Africa. Index of names, political and economic organizations.

929 GUNSBERG, HENRI. Les Chrétiens de gauche ou le parti gris. Paris, J. J. Pauvert, 1966. 117 p. (Libertés, 43)

Polemical attack on efforts of Catholic left and Socialists to form a center opposition party to de Gaulle (in line with Defferre's approach) which author calls the "parti gris," and which author expects to be dominated by clericalism.

930 GURVITCH, GEORGES. Dialectique et sociologie. Paris, Flammarion, 1962. 242 p. (Nouvelle bibliothèque scientifique)

Examination of the dialectic method in thinkers ranging from Plato through Marx, and sociologist's own interpretation of this method (his own designation is 'hyper-empirical dialectics') as the most flexible and undogmatic tool for understanding social reality. Author examines applications of dialectics in sociology, and relations between sociology, history, and individual social sciences.

931 GURVITCH, GEORGES. La vocation actuelle de la sociologie. t. 2. Antécédents et prespectives. 2. éd. refondue et augm.(no. 5), Paris, Presses universitaires de France, 1963. 500 p. (Bibliothèque de sociologie contemporaine) Bibliographical footnotes.

Discussion, under "antecedents," of sociological contributions of Durkheim and Marx. Under "perspectives," sociologist criticizes current French sociological research as following the American model of collecting meaningless statistics in contrast to his own more productive dialectic approach. Two examples of topics that can be studied by his method are industrial society and technocracy, the multiplicity of social time in different types of society, on which he presents his preliminary conclusions.

932 GUYARD, JACQUES. Le miracle français. Paris, Éditions du Seuil, 1965. 123 p. Includes bibliography.

Survey of French economic expansion, 1945-1965, as seen in growth of national product, investment, consumption, price movements. For years of Fifth Republic, European economic integration and price stabilization are stressed.

933 GUPTA, MADAN GOPAL. Government of the Fifth Republic of France. 2d ed. Allahabad, Central Book Depot, 1963. 172 p. Includes bibliography.

Indian political scientist's comprehensive survey of institutions of Fifth Republic and political conceptions underlying the 1958 Constitution. Originally concluded in 1959, this work was revised for 1963 edition to incorporate actual functioning of institutions, election results, constitutional changes, and evaluation of efficacy of Fifth Republic.

934 HACHETTE, FIRM, PUBLISHERS, Paris. 12 mois d'édition juridique, politique, économique, et sociale française. Paris, 1963.

Classified listing of French books published Jan.-Dec. 1962, complemented by list of periodicals, author index. Books on political issues, in particular Algeria, are well represented.

935 HACKETT, JOHN and ANNE-MARIE HACKETT. Economic planning in France, with a foreword by Pierre Massé. Cambridge, Harvard University Press, 1963. 418 p. maps, diagrs. Bibliography: p. 401-416

Major scholarly work on French planning by English economist and his French civil servant wife, carried out with full cooperation of French planning officials. Major sections are: 1) Institutional framework of planning; 2) Planning procedure; 3) Implementation in different sectors; 4) Prospects for Fifth Plan as of early 1963. Extensive bibliography of official documents (laws and statutes, Economic and Social Council, Commissariat au Plan, National Assembly and Senate publications, and periodical literature 1959-1961.

936 HACKETT, JOHN. Economic planning in France: its relation to the policies of the developed countries of Western Europe. New York, Asia Pub. House, 1965. vi, 55 p.

Lecture held in Bombay to familiarize Indian economists with post-war European planning, particularly French application of concept of indicative planning as well as targets for Fifth Plan, with special attention to the problems presented by foreign trade.

937 HAHN, LORNA. North Africa, nationalism to nationhood. Introd. by John F. Kennedy. Washington, Public Affairs Press, 1960. 264 p. Includes bibliography.

American political scientist familiar with North Africa gives history of national independence movement in Tunisia, Morocco, and Algeria. De Gaulle's policy leading to Sept. 1959 self-determination offer is assessed in final chapter. Kennedy's introduction expresses sympathy for nationalist movements in North Africa.

938 HAHN, LORNA. War in Algeria: is confederation the answer? New York, American Committee on Africa, 1958. 32 p. (Africa today pamphlet, 1)

Proposal written shortly before de Gaulle's return to power. Author urges making Algeria part of a North African confederation linked with France and NATO, so that French settlers in Algeria could have some assurance that their rights would be respected.

939 HALEVY, DOMINIQUE. Contre la bombe; pour une doctrine française du renoncement aux armes nucléaires. [Ce texte a été rédigé pour la Féderation française contre l'armement atomique.] Paris, Éditions de Minuit, 1960. 191 p. (Documents). "Quelques livres": 189-190.

Description of international nuclear armaments, control negotiations, current world, European, and French nuclear strategy, followed by plea for French nuclear disarmament and program for step-by-step elimination of nuclear and conventional weapons.

940 HAMADA, HADDAD, (defendant). Le procès du Réseau Jeanson, présenté par Marcel Péju. Paris, F. Maspero, 1961. 251 p. (Cahiers libres nos. 17-18)

Summary of trial of seven Algerians, including Haddad Hamada, and eighteen Frenchmen before Tribunal militaire permanent de Paris, Sept. 1960, for active support of F.L.N. Jeanson himself was convicted in absentia.

941 HAMEL, EMMANUEL. Les atouts française. Paris, Plon, 1958. 239 p. (Tribune libre, 21)

After summarizing all the negative aspects (government instability, housing and trade deficits) author describes results of post-war technological progress and fruits of world-wide French efforts, with specific cases and figures. Study was made in last months of Fourth Republic by non-partisan group.

942 HAMON, LÉO. Discours...2 juin 1959. n.p., 1959. 4 l
(Union démocratique du travail)

On Algerian war and Gaullist policy in Algeria.

943 HAMON, LEO (ed.). Les nouveaux comportements politiques de la classe ouvrière; entretiens de Dijon. Ouvrage publié avec le concours du Centre national de la recherche scientifique. Paris, Presses universitaires de France, 1962. 252 p. (Publications du Centre d'études des relations politiques, Université de Dijon)

Verbatim report of colloquium held at University of Dijon's Centre détudes des relations politiques, Feb. 1960 under the direction of Léo Hamon, who also acted as rapporteur of meeting. Other speakers were André Philip, Pierre Naville, Serge Mallet, trade union leaders from C.F.T.C. and C.G.T. Discussions dealt with changes in workers' demands, political outlook (decline of ideological outlook) party affiliations, trade union participation in political life, changes in workers' way of life.

944 HAMON, LEO. La stratégie contre la guerre. [Préface du Général Charles Ailleret] Paris, B. Gasset, 1966. 319 p.

Revised version of seminar on military strategy given at University of Dijon, prefaced by General Ailleret, French Chief of Staff and "father" of the French atomic bomb, who calls author one of first politicians to recognize value of independent French nuclear force. After analysis of works of strategists de Gaulle and Mao Tse-Tung, Hamon examines threats and possibilities in atomic age and sees world's best chance for peace and stability combined with internal mobility in an oligopoly of nuclear deterrence, in line with Gaullist policy.

FOR ADDITIONAL WORKS BY LEO HAMON, SEE AUTHOR INDEX

945 HANIEL, ERICH. Regierungsbildung und Regierungskrisen in der Verfassungsentwicklung der französischen Vierten Republik. Tübingen, Mohr, 1961. 141 p. Bibliography: p. 134-135.

Constitutional regulations relating executive and legislative branches of the government in 1946 Constitution, and 1951, 1954, and 1958 reforms. Author analyzes manner in which government is formed and overthrown and National Assembly dissolved, with tables for Fourth Republic governments, votes of confidence 1946-1958. Gaullist take-over May-June 1958 is described in epilogue.

946 HARCOURT, FRANÇOIS D'. Demain: La France, l'Europe, le monde. Paris, Hachette, 1965. 269 p. Bibliography: p. 265-266.

Journalist's essays on selected internal and international problems of present-day France (social problems of youth and age, economic problems of agriculture and planning, response to decolonization, nuclear weapons, European unification, aid to underdeveloped areas). Selective bibliography of best popular works in these areas.

947 HARLOW, JOHN S. French economic planning, a challenge to reason. Iowa City, University of Iowa Press, 1966. V, 104. "Further reading": 84-85. Bibliographical footnotes.

Concepts, methods, and achievements of French planning presented for the enlightenment of the American business community. Objectives for Fourth Plan are scrutinized in detail, and appendix summarizes both Fourth and Fifth Plans.

948 HARVARD UNIVERSITY. INTERNATIONAL PROGRAM IN TAXATION. Taxation in France. Prepared by the Law School of Harvary University, International Tax Program, in consultation with the United Nations Secretariat. Chicago, Commerce Clearing House, 1966. lxxi, 1241 p. (World tax series)

Compendium on 1965 taxation system, with lengthy section on international aspects, including list of international agreements. Background material gives useful summary of economic conditions, graphic presentation of organization of ministries concerned with fiscal policy. Excellent up-to-date bibliographies on individual topics. Principal contributors are Martin Norr and Pierre Kerlan.

949 HATZFELD, HENRI and JACQUES FREYSSINET. L'emploi en France. Paris, Éditions ouvrières, Économie et humanisme, 1964. 271 p. tables, diagrs. (Initiation économique 5) Includes bibliography.

Popular work on economic theories of employment, historical and current situation, with statistics up to 1961 in terms of employment structure and government planning and policies affecting employment.

950 HAURIOU, ANDRÉ. Droit constitutionnel et institutions politiques. Paris, Éditions Montchrestien, 1966. 826 p. Includes bibliography.

Historical and functional survey intended for law students of political institutions in Western countries, with 150-page section on institutions of Fifth Republic and their evolution through 1964. Placing French institution within "classic constitutional conception" of Western democracies, author shows how balance is now leaning too far in reinforcing executive power. Good discussion of French electoral system is found in comparative section of work. Extensive up-to-date bibliographies after each chapter, subject and name index.

951 HAVET, JEAN. L'Algérie au carrefour. Paris, 1959. 16 p. (Comité d'action de défense démocratique)

Plea for strategic colonization of Algeria as nucleus for a French United States of North Africa. The comité d'action de défense démocratique was organized by Soustelle.

952 HAYTER, TERESA. French Aid. London, Overseas Development Institute, 1966. 229 p.

Well-rounded survey of French technical and economic assistance, with special sections on aid to different areas, history of the program and current (1965) administration, statistics on economic aid and technical assistance up to 1965. Good list of abbreviations of all agencies connected with assistance program.

953 HAYWARD, JACK ERNEST SHALOM. Private interests and public policy; the experience of the French Economic and Social Council. New York, Barnes and Noble, 1966. viii, 115 p. (Monographs in politics) Bibliographical footnotes.

History of Conseil Economique et Social, its functioning, representation of different economic organizations and conflicts between them within council, influence on economic policy (notably planning) and proposals for merging the council with Senate or making it a tool for democratic planning. Useful list of trade union, professional, business, and agricultural associations.

954 HEDTKAMP, GÜNTER. Planification in Frankreich; Grundlagen, Technik und Erfahrungen. Köln, C. Heymann, 1966. 176 p. tables (1 fold.) diagrs. (FIW-Schriftenreihe, Heft 31) Includes bibliography.

First part of work by German econometrist covers theories and historical background of central government planning and feasibility of input-output analysis in Western economics; second half of study examines critically French planning experience to determine how projections for whole economy and individual branches are established and how accurate they are, how the most recent plans were prepared, and what instruments for the plans' application exist in French institutions. Tables on public investments 1959-1962, maps of new regional planning administrative units and new higher education establishments.

955 HEDUY, PHILIPPE. Au lieutenant des Taglaïts. Paris, Table ronde, 1960. 351 p.

Personal narrative of French reserve officer serving in artillery batallion in Kabyle mountains summer 1958-Dec. 1959. Author, who personally favored May 1958 uprising and remains active in French nationalist groups, gives close-up and convincing view of feelings and general political attitudes of career officers fighting and facing day-by-day violence, alienated from metropolitan French and Gaullist government, which betrays them by negotiations and European settlers in Algeria who hamper their efforts to win war psychologically.

956 HELD, JEAN FRANCIS. L'affaire Moumié. Paris, F. Maspero, 1961. 30 p.

Account of October 1960 poisoning in Geneva of Felix Moumié, extreme leftist nationalist leader in the Cameroons, by an agent of "Main rouge," a terrorist organization representing French and other European colonial interests. See also no. 1013.

957 HERMENS, FERDINAND ALOYS. The Fifth Republic; [a political study of modern France.] Notre Dame, Ind., University of Notre Dame Press, 1960. 90 p. (Notre Dame books) Includes bibliographical footnotes.

Brief analysis of the 1958 Constitution, and first three elections (National Assembly, Senate, municipal) to evaluate Fifth Republic's prospects as a workable political system.

958 HERNU, CHARLES. La colère usurpée. Paris, Editions C. H., 1959. 333 p.

Articles issued in "Les Jacobins" (organ of Club des Jacobins) and other publications 1953-1959, attacking Fourth Republic governments and "le système." Author was elected deputy for Seine Jan. 1956 and supported Mendès-France wing of Radical Party. Last third of volume reflects collapse of Fourth Republic, search for new rallying point of French Left in opposition to de Gaulle (for whom he has personal sympathies).

959 HERVE, PIERRE. Ce que je crois. Paris, B. Grasset, 1958. 183 p.

Explanation of former French Communist's deviation from orthodox Marxism and opinions on specific political problems as of 1957.

960 HIRSCH, ETIENNE. Die französischen Planungsmethoden und ihre Ausdehnung auf den Gemeinsamen Markt. Berlin, Duncker and Humbolt, 1962. 192 p. (Sonderschrift des IFO-Instituts für Wirtschaftsforschung, Nr. 30)

Talk by former head of Euratom as well as of French Planning Commissariat emphasizing compatibility of French planning methods with claims of Common Market economy and desirability of extending such methods to Common Market as a whole.

961 Une Histoire politique de l'armée. V. 2. De de Gaulle à de Gaulle, 1940-1967. By Jean Planchais. Paris, Editions du Seuil, 1967. 380 p. (L'Histoire immédiate) Bibliographical footnotes.

Though only 50 pages of this work on the politics of the French Army under de Gaulle concern its share in the birth of the Fifth Republic and its participation in the Algerian conflict, this will-informed study shows the historical development of the various issues that came to a head after 1958. Planchais, as "Le Monde" specialist on military affairs from 1945 on, had access to Ministry of Defense, parliament, as well as military leaders, of whom book provides convincing sketches. (See also nos. 1466, 1467.)

962 HOFFHERR, RENE. Coopération économique franco-africaine. Paris, Sirey, 1958. 169 p. maps (1 fold.) diagrs. "Bibliographie": p. 149-151.

French modernization program for Africa, particularly development of energy and oil resources, 1956-1957.

963 HOFFMANN, STANLEY. Le mouvement Poujade, avec la collaboration de Michel des Accords, Serge Hurtig, et al. Préf. de Jean Meynaud. Paris, A. Collin, 1956. xxxvi, 417 p. maps, facsims. (Cahiers de la Fondation nationale des sciences politiques, 81) Bibliographical footnotes.

Study of Poujadist movement based on its publications, close examination of Jan. 1956 election and reactions of professional organizations, labor movement, other political parties. Author highlights the place of the movement within the French antiparliamentary tradition and the extent to which it temporarily took over Gaullist votes.

FOR ADDITIONAL WORKS BY STANLEY HOFFMANN, SEE AUTHOR INDEX

964 HORON, A. GOUREVITCH. L'Afrique et le Proche-Orient devant l'agression. Paris, 1959. 24 p. (Comité d'action de défense démocratique)

Dangers of Panarabism and Soviet aggression in North Africa. See also no. 951.

965 HOUART, PIERRE. L'attitude de l'église dans la guerre d'Algérie, 1954-1960. Bruxelles, Le Livre africain, 1960. 121 p. "Chronologie et bibliographie": p. 105-121.

Selected statements, appeals, articles, Nov. 1954-Dec. 1959, by leading French Catholics and Catholic organizations on all aspects of Algerian war and military service.

966 HOUZEL, XAVIER. Les perspectives de développement économique et social en Algérie et la rénovation rurale; mémoire présenté à l'Institut d'études politiques de l'Université de Paris sous la direction de M. Chardonnet. Paris, 1961. 213 l. Includes bibliography.

Land reform, agricultural credit system and rural renovation programs undertaken by French government in Algeria, 1956-1960 in conjunction with the program of general economic expansion of the Constantine Plan, balance sheet of failures and successes after five years (March 1961), recent plans proposed by commission of Algerian deputies in National Assembly and other agricultural specialists. Bibliography gives official texts, reports, and statistics on Algerian agriculture and government activities.

967 HUGHES, HENRY STUART. The obstructed path; French social thought in the years of desperation, 1930-1960. 1st ed. New York, Harper and Row, 1968. xi, 304 p. Bibliographical footnotes.

Discussion on influential historians, philosophers, writers, and anthropologists belonging to a generation cut off from the main stream of Western intellectual life and deeply immersed in ideological conflict revolving around Catholicism and Marxism. Among figures still active in Fifth Republic years are Sartre, Merleau-Ponty, and Lévi-Strauss.

968 HUMBARACI, ARSLAN. Algeria: a revolution that failed; a political history since 1954. New York, Praeger, 1966. xiii, 308 p. maps. Bibliography: p. 196-198.

Comprehensive work on post-independence Algeria, 1962-1965, by sympathetic Turkish journalist stationed in Algeria, covering important facts on governmental changes, economic and social conditions, attempts and failures to implement revolutionary goals of socialism and Arab unity, Franco-Algerian relations, Ben Bella's disgrace and Boumedienne's seizure of

969 HUMPHREYS, THOMAS B. A study on the continuity and change in French military policy from the Fourth to the Fifth Republic; submitted to the United States Naval Academy in partial fulfillment of the requirements for a Trident Scholar program. Annapolis, Md. 1965. 153 l. Bibliography: p. 142-153.

power. Appendix on Algerian press lists and describes French and Arab dailies, weeklies, and periodicals. Useful subject and name index.

Controversies over military policy during Fourth Republic and current French military issues (Algeria, reorganization of national defense, relations with NATO, attitude toward Multilateral nuclear force, nuclear weapons, disarmament) in the wider context of Gaullist international policy, mainly on the basis of newspaper reports and replies to questionnaire by French and American military specialists. Young naval officer seeks to isolate historic and recent elements in US-French frictions.

970 HURST, JEAN-LOUIS. Le déserteur. By Maurienne [pseud.] Paris, Editions de Minuit, 1960. 125 p. (Les Jours et les nuits)

Personal narrative of young French Communist beginning his military service in 1957, stationed in Germany during collapse of Fourth Republic, and being led to desert army in late 1958, because of his opposition to Algerian war together with like-minded non-Communist friends. (For censorship trial against publisher of this novel, see no. 559.)

971 IDIART, PIERRE and REINE GOLDSTEIN. L'avenir professionnel des jeunes du milieu populaire. Paris, Editions ouvrières, 1965. 214 p. (Collection Jeunesse Actualité)

Results of questionnaires, 1963-64 sent to 60,000 boys and girls belonging to Jeunesse ouvrière catholique concerning their educational background, vocational training, and career plans.

972 IDIART, PIERRE. La quantité humaine. Paris, Editions ouvrières, 1962. 245 p. (Collection "Points d'appui")

Reflections on the material and psychological transformations of the French working class since Marx and current viability of Marxism.

973 In search of France. By Stanley Hoffmann et al. Cambridge, Harvard University Press, 1963. xiii, 443 p. Bibliographical references included in "Notes" (p. 409-428)

Essays on adaptations to a modern industrial society of French political institutions, with emphasis on problems of democratization unresolved in Fifth Republic (Stanley Hoffmann) of economy (Charles Kindleberger) of social structures and values (Laurence Wylie and Jesse Pitts) and of foreign policy (Jean-Baptiste Duroselle). French political scientist François Goguel reviews this primarily American approach to French society.

974* INFORMATIONSDIENST, München. French-Algerian relations, München, 1960. 1 env.

Information on Mouvement National Algérien as of June 1960. See also no. 2066.

975 Initiation à l'Algérie. By J. Alazard, S. Bencheneb et al. Paris, Librairie d'Amérique et d'Orient Adrien-Maisonneuve, 1957. xi, 422 p. illus., maps. "Bibliographie sommaire": p. 415-416.

Essays by individual authors on Algeria's past and various aspects of culture, society, economy, administrative organization, with little information beyond 1955.

976 Initiation aux problèmes d'outre-mer; colonisation, décolonisation, sous-développement. By Gilbert Blardone et al. Lyon, chronique sociale de France, 1959. 366 p. (Collection "Savoir pour agir," v. 6) "Bibliographie": p. 351-356.

Collective work under auspices of Chronique sociale de France giving essential facts on colonialism, trend toward decolonization, information on French Community and economic relations within it, specific statements of Catholic hierarchy on colonial questions and problems of social legislation for overseas territories. Useful list of conferences sponsored by Catholic Church on colonial problems and good bibliography.

977 ISENBERG, IRWIN (ed.). France under de Gaulle. New York, H. W. Wilson Co., 1967. 189 p. (The Reference shelf, v. 39, no. 1) Bibliography: p. 178-189.

1965-66 survey of French political life, de Gaulle's personal stand on international issues, Gaullist diplomacy, and France's place in the Atlantic Alliance, composed of short excerpts from 1965-66 articles and books mainly by Americans. Good bibliography of books and articles in English.

978 ISORNI, JACQUES. Ainsi passent les républiques. Paris, Flammarion, 1960. 234 p.

Chronicle of French political life, 1955-1958 from perspective of author's parliamentary experience as an Independent deputy. The book, written in mid-1959, shows stand of author and other parliamentarians toward foreign policy, decolonization, internal party politics, collapse of Fourth Republic and elaboration of new institutions.

979 ISORNI, JACQUES. Les cas de conscience de l'avocat. Paris, Librairie académique Perrin, 1965. 313 p. (Les Cas de conscience)

Personal experiences as defense lawyer regarding ethics of legal practice, particularly when defending cases involving political crimes. Most trials discussed antedate Fifth Republic, except for "barricades" trial and Isorni's own libel trial.

980 ISORNI, JACQUES (defendant). Compte rendu. Le Procès: L'Accusateur public contre Isorni, les 15 et 16 janvier 1965. Paris, Table ronde, 1965. 236 p.

Record of trial before Tribunal de grande instance de la Seine against Isorni and his publisher, La Table ronde, for offense against the chief of State. The incriminated work is his "Jusqu'au bout de notre peine" (see no. 983) in which he excuses O. A. S. political murders by accusing de Gaulle of having instigated the political murder of Admiral Darlan. As an experienced defense lawyer, Isorni speaks in his own defense and attacks de Gaulle's perversion of legal procedure by his setting up special tribunals. Isorni is found guilty.

981 ISORNI, JACQUES (defendant). La défense et la justice, un procès: Le Ministère public accuse Isorni, défendu par Mes. Amiel et Goust et par le bâtonnier Alléhaut. Paris, Flammarion, 1965. 251 p.

Nearly complete verbatim record of trial held before same tribunal (see above) 6/7 March 1964, in which Isorni was prosecuted for libel against Finance Minister Giscard d'Estaing because in the role of defense lawyer for one of the would-be de Gaulle assassins at Petit-Clamart, Isorni had claimed that Giscard d'Estaing had O. A. S. sympathies and had helped pass information to O. A. S. in mid-1961. In libel trial, further information on Finance Minister's character is brought and light shed on intrigues within government at that time, evidence is shown for possible connivance by Giscard d'Estaing with O. A. S., and connections between O. A. S. movement and attempted de Gaulle assassination are established. Isorni was first acquitted, then retried at the end of 1964, acquitted a second time.

982 ISORNI, JACQUES. Hommes de Dieu et hommes du diable. Paris, Flammarion, 1964. 233 p.

Encounters with Franco, Pope John XXIII, in connection with author's visits to Spain and Italy, 1962-1963, to help political refugees fleeing from de Gaulle. Although these are private missions, the author sheds some light on current Spanish relations and Vatican's position toward de Gaulle.

983   ISORNI, JACQUES. Jusqu'au bout de notre peine. Paris, Table ronde, 1963. 228 p.

Account of trials, July 1962-May 1963, of military figures and O.A.S. leaders by their defense lawyer. Includes interview with Salazar August 1962. Annexes reproduce Isorni's defense plea for O.A.S. officers, Sept. 15, 1962, before High Military Tribunal, as well as his own interrogation March 1963. (See also no. 980.)

984   ISORNI, JACQUES. Lui qui les juge. Paris, Flammarion, 1961. 234 p.

Indictment of de Gaulle's Algerian policy and loss of French Empire, (with unfavorable parallels to Pétain's success in saving the Empire) and eye-witness account of three political trials; that of the Jeanson network (pro-F.L.N) the barricades trial, both in 1960, that of the rebellious generals in 1961. Isorni served as defense lawyer in latter two trials. Appendix reproduces his speeches and articles, defense at barricade trial, Nov. 1960, at Alain de Sérigny trial, March 1961, and at General Bigot's trial, June 1961.

985   ISORNI, JACQUES. Pétain a sauvé la France. Paris, Flammarion, 1964. 140 p.

Plea for revision of Pétain conviction (on the strength of his contributions to internal unity and preservation of French Empire) and de Gaulle's recent stand on revision issue.

FOR ADDITIONAL WORKS BY AND ABOUT JACQUES ISORNI, SEE AUTHOR INDEX

986   Itinéraires, chroniques and documents (periodical). L'affaire Pax en France. Paris, 1964. 197 p. (Its Supplément au no. 88)

Issue of Catholic periodical devoted to 1964 controversy around Polish Catholic organization "Pax" and its reception in French Catholic Press. Main target is Catholic periodical "Informations Catholiques internationales" which is accused of deliberately misleading French Catholics by presenting Pax as a pacifist rather than a subversive communist movement. (See also no. 290.)

987   IZARD, GEORGES. Lettre affligée au général de Gaulle. Paris, R. Laffont, 1964. 95 p.

Protest against de Gaulle's post-Algerian war policy of French greatness as expressed in French nuclear strategy and leadership ot anti-U.S. neutralist have-nots. While not a political opponent, author speaks for restless middle-of-the-road Frenchman who sees his country's prosperity threatened by elusive pursuit of greatness.

988   JABHAT AL-TAHRIR AL-QAWMI. Projet de programme pour la réalisation de la révolution démocratique populaire. [Alger? Presses de l'imprimerie spéciale d'al-Chaab, 1962?] 60 p.

Summation of Algerian situation at eve of independence and political, economic, and cultural program adopted by the Conseil National de la Revolution Algérienne (C.N.R.A.) in Tripoli, June 1962. At head of title: Front de libération nationale.

989   JABHAT AL-TAHRIR AL-QAWMI. Projet de statuts du Parti. [Alger, Impr. al-Chaab, 1962?] 21 p.

Role of F.L.N. in independent Algeria, as elaborated at Tripoli congress (see above) and statutes determining its formal organization.

990   JABHAT AL-TAHRIR AL-QAWMI. La question algérienne devant le Conseil de sécurité de l'O.N.U. [Alger?] Editions; Résistance algérienne [1956?] 49 p.

Contains F.L.N. delegate Hussein Ait Ahmed's declaration before Arab Information Center, N.Y. and stenographic record (in French) of 129th session of Security Council, June 26, 1956 at which request by 13 Afro-Asian countries for full discussion of Algerian question is voted down. See also Algerian Front of National Liberation Delegation, New York.

991   JABHAT AL-TAHRIR AL-QAWMI. Règlement de discipline générale et de juridiction militaire. Alger, 1958. 15-16 p.

Regulations for Army of National Liberation adopted by Algerian Provisional Government's Executive Committee April 12, 1958. Text in Arabic and French.

992   JABHAT AL-TAHRIR AL-QAWMI. La révolution algérienne par les textes; documents du F.L.N. présentés par André Mandouze. 3. éd. remise à jour et augm. Paris, F. Maspero, 1961. 218 p. (Cahiers libres, no. 16)

Sourcebook on Algerian revolution composed of brief excerpts from F.L.N. documents, primarily from "El Moudjahid" and addressed to militants rather than as propaganda outside Algeria. Excerpts are arranged by main political themes of revolution, 1954-1961.

993   JABHAT AL-TAHRIR AL-QAWMI. DELEGATION, N.Y. White paper on the application of the Geneva conventions of 1949 to the French-Algerian conflict. New York, Algerian Office, 1960. 85 p.

White paper on violations of international conventions in treatment of prisoners (torture, internment camps) drawn up by the Delegation of the Provisional Government of the Algerian Republic, New York.

994   JABIN, ANDRE. Le guide pratique des élections, en collaboration avec Janine Vacherand. Paris, Editions "Europa," 1967. 351 p. Looseleaf.

First part answers common questions on electoral procedure, second part supplies legal texts for political assemblies, presidency, referenda, professional bodies such as Caisse de Sécurité Sociale through December 1966. See also nos. 777 and 1496.

995   JACOB, ALAIN. D'une Algérie à l'autre. Paris, B. Grasset, 1963. 237 p.

"Le Monde's" special correspondent in Algeria reports events from May 1958 through Algerian independence, with lengthy sections on Jan. 1960 barricades, Generals' putsch and O.A.S.

996   JACQUOT, MICHEL JEAN. La politique douanière et la coopération franco-africaine. Ouvrage honoré par le Ministère de l'éducation nationale. Préf. de François Luchaire. Paris, Documentation africaine, 1963. 221 p. Includes bibliography.

Changes in economic relations between France and its former African colonies, in particular the tariff and preferential trade agreements. Author, who is tariff inspector, shows why common Franco-African tariff for the franc zone is incompatible with Common Market, liberalization of international trade, as well as divergent economic interests of underdeveloped African states. The special problem of Algeria is not covered. Appendices include text of articles of European Economic Community regarding members' overseas territories and of association of African states with Community.

997 JAELIC, JEAN. La droite, cette inconnue. Paris, Sept couleurs, 1963. 415 p.

Very subjective and intuitive attempt to redefine concepts of "Right" and "Left" in terms of deep-rooted human tendencies, identifying the Right with a profoundly Christian, ascetic, aristocratic, generous world view, in opposition to both capitalist and communist materialism, which are to the Left. De Gaulle in this context is viewed as fundamentally to the Left. Author reinterprets European unification, nationalism, patriotism, racism, social reform in the light of this classification.

998 JAFFRE, YVES FREDERIC. Les tribunaux d'exception, 1940-1962. Paris, Nouvelles Editions latines, 1963, c1962. 365 p. Bibliography: p. 358-360.

For Fifth Republic, author summarizes 1960-1962 political trials (barricades, Generals' putsch, Jouhaud, Salan, O.A.S.) describing legal procedure, nature of evidence, outcome, etc. as it appears in published documents on trials. Jaffre himself acted as defense lawyer in censorship trial (see no. 1646).

999 JAFFRE, YVES FREDERIC (ed.). Le procès du Petit Clamart; exposé des faits, débats, dépositions, réquisitoire, plaidoiries. Paris, Nouvelles Editions latines, 1963. 641 p. illus., map, plan, port.

Slightly abbreviated record (first 3 sessions dealing with controversy about court's jurisdiction are only summarized) of trial of Bastien-Thiry and others accused of attempted de Gaulle assassination. In some cases text is more complete than the official stenographic "Compte-rendu" (see no. 143) as in the final defense plea of Bastien-Thiry's lawyers. Photographs from trial.

1000 JAMET, CLAUDE (ed.). Le rendez-vous manqué de 1944; vingt ans après, seize anciens résistants, vichystes, et collaborationnistes confrontent leurs points de vue dans un débat organisé, animé et présenté par Claude Jamet. Paris, Editions France-Empire, 1964. 317 p.

Verbatim record of 1964 round table discussion on six questions concerning participants' attidude during German occupation and current reassessment of this attitude. 20 participants include Vichy officials, collaborationists, and active resistants, with photographs, biographical data on each. Parallels with recent upheavals in Algeria and O.A.S. resistance are drawn by various participants, among whom there is no real government spokesman.

1001 JANON-ROSSIER, CLAIRE. Ces maudits colons Cent trente-deux années d'économie française en Algérie. Préf. de Paul Robert et Marcel Barbut. Paris, Table Ronde, 1966. 255 p.

Detailed description, with facts and figures, of achievements of French colonization in agriculture, agricultural research, and administrative machinery for increasing and improving agricultural output. Author points out that level of agricultural research in pre-1962 Algeria was higher than in France, and that the exodus of agronomists should be put to advantage in the metropolis. The work is based on a dissertation at the University of Aix-en-Provence written by Algerian-born young woman whose grandfather was an outstanding agronomist in Algeria.

1002 JASSERON, GEORGES. Les Harkis en France; scènes et témoignages. Paris, Editions du Fuseau, 1965. 157 p. (Collection les Chemins du réel, 12)

Sketches and anecdotes of individual 'harkis' (Algerians who fought alongside French army against F.L.N.) relocated in France and struggling to adjust to modern society and French bureaucracy. Author was in charge of a relocation center for harkis in Rouen, 1962-3.

1003 JASSERON, ROBERT. "Wilaya métro." Paris, Presses du Mail, 1963. 285 p.

Fictional account, interspersed with excerpts from newspapers describing actual incidents, of French network for supporting F.L.N. in Paris and terrorism carried out by F.L.N. in Paris against Algerian compatriots. Particular targets are the Jeanson network and Catholic intellectuals, who, according to author, were not prosecuted for treason by French government. Introduction by Bachaga Boualam.

1004 JEANSON, FRANCIS. Notre guerre. Paris, Editions de Minuit, 1960. 119 p. (Documents)

Author's justification for his clandestine participation in "Réseau Jeanson," which for three years had been raising money for F.L.N. and encouraging desertions. Writing in the wake of his press conference April 1960, Jeanson addresses himself primarily to critics from Left by justifying his stand as the most effective weapon against fascist tendencies and for assuring Franco-Algerian reconciliation.

1005 JEANSON, FRANCIS. La révolution algérienne; problèmes et perspectives. Milano, Feltrinelli, 1962. 255 p. Bibliography: p. 249-255.

Having actively served Algerian nationalist cause, French philosopher surveys unpolemically social scientists' findings about economic growth possibilities in underdeveloped countries to help Algerians follow a realistic course after independence. Author sees in Algeria a test case for what can be done in a society "mobilized" by a long revolutionary struggle and willing to pursue totally collective goals. Specifically, author discusses modes of agricultural reform, planning, industrialization, education, foreign aid, keeping in mind need for popular participation at all levels. Good bibliography on Algerian economy and theory of economic growth.

FOR ADDITIONAL WORKS BY AND ABOUT FRANCIS JEANSON, SEE AUTHOR INDEX

1006* JEUNE NATION. [Leaflet summoning patriotic Frenchmen to wear mourning during Khrushchev's visit - "the man of Budapest who arms F.L.N." - black armbands or neckties as a sign of protestation.]

1007* JEUNES DE L'U.D.T. (Gaullistes de gauche) [Appeal to the students of the Institut d'études politiques], 1961.

1008 JEUNES DE LA GAUCHE EUROPEENNE. [Documents. Paris, 1963] [14] p.

Organization's statutes, list of regional delegates, members of executive committee, and resolutions presented at Jan. 1963 meeting in Reims.

1009* JEUNESSES INDEPENDANTES DE PARIS. [Appeal to the students studying of the Institut d'études politiques], Paris, 1961. 2 p.

1010 JIMENEZ DE PARGA Y CABRERA, MANUEL. La Quinta República francesa; una puerta abierta a la dictadura constitucional. Madrid, Editiorial Tecnos, 1958. 191 p. diagrs.

Articles published in Madrid newspaper "Ya" May 24 - Sept. 18, 1958, discussing de Gaulle's past views, French political institutions, and the 1958 Constitution, with particular stress on its totalitarian potential.

1011 JOBERT, AMBROISE et al. Chronologie des événements mondiaux de 1945 à 1965. Grenoble, Université de Grenoble, Institut d'études politiques, 1966. 59 p.

Month by month chronology of world politics going up to July 1965 and divided into parallel columns on France, the Atlantic World, the Communist World, and the Third World. Good index helps locate events quickly. Co-authors are Jean Machu, Pierre Boulle, and Jacques Solé.

1012   JOESTEN, JOACHIM. The new Algeria. Chicago, Follett Pub. Co., 1964. vi, 258 p. maps, port.

Swiss-American journalist's sympathetic description of Algerian political history since independence, Ben Bella and the political figures around him, Algerian road to socialism in agriculture and industry, foreign policy and relations with France. Appendices reproduce 1963 constitution, Evian agreements, Tripoli program of June 1962.

1013   JOESTEN, JOACHIM. The Red Hand; the sinister account of the terrorist arm of the French right-wing "ultras"—in Algeria and on the Continent. London, New York, Abelard-Schumann, 1962. 200 p.

Story of counter-terrorism against North African nationalist militants and their European supporters by secret society called Red Hand, emerging in 1952 and replaced a decade later by O.A.S. Most directly involved are French civilian and military secret services and European extremists in North Africa. Activities of Red Hand center in Germany, Switzerland, and Belgium. See also no. 956.

1014   JOHNSTONE, ALLEN W. United States direct investment in France: an investigation of the French charges. Cambridge, Mass., M.I.T. Press, 1965. xv, 109 p. Bibliography: p. 101-106.

Based on thesis written at M.I.T. School of Management by Chrysler International executive on changes in attitude of French government toward American direct investment after August 1962 and rationale behind it. Current status of American investment in France is summarized (Chrysler is largest U.S. firm involved). Author also reports on 1964 interviews with 24 executives of French-based U.S. firms regarding control policies of parent companies.

1015   JOUHAUD, A. L'Algérie deux ans après le référendum. By L'Haque [pseud.] Chatou (S.-and-O.) Association d'études pour l'Afrique du nord, 1960. 23 p.

Attack on Gaullist policy in Algeria since Sept. 1958 referendum for having betrayed hopes of May 1958, giving ground to F.L.N., and risking civil war at home at the same time.

1016   JOUHAUD, EDMOND, (defendant). Le procès d'Edmond Jouhaud; compte rendu sténographique. Paris, A. Michel, 1962. 356 p. (Les Grands procès contemporains)

April 1962 trial of General Jouhaud after his capture in Oran before Haut Tribunal Militaire, the same tribunal before which Generals Challe and Zeller had been tried the previous year. Trial centers on Jouhaud's actions May 1958 and on his participation in O.A.S. 1961-1962. Lengthy autobiographical statement of Algerian-born accused. Among defense witnesses are Léon Delbecque, Alain de Sérigny, Raymond Dronne, Algerian-born wife of Albert Camus. Jouhaud was condemned to death by tribunal but reprieved at last moment.

1017   JOUSSELLIN, JEAN. Une nouvelle jeunesse française. Toulouse, Privat, 1966. 336 p. (Epoque) Bibliographical footnotes.

Characteristics of French rural, working class and student youth, its special problems and support given by youth movements and state agencies. Appendix lists major youth associations.

1018   JOUVE, EDMOND. Le général de Gaulle et la construction de l'Europe, 1940-1966. Préf. de Maurice Duverger. Paris, Librarie générale de droit et de jurisprudence, R. Pichon et R. Durand-Ausias, 1967. 2 v. illus., facsims. (Bibliothèque constitutionnelle et de science politique, t. 25) Includes bibliography.

Major documentary work carried out with the help of government archives on de Gaulle's and Gaullism's foreign and military policy, focused on European unification. V. 1 (881 pages) analyzes over 1500 references to European policy in de Gaulle's published and unpublished writings and statements (tapes were also scanned) between 1906 and 1966 to reconstruct the genesis, contents, and present institutional framework of de Gaulle's and Gaullist European policy, as well as public response thereto. Political chronology, extensive bibliography of books and articles on European unification, subject index round off v. 1. V. 2 (969 pages) contains chronological list of all texts by de Gaulle, selected unpublished de Gaulle texts, 1906-1966, and other documents on government policy, U.N.R. views, official declarations and agreements, 1965 campaign texts on European policy. 300 pages of cartoons from international press reflect world reaction to de Gaulle's European policy, 1950-1966.

1019   JOUVENEL, BERTRAND DE, (ed.). Futuribles; studies in conjecture. Geneva, Droz, 1963-65. 2 v. maps (1 fold.) fold. diagrs.

Studies on the possibilities of predicting political institutions by French and non-French political scientists. Second volume concentrates on forecasting the institutions of an integrated Europe.

FOR ADDITIONAL WORKS BY AND ABOUT BERTRAND DE JOUVENEL, SEE AUTHOR INDEX.

1020   JUIN, ALPHONSE PIERRE. C'étaient nos frères; illus. de Jean Reschofsky. Paris, Presses de la Cité, 1962. 223 p. illus., maps.

Fictional account of fighting in Kabylia, 1960-1961 as seen through the eyes of an Algerian-born officer loyal to the government. Evolution of Gaullist policy in Algeria and issue of army loyalty to the government dominate novel. Author's own views are moderate and, as of Dec. 1961, reckon with successful negotiation with F.L.N.

1021   JUIN, ALPHONSE PIERRE and HENRI MASSIS. L'Europe en question; textes. Paris, Plon, 1958. 11 p. (Tribune libre, 30)

General's essay discusses military strategy for keeping Western Europe free in the new age of nuclear stalemate, while Massis argues in favor of a spiritual, Christian rather than a materialistic unification of Western Europe as the only way to resist both Soviet and U.S. hegemony.

1022   JUIN, ALPHONSE PIERRE and AMAR NAROUN. Histoire parallèle: la France en Algérie, 1830-1962. Paris, Librairie académique Perrin, 1963. 316 p. illus., ports.

Positive and negative views of French colonization and construction in Algeria, dealing only briefly with final years of struggle.

1023   JUIN, ALPHONSE PIERRE. Je suis soldat. Paris, Editions du Conquistador, 1960. 118 p. ports. (Collection "Mon métier")

General's military career and reflections on proper military orientation at a time of nuclear and subversive warfare.

1024   JUIN, ALPHONSE PIERRE. Mémoires. Paris, A. Fayard, 1959-60. 2 v. illus., ports. (Les Grandes études contemporaines)

Final portion of second volume covers General's experiences in NATO 1951-58, his reactions to May 13, 1958 and birth of Fifth Republic, and his views on de Gaulle's Algerian and NATO policy in first year of government.

1025 JUIN, ALPHONSE PIERRE. Le Maghreb en feu. Paris, Plon, 1957. 192 p.

Author's role in emancipation of Tunisia and Morocco and outlook for Algeria in early 1957.

1026 JUIN, ALPHONSE PIERRE. Trois siècles d'obéissance militaire, 1950-1963. Paris, Plon, 1964. 210 p. Bibliographical footnotes.

Three centuries of French military history are reviewed to prove that army as a whole consistently remained loyal to legal government, with final chapter on experiences of Fifth Republic giving a fair interpretation of misunderstanding on Algerian policy between de Gaulle and military leaders. Juin blames Algerian chaos in part on 1961 military rebellion and subsequent participation in O.A.S. of part of officer corps, but insists that this always remained a minority reaction.

1027 Les justices d'exception et la presse française. Paris, Editions Galic, 1962. 159 p. (L'Histoire au jour le jour no. 7)

Newspaper excerpts, June-Sept. 1962, on trials of Salan, Jouhaud, O.A.S. leaders, and treatment of political prisoners.

1028 KAES, RENE. Les ouvriers français et la culture; enquête 1958-1961. Sous la direction de Marcel David. Paris, Dalloz, 1962. 592 p. diagrs.

Study made at Institut du Travail, Strasbourg University, based on questionnaires administered to 572 workers in 14 representative plants all over France to determine workers' attitude toward and direct participation in culture (reading, the arts, leisure activities, scientific information) as a function of social origin, education, sex, etc.

1029 KAHN, EMILE. Au temps de la République, propos d'un républicain... Paris, Ligue des droits de l'homme, 1966. 408 p. port.

1930-1958 speeches and articles of secretary general and president of Ligue des Droits de l'Homme. For 1956 - Jan. 1958 (date of Kahn's death) articles concentrate on Ligue's views on Algerian war.

1030 KANAPA, JEAN. La doctrine sociale de l'église et le marxisme. Paris, Editions sociales, 1962. 317 p. (Marxisme et religion) Bibliographical footnotes.

Juxtaposition of Catholic doctrine and Marxism on such issues as natural law, property, capitalism, class struggle, democracy, organization of economy, state planning, labor movement, and family, with some of pronouncements related to social and economic policies of Fifth Republic. Unfamiliar documentation from French Catholic books and journals for 1958-1961 is analyzed unpolemically, although author's purpose is to prove inadequacy of Church doctrine in dealing with social problems.

1031 KAYSER, JACQUES. De Kronstadt à Khrouchtchev; voyages franco-russes, 1891-1960. Paris, A. Colin, 1962. 291 p. illus., ports., facsims. (Kiosque; les faits, la presse, l'opinion, 19) Bibliography: p. 184-185.

Includes chapter on Khrushchev's visit to France March-April 1960, with excerpts of press reactions to this event in France and abroad.

1032 KAYSER, JACQUES. Le quotidien français. Préf. de Pierre Renouvin. Paris, A. Colin, 1963. 167 p. port., diagrs. (Cahiers de la Fondation nationale des sciences politiques, 122)

Posthumous work by head of Institut français de presse giving methodological tools for classification and comparison of French newspapers, together with data for 12 Parisian and 21 provincial dailies as of 1961.

1033 KELLY, GEORGE ARMSTRONG. Lost soldiers; the French Army and Empire in crisis, 1947-1962. Cambridge, Mass., M.I.T. Press, 1965. x 404 p. Bibliography: p. 382-391.

American political scientist's sympathetic account of French Army's experiences in Indochina and Algeria, based largely on French military journals, with good description of Army's revolutionary war ideology and psychological warfare operations in Algeria, chain of events leading from May 1958 to generals' putsch and O.A.S. Excellent bibliography of books and articles.

1034 KERAMANE, HAFID. La pacification; livre noir de six années de guerre en Algérie. Lausanne, La Cité-Editeur, 1960. 272 p.

Documentation drawn primarily from published sources 1956-1959, notably "El Moudjahid," on the entire range of repressive measures in Algeria and France against Algerians: torture, illegal arrests, concentration camps, war crimes, demonstrating that things have not improved under Fifth Republic.

1035 KESSEL, PATRICK and GIOVANNI PIRELLI. Le peuple algérien et la guerre; lettres et témoignages d'Algériens, 1954-1962. Paris, F. Maspero, 1962. 757 p. (Cahiers libres, no. 41-42-43)

Documentary work on Algerian revolution, most of it not published previously and drawn from private archives, retracing struggle more or less chronologically Jan. 1955 - May 1962 by means of letters of Algerians in prison and camps to either friends or officials. Letters have not been edited. Glossary, list of abbreviations, very extensive name index, and itemized table of contents.

1036 KHEITMI, MOHAMMED RECHID. Les partis politiques et le droit positif français. Préf. de Robert Pelloux. Paris, Librairie générale de droit et de jurisprudence, R. Pichon et R. Durand-Auzias, 1964. 344 p. tables. (Bibliothèque constitutionnelle et de science politique, 9) Includes bibliography.

Doctoral dissertation, University of Lyon, on legal status of political parties in France (public law on associations of July 1, 1901 and subsequent applications). Includes Fifth Republic reforms, through 1964 on such matters as regulation of electoral campaigns by judiciary. Good bibliography, list of laws and decrees for Fifth Republic.

1037 KHELIFA, LAROUSSI. Manuel du militant algérien. Lausanne, La Cité, 1962. 300 p. (Collection "Contribution")

Slightly expanded version of 1957 manual for militants in Algerian liberation struggle giving information about F.L.N. and other nationalist organs, history of Algeria and description of its resources, and history of Algerian nationalism, with post-independence prospects. Manual also gives rudimentary information about political institutions in other countries.

1038 KHROUCHTCHEV EN FRANCE. Paris, Editions de la Librairie du Globe, 1960. 359 p. illus., ports., double map.

French journalist Pierre Hentgen's chronicle of daily events and description of atmosphere during Khrushchev's stay in France, March 23 - April 4, 1960, reproducing Khrushchev's speeches and remarks in extenso in translation, with text of final official communiqué. Many photographs.

1039 KHRUSHCHEV, NIKITA SERGEEVICH. Déclarations et conférence de presse, Paris, 14-19 Mai 1960. Paris, 1960. 31 p. (Collection "Etudes soviétiques") "Supplément à Etudes soviétiques no. 146."

Texts of speeches and press conference at stop-over in France after failure of summit conference.

1040 KHRUSHCHEV, NIKITA SERGEEVICH. Peace in Europe—peace throughout the world; speech of N. S. Khrushchov on the results of his visit to France, at a meeting of Moscow working people, April 4, 1960. London, Soviet Booklets, 1960. 13 p. illus. (Soviet booklet no. 70)

Informal summary of his talks with de Gaulle on Germany, Franco-Russian cooperation, description of his travel impressions.

1041 KRAFT, JOSEPH. The struggle for Algeria. 1st ed. Garden City, N.Y., Doubleday, 1961. 263 p. maps.

American journalist's balanced account of Algerian struggle as seen by settlers, Algerian nationalists, French army, and as reflected in French politics. Author was Algerian reporter for New York Times, London Observer, 1952-1961.

1042 KREBS, KURT. Frankreichs Landwirtschaft in der Europäischen Gemeinschaft. Als Vortag gehalten vor der deutsch-französischen Parlamentarier-Vereinigung des Deutschen Bundestages, Februar 1963. Frankfurt am Main, DLG-Verlag, 1963. 64 p.

Changes in agricultural sector of French Third and Fourth Plan to accommodate Common Market provisions for agricultural products and laws enacted to facilitate transition, 1960-1963. Position of French farmers toward British participation in Common Market is identified.

1043 KULSKI, WLADYSLAW WSZEBOR. De Gaulle and the world; the foreign policy of the Fifth French Republic. [1st ed.] Syracuse, N.Y, Syracuse University Press, 1966. xxi, 428 p. Bibliography: p. 415-420.

Cogent, well-rounded and carefully documented presentation of French international relations under de Gaulle by American scholar and former Polish diplomat, whose research brought him to France 1961-1962, 1965. Book covers de Gaulle's personal philosophy on world affairs, popular sentiments on de Gaulle's views, and evolution and status as of early 1966 of nuclear policy, relations with NATO, Common Market and British membership, Franco-Soviet and Franco-German relations, cooperation with U.N. and underdeveloped countries. Excellent bibliography for major works on Fifth Republic and extensive annotations.

1044 KUNTZ, FRANCOIS. L'officier français dans la nation. Paris, C. Lavauzelle, 1960. xxii, 184 p.

History of officers' relations with nation as a whole from Monarchy to 1939, with epilogue on current (Dec. 1959) integration of officers into national consensus. Author presented this material as lectures before Ecole nationale des officiers de réserve d'Etat Major and is optimistic about officers' acceptance of Gaullist policy in Algeria.

1045 LABIN, SUZANNE. De Gaulle, ou la France enchaînée. Paris, 1965. 39 p.

Critical survey of French relations with communist countries (all improving) and with U.S., England, Germany, NATO, and Common Market (all deteriorating) and indicating a drift into communist camp. Author motivates de Gaulle's foreign policy by his prejudice against U.S. and his personal ambitions and demonstrates that alliance with U.S. fails to endanger French national independence.

1044a KUTZNETSOV, VITALII NIKOLAEVICH. Razvitie marksistskoi filosofii vo Frantsii posle Vtoroi Mirovoi voiny, 1945-1966 gg.; lektsiia. Moskva, Izd-vo Mockovskogo Universiteta, 1962. 62 p. Includes bibliography.

Controversies on Marxist theory and evaluation of Soviet Union involving French Communisty Party figures and Communist intellectuals since World War II.

1046 LACHERAF, MOSTEFA. L'Algérie: nation et société. Paris, F. Maspero, 1965. 346 p. (Cahiers libres, 71-72) Includes bibliography.

Historical and political studies on Algeria, 1830-1963, originally published in "Temps Modernes," "Cahiers internationaux," "Esprit," "Vérité et Liberté," and "El Moudjahid" of which author was editor immediately after independence.

1047 LACOSTE, ROBERT. Views of the French administration on its intentions for Algeria. New York, 1957. 5 l. (Algerian Front of National Liberation Delegation. Publications, series B, no. 4)

FOR ADDITIONAL WORKS BY AND ABOUT ROBERT LACOSTE, SEE AUTHOR INDEX

1048 LACOSTE, YVES, and ANDRE NOUSCHI. L'Algérie, passé et présent; le cadre et les étapes de la constitution de l'Algérie actuelle. By André Nouschi, préf. de Jean Dresch. Paris, Editions sociales, 1960. 462 p. diagrs. Includes bibliographies.

After an inventory of country's attributes and resources for agriculture and industry, history is traced back to pre-Roman times, and stops with 1919. Wealth of detail on pre-colonial era aims to shatter "official legend" that Algeria was nothing before French settlers turned it into productive society.

1049 LACOSTE LAREYMONDIE, MARC DE. Mirages et réalités; l'arme nucléaire française. Paris, Editions de la Serpe, 1964. 215 p. tables, diagrs.

History of French nuclear efforts, 1945-1963 and simple technical description of worldwide nuclear armament and nuclear strategy. French military policy and objectives for 1970 are criticized as unrealistic. Author was directly involved in French nuclear military effort.

1050 LACOUTURE, JEAN. Cinq hommes et la France. Paris, Editions du Seuil, 1961. 370 p.

Political biographies of Ho-Chi-Minh, Habib Bourguiba, Ferhat Abbas, Mohammed V, Sékou Touré and their current relations with France and de Gaulle personally.

1051 LACOUTURE, JEAN. De Gaulle. Paris, Editions du Seuil, 1965. 188 p. illus., ports. (Le temps qui court, 38) Includes bibliography.

Journalist's mildly critical interpretation of de Gaulle's historical role, last two chapters dealing specifically with Fifth Republic and giving a balanced psychological and political summation. Chronology of de Gaulle's life through 1965, good illustrations.

1052 LACROIX, JEAN. Marxisme, existentialisme, personnalisme; présence de l'éternité dans le temps. 5. éd. Paris, Presses universitaires de France, 1962. 1949. 123 p. (Bibliothèque de philosophie contemporaine. Histoire de la philosophie et philosophie générale)

Philosopher's essays on main strands of contemporary French philosophy.

1053 LAFAY, BERNARD. La France retrouvée: de l'impuissance à l'efficacité. Paris, Plon, 1958. 124 p. (Tribune libre, 38)

Editorials in "Bulletin du Centre Républicain" and weekly "L'Heure de Paris" in which deputy from Paris follows collapse of Fourth Republic, Oct. 1956 - May 1958 in terms of North African crises, foreign policy, institutional weaknesses. Concluding section for May 15 - July 14, 1958 expresses confidence in de Gaulle's restoration of French unity.

1054 LAGAILLARDE, PIERRE (defendant). "On a triché avec l'honneur." Texte intégral de l'interrogatoire et de la plaidoirie des audiences des 15 et 16 novembre 1960 du procès des "Barricades." Préf. de Jean Gallot. Paris, Table ronde, 1961. 204 p. port. (on cover) (Collection "L'Ordre du jour")

Pierre Lagaillarde, deputy from Algiers since 1958, in his statement before the court, explains his actions from 1957 to his organization of student revolt in Alger in Jan. 1960, in particular his role in the Comité du Salut Public, May 1958, and his parliamentary activities, as well as those of the other Algerian deputies. Defendant fled to Spain while on parole.

FOR ADDITIONAL WORKS ABOUT PIERRE LABAILLARDE, SEE AUTHOR INDEX

1055 LA GORCE, PAUL MARIE DE. De Gaulle entre deux mondes; une vie et une époque. Paris, Fayard, 1964. 766 p. (Les Grandes études contemporaines) Includes bibliography.

Best documented, comprehensive, and impartial work on de Gaulle published so far, written by political journalist specializing in military affairs. De Gaulle's political personality, life, philosophy, political conduct are situated within an informed account of France's evolution between World War I and 1964 into a highly industrialized state. The pre-World War II years, de Gaulle's wartime role, his R.P.F. experiment, his return to power, and his policies in Fifth Republic (Algeria, political institutions, foreign policy, economic policy) are covered in equal detail. No footnotes or index, sources for each section. For critical review of this work, see no. 593.

1056 LA GORCE, PAUL MARIE DE. La France pauvre. Paris, B. Grasset, 1965. 287 p.

Popular work on plight of special groups of poverty-stricken— the old, immigrants, small farmers and merchants.

1057 LA GORCE, PAUL MARIE DE. La République et son armée. Paris, Fayard, 1963. 708 p. (Les Grandes études contemporaines) Includes bibliography.

Final 150 pages of this history of French army's political personality and involvement in French political life cover Algerian war, participation in and acceptance of philosophy of May 1958 uprising, and reluctant acceptance of defeat in Algeria. English translation is entitled "The French Army; A Military-Political History" (New York, 1963.)

1058 LA LANDE DE CALAN, PIERRE DE, VICOMTE. Renaissance des libertés économiques et sociales. Préf. de Henri Fayol. Paris, Plon, 1963. 327 p.

Study group's justification of free enterprise for contemporary French economy without rejecting society's regulatory and compensatory social responsibility. Proposals for economic democratization through blurring of ownership and employee function within the firm (e.g., Bloch-Lainé's) are rejected in favor of proposals strengthening owner's and workers' proper responsibilities. Government's function is seen as supporter of individual initiative.

1059 LA MALENE, CHRISTIAN DE. La politique extérieure de la France; rapport. Secrétariat général du Conseil national et des Assises nationales, 1963. 56 p.

Speech at U.N.R.-U.D.T. 3rd Assises Nationales, Nice, Nov. 1963, on major elements of Gaullist foreign policy: European unification, Atlantic Alliance, relations with East.

1060 LA MALFA, UGO. Contro l'Europa di de Gaulle; scritti e discorsi a cura di Adolfo Battaglia. Milano, Edizioni di Comunità, 1964. 201 p. (Cultura e realtà, 64)

Speeches in parliament and articles in "Voce repubblicana" (1954-1964) commenting on defeat of European Defense Community and subsequent obstacles put into path of European unification by de Gaulle since his return to power, identifying his nationalist authoritarianism as the most dangerous enemy for European democracy and proposing substitution of Great Britain for France as a member of the European Economic Community. In his lengthy introduction, Adolfo Battaglia emphasizes that de Gaulle has effectively side-tracked European unification.

1061 LAMBERT, DENIS; WERTHEIMER, MARCEL. La paupérisation du secteur traditionnel et les options de croissance de l'économie algérienne, Marcel Wertheimer: Des progrès massifs et rapides sont-ils possibles en milieu agricole traditionnel? Présenté par Maurice Byé. Paris, Presses universitaires de France, 1962. 112 p. (Etudes Tiers monde; problèmes des pays sous-développés)

Both monographs deal with problems of pre-independence Algeria. Lambert argues for giving priority to expansion of traditional agricultural sector in contrast to Constantine Plan. Wertheimer describes efforts of Services agricoles de Grande-Kabylie to improve wheat production. Appendix lists official studies on Algerian economic development.

1062 LA MORANDIERE, F. PORTEU DE. La révolution en sursis; vers une république à trois ordres. Paris, Nouvelles éditions latines, 1961. 188 p.

Analysis of communist revolutionary methods and needed Christian-democratic counterforces, with program for new French political institutions. De Gaulle's government brought only breathing spell, no real reforms.

1063 LAMOUR, PHILIPPE. 60 millions de Français. Paris, Buchet/Chastel, 1967. 305 p. (Ce siècle)

Published version of television program by prominent figure in regional development (notably that of the Rhône Valley) on long-range plans for an economy of sixty million Frenchmen. First part discusses types of growth in industry, agriculture, and service trades most compatible with modern technology, with perceptive sections on housing, tourism, conservation of natural and human resources. Second part concentrates on development of major regions: the Paris area, the North-East, South, and West, while final section raises question of how to administer and finance regional development.

1064 LANCE, PIERRE. Charles de Gaulle, ce chrétien nietzschéen. Paris, Septième aurore, 1965. 170 p.

De Gaulle's writings are dissected to prove his spiritual affinity with Nietzsche's superman. Author sees conflict between Nietzschean conception of French grandeur and Christian-Socialist orientation of his domestic policy (social welfare without far-reaching changes in French social structure), while profound social changes alone would permit realization of political aims.

1065 LANCELOT, ALAIN; ADAM GERARD. Les groupes de pression. I. La pression des groupes, by Alain Lancelot. II. Les organisations syndicales, by Gérard Adam. Paris, 1960. 18 l (Fondation nationale des sciences politiques. Cycle supérieur d'études politiques. Guide de recherches, no. 1) Includes bibliographies.

Review of current research on pressure groups in general and trade unions in particular, with short up-to-date bibliographies.

1066 LANCELOT, MARIE-THERESE. L'étude des administrations publiques en France. Paris, 1960. 19 l. (Fondation nationale des sciences politiques. Cycle supérieur d'études politiques. Guide de recherches, no. 4)

Review of current research on public administration under Fourth and Fifth Republic: books, periodicals, basic documentary sources, study groups.

1067 LANCELOT, MARIE-THERESE. L'Organisation armée secrète; chronologie. Paris, 1963. 2 v. tables. (Fondation nationale des sciences politiques. Centre d'étude de la vie politique française. Série "Documents" no. 2)

V 1 gives chronology of political events, Jan. 1961 - Nov. 1962 O. A. S. action in Algeria and France, anti-O. A. S. countermeasures, v. 2 reproduces chronologically O. A. S. and anti-O. A. S. leaflets, proclamations, and letters, lists victims of O. A. S. attacks by political party and newspaper affiliation.

1068 LANDA, ROBERT GRIGOR'EVICH. Natsional'no-osvoboditel'noe dvizhenie v Alzhire, 1939-1966 gg. Moskva, Izd-vo vostochnoi lit-ry, 1962. 289 p. Includes bibliography.

History of Algerian national liberation movement, 1939-1962, based on standard French literature and Algerian newspapers. Carefully annotated with good bibliography.

1069 LANGLOIS, WALTER G. André Malraux: the Indochina adventure. New York, Praeger, 1966. ix, 259 p. Bibliographical references included in "Notes" (p. 231-252)

Reconstruction of Malraux's expedition to Indochina in the 1920's and its role in laying the foundation for his anticolonial philosophy.

1070 LANGROD, JERZY STEFAN. Some current problems of administration in France today. San Juan, Puerto Rico, School of Public Administration, 1961. 152 p. (Studies in Foreign and comparative public Administration) ML

Based on 1957 lectures, with appendix outlining trends initiated in first months of Fifth Republic and relevant decrees.

1071 LAPONCE, J. A. The government of the Fifth Republic; French political parties and the Constitution. Berkeley, University of California Press, 1961. 415 p. illus., tables. Bibliography: p. 387-400.

Systematic survey of Fifth Republic's new institutions and clear explanation of their actual operation in the first two years. The functioning of the branches of government and of election system, status of major political parties is analyzed with various tabulations.

1072 LAROCHE, FABRICE and FRANÇOIS D'ORCIVAL. Le courage est leur patrie. Paris, Editions Saint-Just, 1965. 238 p. (Collection "Action")

Sketches and episodes portraying dozens of O. A. S. activitists as true revolutionaries of the 1960's. Authors show participation of men outside France, support for O. A. S. from United States. Episodes illustrate connivance of government, police, communists. Laroche is connected with several French nationalist publications (see nos. 1873, 1938, 1940).

1073 LAROCHE, FABRICE. Salan devant l'opinion. Paris, Editions Saint-Just, 1963. 204 p. illus., ports., facsims.

Short biography of General Salan, followed by detailed account of his rôle in Algeria May-June 1958, Sept. 1960-April 1962, his arrest and trial. Author emphasizes general's political vacillations as illustrated in his relations with de Gaulle, Susini, O. A. S. movement. Appendix cites documents on 1957 Bazooka Affair.

1074 LAROCQUE-LATOUR, JACQUES DE. Journal d'un embastillé. By Coral [pseud.]. Paris, Société de presse et d'éditions Saint-Just, 1962. 1 v. of illus.

Cartoons and narrative relating author's arrest, court experiences and year in Bastille prison, June 1961-1962 for participation in so-called "Complot de Paris" at time of April 1961 generals' putsch in Algeria. Events outside prison, such as final stages of Algerian war and height of O. A. S. violence in Paris, are seen through eyes of prisoners. For account of Complot de Paris trial, see Cottaz (no. 410).

1075 LAROCQUE-LATOUR, JACQUES DE. Journal d'un suspect. By Coral [pseud.]. Paris, Editions Saint-Just, 1964. 1 v. of illus. (unpaged)

Continuation of "Journal d'un embastillé" commenting on current events July 1962 - Dec. 1963 by cartoons and text, with emphasis on political trials, chaos in Algeria.

1076 LAROQUE, PIERRE (ed.). Succès et faiblesse de l'effort social français. By Suzanne Grévisse, et al. Préf. et conclusion de Pierre Laroque. Ouvrage publié sous le patronage de la Fondation nationale des sciences politiques. Paris, A. Colin, 1961. 366 p. Bibliography: p. 351-356.

First section examines Fourth and Fifth Republic's social policy and legislation (health, housing, childhood and old age, education, etc.) with numerous tabulations; second part summarizes labor and agricultural policy; final section describes organs and financing of social policy. Extensive bibliography of government documents, periodicals in these areas. Subject index.

1077 LAROUSSE, PIERRE. Petit Larousse; dictionnaire encyclopédique pour tous. Paris, Larousse, 1966. 1795 p. illus. (part col.) ports., maps (part col.) diagrs.

Dictionary brought up to date, with maps of new (1965) departments for Paris area and new French road and airline maps.

1077a LARTEGUY, JEAN. The centurions; tr. from the French by Xan Fielding. 1st ed. New York, E. P. Dutton, 1962. 487 p. ML

Novel of experiences of professional officers - the centurions - fighting for lost causes in Indochina and Algeria, and finally, in their frustration, rising up against French political institutions. "Les prétoriens" (see no. 1079) is a direct sequel. Original French "Les centurions" (Paris, 1960) is not available at Hoover or ML.

1077b LARTEGUY, JEAN. Les dieux meurent en Algérie. Texte de Jean Lartéguy; photos de Marc Flament. Paris, Editions de la pensée moderne, 1960. 1 v. (chiefly illus.) ML

Captions to war scenes by Lartéguy underline degradation brought by war to both French Army and Algerian population and the disintegration of traditional ways.

1078 LARTEGUY, JEAN. Un million de dollars le Viet; la seconde guerre d'Indochine. Evreux, R. Solar, 1965. 317 p. illus.

Based on reportage for "Paris-Match" dealing with journalist and novelist's return visit to Vietnam in autumn 1965, with interesting parallels between this conflict and Algerian war, criticisms of both U. S. and Gaullist policy in Southeast Asia.

1079 LARTEGUY, JEAN. Les prétoriens. Paris, Presses de la cité, 1961. 325 p.

Novelist draws sympathetic picture of group of parachute officers who in historic setting of May 1958 in Algeria (many historical figures such as Salan are also introduced) play a major role in bringing de Gaulle back to power and come close to making government accept integration as practical objective. Background figures include French-Algerian politicians, Algerian nationalists, French Leftists, and other military elements. Story gives glimpses of Algerian war up to end of 1960. This well-written novel was probably the most widely read work of fiction on Algeria. It continues author's "Les centurions" (1077a).

1080 LATTRE, ANDRE DE. Les finances extérieures de la France (1945-1958). Paris, Presses universitaires de France, 1959. xv, 391 p.

Careful study of new mechanisms for international monetary transactions elaborated during Fourth Republic (capital movements, balance of payments shifts) and government controls, as well as international, intra-European, and American efforts through military and economic aid to achieve stabilization of French international balance. Author sees preconditions for balanced accounts achieved under de Gaulle.

1081 LATTRE, ANDRE DE. Politique économique de la France depuis 1945... Paris, Sirey, 1966. 522 p. (Politiques économiques)

Survey of French economic policy, 1945-65, based on elementary course at Institute d'études politiques, Paris. Mechanisms and organs of government control over economy (budgetary, fiscal, and credit policy, wage and price policy) and specific areas of intervention in structure of economy (housing, agriculture, foreign trade capital movement, exchange rates) are examined. Final section summarizes over-all economic history of period.

1082 LAUBADERE, ANDRE DE. Traité élémentaire de droit administratif. 1. éd. entièrement refondue. Paris. Librairie générale de droit et de jurisprudence, R. Pichon et R. Durand-Auzias, 1957. 823 p. Bibliographical footnotes.

Supplement covers constitutional provisions and organic laws affecting administrative law as a result of transfering regulatory authority to Prime Minister, as well as other specific innovations in public law.

1083 LAUDRAIN, MAURICE. La voie française du socialisme; postface de Jacques Duboin. Paris, Maison du livre français, 1963. 142 p.

Attempt to adapt socialist philosophy to an era of automation and affluence through socialized income, state planning, unions of producers and unions of consumers as basic political organizations. First part of book retraces history of French labor movement, second reproduces dialogue with French Communist on points of agreement and difference. Work appeared originally in the 1961 issues of "La grande relève," organ of the Mouvement français pour l'abondance, headed by Jacques Duboin. See also "Perspectives syndicalistes" edited by Laudrain (no. 2048).

1084 LAUNAY, MICHEL. Paysans algériens; la terre, la vigne, et les hommes. Paris, Editions du Seuil, 1963. 430 p.

Description of life of Algerian farmers, Moslem and European, at eve of independence. Author writes from personal observation during military service in Oran region, 1960-1961, and confronts his own impressions with findings of economists, sociologists, and agronomists.

1085 LAURAT, LUCIEN. Frankreichs Weg von der Vierten zur Fünften Republik. Lübeck, M. Schmidt-Römhild, 1960. 91 p. (Zeitgeschehen in historischer Sicht, Heft 5)

French journalist's and socialist politician's explanation of collapse of Fourth Republic through continuing economic and political crises and popular disaffection, much of which is blamed on Communist influence (Mitterand and Mendès-France are characterized as Communist sympathizers, in contrast to S.F.I.O leaders) and praise of Gaullist regime as carrying out Socialist policies of gradual decolonization, European integration, combined with constitutional reform and financial stability.

1086 LAURENT, JACQUES. L'Algérie quand on y est ... By Cecil Saint Laurent [pseud.]. Paris, Livre contemporain, 1958. 246 p.

Slightly fictionalized reportage on psychological climate in Algiers, among troops and in villages of Kabylia in the Spring of 1958, emphasizing friendly relations between Europeans and Moslems to give lie to pessimistic views of French Left and Americans.

1087 LAURENT, JACQUES. Année 40, Londres, De Gaulle, Vichy. Avec la collaboration de Gabriel Jeantet. Paris, La Table ronde, 1965. iv, 414 p. (L'Histoire contemporaine revue et corrigée)

Collection of texts (mainly from published sources) aiming to demonstrate de Gaulle's personal and political motivations other than patriotism in shaping Free French resistance movement and in refusing credit to independently operating resistance inside France, which Vichy government was tacitly supporting.

1088 LAURENT, JACQUES. Mauriac sous de Gaulle. Paris, Table ronde, 1964. 218 p.

Witty polemic over Mauriac's adulatory biography of de Gaulle (no. 1198) taking him to task for his interpretation of recent French history, in which de Gaulle is cast as savior, while Laurent sees nothing significant in any of de Gaulle's actions. De Gaulle is accused of making all of Vichy seem sinful for the very purpose of appearing a savior and applying the same technique in ending Algerian conflict. For this work Laurent was tried for offense to the head of state (see no. 1089).

1089 LAURENT, JACQUES (defendant). Offenses au chef de l'Etat, audiences des 8 et 9 octobre 1965. Paris, Table ronde, 1965. 199 p.

Trial before Tribunal de grande instance de la Seine of Laurent and his publisher for "Mauriac sous de Gaulle" (see above) whose offensive passages are cited extensively and defended by author. Among defense witnesses are many left-wing writers, presidential candidates Tixier-Vignancour and Pierre Marcilhacy, but Mauriac himself declined to appear. Laurent was convicted.

1090 LAURET, RENE. Notre voisin l'Allemand; deux peuples s'affrontent. Paris, Nouvelles éditions latines, 1960. 217 p. (Collection Le XXme siècle) Bibliographical footnotes.

History and current trends in Franco-German relations, with appeals for complete reconciliation. English edition is "France and Germany; the legacy of Charlemagne" (Chicago, Regnery, 1964).

1091 LAURIOL, MARC. L'Algérie angoissée. Alger, Editions Baconnier, 1956. 81 p.

Algerian-born politician's view of Algerian alternatives - integration or withdrawal - in which author explains psychology of European settlers in Algeria to metropolitan French.

1092 LAURIOL, MARC and PHILIPPE MARÇAIS. Au service de l'Algérie française nouvelle. Alger, Impr. Baconnier frères, 1960. 192 p.

Authors' interventions in National Assembly and newspaper articles Dec. 1958 - Jan. 1960 on the themes of French-Algerian unity and Algerian financial problems. Authors were deputies for Algiers and members of parliamentary group "Unité de la République." In appendix report of Algerian deputies, Jan. 1959, on measures for promoting integration.

1093 LAURIOL, MARC. Le Fédéralisme et l'Algérie. Paris, La Fédération, 1957. 37 p. (Comité d'action pour une République fédérale française)

Institutional solution for keeping Algeria French while respecting Moslem and European settlers' autonomy through personal rather than territorial federalism.

1094 LAURIOL, MARC. La politique extérieure de la France en face de la politique mondiale; texte de l'exposé fait à la 24e réunion du Bureau d'études du C.E.P.E.C. le 28 janvier 1964. Paris, Centre d'études politiques et civiques, 1964. 31 p. (Dossiers du CEPEC, 17)

Speech before Centre d'études politiques et civiques (of which General Weygand is honorary president) attacking de Gaulle for underestimating the strength of communist ideology and mistakingly weakening the Atlantic Alliance by seeking reconciliation with U.S.S.R.

1095 LA VARDIERE (commandant). Pour une armée nouvelle, moderne, efficace, française. Paris, Charles-Lavauzelle, 1957. 161 p. tables, diagrs. (part fold.)

Staff officer's detailed proposal for military reorganization, with special plans for establishment of civilian and auxiliary defense forces and a new type of African army.

1096 LAVERGNE, BERNARD. L'hégémonie du consommateur; vers une rénovation de la science économique. 1 éd. Paris, Presses universitaires de France, 1958. 359 p. Bibliographical footnotes.

Economist's critique of classical and neo-classical economic theories of value and production, followed by case for consumer-directed cooperative socialism, which would be the economic equivalent of universal suffrage in a political democracy.

1097 LAVERGNE, BERNARD. Essor et décadence des idées politiques et sociales en France de 1900 à nos jours; souvenirs personnels. Paris, Fischbacher, 1965. 258 p.

Personal reactions of economist and political scientist to events on political scene (French and international) in his lifetime. For post-war era, author traces genesis of East-West conflict, European unification, and explains his personal opposition to dominant orientation on these issues in Fourth Republic, but approval of de Gaulle's conceptions.

1098 LAVERGNE, BERNARD. Problèmes africains; Afrique noire - Algérie - Affaire de Suez. Paris, Larose, 1957. 118 p. Bibliographical footnotes.

Includes discussion on "Algerian problem without illusion" as of mid-1957, in which author sees withdrawal of French to stronghold in Oran and control of corridor to Saharan oil as only realistic way out of never-ending pacification. Algeria is regarded as an economic burden, integration incompatible with Moslem hostility, internal autonomy for most of Algeria as only solution.

1099 LAVIE, LOUIS. Le drame algérien, ou la dernière chance de la France. 3. éd. complétée. Alger, Editions Baconnier, 1956. 140 p. tables.

French-Algerian's arguments supporting Soustelle's position on integration aimed at French public opinion before Jan. 1956 elections.

1100 LAZAREFF, SERGE. Le statut des forces de l'O.T.A.N. et son application en France. Préf. de Charles Rousseau. Paris, A. Pedone, 1964. 548 p. Includes bibliography.

November 1950 agreements and subsequent legal decisions regarding status of NATO military personnel stationed in France.

1101 LEAGUE OF RED CROSS SOCIETIES. Relief action for Algerian refugees in Tunisia and Morocco, 1959-1962; final report. [Report by Marcel Erdmer.] Geneva, 1963. 39 p. illus., map (on lining papers)

Figures on relief operations by several national Red Cross societies and U.N. High Commissioner for Refugees, and information on repatriation assistance after Evian agreement to 120,000 Algerian refugees in Tunisia and another 60,000 in Morocco. Tables give figures for donations from national Red Cross societies and other philanthropic organizations.

1102 LEBESQUE, MORVAN. La loi et le système; chroniques du Canard. Paris, Editions du Seuil, 1965. 312 p. (Collection "L'Histoire immédiate")

Comments on current political and cultural events at home and abroad, mainly 1958-1965, by columnist from satirical weekly "Canard enchaîné," in which articles were originally published.

1103 LE BOURRE, RAYMOND. Le syndicalisme français dans la Ve République. Paris, Calmann-Lévy, 1959. 212 p. (Questions d'actualité)

National secretary of Force Ouvrière, who was instrumental in its splitting off from C.G.T. in 1947, welcomes weakening of political parties under Fifth Republic and encourages unions to press for greater economic democracy and move from a revolutionary ideology to a constructive reformism which accepts both private and collective ownership. Author sheds interesting light on trade unions' unwillingness to support popular front to save Fourth Republic.

1104 LE BRUN, PIERRE. Questions actuelles du syndicalisme. Paris, Editions du Seuil, 1965. 171 p. (L'Histoire immédiate)

Secretary of C.G.T. and member of Conseil économique et social gives personal views on the relative pauperization of the laboring class, the role of trade unions in the national planning process and alternatives for the Fifth Plan options submitted by the government, the proper relation between organized labor and political parties, and steps to accelerate the unification of the fragmented French labor movement. Le Brun, though critical of current economic policies, supports de Gaulle's foreign policies.

1105 LE CALONNEC, J. F. La France et "moi;" ce que de Gaulle pense de la démocratie. Paris, Témoignage chrétien, 1962. 191 p. (Bibliothèque de l'homme d'action)

Book concluded summer 1962 retraces de Gaulle's attitude toward democracy in its widest sense through writings, speeches, actions. De Gaulle's basic democratic faith, stand on political, social, and economic democracy are fairly evaluated and documented. The author's conclusion is that de Gaulle's political philosophy is unlikely to foster French democracy.

1106 LECERF, JEAN. Histoire de l'unité européenne; préf. de Jean Monnet. Paris, Gallimard, 1965. 382 p. (Collection idées)

Popular work on formation of Common Market, Fouchet plan for political union, British membership, membership for associated states, current trends and prospects. Good non-technical bibliography.

1107 LECERF, JEAN. La percée de l'économie française. Postface de Raymond Aron. Paris, Arthaud, 1963. 349 p. illus. (Collection Notre temps, 6) Includes bibliography.

Journalist-economist's history of French economy under different governments from end of World War II through end of Algerian conflict. Aron's postscript evaluates causes for French achievements, prospects for continued 4-5% annual growth, role of planning and Common market as stimulants.

1108 LECOEUR, AUGUSTE. Le partisan. Paris, Flammarion, 1963. 313 p. (L'Actuel)

Political autobiography 1939-1962 of one-time presumptive heir to Thorez, who left French Communist Party in 1955, founding dissenting organ "La Nation socialiste." (See no. 2014.) Final chapters deal with years of de-stalinization and his own integration in Socialist Party during Fifth Republic.

1109 LECTURES FRANÇAISES (periodical). L'Assemblée introuvable; le trombinoscope de la Vème bis. Dessiné par Pinatel.

Paris, 1963. 192 p. illus. Special issue.

Biographies of deputies in National Assembly elected Nov. 1962, preceded by malicious sketches of new Cabinet members and short identification of all political parties and groups of which deputies are members (extracted from Henri Coston's "Partis politiques..." no. 407).

1110 LECTURES FRANÇAISES (periodical). François Mitterand; ou, "Cet homme est dangereux." Paris, 1958. 93 p. "Numéro spécial, octobre 1958."

Collection of articles on Mitterand tracing his political career and involvement in the "affaire des fuites" during his service as Minister of Justice (1957) giving his stand on Algeria and defense of Fourth Republic in May 1958, as well as his willingness to resurrect a popular Front with the communists in September 1958, with the hope of becoming head of the government himself.

1111 LECTURES FRANÇAISES (periodical). Les nouveaux messieurs; les pour et les contre de l'élection présidentielle. Paris, 1966. 64 p. "10e année, no. 106-107, janvier-février 1966."

Biographies of newly appointed Cabinet members, figures for first and second round of presidential election by political affiliation of voters as compared to 1958 election, and lists of persons and organizations supporting different presidential candidates in first and second round, as well as stand of political press during campaign.

1112 LEFEVRE, BERNARD. L'Occident en péril. Paris, Nouvelles éditions latines, 1961. 169 p.

Writing in Paris prison fall of 1960 (for his participation in Jan. 1960 Algerian rebellion) French Algerian politician describes aims and methods of international communist conspiracy in Europe, Asia, and Africa, with considerable details for Algeria. In his crusade against both Marxism and liberalism, Lefèvre envisions a Christian corporate state, for which he gives a constitution and social program. Solution for Algerian problem is seen within framework of a French corporate state.

1113 LEFEVRE, BERNARD. Sur le chemin de la restauration. Paris, Nouvelles éditions latines, 1959. 254 p. "Bibliographie": p. 247-251.

Amplification of principles of a corporative order underlying "Manifesto of 14," promulgated in July 1958 by Algerian Comité du Salut Public, of which author was a member. Program includes elimination of political parties, regional government by communities and professional organizations, a decentralized colonial empire. Opponent of Marxism and liberalism is inspired by political philosophy of Salazar, Catholic integrists.

1114 LEITES, NATHAN CONSTANTIN. The "Europe" of the French. Santa Monica, Calif., Rand Corp., 1965. ix, 41 p. (Rand Corporation Memorandum RM-4584-ISA) Bibliographical footnotes.

Public sentiment on European unification as reflected in public opinion studies, "Le Monde," and "La Nation." Author points to declining nationalist fervor among Gaullists, acceptance of European statehood in principle, but lukewarm popular attitude about steps toward achieving it in near future.

1115 LEITES, NATHAN CONSTANTIN. On the game of politics in France. Unedited advance copy. Santa Monica, Calif., Rand Corp., 1958. v, 181 p. (Rand Corporation Research memorandum, RM-2187-RC) Bibliographical references included in "Notes" (p. 163-181)

Study made for Rand Corporation to disengage rules governing Fourth Republic's parliamentary system in its last years. Malfunctioning of system, i.e., its incapacity to take responsible action, is exemplified, but there is no explicit prediction of its imminent collapse or how it might come about, although manuscript was written Feb.-May 1958. Also issued in slightly different form in French under title "Du malaise politique en France (Paris, Plon, 1958).

1116 LEITES, NATHAN CONSTANTIN. On the game of politics in France. With a foreword by D. W. Brogan. Stanford, Stanford University Press, 1959. xiii, 190 p. Bibliography included in "Notes" (p. 169-181).

In book form, this version reproduces original English text but has June 1958 epilogue following through collapse of parliamentary system and approval of de Gaulle by National Assembly as further evidence of one of the previously analyzed rules of the game, the resort to a "force majeure" for introducing drastic change.

1117 LEMAIGNEN, ROBERT. L'Europe au berceau; souvenirs d'un technocrate. Paris, Plon, 1964. 219 p.

Personal account of author's work as French representative, together with Robert Marjolin, on 9-member Commission of the European Economic Community, the Common Market's executive organ, 1958-1961. Work involved considerable dealings with French politicians in elaboration of French economic European policy.

1118 LENNE, RAPHAEL. Charles de Gaulle, der Erleuchtete. München, Rütten and Loening, 1965. 270 p. ports. Includes bibliography.

Using as sources historians favorable to Pétain, author examines de Gaulle's military and political activities 1940-1945 and leads up to a portrait of a neurotic paranoiac like Hitler, acting out his own psychological needs in his conflicts with friendly nations and statesmen rather than pursuing France's best interests.

1119 LENTIN, ALBERT PAUL. L'Algérie des colonels; journal d'un témoin juin - octobre 1958. Paris, Editeurs Français Réunis, 1958. 98 p. (Petite bibliothèque républicaine)

Algerian-born left-wing journalist's eyewitness account of de Gaulle's first visit to Algeria, his consultations with military leaders and members of Public Safety Committee, and his later trips before September referendum and Constantine speech. Some parts were originally published in "Libération" and "Temps Modernes."

1120 LENTIN, ALBERT PAUL. L'Algérie entre deux mondes. V. 1 Le dernier quart d'heure. Paris, R. Julliard, 1963. 321 p.

"France-Observateur" reporter's eyewitness account of last stages of Algerian decolonization. So far only this first volume, following developments from Nov. 1960 - May 1961, has been published. Author has intimate acquaintance with different segments of Algerian society, ranging from "pieds-noirs," politicians, and students, to Moslems and F.L.N. leaders, as these groups edge closer to the abyss. Political events covered in detail are Jan. 1961 referendum, negotiations with F.L.N., crisis in army.

1121 LENTIN, ALBERT PAUL. Blackmail or partition. New York, 1961. 6 l (Delegation of the Provisional Government of the Algerian Republic, N.Y., Dec. 61-36-5)

1122 LE PREVOST, JACQUES. Défense de l'Algérie. Alger, Librairie Dominique, 1957. 197 p.

Current events radio broadcasts on Radio-Algérie Sept. 1956-July 1957 commenting mainly on North African affairs and U.N. repercussions and defending French in Algeria and French army against foreign and domestic critics.

1123 LERICHE, JOSEPH. Les Algériens parmi nous; essai psycho-sociologique d'après les enquêtes et travaux des Etudes sociales nord-africaines. Paris, Editions sociales françaises, 1959. 231 p. Bibliographical footnotes.

History of North African immigration, investigation of Algerian immigrants' psychology, living and working conditions, permanence of implantation in France, and effectiveness of government and employer measures to facilitate their adaptation to French life.

1124 LERNER, DANIEL, ed. and RAYMOND ARON, ed. France defeats EDC. New York, F. A. Praeger, 1957. xii, 225 p. Bibliographical footnotes.

A study of political attitudes on foreign and military policy in parliament, among political parties and public opinion as illustrated by the defeat of the European Defense Community. Individual chapters are by French political scientists Raymond Aron, Jacques Fauvet, Alfred Grosser, Stanley Hoffmann, Jean José Marchand, Jean Stoetzel, and André Philip. French version "La querelle de la C. E. D." is not at Hoover.

1125 LE ROY, FRANÇOIS, comp. La conduite des affaires étrangères en France; documents. Paris, 1959. iv, 44 l (Centre d'étude des relations internationales. Série D: Textes et documents pour l'étude des relations internationales, no. 1)

Constitutional and legislative texts regulating conduct of foreign affairs, from First through Fifth Republic, the latter only being represented by excerpts from the 1958 Constitution.

1126 LE SAGE, ROGER. Go..! Parachutistes français en Indochine. Préf. du Général Massu. Paris, Editions France-Empire, 1959. 316 p. illus.

Description of parachutists' day-to-day existence during Indochina campaign by administrator of Fédération nationale des parachutistes français.

1127 LE TROQUER, ANDRE. La parole est à André Le Troquer. Paris, Table ronde, 1962. 246 p. illus. (L'Ordre du jour)

Memoirs of former National Assembly president include only a few incidents related to Fifth Republic: his secret negotiations with de Gaulle, May 28, 1958, recollections of National Assembly session accepting de Gaulle's leadership, and explanation of his opposition to Jan. 1961 referendum on Algeria.

1128 LE TOURNEAU, ROGER. Evolution politique de l'Afrique du Nord musulmane, 1920-1961. Paris, A. Colin, 1962. 503 p. maps. Bibliography: p. 479-486.

Political evolution of Morocco, Tunisia, and Algeria treated separately. Algerian section gives a comprehensive survey of nationalist struggle and negotiations with de Gaulle on Algeria through September 1961. Author is pessimistic about prospects of Moslem-European cohabitation. Annotated bibliography for key works on Algeria, documentary sources.

1129 LEULLIETTE, PIERRE. Saint Michel et le dragon; souvenirs d'un parachutiste. Paris, Editions de Minuit, 1961. 358 p.

Personal account of service in parachutist regiment, 1954-1957, reflecting counter-terrorist activities and use of torture by regiment in reaction to growing nationalist strength. Saint-Michel is parachutists' patron saint.

1130 LEVINE, ERIC. The French intellectual and the Algerian War. New York, 1962. 158 l. Bibliography: l. 149-158.

Columbia Ph.D. thesis gives background of April 1960 "Manifeste des 121" on refusal to serve in Algeria, response to manifesto by other French intellectuals and broader segments of public opinion, and further repercussions among opponents of Algerian war through the rest of 1960. Appendix gives English translation of manifesto and other statements. Extensive bibliography of opposition to Algerian war, including periodical literature, pamphlets, and leaflets. For fuller account of this manifesto, see Maspero (no. 1187).

1131 LEVY, YVES. Le problème des modes de scrutin et le fonctionnement de la démocratie; réflexions sur les théories de Maurice Duverger. Paris, M. Rivière, 1956. 41 p.

Analysis of Maurice Duverger's work on political sociology and his practical proposal for a two-stage majority electoral system. Author demonstrates that on the strength of Duverger's own theories, only a single-stage majority ballot would be conducive to a strong, effective government supported by a coherent two-party structure.

1131a LA LIBRAIRIE FRANÇAISE. Livres de l'année. Catalogue général des ouvrages parus en langue française. Paris, Cercle de la Librairie, 1956-1967. ML

Annual catalogue of all French books arranged by topics (e.g., Social sciences and its subdivisions) and followed by a complete author and title listing, plus an index of publishing houses and their addresses having books in that year's catalogue. See also no. 1131b.

1131b LA LIBRAIRIE FRANÇAISE. Tables décennales. Catalogue général des ouvrages parus en langue française entre janvier 1956 et janvier 1966. Paris, Cercle de la librairie, 1967. 4 vols. ML

Two volumes (A-I, J-Z) by authors, two by titles, combining all the entries from the yearly catalogue volumes. Books are not topically arranged. Each volume has over 3,000 pages.

1132 LICHTHEIM, GEORGE. Marxism in modern France. New York, Columbia University Press, 1966. ix, 212 p. Bibliography: p. 199-207.

History, evolution, and present tendencies of Marxist thought in France, as based on study of a wealth of philosophical, political, sociological, and economic writing, which author relates to changes in French political situation since World War II. The author shows how the French Communist Party, the dissident Communists, and the non-Communist Marxists are adapting to a situation in which revolutionary theory has become divorced from the possibility of revolutionary practice. Excellent bibliography on French social thought.

1133 LIGOT, MAURICE. Les accords de coopération entre la France et les Etats africains et malgache d'expression francaise. Préf. de Jacques Foccart. Paris, Documentation française, 1964. 187 p. (Le Monde contemporain) Bibliography: p. 147-150.

Study based on 1963 dissertation describing genesis of cooperation agreements on defense, trade, aid, cultural exchanges, negotiation of agreements, 1956-1960, and current organs of cooperation. Introduction by Jacques Foccart, Secretary for African Affairs, shows place of agreements in the history of decolonization.

1134 LIGOU, DANIEL. Histoire du socialisme en France, 1871-1961. Lettre-préf. de Pierre Mendès-France. Paris, Presses universitaires de France, 1962. viii, 672 p. "Bibliographie générale": p. 639-644.

Final 30 pages deal with Algerian war and developments after May 1958 (S.F.I.O. participation in first de Gaulle Cabinet, 1958-59 elections, founding of P.S.U.).

1135 LINDBERG, LEON N. The political dynamics of European economic integration. Stanford, Calif., Stanford University Press, 1963. xiv, 367 p. tables. Bibliography: p. 351-380.

Interactions of European Economic Community with decision-making process in each of member countries, based in large part on interviews with EEC staff, political and economic leaders responsible for members' policies concerning EEC, 1959-1961.

1136 LINDON, RAYMOND. Le livre du citoyen français, initiation aux problèmes politiques et électoraux, éducation civique. Paris, Flammarion, 1966. 284 p.

Brief history and survey of current political, judicial, and administrative institutions intended as an informal text in civics. The section on voting procedures from the local to the presidential level is especially useful.

1137 LIPIANSKY, EDMOND and BERNARD RETTENBACH. Ordre et démocratie; deux sociétés de pensée: de l'Ordre nouveau au Club Jean Moulin. Préf. de Jean De Soto. Paris, Presses universitaires de France, 1967. 176 p. (Travaux et recherches de la Faculté de droit et des sciences économiques de Paris. Série "Science politique," no. 10) Includes bibliography.

Monographs on two political clubs, the anti-democratic but supranational Ordre nouveau of the 1930's and the Club Jean Moulin. Bernard Rettenbach's study on latter's conceptions of democracy and socialism is based on club's publications.

1138 LIVOIS, RENE DE. Histoire de la presse française. Lausanne, Editions Spes, 1965. 2 v. illus., ports. (part col.) plates (part col., 1 mounted) facsims.

First volume covers pre-1881 period, second volume goes up to 1965, in the form of beautifully illustrated essays on the main aspects of the French press. The essay on the Fifth Republic describes the decline of the daily press in favor of the more specialized weekly and monthly magazine and its highly developed advertising system. A short section surveys confidential news letters (André Noël, etc.). Photographs in text of leading press figures and a biographical dictionary of press figures mentioned in the two volumes.

1138a Livres français de droit, sciences politiques, économiques, sociales et humaines, 1957-1963. Paris, S.P.E.L.D., 1963. 204 p. LL

Selective bibliography of books and periodicals arranged under: law, political science (including elections, political parties, pressure groups, political institutions) economic and social sciences, and human sciences (history, geography, sociology).

1139 LOI, MAURICE. Le désastre scolaire. Paris, Editions sociales, 1962. 308 p. tables.

The "disaster" of the title refers to the degradation of public education under de Gaulle as part of a deliberately antidemocratic approach, in contrast to Soviet example. Author, a mathematics professor and leading figure in Syndicat national de l'enseignement secondaire, presents comprehensive picture of 1961-62 educational situation, budget for public and Catholic schools, figures on students in different types of secondary schools, and deals informatively with Gaullist educational reforms, despite strong ideological bias. French Communist Party's educational program is defined.

1140 LOISEAU, JEAN (pseud.). Pied-noir, mon frère; témoignage d'un francaoui. Paris, Editions France-Empire, 1963. 252 p. illus., facsims. Includes bibliography.

Reminiscences of French aviator stationed in Algeria since 1932 about development of aviation in Algeria and survey of achievements, human and economic, of European settlers, with short biographies of several Algerian-born personalities. Author pleads for repatriates, explaining their feelings of frustration and indignation to indifferent French. Includes 1962 testimonies of repatriates and Algerian clergymen.

1141 LORENZI, HENRI. Les jeunes votent. Paris, Editions C. L. E. D.O.R., 1964. 202 p. illus. (Essais pédagogiques)

Successful experiment in student self-administration carried out in a vocational school in Marseilles for handicapped and low-achieving adolescents, as told by the school's director.

1142 LUCHAIRE, FRANÇOIS. L'Aide aux pays sous-développés... Paris, Presses universitaires de France, 1966. 128 p. (Que sais-je? Le point des connaissances actuelles, no. 1227) Bibliography: p. 125.

Principles and special problems of economic and technical assistance, description of international assistance organs, and state by state survey, with brief section on France.

1142a LUCHAIRE, FRANÇOIS. Droit d'outre-mer et de la coopération... 2e édition... Paris, Presses universitaires de France, 1966. 628 p. ("Thémis"; manuels juridiques, économiques et politiques) Includes bibliographies. LL

Changing political institutions of French Union, French Community, and current economic and technical assistance within structure of new states, with details on Franco-African cooperation agreements, as well as information on arrangements within overseas departments and territories.

1143 LUCHAIRE, FRANÇOIS. Les institutions politiques et administratives des territoires d'outre-mer après la loi-cadre. Paris, Librairie générale de droit et de jurisprudence, 1958. 221-294 p. "Extrait de la Revue juridique et politique de l'Union Française no. 2, avril-juin 1958." Bibliographical footnotes.

Reforms introduced in political institutions of French Union by 1956-57 laws and decrees.

1144 LUDWIGSBURG, GER. DEUTSCH-FRANZÖSISCHES INSTITUT. Deutschland-Frankreich; Ludwigsburger Beiträge zum Problem der deutsch-französischen Beziehungen. Stuttgart, Deutsche Verlags-Anstalt, 1954-1963. 3 v. (Veröffentlichungen des Deutsch-Französischen Instituts, Ludwigsburg, 1-3) Includes bibliography.

Volumes for 1954, 1957, and 1963 consisting of a collection of talks by German and French statesmen and scholars on Franco-German political and cultural relations. 1963 volume includes 1958 lecture on Franco-German relations by Couve de Murville, then French ambassador in Germany.

1145 LUTZ, VERA C. French planning. Washington, American Enterprise Institute for Public Policy Research, 1965. x, 105 p. Bibliography: p. 101.

American economist's critical analysis of French flexible central economic planning, comparing forecasts with actual results in specific industries and gauging prospects of Fifth Plan's reconciling stabilization and growth objectives. Author concludes that French planning has not been a decisive factor in the country's economic growth.

1146 LYAUTEY, PIERRE. L'Armée, ce qu'elle est, ce qu'elle sera. Paris, R. Juillard, 1963. 268 p. illus.

Report on author's personal inspection of French military establishments as of 1963 (airforce, navy, nuclear force, ground forces, military schools) exemplifying current technologically oriented military policy.

1147 LYAUTEY, PIERRE. Claude Barrès; a hero in revolt. Translated from the French by Humphrey Hare. London, Macmillan, 1962. 215 p.

Biography of grandson of nationalist novelist Maurice Barrès, based on his diaries and letters to his family. The biography follows his exploits as a parachutist in the Resistance, in Indochina, and in Algeria, where he died in 1959. The work was published in French as "Un héros révolté: Claude Barrès," but is not at Hoover in original.

1148 LYONS. UNIVERSITE. INSTITUT DES ETUDES ECONOMIQUES. Le financement des entreprises et le Marché commun; colloque université-industrie organisé par l'Institut des études économiques de la Faculté de droit et des sciences économiques de l'Université de Lyon en février 1962 par J. Austruy et al. Préf. de A. Murat. Paris, Dunod, 1963. 150 p. (Bibliothèque d'administration des entreprises)

Most of studies deal with methods of financing and planning of investment for French firms of different types and localities.

1149 MABIRE, JEAN. L'écrivain, la politique et l'espérance. Paris, Editions Saint-Just, 1966. 224 p. (Collection Europe, 1)

Essays originally published in "Esprit public" 1962-1964, defining author's version of a European nationalism to replace French nationalism.

1150 MABIRE, JEAN. Histoire d'un Français: Tixier-Vignancour. Paris, Esprit nouveau, 1965. 222 p.

Written as a campaign document for presidential candidate Tixier-Vignancour in January 1965, the work shows continuity of candidate's affiliation with French Right from support of Action Française through post as Information Minister under Petain, political ostracism in first post-war decade, and glamorous role as defense lawyer for nationalist opponents of de Gaulle.

1151 MACRAE, DUNCAN. Parliament, parties, and society in France, 1946-1958. New York, St. Martin's Press, 1967. xiii, 375 p. Bibliography: p. 354-363.

Analysis of Fourth Republic's governmental instability on the basis of certain hypotheses which author tests through statistical correlation methods. Among the variables are attitudes of political parties and their expression in parliamentary votes, relations between cabinets and Assembly, political attitudes of electorate. Good bibliography.

1152 MACRIDIS, ROY C. (ed.). De Gaulle: implacable ally. With a special introd. by Maurice Duverger. New York, Harper and Row, 1966. xxxv, 248 p.

De Gaulle's policy of national independence, broken down as 1) conditions of independence; 2) margin of independence; 3) French independence, is presented through excerpts from his books, memoirs, major addresses 1958-1964 and 1965 speeches. Editor has used topical rather than chronological approach, with introduction for each of sections. Part 1 covers de Gaulle's philosophy of political and economic reform and decolonization. Part 2 describes de Gaulle's views on French role in international affairs and nuclear policy. Part 3 deals with de Gaulle's specific pronouncements on European integration, German alliance, Atlantic Community, the U.S., the U.N., and the "Tiers-monde." Duverger's introduction underlines outdated and visionary elements in de Gaulle's thinking and diplomacy, weighing his failures and successes as a French statesman of the 1960's.

1153 MACRIDIS, ROY C. and BERNARD E. BROWN. The De Gaulle republic: quest for unity. Homewood, Ill., Dorsey Press, 1960. ix, 400 p. illus. (The Dorsey series in political science) Bibliographical footnotes.

American political scientists' systematic analysis of the factors leading to the birth of Fifth Republic, its constitution, first elections, and new institutions and political allignments through 1959, with Feb. 1960 epilogue.

1154 MADAULE, JACQUES. Histoire de France. V. 3: De la IIIe à la Ve Republique. Edition revue. Paris, Gallimard, 1965. 377 p. (Collection Ideés, 108)

Final 25 pages on first phases of Algerian war, founding of Fifth Republic, and conclusion of Algerian war.

1155 MAINGUY, MAURICE. Le pétrole et l'Algérie. Paris, Editions du Cerf, 1958. 126 p. tables. (Tout monde en parle) Bibliographical footnotes.

Author examines oil exploitation in Algeria to prove that it is not a sufficient justification for continuing Algerian war for the sake of perpetuating French control over Saharan oil, a conclusion that is not modified by May 1958 events.

1156 MAITAN, LIVIO (ed.). L'Algeria e il socialismo. Roma, Samonà e Savelli, 1963. xxxvi, 260 p. (Cultura politica, 3)

Basic documents (in Italian) on first year of Algerian independence; 1962 Tripoli program, 1963 constitution, Ben Bella speeches and statements Nov. 1962 - June 1963, trade union resolutions, experiences of "autogestion" in factories, statements of F.L.N. leaders in conflict with Ben Bella, with explanations of editor.

1157 MALE, GEORGE ALBERT. Education in France. Washington, U.S. Dept. of Health, Education, and Welfare, Office of Education; for sale by the Superintendent of Documents, U.S. Govt. Print. Off., 1963. viii, 205 p. map, tables. (U.S. Office of Education. Bulletin 1963, no. 33) Bibliography: p. 197-205.

Survey of administrative structure of primary, secondary, vocational, and higher education. Changes introduced under Fifth Republic are taken into account, and the many statistics go up to 1962. Curricula in primary and secondary schools are compared with those of U.S. schools. Bibliography lists relevant publications of Ministry of National Education.

1158 MALEVILLE, GEORGES. A l'échelle mondiale; essai d'une Union Française Fédérale. Paris, Librairies Techniques, 1958. 216 p.

Constitutional expert's plan in early 1958 for transforming French Union into a looser federation covering Algeria, tropical Africa, and Madagascar, with considerable internal autonomy, as only viable alternative for abandoning French Empire completely.

1159 MALI, TIDIANE. Une philosophie sur l'affaire Ben Barka... Lyon, Impr. Hettiger, 1966. 96 p. (Pour un monde meilleur)

African-born author's reflections on the prevalence of violence in modern society and the bad example it gives to new nations, as illustrated by Ben Barka's assassination.

1160 MALLET, SERGE. Le Gaullisme et la gauche. Paris, Editions du Seuil, 1965. 266 p. (Collection "L'Histoire immédiate") Includes bibliography.

Articles published in various periodicals June 1958-June 1964 on the question of how the Left can make its opposition to de Gaulle effective, given the generally accepted new political institutions. Author, who is member of P.S.U.'s executive committee, as well as professor of sociology and journalist, sees fight for democratic socialism within framework of modern industry as the most favorable terrain. There are interesting sidelights on internal tendencies and cleavages of P.S.U., as illustrated by excerpt from Jan. 1963 party congress.

1161 MALLET, SERGE. La nouvelle classe ouvrière. Paris, Editions du Seuil, 1963. 265 p. (Collection Esprit: "La cité prochaine")

Case studies sponsored by Club Jean Moulin on the new working class and new trade unionism, carried out 1958-60 in three industries with advanced technologies: the electronic company Bull, with its main factory in Paris and provincial subsidiaries, the Caltex refinery in the Bordeaux area, and the electrical company Thompson-Houston near Paris. Author sees growing interest in sharing managerial function within enterprise and voice in national economic planning in unions representing this new type of workers, as against the Confédération générale du travail, which concentrates on wage demands within firm.

1162 MALLET, SERGE. Les paysans contre le passé. Paris, Editions du Seuil, 1962. 287 p. map.

First part of book describes efforts of Cercle National des Jeunes Agriculteurs (C.N.J.A.) since the beginning of the Fifth Republic to restructure French agriculture along cooperative and trade union lines and integrate it with the trade union movement. In second part, author inspects different agricultural regions in Central and Western France to show impact of increasing mechanization, giving a detailed and vivid picture of a modernizing agriculture.

1163 MALRAUX, ANDRE. Discours 1958-1965. Paris, Action étudiante gaulliste de Paris, 1966. 16 p. port.

Includes following speeches: August 24, 1958 (Paris, on Résistance) May 28, 1959 (Athens, on Greek culture) August 25, 1959 (Brazilia, on modern architecture) March 8, 1960 (U.N.E.S.C.O., on archeology) September 3, 1963 (Paris, on George Bracque) April 18, 1964 (Bourges, on popular culture) May 31, 1964 (Rouen, on Jeanne d'Arc) December 19, 1964 (Paris, on Jean Moulin) September 1, 1965 (on Le Corbusier) and December 15, 1965 (Paris, campaign speech for de Gaulle).

FOR ADDITIONAL WORKS BY AND ABOUT ANDRE MALRAUX, SEE AUTHOR INDEX

1164 MALTERRE, JACQUES and PAUL BENOIST. Les partis politiques français. Paris, Editions du Témoignage chrétien, 1957. 173 p. (Bibliothèque de l'homme d'action)

History and status as of 1956 of major political parties and groups (Communist, Socialist, independent Left, Radicals, M.R.P., R.P.F., Independents, and Poujadists).

1165 MANCERON, CLAUDE. Cent mille voix par jour pour Mitterrand. Paris, R. Laffont, 1966. 316 p. ports.

Historian who participated in Mitterand campaign gives short biography of candidate and information on members of his team (especially Charles Hernu). Main part of volume consists of campaign diary, with excerpts from speeches. Appendices include texts of radio interviews of Louis Aragon and Jean Rostand in support of Mitterand, and of Emmanuel d'Astier and Joseph Kessel in support of de Gaulle, a note on campaign budget, and lists of Mitterand supporters. Numerous photographs of Mitterand and campaign scenes.

1166 MANDRIN, JACQUES. L'enarchie, ou Les mandarins de la société bourgeoise. Paris, Table ronde, 1967. 169 p. (La Table ronde de combat "Les Brulots," 5)

Caustic description of procedures of selection and formation of future civil servants by Ecole nationale d'administration (E.N.A.) founded after World War II and operating in close cooperation with Institut des Sciences Politiques in Paris, which provides most of its students. "Enarchie" refers to rule by the E.N.A.'s corps of graduates. Author proposes alternate methods for training functionaries suited to a socialist and democratic society.

1167 MANEVY, ALAIN. L'Algérie à vingt ans. Paris, B. Grasset, 1960. 236 p.

Purely personal account of young soldier's life in Algeria around 1958.

1168 MANIN, PHILIPPE. Le R.P.F. (Rassemblement du peuple français) et les problèmes européens... Paris, Presses universitaires de France, 1966. xi, 140 p. (Travaux et recherches de la Faculté de droit et des sciences économiques de Paris. Série "Europe," n°3)

1963 political science dissertation tracing R.P.F.'s and de Gaulle's fluctuating views on European unification, 1947-1954. These views ranged from pro-European anti-communism to anti-European neuralism. Sources are de Gaulle's and other party leaders' speeches and party publications.

1169 MANNONI, EUGENE. Moi, général de Gaulle. Paris, Editions du Seuil, 1964. 154 p.

"France-Soir" journalist's impressionistic portrait of de Gaulle through snatches of his speeches and writings. Neither a biography nor a systematic analysis of his writing, it is an attempt to define de Gaulle's unique role in French history and his political personality, as expressed in his conception of nationalism and his relations with military, political parties (including U.N.R.). Author makes strong case for de Gaulle's realism and anti-dogmatism summarized in de Gaulle's leitmotiv of "les choses étant ce qu'elles sont."

1170 MANSELL, GERARD. Tragedy in Algeria. London, New York, Oxford University Press, 1961. 76 p. Includes bibliography.

Brief history of French colonization, political developments from World War II until the end of 1960.

1171 MANUALI, LOUIS. La France face à l'implantation étrangère. Préf. de Olivier Moreau-Neret. Paris, Editions SEF, Société d'éditions économiques et financières, 1967. 129 p. Includes bibliography.

Survey of foreign and particularly American investments in France, 1950-1965, differential study by sectors of French industry, examination of economic and political pros and cons of foreign investments for each sector. Author proposes measures to limit foreign investment for Common Market as a whole. Appendix includes letter of Franz Josef Strauss to Ludwig Erhard praising French attempts to control U.S. investments.

1172 MARC, ALEXANDRE. L'Europe dans le monde. Paris, Payot, 1965. 238 p. (Bibliothèque politique et économique) Bibliographical footnotes.

Includes balance sheet of successes and failures of European federation since beginning of Fifth Republic by one of French spokesmen for federalist movement and evaluation of de Gaulle's personal stand on European federation.

1173 Le Marché commun, chômage ou prospérité? Paris, Editions du Monde ouvrier, 1959. 261 p. illus., ports. (Collection "Problèmes de notre temps")

Description of Common Market's aims, history, institutions and political organs, and comparison of production, wages in France and other Common Market countries. Authors predict that Common Market will not radically affect position of French workers and quotes opinions of socialist leaders in other countries. Union de la Gauche Socialiste, whose point of view is here expressed, urges acceptance of Common Market as starting point toward unified socialist Europe.

1174 La Marche de la France au socialisme, vingt ans après l'interview de Maurice Thorez au "Times" (17 novembre 1946)... Paris, Editions sociales, 1966. 125 p. (Publications de l'Institut Maurice Thorez)

Institut Maurice Thorez publication compiled by George Cogniot, Jacques Chambaz, Henri Claude, Jacques Denis, and Victor Joannes, taking as its starting point a 1946 speech by Thorez insisting on the French Communist Party's democratic rather than Communist objectives. Review of developments in international and French communism since 1946 serves to demonstrate compatibility between communist ideology and non-violent, democratic, and parliamentarian path to socialism in France. Authors, using classic Marxist sources, prove that dictatorship of the proletariat in France implies multi-party state and full civil liberties.

1175 MARCILHACY, PIERRE. Ce que je n'ai pas dit. Paris, R. Laffont, 1966. 207 p.

Lawyer, former senator, defeated presidential candidate, discourses on French life and civilization and touches political questions (de Gaulle's excessive personal power and misinterpretations of French history) only incidentally. These are thoughts he left unexpressed during presidential campaign.

1176 MARCILHACY, PIERRE. Les Chouans de la liberté; vingt années d'observation politique. Paris, Nouvelles éditions latines, 1963. 179 p.

Collection of articles, 1944, 1956-1963, originally published in "Le Monde," "Combat," and political science journals giving the Senator's reactions to the Algerian war, de Gaulle's return to power, the new constitution, and his increasingly negative judgment on the Fifth Republic's institutions and policies.

FOR ADDITIONAL WORKS BY AND ABOUT PIERRE MARCILHACY, SEE AUTHOR INDEX

1177 MARCUS, JOHN A. French party literature. Salt Lake City, 1959. [9] p. Reprinted from Western Political Quarterly, v. 12, no. 1, March 1959, [168]-176 p.

Party by party survey (Communist Party, Communist opposition groups, Union de la gauche socialiste, Parti socialiste, Jeune République, Poujadist movement, Républicains sociaux, Indépendants et Paysans, extremist rightist group connected with May 13 uprising, Mouvement républicain populaire, Radicals with their splinter groups, Union démocratique et socialiste de la Résistance) of their publications, i.e., both regular party organs and important pamphlets. None of the information goes beyond summer 1958.

1178 MARCUS, JOHN T. Neutralism and nationalism in France: a case study. New York, Bookman Associates, 1958. 207 p. Includes bibliography: p. 187-203.

Study completed shortly before May 1958 analyzing how leftist intellectuals' neutralism and R.P.F. nationalism in the 1950's merged in a national consensus of nationalist neutralism embodied in Gaullism, despite the failure of the R.P.F. as a political movement.

1179 MAREC, JEAN PAUL. La ténébreuse affaire Ben Barka. Avant-propos de Jacques Isorni... Paris, Editions des Presses noires, 1966. 253 p. (Les Grandes affaires de ce temps)

Free reconstruction of confusing sequence of events surrounding kidnaping and disappearance of Moroccan exile Ben Barka and abortive efforts of police and tribunals to bring culprits to justice, disclosing at the same time scandalous weaknesses in police and secret services and implicating high government officials. Introduction by Isorni recalls other instances in which de Gaulle sanctioned political murder and illegal acts for his own purposes.

1180 MARKOVIC, TIHOMIR J. L'industrie française de 1789 à 1964. Paris, 1965-66. 3 v. tables. (Cahiers de l'Institut de science économique appliquée, no. 163, 174, 179) Institut de science économique appliquée. Cahiers. Série AF: Histoire quantitative de l'économie française, 4, 6-7.

Methodology of statistical production indices, followed by statistical study of individual industries and total output. A few of series are carried through to 1959.

1181 MARTIN, CLAUDE. Histoire de l'Algérie française, 1830-1962. Paris, Editions des 4 fils Aymon, 1963. 508 p. Includes bibliography.

Detailed, well-informed and well-organized political history of French colonial rule (though leaning toward pro-settler and anti-Gaullist view) with last 80 pages devoted to Algerian evolution from 1958 to independence, but over half of lengthy work tracing the stages of the nationalist upsurge.

1182 MARTIN, MARCEL. Recherche d'une éthique moderne de la vie politique française. Paris, Librairies techniques, 1959. 62 p.

General political principles for an expanding society more and more closely linked to other nations. Author welcomes Fifth Republic's strong executive and emphasis on common purposes and concludes with a new "declaration of rights of man and republican principles."

1183 MARTIN-CHAUFFIER, LOUIS. Algérie an VII: l'examen des consciences. Paris, R. Julliard, 1961. 122 p.

Plea against continued use of torture in Algeria both because of its corrupting influence on French army and of its negative impact on Algerian population. Author, who was French representative on Commission internationale contre le régime concentrationnaire in 1957, accuses de Gaulle of keeping up Fourth Republic's methods and of delaying (Dec. 1960) needlessly the end of the conflict.

1184 MARTINET, GILLES. Le marxisme de notre temps, ou Les contradictions du socialisme. Paris, R. Juillard, 1962. 172 p.

Criticism of orthodox bases of Marxism and French Communism as opposed to his own program for socialist democracy, relations with underdeveloped countries, and European unification. Author who is editor of France-Observateur and leading figure in P.S.U., analyzes fate of left-wing parties outside S.F.I.O. and Communist Party in Fifth Republic. Published in English as "Marxism of our time; or the contradictions of socialism" (New York, 1964).

FOR ADDITIONAL WORKS BY AND ABOUT GILLES MARTINET, SEE AUTHOR INDEX

1185 MASCHINO, MAURICE. L'engagement: le dossier des réfractaires. Paris, F. Maspero, 1961. 133 p. (Cahiers libres, no. 19)

Different types of motivation for refusing military service and deserting and efforts to turn these individual acts into a collective stand against the government's Algerian policy and positive support for F.L.N. and a socialist Algeria. Réseau Jeanson and "Jeune Résistance" are main organizations involved.

1186 MASCHINO, MAURICE. Le refus; récit. Nouv. éd. augm. Paris, F. Maspero, 1960. 202 p. (Cahiers libres, no. 7)

Personal account of French professor teaching in North Africa 1951-1957 and refusing military service in Algeria because of his conviction that French are acting in bad faith.

1187 MASPERO, FRANÇOIS (éd.). Le droit à l'insoumission: "Le dossier des 121." Paris, F. Maspero, 1961. 231 p. (Cahiers libres, no. 14)

Text of Sept. 5, 1960 declaration urging refusal of military service signed by 121 opponents (including publisher Maspero) of Algerian war, complemented by 125 additional signatures containing names of many prominent intellectuals, literary and theatrical figures. Book gives further consequences of declaration, interviews with 12 signers, depositions of Sartre and others at Jeanson trial, text and signatures of two other manifestos, one supporting and the other opposing the main declaration. The latter is a rare public document in which French intellectuals uphold Algerian war and side with French nationalists. See also no. 1130.

1188 MASSE, PIERRE. Le plan; ou, L'anti-hasard. Paris, Gallimard, 1965. 250 p. (Collection Idées)

Essays and public addresses by head of Commissariat Général du Plan on methods and philosophy of French planning, 1959-1965. One essay deals with regional planning.

1189 MASSE, PIERRE, FRANÇAIS BLOCH-LAINE and MASSELIN. Rapport sur la situation des salaires du secteur nationalisée. Paris, Documentation française, 1963. 17 p. tables. [France. Direction de la documentation] Recueils et monographies, no. 43.

March 1963 report to Prime Minister on wages in nationalized industries, giving wage statistics in coal mining, electrical industry, and railroads, 1957 - Jan. 1963, with comparisons to wages in the private sector.

1190 MASSENET, MICHEL. L'angoisse au pouvoir. Paris, Plon, 1959. 109 p. (Tribune libre, 44)

Analysis of Fourth Republic's incapacity to deal with crucial problems of French political life and affirmation of new regime's potential for dealing better with them. A member of Conseil d'Etat in Fourth Republic, Massenet participated in drawing up 1958 Constitution.

1191 MASSENET, MICHEL. Contrepoison; ou, La morale en Algérie. Paris, B. Grasset, 1957. 129 p.

After refuting economic, Christian, and military arguments for withdrawal, author makes moral case for continuing Franco-Algerian symbiosis, admitting the challenge this solution represents to French political institutions in carrying through workable reforms in Algeria. For review of this work, see no. 583.

1192 MASSIGLI, RENE. Sur quelques maladies de l'état. Paris, Plon, 1958. 81 p. (Tribune libre, 27)

Career diplomat's criticism of indecisiveness and instability of government and alienation between Cabinet and civil servants, warning of executive's incapacity to meet challenge of Algeria and Common Market shortly before May 1958.

1193 MASSIP, ROGER. De Gaulle et l'Europe. Paris, Flammarion, 1963. 202 p. (L'Actuel)

Summary and chronology of European unification prior to Fifth Republic, de Gaulle's policies, and current (1963) prospects for communal institutions, political and military integration, reconciliation with Germany, admission of Great Britain to Common Market. Author lucidly analyzes logic and contradictions in de Gaulle's underlying aims. De Gaulle's speeches and writings on European unification before and after 1958 are cited.

1194 MATHEWS, RICHARD KYNASTON. Letters relating to Africa to the Institute of Current World Affairs. Paris, 1962. illus., maps. "Not for publication." Letters, Jan. 12, 1962-Nov. 20, 1963.

January and February 1962 letters from Paris reflect French reactions to final stages of Algerian war, such as the partition proposals, and give biography of Ben Khedda, head of the Algerian Provisional Government. Subsequent letters do not concern French affairs.

1195 MATTEI, GEORGES M. Disponibles; roman. Paris, F. Maspero, 1961. 169 p. (Cahiers libres, no. 26)

Novel based on response to a year's service in Algeria by young reserve officer and attempts to oppose the war after his return to civilian life in 1958.

1196 MATTHEWS, TANYA (SVETLOVA). Algerian A. B. C. London, G. Chapman, 1961. 147 p.

Brief journalistic account of origins and history of Algerian war, generally sympathetic to nationalist cause. Foreword is by Minister of Information of Algerian Provisional Government Mohamed Yazid, Oct. 1961. An identical American edition is entitled "War in Algeria: background for crisis" (New York, 1961).

1197 MAUCORPS, PAUL H., ALBERT MEMMI, and JEAN-FRANCIS HELD. Les Français et le racisme. Avec le concours du Mouvement contre le racisme, l'antisémitisme et pour la paix et la participation de J. Bron, et al. Paris, Payot, 1965. 290 p. (Etudes et documents Payot)

Summary and interpretation by three social scientists of results of questionnaires sent out in 1963 to a cross section of 200 members of the Mouvement contre le Racisme for their testimony on current status of racism in France: its causes, manifestations, counter-measures, with focus on Jewish, North African and black African victims, and impact on their status of national independence in Africa, establishment of Jewish state.

1198 MAURIAC, FRANÇOIS. De Gaulle. Paris, B. Grasset, 1964. 345 p.

Confrontation of author's personal image of de Gaulle with the figure emerging from de Gaulle's public pronouncements (extensively quoted) between 1940 and 1964. Mauriac tries to justify why he, in contrast to fellow-liberals (he was an ardent supporter of de Gaulle's opponent Mendès-France) and leftists, has found de Gaulle's policies unfailingly realistic and farsighted and the institutional changes indispensable. Among the many critical reactions to this work, the most biting is Laurent's "Mauriac sous de Gaulle" (no. 1088).

1199 MAURIAC, FRANÇOIS. Le nouveau Bloc-notes, 1958-1960. Paris, Flammarion, 1961. 420 p.

Novelist's peripatetic weekly comments on political and literary events of January 1958-December 1960, expressing his approval of de Gaulle. The weekly notes originally appeared on the back page of "L'Express," which opposed many of Mauriac's pro-Gaullist views. The collaboration ended in 1960. Index of persons and book titles.

1200 MAVRINAC, ALBERT. Organization and procedure of the National Assembly of the Fifth French Republic. London, Hansard Society for Parliamentary Government, 1960. 39 p.

Short statement of rules and procedures governing National Assembly under Fifth Republic as set down in Constitution and implemented in first year of operations.

1201 MAY, ROGER. La France a la bombe. Paris, Gallimard, 1959. 308 p. (L'Air du temps)

Journalist's survey of civilian and military development of nuclear technology, as of 1959, both in France and in other countries.

1202 MAZE, JEAN. L'anti-système. Paris, A. Fayard, 1960. 319 p. (Les Idées et la vie)

Criticism of political institutions of Fifth Republic by journalist who had previously condemned the Fourth Republic's "système" and now attacks political vacuum created by sclerosis of political parties, the U. N. R.'s lack of program, and the new regime's failure to reform structure of government by decentralization.

1203 MEGRET, MAURICE. La guerre psychologique. Paris, Presses universitaires de France, 1963. 127 p. (Que sais-je? 713)

Almost unrevised from its 1956 edition, which concentrates on the techniques of psychological warfare applied in World Wars I and II, and by the U.S. and Soviet Russia in the course of the cold war. Author warns against danger of making psychological warfare an end in itself, but does not draw directly on recent French experiences.

1204 MEGRINE, BERNARD. La question scolaire en France. Paris, Presses universitaires de France, 1960. (Que sais-je no. 864) ML

Background and provision of December 1959 law on education (Law no. 59-1557, increasing support for private Catholic schools) and arguments on Church-State educational problems by political and other groups involved in the conflict.

1205 MEINICKE-KLEINT, HEINZ. Algerien, Marokko, Tunesien; Unterjochung und Befreiung. Berlin, Dietz, 1965. 355 p. illus., maps (on lining papers) Includes bibliography.

Parallel histories of the three North African countries, with first section on colonization, second on liberation movement and national independence. Author presents stand of international communism on aims and methods best suited for these countries after independence and help given by Communist states.

1206 MEISEL, JAMES HANS. The fall of the Republic; military revolt in France. Ann Arbor, University of Michigan Press, 1962. 309 p. Includes bibliography.

American political scientist's view of politicized army's role in the collapse of the Fourth Republic and the series of crises accompanying the final stages of the Algerian war. Author examines Fascist affinities of certain military doctrines of counter-insurgency, events in Algeria in May 1958, January 1960, April 1961, and the significance of the O.A.S. as a continuation of this revolt against a peaceful society. Since book was concluded in summer 1962, with civil war threat at its height, parallels with collapse of Weimar Republic are not surprising.

1207 MELLOR, ALEC. Histoire de l'anticléricalisme français. Tours, Mame, 1966. 496 p. Bibliography: p. 460-472.

History of anticlerical philosophy and movements going back to middle ages, with short final section on survivals of anticlericalism in French Communist party's stand and battles around school question in Fourth and Fifth Republic.

1208 MELNIK, CONSTANTIN and NATHAN LEITES. The house without windows; France selects a President. Translated from the French by Ralph Manheim. Evanston, Ill., Row, Peterson 1958. 358 p. diagrs., tables. Bibliography: p. 329-335.

Blow-by-blow account of the long drawn-out election of René Coty as President of the French Republic, December 1953, as a small-scale model of the degradation of the Fourth Republic's parliamentary system out of touch with reality and public opinion. The study is part of Rand Corporation's series on French institutions.

1209 MENANT, MICHEL. L'apostolat en jeunesse ouvrière; fondements doctrinaux. Lettre-préf. de Mgr Ancel. Paris, Editions ouvrières, 1965. 239 p. (Eglise et jeunesse, 4) Bibliographical footnotes.

Doctrinal and practical aspects of the work among young French workers carried on by the Jeunesse ouvrière catholique.

1210 MENDERSHAUSEN, HORST. From NATO to independence: reflections on de Gaulle's secession [paper prepared for presentation at a seminar at the Washington Center of Foreign Policy Research]. Santa Monica, Calif., Rand Corporation, 1966. 32 l.

Interpretation of France's withdrawal from NATO as a decisive step in dismembering the Atlantic Alliance and of possible consequences for Franco-German and German-U.S. relations.

1211 MENDES-FRANCE, PIERRE. An analysis of General de Gaulle's policy in Algeria by Pierre Mendès-France, former premier of France. New York, 1960. 3 l. (Delegation of the Provisional Government of the Algerian Republic, N.Y.)

1212 MENDES-FRANCE, PIERRE. Gouverner c'est choisir. V. 3 La politique et la vérité, Juin 1955 - Septembre 1958. Paris, R. Julliard, 1958. 356 p. (Collection La Nef)

Third volume consists of excerpts from speeches before National Assembly, press conferences, etc., arranged under: 1) international relations; 2) economic policy; 3) Algeria and French Union; 4) political institutions (collapse of Fourth Republic, new constitution).

1213 MENDES-FRANCE, PIERRE. La république moderne; propositions. Paris, Gallimard, 1962. 251 p. (Collection Idées, 18)

Proposals for new constitutional structure (such as "gouvernement de législature," transformation of Economic Council into second chamber) for new methods of planning and decentralization. The book is the outcome of Mendès-France's consultation with 4000 local and political leaders throughout France in the course of 1962, a grass-roots consensus on political reform.

FOR ADDITIONAL WORKS BY AND ABOUT PIERRE MENDES-FRANCE, SEE AUTHOR INDEX

1214 MENDES-FRANCE, RENE. Le dur chemin de la paix et le futur contrat social ... Paris, l'auteur, 1967. 71 p.

Scheme for replacing money-centered organization of French society by a form of social contract obliging each member of society to contribute an agreed number of hours of collectively determined labor.

1215 MENGIN, ROBERT. De Gaulle à Londres vu par un Français libre. Paris, Table Ronde, 1965. 345 p. (L'Histoire contemporaine revue et corrigée)

Chronicle of de Gaulle's London years, 1940-1943 by staff member of French Embassy who shared political aims of Free French but refused to place himself under de Gaulle's command. Author's diary highlights intrigues among Free French leaders and constant drive for supreme power by de Gaulle in his relations with collaborators and foreign statesmen. English translation appeared as "No laurels for de Gaulle" (London, 1966).

1216 MENINGAUD, JEAN. La France à l'heure algérienne. Paris, Paris-Livres, 1956. 188 p. plates.

French businessman in Algeria for last decade presents arguments for French Algeria and blames nationalist manifestations on pan-Arabism and Soviet and U.S. intrigues. Steps toward political reform are decried and work of recent Governor Generals in Algeria is praised. Appendix reproduces 1956 appeals for French Algeria, one by University of Algiers students.

1217 MERENS, LOUIS (pseud.). La paix des braves. [Paris?] Esprit nouveau, 1963. 235 p.

Thinly disguised fictional account of months between Evian agreement and Algerian independence, seen through eyes of Algerian-born Frenchman serving in an official capacity. Exodus of Europeans, final O.A.S. operations, the hopeless and tragic violence between nationalist and pro-French, European and Moslem communities are themes of novel, which keeps close to actual events.

1218 MERLE, MARCEL (ed.). Les églises chrétiennes et la décolonisation. Paris, A. Colin, 1967. 517 p. (Cahiers de la

Fondation nationale des sciences politiques, 151) Includes bibliography.

Contributions by individual authors covering Vatican and international Protestant organizations as well as Catholic churches and Protestant hierarchies in France, Germany, England, Belgium, Netherlands, Portugal, and U.S. Lengthy chapter on French Catholic Church analyzes its stand on Algerian war, with many quotations from statements of Catholic hierarchy and Catholic groups. A shorter chapter is devoted to French Protestant churches and position on decolonization.

1219 MERLE, ROBERT. Ahmed Ben Bella. Paris, Gallimard, 1965. 184 p.

Political autobiography as told to French writer in a series of conversations, 1963-64, and reconstructed in chronological sequence and first-person form, covering Ben Bella's years in French Army, participation in the formative stages of the Algerian revolution, prison experiences, and share in peace negotiations and setting up of independent Algerian government, after Ben Bella's disgrace. An English translation is also entitled "Ahmed Ben Bella" (New York, 1967).

1220 MERLEAU-PONTY, MAURICE. Signes. Paris, Gallimard, 1960. 438 p.

Essays on philosophical questions, followed by brief comments on political questions, 1948 - June 1958, the last two giving author's lucid comments on de Gaulle's return to power.

1220a MERRITT, RICHARD L. and DONALD J. PUCHALA (comps.). Western European attitudes on arms control, defense, and European unity, 1952-1963. New Haven, Yale University, Political Science Research Library, 1966. 299 p. LL

Comparative statistics of political attitude in France, West Germany, Italy, and Great Britain on international relations, European policy, and disarmament, based on public opinion surveys done for the United States Information Agency, 1952-1962. For France, the polling was done by Institut français d'opinion publique.

1221 MEYNAUD, JEAN and ALAIN LANCELOT. Les attitudes politiques. Paris, Presses universitaires de France, 1962. 126, [2] p. ("Que sais-je?" Le point des connaissances actuelles, no. 993) "Bibliographie": p. 127.

Popular summary of theories on the formation of political attitudes and ideologies in France and other parts of the world.

1222 MEYNAUD, JEAN. L'élaboration de la politique économique. Aix-en-Provence, La Pensée universitaire, 1959. 228 p. Bibliography: p. 227-228.

1958 course given at the Institut d'études politiques, Aix-Marseille University. Lectures discuss political framework for elaboration of economic policy, nature of economic objectives, choice of measures to bring them about and role of economist. Examples are drawn both from Fourth Republic and foreign experience, with postscript analyzing what modifications can be expected as a result of the 1958 Constitution.

1223 MEYNAUD, JEAN. Les groupes de pression. Paris, Presses, universitaires de France, 1960. 127 p. (Que sais-je?" Le point des connaissances actuelles, no. 895)

Popular summary of role of pressure groups in different kinds of political systems, with some details on innovations brought by Fifth Republic (e.g., Conseil Economique et Social's expanded rôle).

1224 MEYNAUD, JEAN. Nouvelles études sur les groupes de pression en France. Paris, A. Colin, 1962. 448 p. (Cahiers de la Fondation nationale des sciences politiques, 118) Bibliography: p. 420.

Theoretical analysis of pressure groups is combined with a comprehensive presentation of a wide variety of organizations, their aims and methods, access to decision-making process. Although examples are also drawn from outside France, author deals mainly with situation under Fifth Republic. Extensive bibliographical notes after each chapter, author and subject index, list of over 300 groups cited and identified in text.

1225 MEYNAUD, JEAN and ALAIN LANCELOT. La participation des Français à la politique. Paris, Presses universitaires de France, 1961. 122, [1] p. (Que-sais-je? no. 911) "Bibliographie sommaire": p. 123.

Introductory survey of nature and extent of participation of French in political life, with some figures for 1959-61.

1226 MEYNAUD, JEAN. La révolte paysanne. Paris, Payot, 1963. 308 p. (Etudes et documents) Includes bibliography.

Scholarly but non-technical work on basic economic and technological problems facing French agriculture, which led to violent outburst in previous year. Author puts French agricultural dilemma in perspective of situation in all advanced economies, where food demand is inelastic and individual farmers weakly organized. Author describes modernization and cooperative methods of French agriculture and gives detailed account of Fifth Republic's agricultural reforms. Good bibliography.

1227 MEYNAUD, JEAN. Les speculations sur l'avenir; essai bibliographique. Lausanne, 1965. 137 p. (His Etudes de science politique, 12) Includes bibliography.

Bibliographical essay on hundreds of books, periodicals and colloquia predicting the future for one country or mankind, making forecasts for the next decade or the year 2000. The bibliography concentrates on recent works appearing in France and disengages the political significance of the different types of predictions - socialist and libertarian - (such as the inherent conservatism of predictions based on technological innovations bringing in their wake the disappearance of ideologies and the gradual merging of capitalism and communism). Special attention is paid to the periodicals "Prospective" and "Futuribles," the latter edited by Bertrand de Jouvenel and concentrating on the prediction of political and social change (see no. 1019).

1228 MEYNAUD, JEAN. Sport et politique. Paris, Payot, 1966. 323 p. (Etudes et documents Payot) Bibliography: p. 315-318.

Includes description of French participation in different types of sports, athletic organizations, government policy for encouraging physical education, group sports, and international competitions. Author analyzes the political significance of sports for its participants and what advantages the government seeks to gain from athletics. Only the French Communist Party affirms the political role of sports. A large part of the book deals with other European countries and the U.S., as well as with international competitions (Olympics) and their political implications.

1229 MEZERIK, AVRAHM G. (ed.). Algerian developments, 1959: De Gaulle, FLN, UN. New York, International Review Service, [1960?] 60 p. illus. (International review service; analysis and review of international problems, v. 6, no. 55)

September 1958 - September 1959 developments in Algeria, France, and at U.N., with chronology for June 1958 - December 1959 and special chronology for Algerian question at U.N., 1955-1959.

1230 MEZERIK, AVRAHM G. (ed.). The Algerian-French conflict: international impacts, UN action. New York, 1958. 39 p. (International review service, v. 4, no. 43)

Brief history of Algerian war and repercussions at U.N. with chronology 1830-1945.

1231 MEZERIK, AVRAHM G. (ed.). Tunisian-French dispute: Bizerta, Sahara, UN action. New York, International Review Service, 1961. 63 p. illus. (International review service, v. 7, no. 67)

Background of clash with Tunisia over Bizerte and Sahara, Oct. 1961, with chronology of Franco-Tunisian relations 1834-1961.

1232 MICAUD, CHARLES ANTOINE. Communism and the French Left. New York, Praeger, 1963. 308 p. (Books that matter) Includes bibliography.

American scholar's socio-political study of Communists and other left-wing groups completed in large part before 1958, with only final chapters on Fifth Republic and newly founded Parti Socialiste Unifié, but analysis of Communist and Socialist parties, trade unions, relations of intellectuals to political Left is valid for later years as well.

1232a MICHAL, BERNARD (ed.). Les grandes énigmes de la IVe République; v. 3. Avec la collaboration de Edmond Bergheaud et al. [Paris?] Editions de Saint-Clair, 1967. 247 p. plates. (Les Grandes énigmes historiques de notre temps) Includes bibliography.

Volume 3 covers October 1956 - May 1958 episodes, notably capture of Ben Bella, disappearance of Captain Moureau, Sakhiet bombing, and background of May 13, 1958. This final section (100 pages) follows events both in Paris and Algeria, using published inside accounts.

1233 MICHAL, BERNARD (ed.). Les grandes énigmes de la Ve République. Avec la collaboration d'Edmond Bergheaud et al. [Clermont-Ferrand?] Editions de Saint-Clair, 1967. 3 v. illus., ports. (Les Grandes énigmes historiques de notre temps) Includes bibliographies.

Reconstruction of 11 dramatic episodes connected with the liquidation of the Algerian war on the basis of published documents, newspapers, books, and personal archives, by Bernard Michal, Edmond Bergheaud, and six other writers. Vol. 1 covers 1960-1961, vol. 2 January - June 1962, and vol. 3 July 1962 - December 1962. Episodes include the January 1960 and April 1961 uprising in Algeria, negotiations with F.L.N. by French government and O.A.S., as well as the abortive negotiations with Si Salah in June 1960, episodes related to the O.A.S. such as the violent clash between pro-French Algerians and the French army in March 1962, O.A.S. operations in Algeria and Salan's arrest, the attempt on de Gaulle's life at Petit-Clamart, and the arrest of Colonel Argoud. One section describes the power struggle in the first year of Algerian independence. Numerous illustrations.

1234 MICHEL, ANDREE and GENEVIEVE TEXIER. La condition de la Française d'aujourd'hui. Genève, Gonthier, 1964. 2 v. (Collection Femme) Includes bibliography.

First volume deals with myths surrounding woman and realities of woman's position in French family, professions, political life. Second volume describes pressure groups aiming to keep women in their traditional role (e.g., Catholic Church, professional and employer groups) and groups advocating greater equality (political parties, unions, family planning groups). Outlook for family planning, fuller integration into economic life is analyzed.

1235 MICHEL, ANDREE. Les travailleurs algériens en France. Préf. par Pierre Laroque. Paris, Centre national de la recherche scientifique, 1956. 238 p. illus., maps (part fold.) (Travaux du Centre d'études sociologiques) Bibliography: p. 227-234.

Sociologist's investigation, based on official documents and 1955-56 interviews of Algerians in Paris area and Eastern France, on nature of employment qualifications, conditions of work, salary, housing. Author's thesis is that the stereotypes of the "backward natives" have been transferred directly from colonial situation to Algerian migrants and serve as self-justification for prevalent segration and discrimination as well as latent antagonism. Study also examines causes and nature of emigration and rate of return. Extensive bibliography includes many documentary studies.

1236 MICHEL, FRANÇOIS. Christ et croissant pour l'Algérie nouvelle. Manifeste pour une paix humaine, un monde meilleur! Paris, L. Soulanges, 1962. 168 p.

Rambling comments on possibilities of Algerian peace and other international issues by former naval officer and devout Catholic. As of Sept. 1961, author supports de Gaulle, whom he considers only one capable of ending Algerian conflict. Though favoring self-determination and an Algerian state, author proposes continued presence of a Franco-Algerian army to prevent control by F.L.N. and take-over of international communism.

1237 MICHEL, HENRI. Histoire de la France libre. Paris, Presses universitaires de France, 1963. 126 p. ("Que sais-je?" Le Point des connaissances actuelles, 1078) Includes bibliography.

De Gaulle occupies center of stage in this popular history of the French resistance.

1238 MICHELAT, GUY and JEAN PIERRE THOMAS. Dimensions du nationalisme; enquête par questionnaire (1962). Préf. de Raoul Girardet. En appendice: Analyse hiérarchique et indice de transivité, par Raymond Boudon. Paris, A. Colin, 1966. xiii, 184 p. diagrs. (Cahiers de la Fondation nationale des sciences politiques. 143)

Results of Jan.-Feb. 1962 questionnaires on different varieties of nationalism and correlations with other political attitudes answered by 223 students of Paris, Strasbourg, Grenoble Institutes of Political Studies. Study, which was carried through at height of polarization on Algerian conflict, not surprisingly shows strong correlations between identification with Right and nationalist ideology.

1239 MICHELET, EDMOND. Contre la guerre civile. Paris, Plon, 1957. vii, 104 p. (Tribune libre, 13)

Analysis of the alignment of political parties and movements with respect to the Algerian conflict (French and French-Algerian neo-Nazis, the old and new-style Right, as exemplified by Raymond Aron's rationalist argument for withdrawal from Algeria, the Communists, and the Catholic and Mendesist Left) in the face of the Army's emotional commitment to keeping Algeria French while improving the lot of the non-Europeans. The failure to face the facts of the war and the vacillations of the successive governments raise the specter of a civil war between the impassioned defenders of French Algeria and those passively or actively advocating Algerian independence. Only de Gaulle is seen capable of renovating political institutions and rallying popular unanimity behind a positive and generous, yet firm Algerian policy

1240 MICHELET, EDMOND. Le Gaullisme, passionante aventure. Paris, Fayard, 1962. 170, [1] p. Bibliography: p. 163-171.

History of the Gaullist movement 1940-1962, seeking its spiritual roots and conceptual unity through the resistance, the beginning of the Fourth Republic, the R.P.F., and the Fifth Republic. Author spent war years in concentration camp, became deputy in 1945, Minister of Justice after 1958. Work contains interesting analysis of Bidault's political role in creation of M.R.P. and on the attitude of other Gaullists such as Soustelle, Vallon, and Debré.

1241 MIGNON, ERNEST. Les mots du général. Préf. de Jean Cau. Illus. de Jacques Faizant. Paris, A. Fayard, 1962. 152 p. illus.

Collection of brief anecdotes ('bons mots') illustrating de Gaulle's personality and political philosophy and spanning his entire public career. Anecdotes are arranged by topics such as: De Gaulle and politics, de Gaulle and the army, de Gaulle and diplomacy, de Gaulle and his ministers. Stories are authentic or at least plausibly attributable to de Gaulle, neither flattering nor systematically hostile.

1242 MIGNOT, ELIE. Der Kampf der Kommunistischen Partei Frankreichs gegen den Kolonialismus und für den Frieden in Algerien. Berlin, Dietz, 1959. 38 p. (Internationale Reihe)

Attitude of Parti Communiste Français toward Algerian war and F.L.N. and critical stand on Gaullist Algerian policy for failing to bring war to an end.

1243 MINGUET, RENE. Histoire du futur; la France dans 20 ans. Paris, Entreprise moderne d'édition, 1965. ix, 300 p. maps.

Businessman and planner studies each of nine major regions of France, examining local population, agriculture and industrial production, and prospects for new developments.

1244 MITTERRAND, FRANÇOIS. Le coup d'état permanent. Paris, Plon, 1964. 279 p. (Collection "Les débats de notre temps")

Subversive origins and unlawful functioning of Fifth Republic are subjected to virulent attack by one of leading spokesmen of democratic opposition to de Gaulle, Minister of the Interior under Mendès-France, later Minister of Justice and currently deputy. De Gaulle is accused of having exploited and aggravated weaknesses of previous regime and step by step turned the Fifth Republic into a police state, securing his unlimited personal rule by debasing the very institutions he himself approved in the 1958 Constitution. Author discusses at length changes in French judicial organs and the recent establishment of the Cour de Sûreté for political crimes.

1245 MITTERRAND, FRANÇOIS. François Mitterrand répond aux questions. Paris, 1966. 30 p. (Les Cahiers de la Convention des institutions républicaines, 6) "Supplément à 'Combat républicain,' no. 22, décembre 1966."

Complete text of Sept. 1966 radio discussion with Jacques Fauvet and answers to listener questions on Fédération de la gauche démocrate et socialiste's stand on a wide range of international and domestic issues.

1246 MITTERRAND, FRANÇOIS. Un plan pour la Féderation. Paris, 1966. 38 p. (Les Cahiers de la Convention des institutions républicaines, 1) "Supplément à "Combat républicain," no. 14, mars 1966."

Mitterrand address before March 1966 meeting of Convention des institutions républicaines and subsequent interview concerning prospects for unifying Left through the Fédération de la gauche démocratique et socialiste, of which he is president and of which Convention is one of three major adherents.

1247 MITTERRAND, FRANÇOIS. Présence française et abandon. Paris, Plon, 1957. 240 p. (Tribune libre, 12)

History of France's involuntary retreat from Indochina, Morocco, and Tunisia and plea for wider application of the "loi-cadre" granting greater autonomy to sub-Saharan Africa. Mitterrand defends the wisdom of Mendès-France's and Edgar Faure's North African policies as the only way to preserve some sort of French presence. The Algerian situation is not specifically mentioned.

FOR ADDITIONAL WORKS BY AND ABOUT FRANÇOIS MITTERRAND, SEE AUTHOR INDEX

1248 MOCH, JULES SALVADOR. Non à la force de frappe. Paris, R. Laffont, 1963. 270 p.

Socialist politician's case against French and multinational nuclear force. Moch served as French delegate to disarmament conferences for a decade and advocates disarmament as the only solution, giving concrete possibilities for this approach, with supporting arguments from papal "Pacem in Terris." Book describes formation, March 1963, of the Ligue nationale contre la force de frappe, reproducing text of its appeal and first signers.

1249 MOCH, JULES SALVADOR. Paix en Algérie en 1961. Paris, R. Laffont, 1961. 270 p.

Balanced review of Algerian problem within context of Fourth and Fifth Republic and its repercussions in the United Nations precedes proposals for peace settlements that might be acceptable to both Algerian communities, after failure of Melun negotiations.

1250 MOCH, JULES SALVADOR. Socialisme vivant; (dix lettres à un jeune) Paris, R. Laffont, 1960. 203 p. (Problèmes sociaux de l'âge atomique, 1)

Up-dating of Socialist doctrines in form accessible to the young and reassessment of such concepts as the class struggle, relations with communism, non-socialist democrats, while insisting on the continuity of Socialist moral inspiration. The ideas were the outcome of S.F.I.O's Groupe d'Etudes Doctrinales, set up in 1959, which published its theses and debates in the "Revue Socialiste."

1251 MOHLER, ARMIN. Die französische Rechte; vom Kampf um Frankreichs Ideologienpanzer. München, Isar Verlag, 1958. 86 p. (Konservative Schriften, Bd. 3) "Kritische Bibliographie": p. 74-86.

Essay on dying out of old rightist movements, the immobilism of the forces clinging to the status quo, and the scattered little groups that may serve as a rallying point for a new Right. Among movements with potential new right are Gaullism and Mendesism, which, as of early 1958, seemed to have failed. Author is Swiss-born journalist stationed in France as foreign correspondent, with personal ties to German conservatives as former secretary of Ernst Juenger.

1252 MOHLER, ARMIN. Die Fünfte Republik; was steht hinter de Gaulle? München, R. Piper, 1963. 331 p. tables. (Piper Paperback) "Kritische Bibliographie": p. [224]-295.

Systematic analysis of major political forces at work in the founding, functioning, and opposition to Fifth Republic. In addition, work provides excellent reference tools for first four years of Fifth Republic: 1) detailed chronology of Gaullism prior to and during Fifth Republic; 2) sketches of main political organizations; 3) a key to new political vocabulary; 4) annotated, topically arranged bibliography of about 1000 books and articles; 5) lists of newspapers and periodicals and their political orientation. Index of persons and authors mentioned in bibliography.

1253 MOINE, ANDRE. Après "Pacem in terris"; chrétiens et communistes. Paris, Editions sociales, 1965. 179 p. ("Politique et religion")

Possible areas of cooperation between Communist parties and Catholic Church in the wake of the Vatican's new conciliatory attitude.

1254 MOINET, BERNARD. Journal d'une agonie ... Préf. de Jean-Louis Tixier-Vignancour. Paris, Editions Saint-Just, 1965. 240 p. plates.

Diary, Dec. 1961-April 1962, of French army captain stationed in Algeria since 1957 and recording his impressions of final months of violence in Oran, involving O.A.S., F.L.N., but also police and military forces loyal to the government. As an officer uncompromised by political rebellion, author had testified as defense witness in Salan trial, describing the vicious behavior of government troops against European population, and the book as a whole is to bear witness to the stages that actually lead to Algerian independence to counteract official Gaullist version in which O.A.S. alone is responsible for all violence. Appendices reproduce contradictory de Gaulle declarations on Algeria, 1958-1961, text of Evian agreements, O.A.S., F.L.N., and P.S.U. leaflets.

1254a MOLCHANOV, NIKOLAI NIKOLAEVICH. Vneshniaia politika Frantsii (Piataia respublika) Moskva,Izd-vo In-ta mezhdunarodnykh otnoshenii, 1961. 118 p. (Venshniaia politika, mexhdunarodnye otnosheniia)

Continuity and change in Fifth Republic's foreign policy, 1958-1961, with chapters on participation in NATO, relations with West Germany and the Soviet Union, European policy.

1255 MOLLET, GUY. L'Armée et la nation [une série d'articles publiés dans le "Populaire de Paris" du 22 février au 6 mars 1960]. Arras, Société d'éditions du Pas-de-Calais, 1960. 38 p.

Secretary general of Parti socialiste's recapitulation of party's military doctrine, psychological and political explanation of current demoralization and divisions in army, and favorable comments on Gaullist military and Algerian policy.

1256 MOLLET, GUY. Bilan et perspectives socialistes. Paris, Plon, 1958. 223 p. (Tribune libre, 18)

Public addresses given throughout France December 1957 explaining Mollet's and the Socialist Party's stand on the cold war, disarmament, the French Union, Algeria, economic and social programs, and the party's attitude toward political collaboration with the Communist party and other parties.

1257 MOLLET, GUY. 13 [i.e., Treize] mai 1958 - 13 mai 1962. Paris, Plon, 1962. 244 p. (Tribune libre, 63)

Socialist politician's speeches in the National Assembly and at S.F.I.O. meetings, interviews, articles, letters topically arranged as follows: birth of the Fifth Republic, international affairs, Algeria, internal affairs, ideological problems. The original texts are unaltered but connected by author's 1962 comments.

FOR ADDITIONAL WORKS BY AND ABOUT GUY MOLLET, SEE AUTHOR INDEX

1258 MONGE, RENE. Le travailleur espagnol et la famille espagnole en France. El trabajador español y la familia expañola en Francia. Paris, Service social d'aide aux émigrants, 1966. 71 p.

Bi-lingual questions and answers on social services, status of immigrants, labor laws applicable to Spanish workers.

1259 MONGE, RENE. Le travailleur italien en France et la famille italienne en France. Il lavoratore italiano [e] la famiglia italiana in Francia. Paris, Service social d'aide aux émigrants 1966. 71 p.

Same as above for Italian workers.

1260 MONGE, RENE. Le travailleur portugais et la famille portugaise en France. O trabalhador português a família portuguesa en França. Paris, Service social d'aide aux émigrants, 1966. 69 p.

Same as above for Portuguese workers.

1261 MONNERVILLE, GASTON. Le Sénat: institution fondamentale d'une république démocratique. 2. éd. Paris, Editions SERPIC, 1965. 58 p. port.

Lectures by Senate president at various student gatherings during 1964 explaining history, function, representativeness and possible reform of Senate under 1958 Constitution.

1262 MONNET, JEAN. Address at the opening ceremony of the Second World Congress of Man-made Fibres, London, 1 May, 1962. London, 1962. 9 l.

Speech on European economic integration.

1263 MONNET, JEAN. Address when receiving the Freedom Award in New York on January 13, 1963. New York, 1963. 9 p.

Speech on Atlantic partnership.

1264 MONNET, JEAN. La Communauté européenne et l'unité de l'Occident. Lausanne, Ecole des H.E.C., Université de Lausanne, 1961. 10 p.

Speech on Atlantic partnership.

1265 MONNET, JEAN. La Communauté européenne et la Grande-Bretagne. Lausanne, Centre de recherches européennes, Ecole H.E.C., Université de Lausanne, 1958. 15 p.

October 1957 speech at Harrogate on European Free Trade Association and Common Market relations, urging patience on all sides.

1266 MONNET, JEAN. L'Europe et l'organisation de la paix. Lausanne, Centre de recherches européennes, Ecole des H.E.C., Université de Lausanne, 1964. 14 p. port.

February 1964 address at Bad Godesberg on U.S.-European partnership in terms of trade and weapons (such as the multilateral nuclear force) as fundamental tool for reducing international tensions.

1267 MONNET, JEAN. Speech at the commencement ceremonies, Dartmouth College, New Hampshire, U.S.A., June 11th, 1961. [n.p., 1961] 10 l.

Speech on Atlantic partnership.

1268 MONTAGUT, PIERRE and HENRI BISSARDON. L'Algérie: ses problèmes. Lyon, Editions des Deux-fleuves, 1961. 168 p. (Collection Choc)

Brief popular work on Algerian political history and some of the country's basic economic and demographic problems, the effects of the war and Constantine Plan, composition of European population in Algeria as of July 1961. Authors come out in favor of Algerian independence.

1269 MONTEIL, VINCENT. Les officiers. Paris, Editions du Seuil, 1964. 191 p. illus. (Le Temps qui court, 8)

History of French officer corps, 1815-1963, with final 25 pages devoted to drama of professional soldiers under Fifth Republic in Algeria and later as members of O.A.S. Author, who is unsympathetic to rebellious officers, briefly explains their psychological motivations as well as those of the officers who resisted the nationalist intoxication.

1270 MONTPEYROUX, ANDRE DE BROUSSE BRETAGNE, MARQUIS DE. Pour la France faut-il suivre Salan? Par de Montpeyroux Brousse (El Ghoul) [Bruxelles, 1961]. 154 p. illus.

Member of OA.S. recently escaped from Paris prison, a former local councilman in Central France having served in Algeria, reviews fight to preserve French Algeria since 1958 and attacks other defenders of French Algeria like Soustelle and Lagaillarde as ineffective and January 1960, April 1961 uprisings as ill-advised.

1271 MONTVALLON, PIERRE DE. Le prince qui nous gouverne. [By] Piem [pseud.]. Paris, Editions Témoignage chrétien, 1960. 63 p. chiefly illus.

Thematically arranged cartoons on de Gaulle, 1958-1960. Author is political cartoonist for "Témoignage chrétien."

1272 MONTVALON, ROBERT DE. Ces pays qu'on n'appellera plus colonies. Paris, Editions T.C., 1957. 108 p. (Bibliothèque de l'homme d'action)

Essays on changes in the colonial situation and adaptation thereto by the Catholic Church in giving greater autonomy to native Catholics and taking part in the colonies' economic development.

1273 MORICE, ANDRE. Les fellagha dans la cité. Nantes, Editions de la Société d'Editions du P.O., 1959. 140 p.

1957 Defense Minister's evidence against the French Communist Party and the "defeatist" press (primarily "Express" and "France-Observateur") for giving aid and comfort to the F.L.N. and the cause of Algerian independence. Evidence consists of excerpts from Communist publications and "defeatist" press on Algerian war, with comments by author and other political figures for 1957 - December 1958.

1274 MORIZOT, JEAN. L'Algérie kabylisée. Préf. de Pierre Rondot. Paris, J. Peyronnet, 1962. 163 p. plates, maps. (Cahiers de l'Afrique et l'Asie, 6) Bibliographical footnotes.

Kabylia's social and economic evolution, 1830-1961 by former French administrator of the area. Kabylia, which was left nearly totally outside settlers' orbit, played a leading role in revolution and author speculates on part Kabylia's intellectual elite will play after independence.

1275 MORLAND, BARANGE and MARTINEZ. Histoire de l'Organisation de l'armée secrète. Paris, R. Julliard, 1964. 605 p.

Antecedents of O.A.S. are retraced to beginning of Algerian revolution in tie-up between some of French military leaders with French-Algerian activists. History of O.A.S. is carried through until movement's dissolution both in France and Algeria in early 1963. The intricate story is told with a profusion of names and details (no name index). Appendices reproduce O.A.S. and Conseil national de la Résistance (C.N.R.) directives, Sept. 1961 - Jan 1963.

1276 MOSSE, ROBERT. Bibliographie d'économie politique 1945-1960, 1960-1962. Avec la collaboration de Michel Potier. Paris, Sirvey. 2 v.

Classified bibliography of French publications in economics, but not exclusively about France. Author and subject indices. V. 1 covers 1945-1960, v. 2 1960-1962. The 891 items of the second volume all relate to the Fifth Republic.

1277 MOTHE, DANIEL. Militant chez Renault. Paris, Editions du Seuil, 1965. 233 p. (Collections Esprit. "La Cité prochaine.")

Revealing case study of labor relations in France's largest nationalized industry, based on the author's personal experience there as a skilled worker and union representative. Workers' attitudes toward work, unions, larger political problems, the relation between union "militants" and workers on the one hand, labor organizations on the other, the effect of changing economic conditions and legislation on labor relations as a whole are perceptively described. Author emphasizes that union hierarchy, notably that of C.G.T. no longer symbolizes real worker experiences and adds to depersonalization of workers' life experience. Participation in work decisions and growing responsibility rather than vague revolutionary goals and demands limited to higher wages and shorter hours are seen as the only answer to growing worker alienation.

1278 MOTLEY, MARY (pseud.). Home to Numidia. London, Longmans 1964. 227 p.

Personal narrative of English woman's life in Kabylia, at the edge of Saharan desert during pre-World War II years, beginning of Algerian war, summer of 1961, after May 1962. Author's close ties to Moslem childhood friends as well as acquaintance with some French Algerians in Algiers permit her to see conflict from different angles, although author refuses to become involved in political conflict.

1279 MOUILLARD, MAURICE. La mystification du 13 mai au 28 septembre. Paris, Editions sociales, 1958. 283 p.

Communist interpretation of the birth of the Fifth Republic, attacking four myths of its supporters: that de Gaulle shielded France from fascism, that integration and fraternization in Algeria can be achieved through counter-revolutionary psychological warfare, that the evils of the old parliamentary "système" have been exorcized, and that the new constitution has renovated French political institutions. Results of the September referendum are seen as an expression of popular wishful thinking.

1280 MOUILLESEAUX, LOUIS (ed.). Histoire de l'Algérie; textes de Jean Lassus et al. Paris, Productions de Paris 1962. 452 p. illus., ports., map.

Illustrated history of Algeria going back to antiquity, and presenting favorable picture of French conquest, with short sections on recent French efforts to modernize country, chronology of war, prospects for a new Algeria as of early 1962. Chapters are by different authors, including Georges Marçais, and Jean Farran.

1281 MOUREAU, MAURICE. Des Algériens accusent... Paris, Editions du Scorpion, 1959. 156 p. (Collection Alternance)

Algerians currently living in France but having left their birthplace after the outbreak of the revolution, tell their personal experiences and explain their attitudes toward the Algerian war. All of them support Algerian independence.

1282 MOUSSA, PIERRE. Les chances économiques de la communauté franco-africaine. Paris, A. Colin, 1957. 271 p. illus. (Cahiers de la Fondation nationale des sciences politiques, 83) "Bibliographie": p. 215-216.

Industry by industry assessment of economic interactions between France and African colonies followed by comparison of French efforts to help African industrialization with that of other European countries and proposals for new economic programs speeding up industrialization.

1283 MOUVEMENT CONTRE L'ARMEMENT ATOMIQUE. [Publications of the Mouvement contre l'armement atomique, including no. 5-10 of the periodical "Alerte atomique," and materials relating to disarmament collected by the Movement. Paris, 196-] 1 envelope, bound.

Mainly 1965-66 material (leaflets, appeals, newsletters) opposing French nuclear weapons and Vietnam war. (For earlier protest against French bomb, see French Fifth Republic Collection, Box 1, part 4.)

1284* MOUVEMENT DE LA JEUNESSE COMMUNISTE DE FRANCE. [Appeal to French Youth during April 1961 generals' putsch]

1285* MOUVEMENT DE LA PAIX. Le péril atomique. [Paris, 1958] [8] p.

1286* MOUVEMENT DE SAINT-CERE. Congrès des 10, 11, 13 avril 1958. St-Céré (Lot), 1958. 5 p.

Congress resolutions sanction new political regime, by violence if necessary.

1287* MOUVEMENT FEDERALISTE FRANÇAIS. Les impératifs de l'économie française. [Paris, Fédération, 1959?] 19 p.

1288* MOUVEMENT POUJADE. ECOLE DES CADRES. [Material on party's school for political education, July 1958] Capdenac (Aveyron)

FOR ADDITIONAL PUBLICATIONS BY AND ABOUT MOUVEMENT POUJADE, SEE AUTHOR INDEX

1289* MOUVEMENT POUR LE TRIOMPHE DES LIBERTES DEMOCRATIQUES. [Appeal to let Messali Hadj return to Algeria] [Paris, 1961?]

1290 MOUVEMENT REPUBLICAIN POPULAIRE. CONGRES NATIONAL. Compte-rendu sténographique des congrès nationaux; reproduction de documents appartenant aux archives du M. R. P. (Paris). [Paris, 1944-1962] Microfilm copy (positive) of typescript made by Service international de microfilms, Paris.

Nineteen volumes of documents on each of the 19 national congresses, reproduced on 17 reels of microfilm. (Reel 1 and 13 each cover two congresses, otherwise each reel covers one congress), under the guidance of the Fondation nationale des sciences politique, which also drew up a table of contents for the first 15 reels, available in mimeographed form at the Hoover Institution. Congresses held since beginning of Fifth Republic are on reels 13-17.

1291 MOUVEMENT REPUBLICAIN POPULAIRE. 21. CONGRES NATIONAL, LE TOUQUET, 1964. 21e congrès national du M. R. P., Le Touquet, 7-8-9 mai 1964. Paris, 1964. 5 v. in 1. (Action civique et politique, no. 11) In portfolio.

Speakers Jean Lecanuet, Joseph Fontanet, Jean Mastias, Maurice Blin, and André Monteil outline party program on domestic and foreign policy.

1292 MOUVEMENT REPUBLICAIN POPULAIRE. 22. CONGRES NATIONAL, VICHY, 1965. 22e congrès national du M. R. P., Vichy, 27-28-29 mai, 1965. Paris, 1965. 4 v. in 1. (Action civique et politique, no. 15) In portfolio.

Speakers Joseph Fontanet, Pierre Abelin, Jean Lecanuet, and Pierre Pflimlin report on party's domestic and foreign policy program and discuss M. R. P.'s support of Gaston Defferre's presidential candidacy.

1293* MOUVEMENT REPUBLICAIN POPULAIRE. SECRETARIAT GENERAL. Statuts nationaux. Paris, 1957. 15 p.

FOR ADDITIONAL PUBLICATIONS BY AND ABOUT THE MOVEMENT REPUBLICAIN POPULAIRE, SEE AUTHOR INDEX

1294 MÜLLER, HANS DIETER (ed.). Die Force de frappe: Europas Hoffnung oder Verhängnis? Olten, Walter-Verlag, 1965. 124 p. (Walter Texte und Dokumente. Analysen) Bibliographical footnotes.

Two German political experts, Georg Picht and Carl Friedrich von Weizsaecker and two Frenchmen, political scientist Alfred Grosser and statesman Paul Reynaud, give their views of de Gaulle's policy of nuclear armament and Franco-German relations. Picht's essay covers military strategy in some detail and presents theories of U.N.R. and military leaders. Only Grosser has some sympathy for de Gaulle's rejection of the Atlantic Alliance and search for an independent strategy. In Appendix 1964 statements by de Gaulle, Couve de Murville and General Ailleret documenting above essays.

1295 MUENCHHAUSEN, THANKMAR, FREIHERR VON. Ziele und Widerstaende der franzoesischen Algerienpolitik von 1945-1958. Muenchen, 1962. XV, 441 p. Bibliography: p. 419-441 ML

Heidelberg doctoral dissertation, giving brief history of Algerian colonization and nationalism, as well as abortive reforms prior to 1954. Main part of dissertation shows role of Algerian question in last years of Fourth Republic, with detailed and systematic presentation of Algerian policy of successive governments, views of Army, political parties, and public opinion toward Algerian question, the war, and May 1958 uprising.

1296 MULLER, JEAN. De la pacification à la répression; le dossier Jean Muller. [Extrait des lettres durant sa vie de soldat en Algérie, juin - oct., 1956.] Paris, 1957. 29 p. (Cahiers du Témoignage chrétien, 38)

Letters to personal friends by young French officer, who had been active in various youth movements but not politically affiliated, and who was killed in action in Algeria October 1956. Letters describe pacification measures, use of torture, internment camps.

1297 MUNDT, TITO. De Gaulle, el gran solitario. Santiago de Chile, Zig-Zag, 1964. 234 p.

Chilean journalist's impressionistic political biography of de Gaulle shortly after his visit of state to South America.

1298 MURATET, ROGER. On a tué Ben Barka. Paris, Plon, 1967. 380 p. plates. Bibliographical footnotes.

Outcome of a yearlong investigation of Ben Barka affair by French correspondent in Morocco, who interviewed at length all persons connected directly with drama and with judicial procedure. Work not only reconstructs in detective story style the strands of the murder, but clarifies Moroccan and French context. Author concludes that Moroccan government alone bears blame, French police are exonerated. Story is carried through March 1967.

1299 MURCIER, ALAIN. Was will de Gaulle, die Sphinx Frankreichs? Diessen/Ammersee, W. Tucher, 1965. 159 p. (Aktuelle Taschenbücher)

French journalist's explanation of de Gaulle's current views on European unification, Atlantic Alliance, military strategy, and international relations.

1300 MURY, GILBERT. Essor ou déclin du catholicisme français? Paris, Editions sociales, 1960. 317 p. (Maxisme et religion) Bibliographical footnotes.

Sociological and statistical description of urban and rural Catholic institutions based on Catholic studies but viewed in line with Marxist philosophy.

1301 MUS, EMILE. Guerre sans visage; lettres commentées du sous-lieutenant Emile Mus [par son père, Paul Mus] Paris, Editions du Seuil, 1961. 187 p. port. (Collections "Esprit." La condition humaine)

Factual, non-political letters documenting young French officer's service in parachute regiment 1958-July 1960. The letters are introduced by a lengthy commentary written after his son's death by economist Paul Mus, who sees them as an expression of inadequate communication between the army and metropolitan France.

1302* MUSEE DE L'HOMME. BIBLIOTHEQUE. Liste des acquisitions, 1960. Paris, Musée de l'homme, 1961. 59 l.

1303* MUSLIM STUDENTS' FEDERATION. INFORMATION DEPT., LONDON. Life in Algeria. 3rd ed. [London, 1960] 36 p.

Report of 1959 study trip to Algeria summarizing facts of political and economic situation, and interpreting French policies, notably the Constantine Plan, favorably.

1304 NAEGELEN, MARCEL EDMOND. L'Hexagonie; essai fantaisiste d'histoire contemporaine. Paris, Presses du Mail, 1963. 220 p.

Thinly veiled satire on recent French history (abandonment of Algeria) and de Gaulle.

1305 NAEGELEN, MARCEL EDMOND. Mission en Algérie. Expériences et opinions d'un gouverneur général. Paris, Flammarion, 1962. 314 p.

Socialist politician's experiences as Algerian governor general, 1948-1951 and his efforts to implement 1947 political statute for Algeria, with some comments on political evolution during Fifth Republic. Author urges continued French responsibility for Algeria and peaceful cohabitation of the two communities, though admitting as of March 1962 that integration is impossible.

1306 NAEGELEN, MARCEL EDMOND. Une route plus large que longue. Paris, R. Laffont, 1965. 345 p. ("L'Histoire que nous vivons")

Presentation of political situation in Algeria before Fifth Republic, explanation of steps leading to Evian Treaty, analysis of its provisions and their subsequent abrogation (without French protest). Fate of French Algerians who tried to cooperate with new regime and their gradual disillusion with Ben Bella regime is traced and treatment of those who returned to France, as well as current status of Algerian workers in France is described. Though author blames Gaullist policy for the present chaos, he is more moderate than many Gaullist opponents and tries to apportion some responsibility to O.A.S. for producing Algerian fiasco.

1307 NANIA, GUY. Un parti de la gauche: le PSU; préf. d'Edouard Depreux. Draveil, (S.-O.), Librairie Gedalge, 1966. 299 p. illus. Includes bibliography.

Study based on doctoral dissertation and carried out with cooperation of Parti Socialiste Unifié, which gave unlimited access to files. Author retraces precursors to party's founding in April 1960 by giving history of its constituent organizations, the Union de la Gauche Socialiste and other miniscule leftist groups, the Tribune du Communisme, the post-1958 Union des Forces Démocratiques, and the S.F.I.O. dissident Parti Socialiste Autonome. The party's inner functioning, conflicts, program and action, sociology of membership and leaders, publications, and political prospects are examined in great detail and without favorable bias. Appendix reproduces party's statutes and charter. Name index.

1308 NANTET, JACQUES. Pierre Mendès-France. Paris, Editions du Centurion, 1967. xx, 272 p. ports. (Hommes présents) Includes bibliography.

Political biography, with last 20 pages summarizing Mendès-France's opposition to Fifth Republic, his current views, and his successful campaign as deputy for Grenoble area, March 1967. Bibliography lists all of Mendès-France's publications.

1309 NAROUN, AMAR. Ferhat Abbas; ou Les chemins de la souveraineté. Paris, Denoel, 1961. 183 p. (Petits précis sur les hommes et les questions du jour, 1)

Political and ideological biography of Ferhat Abbas leading to his commitment to nationalist revolution by personal friend of Algerian nationalist. There are also sketches of Ahmed Boumendjel and Ahmed Francis, friends of Ferhat Abbas and the author.

1310 NATHAN, ROBERT. Vers l'Europe des réalités. Paris, Plon, 1963. 193 p.

Arguments favoring admission of Great Britain into the Common Market.

1311 NATION FRANÇAISE (periodical). Ecrits pour une renaissance, par le groupe de la Nation française: Pierre Andreu et al. Paris, Plon, 1958. viii, 233 p. (Tribune libre, 19)

Individual essays by principal collaborators of "Nation française," founded in 1955, on future of nationalism, proposals for a strong state, Algerian question. The essays date from 1957-58, foresee end of Fourth Republic, are anti-parliamentarian but moderate on Algerian question. Among contributors are Jules Monnerot, Pierre Boutang, Jean Brune. For "Nation française" see no. 2013.

1312 NATION FRANÇAISE (periodical). Livre blanc de notre honte et la passion des harkis. Paris, 1962. 16 p. "Supplément au no. 371."

Fate of Moslem auxiliary troops (the "harkis") after Algerian independence as described in court testimony of editors of "Nation française" and "Esprit public," indicted for fomenting military disobedience in Algeria.

1313 NATIONAL INSTITUTE OF ECONOMIC AND SOCIAL RESEARCH. Economic planning in France; record of a conference organized by the National Institute of Economic and Social Research in London, 20-22 April, 1961. London, 1961. 207-237 p. (PEP pamphlets, no. 454)

Abbreviated text of speech by Pierre Massé, head of Commissariat général du plan, on the guiding ideas behind French planning and summaries of speeches of other French planning officials. Conclusions compare French and British methods.

1314 NAVILLE, PIERRE. La classe ouvrière et le régime gaulliste. Paris, Etudes et documentation internationales, 1964. 489 p. (Questions du socialisme, 1)

Articles written 1953-1963 for "Perspectives socialistes," "Tribune du peuple," "Tribune socialiste," "Tribune Marxiste," "Nouvel Observateur," "Cahiers du Centre d'études socialistes," and a few lectures and scholarly articles on the problems of the French labor movement in a modern industrial society. Though some topical articles on the Union de la Gauche socialiste, the P.S.U. and the Communist Party, the Algerian war, and international communism deal more specifically with political matters, the title of the book is misleading.

1315 NAVILLE, PIERRE. L'intellectuel communiste (à propos de Jean-Paul Sartre) Paris, M. Rivière, 1956. 64 p.

Non-Communist Marxist's discussion of the function of the intellectual in Marxist theory and French practice and refutation of Sartre's philosophical justification of blind allegiance to the French Communist Party, at the very time when international communism was going through its first de-stalinization phase. Author assesses prospects of de-stalinization in French communist leadership, as exemplified by Pierre Hervé's revolt. The essay was originally published in 1956 issues of "Lettres nouvelles."

1316 NAVILLE, PIERRE. Vers l'automatisme social? Problèmes du travail et de l'automation. Paris, Gallimard, 1963. 258 tables. (Problèmes et documents) Includes bibliographical references.

Sociologist's study of the penetration of automation into French industry around 1960, automation's effect on work organization and the workers' sense of alienation, with stress on automation's constructive implications.

1317 LA NEF (periodical). 12 hommes politiques répondent à 12 questions. Paris, Julliard, 1965. 223 p. "Cahier trimestriel ... octobre-décembre 1965, nouvelle série, cahier no. 24-25."

Full and thoughtful answers shortly before presidential election to 12 questions on foreign and European policy, political institutions, economic, social, and educational issues by three presidential candidates (Jean Lecanuet, Pierre Marcilhacy and François Mitterand) Michel Debré as Gaullist spokesman, Emmanuel d'Astier as Gaullist supporter from the left, uncommitted center politicians Jacques Duhamel, Edgar Faure and Maurice Faure, outspoken opposition leaders Gilles Martinet (P. S. U.) Guy Mollet (S. F. I. O) and Waldeck-Rochet (P. C. F.) and political scientist Georges Vedel. Disagreement is fundamental only on European question, while opposition to Gaullist institutions has subsided and is muted on relations with U. S., domestic policy.

1318 LA NEF (periodical). Histoire de la guerre d'Algérie, suivie d'une histoire de l'O.A.S. Paris, Julliard, 1963. 191 p. "La Nef, nouvelle série, numéro spécial, cahier nos. 12-13, octobre 1962-janvier 1963."

Retrospective articles by ten authors on different aspects of the Algerian war: chronology, F. L. N. and pied-noir mentality, reactions to the war of French intellectuals and Catholics, the course of negotiations, and the disappointment of liberal French opinion with chaotic conditions after Algerian independence. The second part is by Paul Marie de la Gorce, giving detailed history of the origins, formation, successes and failures of the O. A. S. in Algeria, December 1960 - June 1962.

1319 LA NEF (periodical). La police en France. Paris, Julliard, 1963. 158 p. (Its n. s. Cahier no. 14)

First part, by Nef editors, on specific functions of police, second by individual authors, among them François Mitterand and Constantin Melnik, commenting on the police's rôle in the Fifth Republic. Mitterand sees trend toward police state, in contrast to Melnik, who predicts police's anti-subversive function subsiding after O. A. S. dissolution.

1320 NEGRI, GUGLIELMO. Verso la Quinta repubblica; l'evoluzione constituzionale contemporanea in Francia. Pisa, Nistri-Lischi, 1958. 91 p.

Constitutional reform from founding of Fourth Republic to May 1958.

1321 NERA, GILLES. La Communauté. Paris, Presses universitaires de France, 1960. 126 p. illus. ("Que sais-je?" Le point des connaissances actuelles, no. 428)

History, institutions, operations and underlying political conception of French Community, seen in an optimistic light before the institution's disintegration.

1322 Neuf thèses de l'opposition de gauche. Paris, Nouvelles éditions sociales et internationales; Edition Librairie de l'Etoile, 1966. 132 p.

Collective work by an unidentified group of communist dissidents critical of all strands of French Marxism (the Communist Party, the pro-Chinese, and the revisionist) for indirectly strengthening the Gaullist regime and offering no means of revolutionizing workers in a technologically advanced society.

1323 NICOL, AXEL. La bataille de l'O.A.S. Paris, Sept couleurs, 1962. 217 p.

Personal experiences of French businessman recently settled in Algeria who was drawn to O. A. S. in early 1961 and was active as a militant until July 1962. His responsibility was to publish O. A. S. posters, and he knew O. A. S. leaders from personal contact.

1324 NICOLET, CLAUDE. Pierre Mendès-France; ou, Le métier de Cassandre. Préf. de Pierre-Henri Simon. Paris, R. Julliard, 1959. 252 p.

Sympathetic political biography of Mendès-France, concentrating on his efforts, after his short career as prime minister, to galvanize the Radical Party into a dynamic force in French political life. A final section describes Mendès-France's and the author's own stands at the birth of the Fifth Republic. In his lengthy introduction, Pierre-Henri Simon defends Mendès-France, whose policies he only partially approves, against recent slander and emphasizes the similarities between de Gaulle's and Mendès-France's basic objectives, hoping to see them eventually join forces.

1325 NICOLLE, PIERRE. Algérie perdue; préf. du Bachaga Boualam. Lagny-sur-Marne, Editions d'Histoire et d'Art, 1965. 263 p. (Les Chemins du réel, 16)

Algerian history from origins to independence interpreted from French Algerian view point, and stressing vacillations in Gaullist policy and gradually accelerating deterioration leading to O. A. S. violence and catastrophy of European exodus. Author is Frenchman settled in Algeria since 1950. The book was actually written in the wake of Algerian independence.

1326 NOEL, LEON. Notre dernière chance. Paris, Librairie Gedalge, 1956. 198 p.

Analysis of French political institutions by jurist and Gaullist deputy in National Assembly, 1951-1955, with proposals for political and constitutional reforms, many of which were incorporated in 1958 constitution. Author also describes fate of R. P. F. in parliament up to dissolution in December 1955.

1327 NORA, PIERRE. Les Français d'Algérie. Introd. par Charles-André Julien. Paris, R. Julliard, 1961. 252 p.

Implacable dissection of European settlers' mentality, viewed historically and in the context of the Algerian war, as well as their relations with the French Army and French political life as a whole. Author, a French historian teaching at an Algerian lycée 1958-1960, provides one of the most penetrating and closely observed pictures of the settlers' world and thereby explains how the Algerian conflict took the shape it did. Author shares Sartre's and Fanon's interpretation of the colonial situation, but is concerned with its effect on the ruling group. Writing before April 1961, he sees no possibility of altering settlers' mentality other than the granting of independence.

1328 Normandie, en avant; cahiers du Neuvième d'infanterie, régiment de chasseurs parachutistes, publiée par l'Association des anciens. v. 3. Cinq ans dans le Constantinois, 1956-1960 et ailleurs. [1961]- v. 4. De Djidjelli à Moscou, de Moscou à Djidjelli, 1664, 1812, 1962, puis Toulouse, 1962-1965. [1966]. Rédacteur en chef Albert A.-J. Leclerc. Paris, illus., plates, ports., maps (part fold.) facsims.

Quarterly journal published by veterans of 9th Infantry Regiment, whose issues for 1956-1960 are collected as vol. 3 and for 1961-1965 as vol. 4. In addition to historical information about the regiment, the journal is devoted to a regimental diary of the newly reconstituted 9th Régiment d'Infanterie chasseurs parachutistes, following its exploits in the Constantine and other parts of Algeria June 1956 - November 1962, when it is moved back to the French mainland. There are news of its members and eulogies on some of its officers killed in action (e. g., Claude Barrès, June 1959) as well as notices of military instructions, shifting of officers, reorganization of larger units in the wake of the April 1961 putsch.

1329 NOUREDDINE, MEZIANE. Un Algérien raconte... Paris, Editions du Seuil, 1960. 344 p.

Oct. 1958-July 1959 prison diary of Kabylian, who had been arrested in Paris for F. L. N. support. Diary describes prison conditions and discussions among Algerian inmates.

1330 NOUSCHI, ANDRE. La naissance du nationalisme algérien. Paris, Editions de Minuit, 1962. 162 p. (Documents) Bibliography: p. 8-12.

Carefully documented, scholarly presentation of political, legislative, economic, and social evolution in Algeria, 1914-1954, resulting in demands for national independence rather than full French citizenship. Continuation of Y. Lacoste's "L'Algérie, passé et present" (no. 1048).

1330a NUNEZ GARCIA SANCO, ANTONIO. La conception européenne du général de Gaulle d'après ses discours ... Nancy, Centre européen universitaire, 1966. viii, 72 p. (Université de Nancy. Publications du Centre européen universitaire. Collection des mémoires, no. 21) Bibliography: p. 69.

Analysis of de Gaulle's stand on European integration and of his own long-range objectives for a federation of European states led by France on the basis of his speeches and press conferences 1958-1965, from which many excerpts are reproduced.

1331 L'O. A. S. et la presse française. Paris, Editions Galic, 1962. 158 p. (L'Histoire au jour le jour no. 1)

Excerpts from Paris and regional dailies on activities of O. A. S., August 1961 - May 1962, reflecting rapid rise and decline of the organization.

1332 OAS parle. Paris, R. Julliard, 1964. 355 p. illus., facsims., ports. (Collection Archives, 10)

Original O. A. S. archival collection from its staff headquarters, anonymously turned over to publisher by person connected with O. A. S. movement. The archive consists of O. A. S. leaders' correspondence, proclamations, directives, appeals, leaflets, memoranda, constitutional projects, June 1961 - June 1962. Introduction, chronology, biographical notes on principal participants complement original documents.

1333 O'BALLANCE, EDGAR. The Algerian insurrection, 1954-62. Hamden, Archon Books, 1967. 231 p. maps.

American journalist's military and political history of Algerian war, seen from both the French and the nationalist side. It is author's contention that the methods of revolutionary warfare used by Algerian nationalists were not successful militarily, that the revolution did not have genuine popular support among Moslem population, though there was no question of a Communist-controlled movement, and that victory was due to political and diplomatic factors. Work is based on published sources, some of them dealing retrospectively with the Algerian conflict. Good list of abbreviations.

1334 O'BALLANCE, EDGAR. The story of the French Foreign Legion. London, Faber and Faber 1961. 270 p. illus., maps.

History of Foreign Legion, with one short chapter on its military actions in Algerian war.

1335 OLIVI, BINO. L'Europa difficile; saggi. Introd. di Roberto Ducci. Milano, Edizioni di Comunità, 1964. 188 p. (Cultura e Realtà, 65) Bibliographical footnotes.

Essays by Italian staff member of European Economic Commission confronting different visions of European unification, notably Monnet's and de Gaulle's.

1336 OPPERMANN, THOMAS. Die algerische Frage; rechtlich-politische Studie. Stuttgart, W. Kohlhammer, 1959. xvi, 225 p. maps. (Untersuchungen zur auswärtigen Politik, Bd. 1)

Major scholarly work on the origins of the Algerian conflict in terms of the institutional and legal framework that had been imposed by the French government on the country's social and economic reality to consolidate the symbiosis of a European minority and a Moslem majority. Author briefly describes the Fifth Republic's impact on this long-standing conflict, the international status of the Algerian provisional government, and international proposals for ending war.

1337 ORGANISATION COMMUNE DES REGIONS SAHARIENNES. La situation du logement dans les départements sahariens; données statistiques. Association auxiliaire pour l'urbanisme en pays sous-développés ou arides (A. U. X. U. S. D. A.), 1961. 3 v. of tables.

Statistics for different types of dwellings in Sahara, based on information from Algerian statistical service.

1338 ORGANISATION COMMUNE DES REGIONS SAHARIENNES. BUREAU D'ETUDES STATISTIQUES, ECONOMIQUES ET SOCIALES. L'énergie électrique au Sahara [document annexe au bulletin spécial consacré à l'énergie électrique au Sahara. Paris? 1962?] 19 p. diagrs.

Statistics for Saharan power production and consumption, 1960.

1339 ORGANISATION COMMUNE DES REGIONS SAHARIENNES. GROUPE DE TRAVAIL NO. 3. DEVELOPPEMENT INDUSTRIEL. Les données techniques du problème de la construction au Sahara. [n. p., 1961]. 61 l. tables.

Report on housing needs in Sahara end of 1961.

1340 ORGANISATION COMMUNE DES REGIONS SAHARIENNES. SERVICE DES RELATIONS PUBLIQUES ET DE L'INFORMATION. OCRS. [Organisation commune des régions sahariennes. Rédaction: Raymond Postal]. Paris [1962?] 1 v. (unpaged) in portfolio.

Report on organization's contribution to Saharan economic infrastructure and oil industry, April 1958 - April 1962, with list of members. For other publications of the Organisation commune, see nos. 1962, 2030, 2031.

1341* ORGANISATION DE L'ARMEE SECRETE (O. A. S.). [Leaflets distributed]. 1 env., 4 leaflets.

1342 ORGANISATION DE L'ARMEE SECRETE (O. A. S.). [Miscellaneous publications of the Organisation de l'armée secrète. Alger, etc., 1961-62]. 1 envelope in folder.

Includes about 45 items consisting of broadsides, appeals, clandestine news letters distributed in metropolitan France and Algeria Nov. 1961 through April 1962. Identifiable organizations are: O. A. S. France Mission III, O. A. S. Direction centrale, O. A. S./Metro/A. P. P. (its "Consignes générales et directives d'organisation") Union pour la défense de l'Occident, Conseil National de la Résistance, all active in France. For Algeria, there are O. A. S. Est-Algérien, O. A. S.-Alger, and O. A. S. Légion. Other interesting individual items are "Les Centurions, publication de l'O. A. S. réservée aux officiers et cadres," (no. 8, printed in Italy), a communication between Spanish exiles Col. Argoud, Col. Lacheroy, Pierre Lagaillarde, Joseph Ortiz and O. A. S. headquarters in Algeria, a letter from General Salan to Michel Debré, Jan. 1962, and a letter by A. de B. Montpeyroux, a former local politician exiled because of his O. A. S. activities.

1343* ORGANISATION DE L'ARMEE SECRETE (O. A. S.). [Typed copy of leaflet stating the aims and purposes of the O. A. S. December 1961.] 4 p.

Leaflets answer questions as to O. A. S. membership, methods, and over-all objectives.

FOR ADDITIONAL PUBLICATIONS BY AND ABOUT THE ORGANISATION DE L'ARMEE SECRETE, SEE AUTHOR INDEX

1344 ORMESSON, WLADIMIR, COMTE D'. Les vraies confidences. Paris, Plon, 1962. 273 p.

Diplomat's autobiography including two illuminating chapters on the continuities in de Gaulle's personality, political philosophy and policies under the Fifth Republic.

1345 ORTIZ, JOSEPH. Mes combats; carnets de route 1954-1962. Paris, Editions de la Pensée moderne, 1964. 311 p.

Diary of leading French Algerian politician, originally in Poujadist movement in Algiers, who organized resistance to negotiation with F.L.N. as early as 1956. Diary describes his involvement in 1957 "bazooka affair," May 13, 1958, his founding and organizing of the Front National Français before the November 1958 elections, and his part in the January 1960 barricades. After his escape to Spain to avoid arrest, Ortiz witnessed dissensions in French nationalist camp, but took no active part in generals' putsch or O.A.S.

1346 OSSWALD, KLAUS-DIETER, ULRICH KÖHLER and WERNER RUF. Frankreichs Entwicklungshilfe; Politik auf lange Sicht? Köln, Westdeutscher Verlag, 1967. xii, 321 p. (Ordo politicus, Bd. 6) Bibliography p. [319]-321.

Survey of forms and organs of French aid to underdeveloped countries in Fourth and Fifth Republic, examination of official and unofficial justification of aid and criticism of policy. Government's attitude toward international and regional (Common Market) forms of aid is analyzed. Good bibliography.

1347 OUZEGANE, AMAR. Le meilleur combat. Paris, Julliard, 1962. 307 p. Bibliographical footnotes.

History of struggle for Algerian independence both before and since founding of F.L.N. The author, writing in Paris prison March 1962, is proposing to rebut the article by the first secretary of the Algerian Communist Party published in "Kommunist" Nov. 1960 on the Algerian revolution (see no. 1364) and explains to his fellow Algerians why, in contrast to French and Algerian Communist Party, the F.L.N. stressed Arabism, Islam, and national rather than class unity. Author became Minister of Agriculture after independence.

1348 PADO, DOMINIQUE. 13 mai; histoire secrète d'une révolution. Paris, Editions de Paris, 1958. 155 p.

Anecdotal chronicle of May 13 - June 4, 1958, shifting from Algiers to Paris and sympathetic to aims of Algerian uprising. Selected documents (letters, telegrams, speeches) in appendix.

1348a PAGE, A. Economie politique. Paris, Dalloz, 1966. 139 p.

Introductory course in economics for university students concentrating on theory rather than French reality.

1349 PAILLAT, CLAUDE. Dossier secret de l'Algérie. Paris, Livre contemporain [1961-1962]. 2 v.

Tome I, written at the height of the civilian-military struggle, emphasizes growing misunderstanding on the Algerian question from May 1958 to April 1961. Author shows intrigues on both Algerian nationalist and French military and civilian side, giving portraits of many participants, reconstructing conversations and reproducing letters (without giving sources). Tome II, concluded after Algerian independence, goes back to the beginning of the nationalist rebellion and leads up to May 1958, following day-to-day tactics of the nationalists and strategy of French military and political leaders in Algeria and Paris. Author's sympathies are with French Algeria and army.

1350 PAILLET, MARC. Gauche, année zéro. Paris, Gallimard, 1964. 372 p. (Collection Idées, 49) ML

Prospects for a new alignment of French left and proposals for economic, political, institutional reform, following criticism of Gaullist efforts in this area.

1351 PAJAUD, HENRI. La révolution d'Alger. Paris, Les 4 fils Aymon, 1958. 153 p. illus., ports.

Journalistic account covering events in Algeria February - June 6, 1958. Author tries to capture emotions sweeping French in Algeria and leading to de Gaulle's return to power, in which author sees fulfillment of generous aspirations. Photographs of demonstrations from Army Cinematographic Service.

1352 PAPON, MAURICE. L'ère des responsables. Paris, A. Fayard, 1960. 186 p. (Les idées et la vie)

Reflections on problems of administrative responsibility drawing parallels between theory of industrial management (problems of excessive specialization, overburdening of executive, need for outside consultants, forecasting techniques) and government bureaucracy. Author's varied administrative experience includes service as head of Paris police in Fifth Republic.

1353 PARET, PETER. French revolutionary warfare from Indochina to Algeria, the analysis of a political and military doctrine. New York, Published for the Center of International Studies, Princeton University, by F.A. Praeger, 1964. vi, 163 p. illus., maps. (Princeton studies in world politics, 6) "A select bibliography of writings on guerre révolutionnaire": p. 157-163.

Theory and practice of revolutionary and counterrevolutionary warfare, as evolved by French Army after its defeat in Indochina and leading up to army revolts in 1961 and O.A.S. Specifically, author examines methods of psychological warfare and the use of S.A.S. units in Algeria to win over population. The theory is seen in the setting of French military philosophy and its successes and failures and political implications are assessed to establish its wider applicability.

1354 PARIS. BIBLIOTHEQUE NATIONALE. DEPARTEMENT DES PERIODIQUES. Catalogue collectif des journaux quotidiens d'information générale, publiés en France métropolitaine de 1957 à 1961. Paris, 1962. 129 p.

Alphabetical list of Paris and regional dailies, giving location in French depository libraries and archives, with approximate dates of collections. Separate list, with addresses, of over 150 depositories.

FOR ADDITIONAL PUBLICATIONS BY PARIS. BIBLIOTHEQUE NATIONALE, SEE AUTHOR INDEX

1355 PARIS. COLLEGE COOPERATIF. Planification et volontariat dans les développements coopératifs; quinzaine d'études, 15-27 janvier 1962, organisée par le Collège coopératif, sous la direction de Henri Desroche. Paris, Mouton, 1963. 422 p. (Recherches coopératives, 3)

Includes talks on French experience of cooperative agriculture with respect to the extension of credit and government price stabilization programs.

1356 PARIS. ECOLE NORMALE SUPERIEURE. L'histoire sociale, sources et méthodes; colloque de l'Ecole normale supérieure de Saint-Cloud, 15-16 mai 1965. Paris, Presses universitaires de France, 1967. 298 p.

Colloquium on sources of documentation and methods of exploiting them for past and contemporary social history, with special listing of documentary sources for current information and possibilities of machine retrieval of data.

1357 PARIS. INSTITUT FRANÇAIS D'OPINION PUBLIQUE. Les aspirations des jeunes français de 16 à 24 ans; contribution à une étude sur les aspirations de la jeunesse européenne, juin à décember 1961. Paris, 1962. 2 v. Loose-leaf.

Item by item results of questionnaires given to 1523 young men and women throughout France July-August 1961 covering attitudes toward and level of education, professional goals, attitudes on family, political issues, standard of living, and moral and ethical questions, as well as nature of leisure activities. The study was made for the Bureau Européen de la jeunesse et de l'enfance.

1358 PARIS. INSTITUT POUR L'ETUDE ET LE DEVELOPPEMENT DE L'INDUSTRIE EN ALGERIE. Etude sur le développement industriel de l'Est algérien. Résumé d'une étude de branche [Paris, 1960?] 43 p. (Caisse d'équipement pour le développement de l'Algérie. Guide de l'industriel)

Inventory of available material and human resources in this poorest region of Algeria and proposals for industrial investment within the framework of the Constantine Plan.

1359 PARIS. UNIVERSITE. INSTITUT D'ETUDES POLITIQUES. La désignation des candidats à l'élection du président de la République; étude de Didier Cultiaux et al. Paris, Centre d'études et de documentation, 1966. 45 p. (La Participation des citoyens, 2) Etudes et documents de la Nouvelle revue politique, série C no. 2)

Contributions by political science students examining the mechanism whereby certain candidacies were successfully (or unsuccessfully) advanced before the election and showing the role of parties and political clubs in taking the initiative.

1360 PARIS. UNIVERSITE. INSTITUT DES SCIENCES SOCIALES DU TRAVAIL. Evolution des modes de rémuneration; étude sociologique de la résistance et de l'aspiration au changement; recherche sociologique effectuée dans les mines de fer à la demande de la Haute autorité de la Communauté européenne du charbon et de l'acier. Bruxelles, 1962. 101 p.

Results of interviews with management, questionnaire survey of union leaders and workers in 25 French iron mines on attitudes toward variable as against fixed monthly wages and on the three groups' larger social perspective.

1361* LA PARISIENNE (periodical). La droite. Paris, 1956. 115 p. October 1956 issue.

Essays by Jacques Laurent, Emanuel Beau de Loménie, Pierre Boutang, Emmanuel Berl, Pierre Andreu, Paul Sérant, and Julien Segnaire defining the meaning of "the Right" as a political movement and psychological orientation. Includes poll of Paris students on their image of the Right.

1362 PARODI, JEAN-LUC. Les rapports entre le législatif et l'exécutif sous la Ve République. Paris, Fondation nationale des sciences politiques, 1962. 56 l (Centre d'étude de la vie politique française, Série "Recherches" no. 1) Bibliography 1. 51-56. ML

Constitutional interpretation of executive and legislative power, parliamentary clashes with executive branch and decisions of Constitutional Council. For 1958-1961, specific instances of conflicts are analyzed, as are exceptional powers granted to de Gaulle.

1363 Le Partage des bénéfices, expansion et inégalités en France. Paris, Editions de Minuit, 1966. 444 p. (Le Sens commun)

Results of joint colloquium by sociologists and economists held June 1965 in Arras under the direction of Pierre Bourdieu and Alain Darbel. Essays by individual participants shed light on different aspects of the changes in French society and economy since World War II under the impact of rapid economic growth. Contributions deal with measurement of economic growth, consumption changes, demographic evolution, changes in pattern of employment, female labor. Economists and sociologists give partial answers to the question whether inequalities have been reduced by studying income distribution, social mobility, distribution of capital, preservation of cultural heritage via educational system.

1364 PARTI COMMUNISTE ALGERIEN. Alzhirskii narod pobedit. [Perevod s frantsuzskogo] Moskva, Gos. izd-vo polit. lit-ry, 1961. 82 p.

Role of Algerian Communist Party in advancing cause of Algerian independence during 1960, especially by mobilizing worker and international support. Pamphlet is an annotated Russian translation, published at the end of 1961, of an article by the Algerian Communist Party that appeared in the Russian press November 1960. This is the article contested by Ouzegane (see no. 1347).

FOR ADDITIONAL PUBLICATIONS BY AND ABOUT THE PARTI COMMUNISTE ALGERIEN, SEE AUTHOR INDEX

1365* PARTI COMMUNISTE FRANÇAIS. Aide-mémoire du propagandiste; activité parlementaire, 2 janvier 1956-15 février 1958. Paris, 1958. 43 p.

Summary of bills on social legislation introduced by Communist deputies and breakdown of votes by parties on key issues.

1366 PARTI COMMUNISTE FRANÇAIS. Algérie: le "cessez-le-feu" est une victoire des forces de paix; faits et documents. Paris, 1962. 23 p. illus.

Summary of Algerian war and role of French Communist Party in advocating peace and Algerian independence.

1367* PARTI COMMUNISTE FRANÇAIS. Allemagne: 10 questions. Paris, 1959. 4 p.

Plea for summit conference to settle German question.

1368 PARTI COMMUNISTE FRANÇAIS. Aux ingénieurs et cadres techniques; présentation du programme de restauration et de rénovation de la démocratie. Paris, 1962. 22 p.

February 1962 summary of party's political and economic program as formulated at its 15th and 16th congresses, to serve as a basis for joint action with other anti-Gaullist parties.

1369 PARTI COMMUNISTE FRANÇAIS. L'avenir démocratique de la France; problèmes actuels. Paris, 1962. 63 p.

Party's stand on political reform, as expressed by Waldeck Rochet at a May 1962 public meeting, answers by Rochet and Jacques Duclos to questions on various internal and foreign policy issues, and excerpts from current "L'Humanité" editorials.

1370 PARTI COMMUNISTE FRANÇAIS. La CFTC et la "planification démocratique;" ce qu'en pense le Parti communiste français. Paris, 1962. 22 p. illus. "Supplément au no. 4 (nouvelle série) du Bulletin de propagande et d'information du Parti communiste français."

Attack on Confédération française des travailleurs chrétiens' pamphlet on democratic planning.

1371* PARTI COMMUNISTE FRANÇAIS. Contre les 350 ordonnances. "L'infanterie" se défend...; bilan de la politique gaulliste. 3rd ed. Paris, 1959. 15 p.

Propaganda for April 1959 cantonal elections.

1372 PARTI COMMUNISTE FRANÇAIS. Deux années de lutte pour le front unique; recueil des propositions d'unité d'action adressées...au Parti socialiste S.F.I.O. Paris, 1957. 31 p.

Appeals and letters, Dec. 1955-Oct. 1957, addressed to S.F.I.O.

1373* PARTI COMMUNISTE FRANÇAIS. Du XIVe au XVe congrès du Parti communiste français; trois années de lutte pour l'unité ouvrière et l'union des républicains; recueil de documents et propositions d'unité d'action adressées par le Parti communiste français au Parti socialiste S.F.I.O. at aux partis de gauche. Paris, 1959. 77 p. Supplément aux Cahiers du communisme, no. 5.

Same as 1372 for Feb. 1958 - Ap. 1959 focused on opposition to de Gaulle's return to power, elections and Sept. 1958 referendum.

1374 PARTI COMMUNISTE FRANÇAIS. Frantsuzskoi kommunisticheskoi partii 40 let. Moskva, Gospolitizdat, 1961. 81 p.

Article by Maurice Thorez reviewing French Communist Party's history, followed by theses of the Party.

1375* PARTI COMMUNISTE FRANÇAIS. [Leaflets concerning the assumption of power by de Gaulle, May, 1958] 1 env.

Appeals to resist fascist plot.

1376* [PARTI COMMUNISTE FRANÇAIS]. [Letters by party leaders] Paris, 1958. 1 env.

3 leaflets, Feb. 1958 reproducing Thorez' letters to Mollet and Duclos letter to 4 large trade unions appealing for joint action.

1377 PARTI COMMUNISTE FRANÇAIS. Le logement; des précisions, des solutions. Paris, 1962. 16 p. (Its Problèmes de notre temps)

1378* [PARTI COMMUNISTE FRANÇAIS]. Marseille souffre, lutte, espère. Paris, 1958. 23 p.

Election propaganda for Feb. 1958 by-election in Marseille.

1379* PARTI COMMUNISTE FRANÇAIS. Paix en Algérie! Paris, 1958. 12 p.

After bombing of Sakiet-Sidi-Youssef Feb. 1958.

1380 PARTI COMMUNISTE FRANÇAIS. Le Parti communiste français dans la lutte contre le colonialisme; recueil de textes présentés et commentés par Monique Lafon. Paris, Editions sociales, 1962. 217 p.

Speeches and articles by leading members of Parti communiste français on war in Indochina, decolonization in Africa, during the Fourth and Fifth Republic, and the Algerian war. Final section contains messages of Communist leaders in newly independent African states.

1381 PARTI COMMUNISTE FRANÇAIS. Pour une démocratie véritable. Paris, 1962. 14 p. illus.

Pamphlet opposing October 1962 referendum on presidential election.

1382* PARTI COMMUNISTE FRANÇAIS. Problèmes de notre temps, faits et documents: Les partis socialistes devant le péril mortel des armes atomiques. [Paris, 1958?] 15 p.

1383* PARTI COMMUNISTE FRANÇAIS. Le programme national. Paris, 1958. 3 p.

Propaganda for April 1958 cantonal elections.

1384 PARTI COMMUNISTE FRANÇAIS. La question allemande. Paris, 1959. 14 p. (Problèmes actuels.)

1385 PARTI COMMUNISTE FRANÇAIS. Vers l'avenir. Paris, 1962. 15 p. illus.

Campaign pamphlet for November 1962 general elections.

1386* PARTI COMMUNISTE FRANÇAIS. Une victoire du peuple de France sur la rébellion fasciste; appels et documents du Parti communiste français, 22-27 avril 1961. Paris, 1961. 22 p.

Appeals opposing Generals' putsch by P. C. F. central committee and deputies.

1387* PARTI COMMUNISTE FRANCAIS. [Unlisted material.] 1 env.

1957 appeal to end Algerian war.

1388* PARTI COMMUNISTE FRANÇAIS. BUREAU POLITIQUE. [Leaflets dealing with political issues under the de Gaulle regime] 1 env.

Mainly spring 1961.

1389* PARTI COMMUNISTE FRANÇAIS. COMITE CENTRAL. Ecole élémentaire du Parti communiste français. 4 v.

Contents: [1] Cogniot, Georges: Le Parti communiste instrument décisif de la classe ouvrière dans la lutte pour le pain, pour la paix, pour le socialisme. [2] La paupérisation de la classe ouvrière. [3] La lutte pour la paix. [4] Le front unique.

1390* PARTI COMMUNISTE FRANÇAIS. COMITE CENTRAL. La journée internationale des femmes en 1958. Paris, 1958. 4 p.

April 1958 cantonal election propaganda.

1391 PARTI COMMUNISTE FRANÇAIS. COMITE CENTRAL. Problèmes du mouvement communiste international. Paris, 1963. 95 p. (Its Documents)

Documents on Parti communiste français' stand on international communism, particularly disagreement with Chinese Communists, 1960-1962, including exchanges with Chinese Communists, Thorez statements and speeches within the party and at international communist conferences.

1392 PARTI COMMUNISTE FRANÇAIS. COMITE CENTRAL. Rapport du Comité central, présenté par Waldeck Rochet. Paris, 1961. 90 p. "Supplément au no. 5.195 de l'Humanité."

Report on party's activities, programs, internal leadership conflict over democratic centralism, 1959-1961, presented to party's XVIth Congress.

1393 PARTI COMMUNISTE FRANÇAIS. COMITE CENTRAL. 3 années de lutte pour l'union des forces ouvrières et démocratiques. Pour le pain, pour la paix, pour la démocratie. Rapport d'activité du Comité central. Paris, 1964. 295 p. "Supplément au Bulletin de propagande et d'information no. 1, janvier 1964."

Communist party Central Committee's report before 17th Congress on party's activities, 1961-64 among workers, youth, farmers, in parliament and municipalities. Report gives interesting information on current organizational structure, finances, training of party cadres, Communist press and other propaganda media.

1394 PARTI COMMUNISTE FRANÇAIS. COMITE CENTRAL. L'union pour une France démocratique indépendante, pacifique et prospère. Rapport du Comité central, présenté par Waldeck Rochet, Secrétaire général du Parti communiste français. Paris, 1967. 90 p. "Supplément aux 'Cahiers du communisme,' no. 1, janvier 1967."

Central Committee's report to 18th Communist Party Congress, Jan. 1967, on party's positions since 17th Congress, including electoral alliance with Federation de la gauche démocrate et socialiste, attempts to elaborate a common program for the legislative elections, and doctrinal convergence with non-Communist left.

1395 PARTI COMMUNISTE FRANÇAIS. COMITE CENTRAL. Conférence, Ivry, 1963. Les étudiants communistes face aux grands problèmes de notre époque. Paris, 1963. 123 p.

Disagreements with Union des étudiants communistes are discussed at a meeting between individual central committee members, including Louis Aragon, Roger Garaudy, Maurice Thorez,

Guy Besse and a spokesman for the student organization.

1396 PARTI COMMUNISTE FRANÇAIS. COMITE CENTRAL. CONFERENCE, IVRY, FEB., 1961. Le Parti va vers son XVIe congrès. Rapport présenté par Waldeck Rochet. Discours de Maurice Thorez. Résolutions. Ivry, 23-24 février 1961. Paris, 1961. 63 p. (Les Travaux du Comité central du Parti communiste français)

Speeches by Waldeck Rochet and Maurice Thorez on recent internal opposition.

1397 PARTI COMMUNISTE FRANÇAIS. COMITE CENTRAL. CONFERENCE, IVRY, JAN. 1961. Pour une juste orientation de la lutte pour la paix et la démocratie. Rapport présenté par Waldeck Rochet. Discours de Maurice Thorez. Documents du Comité central et du Bureau politique. Ivry, 13-14-15 janvier 1961. Paris, 1961. 61 p. (Les Travaux du Comité central du Parti communiste français)

Analysis of results of January 1961 referendum on Algeria, which party had opposed.

1398 PARTI COMMUNISTE FRANÇAIS. COMITE CENTRAL. CONFERENCE, MALAKOFF, 1962. Ecarter tout ce qui divise, ne retenir que ce qui unit. Rapport présenté par Waldeck Rochet. Intervention de Maurice Thorez. Résolutions. Malakoff, 13-14 décembre 1962. Paris, 1963. 47 p. (Les Travaux du Comité central du Parti communiste français)

Analysis of results of October 1962 referendum and November 1962 legislative elections and prospects for unification of Left.

1399* PARTI COMMUNISTE FRANÇAIS. COMITE CENTRAL. SECTION DE PROPAGANDE. Documents: Déclaration des partis communistes et ouvriers des pays socialistes; manifeste pour la paix de 64 partis communistes et ouvriers; résolution du Comité central du Parti communiste français du 5 décembre 1957. Paris, 1957. 32 p.

1400 PARTI COMMUNISTE FRANÇAIS. COMMISSION D'HISTOIRE. Histoire du Parti communiste français; manuel [élaboré par la Commission d'histoire auprès du Comité central du Parti communiste français, sous la direction de Jacques Duclos et François Billoux] Paris, Editions sociales, 1964. 774 p.

Last 50 pages of this official history cover May 1958 - 1964, concentrating on party congresses and conferences.

1401 PARTI COMMUNISTE FRANÇAIS. COMMISSION D'HISTOIRE. Karl Marx, son oeuvre et le mouvement ouvrier. Paris, 1964. 31 p. illus., ports., facsims.

Photographs and descriptive material on Karl Marx exhibit organized 1963 in Paris by French Communist party's Commission d'histoire for the 80th anniversary of Marx's death. Pamphlet includes information on Communist Centre de Documentation du Mouvement Ouvrier.

1402 PARTI COMMUNISTE FRANÇAIS. CONFERENCE NATIONALE, GENNEVILLIERS, 1963. Donner au peuple de France un Parti communiste encore plus grand et plus fort. Rapport de Georges Marchais. Discours de clôture de Waldeck Rochet. Résolution et appel pour la souscription nationale, Gennevilliers, 2-3 février 1963. Paris, 1963. 108 p. "Supplément aux "Cahiers du communisme" no. 1-2 janvier-février 1963."

Reorganization proposals for making party's work more effective, from cells to mass organizations, with current figures on membership in different parts of France and finances.

1403 PARTI COMMUNISTE FRANÇAIS. CONGRES NATIONAL. Rapports, interventions et documents. 14e-18e. Congrès, 1956, 1959, 1961, 1964, 1967. Paris. 5 vols., illus., ports. Published as supplementary issues of "Cahiers du communisme," 1956-1967.

These are the complete proceedings of the party congresses.

1404* PARTI COMMUNISTE FRANÇAIS. ELECTION, 1958. [Unlisted material.]

Leaflets for April 1958 cantonal elections.

FOR ADDITIONAL PUBLICATIONS BY AND ABOUT THE PARTI COMMUNISTE FRANÇAIS, SEE AUTHOR INDEX AND SUBJECT INDEX

1405 PARTI COMMUNISTE INTERNATIONALISTE (FRANCE). Après De Gaulle? Paris, 1961. 34 p. ("La Verité des travailleurs" numéro spécial)

History of Fifth Republic as a reflection of the Parti communiste français' failures, first in its Algerian policies and then in its ineffective opposition.

1406* PARTI D'UNION DE LA GAUCHE SOCIALISTE. Congrès d'unification, 8 décembre 1957, textes de Base. 2nd ed. Paris, 1958. 63 p.

This party was constituted in December 1957 by uniting the following groups: Nouvelle Gauche, Mouvement de libération du peuple, groups of the Action socialiste, the Unité socialiste and about 60 % of the Jeune République. It merged in 1960 with Parti socialiste unifié. Texts included are statutes and program of new party, membership list of executive committee. For party publications, see nos. 2004 and 2046. See also no. 1307 for party history.

FOR ADDITIONAL PUBLICATIONS BY AND ABOUT THE PARTI D'UNION DE LA GAUCHE SOCIALISTE, SEE AUTHOR INDEX

1407 PARTI REPUBLICAIN RADICAL ET RADICAL-SOCIALISTE. CONGRES. Compte rendu sténographique des congrès nationaux, 36-59, 1944-1962.

11 reels of positive microfilm reproducing documents in Paris archives of Parti républicain radical et radical socialiste, filmed by the Service international de microfilm under the direction of the Fondation nationale des sciences politiques for its series: Documentation sur les partis politiques français. The documentation for each congress is much more extensive than the Party's published reports. Reels 10 and 11 cover the 1957-1962 congresses. For item by item listing of contents, see the Fondation nationale des sciences politiques index (no. 646).

1408 PARTI REPUBLICAIN RADICAL ET RADICAL SOCIALISTE. CONGRES, 61st, ARCACHON, 1964. 61e congrès du Parti radical et congrès du Rassemblement démocratique, 25 au 27 septembre, 1964. Paris, B.I.R.S., 1965. 122 p. illus., ports. (Bulletin d'information radical-socialiste, no. 52, avril, 1965)

Texts of speeches and resolutions for Radical party congress and for the subsequent congress of the Rassemblement démocratique, the parliamentary group to which the Radical deputies belonged.

1409 PARTI REPUBLICAIN RADICAL ET RADICAL SOCIALISTE. CONGRES. 62d, LYON, 1965. 62e congrès national, Lyon, 22 et 23 octobre 1965. Paris, B.I.R.S., 1965. 68 p. illus., ports. (Bulletin d'information radical-socialiste, no. 56, avril, 1965)

Texts of speeches and resolutions, including debate on joining the recently formed Fédération de la gauche démocrate et socialiste and supporting Mitterand candidacy, both of which congress approved.

FOR ADDITIONAL PUBLICATIONS BY AND ABOUT THE PARTI REPUBLICAIN RADICAL ET RADICAL-SOCIALISTE, SEE AUTHOR INDEX

1410* PARTI SOCIALISTE. De la révolution d'octobre au règne de Monsieur "K"; 1917-1957, quarante ans d'attentat contre le socialisme. Paris, Librairie des municipalités, 1957. 30 p. Supplément au Bulletin intérieur no. 95, Sept. 1957.

1411 PARTI SOCIALISTE. CONFERENCE NATIONALE D'INFORMATION, CLICHY, 1965. Pour préparer utilement le 55ème Congrès national, Clichy, 3 au 6 juin 1965; thèmes de discussion élaborés à la Conférence nationale d'information, Clichy, 3-4 avril, 1965. Paris, 1965. 207 p. (Parti socialiste. Bulletin intérieur, no. 136)

Among topics of discussion is the possibility of federation with other leftist parties and groups.

1412 PARTI SOCIALISTE. CONGRES NATIONAL. Rapports, 40-55, 1948-1965. Paris, Librairie populaire. Published as no. 32-135 of Parti socialiste. Bulletin intérieur.

These are not texts of speeches at congresses, but only reports of party's executive committee submitted ahead of the congresses.

1413* PARTI SOCIALISTE. CONSEIL NATIONAL, PUTEAUX, MAY 12, 1957. Conseil national de Puteaux du 12 mai 1957; discours prononcés par Pierre Commin, Robert Lacoste, Guy Mollet. Paris, 1957. 64 p. Supplément au Bulletin intérieur no. 95, juin 1957.

Includes speech by Robert Lacoste then Algerian Governor General, defending government's Algerian policy.

1414* PARTI SOCIALISTE. ELECTIONS CANTONALES, 4 JUIN 1961. Arguments et ripostes. Paris, 1961. 30 p. (Librairie des municipalités) Supplément à la "Documentation socialiste."

FOR ADDITIONAL PUBLICATIONS BY AND ABOUT THE PARTI SOCIALISTE (S.F.I.O.) SEE AUTHOR INDEX AND SUBJECT INDEX

1415* PARTI SOCIALISTE AUTONOME. Documents et textes... Paris, 1959. 32 p. (Tribune du socialisme. Supplément no. 25)

Parti socialiste autonome was founded in September 1958 after dissidents broke away from Parti socialiste because of majority approval of Gaullist regime and Algerian war. It was joined by Pierre Mendès-France and other dissidents from Radical Party in July 1959. In April 1960, party merged with other groups to form Parti socialiste unifié. Texts reproduced include material from party's first congress, adhesion of Mendès-France, and preliminary text for fusion to form Parti socialiste unifié.

1416* PARTI SOCIALISTE AUTONOME. CONGRES NATIONAL MONTROUGE 1959. Le premier congrès national du Parti socialiste autonome, Montrouge, 1-2-3 mai 1959; discours d'Edouard Depreux, Oreste Rosenfeld, André Philip. Paris, Editions du Parti socialiste autonome, 1959. 58 p. (Tribune du socialisme. Supplément nos. 19-20)

Only text of speeches.

1417* PARTI SOCIALISTE UNIFIE. 1er novembre 1954-1er novembre 1961;[protest against war in Algeria.] Paris, 1961. 1 p.

1418* PARTI SOCIALISTE UNIFIE. Qu'est-ce que le P.S.U.; pour le Front socialiste. Paris, 1960. 15 p.

Appeal to all socialist parties to help end Algerian war and text of resolution adopted by party's first congress.

1419* PARTI SOCIALISTE UNIFIE. Unlisted material. Paris.

April 1961 leaflets.

1420* PARTI SOCIALISTE UNIFIE. CONGRES D'UNIFICATION, ISSY-LES MOULINEAUX, 1960. Textes et documents du Congrès d'unification. Paris, 1960. 48 p.

Party was founded April 1960 as a result of the fusion of the Parti d'union de la gauche socialiste, the group centering around Tribune du communisme, and the Parti socialiste autonome. For details, see Nania (no. 1307). Included here are program of congress and speeches by Gilles Martinet, Jean Poperen, and Edouard Depreux.

FOR ADDITIONAL PUBLICATIONS BY AND ABOUT THE PARTI SOCIALISTE UNIFIE, SEE AUTHOR INDEX

1421 PARTURIER, FRANÇOISE. Marianne m'a dit.... Paris, Nouvelles éditions de Paris, 1963. 101 p. illus.

France's clandestine and official love affair with de Gaulle, 1940-1963, cartoons and text retracing the ups and downs of de Gaulle's relations with French public opinion.

1422 PATRIE ET PROGRES. Cahier no. 1-3. Paris, 1961. 3 v. "Supplément."

Cahiers edited by Jacques Gagliardi. Cahier 1 (Dec. 1961) on economic planning, Cahier 2 (May 1962) on political institutions and Cahier 3 (Nov. 1962) on international relations express impatience with slowness of Gaullist reforms in these areas. See also nos. 1885, 2040 for later publications.

1423 PAUTARD, ANDRE. Mohammed, l'Algérien mon ami. Illus. de l'auteur. Paris, Editions ouvrières, 1962. 151 p. illus., maps., plans. Bibliography: p. 143-145.

Popular survey of Algerian civilization, written to give French workers a better understanding of their Algerian fellow-workers and speed up French-Algerian reconciliation. Includes short history of Algerian nationalism and Algerian war.

1424 PAWERA, JOHN C. Algeria's infrastructure; an economic survey of transportation, communication, and energy resources. New York, F. A. Praeger, 1964. 234 p. illus., maps. (Praeger special studies in international economics). Bibliography: p. 232-234.

Sector by sector survey, based mainly on pre-independence data, of Algerian highways, railroads, airlines, shipping, pipelines, oil and other energy sources.

1425 Les pays d'outre-mer de la République française, la Communauté et les accords d'association, par X.X.X. Paris, Librairie générale de droit et de jurisprudence, 1960. 86 p. (Extrait de la Revue juridique et politique d'outremer nos. 1, 3 et 4, 1959)

Innovations of 1958 Constitution regarding overseas territories and departments, with detailed enumeration, by articles of the constitution, of the jurisdiction and political and judicial organs of the French Community.

1426 PEIKERT, HELMUT. Frankreichs Wirtschaft heute; Struktur und Tendenzen. Wiesbaden, Krauskopf, 1961. 225 p. diagrs., tables. Bibliography: p. 214-215.

Survey of French economy, describing Plans I-III, structure of economy, through 1960, with international comparisons, and giving a summary of Fifth Republic's economic reforms. Author is secretary general of Franco-German Chamber of Commerce and work is prefaced by Ludwig Erhard and Jacques Rueff.

1427 PEILLARD, JEAN. La pacification de l'Algérie et la conscience française. Alger, Editions Baconnier, [1956?] 69 p. tables.

Justification of French colonialization and pacification measures by French Catholic residing in Algeria in reply to questions of Catholic friends in France. Author claims that army is protecting Moslem masses from Cairo-led nationalists.

1428 PEJU, PAULETTE. Les harkis à Paris. Dossier présenté par Paulette Péju. Paris, F. Maspero, 1961. 116 p. (Cahiers libres, no. 23)

Documents reproducing complaints of Algerians living in France about incidents in which they were terrorized by the harkis, January - April 1961. The harkis, Moslem auxiliary forces serving both in French Army and police, were introduced to Paris in 1960 by police prefect Maurice Papon to break the F. L. N. Paris network without involving Paris police in terrorism.

1429 PELLENC, MARCEL. La France le dos au mur. Paris, Nouvelles éditions latines, 1956. 170 p.

Survey of France's economic ills (with emphasis on inflation and rural poverty) by French Senator and author of report for the Senate Finance Commission in mid-1956, including an estimate of costs of peacetime investment in Algeria to provide moderate economic growth, amounting to more than current military costs.

1430 PEMBERTON, JOHN E. How to find out about France; a guide to sources of information, by John E. Pemberton. Oxford, New York, Pergamon Press, 1966. xvi, 199 p. illus. (part fold. col.) fold. col. maps. (The Commonwealth and international library. Library and technical information division)

Annotated bibliography on reference works and basic textbooks covering the main aspects of French culture, government, economics, press, scientific documentation.

1431 PENICAUD, JEAN PHILIPPE. La doctrine du néo-nationalisme français. T. 1. La philosophie. Saint-Sulpice-Laurière (Haute-Vienne) L'Avenir de la France, 1963. 189 p.

Reflections on human nature, technical progress, and the reconciliation of the two by a government of "supermen."

1432 PEOPLE'S DAILY, PEKING. D'où proviennent les divergences? Lausanne, Editions de la Cité, 1963. 302 p.

Six essays from Chinese press, spring 1963, commenting on attacks by French, Italian, and U. S. Communist parties against Chinese Communism. The first of the essays is published separately in English as "Whence the Differences?" (Peking, 1963)

1433 PERCHE, MAURICE (ed.). 3 documents sur la défense de l'école et de la laïcité. Paris, 1963. 16 p. "Supplément au numéro 116 de 'L'école et la nation.'"

1954, 1961, 1962 resolutions of Parti Communiste Français opposing additional state subsidies to Catholic schools.

1434 PEREZ, GILBERT (ed.). Recueil des journaux d'Algérie; sélection du 2 novembre 1954 au 4 juillet 1962. [Marseille? 196-]. 2 v. facsims.

Volumes consist of facsimile reproductions of entire issues of the three leading European settler dailies from Algiers: "Echo d'Alger," "Journal d'Alger," Dépêche quotidienne d'Algérie" selected from the key periods of the Algerian war, such as May 1958, January 1960, April 1961, and March 1962. The second volume begins with January 1960. Issues of "Echo d'Alger" stop with April 1961.

1435 PERIOT, GERARD. 2e classe en Algérie. Paris, Flammarion, 1962. 282 p.

Personal narrative of young political scientist serving as conscript in Algeria 1958-1960. Author gives a first-hand description of army's pacification methods - regroupment camps, education program, enforced voting, torture - and its pervading self-deception to conceal its failure in winning over population. Author witnesses de Gaulle's 1960 "tour des popotes."

1436 PERRAULT, GILLES. Les parachutistes. Paris, Editions du Seuil, 1961. 189 p.

Socio-psychological study of this elite corps of the French army, tracing parallels between its indoctrination and that given to Nazi youth corps: the myth of physical superiority, the glory of non-rational violence, specifically catering to the adolescent. Author warns of making parachute troops scapegoats for excesses of Algerian war and turning them into complete fascists by making them social outcasts.

1437 PERROT, MICHELLE and ANNIE KRIEGEL. Le Socialisme français et le pouvoir. Paris, Etudes et documentation internationale, 1966. 223 p. (Cahiers du Centre d'études socialistes, no 58-64) Bibliographical footnotes.

Michelle Perrot's monograph deals with the pre-World War I Socialist Party, that of Annie Kriegel with the history of the French Communist Party from its founding to August 1966, giving a refined and well-documented analysis of the party's philosophical, tactical, and sociological shift toward polycentrism and pluripartism, culminating in the endorsement of Mitterand as presidential candidate and pointing toward a long-range integration in a social-democratic movement. Good bibliographical footnotes.

1438 PERROUX, FRANÇOIS, (ed.). L'Algérie de demain; étude. Paris, Presses universitaires de France, 1962. 262 p. Numéro hors série de Tiers monde.

Algerian economic and social prospects in the wake of the signature of the Evian agreements, as seen by economists, sociologists, and jurists. Topics treated are: education, migration, economic development, Franco-Algerian economic co-operation, and exploitation of the Sahara. Among studies are those by Pierre Bourdieu, Michel Massenet, and George Lavau.

1439 PERROUX, FRANÇOIS. Le IVe plan français, 1962-1965. Préf. de Pierre Massé. Paris, Presses universitaires de France, 1962. 126, [1] p. (Que sais-je, no. 1021) Bibliography: p. [127]

Critical examination of Fourth Plan, which was about to be launched, by economist and prominent member of Economic and Social Council. German translation: "Frankreichs Wirtschaftsprojektion; der IV. franzoesische Plan, 1962-1965" (Berlin, 1964)

1440 PERROUX, FRANÇOIS, (ed.). Problèmes de l'Algérie indépendante; étude présentée par François Perroux. Paris, Presses universitaires de France, 1963. 207 p. map. "Numéro hors série de Tiers monde."

Prospects for agricultural reform, industrialization, oil exploitation, formation of professional class, university education in Algeria are analyzed in the light of the massive European exodus. Chapter on agriculture is by René Dumont, that on Franco-Algerian cooperation by Yves Chaigneau, liberal former French governor general in Algeria.

1441 PERROUX, FRANÇOIS. Les techniques quantitives de la planification. Paris, Presses universitaires de France, 1965. 315 p. diagrs.

Methods of calculating and predicting primary and secondary effects of public and private investments in promoting economic growth as an analytic tool for national planning.

1442 PERRUCHOT, HENRI. La France et sa jeunesse. Dessin de Jean Randier. Paris, Hachette, 1958. 208 p. illus. (Les Grands problèmes)

Journalist's interpretation of results of 1957 survey on attitudes of French youth toward politics, moral and aesthetic values, education, leisure.

1443 PETAIN, HENRI PHILIPPE BENONI OMER. Pétain, toujours présent; sous la direction de Henry Coston. Avec la collaboration de Jacques Isorni. Paris, 1964. 157 p. "Lectures françaises. Numéro spécial, janvier 1964."

Pétain biography, excerpts from his speeches summing up his political thoughts, as well as contemporary and current judgments on his achievements.

1444 PEUREUX, GERARD. Le Haut-Conseil de l'Union française, sa constitution et son oeuvre (1946-1958) avec la publication de documents inédits et un appendice sur le Conseil exécutif de la Communauté. Préf. de Pierre Lampué. Paris, Librairie générale de droit et de jurisprudence, 1960. 272 p. (Bibliothèque de droit public, t. 24) Bibliography: p. 247-260.

History of French Union's executive organ, the Haut Conseil, and its successor under the Fifth Republic, the French Community's executive council, as established by the 1958 Constitution. Good bibliography of documents, books, and articles on French Union.

1445 PEYREFITTE, ALAIN. Faut-il partager l'Algérie? Paris, Plon, 1961. 362 p. (Tribune libre, 61)

Minister of information's serious study of the possibilities of regrouping the "Algériens-français" and "Franco-Musulmans" in the Western part of Algeria, turning the Sahara into a separate entity, and making the remainder completely independent. Author surveys results of such compromise partitions elsewhere. This solution is proposed as an alternative in the face of F.L.N. intransigeance in negotiations and as an effective pressure to make them accept compromise terms. Author is ostensibly speaking only for himself, not de Gaulle.

1446 PEYREFITTE, ALAIN. Rue d'Ulm; chroniques de la vie normalienne. Introd. de Georges Pompidou. Nouvelle éd., rev. et augm. Paris, Flammarion, 1963. 413 p.

Commemorative volume consisting of personal recollections of years at Ecole Normale Supérieure by some of its prominent graduates, among whom author.

1447 PEYREFITTE, ROGER. Les juifs. Paris, Flammarion, 1965. 514 p.

Fictionalized fresco of French Jewry in Fifth Republic by French novelist, bringing together a conglomeration of facts and hearsay on Jewish high society and the position of assimilated and orthodox Jews in France during the German occupation, in the Fourth and Fifth Republic. One chapter is an interview with Mendès-France, other chapters shed light on current forms of antisemitism and the reactions of the French clergy to recent papal gestures toward Christian-Jewish reconciliation, positions of French free masonry.

1448 PFLIMLIN, PIERRE and RAYMOND LEGRAND-LANE. L' Europe communautaire. Paris, Plon, 1966. 398 p.

Popular work on history and development of common European institutions by M.R.P. leader. Despite his personal commitment to European integration, author realistically reviews current situation (late 1965) and Gaullist policies to see what remains valid of original motivation for European unification. Note especially chapters on gropings toward common political institutions since 1958.

1449 PHILIP, ANDRE. Counsel from an ally; reflections on changes within the Atlantic community. Columbia, University of Missouri Press, 1966. xi, 79 p. (The John Findley Green Foundation lectures, 1965)

Lectures on current (mid-1965) French political scene, modernization of its society, and French stand on Common Market, Atlantic Alliance, international trade, and American foreign policy (particularly the war in Vietnam). As a spokesman for his country, Philip rarely criticizes his government except on its nuclear strategy.

1450 PHILIP, ANDRE. La gauche; mythe et réalités. Paris, Aubier, Editions Montaigne, 1964. 228 p.

Essays and lectures, by socialist politician and scholar 1960-1964, defining socialist attitude toward key issues of international relations (Atlantic Alliance, European unification, admission of Great Britain) and internal French political institutions in the light of the evolution of modern French society. Author advocates founding of a constructive socialist democratic party encompassing the new left, for which he considers Gaston Defferre as an acceptable spokesman in the coming presidential elections.

1451 PHILIP, ANDRE. Pour un socialisme humaniste. Paris, Plon, 1960. v, 234 p. (Tribune libre, 55)

Assessment of Gaullist institutions, economic, social and education policies, international relations, conduct of the Algerian war demonstrating that the first year of the Fifth Republic has brought no vital improvements. Second part of volume sets goals for a new socialist party resting on common democratic values.

1452 PHILIP, ANDRE. Le socialisme trahi. Paris, Plon, 1957. 240 p. (Tribune libre, 1)

Indictment of Mollet government for its betrayal of democratic and socialist principles in continuing Algerian war (with extended discussion of Algerian question) and of Socialist party as such for its ossification. Author appeals for a new labor party along the British model.

1453 PHILIP, ANDRE. Les Socialistes. Paris, Editions du Seuil, 1967. 256 p. (Politique, v. 9) Bibliography: p. 245-246.

Evolution of Parti socialiste from its birth through 1967, with short but penetrating observations on the Mollet government, the party's share in the end of the Fourth Republic and its attitude toward the founding of the Fifth Republic, the party's current organization and membership, the position of democratic socialism with respect to French social structure and world problems. The author left the party in 1956 because of disagreements with Mollet on Algerian policy.

FOR ADDITIONAL WORKS BY ANDRE PHILIP, SEE AUTHOR INDEX

1454 PICKLES, DOROTHY MAUD. Algeria and France; from colonialism to cooperation. New York, Praeger, 1963. 215 p. (Books that matter) Includes bibliography.

Balanced account of France's efforts to cope with the Algerian problem, 1954-1962, with main portion devoted to de Gaulle's tactics and an evaluation of his policy's successes and side effects.

1455 PICKLES, DOROTHY MAUD. The Fifth French Republic. New York, Praeger, 1960. 222 p. (Books that matter) Bibliographical footnotes.

Summary of the Fifth Republic's institutions and the rationale behind their operation: provisions of the 1958 Constitution, the electoral system, political parties, parliament and executive, the presidency, French Community and Algerian policy, as they emerge after one year's operation.

1456 PICKLES, DOROTHY MAUD. The Fifth French Republic: institutions and politics. Rev. [i.e. 2d] ed. New York, Praeger, 1962. 261 p. (Books that matter)

New edition covers development of policy in French Community, Algeria, defense up to 1962.

1457 PICKLES, DOROTHY MAUD. The uneasy entente: French foreign policy and Franco-British misunderstandings. London, New York, etc., issued under the auspices of the Royal Institute of International Affairs (by) Oxford U.P., 1966. vi, 180 p. (Chatham House essays, no. 13)

French foreign policy (European unification, Atlantic Alliance, Franco-German and Franco-Russian relations) and de Gaulle's "grand design" for world affairs and methods of diplomacy are reviewed to show extent of national consensus in these areas and divergences with British views.

1458 Les pieds-noirs et la presse française. Paris, Editions Galic, 1962. 159 p. (L'Histoire au jour le jour no. 3)

Excerpts from daily press (mainly regional) February - June 1962 on exodus of European settlers from Algeria.

1459 PIERCE, ROY. Contemporary French political thought. London and New York, Oxford University Press, 1966. 276 p. Includes bibliography.

This study is limited to a critical analysis of the writings of six political thinkers influential in France after World War II: Emanuel Mounier, Simone Weil, Albert Camus, Jean-Paul Sartre, Bertrand de Jouvenel, and Raymond Aron. Although the latter three have taken active part in the controversies of the Fifth Republic, their stand on concrete political questions is not presented here.

1460 PIGANIOL, PIERRE and LOUIS VILLECOURT. Pour une politique scientifique. Préf. du docteur André Cournand. Paris, Flammarion, 1963. 299 p. illus., tables. (Nouvelle bibliothèque scientifique) Bibliography: p. 293-296.

Includes survey of French scientific research organs and institutions (governmental, academic, and industrial) and budget allocated for research in Fourth Plan. Authors were members of governmental study group on the promotion of scientific research.

1461 PIGE, FRANÇOIS. Radiodiffusion et télévision au Maghreb... Paris, Fondation nationale des sciences politiques, 1966. 183 p. maps. (Centre d'étude des relations internationales. [Publications] Série G. Etudes maghrébines, no. 6).

Separate sections on Algeria, Morocco, and Tunisia, describing evolution of radio and television networks and programming before and since independence.

1462 PINDER, JOHN. Europe against de Gaulle. New York, Praeger, 1963. viii, 160 p. Bibliographical footnotes.

British author's argument in favor of Monnet's conception of European federation and Atlantic partnership. Writing in the wake of Great Britain's failure to win Common Market membership, author violently attacks de Gaulle's "chauvinistic nationalism" and urges setting up of a Defense and Political Community by U.S. and Great Britain as a counter-strategy.

1463 PINEAU, CHRISTIAN. The Algerian problem; address...before the Political Committee of the U.N. General Assembly on February 4, 1957. New York, 1957. 38 p. (France. Ambassade, U.S. Service de presse et d'information) Speeches and Press Conferences, no. 37.

1464 PINEAU, CHRISTIAN. Brighter prospects in Algeria; address before the Political Committee of the U.N. General Assembly on November 27, 1957. New York, 1957. 18 p. (France. Ambassade, U.S. Service de presse et d'information)

1465 PINNING, GERMAN. Wer steht hinter de Gaulle? Näheres über Technokraten und Synarchisten. Pähl (Oberbayern) Verlag Hohe Warte, F.v. Bebenburg, 1959. 149 p. map, diagr., facsims. "Quellennachweis": p. 141.

Attempt by German follower of Mathilde Ludendorff to uncover continuity between the Mouvement synarchiste révolutionnaire of the 1930's and the aims and tactics of the technocrats (e.g., Chaban-Delmas) backing de Gaulle. Author sees technocrats' influence in the overthrow of the Fourth Republic and shows similarities between 1958 Constitution and synarchist conceptions.

1466 PLANCHAIS, JEAN. Le malaise de l'armée. Paris, Plon, 1958. 114 p. (Tribune libre, 16)

Essays by "Le Monde's" military expert written in the spring of 1958 and analyzing the causes of the army's demoralization through colonial defeats and the split between professional soldiers on the one hand, politicians and French society at large on the other. Although author fails to predict the imminent intervention of the military, he indicates their impatience with the existing regime. For more extensive treatment, see "Une histoire politique de l'armée" (no. 961) second volume of which was contributed by Planchais.

1467 PLANCHAIS, JEAN. L'Armée. Paris, Buchet/Chaste, 1959. 159 p. illus., ports. (Collection "Où en est" [6])

Status of French armed forces as of late 1959 (ground, naval, and air forces, military schools) and relations of military with civilian government since advent of Fifth Republic. Short sketches of chiefs of staff.

1468 PLANHOL, XAVIER DE. Nouveaux villages algérois; Atlas blidéen, Chenoua, Mitidja occidentale. Paris, Presses universitaires de France, 1961. 120 p. illus., maps (part fold.) (Publications de la Faculté des lettres et sciences humaines d'Alger, 39)

Study, done with help of French Army staff, of population resettlement in foothills of Atlas and in Mitidja plains, 1957-1960, as part of the Army's pacification program. Study describes structure of new villages, nature of dwellings in new settlements, and prospects for permanence.

1469 PLASCHKE, HERBERT and DIETER KLEIN. Bonn-Paris; Achse der Monopole. Berlin, Dietz, 1964. 161 p. diagr. (Internationale Reihe) Bibliographical footnotes.

Attack on Franco-German agreements as collusion between French and German big business interests, particularly in the armament industry. Authors point out divergence between French and German economic and military aims. Includes list of executive committee members for both countries of an East German and French goodwill society.

1470 PLENIER, J. Oh! Monsieur l'archiprêtre [un curé d'Algérie parle à ses paroissiens.] Toulouse, Privat, éditeur, 1961. 184 p.

Weekly sermons, reprinted from parish bulletin of Rio-Salado near Oran, dealing with everyday questions of Christian morality, Catholic activities in France and Algeria. Some of sermons advise on proper conduct in a small Algerian town in the context of broader problems of French settlers in Algeria between 1957 and 1960.

1471 PLUM, WERNER. Algerische Dichtung der Gegenwart. Nürnberg, Glock und Lutz, 1959. 151 p. "Literaturhinweise": p. 146-148.

Characteristics of contemporary Algerian literature (Arab heritage, French education, nationalist inspiration) and discussion of individual writers including Katab Yacine, Mohammed Dib, Malek Haddad, Assid Kjebar, Jean Amrouche, Mouloud Feraoun, and Mouloud Mammeri, with list of post-World War II Algerian French-language novels.

1472 PLUM, WERNER. Gewerkschaften im Maghreb: UGTT - UMT - UGTA. Hannover, Verlag für Literatur und Zeitgeschehen, 1962. 120 p. map. (Schriftenreihe der Forschungsstelle der Friedrich-Ebert-Stiftung. A. Sozialwissenschaftliche Schriften) Includes bibliography.

History, economic, social, political, and educational program as well as international ties of trade unions in each of the three North African countries. Excellent up-to-date bibliography on economic and social questions in Algeria and union publications.

1473 PLUMYENE, JEAN and RAYMOND LASIERRA. Le complexe de gauche. Paris, Flammarion, 1967. 206 p. (Le meilleur des mondes) Bibliographical footnotes.

Malicious composite portrait of the young French Leftist, the rebel and masochist, whom the authors define as a spiritual "illegitimate child" rejecting all that the father figure represents. The portrait is filled in by means of quotations from existentialist novels and movies, Simone de Beauvoir's memoirs, excerpts from "Temps Modernes" and "France-Observateur," highlighting the political clichés carried on from the French Revolution, up-dated for the Algerian war and Castroism, but penetrating also into areas of behavioral conformity.

1474 PLUMYENE, JEAN and RAYMOND LASIERRA. Les fascismes français, 1923-1963. Paris, Editions du Seuil, 1963. 315 p. (L'Histoire immédiate au seuil) Includes bibliography.

Final forty pages deal with fascist manifestations growing out of the Algerian conflict: European settlers' ideology, the psychological warfare concepts in the Army, the counterrevolutionary movement of George Sauge, and finally the O.A.S. Includes chronology of fascist movements, 1922-1963.

1475 POERNER, ARTHUR JOSE. Argélia: o caminho da independência. Prefácio de Otto Maria Carpeaux. Rio de Janeiro Civilização Brasileira, 1966. 127 p. illus., ports. (Coleção Documentos da história contemporânea, v. 20)

Brazilian journalist's sympathetic history of Algerian independence movement and political evolution 1962-1965, seen against the background of Brazil's own colonial burdens.

1476 POKROVSKII, ALEKSANDR IVANOVICH. Frantsuzskaia burzhuaznaia politicheskaia ekonomiia. Obnovlenie ili krizis? Moskva, Izd-vo Instituta mezhdunarodnykh otnoshenii, 1961. 244 p. Includes bibliography.

Review of post-World War II French economic writing, with emphasis on whether violent economic fluctuations had been eliminated.

1477 POLITICAL AND ECONOMIC PLANNING. Aspects of European integration; an Anglo-French symposium of essays and comments produced in collaboration by Political and Economic Planning, London, and the Institut de science économique appliquée, Paris, London, 1962. 140 p. tables.

Debate between French and English economists on implications of Great Britain's joining Common Market in terms of agricultural policy, relations with overseas territories and developmental aid, and harmonization of economic policies.

1478 POUJADE, PIERRE. Premières réflexions internationales. Saint-Céré (Lot), 1961. 4 p. (Mouvement Poujade.)

Appeal by Poujade mouvement for creating an "Internationale nationaliste occidentale" January 1961 to defend Occident against communism. See also Mouvement Poujade in Author Index.

1479 POUJADE, ROBERT. Les Républicains sociaux et la jeunesse; rapport... Paris, Centre national des jeunes républicains sociaux, 1957. 7 p. (Républicains sociaux. 2nd Congress. Bordeaux, 1957)

1480 POULAIN, JEAN CLAUDE. L'Eglise et la classe ouvrière. Paris, Editions sociales, 1960. 186 p. (Politique et religion)

Catholic Church's social doctrine and political organs and Church's current drive to capture working class allegiance, as seen from French Communist Party's point of view.

1481 Pour ou contre la force de frappe; déclarations du Général de Gaulle; opinions et commentaires d'Etienne Anthérieu et al. Paris, J. Didier, 1963. 269 p. (Collection forum)

Three de Gaulle speeches (Nov. 1959, Jan. and April 1963) stating his nuclear policy, followed by views and comments of 24 French and 9 foreign politicians, dating mainly from spring 1963. Only U.N.R. leaders and government ministers, as well as General Gallois, come out in support of nuclear weapons, while politicians from all other parties are opposed.

1482 Le pouvoir personnel et la presse française. Paris, Editions Galic, 1962. 158 p. (L'Histoire au jour le jour no. 8)

Press excerpts July - Sept. 1962 arguing for and against popular election of president at the eve of the Oct. 1962 constitutional referendum, with a few earlier statements on the dangers of personal power.

1483 POZZO DI BORGO, LOUIS. Algérie d'hier et d'aujourd'hui. Paris. Editions du Conquistador, 1957. 134 p.

Royalist French Algerian's criticism of concessions made in Algeria by Fourth Republic, resulting in deterioration of Algerian society as compared to early colonial days.

1484 PRELOT, MARCEL. Pour comprendre la nouvelle constitution; études et documents. 2. éd. rev. Paris, Editions du Centurion, 1959. 191 p. (Collection "Le poids du jour")

Professor of constitutional law and president of National Assembly's committee on constitutional reform situates new constitutional provisions in historical context for readers of "La Croix" at the eve of the 1958 constitutional referendum. Documents are the juxtaposed preliminary and final version of the 1958 constitution. Revised edition, concluded February 1959, has a new chapter on the functioning of the new institutions.

1485 Présence de Jean Bastien-Thiry. Paris, Editions du Fuseau, 1966. 110 p. port.

Declaration by Jean Bastien-Thiry at his trial, February 2, 1963 (for full trial record, see no. 143) followed by 27 articles from French press, March-April 1963, condeming his hasty execution.

1486* PRESSES NATIONALES ASSOCIEES. Courrier personnel spécial, 1 août 1958, Liège. 1 env. mimeographed.

Newsletter and annexed studies and documents on May 1958 events in Algeria by Belgian journalist Pierre Joly, who had been in close touch with activist civilian and military elements in Algeria. Newsletter and documents contain source material on background, 1956-1958, on May 13, 1958 in Algeria, the personalities involved in Comité du Salut Public d'Alger, and General Lionel Chassin's Mouvement Populaire du 13 Mai (M.P. 13).

1487* PREUVES: REVUE MENSUELLE (periodical). L'éveil de l'Afrique noire; trois conférences-débats... Paris, 1958. 47 p. Supplément au no. 88, juin 1958.

One lecture on colonization of Africa, one on colonies' social structure, one on roads to independence.

1488 PREZELIN, JACQUES. Roger Louis raconte ses reportages pour Cinq colonnes à la une. Monaco, Paris, R. Solar, 1966. 287 p. illus.

Interview with television documentary producer Roger Louis, who tells about incidents connected with the filming of certain programs, notably a documentary on the events in Algeria, April 1961, which focused on a discussion with a European settler, a doctor, epitomizing the reactions of Europeans of goodwill in Algeria for the French spectator. Roger Louis gives interesting information on the early days of French television.

1489 PRIESTER, EVA. In Algerien sprechen die Gewehre; der Freiheitskampf eines Volkes. Berlin, Dietz, 1959. 270 p. illus., map.

Eyewitness report, 1958-59, of East German journalist on Algerian nationalist combattants and refugees in Tunisia, as well as sufferings of Algerian people.

1489a Le procès Salan et la presse française. Paris, Editions Galic, 1962. 155 p. (L'Histoire au jour le jour, no. 2)

Reactions in Paris dailies and opinion press to Salan's arrest, April 21, 1962 and to the daily court sessions and final verdict, May 1962.

1490 PROMOTIONS (periodical). La coopération technique. Paris, 1962. 151 p. "Numéro spécial."

Introductory essay by Minister for Cooperation Raymond Triboulet on French aid to Africa and discussions by officials responsible for aid administration on how to improve technical aid to underdeveloped countries.

1491 PUCHEU, RENE. Le journal, les mythes et les hommes. Paris, Editions ouvrières, 1962. 183 p. tables. (Collection "Vivre son temps," 3) Bibliographical footnotes.

Ways in which daily press caters to public's preferences for melodrama and human interest news and specific methods of distorting news used by papers with varying political orientation, with useful figures for circulation and type of readers of major dailies.

1492 PURTSCHET, CHRISTIAN. Le Rassemblement du peuple français, 1947-1953. Préf. de C.-A. Colliard. Avent-propos de Marcel Prélot. Paris, Cujas, 1965. xxii, 401 p. Includes bibliography.

History of R.P.F. based on the party's own archives, presenting R.P.F.'s methods and doctrine and views of its leaders. Although chronologically limited to pre-1958 period, there is continuity of leadership and doctrine into Fifth Republic. Marcel Prélot's preface relates his personal experiences in the party.

1493 PURTSCHET, CHRISTIAN and ANDRE VALENTINO. Sociologie électorale en Afrique du Nord. Préf. de Georges Burdeau. Paris, Presses universitaires de France, 1966. 234 p. (Travaux et recherches de la Faculté de droit et des sciences économiques de Paris. Série "Science politique," no. 7) Includes bibliography.

The monograph by Valentino deals with the 1962 Moroccan referendum. The Purtschet monograph, based on a 1960 dissertation, concerns the Nov. 1958 election for deputies to National Assembly from the 18 Algerian electoral districts, which author observed at first hand, with access to all official electoral documentation. For this first (and last) general election, author describes candidates, voter psychology (based on author's questionnaires) campaign and role of army, official control mechanism for election, results, and sketches of 69 successful candidates. In assessing election as one step in selecting representative, democratically chosen political leaders indispensable for de Gaulle's policy of Algerian self-determination, author concludes that it failed to achieve its objective.

1494 QUIEDEVILLE, ROGER. La nouvelle Constitution (1958) La Communauté française. Paris, Foucher, 1959. 19 p.

Popular summary of principles and provisions of 1958 Constitution and composition and operation of French Community.

1495 QUILLIOT, ROGER. La société de 1960 et l'avenir politique de la France. Paris, Gallimard, 1960. 199 p. (Problèmes et documents)

Evolution of French society, with some up-to-date statistics, as seen by political scientist seeking a program for the French Left better adapted to current conditions and neither systematically anti-communist nor anti-Gaullist. Author later headed "Horizon 80," which sponsored Defferre's presidential candidacy.

1496 RABANY, CHARLES GUILLAUME. Guide général des élections. Nouv. éd., entièrement refondue et mise à jour au 1er juillet 1957 par André Jabin. Préf. de Roger Farçat. Paris, Berger-Levrault, 1957. viii, 447 p.

Technical provisions for elections, as established by judicial decisions in contested elections regarding such matters as voter registration, declaration and elegibility of candidates, election day procedures. The original 1928 edition was completely revised and brought up to date. Work does not discuss the electoral system as such.

1497 RABIL, ALBERT. Merleau-Ponty, existentialist of the social world. New York, Columbia University Press, 1967. xviii, 331 p. Bibliography: p. 301-325.

Philosopher's life and works, explaining his interpretation and movement away from Marxism, as well as his gradual estrangement from his fellow-existentialist Sartre. Complete bibliography of philosopher's writings.

1498 Racconti di bambini d'Algeria; testimonianze e disegni di bambini profughi in Tunisia, Libia e Marocco. La ricerca delle testimonianze e dei disegni è stata condotta da un'équipe del Ministero delle informazioni del Governo provvisorio della Repubblica algerina. Traduzione di Giovanni Pirelli. Torino, G. Einaudi, 1962. 152 p. illus. (part col.) (Saggi, 307)

Brief oral or written autobiographies of nearly 100 Algerian refugee children in Morocco, Tunisia, Libya, and near Algerian border, complemented by expressive drawings.

1499 RAHMANI, ABDELKADER. L'affaire des officiers algériens. Paris, Editions du Seuil, 1959. 171 p.

Personal narrative of Algerian career officer serving in French army since 1945 whose efforts to halt French repression in Algeria after 1956 by writing to President of the Republic and contacting French politicians ended with his imprisonment, together with fellow Algerian officers. Liberated by de Gaulle in fall 1958, Rahmani has hopes in de Gaulle's understanding for Algerian national aspirations.

1500 RAINVILLE, JEAN MARIE. Condition ouvrière et intégration sociale. Paris, Editions ouvrières, 1967. 230 p. (Collection "L'Evolution de la vie sociale") Includes bibliography.

Canadian sociologist's study based on small sample of workers in a predominantly working class district in the outskirts of Paris, to determine: attitude toward work, standard of living and consumption patterns, education of children, social relations, use of leisure. Results show incoherence in behavior and attitudes resulting from clash between traditional working-class outlook and partial acceptance of mass consumption society.

1501 RAISSAC, GUY. Un combat sans merci; l'affaire Pétain-de Gaulle, 1966. 527 p. plates, ports. Includes bibliography.

Author was secretary general of archives of the Haute Cour de

Justice, and many of its documents are presented on the conflict between de Gaulle and Pétain, de Gaulle and Giraud. Some of the interviews with participants took place after 1958, although the material itself stops with 1945.

1502 RAMADIER, PAUL. Les socialistes et l'exercice du pouvoir; préf. de J. Paul-Boncour. Paris, R. Laffont, 1961. 282 p. (Problèmes sociaux de l'âge atomique, 4)

Guidelines of Socialist policy on such issues as social security, worker participation in industry, nationalization, planning, democracy, viewed in their historical perspective.

1503 RANGER, JEAN. L'étude des élections en France. Paris, 1961. 26 l. (Fondation nationale des sciences politiques. Cycle supérieur d'études politiques. Guide de recherches, no. 7) Bibliography: l. 14-26.

Most of studies cited deal with pre-1958 elections, but some of the references point to documentary sources for elections under Fifth Republic.

1503a REALITES (periodical). France: a youthful nation rebuilds its future. Clichy, France, 1965. 63 p. illus.

Handsomely illustrated survey of recent scientific, technological, (communications, transportation, power, construction, medicine) economic, social welfare, and cultural advances.

1504* REALITES (periodical). "If God lets me live..."; What the West doesn't understand about de Gaulle. Paris, 1960. 11 p. Special reprint from the issues of March and April 1960, pp. 40-43 and 58-64.

On de Gaulle's methods and ideas of government.

1505 RECHERCHES INTERNATIONALES A LA LUMIERE DU MARXISME. L'Europe. Paris, 1966. 210 p. "Mars-avril 1966; numéro 52."

Analysis of different facets of European integration, relations between Western and Eastern Europe by Soviet, French, German, and Italian authors. An introductory essay by Jacques Duclos states position of French Communist Party on European economic integration and the Atlantic Alliance.

1506 RED CROSS. INTERNATIONAL COMMITTEE, GENEVA. The ICRC and Algerian conflict, March 1955 - December 1959. [Geneva? 1959] 27 l.

Report on International Red Cross intercessions, 1955-1959, in favor of Algerian prisoners, refugees, displaced persons, French and other prisoners of war in F.L.N. hands.

1507 REIMBOLD, JEAN. Pour avoir dit non, 1960-1966. Paris, Table ronde, 1966. 239 p.

Personal narrative of French O.A.S. activist, whose political career began by organizing R.P.F. group in Morocco in 1950's. Progressively disillusioned with Gaullists and de Gaulle's colonial policy, Reimbold founded Union pour la présence française in Morocco. After de Gaulle's return to power, Reimbold's opposition first took legal form through Union pour l'Algérie française in Southern France, then became clandestine. His O.A.S. activities and ties with Conseil national de la Résistance led to his condemnation in absentia and capture in Sept. 1964. Book, written in prison, describes condition of fellow political prisoners.

1508 REMOND, RENE. La droite en France de la première restauration à la V-e République. 2. éd. rev. et augm., Paris, Aubier, Editions Montaigne, 1963. 409 p. maps. (Collection historique) Bibliography: p. 374-398.

Although only final 40 pages deal with Fifth Republic, the Gaullist ideology is fitted into the previously developed schematism of the French Right by assimilation with Bonapartism, i.e., the search for stability through strong government, with technocratic leanings, sympathy for direct democracy, a quest of national greatness through unity. This rightist current is contrasted with the philosophy of the libertarian right, with which Independents are identified. Among documents is the text of "Manifeste des 14 membres du Salut Public d'Alger," July 23, 1958.

FOR ADDITIONAL WORKS BY RENE REMOND, SEE AUTHOR INDEX

1509 RENCONTRE SOCIALISTE DE GRENOBLE, 1966. Débats et controverse, 30 avril-1er mai, 1966. Paris, 1966. 64 p.

Meeting sponsored by Parti socialiste unifié, Communist opposition groups, trade unionists, and several political clubs. Major address by Mendès-France is followed by debate on preliminary reports outlining a common program for the French Left on political institutions, foreign and European policy, economic institutions, and economic policy.

1510 RENCONTRE SOCIALISTE DE GRENOBLE, 1966. Rapports préparatoires. Paris, G. Leprieur, 1966. 68 p. illus.

Appeal of organizing committee and preliminary proposals by committee on joint Left program (see above).

1511 RENCONTRE SOCIALISTE DE GRENOBLE, 1966. COMITE D'INITIATIVE AUX DELIBERATIONS DES COLLOQUES SUR LA VIE REGIONALE EN FRANCE. Décoloniser la province; rapport général. [Paris, 1966?] 41 p.

Separate report on regional inequities and possibilities for decentralization and promotion of provinces by means of new political institutions giving greater power to regional units, despite French Left's traditional bias in favor of centralization.

1512 Répertoire de la presse et des publications périodiques françaises. 3rd. ed. 1964; 4th. ed. 1968.

Catalogue of all currently published French newspapers and periodicals (ca 15,000) prepared by the Periodical Division of the Bibliothèque Nationale, Paris, under the direction of Henri F. Raux for the first three editions, Mmes Coisel, Beulé, and Van der Sluijs for the fourth edition. First edition (1958) covers 1956-57 and is at Main Library. Third edition (1964) covers 1960 - August 1963, and fourth edition (1968) covers August 1963 - December 1966. All publications listed are deposited at Bibliothèque Nationale. The main part of the catalogue is divided into 16 types of periodicals, of which these are of special interest: general information newspapers and periodicals (including information bulletins and confidential letters); legal, political, international affairs, economic, and social science periodicals. For each publication, title, subtitle, place of publication, initial date under that title, director of publication, address, format, cost, and sometimes circulation figures are given. The catalogue is complemented by a name, organization and title index. The latter lists periodicals that have ceased publication since the earlier "Répertoire" edition.

1513* REPUBLICAIN SOCIAUX. Devant le traité instituant la Communauté Européenne de l'Energie Atomique (EURATOM) Paris, 1957. 8 p. (Note d'information du Centre national des Républicains sociaux, no. 21)

Reviews party's objections to various phases of European unification as well as specific drawbacks of EURATOM.

1514 REPUBLICAINS SOCIAUX. 2nd CONGRESS, BORDEAUX, 1957. 2e congrès national; rapports soumis aux fédérations départementales. Bordeaux, 1957. 1 portfolio.

Feb. 1957 report on economic questions and party statutes.

FOR ADDITIONAL PUBLICATIONS BY AND ABOUT THE REPUBLICAINS SOCIAUX, SEE AUTHOR INDEX

1515 RETOURNARD, FRANÇOIS. Les institutions de la France. Paris, Bloud et Gay, 1959. 122 p. (Manuels d'enseignement technique)

Civics textbook on French political organization, emphasizing the changes brought by the 1958 Constitution. Chapters cover the constitution, role of the executive, parliament, local administration, judiciary, financial structure, French Community.

1516 RETOURNARD, FRANÇOIS. Le rôle et l'influence de l'Assemblée des présidents des conseils généraux dans la vie publique française depuis 1946. Paris, 1964. 115 p. diagrs. (Fondation nationale des sciences politiques. Centre d'étude de la vie politique française. Série [C]: Recherches, no. 2) Includes bibliography.

This Assembly, drawn from local government leaders, was founded in 1946. Study shows their representation in National Assembly, scope of action in local government and regional economic development in Fourth and Fifth Republic.

1517 REVEL, JEAN FRANÇOIS. Contrecensures: politique, religion, culture de masse, art et critique d'art, enseignement, avant-garde, philosophie et sciences humaines, auteurs incompris, antisémitisme. Paris, J.-J. Pauvert, 1966. 389 p. illus., ports.

1958-1966 essays on political and cultural topics, arranged by subject, originally published mostly in "l'Express," "France-Observateur," and "Figaro littéraire." The political commentary reflects a consistent opposition to de Gaulle. Most of the essays on religion, education, literature, art, and sociology are book reviews.

1518 REVEL, JEAN FRANÇOIS. En France; la fin de l'opposition. Paris, Julliard, 1965. 201 p.

Diatribe against French nation as a whole, in particular left-wing intellectuals, for its willing accommodation to an autocratic, non-parliamentary regime without respect for its own laws, on the simple excuse that its excesses are not as severe as Fascism's, while secretely admiring the efficacy of a centralized bureaucracy. Author illustrates authoritarian features such as mass media control, repression of demonstrations, attacks growing income inequalities accompanying economic progress (for which he credits modern industrial society rather than de Gaulle). Many of these themes were to be taken up in presidential campaign by Mitterand. For a more explicit critique of 5th Republic, see Revel's contribution in no. 419.

1519 REVEL, JEAN FRANÇOIS. Le style du général; essai sur Charles de Gaulle, mai 1958-juin 1959. Paris, R. Julliard, 1959. 179 p.

Dialogue between French novelist (author) and fictitious friend from abroad irreverently dissecting de Gaulle's utterances May 1958 - June 1959 to destroy the myth of his literary and oratorical skill. Personality foibles, such as egocentricity, as well as political fallacies are highlighted through careful textual criticism, though de Gaulle's political philosophy and policies are not directly attacked.

1520 REVERDY, JEAN CLAUDE. Recherche sur les attitudes du sous-prolétariat algérien à l'égard de la société urbaine. Alger-Aix-en-Provence, 1963. 71 p.

1961-62 case study for Centre africain des sciences humaines appliquées, abruptly terminated by April 1962 O.A.S. violence, on attitudes of several hundred inhabitants of a small "bidonville" in the heart of Algiers. Results based on interviews and statistical study show differences between adults with close rural ties and completely rootless young, alienation of both generations from life of city, hatred of Europeans, and likely problems after independence, which may leave them just as alienated.

1521 La révolution algérienne, par le peuple et pour le peuple. L'Armée de la libération nationale. Tunis, 1960. 15 p. of illus.

Photographic presentation of Army of National Liberation in action distributed by Algerian Provisional Government's Ministry of Information, May 1960, presumably from Tunis.

1522 REVUE DE L'ACTION POPULAIRE. Démocratie aujourd'hui. By P. Antoine et al. Paris, Spes, 1963. 188 p. (Bibliothèque de la recherche sociale)

Eight contributions drawn from 1960-62 issues of "Revue de l'action populaire" on the theory and practice of democracy, including two on the experience of the Fifth Republic, Jean-Louis Quermonne's on the new political institutions, and François Bloch-Lainé's on the prospects for popular participation in the economic decision-making process.

1523 REVUE DES DEUX MONDES. Les pieds-noirs; la question du jour. Paris, 1961. 63 p. illus., ports. (Its Les Documents, no. 18) Bibliography: p. 63.

History of French colonization in Algeria (following the pattern of American pioneers) aiming to clarify the attitudes of European settlers in 1961. Current situation of settlers is summarized by demographic, professional, and income statistics, with a representative geneology for a settler family. Useful glossary.

1524 REVUE FRANÇAISE DE SOCIOLOGIE. Guerre, armée, société. Paris, Julliard, 1961. 159 p. "Numéro spécial, avril-juin 1961. Deuxième année. no. 2."

About half of this special issue deals with French society and the army, with articles on political attitudes and motivations of candidates to the different military schools and study on the ties between counter-revolutionary, anti-communist Catholic movements centered around "Cité catholique" and "Le Verbe" and military elements.

1525 REVUE GENERALE DES SERVICES DE POLICE. Organisation des services de police. Paris, 1961. 31 p.

Instructional manual for internal police use giving history of police and the current organizational framework and functions of its main branches: Sûreté Nationale, Préfecture de police (Paris) and Gendarmerie nationale, all of them subordinated to the Ministry of the Interior.

1526 REVUE MILITAIRE D'INFORMATION. L'enseignement français. Présentation, aspects et perspectives, par J. Sarrailh et al. Paris, 1959. 110 p. illus. Issue no. 304 for April, 1959. "Bibliographie": p. 81.

Collection of articles by educators and administrators surveying all types of French education as of 1958-59 (primary, secondary, technical, adult, popular, university, and military, with the education of the country's youth before military service.

1527 REVUE MILITAIRE D'INFORMATION. La guerre révolutionnaire; données et aspects, méthode de raisonnement, parade et riposte, par Ximenès et al. Paris, 1957. 111 p. illus., ports., maps. Issue no. 281 for February-March, 1957. "Bibliographie sur la guerre révolutionnaire": p. 110-111.

Officers' discussion of encounters with revolutionary wars in Indo-China and North Africa and elaborate counter-measures. This is one of the early instances of military debate on psychological warfare (action psychologique). Colonel C. Lacheroy introduces the individual essays.

1528 REY, BENOIST. Les égorgeurs. Paris, Editions de Minuit, 1961. 97 p. (Documents)

Personal diary of service in commando unit in Algeria (Constantine area) September 1959 through October 1960, emphasizing cruelty of pacification operations.

1529 REYGASSE, RENE, 1911. Témoignage d'un "ultra" sur le drame algérien. Paris, Editions "Témoignage chrétien," 1960. 79 p. ("Documents")

Author is fourth-generation Algerian from a family of government officials and himself administrator of native settlements. Author speaks for French Algerians who refuse to abandon their native land and seeks solution in direct reconciliation between F. L. N. and "ultras" like himself, who together make up 90% of the Algerian population and must perforce be the building blocks of a new state. Abuses of French administration before de Gaulle (such as election frauds, false promises, and pacification measures) are blamed for sharpening discord between the communities - author believes that European settlers might have accepted Algerian autonomy before 1945 massacres. De Gaulle is blamed for not following up the possibilities of reconciliation with Algerian nationalists after May 1958.

1530 REYNAUD, JEAN DANIEL. Les syndicats en France. Paris, A. Colin, 1963. 289 p. (Collection U/Série "Société politique")

Scholarly survey of different aspects of French trade unionism, historical and contemporary (through 1963) with documents illustrating each topic.

1531 REYNAUD, PAUL. Et après? Paris, Plon, 1964. 204 p.

Imaginary dialogue permitting author to retrace his contributions to parliamentary reform in Fourth Republic (proposal for automatic dissolution to increase governmental stability) and his fight against de Gaulle's metamorphosis of the Fifth Republic's constitution (which author helped to draw up) into an instrument of personal power. Reynaud reiterates his opposition to the 1962 referendum on the election of the president and offers his own counter-proposal of directly electing the prime minister.

1532 REYNAUD, PAUL. La politique étrangère du Gaullisme. Paris, R. Julliard, 1964. 269 p.

Detailed criticism of de Gaulle's foreign policy between the end of the Algerian war and spring 1964: European unification, NATO, nuclear weapons, relations with Germany, Great Britain, U. S., Russia, China, underdeveloped countries as illustrations of de Gaulle's lack of realism in seeking French greatness through anti-Americanism and isolation from European democracies. Reynaud blames de Gaulle's unfortunate personal experiences for his foreign policy orientation.

1533 RIBEAUD, PAUL. Barricades pour un drapeau. Paris, Table ronde, 1960. 233 p. illus., ports. (L'Ordre du jour)

Eyewitness account of January 1960 uprising of Algerian students by journalist for Paris-Match, with contacts among French-Algerian politicians. Journalist suspects Communist plot behind removal of General Massu from Algeria, in which Joseph Ortiz was an unwitting collaborator.

1534 RIDLEY, FREDERICK F. and JEAN BLONDEL. Public administration in France. Introduction by Peter Campbell. London, Routledge and Kegan Paul, 1965. xvi, 336 p., maps. Bibliography: p. 323-327. ML

Comprehensive and clearly written account of the framework of French administration (role of president and government, the civil service, ministries, and local government) and the different types of services rendered by public administration (justice, police, financial and economic control, planning, nationalized industries, education, and welfare). Authors describe current organization, but also indicate evolution in each area.

1535 RIEUNIER, RENE. Réquisitoire contre le mensonge. Paris, Nouvelles Editions latines, 1962. 384 p.

History of France, 1940-1962, written by engineer at Michelin and organizer of the union Ingénieurs et Cadres during Vichy regime. Author presents de Gaulle as a forger of divisions since his first appearance on national scene in 1940, not a symbol of French unity. Over half of book is devoted to Fifth Republic: its origins, the intensification of de Gaulle's "monocracy" and his perjury in connection with Algeria, leading up to the military and O. A. S. trials, which coincided with the writing of the book, and which are treated in full. This violent indictment of de Gaulle brought the author to court for offense against the chief of state (see no. 1646).

1536 RIGAUD, JACQUES, (ed.). Débat sur la France de demain. Le Manifeste des cinq, et les commentaires des cent. Paris, Julliard, 1961. 250 p.

Propositions about France's long-range orientation with respect to economic, social, educational, and foreign policy objectives, as expressed in a manifesto drawn up by four journalists: Alfred Max (Réalités) Michel Drancourt (Entreprise) Danielle Hunebelle (Réalités and Le Monde) and François Fontaine (Information Service, European Communities) together with General Pierre Gallois. Comments by hundred identified members of French political, industrial, administrative and intellectual elite, covering whole range of political spectrum, are summarized by topics and critically presented by political scientist Jacques Rigaud. The main controversy concerns the manifesto's technocratic orientation.

1537 RISPY, FRANZ. Sie klagen an! Erschütternde Tatsachenberichte geflüchteter Fremdenlegionäre über die Tragödie von Algerien. Zürich, Riza-Verlag, 1958. 112 p. plates, ports.

Swiss Foreign Legion officer's eyewitness account of pacification in Algeria, 1957 - April 1958, describing use of torture and other forms of violence. Shorter statements by other Foreign Legion deserters with a special section on forced recruiting of Hungarian refugees into Legion.

1537a ROBEQUAIN, CHARLES. Madagascar et les bases dispersées de l'Union française (Comores, Réunion, Antilles et Guyane, Terres Océaniennes, Côte des Somalis, Saint-Pierre et Miquelon, Iles Australes, Terre Adélie) Paris, Presses universitaires de France, 1958. 586 p. illus., maps, diagrs. (Pays d'outre-mer; colonies, empires, pays autonomes. 4. sér.: Géographie de l'Union française, 3) "Bibliographie": p. 541-572.

Physical geography, resources, economy of Madagascar, to which over half of volume is devoted, and each of French possessions in the West Indies, the Pacific, and off the African coast. After dissolution of French Union, Madagascar joined French Community and later became Malagasy Republic, while remaining areas became overseas territories and departments. Extensive bibliography of books and articles.

1538 ROBERTSON, ARTHUR CLENDENIN. La doctrine du général de Gaulle. Paris, A. Fayard, 1959. 318 p. (Les Idées et la vie) "Bibliographie": p. 309-318.

Study, by one of his American admirers, of de Gaulle's ideas as expressed in his published works, speeches, and political actions up to 1951. Written originally as a 1954 doctoral dissertation at the University of Strasbourg, the work was not revised to take into account de Gaulle's more recent political role.

1539 ROBINET DE CLERY, ADRIEN. De la Quatrième à la Cinquième République; aperçu sur l'histoire constitutionnelle de la France contemporaine de février 1956 à septembre 1958, avec le texte intégral de la Constitution de 1958. München, M. Hueber, 1958. 32 p.

Text of 1958 Constitution, preceded by explanatory note on end of Fourth Republic and followed by a summary of constitution's new provisions.

1540 ROCHET, WALDECK. Ceux de la terre. Paris, Editions sociales, 1963. 370 p. plates.

Description of growing mechanization of French agriculture, peasant discontent, and increasing capitalist control over agriculture under de Gaulle, with current Communist party program for agriculture and activity in rural France.

1541 ROCHET, WALDECK. Le marxisme et les chemins de l'avenir. Paris, Editions sociales, 1966. 93 p.

Speech at March 11-13, 1966 meeting of the central committee of the Parti communiste français. Rochet reviews current philosophical criticisms and problems of Marxism, relations with intellectuals, and possibility of passage to socialism by methods acceptable to social democratic parties. Resolutions of central committee supporting speech follow.

1542 ROCHET, WALDECK. Les raisons du soutien communiste à François Mitterand; rapport de Waldeck Rochet, Sécretaire général du Parti. Résolution, Drancy, 23 septembre 1965. Paris, 1965. 31 p. "Supplément à l'Humanité-dimanche' du 26 septembre 1965."

Speech before central committee of Parti communiste français urging common presidential candidate and demonstrating that Mitterand's views on economy, Atlantic Alliance, European unification are not unacceptable. Resolution supporting speech follows.

FOR ADDITIONAL WORKS BY WALDECK ROCHET, SEE AUTHOR INDEX

1543 ROGATI, ELIO. La seconda rivoluzione algerina. Roma, Opere nuove, 1965. 234 p. (Testimonianze, 1)

Sympathetic study of post-independence Algeria, 1962-1964, concentrating on: 1) political issues (such as the role of the F.L.N. and trade unions, drawing up the constitution, outlawing the Communist party, improvising foreign policy); 2) agricultural self-administration; 3) cultural and religious accommodations. Documents in Italian include the text of the constitution, statutes of F.L.N., and decree on agricultural self-administration.

1544 ROMAINS, JULES. Les hauts et les bas de la liberté; suprêmes avertissements, retrouver la foi; nouvelles inquiétudes. Paris, Flammarion, 1960. 268 p.

Collection of political essays, 1939-1960, the last two of which deal with Fifth Republic's anti-parliamentarian orientation.

1545 ROMEUF, JEAN. Les salaires et les revenus du travail en France (1958) Présentation par Emile Roche. Paris, Publications économiques et sociales, 1958. 80 p. tables. Supplement to Les Cahiers économiques, janvier-mars 1958. Pub. by Institut d'observation économique, Paris.

Statistics on wage earners in different wage brackets, divided by major types of employment and discussion and typical figures of incomes for wage earners broken down into: artisans, liberal professions, technical and managerial personnel, civil servants, white and blue collar workers, farmers, household servants, merchant marine. These are not final statistical data, but a useful survey of economic status as of January 1958.

1546 RONFANI, UGO. Perchè de Gaulle. Bari, Laterza, 1965. 306 p. (Libri del tempo, no. 90)

Well-informed analysis of forces in French political life that brought de Gaulle back to power and have kept him in office, de Gaulle's philosophy of national greatness, the individuals around de Gaulle and U.N.R. leadership, economic and institutional reforms, cultural objectives, foreign policy, unresolved problems and chances of survival of Fifth Republic. Most of the material concerns the post-Algerian war period and goes up to the end of 1964.

1547 ROSENSTIEL, FRANCIS. Le principe de "supranationalité;" essai sur les rapports de la politique et du droit. Paris, A. Pedone, 1962. 134 p. Includes bibliography.

Jurist's demonstration that "supranationality" as exemplified by the European Communities has neither a political nor a juridical foundation, and that functional integration cannot by itself be a stage to political federalism. Author warns of turning the Communities' technocrats, as a result of the political vacuum, into politicians in spite of themselves.

1548 ROSFELDER, ANDRE. L'Algérie à bâtir. Alger, Baconnier, 1959. 147 p.

Case for Algerian integration by fourth-generation French-Algerian petroleum specialist, who participated in May 1958 revolt. While admitting the validity of the world-wide decolonization movement, author argues that it is both desirable and possible within the institutional framework of the Fifth Republic, the fraternization initiated May 1958, and the massive investment program envisaged by the Constantine Plan to keep Algeria in the French orbit. In answer to the French Left, author insists that this, rather than independence, is the constructive and generous answer to the Algerian problem.

1549 ROUABLE, MAURICE. Précis de géographie: France et Communauté. Préparation aux C.A.P. commerciaux, B.E.C. 1re partie, B.E.I. 1re partie. 2. éd. Paris, Dunod, 1962. 105 p. illus. (Bibliothèque de l'enseignement technique)

Teaching manual summarizing physical geography, population, agricultural and industrial output for each of 20 regions of France, and giving the same information for Algeria, Sahara, West and Equatorial Africa, Madagascar, and smaller French overseas departments.

1550 ROUANET, PIERRE. Mendès-France au pouvoir, 18 juin 1954-6 février 1955. Paris, R. Laffont, 1965. 570 p.

Though limited to 1954-55, work sheds light on subsequent decolonization problems.

1551 ROUGIER, LOUIS AUGUSTE PAUL. L'erreur de la démocratie française. Paris, Editions l'esprit nouveau,1963. 270 p.

Criticism by French political philosopher of political systems of Fourth Republic (parliamentary omnipotence leading to government impotence) and Fifth Republic (government omnipotence leading to police state) and a plea for a government of law, in which neither parliament nor the head of state has unlimited power.

1552 ROUX, DOMINIQUE DE. Charles de Gaulle. Paris, Editions universitaires, 1967. 124 p. (Classiques du XXe siècle 92) Includes bibliography.

Comments on de Gaulle's philosophy of history and his visions of French and West's historical destiny, as illustrated in de Gaulle's Memoirs and other historical and military writings. Good bibliography of books on de Gaulle and Gaullism.

1553 ROVAN, JOSEPH. Une idée neuve: la démocratie. Paris, Editions du Seuil, 1961. 206 p.

Reflections on decline of democracy in France in recent history and suggestions for its renovation through new forms of democratic participation suitable for a highly technological society and the political framework of the Fifth Republic.

1554 ROY, JULES. Autour du drame. Paris, R. Julliard, 1961. 224 p.

Article series on Algeria that first appeared in "L'Express" and "Le Monde," June 1960-June 1961. Author travelled in Algeria in 1960 and reports on French Army, European activists, Algerian nationalist leaders, but was in Paris during April 1961 putsch and trial of General Challe, which are also covered. Prospects for peace, as seen from Algeria, are weighed.

1555 ROY, JULES. La guerre d'Algérie. Paris, R. Julliard, 1960. 215 p.

Personal experiences of Algerian-born French writer and close friend of Camus, who returns to Algeria after Camus' death to form his own opinion of the conflict. He is exposed to pro-French views when he visits his own "poor settler" family in a Kabylian village, talks to Europeans in Algiers, Bône, in a prosperous farm community, and to an army captain at a Tunisian border area; for the Algerian nationalist view, he sees a 'pacified' Kabylian village and a Tunisian refugee camp. Out of his shocked reactions comes an impassioned plea for negotiations with F.L.N. and peace at all costs, in the face of military intransigence and growing desperation among European settlers (summer 1960).

1556 ROY, MAURICE. Evolution des relations économiques entre les pays du Marché commun et les états associés d'Afrique et Madagascar. Aix en Provence, "La Pensée universitaire," 1964. 419 p. map. Includes bibliography.

Scholarly study of commercial exchanges, investment, and technical assistance between Common Market countries and former French colonies in Africa, 1958-1961. Good bibliography of books, articles and documents.

1557 RUBINSKII, IURII IL'ICH. Piataia respublika; politicheskaia bor'ba vo Frantsii v 1958-1963 godakh. Moskva, Mezhdunarodnye otnosheniia, 1964. 385 p.

Well-informed and widely documented political history of Fifth Republic by Russian author, with detailed information on the evolution of French political parties and the different stages of the Algerian conflict. Sources are not only Communist, but whole range of newspapers and periodicals, standard academic studies on Fifth Republic.

1558 RUDEL, CHRISTIAN. Mon village à l'heure de l'expansion. Paris, Editions ouvrières, 1965. 157, [3] p. (Collection "Réalisations") Bibliography: p. 158.

Proposals for ending rural exodus and renovating village life by a variety of measures for local economic development, such as specialized agriculture and industry, reforestation, tourism.

1559 RUEFF, JACQUES. L'âge de l'inflation. 3. éd. Paris, Payot, 1963. 144 p. (Etudes et documents Payot)

Collection of talks and articles, 1932-1961, on the advantages of the international gold standard over the gold exchange standard introduced after World War I and again after World War II. For Fifth Republic, 1961 talk warns of possible analogies with 1929 with respect to dollar over-extension.

1560 RUEFF, JACQUES. Le lancinant problème des balances de paiements. Paris, Payot, 1965. 233 p. (Etudes et documents Payot)

Case studies of balance of payment disequilibria (1928, 1933, 1949, and 1963) and theoretical treatment demonstrating the defects of the international monetary mechanism, which are currently causing disequilibrium in U.S. balance of payment, just as, ten years earlier, it was causing a chronic dollar shortage.

FOR ADDITIONAL WORKS BY AND ABOUT JACQUES RUEFF, SEE AUTHOR INDEX

1561 RUFFRAY, PATRICK DE. Décoloniser les provinces, conversations régionalistes en Poitou-Charentes. Poitiers, S.F.I.L. et impr. M. Texier réunies, 1967. 240 p. maps.

Problems of reanimating life in rural and declining South-West of France, underlining the importance of changing ecclesiastic structure in rural areas.

1562 SAADIA and LAKHDAR. L'aliénation colonialiste et la résistance de la famille algérienne. Lausanne, La cité, 1961. 195, [1] p. (Contribution) "Index des livres cités": p. 196.

Algerian sociologist's study of French colonialism's pressure to bring about voluntary submission of Algerians to French civilization by naturalization, conversion to Christianity, military service, prostitution, inter-marriage and emigration, and the resistance of the Algerian family to these efforts. Study is preceded by a violently anti-French introduction by Ferhat Abbas.

1563 SAHLI, MOHAMED C. Décoloniser l'histoire; introduction à l'histoire du Maghreb. Paris, F. Maspéro, 1965. 148 p. (Cahiers libres, 77)

Critique of French historians' and sociologists' biased presentation of Algeria's colonial and pre-colonial history and French assimilation efforts.

1564 SAINDERICHIN, PIERRE and JOSEPH POLI. Histoire secrète d'une élection, 5-19 décembre 1965. Paris, Plon, 1966. 252 p.

Non-partisan inside history of presidential campaign by a political journalist and a television producer with all the intrigues involved in the different candidacies, notably Pinay's and de Gaulle's. Of special interest is the role of television in the campaign and the reaction to this medium by the different candidates.

1565 SAINT MARC, MICHELE. Zone franc et décolonisation. Avant-propos de Robert Buron. Préf. de Jean Weiller. Paris, Société d'édition d'enseignement supérieur, 1964. 259 p. illus. (Développement économique, 10) Bibliography: p. 249-253.

Study (based on 1963 dissertation at University of Paris) on the history of the franc zone during the period of decolonization, 1956-1962, showing what new forms of economic and monetary cooperation between France and its former colonies (Morocco, Tunisia) and former members of the French Community are replacing colonial control.

1566 SAINT-ROBERT, PHILIPPE DE. Le jeu de la France, essai. Paris, Julliard, 1967. 253 p. Bibliographical footnotes.

Coherent exposition of Gaullist principles of national independence. Gaullist European policy, rejection of the Atlantic Alliance relations with Germany, and above all a closely argued explanation of Gaullist rejection of U.S. domination in Western Europe, going back historically to inept U.S. intervention after the two world wars and its current delusions of grandeur in Latin America and Asia. In contrast, there are shown to be many convergent interests with Soviet Union. Author is one of editors of "Télégramme de Paris," (see no. 2109).

1567 SAINTE LORETTE, LUCIEN. Rapports sur les affaires étrangères. [Paris, Secrétariat général du Conseil national et des Assises nationales de l'UNR-UDT, 1963]. 7, 8, 4 p.

Speech at May 1963 Conseil National de l'U.N.R.-U.D.T. explaining Gaullist policy for European political and economic integration. Annexed speech by Jean de Lipkowski motivates refusal to admit Great Britain into Common Market.

1568 SALAN, RAOUL, (defendant). Le procès de Raoul Salan; compte rendu sténographique. Paris, A. Michel, 1962. 555 p. (Les Grands procès contemporains)

Major document on Algerian problem, Gaullist Algerian policy, and O. A. S. emerging from Salan's lengthy explanatory statement (he refused to answer questions) Tixier-Vignancour's eloquent defense, declarations of witnesses Michel Debré, François Mitterand, Christian de Malène, René Coty, cited by the defense, and government witnesses General Ailleret and Governor General Morin. Salan, captured in Algeria April 20, 1962, was brought before the Haut Tribunal militaire de Paris, the same tribunal which had just sentenced to death General Jouhaud. Salan was indicted both for his participation in April 1961 putsch and his leadership of the O. A. S. and tried May 15-23, 1962. Trial also sheds light on Bazooka affair (attempted murder of Salan, Jan. 1957) and May 1958.

FOR ADDITIONAL WORKS ABOUT RAOUL SALAN, SEE AUTHOR INDEX

1569 SALLANTIN, XAVIER. Essai sur la défense. Paris, Desclée de Brouwer, 1962. 188 p. illus. (Questions actuelles)

Philosophy of defense of West against Communism seen both as a negative process (military strategy) and a constructive answer to world problems, in which the negative military anti-communist point of view must not be allowed to obscure other considerations.

1570 SALLERON, LOUIS. La France est-elle gouvernable? Propos politiques et civiques. Paris, L'Esprit nouveau, 1963. 409 p.

Series of studies written mainly 1957-1960 for Centre d'études politiques et civiques (C. E. P. E. C.) on a broad range of political questions, the army, communism, socialism, religion. The center, founded in 1954, was intended to combat the decay of French political institutions and restore a strong government. Final essay, May 1963, sums up the center's program.

1571 SALLERON, LOUIS. Pouvoir et propriété dans l'entreprise; sur un livre de M. Bloch-Lainé. Paris, 1963, 27 p. "Tiré à part d'Itinéraires, numéro 75."

Condemnation of Bloch-Lainé's proposals for reforming legal status of firms presented in his "Réforme de l'entreprise" as contrary to Catholic doctrine of the rights and responsibilities of private property and implying a reinforcement of technocracy. Salleron expresses views in line with those of extremely conservative Cité catholique. For a comparable criticism of Bloch-Lainé, see no. 356.

1572 SALYCHEV, STEPAN STEPANOVICH. Ideologiia i politika frantsuzskoi sotsialisticheskoi partii, 1944-1964 gg. Moskva, Mysl', 1966. 503 p. Includes bibliography.

Carefully documented political history of Parti Socialiste in Fourth and Fifth Republic and analysis of the political and economic theories of party thinkers such as Jules Moch, Lucien Laurat, André Philip, Roger Quilliot, with emphasis on their anti-communist as well as anti-Marxist character. Last 150 pages dealing with Fifth Republic period discuss party's current program, its opposition role, and prospects of collaboration with communists, as illustrated by 1965 presidential campaign. Good bibliography of Socialist sources and both French and Russian literature.

1573 SANGUINETTI, ALEXANDRE. La France et l'arme atomique. Paris, R. Julliard, 1964. 122 p.

Military and economic argument in favor of French nuclear weapons, which might later be jointly controlled by European Community. Author, who is vice-president of National Assembly's Commission of National Defense, explains motivation of Gaullist military policy centering around nuclear deterrent, elimination of large land armies and compulsory military service, to be replaced by a highly trained professional army of about half a million and 'peace corps' type six-months' service for all 18-year olds.

1574 SANGUINETTI, ALEXANDRE. Rapport sur la politique militaire. [Paris, Secrétariat général du Conseil national et des Assises nationales, 1963] 34 p.

Speech by vice-president of National Defense Committee of National Assembly at U. N. R. -U. D. T. 3rd Assises Nationales, Nice, Nov. 1963, giving rationale behind government's military strategy of combining nuclear deterrent with small professional army.

1575 SANTINI, ANDRE. L'aide de l'état à la presse. Préf. de C.-A. Colliard. Paris, Presses universitaires de France, 1966. 95 p. (Travaux et recherches de la Faculté de droit et des sciences économiques de Paris, Série "Droit public," no. 3) Includes bibliography.

Analysis of different forms of press subsidies by Ministry of Information during Fourth and Fifth Republic, with special data on "Le Monde" finances, as of May 1964.

1576 SARNE, DANIEL. L'affaire Ben Barka. Paris, Table ronde, 1966. 233 p. (Vérité, justice)

Chronological account of Ben Barka's kidnaping and disapearance, police and court handling of the case, October 1965-March 1966. Introductory essay by Jean-Marc Varaut takes Ben Barka case as a starting point for bringing out the deterioration of justice under Fifth Republic and steps toward a totalitarian state, in which not only the functioning of the police and the so-called parallel police but the integrity of Minister of the Interior and other high-ranking officials are called into question.

1577 SARTRE, JEAN PAUL. Colonialisme et néo-colonialisme. Paris, Gallimard, 1964. 253 p. (His Situations, 5)

Articles originally published in "Temps modernes" and "Express" dealing with decolonization, Algerian war, and termination of conflict, as well as opposition to de Gaulle's return to power and arguments against 1958 and 1961 referenda.

1578 SARTRE, JEAN PAUL. Critique de la raison dialectique, précédé de Question de méthode. t. 1. Théorie des ensembles pratiques. Paris, Gallimard, 1960. 755 p. (Bibliothèque des idées)

First part of Sartre's most serious attempt at reinterpreting Marxism in the existentialist framework.

FOR ADDITIONAL WORKS BY AND ABOUT JEAN PAUL SARTRE, SEE AUTHOR INDEX

1579 SAUDI ARABIA. AL-BIʿ THAT LADA AL-UMAM AL-MUTAHIDAH. Statements made during the 14th session of the United Nations General Assembly by His Excellency Mr. Ahmad Shukairy, Minister of State for United Nations Affairs. Prepared by the Saudi Arabian Mission to the United Nations. New York, 1960. 129 p.

Statements on disarmament and protests on French nuclear tests in the Sahara and on Algerian war.

1580 SAUGE, GEORGES. Echec au communism. 3. éd., rev., corr. et augm. Paris, Iles d'or, 1963. 230 p.

Popular lectures on the essence of Marxism-Leninism, the Communist party apparatus and its strategy, illustrated by quotations from Communist thinkers and political leaders (with biographical notes on each) on such topics as the class struggle, communism and religion, parliamentary government, peace. Third edition analyzes CPSU's XXII Congress (1961) according to the same topics. The author, founder of lay Catholic Centre d'Etudes Supérieures de Psychologie Sociale, whose prime aim is to counter onslaught of communism and for which these lectures were prepared, gives appropriate Christian counter-arguments and cites May 1958 events as the first appropriate counterrevolutionary response to communist strategy.

FOR ADDITIONAL WORKS BY AND ABOUT GEORGES SAUGE, SEE AUTHOR INDEX

1581 SAUREL, LOUIS. La Légion étrangère; préf. d'Alain Decaux. Paris, Editions Rouff, 1965. 190 p. (Dossiers de l'histoire, 3) Includes bibliography.

History of Foreign Legion's deployment, with last 20 pages clarifying its participation in April 1961 putsch in Algeria.

1582 SAUVY, ALFRED. La montée des jeunes. Paris, Calmann-Lévy, 1959. 264 p. (Questions d'actualité)

Evolution of French demography since World War II and the effects of the rise in birth rates on educational, housing, employment needs, and the relative needs of French and Algerian youth.

1583 SAUVY, ALFRED. Mythologie de notre temps. Paris, Payot, 1965. 297 p. illus. (Etudes et documents Payot) Bibliographical footnotes.

Study of public opinion and its lack of responsiveness to the results of statistical observation, particularly in the economic realm (relation between mechanization and employment, housing Malthusianism). The myths on which political parties build their philosophy and actions are also examined, as is the problem of rational leadership in the face of collective myths.

1584 SAUVY, ALFRED. L'opinion publique. Paris, Presses universitaires de France, 1956. 127 p. ("Que sais-je?" Le point des connaissances actuelles [70])

Popular work on the formation and measurement of public opinion, in particular political attitudes, but with few current examples.

1585 SAUVY, ALFRED. Le Plan Sauvy, commenté par Pierre Le Brun, Pierre Mendès-France et al. Paris, Calmann-Lévy, 1960. 220 p. (Questions d'actualité)

Sauvy's proposals, first published in "Express" March-June 1960, for a "progressive" economic policy covering housing, agriculture, education, health, aid to underdeveloped areas, etc. Author is both a demographer and a member of the Conseil Economique et Social. His proposal is followed by comments from 8 persons, mainly trade union members of the Conseil Economique et Social, as well as Mendès-France.

1586 SAVAGE, CATHARINE. Malraux, Sartre, and Aragon as political novelists. Gainesville, University of Florida Press, 1964. 64 p. (University of Florida monographs. Humanities, no. 17) Bibliographical footnotes.

Analysis of representative political novels by each of these authors.

1587 SAVARY, ALAIN. Nationalisme algérien et grandeur française. Paris, Plon, 1960. 204 p. illus. (Tribune libre, 54)

Analysis of the real cost of Algerian integration in terms of the country's political, economic, demographic, and sociological situation and demonstration of the incompatibility between carrying through a consistent integration policy and true French national greatness. Author, secretary of state in charge of Moroccan and Tunisian affairs in Mollet government and one of the founders of the Parti Socialiste Autonome, advocates immediate negotiations with F.L.N. to assure a 10-year transition from present political institutions to independence. He is critical of de Gaulle's proposals for self-determination, for which he feels Algeria is not ready in the wake of the bitter struggle. This closely-reasoned argument for Algerian independence is one of the most frequently cited works in the controversy.

1588 SCHAEFER, RENE. Révolution en Algérie. Paris, Editions France Empire, 1956. 414 p. maps, tables.

Explanation of a collective Algerian consciousness as a result of the social and economic disintegration of traditional society, with a carefully documented description of the dynamics of the Algerian economy. Only by recognizing the deep roots of this revolution and taking charge of its goals can France prevent a "national" war and communist take-over. Author, who has spent many years in Algeria, insists that external support of Algerian nationalism is only a minor factor.

1589 SCHEER, MAXIMILLIAN. Algerien; Jugend im Feuer. Berlin, Verlag der Nation, 1959. 94 p. illus.

Sketches of young Algerian nationalists and reception of young visitors in German Democratic Republic.

1590 SCHEINMAN, LAWRENCE. Atomic energy policy in France under the Fourth Republic. Princeton, N.J., Princeton University Press, 1965. xxiv, 259 p. Bibliography: p. 224-244.

Final chapters describe continuity and change in French atomic policy, both military and civilian, under Fifth Republic. Exhaustive bibliography, some of it covering post-1958 period.

1591 SCHENK, FRITZ. Zehn Jahre Deutsch-Französisches Institut, Ludwigsburg, gegründet am 2. Juli 1948; Tätigkeitsbericht. Ludwigsburg, 1958. 40 p.

Review of Institute's activities, including list of publications and names of participating German and French private and governmental organizations supporting cultural exchanges.

1592 SCHEUER, GEORG. Marianne auf dem Schafott; Frankreich zwischen gestern und morgen. Wien, Europa Verlag, 1966. 335 p. (Europäische Perspektiven)

Political history of Fifth Republic and its antecedents, concluding with 1965 election. Author, a Paris correspondent for German and Austrian press, demonstrates, through vicissitudes of political life, the tenacity of French democratic forces.

1593 SCHMILL, ERICK. Les investissements étrangers en France. Paris, Editions Cujas, 1966. 136 p. (Connaissances de l'économie, 2)

Brief survey of foreign investments in France and changing attitudes of French government toward them.

1594 SCHMITT, WALTHER E. Zwischenrufe von der Seine; die Entwicklung der Europa-Politik und das deutsch-französische Verhältnis. Stuttgart, W. Kohlhammer, 1958. 207 p.

German parliamentarian's analysis of French political parties' vacillations and objections with respect to European unification and closer ties with Germany and final acceptance of the Common Market.

1595 SCHNEIDER, BERTRAND. La Ve république et l'Algérie; documents et confrontations. Paris, Editions Témoignage chrétien, 1959. 157 p. (Bibliothèque de l'homme d'action) "Petite bibliographie objective": p. 152-153.

Summary of measures of successive French governments, military actions and negotiations, proposed solutions, 1954-1958 as a background for de Gaulle's Algerian policy in first 9 months of Fifth Republic, with emphasis on Constantine Plan. Author estimates costs of integration to be beyond what France

1596 SCHNEIDER, FERNAND MARIE THIEBAUT. Stratégie pour l'Occident, l'U.R.S.S. dans l'O.T.A.N.? essai politique et militaire. Paris, Charles-Lavauzelle et Cie, 1965. x, 214 p. illus. Bibliography: p. 207-211.

Systematic exposition of present nuclear and conventional military status of East-West confrontation, political and economic factors affecting NATO and the Atlantic Alliance as a whole and examination of best strategic responses. Author summarizes opinions of 16 military theorists in France, U.S. and Germany on these points. De Gaulle's military policy is mentioned but not directly criticized. Author is retired officer who had been attached to NATO staff. Problems of revolutionary wars, as exemplified by current Vietnamese conflict are stressed. Good bibliography of recent articles.

1597 SCHOENBRUN, DAVID. As France goes. New York, Harper, 1957. 341 p.

American journalist's history of the Fourth Republic, evolution of French Union and European unification, complemented by a survey of political parties and the parliamentary system, as well as other aspects of French civilization. Author balances deterioration against signs of renewed vigor.

1598 SCHOENBRUN, DAVID. The three lives of Charles de Gaulle. New York, Atheneum, 1966. 373 p. Bibliographical footnotes.

Biography in three parts: pre-World War II, World War II, and post-May 1958. Author had frequent interviews with de Gaulle during years as reporter in London and recently as CBS correspondent in France. The most revealing sections are on de Gaulle's current foreign policy and relations with U.S. statesmen; the author had a long interview with Eisenhower on his dealings with de Gaulle, both during the war and after 1958.

1599 SCHOLL-LATOUR, PETER. Im Sog des Generals; von Abidjan nach Moskau. Stuttgart, Deutsche Verlags-Anstalt, 1966. 363 p.

German television correspondent stationed in Paris reports in diary form political developments (internal and foreign) between July 1965 and July 1966, with the spotlight on de Gaulle himself at home and on his travels. Having been stationed in Indochina and the Congo previously, author is well-informed on colonial questions. Dominant themes are presidential election, North African crises, French withdrawal from NATO, de Gaulle's visit to Russia.

1600 SCHUMAN, ROBERT. Pour l'Europe. Paris, Editions Nagel, 1963. 209 p. ports., facsim. (Ecrits politiques)

Summation, based on notes, speeches, and articles, of guiding principles underlying his promotion of European unification.

1601 SCHWARTZENBERG, ROGER GERARD. La campagne présidentielle de 1965. Préf. de Georges Vedel. Paris, Presses universitaires de France, 1967. 182 p. (Travaux et recherches de la Faculté de droit et des sciences économiques de Paris. Série "Science politique," no. 13) Bibliographical footnotes.

Interpretation of six months of presidential campaign, June through December 1965 to see its effect on the personalization of political activity (how the issue itself was used and how it influenced the style of the campaign) the extent to which political programs were affected (reduction of demagogic extremism by all contenders) and the response to this innovation by political parties (movement toward large political formations of center left and right). Analysis is carried through up to March 1967 elections. Author is convinced that the degree of political concentration demonstrated during the presidential election would make a presidential regime viable but is not sufficient to make a parliamentary regime along the lines of the British system workable.

1602 SEBASTIEN, A. and J. PHILIPPE. Pétain, de Gaulle. Pourquoi amis? Pourquoi ennemis? Etude psychologique. Paris, Union du livre, 1965. 109 p. facsims.

Psychological explanation on the basis of astrological and graphological evidence, of the hostility between de Gaulle and Pétain, notwithstanding the fact that after 1944 de Gaulle took over Pétain's collective image. Astrological evidence points to de Gaulle's retirement in 1965-66.

1603 SECRETAIN, ROGER. Chroniques III. Orléans, Edition de "La République du centre," 1961. xx, 455 p.

Collection of 80 short articles by editor-in-chief of Orléans newspaper "La République du Centre" from his defeat as U.D.S.R. deputy by Poujadists in January 1956 to January 1961. Over half the articles deal with internal politics: the decay of the Fourth Republic, appeal to de Gaulle, establishment and problems of the new regime, seen from a basically favorable point of view. One short section deals specifically with Algeria, February 1956 - January 1961.

1604 SECRETARIAT SOCIAL D'ALGER. L'Algérie et sa jeunesse. Alger, 1957. 432 p. diagrs. (1 fold.) tables. (Etudes du Secrétariat social d'Alger, 3)

Sociological and statistical studies by individual authors on Algerian youth, their education, standard of living, employment, and more detailed regional studies. Secrétariat Social makes its own proposals on educational reforms. Secrétariat Social, a Catholic study group, is dedicated to improving social conditions for the two Algerian communities.

1605 SECRETARIAT SOCIAL D'ALGER. L'Algerie surpeuplée; orientations pour une politique de population. Alger, Editions du Secrétariat social d'Alger, 1958. 318 p. diagrs. (Its Etudes, 4) Bibliographical footnotes.

Historical study of demographic development in Algeria and consideration of different methods of reducing the birth rate which are in harmony with the organization's Catholic ethics and still capable of breaking the vicious cycle of overpopulation-underdevelopment.

1606 SECRETARIAT SOCIAL D'ALGER. Au service de l'industrialisation de l'Algérie; la micro-industrie. Alger, 1959. 158 p. tables, diagrs.

Study of preconditions in Algeria for large-scale industrialization, as proposed by Constantine Plan (quantity and quality of available manpower, social and cultural obstacles). Micro-industry is viewed as the best answer for rural Algeria's under-development, to be combined with modern industries for Algeria's modern sector.

1607 SECRETARIAT SOCIAL D'ALGER. La cohabitation en Algérie. Alger, 1956. 204 p. fold. map. (Etudes du Secrétariat social d'Alger, 2)

Studies by various authors on the 1956 status of relations between the two ethnic communities - legal, economic, and statistical. As analysis shows, this is more a case of juxtaposition than of association between two groups.

1608 SECRETARIAT SOCIAL D'ALGER. Les commissaires au développement; chevilles-ouvrières de la lutte contre le sous-développement. Alger, 1961. 79 p. (Its Etudes, 6)

Secrétariat Social's proposal for promoting economic development by sending individual agents to work in local communities to act as a catalyzer.

1609 SECRETARIAT SOCIAL D'ALGER. De l'Algérie originelle à l'Algérie moderne; éléments de sociologie culturelle au service de l'éducation de base. Alger, 1961. 94 p.

Essays on Algerian culture and possibilities of making necessary adaptation to a modern society. This study served as background for the proposal to send agents to local communities (see above).

1610 SECRETARIAT SOCIAL D'ALGER. Le sous-développement en Algérie. Alger, 1959. 193 p. (Etudes du Secrétariat social d'Alger, 5)

Essays by individual authors, among them Pierre Bourdieu, on the cultural and economic aspects of underdevelopment, as of late 1958, and Secrétariat Social's proposed remedies.

1611 SETTIER, FRANÇOIS. Stratégie de la lutte sociale: France, 1936-1960. Paris, Economie et humanisme, Editions ouvrières, 1961. 349 p. (Collection "Relations sociales") "Bibliographie": p. 344.

Study made in collaboration with University of Aix-Marseilles' Centre d'étude des relations sociales on French labor law, state intervention in enterprises, and labor relations (collective bargaining, co-determination of factory administration, position of trade unions, minimum wage and other wage policies, strikes, and arbitration) with most of the material dealing with the Fourth Republic. Author stresses contradiction between governmental welfare policy and recognition of the sanctity of private property.

1612 SEMAINE DE LA PENSEE MARXISTE; CONFRONTATIONS ET DEBATS. L'homme chrétien et l'homme marxiste. [By] Père Cardonnel, Jeannette Colombel et al. Paris, La Palatine, 1964. 268 p.

Three debates organized by Centre d'études et de recherches marxistes (see no. 844) on materialism and transcendence, praxis and morality, and the Reformation in its Christian and human meaning by three Jesuits, two protestant theologians and Communist philosophers, including Antoine Casanova, Gilbert Mury, and Roger Garaudy. The aim of the discussion is to look for a common ground between Marxist doctrine and Christian theology.

1613 SEMAINE DE LA PENSEE MARXISTE. 4th, PARIS, 1965. Femmes du XXe siècle. Préf. de Roger Garaudy. Paris, Presses universitaires de France, 1965. 234 p. Bibliographical footnotes.

Discussion between communists and non-communists on the rôle of women in French society, their professional and political participation (for instance number of women in different branches of the government) with extensive figures on current practices. In the section "woman and love" views favorable to family planning are refuted by communist spokesmen.

1614 SEMAINE DE LA PENSEE MARXISTE, PARIS, 1966. Démocratie et liberté, Semaine de la pensée marxiste (Paris, 9-15 mars 1966) Préface de Roger Garaudy. Paris, Editions sociales, 1966. 251 p. Bibliographical footnotes.

Discussion bringing together Communist party leaders (Jacques Duclos, Waldeck Rochet) and theoreticians with other political leaders of the left (François Mitterand, S.F.I.O, Radical, Catholic figures) on democratization of political, economic, and educational institutions and the place of liberty in Marxist philosophy. Communist acceptance of multiparty democracy and agreement on socialist and democratic goals of all participants is stressed.

1615 SEMAINE DES INTELLECTUELS CATHOLIQUES, 1958. La conscience chrétienne et les nationalismes; Semaine des intellectuels catholiques, 5 au 11 novembre 1958. Organisée par le Centre catholique des intellectuels français. Paris, P. Horay, 1959. 286 p.

Discussion of 20th century nationalism not limited to French relations with colonies and underdeveloped nations but extending to all of Western civilization; role of Catholic Church, communism, technology in era of decolonization. Biographical notes on participants, some French, others from French Empire.

1616 SEMAINE SOCIALE DE FRANCE, 49th, STRASBOURG, 1962. L'Europe des personnes et des peuples. Lyon, Chronique sociale de France, 1962. 415 p.

Among talks related to current French problems are Philippe Farine's on French attitudes toward European unification, Pierre Bauchet's on regional planning within the European Community and Georges Desmotte's on the status of immigrant workers.

1617 SEMAINE SOCIALE DE FRANCE. 50th, CAEN, 1963. La société démocratique; compte rendu in extenso. Lyon, Chronique sociale de France, 1963. 398 p.

Colloquium revolves around forms that participation in community affairs by individuals can take in contemporary society and how democracy in France can resolve tension between personal fulfillment and social achievements. Emphasis is on fostering participation through new mediating structures, such as local government, trade unions and through economic democratization. Some of talks discuss prospects of political parties, political versus technical decisions. Good up-to-date bibliographies after some of the talks. Among 20 speakers are political scientist René Rémond, theologian J. Y. Calvez, civil servant Roger Grégoire, secretary general of Secrétariats Sociaux Henri Théry, C.F.T.C. vice-president André Jeanson.

1618 SEMAINE SOCIALE DE FRANCE, 53d, NICE, 1966. L'Opinion publique. [By] Alain Barrère, Jean-Christian Fauvet, Jacques Antoine, Paul Vibert, et al. Lyon, Chronique sociale de France, 1966. 415 p. Bibliographical footnotes.

Lecture series on measurement of public opinion (techniques of public opinion polls), impact of mass media (radio, television, press, advertising), public opinion as part of the democratic process, legal status of communication media, with list of relevant laws for radio and television. Several talks deal with public opinion of and within Catholic Church. Talk on legal status of communication media has good bibliography.

1619 SENECHAL, MICHEL. Droits politiques et liberté d'expression des officiers des forces armées. Préf. de Roland Drago. Paris, R. Pichon et R. Durand-Auzias, 1964. 321 p. (Bibliothèque de droit public, t. 55) Includes bibliography.

Legislative history of army officers' and reserve officers' civil rights (right to vote, right to hold elective offices, party membership, freedom of expression) from First to Fifth Republic, examination of existing restrictions in military practice and obstacles to full integration in civilian society. Implications of this lack of integration during periods of civilian-military opposition, as exemplified by April 1961 putsch, are examined.

1620 SENGHOR, LEOPOLD SEDAR, PRES. SENEGAL. Réception du général de Gaulle à l'Assemblée fédérale du Mali, Dakar, le 13 décembre 1959. Dakar, 1959. 25 p.

In addition to Senghor's speeches, includes de Gaulle's speech delivered before Mali National Assembly at the eve of the new federation's independence.

1621 SERANT, PAUL. La France des minorités. Paris, R. Laffont, 1965. 411 p. maps. (Collection L'Histoire que nous vivons) Bibliography: p. 409-412.

History and current status of separatist movements among ethnic minorities in metropolitan France (Alsace-Lorraine, Basque, Breton, Flemish, Occitanian areas) in the context of the experiences of Algerian repatriates. Author highlights the problems inherent in France's extremely centralized government confronted with this diversity and what might be done within a federal European organization.

1622 SERANT, PAUL. Gardez-vous à gauche. Paris, Fasquelle, 1956. 144 p. (Collection "Libelles") Bibliographical footnotes.

Attack on two main non-Communist Leftist orientations currently attracting young bourgeois disciples: the technocratic Left of Mendès-France and the revolutionary Left of Sartre, both of which betray the Left's traditional humanism and anti-totalitarianism, since they fail to condemn vigorously communist totalitarianism, with which they have latent affinities.

1623 SERANT, PAUL. Où va la droite? Préf. de Marcel Aymé. Paris, Plon, 1958. 172 p. (Tribune libre, 20)

Philosophical and ideological trends of the French Right, as of early 1958, and plea for revision of its nationalist, anti-democratic mythology.

1624 SERANT, PAUL. Le romantisme fasciste; étude sur l'oeuvre politique de quelques écrivains français. Paris, Fasquelle, 1959. 321 p. "Bibliographie": p. 309-321.

Political thought of six French fascist writers prominent in pre-World War II and during German occupation: Pierre Drieu La Rochelle, Robert Brasillach, Lucien Rebatet, Louis-Ferdinand Céline, Abel Bonnard, and Alphonse de Chateaubriant. None of the survivors play a current political rôle.

1625 SERIGNY, ALAIN DE, (defendant). Un procès. Paris, Table ronde, 1961. 455 p. (L'Ordre du jour)

Summary and excerpts from June-September 1960 trial before the Tribunal militaire permanent de Paris for participation in the "Barricades" uprising in Algiers, January 1960. Alain de Sérigny, editor of "L'Echo d'Alger" is one of the accused, but only the final section of the book deals specifically with his case. Others indicted are Pierre Lagaillarde, Bernard Lefèvre, Jean-Jacques Susini. Excerpts are grouped around such topics as "the army speaks," "the political climate" "the plot," "the shooting."

1626 SERIGNY, ALAIN DE. La révolution du 13 mai, avec les témoignages inédits de ses principaux acteurs. Paris, Plon, 1958. 184 p. illus., ports., facsim.

Eyewitness account, March - June 6, 1958, by one of leading actors in May 1958 uprising, with excellent photographs taken from "L'Echo d'Alger" including some of the Committees of Public Safety, some of whose declarations are also reproduced. For "Echo d'Alger" edited by Sérigny, see no. 1918.

1627 SERVAN-SCHREIBER, JEAN JACQUES. Lieutenant en Algérie. Paris, R. Julliard, 1957. 276 p.

Personal narrative of combat experiences in Algeria, summer 1956-spring 1957 under General de la Bollardière and Colonel Barberot (see no. 132) by "Express" editor serving as reserve officer. Author emphasizes controversy between his superiors, who adhered to constructive pacification measures, and military hierarchy insisting on counter-terrorism, the approach which was to prevail. Description of fellow officers, discussions among them of goals and methods, relations with civilian authorities, European settlers is only slightly fictionalized. Comments by several officers sharing author's experiences conclude book, one of the most provocative on the conduct of the Algerian war.

1628 SERVAN-SCHREIBER, JEAN JACQUES, (ed.). Rencontres: Nenni, Bevan, Mendès France; février 1959. Paris, R. Julliard, 1959. 188 p. ports.

Text of three days' conversations, initiated by "L'Express" and in the presence of its editor Jean-Jacques Servan-Schreiber between the most prominent French, Italian, and British spokesmen for the non-Communist Left: Pierre Mendès-France, Pietro Nenni, and Aneurin Bevan. The free-flowing exchanges were rearranged by the editor to fall into the following topics: prospects of the European Left and possibilities of alliances with communist parties; planning and democracy; the Atlantic Alliance and relations with the U.S.; the Common Market; decolonization and aid to underdeveloped countries.

1629 SERVIER, JEAN. Demain en Algérie. Paris, R. Laffont, 1959. 175 p.

Analysis of social conditions in Algeria and reforms France could still carry through, primarily in returning a major part of the economy to communal control. Author, an Algerian-born ethnologist specializing in Berber civilization, who had been active on pilot collective farms in Kabylia 1956-1958, demonstrates that the Algerian bourgeoisie, whether pro-French or nationalist, is the main obstacle to progress and that the Algerian revolution is the product of the nationalist bourgeoisie's desire to wrest control from the French without helping the peasant masses.

1630 SHCHIROVSKII, IURII VLADIMIROVICH. Bor'ba Frantsuzskoi kommunisticheskoi partii protiv voiny v Alzhire. Moskva, Izd-vo VPPI i AON, 1962. 150 p.

French Communist Party's opposition to Algerian war, 1954-1961, based on French Communist press, material from party congresses, and a few items from material intended for internal party circulation, as well as Algerian Communist sources.

1631 SHEAHAN, JOHN. Promotion and control of industry in postwar France. Cambridge, Harvard University Press, 1963. 301 p. Includes bibliography.

Economic policies (price control, planning, nationalizations, incentives and protective measures) and results in specific French industries during 1950's compared to U.S. Individual industries covered in detail are aluminum, steel, automobiles, and textiles, with emphasis on changes in production methods and productivity and overall economic growth. Good bibliography for government publications on economic developments, bibliographies on individual topics.

1632 SICARD, MAURICE IVAN. Histoire de la Collaboration. [By] J. Saint-Paulien, pseud. Paris, Esprit nouveau, 1964. 610 p.

History of collaboration during German occupation and subsequent purges by secretary of Doriot's Parti Populaire Français, demonstrating that collaborationists were more consistent than de Gaulle in seeking Franco-German reconciliation. Index of names.

1633 SICE, STANISLAUS. La France requiert contre ses institutions. Préf. du général Weygand. Paris, A. Bonne, 1959. 323 p.

Indictment of institutions of French parliamentary system, views on European integration, Arab nationalism, international relations composed of articles written between 1950 and 1957. Author defends thesis of strong government, firm colonial policy, sound finances.

1634 SIEFER, GREGOR. Die Mission der Arbeiterpriester; Ereignisse und Konsequenzen. Ein Beitrag zum Thema: Kirche und Industriegesellschaft. Essen, H. Driewer, 1960. 335 p. "Literaturverzeichnis": p. 308-326.

Sociological study on worker priest movement in France both before and after its official dissolution, and on new attempts to reach workers through "missions ouvrières." Good bibliography.

1635 SIEGFRIED, ANDRE. De la IVe à la Ve république au jour le jour. Paris, B. Grasset, 1958. 321 p.

Annual introductory comments to "Année politique" 1945-1958, plus analyses, written originally for "Le Figaro," on different aspects of the Fourth Republic and the transitional period between June and November 1958. Of particular interest are political sociologist's explanations for collapse of Fourth Republic and his reactions to the new constitution.

1636 SIEGLER, HEINRICH, FREIHERR VON. Kennedy oder de Gaulle? Probleme der Atlantik- und Europapolitik. Versuch einer Klarstellung jener Probleme und Differenzen, die durch das Abkommen von Nassau und das Scheitern der Brüsseler Verhandlungen über den Beitritt Grossbritanniens zur EWG offenbar wurden. Bonn, Siegler, Verlag für Zeitarchive, 1963. 161 p. illus., tables.

A continuation of "Dokumentation der Europaeischen Integration 1946-1961" giving background to NATO and nuclear weapons impasse between France and U.S. and refusal of Great Britain's Common Market membership, with principal political declarations on these questions July 1962-April 1963, current editorials, and cartoons.

1637 SIEMON, HUGUES. Frankreich stellt die Uhren um. Köln, Westdeutscher Verlag, 1960. 236 p. Bibliographical footnotes.

French-born sociologist's interpretation (for German readers) of political climate and dynamic factors of contemporary France. Topics discussed are specific nature of nationalism in the context of the Fifth Republic, in particular with respect to Algeria, army's mentality and meaning of the doctrine of psychological warfare, documented by Colonel Lacheroy's July 1957 speech on the subject.

1638 SIMON, PIERRE HENRI. Contre la torture. Paris, Editions du Seuil, 1957. 124 p.

Catholic novelist's plea against using torture and other forms of repression violating international rules of war. Includes excerpts from officers' letters and diaries documenting repression in Algeria. For review of this work, see no. 583.

1939 SIMON, PIERRE HENRI. Portrait d'un officier; récit. Paris, Editions du Seuil, 1958. 174 p.

Personal narrative, in fictional form, of a career officer's resignation from the army as a result of his repugnance against the aims and methods of war in Algeria.

1640 SOCIALISME OU BARBARIE; ORGANE DE CRITIQUE ET D'ORIENTATION REVOLUTIONNAIRE, (periodical). La crise française et le gaullisme. Paris, 1958. 103 p. "Volume V, juillet-août 1958."

Four articles commenting on the collapse of the Fourth Republic and de Gaulle's return to power from syndicalist point of view. Authors, who are critical of Communists' and Social ists' purely negative defense of democracy, claim that workers failed to identify with Fourth Republic. Authors are optimistic about de Gaulle's mastering Algerian crisis without civil war. Appendix contains eyewitness accounts of worker reactions, May 13-28, 1958 in various factories and reproductions of leaflets distributed by worker groups.

1641 SOCIETE FRANÇAISE DE SOCIOLOGIE. 1. COLLOQUE, PARIS, 1965. Tendances et volontés de la société française; études sociologiques publiées sous la direction de Jean-Paul Reynaud. Paris, S.E.D.E.I.S., 1966. 501 p. (Futuribles, 5)

Selected and revised contributions from colloquium of Société française de Sociologie bringing together sociologists and other social scientists. Focus of conference are transformations in French economic and social structures and public opinion with respect to these changes. Short bibliographies after each chapter.

1642 SOCIETE GENERALE POUR FAVORISER LE DEVELOPPEMENT DU COMMERCE ET DE L'INDUSTRIE EN FRANCE. Exercices 1963-1965. Paris. 3 v. diagrs.

Investment company's annual reports, with survey of French industrial output, foreign trade, stock market fluctuations.

1643 SOCIETE NATIONALE DES CHEMINS DE FER FRANÇAIS. Activité et productivité de la S.N.C.F., 1938-1962. Paris, 1963. 44 p. tables, diagrs.

Includes charts and statistics on 1962 traffic. S.N.C.F. was established in 1938.

1644 SORAS, ALFRED DE. Documents d'église et options politiques; points de vue sur "Verbe" et sur la "Cité catholique." Paris, Editions du Centurion, 1962. 123 p.

Description of the aims, methods, and supporters of the counter-revolutionary lay Catholic organization Cité Catholique, whose organ is "Le Verbe." Author criticizes their position as a misinterpretation of the Catholic Church's social doctrine. For "Le Verbe" see no. 2125.

1645 SORAS, ALFRED DE. L'Eglise et l'anticolonialisme. Paris, Action populaire, 1957. 50 p. (Collection "Orientations," 2) Bibliography: p. 40-50.

Stand of Catholic Church on 1) the historical justification of colonization 2) the achievements of colonization 3) the current need for decolonization, as expressed by papal pronouncements and statements of French overseas bishops, 1955-1957.

1646 SORLOT, FERNAND, (defendant). Offense au Chef de l'état; le procès du "Réquisitoire;" compte rendu des débats. Avant-propos de René Rieunier. Paris, Nouvelles éditions latines, 1964. 219 p.

January 1964 trial before Tribunal de grande instance du Département de la Seine of editor (Fernand Sorlot) and author (René Rieunier) of "Réquisitoire contre le mensonge," in the course of which the objectionable passages in the book are closely analyzed (see no. 1535). Defense lawyer is Yves-Frédéric Jaffre. The accused were found guilty.

1647 SOUSTELLE, JACQUES. Aimée et souffrante Algérie. Paris, Plon, 1956. 307 p. illus., ports., facsims.

Experiences as governor general of Algeria, February 1955-January 1956, leading up to author's conclusion that integration alone can solve Algerian problem. Appendix includes Soustelle speeches in Algeria.

1648 SOUSTELLE, JACQUES. Conférence de presse tenue par Jacques Soustelle le 18 décembre 1961 à Paris. Paris, 1961. 15 p.

Soustelle's views on resistance to de Gaulle's Algerian policy and place of O.A.S. therein.

1649 SOUSTELLE, JACQUES. Le drame algérien et la décadence française; réponse à Raymond Aron. Paris, Plon, 1957. 70 p. (Tribune libre, 6)

Impassioned counterarguments in favor of Algerian integration in answer to Raymond Aron's "La tragédie algérienne," which urged recognition of the historical inevitability of withdrawal from Algeria. (See no. 83.)

1650 SOUSTELLE, JACQUES. [Editorials reprinted from "Voici pourquoi" and other journals, 1961] 1 env.

April 1961 attacks on Gaullist Algerian policy and on first proposals for constitutional reform regarding presidential election initiated by U.N.R.

1651 SOUSTELLE, JACQUES. L'espérance trahie, 1958-1961. Paris, Editions de l'Alma, 1962. 326 p.

Political memoirs, May 1962, retracing author's part in de Gaulle's return to power, the evolution of de Gaulle's Algerian policy from firm commitment toward a French Algeria before May 1958 to agreement with F.L.N. and the simultaneous change in the views of other leading Gaullists, as against author's own gradual withdrawal from government functions, exclusion from U.N.R., founding of groups like the Centre d'Information sur les problèmes de l'Algérie et du Sahara and the Colloque de Vincennes, and his full opposition to regime at time of writing.

1652 SOUSTELLE, JACQUES. Il faut poursuivre jusqu'à la victoire la bataille pour l'Algérie française. Paris, 1958. 2 p. Supplément à La Vérité sur l'Algérie, no. 15.

Justification of favorable vote on reform of Algerian electoral system approved January 1958 as a step toward greater integration within French political institutions.

1653 SOUSTELLE, JACQUES. Jacques Soustelle vous parle... Paris, 1967. 12 p. (Grands discours français et internationaux)

Soustelle was campaigning for seat in National Assembly and delivered this speech from exile Feb. 1967, reiterating his reasons for opposing de Gaulle's Algerian policy.

1654 SOUSTELLE, JACQUES. L'Orient, foyer de guerre; conférence... le 23 novembre 1956 au Théâtre des ambassadeurs sous les auspices des Conférences des ambassadeurs. Paris, 1956. 26 p. (Grands discours français et internationaux, n.s., 9)

Justification for French defense of Algeria against onslaughts os Pan-Arabism and Soviet expansion.

1655 SOUSTELLE, JACQUES. La page n'est pas tournée. Paris, Table ronde, 1965. 237 p.

Indictment of the results of Gaullist policy in Algeria on the basis of a detailed account of events there since independence, followed by attack on three books defending de Gaulle's handling of the Algerian problem; namely those of Terrenoire, Buron, and Mauriac (nos. 261, 1198, and 1681). Although Algerian betrayal is at heart of Soustelle's opposition to Gaullist regime, he voices his disapproval of transformation of U.N.R. since 1958 and seeks to rally opposition to de Gaulle, including those who reject his economic and European policy, for the coming presidential election. Author was living in exile at time of writing.

1656 SOUSTELLE, JACQUES. Le Sahara d'aujourd'hui et la France de l'an 2000; conférence prononcée... le mardi 26 mai 1959 au Théâtre des ambassadeurs sous les auspices des Conférences des ambassadeurs. Paris, 1959. 25 p. port. (on cover) (Grands discours français et internationaux. n.s., 22)

Prospects for Saharan oil exploitation and development of atomic energy. Soustelle was speaking as Minister for the Sahara and Atomic Energy.

1657 SOUSTELLE, JACQUES. Sur une route nouvelle. Paris, Editions du Fuseau, 1964. 315 p. (Les Chemins du réel, v.2)

Defense of author against charges of fascism and description of the persecution to which he had been personally subjected since 1960, when he publicly went into opposition, followed by an attack on de Gaulle's Algerian policy, its failures since 1962, as well as criticism of his personal dictatorship, economic, European, and nuclear policy. English edition, "A new road for France", New York, 1965, also covers 1964 developments, appealing to American sentiments and stressing that anti-communism rather than right-wing philosophy underlies his criticism of de Gaulle. Author was living in exile at time of writing.

FOR ADDITIONAL WORKS BY AND ABOUT JACQUES SOUSTELLE, SEE AUTHOR INDEX

1658 SOUTY, PIERRE, (ed.). Documents sur la Constitution de la Ve République, législation et jurisprudence, recueillis, classés et annotés. Paris, Editions Montchrestien, 1964. 147 p.

1959-June 1963 decisions of Conseil Constitutionnel, Conseil d'Etat, Cour de Cassation, Cour d'appel de Paris, Haut Tribunal militaire in relation to 1958 Constitution and its applications, with texts of constitution and ordinances composing organic law of Fifth Republic.

1659 SPAIN. OFICINA DE INFORMACION DIPLOMATICA. Spain and France, May, 1964. Madrid, 1964. 179 p. ports., facsims.

French Foreign Minister Couve de Murville's visit of state, as reflected in speeches, press conferences, and final communiqué, as well as in reports and comments from the world press.

1660 SPEARS, SIR EDWARD LOUIS. Two men who saved France: Pétain and De Gaulle. New York, Stein and Day, 1966. 222 p. map.

Petain's role in saving France is illustrated by his manuscript on his part in suppressing French Army mutinies in summer 1917 (it was given to Spears in 1930's as documentation for a World War I military history). For de Gaulle, author, who was in constant contact with him as Churchill's personal delegate, describes decisive role in crystallizing French resistance during summer of 1940, indicating at the same time how the experience indelibly marked de Gaulle's personality.

1661 STAUB, HANS O. Charles André Marie-Joseph de Gaulle, Träumer oder Realist? Luzern, C.J. Bucher, 1966. 198 p. illus., ports.

Personal and political biography, through August 1966, with excellent illustrations. Author examines de Gaulle's attitude toward Europe, analyzes his style of government. The title exemplifies author's ambivalent judgment on de Gaulle's impact on world politics.

1662 STAUB, HANS O. Frankreich zwischen gestern und morgen. Olten, Walter-Verlag, 1963. 257 p. (Walter Paperbacks: Die Diskussion) Bibliography: p. 252-253.

Swiss correspondent's survey of recent French history, 1945-1963, grouped around these themes; 1) Aftermath of World War II; 2) Decay of Fourth Republic; 3) Indochina and North Africa; 4) Algerian rebellion, Algerian question, O.A.S. (author was stationed in North Africa 1959-1961); 5) Foreign, European, and nuclear policy; 6) Nature of Gaullist regime.

1663 STITZER, KARL. Die Götter aus Frankreich. Berlin, Kongress-Verlag, 1960. 175 p. illus.

Episodes from Algerian conflict, 1956-1959, illustrating atrocities committed by French army and police on the one hand, various forms of protests by French soldiers and French Communist Party on the other. Book includes version of Bellounis affair.

1664 STOETZEL, JEAN. Les sondages de l'élection presidentielle de 1965. Paris, 1966. 147-156 p. Detached from Revue française de sociologie, vol. 7, no. 2, April-June 1966.

Text of lecture at Fondation nationale des sciences politiques Jan. 1966 confronting pre-election polls with actual election results.

1665 STRUCTURES ET CONJUNCTURE ECONOMIQUES (periodical). Le logement: analyse de la situation foncière actuelle et ébauche d'une politique réaliste en ce domaine. Le problème foncier. Remarques sur le financement du logement. Paris, Société d'études et d'édition Jean Moulin, 1965. 147 p. Issue for spring 1965.

Club Jean Moulin's proposals for solving housing shortage through changes in legal status of urban land and through better credit system.

1666 SUFFERT, GEORGES. Les Catholiques et la gauche. Paris, F. Maspero, 1960. 190 p. (Cahiers libres, no. 4)

"Témoignage chrétien" editor's survey of Catholic outlook on Algeria, school problem, and of the position and activities of various left-oriented Catholic action groups and periodicals 1945-1959. Last third of book is devoted to author's personal experiences 1958-59 with Catholic action groups in small towns all over France.

1667 SUFFERT, GEORGES. De Defferre à Mitterrand; la campagne présidentielle. Paris, Editions du Seuil, 1966. 191 p.

Early stages of presidential campaign seen through the eyes of active backer of Gaston Defferre's candidacy and advocate of the institution of presidential election. As secretary general of Club Jean Moulin in 1963-65, and frequent contributor to "L'Express," author gives inside information on operation of the political clubs and attempted unification of the Left around Colloques socialistes and Defferre candidacy, as well as on circle around Defferre. Only Mitterand and Lecanuet campaign are discussed.

1668 SULZBERGER, CYRUS LEO. The test: De Gaulle and Algeria. New York, Harcourt, Brace and World, 1962. 228 p.

Correspondent's political history of the Fifth Republic largely published in the "New York Times," 1958-May 1962, focused on de Gaulle's struggle with the army and the O.A.S. Author was stationed in Paris and had a number of interviews with de Gaulle, whom he admires.

1669 SUSINI, JEAN JACQUES. Histoire de l'O.A.S. t. 1. Avril-septembre 1961. Paris, Table ronde, 1963. 396 p.

Only volume published so far on author's participation in founding of O.A.S. at the time of the generals' putsch in Algeria and organization's operation in Algeria in its first half year. As General Salan's aide first in Spain, then in Algeria, author has inside information on leadership conflicts within O.A.S. and draws on O.A.S. archives, which are in his hands, for texts of speeches, letters, messages, and leaflets.

1670 SVOBODA, KAREL. La notion de droit économique; étude sur les conceptions récentes du droit économique en France et dans les pays socialistes. Nancy, 1966. 79 p. (Université de Nancy. Publications du Centre européen universitaire. Collection des mémoires, no. 18) Includes bibliography.

Section on France in this thesis by Eastern European student outlines rationale for state intervention in economy under 'monopoly capitalism' of post-war years, summarizes economic legislation, and describes different accommodations of concept of economic law within French legal theory.

1671 SYMOURS, EDOUARD CONNEAU. Où va la France? Tourcoing, Editions Flandre-Artois, 1960. 249 p. diagrs., facsims.

Astrological predictions for France and the world, with lengthy horoscope for de Gaulle and shorter ones for other politicians.

1672 SYNDICAT NATIONAL DE L'ENSEIGNEMENT SUPERIEUR. Halte aux assasins de l'O.A.S.! Paris, 1961. 2 p.

Handbill issued on December 6th 1961, conjointly with the Fédération de l'Education nationale (F.E.N.)

1673 SZOKOLOCZY-SYLLABA, JANOS. Les organisations professionelles françaises et le Marché commun. Paris, A. Colin, 1965. xii, 372 p. (Cahiers de la Fondation nationale des sciences politiques, 133) Includes bibliographical footnotes.

Ph.D. thesis at University of Geneva under Jean Meynaud investigating the influence of pressure groups on political processes, in this case the Common Market. Author separately studies the reactions of textile, electric construction, and automotive business associations to the different phases of Common Market negotiations. Final section shows attitude of Conseil National du Patronat Français toward changes brought about by economic integration and Fifth Republic economic policy. Extensive documentation for each section in bibliographical notes.

1674 TAIX, GABRIEL. La France au seuil de l'ère atomique. Paris, A. Fayard, 1958. 209 p.

August 1958 review of economic, social, and political ills that lead to collapse of Fourth Republic and assorted proposals (such as birth control, accelerated decolonization) to bring country in line with "atomic age." Author questions de Gaulle's ability to make necessary changes.

1675 TAY, HUGUES. Le régime présidentiel et la France; étude d'histoire des idées juridiques et politiques. Préf. de Robert Pelloux. Paris, Librairie générale de droit et de jurisprudence, R. Pichon et R. Durand-Auzias, 1967. x, 334 p. (Bibliothèque constitutionnelle et de science politique, t. 27) Includes bibliography.

Historical survey of proposals to introduce the American type of presidential regime in France, with half of the volume devoted to the period after 1956. For the latter period, the author presents in detail the suggestions of political scientists Maurice Duverger and Georges Vedel and of the Club Jean Moulin, as well as the reception of these proposals by individual politicians and political parties. The author analyzes possible dangers in carrying out the reform and the extent to which the more fluid political institutions of the Fifth Republic, which have been qualified as "pseudo-presidential" satisfy more effectively the aim of introducing a workable democracy in a multiparty state like France. Extensive bibliography of articles for post-1956 period.

1676 Les techniciens de l'agriculture algérienne vous présentent aspects et réalités de l'Algérie agricole. Alger [1957?] 148 p. (Association des anciens élèves de l'Institut agricole d'Algérie)

Propaganda booklet by French Algerian agronomists addressed to metropolitan France describing French contributions to Algerian agriculture and studying individual regions of Algeria. Photographs and statistics.

1677 TEILLAC, JEAN. Autogestion en Algérie. Paris, J. Peyronnet, 1965. 68 p. (Paris. Université. Centre de hautes études administratives sur l'Afrique et l'Asie modernes. Recherches et documents, 2)

History of self-administration in Algerian agriculture and industry, 1962-1964, its organization, scope, preliminary results, and long-run prospects, giving evidence of capital deterioration in agriculture and regression to more primitive and less commercially competitive forms of production.

1678 TEINDAS, GEORGES and YANN THIREAU. La jeunesse dans la famille et la société modernes. Paris, Editions françaises sociales, 1961. 2 v. (558 p) illus.

V. 1 gives results of authors' (both secondary school teachers) tests and questionnaires for groups of adolescent apprentices and lycée students on use of leisure, artistic tastes, professional ambitions. Authors show deterioration of mechanical abilities for apprentices, rising age level in secondary schools, lack of differentiation between two groups in questionnaire responses. V. 2 explains results by conditioning of youth in technically oriented, mass consumption society, changes in family structure, incapacity of schools, faced with increasing enrollment, to counteract these pressures successfully and consequent deterioration of education. Authors describe in detail attempts to introduce new pedagogic methods in secondary schools.

1679 TEMOIGNAGE CHRETIEN. La faim au ventre; les réfugiés algériens au Maroc et en Tunisie. Paris, 1960. 44 p. (Its Cahiers, 41)

Appeal for half million Algerian refugees in Morocco and Tunisia, with 1959 report of International Red Cross.

1680 TEMOIGNAGE CHRETIEN. Nouveaux témoignages sur la guerre d'Algérie. Le rapport de la Croix-rouge. Terrorisme et contre-terrorisme. Paris, 1960. 61 p. (Its Cahiers, 39)

International Red Cross November 1959 report on detention camps and Témoignage chrétien's own appeals to French authorities as well as F.L.N. to stop terrorism.

1681 TERRENOIRE, LOUIS. De Gaulle et l'Algérie; témoignages pour l'histoire. Paris, Fayard, 1964. 252 p.

Evolution of de Gaulle's thinking on Algerian question between 1955 and Evian agreement, successive measures taken after 1958, and repercussion on politics inside U.N.R. Author was Minister of Information for most of this period as well as U.N.R. leader and gives inside account both of split within U.N.R. over Algeria and of the government response to the 1960 and 1961 uprisings in Algeria and the various rounds of peace negotiations. Author's main aim is to refute charges of de Gaulle's betrayal of his original Algerian position by showing the consistency of his policy. For critical reviews of this work, see nos. 593, 1655.

1682 TESSON, PHILIPPE. De Gaulle Ier [La révolution manquée. Histoire du premier gouvernement de Gaulle, août 1944-janvier 1946] Paris, A. Michel, 1965. 266 p. plates, ports. (Histoire du XXe siècle)

"Combat" editor's history of the 18-months period in which de Gaulle failed to carry through the program of political and social renovation on which Resistance leaders had agreed, thus leaving this task for his second period in power.

1683 THEOLLEYRE, JEAN MARC. Ces procès qui ébranlèrent la France. Paris, B. Grasset, 1966.

Description of the most dramatic political trials connected with decolonization. First group of trials covers individual opposition to colonialism during the Fourth Republic, second group summarizes trials of opponents and defenders of Algerian war: the Jeanson trial on the one hand, the barricades, Salan, and O.A.S. trials on the other.

1684 THIERS, ANDRE. Quarante ans d'erreurs monétaires; ou, Les quinze dévaluations du franc. Paris, Nouvelles éditions latines, 1966. 268 p.

History of 15 devaluations of French franc, 1926-1966, the last two actual devaluations having taken place in Fifth Republic, followed by an examination of French financial, monetary, and general economic situation 1965-66 to show that new pressures for a 16th devaluation are developing in the system. Author is critical of Gaullist "prestige" and technocratic orientation and rejects the interpretation of financial expert Jacques Rueff that a return to the gold standard would eliminate inflation in France, giving his own proposals for monetary reform.

1685 THIRIART, JEAN. Un empire de 400 millions d'hommes: l'Europe. Bruxelles, 1964. 318 p. port.

Guidelines for a European nationalism extending from Portugal to the Russian border, independent and equal to both Russia and the U.S., and having withdrawn from the U.N. Author, a Belgian who supported the O.A.S., wants to use his experiences to form cadres for a national European party, the only form of nationalism able to cope with the contemporary political situation. Spanish edition entitled "Arriba Europa! Una Europa unida: un imperio de 400 milliones de hombres" (Barcelona, 1965). For a criticism of this approach from the traditional nationalist view, see Assac (no. 90).

1686 THIRIART, JEAN. La grande nation; 65 thèses sur l'Europe [L'Europe unitaire, de Brest à Bucarest. Définition du communautarisme national-européen] Bruxelles, 1965. 80 p.

Principles of communitarian European nationalism encompassing all of Europe up to the Russian border, as a substitute for narrower nationalisms having become outdated as a result of decolonization. This European nationalism is equally hostile to the U.S.S.R. and U.S. and seeks independence from both. Author is editor of "Nation-Europe." Appendix gives list of all his articles. See also nos. 1940, 1990, 2011, 2012.

1687 THOREZ, MAURICE. Au Comité central du Parti communiste français réuni à Gennevilliers le 25 mars 1958. Paris, 1958. 4 p. (Parti communiste français. Comité central)

Appeal for a common front of workers and democrats against Fascist threat and proposal for popular front government to end Algerian war.

1688 THOREZ, MAURICE. Lénine et la France; [article] [Paris?] 1960. 22 p. (Parti communiste français) Supplément aux Cahiers du communisme, avril 1960.

Lenin's teachings and their application to current French situation.

1689 THOREZ, MAURICE. Marcel Cachin, la leçon d'une vie; discours à l'assemblée des communistes parisiens... 23 février 1958. Paris, 1958. 18 p. (Parti communiste français. Comité central. Section de propagande)

1690 THOREZ, MAURICE. La paupérisation des travailleurs français. Préf. d'Henri Claude. Paris, Editions sociales, 1961. 156 p.

Collected articles, 1955-1957, with comments on viability of their conclusions for first years of Fifth Republic.

1691 THOREZ, MAURICE. Oeuvres choisies en trois volumes. Paris, Editions sociales, 1965. 3 v.

First two volumes go up to 1950, vol. 3 covers years until Thorez' death in 1964. V. 3 consists of speeches before Communist Party's central committee, political rallies, international communist conferences and a few prefaces illustrating Thorez' views on Communist doctrine, developments in international communism, specific stands of party on current political issues (1958-1964). Final section is devoted to full reproduction of autobiographical "Fils du peuple" concluded Feb. 1960, of which final chapter deals with Fifth Republic.

1692 THOREZ, MAURICE. Oui à la paix, non à de Gaulle; discours au Comité central, Ivry, 22 mars 1962. Paris, 1962. 11 p.

Speech supporting April 1962 referendum approving Evian agreements.

1693 THOREZ, MAURICE. Ressemblons toutes les forces pour la dure bataille contre le pouvoir personnel; discours de clôture à la Conférence fédérale de Paris le 31 mai 1959. Paris, 1959. 15 p. (Parti communiste français)

Attack on Gaullist regime and defense of Communist Party's stand on Algerian war.

1694 THOREZ, MAURICE. Textes choisis: la France au péril du militarisme allemand. Préf. de Jacques Duclos. Paris, 1962. 100 p.

1939-1961 speeches before Communist party congresses and central committee, only last four of which were delivered after 1958 on the subject of Gaullist Franco-German policy.

1695 THOREZ, MAURICE. Textes choisis sur l'Algérie; préf. de Léon Feix. Paris, Parti communiste français, 1962. 140 p.

Speeches before French Communist Party's central committee and congresses and articles on Algerian problem, 1937 - March 1962, selected to show the continuity of the party's stand.

1696 THOREZ, MAURICE. Textes choisis sur la démocratie 1936-1961. Préf. de Waldeck Rochet. Paris, Editions du Parti communiste français, 1962. 96 p.

Excerpts from speeches at French Communist Party congresses and central committee meetings, press interviews, and articles, 1936-May 1961 (about half 1958 -) appealing for unity of action with other democratic elements.

1697 THOREZ, MAURICE. Textes choisis sur la jeunesse; préf. de P. Laurent. Paris, Parti communiste français, 1962. 97 p.

1945-1960 speeches to Communist youth organizations: Union des jeunesses communistes, Union des jeunes filles de France, Union de la jeunesse agricole de France, Union des étudiants communistes de France.

FOR ADDITIONAL WORKS BY AND ABOUT MAURICE THOREZ, SEE AUTHOR INDEX

1698 THORP, RENE WILLIAM. Vues sur la justice. Paris, R. Julliard, 1962. 270 p.

Essays by French jurist and president of Association pour la Saufgarde des Institutions judiciaires et la Défense des Libertés individuelles, founded 1957 by members of the legal profession to prevent legal abuses in wake of Algerian war. One section concerns miscarriages of justice during Algerian war and Association's counter-measures, one covers changes in judicial institutions under Fifth Republic; final section consists of speeches before Lawyers' Association on technical legal problems.

1699 TIARET, ALGERIA (DEPT.) CONSEIL GENERAL. Le Département de Tiaret. Paris, 1962. 202 p. illus. (part col.) map.

Description of the different regions of this Algerian department (set up only in 1956) lying between Orania and the Sahara with a largely Moslem population. Agriculture, modernization programs, small industry, housing and schools are presented with beautiful photographs. Though completed in early 1962, the volume gives no evidence of war and imminent independence.

1700 TILLION, GERMAINE. L'Afrique bascule vers l'avenir; l'Algérie en 1957 et autres textes. Paris, Editions de Minuit, 1961. 177 p. (Documents)

Reprint of "L'Algérie en 1957," followed by revised conclusions, as well as some short studies on education and agriculture written in 1955 while author was organizing the Centres Sociaux in Algiers.

1701 TILLION, GERMAINE. L'Algérie en 1957. Paris, Editions de Minuit, 1957. 121 p. (Documents)

Short exposé originally written for Association des Déportées et des Internées de la Résistance on Algerian question as of 1956 by French ethnographer, who had studied country in 1930's and had returned there in 1955. Author shows impact of modern civilization, as represented by French colonization, on an archaic society capable of feeding a few million people, which she summarizes as "clochardization." Since the country is seen incapable of surviving without massive French help for industrialization, education, technical advances, combined with large-scale emigration of Algerian workers to France, author considers Franco-Algerian symbiosis the only way of averting an economic catastrophe.

1702 TILLION, GERMAINE. Les ennemis complémentaires. Paris, Editions de Minuit, 1960. 218 p. (Documents)

Psychological and sociological components of Algerian war in France, among Moslem and European elements in Algeria, demonstrating comparable irrationalities on opposing sides and the senselessness of the victory being pursued. Work includes author's testimony in favor of Saadi Yacef, politico-military head of F.L.N. in Algeria at the time, with whom she had discussions in summer 1957 on terrorism against civilians.

1703 TILLION, GERMAINE. "The unsolved problem of Algeria." New York, 1960. 5 l. (Delegation of the Provisional Government of the Algerian Republic, N.Y., distr.)

Reproduces speech broadcast over BBC Jan. 1960 commenting on unresolved contradictory demands of French settlers and Algerian nationalists after barricade uprising.

1704 TISSIER, JACQUES. Le gâchis. Paris, Editeurs français réunis, 1960. 137 p.

Personal narrative of military service in Algeria, 1957-58, showing typical French soldier's reaction to operations in Algerian battlefield, disgust at stupidity of war, and resentment of bad treatment of Moslems.

1705 TIXIER, JEAN LOUIS, RICHARD DUPUY, and LE CORROLLER. Défense de Bastien-Thiry. Paris, Presses du Mail, 1963. 208 p.

Defense speeches by Tixier-Vignancour, Dupuy, and Le Corroller at Jan. 28 - March 4, 1963 trial before the Cour militaire de justice of Col. Bastien-Thiry for his part in attempted de Gaulle assassination August 1962. Tixier eloquently recreates psychological climate of violence at end of Algerian war to motivate defendant's conduct. Text of defense speeches is more complete than in stenographic record of trial (see no. 143).

1706 TIXIER, JEAN LOUIS. J'ai choisi la défense. [By] Jean-Louis Tixier-Vignancour. Plaidoiries présentées par Jean-Marc Varaut. Préf. du bâtonnier Jacques Charpentier. Paris, Table ronde, 1964. xxv, 286 p. port.

Defense pleas, reproduced in full, with introductory notes, for the following political trials: affaire des fuites (1956), prosecution against "Rivarol" (1959), barricades trial (Nov. 1960), Salan trial (May 1962), trial of O.A.S. leader Lieut. Degueldre (June 1962), trial of Col. Bastien-Thiry (Feb. 1963), and trial of fellow lawyer Jacques Isorni (July 1963). Preface gives history of political tribunals, 1944-1963.

FOR ADDITIONAL WORKS BY AND ABOUT JEAN LOUIS TIXIER, SEE AUTHOR INDEX.

1707 TOURNOUX, JEAN RAYMOND. Carnets secrets de la politique. Paris, Plon, 1958. 177 p.

May - October 1958 episodes highlighting de Gaulle's approach to Algerian question and relations with U.N.R. Journalist author claims documentary backing for quoted conversations and anecdotes and reproduces report by Algerian Governor General to Minister of the Interior, end of May 1958, on events in Algeria May 13-17.

1708 TOURNOUX, JEAN RAYMOND. L'histoire secrète; la Cagoule, le Front populaire, Vichy, Londres, Deuxième bureau, l'Algérie française, l'O.A.S. Paris, Plon, 1962. 396 p. illus., ports., facsims.

Last third of volume, which concludes with October 1962, deals with counterrevolutionary movements from 1954 on, including O.A.S. Author shows continuity of methods and psychology between pre-1939 fascist Comité secret d'action révolutionnaire (the Cagoule) and O.A.S. giving interesting insights into de Gaulle's attitude toward Cagoule. Seventy pages of secret documents and unpublished texts, a few of which concern secret negotiations between de Gaulle and F.L.N. in spring 1960.

1709 TOURNOUX, JEAN RAYMOND. Pétain et de Gaulle. Paris, Plon, 1964. 556 p. plates, ports., facsims. Bibliographical notes at end of chapters.

Psychological portrait of de Gaulle sketched by a series of anecdotes from childhood through retirement from politics in 1946 and account of his originally warm and, after 1938, hostile relations with his superior Pétain. Appendix reproduces unpublished documents on which text is based, drawn from several private archives, including complete text of de Gaulle's comedy "Une mauvaise rencontre" (1905).

1710 TOURNOUX, JEAN RAYMOND. Secrets d'état: Dien Bien Phu. Les Paras. L'Algérie. L'affaire Ben Bella. Suez. La Cagoule. Le 13 mai. De Gaulle au pouvoir. Paris, Plon, 1960. 514 p.

Origins of counter-revolution (Cagoule, defeat in Indochina, Suez expedition, Gaullist antiparliamentarianism, Algerian secret organizations May 1956-May 1958, including both military and civilian plotters) and de Gaulle's accession to power, documented by unpublished archives and personal diaries of participants, on the basis of which author reconstructs episodes, conversations. Annex reproduces speeches, letters, reports, such as text of de Gaulle's speech March 27, 1958 before veterans committee, Salan, Lacoste speeches May 1958, incidents and conversations illustrating de Gaulle's stand on Algeria, army, institutions. Careful index.

1711 TOURNOUX, JEAN RAYMOND. La tragédie du Général. Paris, Plon, 1967. 697 p.

Political biography of de Gaulle, 1946-1967, reconstructing his public and private stand and tactics on the issues of the day during his years of leadership of the R.P.F., his retirement from political activity, and as head of the government of the Fifth Republic. By using published sources (de Gaulle's, political figures' writings, etc.) inside information, and author's personal interviews with de Gaulle (notably January 1958 and April 1962) author is able to tell his story through de Gaulle's conversations and quotations, with a minimum of commentary by author. Areas treated in most detail are his stand on Germany, the Atlantic Alliance, French Canada, East-West relations, illustrating de Gaulle's frequent reversals of opinion and his basic continuity of thought. Appendices reproduce various documents, including private communication of socialist politician Felix Gouin to his party criticizing proposed 1958 constitution, an interview between Oran journalist Pierre Laffont and de Gaulle November 1960, and several documents on Colonel Bastien-Thiry.

1712 TRAHARD, PIERRE. Césarion; satire. Illus. de Marc Flament. Paris, Editions de la Pensée moderne, 1965. 122 p.

Thinly veiled satirical poems directed against de Gaulle and some of his collaborators, with cartoon illustrations. Author is a professional poet without evident political affiliations.

1713 Travail et travailleurs en Algérie. Données statistiques par Alain Darbel et al. Etude sociologique par Pierre Bourdieu Paris, Mouton, 1963. 566 p. plates, tables (1 fold.) (Maison des sciences de l'homme. Recherches méditerranéennes. Documents, 1)

1961 investigation of selected Algerian workers in Algeria and France on types of employment, income, under- and unemployment of workers. Bourdieu's sociological study, which takes up half the volume, is based on same sample and brings out attitude toward work with the help of many direct quotations.

1714 TRIBOULET, RAYMOND. Des vessies pour des lanternes. Vire, Editions Lecvire, 1958. 68 p.

Analysis of forces blocking institutional reforms for creating a strong government, written by Social Republican deputy May 1958, with plea for de Gaulle's return to power.

1715 TRINQUIER, ROGER. La bataille pour l'élection du président de la République. Montargis, (Loiret) 1965. 188 p.

Sept. 1964 strategy for defeating de Gaulle in the coming presidential election through unity of right and left political forces. Former military leader underscores the de Gaulle-Communist alliance by demonstrating that their policies are in harmony, and that the Communists secretely support de Gaulle.

1716 TRINQUIER, ROGER. Le coup d'état du 13 mai. Paris, Editions l'Esprit nouveau, 1962. 270 p. plates, ports.

History of events in Algeria, May 1958, as seen through the presently disillusioned eyes of Colonel Trinquier. Author, Salan and Massu aide in 1957-58, was one of military leaders actively promoting French-Algerian integration to win over Moslems. Swept into Comité du Salut Public in Algiers, together with Massu, author describes his own actions and machinations of Gaullist politicians on the spot who chanelled the movement for basic institutional reforms and integration into a mere Gaullist coup d'état, leaving main objectives unaccomplished.

1717 TRINQUIER, ROGER. L'état nouveau, la solution de l'avenir. Paris, Nouvelles editions latines, 1963. 152 p.

Program of the Association pour l'Etude de la Réforme des Structures de l'Etat founded in Nov. 1961 by the former colonel and designed to bring nationalist thinking in line with the contemporary French situation through a legal revolution of the country's institutions, to establish "un état nouveau." The organization's organ, entitled first "A.E.R.S.E." and later "Etat nouveau," was published in 1963 and is available at the Hoover Institution (see no. 1930). See also no. 106.

1718 TRINQUIER, ROGER. La guerre moderne. Paris, Table ronde, 1961. 196 p. (L'Ordre du jour)

General theory of how to prepare and fight defensively and offensively under conditions of revolutionary wars, in which enemy applies any and all violent and non-violent means to subvert the established regime and replace it by another. Colonel Trinquier, drawing on his experiences in Indochina and Algeria, where he served continuously 1945-1960 as a parachutist, draws up organizational, psychological, social welfare, political, as well as military countermeasures effective in this type of struggle and insists that they must all be used to win, even if they violate legal and ideological standards of Western democracies. An English edition is entitled "Modern warfare; a French view of counterinsurgency (New York, 1964), and a Spanish edition is entitled "La guerra moderna y la lucha contra las guerrillas" (Barcelona, 1965).

1719 Troisième colloque universitaire sur les solutions du problème algérien. N.p. [Jan. 1958] 14 p.

Final report stating arguments for Algerian independence and steps to end war.

1720 TRON, LUDOVIC. Métamorphoses de la France, 1950-1970; essai. Paris, R. Julliard, 1961. 172 p. illus.

French Senator's diagnosis of blockages in economy and proposed reforms to keep it competitive until new population wave reaches working age. Author touches only incidentally on Algeria and discusses nuclear weapons controversy in terms of economic feasibility.

1721   TRON, LUDOVIC. Opposition à Sa Majesté. Paris, R. Julliard, 1964. 188 p.

Collection of short articles, 1958 - January 1964 originally published in "Combat," "Le Monde," "Dépêche du Midi," and Senate debates illustrating author's growing opposition to de Gaulle for his failure to reform institutions fundamentally and welcoming Defferre's candidacy for a center-left democratic opposition.

1722   UBOLDI, RAFFAELLO. Servizio proibito. Torino, G. Einaudi 1958. 123 p.

Winter 1957 eye-witness report by journalist for "Avanti" on Army of National Liberation's military operations on Tunisian border and on its military leaders.

1723* UNION DEMOCRATIQUE DU TRAVAIL. L'Union démocratique du travail vous parle... Paris, 1960. 46 p. Numéro hors série de Notre république.

Party's stand on major domestic and foreign policy issues a year after its founding, April 1959.

1724* UNION DEMOCRATIQUE DU TRAVIL. CONVENTION NATIONALE, 1 ERE, PARIS (?) 1960. [Motion and reports] [Paris] 1960. 1 folio.

Speakers at this June 1960 congress are Louis Vallon, Léo Hamon, Jacques Debu-Bridel, Roland Pré, Christiane Marcilhacy, Gilbert Grandval, and Pierre Billotte.

1725* UNION DEMOCRATIQUE DU TRAVAIL. CONVENTION NATIONALE, 2e, APRIL 1961. [Reports] Paris, 1961. 1 env.

Speakers are Louis Vallon, Pierre Billotte, Christiane Marcilhacy, Alain Dutaret, and René Capitant.

FOR ADDITIONAL PUBLICATIONS BY THE UNION DEMOCRATIQUE DU TRAVAIL, SEE AUTHOR INDEX. AFTER NOV. 1962, PARTY FUSED WITH U.N.R. TO BECOME U.N.R.-U.D.T.

1726* UNION DES ETUDIANTS COMMUNISTES DE FRANCE. [Appeals to students dealing with political issues under the de Gaulle regime] 1 env.

1960-61 leaflets to end Algerian war and resist Generals' putsch.

1727   UNION DES PARACHUTISTES ANCIENS COMBATTANTS. Historique de parachutisme. 3. éd. Besançon, 1963. 69 p. illus.

Role of French parachute troops (founded 1936) in invasion of North Africa as part of 1. régiment des chasseurs parachutistes (1. R.C.P.) and later deployment in Algeria, 1955-57. Numerous illustrations.

1728* UNION ET FRATERNITE FRANÇAISES. Communiqué: Le Mouvement Poujade (Union et fraternité françaises), Limoges, 1962 2 p.

Condemnation of just concluded Evian agreement.

1729   Union française. 1953-1958. Paris, R. Julliard. 6 v. maps. Director: 1953-1958, G. Oudard.

Yearbook surveying annual evolution of institutions of French Union (laws, decrees regarding political institutions, economic and social policy in overseas departments and territories, operations of overseas aid) 1953 - June 1958. Each member of French Union is also covered individually.

1730* UNION GENERALE DES TRAVAILLEURS ALGERIENS. Memorandum on the Algerian war and the French repression against the Algerian workers, unionists, and their families. Cairo, Costa Tsoumas and Co. 1959 38 p.

Appeal to international labor movement to protest against persecution of U.G.T.A. in Algeria, 1956-1959 and the recent assassination of its Secretary General. See also its "Ouvrier algérien" (no. 2033).

1731   UNION INTERNATIONALE DES ASSOCIATIONS PATRONALES CATHOLIQUES. Perspectives humaines et économiques du Marché commun; la conférence européene de l'U.N.I.A.P.A.C., juin 1958. Paris, 1958. 95 p. (Documents et commentaires; cahiers du Centre chrétien des patrons et dirigeants d'entreprise français, no. 115; nouv. sér., no. 23)

Speeches from inter-European conference, with lengthy exposé by representative of Centre chrétien des Patrons et Dirigeants d'Entreprise Français on impact of Common Market on social policy for France and overseas territories and necessary countermeasures by French government.

1732* UNION NATIONALE DES COMBATTANTS D'AFRIQUE FRANÇAISE DU NORD. [Posters 1958]

Posters urging "yes" vote on Sept. 1958 referendum. On microfilm with U.N.R. posters.

1733* UNION NATIONALE DES ETUDIANTS DE FRANCE. [Appeals to students dealing with political issues under the De Gaulle regime.] 1 env.

Includes pamphlet on student syndical movement and history and organization of U.N.E.F., as well as leaflets on resistance to Generals' putsch.

1734   UNION NATIONALE DES ETUDIANTS DE FRANCE. Enseignement supérieur; document préparatoire au Congrès de l'U.N.E.F. Paris, 1963. 65 p.

Critical examination of teaching methods in French universities in the light of their real functions. This document is to serve as a starting point for 1963 U.N.E.F. Congress on educational reforms.

1735   UNION NATIONALE DES ETUDIANTS DE FRANCE. 48th CONGRESS, GRENOBLE, 1959. Le syndicalisme étudiant et le problème algérien. Lille, 1960. 91 p.

Pamphlet reporting results of a study on repercussions of Algerian war on French and Algerian students, covering such points as splits in French student movement, consequences for Algerian and French students, restrictions of civil liberties. Resolutions of April 13, 1960 U.N.E.F. Congress are reproduced.

1736   UNION NATIONALE DES ETUDIANTS DE FRANCE. SECRETARIAT. Le désarmement; note préparatoire à la Commission internationale du 52ème congrès de l'U.N.F.F., Dijon, 7-13 avril 1963. Paris, 1963. 21 p. "Supplément spécial."

Indictment of French military policy, particularly the nuclear force de frappe, followed by appeal to support existing organizations for disarmament.

FOR ADDITIONAL PUBLICATIONS BY THE UNION NATIONALE DES ETUDIANTS DE FRANCE, SEE AUTHOR INDEX.

1737   UNION POUR LA NOUVELLE REPUBLIQUE. Statuts de l'U.N.R. Paris, Secrétariat général du Conseil national. 10 l. [1959?]

U.N.R.'s original statutes.

1738   UNION POUR LA NOUVELLE REPUBLIQUE. 2. Assises nationales, Strasbourg, 1961. Rapports. Paris, 1961. 1 v. (various pagings)

Individual reports to national congress, March 1961, by members of government and party officials, on U.N.R.'s political philosophy (including proposal for election of French president) elimination of internal dissidence, international, NATO, and European policy, stand on Algerian war, in short, a review of three years of Gaullist policy, followed by proposals for economic and social reforms. For 1963 Assises nationales, see nos. 284, 318, 1059, 1567, 1574.

1739* UNION POUR LA NOUVELLE REPUBLIQUE. [Posters 1958]

Posters for Nov. 1958 election, with two posters of Convention républicaine, a leftist Gaullist party, on microfilm.

FOR ADDITIONAL PUBLICATIONS BY AND ABOUT THE UNION POUR LA NOUVELLE REPUBLIQUE, SEE AUTHOR AND SUBJECT INDEX

1740 UNION SOCIALE D'INGENIEURS CATHOLIQUES. SECTION D'ALGER. Guide de l'ingénieur en Algérie. Paris/Alger 1956. 19 p.

Information on Algeria's European and non-European workers furnished by Secrétariat Social d'Alger.

1741 UNITED ARAB REPUBLIC. MASLAHAT AL-ISTI 'LAMAT. Un dialogue fructueux. Texte des discours échangés entre les responsables égyptiens et M. André Malraux, Ministre d'Etat français...au cours de sa visite en République Arabe Unie, 21-28 mars, 1966, Le Caire, Dép. de l'information, 1966. 59 p. illus.

Includes text of press conference in which Malraux discusses resumption of diplomatic relations with the United Arab Republic.

1742 VACHER-DESVERNAIS, JEAN. L'avenir des Français d'outre-mer; préf. d'Emile Roche. Paris, Presses universitaires de France, 1962. 154 p.

History of the decolonization of the French Empire, bringing 300,000 repatriates back to France before Algerian independence, as compared to the experiences of other colonial powers and that of Germany and Finland after World War II. Author analyses December 1961 law on repatriation (text in appendix) and possibilities of guarantees for European community in an independent Algeria (book concluded spring 1962).

1743 VALLON, LOUIS. Discours...2 juin 1959. n.p., 1959. 3 l. (Union démocratique du travail)

1744 VALLON, LOUIS. La France fait ses comptes. Préf. de Pierre Mendès-France. Post-face de François Perroux. Paris, Presses universitaires de France, 1958. xxiii, 158 p. tables.

Explanation of national accounting methods, with figures for 1957, projections for 1961.

1745 VALLON, LOUIS. Le grand dessein national. Paris, Calmann-Lévy, 1964. 217 p. (Questions d'actualité)

Assessment of Fifth Republic's achievements in main areas of national policy: national defense, atomic weapons, decolonization, Algeria, institutional reform, economic policy, foreign and European unification policy. Author is left-wing Gaullist parliamentarian.

FOR ADDITIONAL WORKS BY AND ABOUT LOUIS VALLON, SEE AUTHOR INDEX

1746 VALLUY, ETIENNE JEAN. Honneur et patrie; nation et supranation. Paris, Nouvelles éditions latines, 1964. vi, 223 p.

Reprints of articles published in "Revue des deux mondes" 1961-1963, with 1964 conclusion. Topics are: 1) French army's dilemna in its Algerian mission, in wake of April 1961 revolt, with replies to letters; 2) proposals for military reorganization based on professional and volunteer personnel, with new officer training goals and institutions (summer 1962); 3) cold war status and nuclear power balance end of 1962; 4) collaboration between University and Army (February 1963); 5) NATO crisis and nuclear partnership (fall 1963). Retired NATO general seeks to conciliate military and civilian, Gaullist and anti-Gaullist views.

1747 VALLUY, ETIENNE JEAN. Se défendre? Contre qui? Et comment? Paris, Plon, 1960. 236 p. (Tribune libre, 59)

Platonic dialogues, confronting French military expert's, diplomat's, Christian's, Communist's, etc. viewpoints toward French national and international defense. Recently retired French NATO general includes description of NATO operations, urging European unification within Atlantic Alliance and concentration on anti-communist defense in current expansive phase of communist movement.

1748 VANUXEM, PAUL FIDELE FELICIEN. Les contes du temps perdu. Paris, Au fil d'Ariane, 1964. 1 v. (unpaged) illus.

Children's stories dedicated by recently liberated author (see below) to children of his former fellow-prisoners. There are no obvious political allusions.

1749 VANUXEM, PAUL FIDELE FELICIEN, (defendant). Le procès Vanuxem [editeur: Jean Gauvin] Paris, Editions Saint-Just, 1963. 283 p.

Trial before Cour de Sûreté, Paris, Sept. 1963, of three presumed O.A.S. leaders: General Vanuxem, Colonel de Blignière, and Maurice Gingembre. The first two accused pleaded mistaken identity, and only the third, a young industrialist, admitted his role as O.A.S. treasurer. Work reproduces text of accusation, defense pleas for three accused, documents presented by prosecution on O.A.S. operations, such as Godard report and correspondence between Gingembre and Colonel Argoud. Editor, who knows Vanuxem personally, gives background of O.A.S. plot in Madrid and adds documents on mistreatment of O.A.S. prisoners. All three accused were sentenced, but Vanuxem, whose confusion with O.A.S. leader known as "Verdun" was clarified, was released some time later. He had been imprisoned for over two years without trial. See also no. 279.

1750 VARIN D'AINVELLE, MADELEINE. La presse en France; genèse et évolution de ses fonctions psycho-sociales. Paris, Presses universitaires de France, 1965. 253 p. (Université de Grenoble. Publications de la Faculté des lettres et sciences humaines, 37) Includes bibliography.

History of French journalism going back to 17th and 18th century, with short sections bringing up to date the press's double evolution as a political and mass information medium, with current (1963-64) examples. Extensive bibliography.

1751 VAUCHER, GEORGES. Le plan de Constantine et la république algérienne de demain; indépendance politique et indépendance économique. Neuchâtel, Editions de la Baconnière, 1961. 109 p. (Problèmes africains)

Evaluation of real achievements and shortcomings of Constantine Plan on basis of French statistical services and reactions of Algerian national leaders. Author demonstrates that main failure is political, in that the plan did not galvanize the desire of Algerian elites and masses to maintain economic ties with France. Writing for the Afro-Asian Organization for Economic Co-operation in Cairo in early 1961, author determines which aspects of the plan and methods of collaboration would be applicable even for independent Algeria.

1752 VEDOVATO, GIUSEPPE. L'Association à la Communauté économique européenne des états africains et malgache. Heule,

Belgique, Editions UGA, 1964. 25 p. (Université internationale de sciences comparées, Luxembourg. Centre international d'études et de recherches européennes. Conférences, 1964)

Summary of terms of July 20, 1963 agreement between Common Market and 18 African states (mainly former members of French Community) replacing terms annexed to Rome Treaty of 1957. New agreement makes African states associates and offers economic assistance.

1753 VERGES, JACQUES. Le crime de colonialisme; colloque de Rome, 2, 3, 4 février 1962. Paris, 1962. 15 p.("Les Temps modernes," no. 190)

Speech of French lawyer Jacques Vergès at second international colloquium of jurists on Algeria (see no. 369 for first colloquium) on general question of decolonization. Pamphlet also includes text of colloquium's resolutions, which spell out its support for an independent, unpartitioned Algeria.

1754 VERGES, JACQUES, MICHAEL ZAVRIAN, and MAURICE COURREGE. Les disparus; le Cahier vert. Postface de Pierre Vidal-Naquet. Ce document a été établi en collaboration avec le Comité Maurice Audin et le Centre d'information pour la défense des libertés et de la paix. Lausanne, La Cité éditeur, 1959. 116 p. facsims., diagrs.

List compiled by three French defense lawyers for Algerian nationalists, identifying 175 Algerians who disappeared during the battle of Algiers, spring 1957, followed by letters from families of disappeared, addressed to International Red Cross. Postscript by Vidal-Naquet reconstructs context within which these illegal acts took place.

1754a VERGES, JACQUES, MICHEL ZAVRIAN, and MAURICE COURREGE. Le droit et la colère. Paris, Editions de Minuit, 1960. 174 p. (Documents)

Defense lawyers of Algerian nationalist prisoners describe deterioration of justice in arrest and trials of military prisoners and other Algerians under suspicion of aiding rebellion; their main target is the February 1960 decree transferring jurisdiction over all non-Europeans in Algeria to military tribunals. Text of decree in appendix. For other works by Vergès on treatment of Algerian nationalists, see nos. 164, 460, 877.

1755 VERMEERSCH, JEANNETTE. Les femmes dans la nation; textes choisis. Paris, Parti communiste français, 1962. 220 p.

Speeches and reports by wife of Maurice Thorez to Parti Communiste Français' central committee 1947-1961, including 1959 speech on peace in Algeria and 1961 speech on 25th anniversary of Communist Union des jeunes filles de France.

1756 VERMEERSCH, JEANNETTE. Organiser les travailleuses qui occupent une place décisive dans la nation; rapport au Comité central, Ivry-sur-Seine, 25-26-27 novembre 1961. Paris, 1961. 61 p.

Communist party's appeal to women workers to join party's women organization Union des femmes françaises, while pointing out weaknesses in party's existing program for organizing women.

1757 VERMEERSCH, JEANNETTE. Pour la défense des droits sociaux de la femme et de l'enfant, rapport et conclusions à la Réunion des responsables du travail parmi les femmes, Nanterre, 24-25 octobre 1964. Paris, Parti communiste français, 1964. 61 p.

Report on current living conditions of women workers, Communist party's demands for 40-hour week and maintenance of existing social security provisions. Efforts of Union des femmes françaises, the Communist women's organization, are reviewed.

1758 VETLANIN, VLADIMIR ALEKSEEVICH. Frantsiia i Zapadnaia Germaniia v "obshchem rynke." Moskva, Izd-vo In-ta mezhdunarodnykh otnoshenii, 1962. 206 p. Bibliographical footnotes.

Effects of Common Market on French economy, Franco-German relations, intra-European trade. Common Market is presented as the tool of Franco-German big business.

1759 VIALET, GEORGES. L'Algérie restera française. Paris, Haussmann, 1957. 271 p. fold. col. maps, tables.

Case for keeping Algeria French (in the wake of the Suez affair) while rejecting all steps toward autonomy, making integration, combined with reform of communal administration in Algeria, the basis for eventual stabilization. Author, who considers only small minority favorable to independence, makes striking comparisons between Algerian standards of living and those in other Mediterranean and Arab countries.

1760 VIANSSON-PONTE, PIERRE. Les gaullistes; rituel et annuaire. Paris, Editions du Seuil, 1963. 189 p. (Collection "L'Histoire immédiate.")

Facetious but perceptive essay on de Gaulle's political style and its ceremonial manifestations, followed by a biographical dictionary of 120 prominent former and current supporters of de Gaulle, with 1-4 page thumbnail sketches giving their political career and present position.

1761 VIANSSON-PONTE, PIERRE. Les politiques. Paris, Calmann-Lévy, 1967. 280 p. (Questions d'actualité)

Summation of Fifth Republic's evolution from its founding to the 1967 general elections and fair-minded evaluation of the regime's successes and failures in the Algerian question, foreign affairs, the reform of political, social, and economic institutions. Month-by-month chronology of political evolution, May 1958 - Dec. 1966. Additional title is "Bilan de la Ve République."

1762 VIANSSON-PONTE, PIERRE. Risques et chances de la Vème République. Paris, Plon, 1959. v, 76 p. (Tribune libre, 53)

Changes in machinery of power and new balance of political forces after first year of Fifth Republic, as seen by head of "Le Monde" political service. Author examines de Gaulle's method of government, the function of the cabinet, parliament, U.N.R., role of press and radio.

1763 VIARD, PAUL EMILE. Traité élémentaire de droit public et de droit privé en Algérie. Alger, Faculté de droit et des sciences économiques, 1960. Tables, fold. map. (Bibliothèque de la Faculté de droit et des sciences économiques d'Alger, v. 37) "Bibliographic": p. 23 26.

V. 1, the first part of this study on Algerian constitutional law, entitled "Les caractères politiques de l'Algérie" (151 p.) describes reforms in political representation resulting from 1958 Constitution and analyzes 1958 referendum. V. 2 "Le régime législatif de l'Algérie" is not at Hoover Institution.

1764 VIARD, RENE. La fin de l'empire colonial français. Préf. de Paul Antonini. Paris, G. P. Maisonneuve et Larose, 1963. 160 p.

Brief history of French Union, French Community, and current combination of independence and economic and cultural assistance, impartially assessing merits of colonial institutions and of current arrangements.

1765 VIDAL-NAQUET, PIERRE. L'affaire Audin; préf. de Laurent Schwartz. Paris, Editions de Minuit, 1960. 100 p. port. (Documents)

Account of arrest and subsequent disappearance, June, 1957, of Maurice Audin, mathematics professor at University of Algiers, known as member of Algerian Communist Party and friend of Henri Alleg. See Maurice Audin in Author Index for other accounts.

1766 VIDAL-NAQUET, PIERRE, (ed.). La raison d'état; textes publiés par le Comité Maurice Audin. Paris, Editions de Minuit, 1962. 330 p. (Documents)

Source book on repressive measures exacted by French military and civilian agencies in Algeria, 1954-1962, in the form of 40 chronologically arranged and annotated documents (not intended for publication), issued by military figures, magistrates, police officials, and members of French control commissions who had to act as representatives of state in repression of Algerian rebellion. Vidal-Naquet's lengthy introduction reviews the varied source material on torture, maladministration of justice, police measures in Algeria during the years of conflict, constituting a bibliography on repression during the Algerian war.

1767 VIDIASOVA, LIUBOV' MIKHAILOVNA. Frantsiia. Moskva, Znanie, 1963. 47 p. (Novoe v zhizni, nauke, tekhnike Seriia 7. Mezhdunarodnaia, no. 7)

French foreign relations with U.S., Great Britain, Germany, Soviet Union 1962-63, followed by text of Khrushchev and Malinovsky interviews on French television Feb. 1963.

1768 VINATREL, GUY. Communisme et franc-maçonnerie. Paris, Presses continentales, 1961. 182 p.

Author, as a freemason, rejects possibility of collaboration between freemasonry and communism because of opposing doctrine and methods. He buttresses arguments pointing to attacks on freemasonry both by French Communist party and Communist governments. Very little recent material.

1769 VINOT, PIERRE. Expansion et monnaie saine dans une société de liberté. Paris, Nouvelles Editions latines, 1960. 383 p. illus. (Bibliothèque de l'économie réaliste)

Gathering of government officials and industrialists at the Colloque de La Brévière, June 20-21, 1959, on the fairest and least inflationary wage distribution for economy and within companies. Vinot, a specialist on standard of living and consumption studies, pleads for revision of notion of minimum wages irrespective of family situation, in favor of minimum consumption units. Vinot describes the work on French consumption behavior of the Centre d'études de la Consommativité.

1770 VIORST, MILTON. Hostile allies: FDR and Charles de Gaulle. New York, Macmillan, 1965. viii, 280 p. Bibliography: p. 251-256.

A study of U.S.-French relations, 1940-1945, based primarily on American military and diplomatic sources, with some references to later conflicts between de Gaulle's and America's foreign policy stemming from clashes between de Gaulle and Roosevelt. Good bibliography.

1771 VIRIEU, FRANÇOIS HENRI DE. La fin d'une agriculture. Paris, Calmann-Lévy, 1967. 291 p. (Questions d'actualité) Bibliographie sommaire.

Impartial evaluation of successes and failures of Gaullist agricultural policies, including Common Market negotiations, and of the role of old and new agrarian organizations in winning a fair share of the national product for agriculture. Agricultural chronology, Dec. 1958 - Dec. 1966. Additional title: "Bilan de la Ve République."

1772 VISINE, FRANÇOIS. L'économie française face au Marché commun. Préf. de René Courtin. Paris, R. Pichon et R. Durand-Auzias, 1959. vi, 113 p. tables. (Collection d'études économiques, 38) "Bibliographie sommaire" p. 103-104.

Favorable assessment of impact of Common Market on French economy based on October 1958 report for Campagne européenne de la jeunesse.

1773 VOLKERT, HEINZ PETER. Die Präsidentschaft der V. Republik in Frankreich. Mainz, 1963. Microfilm copy (negative) xii, 169 p. Includes bibliography.

Doctoral dissertation, Johann Gutenberg University, Mainz on the history of the presidency in France, constitutional provisions and specific powers of the French president in previous republics and in 1958 constitution, demonstrating by parallelisms that the constitutional authority vested in de Gaulle is historically unprecedented.

1774 VOOG, ROGER. Les institutions de la France et de la Communauté. Supplément à l'Initiation civique et à l'Initiation aux problèmes d'outre-mer, Collection "Savoir pour agir." Lyon, Editions Chronique sociale de France, 1959. 38 p.

Summary of 1958 constitution and of status of French Community after Sept. 1958 referendum.

1775 VOSSEN, FRANTZ. De Gaulle; Chronik einer Berufung. München, R. Piper, 1963. 224 p.

Journalist's assessment of de Gaulle's personality and the inner logic of de Gaulle's Algerian and European policy and his relations with military, political parties.

1776 VOYENNE, BERNARD. La presse dans la société contemporaine. Paris, A. Colin, 1962. 327 p. illus., map. (Collection U: Série "Société politique") Includes bibliographies.

Survey of mass communication media (dailies, weeklies, radio and television, press agencies) with statistics for France on such matters as production costs of newspapers, circulation figures, income from advertisement, government subsidies, audiences. Appendix gives circulation figures for different types of French publications and French-language press outside France. Selected texts and bibliographies for each chapter.

1777 VULERT, PIERRE. Vers l'avenir; nouvelles conceptions économiques et sociales. Paris, R. Pichon et R. Durand-Auzias, 1959. 199 p.

Treatise on market economy and proposals for making French economy function more rationally through greatly expanded government intervention.

1778 WACHTEL, DENNIS FAY. De Gaulle and the invasion of North Africa. St. Louis, Mo., 1964. Microfilm copy (positive) of typescript made by University Microfilms, Ann Arbor, Mich. 314 l. Includes bibliography.

St. Louis University Ph.D. thesis, largely based on official American and anti-Gaullist French documents, reviewing de Gaulle's role in World War II (position in resistance, relations with Vichy leaders and U.S. and British governments) as a background to his participation in North African invasion and subsequent maneuvering for control of French government in North Africa. The author emphasizes de Gaulle's success by sheer force of will rather than popularity with either North Africans or Allies.

1779 WAHL, NICHOLAS. The Fifth Republic; France's new political system. New York, Random House, 1959. 130 p. (Studies in political science, PS31) Bibliography: p. 93-95.

One of earliest surveys in English of Fifth Republic. Harvard professor bases his analysis of de Gaulle's and Debré's motivations in establishing the new institutions on talks he had with them in 1957 and 1958.

1780 WEINSTEIN, ADELBERT. Das ist de Gaulle; Anspruch und Wirklichkeit, Versuch eines Porträts. Düsseldorf, Eugen Diedrichs Verlag, 1963. 99 p.

De Gaulle's personality and political strategy as seen by one of editors of "Frankfurter Allgemeine Zeitung" in the wake of de Gaulle's triumphal visit to Germany.

1781 WEINSTEIN, BRIAN G. Training programs in France for African civil servants. Boston, 1964. 71 l. Includes bibliography.

Study made for the Agency for International Development in summer of 1963.

1782 WEISENFELD, ERNST. De Gaulle sieht Europa. Reden und Erklärungen 1958-1966. Frankfurt a. M., Fischer Bücherei, 1966. 172 p. (Fischer-Bücherei, 813)

Chronologically arranged excerpts from de Gaulle's speeches and statements grouped around the themes of independent military strategy, European integration, Franco-German relations, views on European unity beyond "Little Europe."

1783 WERTH, ALEXANDER. De Gaulle, a political biography. Harmondsworth, Middelsex, Eng. Penguin Books, 1965. 391 p. (Political leaders of the twentieth century) Includes bibliography.

De Gaulle's role in French history since before World War II seen from the perspective of his seven years as head of the Fifth Republic, with main chapters devoted to Liberation, R. P. F., return to power in 1958, Algeria, and foreign policy since 1962. Author, an English journalist, is not uncritical, but gives sympathetic portrait of statesman and credits him with substantial political achievements. No original sources.

1784 WERTH, ALEXANDER. The De Gaulle revolution. London, R. Hale, 1960. xiv, 404 p. Bibliographical footnotes.

Origins, birth, and consolidation of Fifth Republic through December 1958, as seen by Paris-based British journalist with little sympathy for de Gaulle.

1785 WERTH, ALEXANDER. Lost statesman, the strange story of Pierre Mendès-France. New York, Abelard-Schuman, 1958. xix, 428 p. port., map.

Political biography of Mendès-France, emphasizing colonial evolution 1954-1957 and Mendès-France's lonely fight against the Mollet government's Algerian policy.

1786 WESTERN EUROPEAN UNION. COMMITTEE ON DEFENCE QUESTIONS AND ARMAMENTS. France and NATO. La France et l'O. T. A. N. Brief prepared by L. Radoux, rapporteur. Paris, 1967. 93 p.

Texts of NATO agreements, speeches and letters by de Gaulle and replies of American statesmen, 1958-1965, and 1966 exchanges between France and other NATO governments on NATO reorganization.

1787 WEYGAND, MAXIME. Histoire de l'armée française. Paris, Flammarion, 1961. 493 p. illus., ports., maps.

Last chapter of this military history describes glorious role of French army in Indochinese and Algerian war and its technical adaptation, as of Oct. 1960 to both subversive and atomic wars.

1788 WHITE, DOROTHY SHIPLEY. Seeds of discord: De Gaulle, Free France, and the Allies. Syracuse, N. Y., Syracuse University Press, 1964. xi, 471 p. ports. Bibliographical references included in "Notes to chapters" (p. 369-451)

Well-documented and fair-minded study of de Gaulle's rôle in early years of World War II, leading him to his fixed distrust of Great Britain and the U. S. Author interviewed many of participants.

1789 Who's who in France, Paris. 1953-54, 1967-68. Paris, J. Lafitte. 2 v.

Bi-annually published biographical dictionary, edited by J. Lafitte and S. Taylor. 1953-54 is first, 1967-68 is eighth edition. Complete set at Main Library. 1967-68 has list of deputies, as of April 1967.

1790 WIATR, JERZY J. Militaryzm a demokracja; szkice o politycznej roli armii w powojennej Francji. Warszawa, Wydawn. Ministerstwa Obrony Narodowej, 1966. 351 p. Bibliographic footnotes.

Evolution of French military-civilian relations after 1945, centered on the conflict between military leaders and de Gaulle. Author also examines Gaullism as a political doctrine and de Gaulle's more recent policy of military independence, as expressed in modernization of army and development of nuclear weapons, which author treats sympathetically. Summaries in Russian and French.

1791 WILLARD, CLAUDE. Socialisme et communisme français. Paris, A. Colin, 1967. 158 p. (Collection U2) Includes bibliography.

Political history of French labor movement from 19th century to present, with final pages on Fifth Republic identifying electorate of the two main labor parties.

1792 WILLIAMS, PHILIP MAYNARD and MARTIN HARRISON. De Gaulle's Republic. London, Longmans, 1960. vii, 279 p. diagrs. Bibliographical footnotes.

Fall of the Fourth Republic, transition to Fifth Republic, new political leaders, functioning of new institutions and Gaullist policies during 1959. Epilogue covers Jan. 1960 Algerian uprising and concomitant degradation of parliamentary power.

1793 WILLIAMS, PHILIP MAYNARD. Politics in post-war France; parties and the constitution in the Fourth Republic. 2d ed. London, New York, Longmans, Green, 1958. xxvii, 506 p. maps, diagrs., tables. Bibliography: p. ix-xi.

Basic work on political system and parties of Fourth Republic, study stops with 1955, except for appendices which carry work through 1956.

1794 WILLIS, FRANK ROY, (ed.). De Gaulle, anachronism, realist, or prophet? New York, Holt, Rinehart and Winston, 1967. 122 p. (European problem studies) Bibliography: p. 120-122.

Collection of 17 readings from books on de Gaulle, (French, English, German, and American) covering de Gaulle's political career before and after 1958. All selections are in English, either originally or translated by the editor, representing a wide range of opinions on de Gaulle's achievements.

1795 WILLIS, FRANK ROY. France, Germany, and the new Europe, 1945-1963. Stanford, Calif., Stanford University Press, 1965. xiv, 397 p. Bibliography: p. 373-387.

Final 50 pages deal with Gaullist policy regarding the Common Market and admission of Great Britain as well as Franco-German relations. The epilogue brings these topics up to date through end of 1964. The author is especially successful in his treatment of the complex Franco-German controversy over agricultural products. Extensive bibliography on European integration and Franco-German relations, including government reports, list of interviewed leaders, 20 of whom are French. A revised and expanded edition "France, Germany, and the New Europe, 1945-1967" (Stanford, 1968) has a 50-page final chapter for the years 1963-67, in which Germany and France are shown to drift apart again.

1796 WILTZ, VICTOR. Lettre ouverte au général de Gaulle, Président de la République. Paris, 1964. 18 p.

Letter to de Gaulle, May 1964, congratulating him on his efforts to detach Latin America from American hegemony, followed by reprint of author's 1951 pamphlet proposing a Latin Union as a cornerstone for a European third force.

1797 WOLFE, THOMAS W. Soviet commentary on the French "force de frappe." Santa Monica, Calif., Rand Corp., 1965. ix, 29 p. (Rand Corporation, Memorandum RM-4359-ISA) Bibliographical footnotes.

Summary of Soviet reactions to the development of independent French nuclear weapons, 1963-64, showing Soviet ambivalence, based on approval of French independence from U.S. and fear of a Franco-German alliance.

1798* WORONOFF, SERGE. [Correspondence from Serge Woronoff, a member of the Foreign Policy Commission of the Parti d'Union de la Gauche Socialiste containing points of view and statements of policy of the new French party.] Paris, 1958. 3 p.

July 1958 letter to Hoover Institution explaining how the Union de la Gauche Socialiste was constituted and what are its main objectives.

1799 WRIGHT, GORDON. France in modern times: 1760 to the present. Chicago, Rand McNally, 1960. 621 p. illus. (Rand McNally history series)

Brief final chapter on Fifth Republic.

1800 WRIGHT, GORDON. Rural revolution in France; the peasantry in the twentieth century. Stanford, Calif., Stanford University Press, 1964. xi, 271 p. illus., ports., maps. Bibliography: p. 251-259.

History, based on author's extended research in rural France in 1950-51 and early 1960's, of political movements of French peasantry from the Third to the Fifth Republic. Last chapter describes changes in mentality and organizational pattern of agrarian leadership, complemented in appendix by description of farm life in six villages. List of periodicals devoted to agrarian politics and abbreviations of peasant organizations.

1801 WULLUS, ARMAND. Français et Allemands: ennemis héréditaires? Une synthèse de l'histoire européenne [par] J. Wullus-Rudiger [pseud.] Bruxelles, Brepols, 1965. 303 p. maps.

Final chapters summarize de Gaulle's steps toward Franco-German reconciliation and subsequent oscillations in the two countries' relations, 1962-1965.

1802 WURMSER, ANDRE. Mais...dit André Wurmser... Préf. d'Etienne Fajon. Paris, Editeurs français réunis, 1961. 305 p.

Collection of humorous articles covering a wide variety of political, cultural, daily-living topics, selected from journalist's daily column in "L'Humanité," March 1955 - July 1961. Political issues are not emphasized.

1803 YACEF, SAADI. Souvenirs de la bataille d'Alger, décembre 1956 - septembre 1957. Paris, R. Julliard, 1962. 122 p.

Memoirs of this dramatic episode of Algerian war by one of leading F.L.N. participants. (See also Germaine Tillion's report on her discussion with Yacef about F.L.N. terrorism during this operation, no. 1702.)

1804 YAZID, MOHAMED. Press conference by Mr. M'hammed [sic] Yazid, Minister of Information of the Provisional Government of the Algerian Republic, Tunis, May 4, 1962. New York, 1962. 2 l. (Delegation of the Provisional Government of the Algerian Republic, N.Y.) Doc. 62-9-E.

Support for Provisional Executive in carrying out Evian agreement.

1805 YSQUIERDO, ANTOINE. Une guerre pour rien. Paris, Table ronde, 1966. 247 p.

Personal narrative of Foreign Legionnaire, who participated in Algerian war, 1955-1961 in First Parachutist Regiment, giving glimpses of military operations at the different stages of the war.

1806 ZAMORA RODRIGUEZ, TOMAS. La presidencia del gobierno en Francia. Madrid, 1965. 222 p. fold. diagrs. (Colección Instituciones políticas) Includes bibliography.

Spanish doctoral dissertation tracing constitutional provisions on presidency from the Third to the Fifth Republic and emphasizing the trend toward increasing executive authority in all contemporary political institutions. Extensive bibliography of books and articles.

1807 ZEHM, GÜNTER ALBRECHT. Historische Vernunft und direkte Aktion; zur Politik und Philosophie Jean-Paul Sartres. Stuttgart, E. Klett, 1964. 230 p. (Frankfurter Studien zur Wissenschaft von der Politik, Bd. 1) Bibliography: p. 220-230.

Analysis of Sartre's literary, political, and philosophical writings highlighting his fluctuating relations with French Communist party and Marxism. Bibliography gives complete list of Sartre's writings, including articles, prefaces, etc.

1808 ZIEBURA, GILBERT. Die V. Republik; Frankreichs neues Regierungssystem. Köln und Opladen, Westdeutscher Verlag, 1960. 333 p. map., tables, diagrs. (Die Wissenschaft von der Politik, Bd. 12) "Bibliographischer Hinweis": p. 318-332.

A source book on the political regime of the Fifth Republic, combining a historical view of the origins of the new institutions and Gaullist doctrine with a detailed analysis of the individual branches of the government (executive, legislative, judicial, administrative, organs of the French Community). For each institution, author gives relevant constitutional provisions and ordinances, current facts (1959-60) on persons in office and election results, accompanied by pertinent statements of de Gaulle, other Gaullists, opponents, African politicians (re French Community) and political scientists. Annotated bibliography for each section.

1809 ZÜRN, PETER. Die republikanische Monarchie; zur Struktur der Verfassung der V. Republik in Frankreich. München, C. H. Beck, 1965. xx, 347 p. (Münchener Studien zur Politik, 5. Heft) Includes bibliography.

Major scholarly work, based on a doctoral dissertation written under Georges Vedel and Theodor Maunz, on the origins, genesis, and organs of the constitution of the Fifth Republic, taking into account the entire literature in the field. Author takes up conception of presidency, prime minister, ministers, parliament, appointed councils, law-making process, with article by article documentation. Following up constitutional evolution through November 1962 to discover its functioning, author notes a built-in tendency toward presidential absolutism (the monarchistic element of the title). Extensive bibliography of books, articles, French dissertations.

Part II: Serial Publications

Publications listed in this section can be located in the French newspaper and French-language serials catalogues, with the following exceptions: serials designated M. L. (Main Library, Stanford) and L. L. (Law Library, Stanford) as well as serials followed by an asterisk (government and organizational publications, newspapers not published in France, which can be located in other special Hoover Institution catalogues).

Unless the month is specified, the initial date is January and the terminal date December. When a serial file pre-dates 1956, it is traced back to its last uninterrupted period. A broken file is indicated by brackets, but isolated missing issues are not taken into account.

Separately catalogued individual issues of periodicals (e. g., Défense de l'Occident, Lectures françaises, etc.) are listed in Part I. Three special microfilmed newspaper collections are itemized in Part I, no. 811(e) - (g). Microfilmed newspapers available on Interlibrary Loan from the Center for Research Libraries, Chicago, are listed at the end of Part II.

Title changes can be traced through the Title Index.

1810* ACADEMIE DES SCIENCES D'OUTRE-MER. Comptes rendus mensuels des séances de l'Académie des sciences d'outre-mer. 1941 - 1967+. Paris. Irreg-monthly. Until 1957, society titled Académie des sciences coloniales.

Important forum for discussions on Africa, decolonization, technical assistance, and relevant books on these topics.

1811 L'Action européenne fédéraliste; bulletin intérieur périodique du Centre d'action européenne fédéraliste (A. E. F.). Ap/My 1957 - S/O 1958. Paris. Bi-monthly.

1812 L'Action fédéraliste européenne; publication mensuelle des Fédéralistes européens. My 1956 - Ag/S 1959// Paris. Bi-monthly. European Union of Federalists. Superseded by Fédéralisme européen (no. 1944).

1813 L'Action laïque. Revue mensuelle de la Ligue française de l'enseignement. F 1961 - D 1963// Paris. Monthly. Superseded by Pourquoi (no. 2055).

Articles on education and educational legislation.

1814 Action libertaire. Organe de la section française de la Fédération internationale des jeunesses libertaires. Ap - D 1964. Paris. Quarterly.

1815 L'Action municipale; au service des municipalités de France. 1956 - F 1966. Paris. Monthly.

Published by centrist organization of municipal councillors.

1816 L'Actualité de l'histoire; tables analytiques. Paris. Institut français d'histoire sociale.

Tables of content for 1952-1960 of Institute's Bulletin trimestriel. For periodical see no. 2008.

1817 Afrique. N 1961 - Je 1962; My 1963 - 1967+. Paris. Monthly.

1818 Afrique contemporaine. Documents d'Afrique noire et de Madagascar. Ap/My 1962 - 1967+. Paris. Bi-monthly. France. Direction de la documentation.

1819 L'Afrique et l'Asie. 1953 - D 1967+. Paris. Quarterly. Association des anciens du Centre des hautes études d'administration musulmane.

Emphasis on problems of technical and economic development.

1820 L'Afrique française. Bulletin du Comité de l'Afrique française et du Comité du Maroc. 1954 - Ja/Mr 1960// Paris. 6 a year.

Organ of French administrators in French Africa.

1821 Alger républicain. Jl 1962 - Je 1965// Algiers. Daily.

Organ of Algerian Communist Party, edited by Henri Alleg.

1822 Alger revue. Revue municipale. 1954 - 1961. Algiers. 3 issues a year after 1956.

Official Algiers publication in agreement with official French policy and giving information on local and Algerian economic affairs and social life of the city.

1823* ALGERIA. Journal officiel. 1953 - Jl 1958// (On microfilm.) Algiers. Superseded by ALGERIA. LAWS, STATUTES, ETC. Recueil des actes administratifs (no. 1830).

1824* ALGERIA. Journal officiel de l'Etat Algerien. Jl - S 1962// (On microfilm.) Algiers. Superseded by ALGERIA. Journal officiel de la République algérienne démocratique et populaire, O 1962 (no. 1825). Supersedes ALGERIA. LAWS, STATUTES, ETC. Recueil des actes administratifs de la délégation générale du gouvernement (no. 1830).

1825* ALGERIA. Journal officiel de la République algérienne démocratique et populaire. O 1962 - 1967+. (On microfilm.) Algiers. Supersedes ALGERIA. Journal officiel de l'état algérien (no. 1824).

1826* ALGERIA. GOUVERNEUR GENERAL. SERVICE D'INFORMATION. Documents algériens. Série économique. 1953 - F 1960. Algiers. Irregular.

1827* ALGERIA. GOUVERNEUR GENERAL. SERVICE D'INFORMATION. Documents algériens. Série monographies. 1948 - N 1958. Algiers. Irregular.

1828* ALGERIA. GOUVERNEUR GENERAL. SERVICE D'INFORMATION. Documents algériens. Série politique. 1946 - 1957. Algiers. Irregular.

1957 issue on radio and television in Algeria.

1829* ALGERIA. GOUVERNEUR GENERAL. SERVICE D'INFORMATION. Documents algériens. Série sociale. Ja - D 1958. Algiers. Monthly.

1830* ALGERIA. LAWS, STATUTES, ETC. Recueil des actes administratifs de la Délégation générale du gouvernement (Algiers). Jl 1958 - Je 1962 // (On microfilm.) Algiers. Supersedes ALGERIA. Journal officiel (no. 1823). Superseded by ALGERIA. Journal officiel de l'état algérien (no. 1824).

1831* ALGERIA. MINISTERE DE COMMERCE. Bulletin économique et juridique. Revue mensuelle de l'Office algérien d'action commerciale. 1948 - D 1956; 1961 - My 1962; F - Ag 1963 // Algiers. Suspended Je - D 1962. Weekly supplements for Mr - Je 1962.

   1963 publication edited by Algerian Republic government.

1832* ALGERIE PRESSE SERVICE. Bulletin politique. Ja - My 1962. Tunis. Daily.

   News service covering events in Algeria and developments concerning Algerian Provisional Government and other nationalist organizations in exile.

1833 L'Algérien en France. Journal mensuel édité par le Parti Communiste français. 1956 - O/N 1960. Paris.

1834 Appel de la France. Journal de l'O.A.S. [1961 - 1962]. Brussels. Supplement to Nation Europe. See also Appel de la France published in France.

1835 Appel de la France. Journal du Conseil national de la résistance. S - N 1962. Clandestine. See also Appel de la France published in Belgium.

1836 Appel pour l'Europe. [1958 - Je 1960]. Paris. Monthly.

   Pro-European unification articles for press quotation.

1837 Arguments. [1958 - 1962//] Paris. Quarterly.

   Political and philosophical issues, with frequent articles on Marxism.

1838 L'Armée française. Revue de la Confédération nationale des réserves, de la Fédération des officiers de réserve républicaine et de la Fédération des sous-officiers de réserve républicaine. Ag/S 1960 - Jl/Ag 1963. Paris. Annual. See also no. 1945.

1839 Articles et documents. 1954 - 1967+. Paris. France. Direction de la documentation. Bi-daily.

   Translations of articles of international interest from the foreign press. For France, it reproduces all the official government declarations and speeches, notably de Gaulle's. Annual index 1966-. See also nos. 1912-1914.

1840* ASSOCIATION DES CADRES DIRIGEANTS DE L'INDUSTRIE POUR LE PROGRES SOCIAL ET ECONOMIQUE. Bulletin. Ap 1959 - 1967+. Paris. Monthly.

   Organization also known as Acadi. Discussions of social and economic issues.

1841* ASSOCIATION NATIONALE POUR LE SOUTIEN DE L'ACTION DU GENERAL DE GAULLE. Bulletin hebdomadaire de presse. N 1961 - 1967+. Paris.

   Public relations organ of government popularizing Gaullist policies.

1842* ASSOCIATION POUR L'ETUDE DES PROBLEMES D'OUTRE-MER. Bulletin. 1953 - 1967+. Paris. 6 a year.

   Concentrates on economic and political developments in Africa.

1843* ASSOCIATION POUR L'ETUDE DES PROBLEMES D'OUTRE-MER. [Report.] De la part de MM. Leglise et Rey. Ja/F - Ap/Jl 1960; 1961 - 1967+. Paris. 6 a year.

   Complements its Bulletin.

1844 Avenirs. My/Je 1964 - D 1965. Paris. Monthly. Bureau universitaire de statistique et de documentation scolaires et professionnelles.

1845* BANQUE NATIONALE POUR LE COMMERCE ET L'INDUSTRIE. Bulletin d'information économique. 1954 - Ap 1966. Paris. Monthly.

1846 Biblio. Répertoire bibliographique de tous les ouvrages parus en langue française dans le monde. 1948 - 1967+. Paris. ML

   Cumulative annual issues using catalogue-dictionary format (combining author, title, and subject entries alphabetically).

1846a Bibliographie de la France. 1955 - 1967+. Paris. Weekly. ML.

   Books published in France and deposited at Bibliothèque nationale during that week. Works in each issue are topically arranged with annual Author Index. Monthly supplements for periodicals, atlases, government publications.

1847 Bibliographie sélective des publications officielles françaises. 1952 - D 1958; O - N 1960; 1960 - 1967+ (in ML). Paris. Fortnightly. Comité de coordination pour la documentation des sciences sociales, publ. by France. Direction de la documentation.

   Includes: documents administratifs and bulletin des sommaires. Each issue is topically arranged. No cumulative index.

1848 Le Bled: hebdomadaire militaire d'information. My 1958 - Je 1960; D 1961 - D 1962 // Algiers-Paris. Pub. trans. to Paris early in 1960. Superseded by Tam. Bimensuel des forces armées (no. 2107).

1849 Le Bulletin. Documents et recherches. D 1955 - Je/Jl 1957 // Paris. Monthly. Superseded by La Lettre (no. 1998).

   Catholic leftist publication. See also Chatagner, J. (no. 326) for editorial correspondence after Bulletin's discontinuance.

1850 Bulletin analytique de documentation politique, économique et sociale contemporaine. 1946 - 1967+. Paris. Bi-monthly or monthly. Fondation nationale des sciences politiques.

   Bibliography of articles topically arranged by countries and international organizations.

1850a Bulletin critique du livre français. 1958 - 1967+. Paris. Monthly. ML

   Short reviews of selected French publications in all fields and contents of leading periodicals.

1851 Le Bulletin d'André Noël. Synthèse hebdomadaire des problèmes politiques français et internationaux. Je 1958 - 1967+. Maisons-Alfort (Seine) Title varies: Lettres d'information politique et économiques; Lettre d'André Noël.

   Confidential newsletter with much inside information on French political life and favoring nationalist opposition to de Gaulle. After Noël died Ag 1964, Mme Noël took over publication.

1852 Bulletin d'information marxiste-leniniste. Jl/Ag 1964. Clichy.

1853 Bulletin d'information radical-socialiste. Mr 1951 - N 1958; S 1964 - 1967+. Issues on national congresses 1959-1962. Paris. Bi-monthly. Parti républicain radical et radical-socialiste.

1854 Bulletin de l'Afrique noire. Je 1959 - N 1963; D 1966 - 1967+. Paris. Weekly.

1855 Bulletin de liaison des Comités pour la formation d'une Association populaire franco-chinoise. O 1963. Paris.

1856 (Omitted.)

1857 Bulletin hebdomadaire d'information et de documentation; mouvement de Saint-Céré. Ap, My 1956; F 1957 - Ag 1958. Capdenac. Union de défense des commerçants et artisans.

1857a Bulletin législatif Dalloz: lois, décrets, arrêtés, circulaires, etc. 1918 - 1967-. Paris. Monthly. LL

Verbatim text of all laws promulgated during that month, supplemented by annual subject index.

1858 Bulletin mensuel de statistique d'outre-mer. [Jl/Ag 1947 - Ap 1956]; 1957 - D 1960. Paris. Quarterly. France. Ministère des finances et des affaires économiques. Institut national de la statistique et des études économiques. ML

1859* BUREAU POLITIQUE DE MGR LE COMTE DE PARIS. Bulletin mensuel d'information. F 1957 - 1967+.

Analysis of current political issues, usually pro-Gaullist.

1860 Cahiers d'études africaines. Ja 1960 - 1967+. Paris. Quarterly. Ecole pratique des hautes études, Sorbonne. VIe section: sciences économiques et sociales.

1861 Cahiers d'outre-mer. Ja/Mr 1960 - 1967+. Bordeaux. Quarterly. Institut de géographie de la Faculté des lettres de Bordeaux.

1862 Les Cahiers de la République: revue bi-mestrielle de politique. D 1956 - Ap/My 1963// Paris. Bi-monthly. Superseded by Courrier de la république (no. 1902).

Organ of Pierre Mendès-France.

1862a Cahiers de sociologie économique. 1959 - 1966. Le Havre. 2 a year. Université de Caen. Centre de recherches et d'études de psychologie des peuples et de sociologie économique. ML

1863 Les Cahiers du Comité de Vincennes. S 1961. Paris.

Organ of Comité de Vincennes, which was organized at Colloque de Vincennes (see no. 364).

1864 Cahiers du communisme: revue mensuelle du Parti communiste français. 1947 - 1967+. Paris.

Special issues on party congresses included. (See nos. 1394, 1402, 1403.)

1865 Cahiers du communisme révolutionnaire. Organe du Parti communiste révolutionnaire de France. Jl 1964, 1967+. Paris. Irregular.

1866 Les Cahiers français: documents d'actualité. 1956 - 1967+. Paris. Monthly.

France. Direction de la documentation. Monthly monographs on French political, economic, social and cultural problems.

1866a Cahiers internationaux de sociologie. 1961 - 1967+. Paris. 2 a year. ML

Includes articles on French sociology and Marxism.

1867 Cahiers reconstruction. Pour un socialisme démocratique par la critique sociale. N 1953 - 1967+. Paris. Bi-monthly.

Organ of political club with socialist leanings.

1868 Cahiers universitaires. Ap - My/Je 1965; N/D 1966. Paris.

Organ of nationalist student movement and connected with Europe-Action (no. 1938).

1869 Carrefour; la semaine en France et dans le monde. 1944 - 1967+. (On microfilm.) Paris. Weekly. ML

1870* CENTRE D'ETUDES SOCIALISTES. Cahiers. 1961 - 1967+. Paris. Bi-monthly.

Each issue is on a special topic concerning French social, economic, and political affairs, on Marxism and international labor movement from a socialist perspective.

1871 CENTRE D'ETUDES SUPERIEURES DE PSYCHOLOGIE SOCIALE. Lettre d'information. Ja - Je 1961. Paris. Weekly.

Militant Catholic group, headed by Georges Sauge, whose main purpose is anti-communist propaganda. May be actively related to Cité catholique (see no. 1524).

1872* CENTRE D'INFORMATION CIVIQUE. Bulletin d'informations générales. D 1964 - 1967+. Paris. Quarterly.

Semi-official organization distributing information on public affairs.

1873* CENTRE D'INFORMATION CIVIQUE. Etudes. 1964 - 1967+. Paris. Monthly.

Each issue devoted to documented study of foreign affairs and domestic questions.

1874* CENTRE DES HAUTES ETUDES AMERICAINES. Bulletin économique. Ja 1966 - Jl 1967// Paris. Weekly.

Reports on French and foreign economic conditions.

1875* CENTRE DES HAUTES ETUDES AMERICAINES. Lettre. Mr 1965 - Jl 1967// Paris. Weekly.

Center grants degrees in American studies. Newsletters on internal French and U.S. affairs, rest of America, international developments. Last editor was Fabrice Laroche. Anti-Gaullist, pro-U.S., anti-Communist.

1876* CERCLE TOCQUEVILLE. Information. S 1964 - F 1965. Lyon. Monthly.

Political club's newsletter.

1877 Chroniques d'outre-mer. 1951 - D 1958// Paris. Monthly. France. Direction de la Documentation and Ministère de la France d'outre-mer. Superseded by Chronique de la Communauté (no. 1878).

1878 Chroniques de la Communauté. Ap 1959 - D 1960// Paris. Quarterly. France. Direction de la documentation. Supersedes Chroniques d'outre-mer (no. 1877).

1879 Chroniques étrangères: Allemagne: 1946 - 1967+; Espagne: 1945 - 1967+; Etats Unis: 1945 - 1967+; Grande Bretagne: 1945 - 1967+; Italie: 1945 - 1967+; U.R.S.S.: 1945 - 1967+. Paris. Monthly. France. Direction de la documentation.

Press summaries on political, economic, cultural developments in each country.

1880 Chronologie internationale; supplément bi-mensuel aux Notes et études documentaires. 1956 - D 1963// Paris. Semi-monthly. France. Direction de la documentation.

Chronology of national and international events, by country. For detailed description, see no. 335. See also no. 2016 for Notes et études documentaires.

1881 Chronologie politique africaine. 1961 - 1967+. Paris. Bi-monthly. Fondation nationale des sciences politiques. Centre d'étude des relations internationales.

1882   Citoyens "60." Cahiers d'éducation politique, économique et sociale. O/N 1963 - 1967+. Paris. Quarterly. Citoyens "60."

Accompanied by monthly newsletter, Organ of political club Citoyens "60."

1883*   CLUB DEMOCRATIE NOUVELLE. CENTRE D'ETUDES ET DE RECHERCHES POLITIQUES ET ECONOMIQUES. Journal. 1964 - Ap 1967. Marseille.

This political club promoted the presidential candidacy of Marseille mayor Gaston Defferre. See also nos. 345-348 for Club's special studies.

1884*   CLUB JEAN MOULIN. Bulletin. 1961 - 1967+. Paris. Monthly or bi-monthly. Irregular supplements entitled Document établi.

For other publications of Club Jean Moulin, see Author Index.

1885   Combat. Le journal de Paris. D 1963 - 1967+. Paris. Monthly issue containing Patrie et progrès. See no. 2040.

FOR COMBAT. LE JOURNAL DE PARIS, SEE ALSO NEWSPAPERS ON MICROFILM LIST.

1886   Le Combat républicain. O 1957 - Mr 1958. Paris. Semi-monthly. Union démocratique et socialiste de la résistance.

Edited by François Mitterrand.

1887   Combat républicain. O 1965 - 1967+. Paris. Monthly. Fédération de la gauche démocrate et socialiste.

Edited by François Mitterrand and used as his campaign organ in bid for presidency. For supplements, see nos. 395-400, 574-577, 1245, 1246.

1888   Le Combat syndicaliste. Organe officiel de la Confédération nationale du travail. Section française de l'Association internationale des travailleurs. N 1962 - 1967+. Paris. Weekly. In French and Spanish. Subtitle varies.

1889   Le Combattant; organe du Front de libération nationale. 2 special issues 1957. Clandestine, issued also as El-Moudjahid (no. 2005) concurrently with that title in newspaper form.

1890*   COMITE FRANCAIS POUR L'UNION PAREUROPEENNE. Bulletin mensuel d'information. N 1960 - 1967+. Paris. Irregular.

Committee has several Gaullist members and acts as spokesman of government's European policy.

1891*   COMITE NATIONAL POUR L'AMENAGEMENT DU TERRITOIRE FRANÇAIS. Bulletin d'information. D 1964 - 1967+. Paris. Monthly.

Semi-official organization concerned with regional planning. Published by Centre d'information civique.

1892*   COMITE NATIONAL POUR LA PREPARATION A L'ELECTION PRESIDENTIELLE. Bulletin d'information. N 1963 - N 1965// Paris. Monthly. Published by Centre d'information civique, a semi-official organization.

1893   Communauté France-Eurafrique. My 1950 - O 1962. Paris. Monthly. Entitled Union française et parlement through F 1959, Revue de la Communauté France-Eurafrique through Jl/Ag 1960. Title changed to France-Eurafrique April 1963 (see no. 1969a).

1894   Communautés et continents. Ja/Mr 1959 - 1967+. Paris. Quarterly. Comité central français pour l'outre-mer. Supersedes Nouvelle revue Française d'outre-mer (no. 2024).

Covers French aid to former colonies.

1895   Communes d'Europe. Bulletin international du Conseil des communes d'Europe. S/O 1958 - Ag/S 1959. Paris. Monthly. Council of Europe.

1896   Le Communiste. Mensuel de la tendance révolutionnaire du Parti communiste français. D 1956 - 1967+. Paris. Monthly.

Communist opposition organ.

1897   Connaissance de l'Afrique. Bulletin d'information du cercle universitaire "Connaissance de l'Afrique." Ap 1965, My/Je - Jl/Ag 1966. Paris.

1898*   CONSEIL NATIONAL DE LA RESISTANCE. COMITE EXECUTIF. France presse-action. Agence centrale d'information et de propagande du C. N. R. O - N 1962. N. p. Clandestine. Weekly. Délégation en métropole O. A. S. /Métro.

1899   Le Contrat social; revue historique et critique des faits et des idées. Mr 1957 - 1967+. Paris. Bi-monthly.

Concentrates on developments of international communism. See also no. 1929.

1900   Coopération technique. 1965 - 1966. Paris. Quarterly. Institut d'étude du développement économique et social.

Edited by François Perroux.

1901   Le Courrier de la nouvelle république. 1960 - 1962// Paris. Weekly. Superseded by La nation (no. 2010).

Internal bulletin of U. N. R. which continues no. 2122.

1902   Le Courrier de la République. F 1959 - N 1960; N 1963 - 1967+. Paris. Monthly.

Ceased publication N 1960. Resumed publication under this title as continuation of Cahiers de la république, organ of Pierre Mendès-France (no. 1862).

1903   Courrier des démocrates. My 1964 - Ag 1967// Paris. Monthly. Superseded by Démocratie moderne (no. 1908a).

Organ of Centre démocrate (see Author Index) active in support of Jean Lecanuet's presidential candidacy.

1904   Courrier européen. Ap 1952 - 1967+. Paris. Monthly. Organisation française du Mouvement européen.

FOR LA CROIX, PARIS, SEE NEWSPAPERS ON MICROFILM LIST

1905   Cuba sí. [1963 - 1967]. Paris. Quarterly. Association France-Cuba.

Revolutionary leftist organ.

1906   Le Débat communiste. Bulletin mensuel. Mr 1962 - 1966// Paris. Amicale des anciens membres du Parti communiste français. Superseded by Unir-débat (no. 2123).

1907   Découvertes. Cahiers mensuels. F 1964 - 1967+. Lisbon. In French.

Organ of exiled French nationalists. Edited by Ploncard d'Assac. See also no. 2134.

1908   Défense de l'Occident. Revue mensuelle, politique, littéraire et artistique. F - Mr 1963. Paris.

Nationalist orientation. For special issues, see nos. 455-459.

1908a   Démocratie moderne. L'hebdomadaire des démocrates. S 1967 - 1967+. Paris. Supersedes both Courrier des démocrates (no. 1903) and Forces nouvelles (no. 1948).

Organ of Centre démocrate.

1909 Démocratie nouvelle. Revue mensuelle de politique mondiale. 1965 - 1967+. Paris.

Closely tied to Parti communiste français.

1910 Démocratie 65. Ja - D 1965. Paris. Weekly.

Called Démocratie 66 J - Mr 1966, then absorbed in Populaire de Paris (no. 2052a). Closely tied to Parti socialiste even before merger.

FOR DEPECHE DU MIDI, TOULOUSE, SEE NEWSPAPERS ON MICROFILM LIST

1911 Développement et civilisations. Organe du Centre international de recherche et de formation en vue du développement harmonisé. S 1964 - 1967+. Paris. Quarterly.

Edited by François Perroux.

1912 Documentation française. Catalogue méthodique. 1945 - 1956/60. Paris. France. Direction de la documentation.

Arranged by country and subject covering selected publications by Direction de la documentation. 1956/60 is in a single volume.

1913 Documentation française. Index général. 1948 - 1967+. Paris. France. Direction de la documentation.

Cumulative annual index covering all France. Direction de la documentation serials (see Author Index). It is arranged by country and subject. Under "France" such topics as administration, economy, education, political figures, foreign and domestic politics are well documented.

1914 Documentation française. Tables mensuelles. 1951 - 1967+. Paris. France. Direction de la documentation.

This is a selective list around specific topics of Direction de la documentation publications.

1915 La Documentation française illustrée. My 1960, Je 1961, Jl 1962. Paris. France. Direction de la documentation. See also nos. 505, 747, 752-754.

1916 Les Documents politiques, diplomatiques et financiers. 1945 - 1967+. Paris. Monthly. Agence indépendante d'informations internationales.

Edited by Roger Mennevée, with inside information on politics and business.

1917 Dossiers pour notre temps. [Je/Jl 1963 - Mr 1964]. Paris. Monthly.

Catholic information bulletin on social and economic questions.

1918* L'Echo d'Alger. 1957 - Ap 1961// Algiers. Daily.

Editor is Alain de Sérigny (see nos. 1625, 1626).

1919 L'Ecole et la nation. S 1957 - 1967+. Paris. Monthly. Parti communiste français.

1920 L'Economie. Journal d'informations industrielles, financières et agricoles du monde entier. 1945 - 1967+. Paris. Weekly. Includes supplements, except Outre-mer africain, which is listed separately (no. 2032).

1921 Economie appliquée. 1953 - 1967+. Paris. Quarterly. Institut de science économique appliquée. ML

1922 Economie et politique; revue marxiste d'économie. Jl 1957 - 1967+. Paris. Monthly.

Closely tied to Parti communiste français. Deals with theoretical problems of Marxist economics.

1923 Ecrits de Paris; revue des questions actuelles. F 1948 - 1967+. Paris. Monthly.

Conservative, anti-Gaullist orientation.

1924* L'Effort algérien. 1958 - N 1960// Algiers. Weekly.

Catholic publication close to Algerian Archbishop Duval.

1925 Entreprise; l'hebdomadaire de l'homme qui réussit. 1959 - D 1963. Paris.

Magazine concentrating on business scene.

1926* L'Espoir - Algérie. [1957 - Je 1962]. Algiers. Fortnightly/ irregular.

Organ of liberal European settlers, interrupted My 1957 - Ap 1960, S 1961 - My 1962, with final issue welcoming Algerian independence.

1927 Esprit. 1946 - 1967+. Paris. Monthly.

Cultural and political issues of general interest.

1928 Esprit public. D 1961, F 1962; N 1962 - S 1963; Ja 1965 - F 1966// Paris. Weekly, then monthly.

Organ of nationalist opposition to de Gaulle, with contributions from spokesmen for French Algeria.

1929 Est et Ouest. 1954 - 1967+. Paris. Fortnightly. Association d'études et d'informations politiques internationales.

Edited by Georges Albertini. Anti-communist organ, sharing many of collaborators of Contrat social (no. 1899).

1930 Etat nouveau. Tribune de l'Association pour l'étude de la réforme des structures de l'état. F 1963 - N 1964// Paris. First issues entitled AERSE (no separate file).

Edited by Col. Roger Trinquier (see no. 1717). Aim is to replace Gaullist regime. For Association's program, see no. 106.

1931 L'Etincelle. Hebdomadaire du Parti communiste guadeloupéen. [1964 - 1967+]. Pointe-à-Pitre.

1931a L'étincelle. No. 4 [1962/3]. Brussels.

May be continuation of Vive le Léninisme (no. 2130).

1932 Etudes. 1955 - 1967+. Paris. Monthly. ML

General information journal published by Pères de la Compagnie de Jésus.

1933 Etudes méditerranéennes. [Autumn 1957 - 1963// Paris. Semi-annual.

Forum for moderate Algerian nationalist leaders such as Ferhat Abbas and French favorable to African independence like Jules Roy. Articles deal not only with North Africa but with Near East.

1934 L'étudiant algérien; bulletin intérieur. Jl, Ag 1958. Tunis. Union générale des étudiants musulmans algériens. See also no. 865.

1935 L'Etudiant d'Afrique noire. Organe de la Fédération des étudiants d'Afrique noire en France. Ap/My 1963, Je/Jl 1964. Paris. Quarterly.

1936　Etudiant de France. [D 1963/Ja 1964 - 1967+]. Paris. Union nationale des étudiants de France. Also titled 21/27.

1937　Europe. Revue mensuelle. 1946 - 1967+. Paris.

Literary and cultural articles.

1938　Europe Action. 1963 - N 1966. Paris. Monthly.

Edited by Fabrice Laroche. Nationalist opposition to de Gaulle close to O. A. S. and organ for Tixier-Vignancour in his presidential campaign.

1939　Europe action hebdomadaire. 1964 - 1967+. Paris. Supplement to Europe action.

1940　L'Europe combattante. Ag, O 1964. Brussels.

Jean Thiriart ed. Supplement to Jeune Europe (no. 1990).

1941　L'Europe en formation. Bulletin mensuel d'information. Mr 1960 - Jl 1961; Mr 1962 - 1967+. Paris. Monthly. Centre international de formation européenne.

1942　Europe - France - Outre-mer. Revue internationale. 1951 - 1967+. Paris. Monthly. Titled changed Oct. 1958 from France outre-mer (no separate file).

Focuses on economic development in French Africa.

1943　Express. My 1953 - 1967+. Paris. Weekly except 1955.

Good coverage of current political affairs. Leftist orientation.

1944　Fédéralisme européen; publication mensuelle du Mouvement fédéraliste européen. O 1959 - 1967+. Paris. Monthly. Supersedes L'Action fédéraliste européenne (no. 1812).

1945*　FEDERATION DES OFFICIERS ET SOUS-OFFICIERS DE RESERVE REPUBLICAINS. L'Officier et le sous-officier de réserve. D 1960 - D 1964/Ja 1965// Paris. Quarterly. See also no. 1838.

FOR LE FIGARO, PARIS, SEE NEWSPAPERS ON MICROFILM LIST

1946　Figaro littéraire. 1961 - 1967+. Paris. Weekly. ML

1947　FONDATION NATIONALE DES SCIENCES POLITIQUES. BIBLIOTHEQUE. Liste mensuelle des ouvrages entrés. 1952 - 1967+. Paris.

Mimeographed acquisitions list, by subjects.

1948　Forces nouvelles; hebdomadaire national du Mouvement républicain populaire. O 1958 - S 1967// Paris. Weekly. Superseded by Démocratie moderne (no. 1908a).

1949　Force ouvrière. 1947 - Je 1958. Paris. Weekly.

Publication of trade union organization by that name.

FOR FORCE OUVRIERE, PARIS, SEE ALSO NEWSPAPERS ON MICROFILM LIST

1950*　FRANCE. AMBASSADE. U. S. SERVICE DE PRESSE ET D'INFORMATION. Community affairs. F 1959 - Je 1960. New York. Irregular.

On French Community.

1951*　FRANCE. AMBASSADE. U. S. SERVICE DE PRESSE ET D'INFORMATION. French affairs. 1953 - 1967+. New York. Irregular.

Important current documentation on French political life, with excellent coverage on elections.

1952*　FRANCE. AMBASSADE. U. S. SERVICE DE PRESSE ET D'INFORMATION. Release. 1956 - 1961. New York. Irregular.

Important news releases.

1953*　FRANCE. AMBASSADE. U. S. SERVICE DE PRESSE ET D'INFORMATION. Selected list of recent acquisitions. 1956 - Ja 1965. New York. Annual.

1954　FRANCE. AMBASSADE. U. S. SERVICE DE PRESSE ET D'INFORMATION. Speeches and press conferences. [1953 - 1967]. New York. Irregular.

Translations of all General de Gaulle's press conferences and selected speeches and press conferences by Couve de Murville, Pompidou, Debré.

1955　FRANCE. ASSEMBLEE NATIONALE. 1946 -. Annales. Documents parlementaires. v. 1-5; 1959/60 - 1962; v. 1 - 1962/3 - 1967. Paris. Imprimerie des journaux officiels. Part of Journal officiel. ML

1956　FRANCE. ASSEMBLEE NATIONALE. 1946 -. Débats. D 1958 -. Paris. Imprimerie des journaux officiels. Part of Journal officiel. ML

See also no. 1967 for Senate debates.

1957*　FRANCE. COMITE D'HISTOIRE DE LA DEUXIEME GUERRE MONDIALE. Bulletin. 1952 - N 1965. Paris. Monthly.

1958　FRANCE. CONSEIL ECONOMIQUE ET SOCIAL. Avis et rapports. 1965 - 1967+. Paris. Imprimerie des journaux officiels. Part of Journal officiel. ML

1959*　FRANCE. INSTITUT NATIONAL DE LA STATISTIQUE ET DES ETUDES ECONOMIQUES. Bulletin bibliographique. 1963 - 1967+. Paris. France. Ministère de la Coopération. Ministère des finances et des affaires économiques.

Annotated bibliography on political and economic affairs, notably African.

1960*　FRANCE. INSTITUT NATIONAL DE LA STATISTIQUE ET DES ETUDES ECONOMIQUES. Bulletin de conjoncture d'outre-mer. My 1963 - N 1964. Paris. Irregular.

1961*　FRANCE. MINISTERE DE LA COOPERATION. ETUDES GENERALES ET DE LA DOCUMENTATION. AFFAIRES ECONOMIQUES ET FINANCIERES. Bulletin bibliographique mensuel. 1964 - 1967+. Paris. After 1966, published by Secrétariat d'Etat aux affaires étrangères chargé de la coopération.

Annotated bibliography on Africa and economic development.

1962*　FRANCE. MINISTERE DU SAHARA. Bulletin officiel de l'Organisation commune des régions sahariennes. S 1957 - D 1958// Paris. Monthly.

Laws and statutes for Sahara. Superseded by FRANCE. MINISTRE DELEGUE AUPRES DU PREMIER MINISTRE. Bulletin officiel (no. 1965).

1963*　FRANCE. MINISTERE DU SAHARA, DES DEPARTEMENTS D'OUTRE-MER ET DES TERRITOIRES D'OUTRE-MER. Bulletin officiel. F 1960 - Je 1962// Paris. Semi-monthly.

Supersedes FRANCE. MINISTRE DELEGUE AUPRES DU PREMIER MINISTRE (no. 1965) and similarly arranged. Superseded by FRANCE. MINISTRE D'ETAT CHARGE DES DEPARTEMENTS, ETC. (no. 1964).

1964*　FRANCE. MINISTRE D'ETAT CHARGE DES DEPARTEMENTS ET DES TERRITOIRES D'OUTRE-MER. Bulletin officiel. Jl 1962 - 1967+. Paris. Semi-monthly.

Laws and Statutes for overseas territories and departments. Supersedes FRANCE. MINISTERE DU SAHARA, DES DEPARTEMENTS D'OUTRE-MER ET DES TERRITOIRES D'OUTRE-MER. Bulletin officiel (no. 1963).

1965* FRANCE. MINISTRE DELEGUE AUPRES DU PREMIER MINISTRE. Bulletin officiel. 1959 - F 1960// Paris. Semi-monthly.

Supersedes FRANCE. MINISTERE DU SAHARA. Bulletin officiel (no. 1962) and contains laws and statutes for Sahara (Pt. 1) for overseas departments (Pt. 2) and general texts (Pt. 3). Superseded by FRANCE. MINISTERE DU SAHARA... (no. 1963).

1966* FRANCE. SECRETARIAT GENERAL DU GOUVERNEMENT. DIRECTION DE LA DOCUMENTATION. INSTITUT NATIONAL DE LA STATISTIQUE ET DES ETUDES ECONOMIQUES. Bulletin hebdomadaire de statistique. 1949 - D 1964// Paris. Weekly.

1967 FRANCE. SENAT. 1958 - Comptes-rendus des débats. D 1958 - 1967+. Paris. Imprimerie des journaux officiels. Part of Journal officiel. ML

1968 France actuelle. A fortnightly report for Americans on modern France and the French Union. Ag 1958 - 1967+. Paris. Comité France actuelle. In English.

1969 France-Algérie. Ja 1964 - 1967+. Paris. Monthly. Association France-Algérie.

Semi-official organ for cultural cooperation.

1969a France - Eurafrique. N 1966 - 1967+. Paris. Monthly. Supersedes Communauté France-Eurafrique (no. 1893).

1970 France-Forum. F 1957 - D 1960; F 1964 - 1967+. Paris. Monthly.

Loosely connected with M.R.P., and serving as forum for political and economic issues.

1971 France horizon. Organe officiel de l'Association nationale des Français d'Afrique du Nord et d'outremer et leurs amis. S/O 1962 - 1967+. Paris. Monthly.

1972 France indépendante. 1954 - N 1962// Paris. Centre national des Indépendants et Paysans. Weekly. Superseded by Journal des Indépendants (no. 1996).

1973 France nouvelle. Hebdomadaire central du Parti communiste français. 1959 - 1967+. Paris. Weekly.

For special issues, see nos. 804, 805.

1974 France-Observateur. 1951 - N 1964. Paris// Weekly. Title changed to Nouvel observateur (no. 2021).

General information magazine with leftist orientation.

FOR FRANCE-SOIR, PARIS, SEE NEWSPAPERS ON MICROFILM LIST

1975 France today. S 1961 - D 1962// New York. Monthly. American Committee for France and Algeria. Superseded by Today in France (no. 2114).

Edited by B. Protter. Anti-Gaullist, pro-French Algeria, in close touch with Soustelle.

1976 France-U.R.S.S. 1951 - 1967+. Paris. Monthly.

Organ of France-U.R.S.S., a group favorable to Franco-Soviet rapprochement, with Gaullist, Socialist, and Communist members.

1977 Fraternité française; la tribune de Pierre Poujade. 1956 - 1967+. Paris-St. Céré. Weekly. Union pour la défense des commerçants et artisans.

1978 Fraternité française matin; la tribune de Pierre Poujade. [Je - Jl 1958]. Limoges. Daily.

1979* Free Algeria. News bulletin. 1956 - 1959. New York. Weekly. Algerian Front of National Liberation.

1980 Gauche européenne; fédération et démocratie sociale. Ap 1954-Jl 1958// Paris. Monthly. Mouvement socialiste pour les états unis d'Europe. See also no. 1991.

1981* Hebdo-coopération. Mr 1963 - 1965. (On microfilm.). Algiers. Weekly.

Originally published as Cooperation by Association de Sauvegarde. Accords d'Evian. O 1963 - D 1964 entitled Coopération-hebdo, thereafter Hebdo-coopération. Organ of French settlers remaining in independent Algeria. Edited by R. A. Soyer.

1982 Hommes et organisations d'Afrique noire. 1963 - 1967+. Paris. Fortnightly. Documentation africaine.

1983 Horizon 80. Jl/Ag 1964 - Ap 1965// Paris. Monthly.

Organ for Gaston Defferre's presidential candidacy published by political club Horizon 80.

FOR L'HUMANITE, PARIS, SEE NEWSPAPERS ON MICROFILM LIST

1984 L'Humanité dimanche. Magazine du Parti Communiste français. D 1965 - 1967+. Paris. Weekly.

1985 Industries et travaux d'outremer. 1955 - 1967+. Paris. Monthly.

Economic development in French Union, French Community and African states.

1986 Information agricole. O 1961 - D 1967+. Paris. Fortnightly, monthly F 1966 on.

Organ of Fédération nationale des syndicats d'exploitants agricoles (F.N.S.E.A.).

1987 Informations catholiques internationales. [Je 1955 - 1967+]. Paris. Fortnightly.

1988 Interafrique presse. Bulletin hebdomadaire. F 1961 - 1967+. Paris. Weekly.

1989 Jeune Afrique. Hebdomadaire international. O 1960 - 1967+. Tunis. Called Afrique action (no separate file) until N 1961. Before 1962, often spokesman of Algerian nationalism. Follows closely North African political developments.

1990 Jeune Europe. Organisation européenne pour la formation d'un cadre politique sous la direction de Jean Thiriart. Je 1962-Ja 1967. Brussels. Weekly.

Supplemented by Europe combattante (no. 1940). Supersedes Nation Europe Ja 1963 (no. 2011).

1991 Jeune gauche. Organe des Jeunes de la Gauche européenne. Ap - Ag 1963. Paris. Bi-monthly. See also no. 1008.

1992 Jeune république. Tribune de la gauche française. [My 1957 - 1967+]. Paris. Bi-monthly.

Organ of Jeune République splinter group which failed to merge with Parti d'union de la gauche socialiste.

1993 Jeune révolution. O - N 1963. Clandestine. Weekly. Conseil national de la révolution. Directoire révolutionnaire provisoire. Organisation de l'armée secrète.

1994　Jeunes travailleurs. S/O 1964 - Ja/F 1965. Paris. Bi-monthly. Centre national d'information d'études et d'action sociale pour les jeunes travailleurs.

Semi-official information center for young workers on employment and vocational training.

1995　Jeunesse an 2000. Culture et loisirs. O 1965 - 1967+. Paris. Monthly.

1996　Journal des indépendants. L'Hebdomadaire du Centre national des indépendants et des paysans. O 1963 - 1967+. Paris. Weekly. Supersedes France indépendante (no. 1972).

1997　Justice. Hebdomadaire du Parti communiste martiniquais. [1964 - 1967]. Fort-de-France.

1998　La Lettre. D 1959 - 1967+. Paris. Monthly. Supersedes Le Bulletin.

Leftist Catholic organ on international relations, aid to former colonies, liberalization within Church.

1999　Luttes; organe de combat des Jeunesses Socialistes S. F. I. O. 1952 - O 1957; 1961 - Ja 1963. Paris. Irregular-fortnightly.

2000　Maghreb. Documents Algérie, Maroc, Tunisie. 1964 - 1967+. Paris. Published jointly by Fondation nationale des sciences politiques's Centre d'étude des relations internationales and France. Direction de la documention.

2001*　MAISON DES AGRICULTEURS FRANÇAIS D'ALGERIE. Bulletin d'information. 1964 - 1967+. Paris. Monthly.

Organ of French repatriates from Algeria.

2002　Marchés tropicaux et méditerranéens. 1945 - 1954; D 1961, S 1964; 1966 - 1967+. Paris. Weekly.

FOR LE MONDE, PARIS, SEE NEWSPAPERS ON MICROFILM LIST

2003　Le Monde. Sélection hebdomadaire. D 1958 - 1967+. Paris. Weekly.

Important articles selected from daily paper with excellent coverage of domestic and international developments.

2004　Le Monde ouvrier. S 1956 - D 1957// Paris. Weekly. Mouvement de libération du peuple.

Superseded by Tribune du peuple (no. 2117), published by Parti d'Union de la Gauche Socialiste, with which Mouvement de libération du peuple merged.

2005*　El Moudjahid; organe central du Front de libération nationale algérienne, la révolution par le peuple et pour le peuple. Ag 1957 - Je 1959 (2. ed.); Je 1961 - Ap 1962. Clandestine, Tunis? Distr. in New York. 1 - 2 issues monthly.

In French. Supersedes Résistance algérienne (no 2067). For Arabic edition, see al-Mujahid (no. 2009). See also Le Combattant (no. 1889) issued concurrently and also titled Moudjahid.

2006*　MOUVEMENT FEDERALISTE EUROPEEN. PARIS. Bulletin européen d'informations. My 1958 - Ja 1959. Paris. Bi-monthly.

2007　MOUVEMENT NATIONAL ALGERIEN. Bulletin d'information. Jl 1960. Algiers (?)

Discusses Mouvement national algérien's rôle in peace negotiations. See also no. 2066.

2008　Le Mouvement social. Bulletin trimestriel de l'Institut français d'histoire sociale. 1953 - Jl/S 1960 (on microfilm); O 1960/Mr 1961; Jl/S 1962 - 1967+. Paris. Quarterly.

For 1951 - 1960 table of contents, see no. 1816.

2009*　al-Mujahid. Ag 1957 - Ap 1962. Tunis. Arabic edition of El-Moudjahid. See no. 2005.

2010　La Nation. [S 1962 - 1967+]. Paris. Daily. Union pour la nouvelle république. Supersedes Courrier de la nouvelle république (no. 1901).

2011*　Nation Europe; pour une Europe de Brest à Bucarest. Jl 1960 - D 1962// Brussels. Weekly. Also published under title Europe-Afrique and Belgique-Afrique, Nation-Belgique.

Edited by Jean Thiriart. Disseminated clandestine O. A. S. material. Superseded by Jeune Europe (no. 1990). See also no. 1834.

2012　La Nation européenne. O/D 1965 - N 1966. Paris. Monthly.

Edited by French sympathizers of Jean Thiriart (see no. 1990). European nationalist views.

2013　La Nation française. Ag 1961 - F 1963. Paris. Weekly.

Edited by Pierre Boutang. See also nos. 1311, 1312. Forum for both Gaullist and anti-Gaullist French nationalism.

2014　La Nation socialiste; organe du Mouvement communiste démocratique et national. My 1956 - D 1962// Paris. Monthly.

Edited by Auguste Lecoeur (see no. 1108).

FOR NEW YORK HERALD TRIBUNE, PARIS, SEE NEWSPAPERS ON MICROFILM LIST

2015　La Nef; revue mensuelle. 1961 - 1967+. Paris. ML

Quarterly since 1960. For special issues see nos. 1317-1319.

2016　Notes et études documentaires. 1945 - 1967+. Paris. Bi-daily. France. Direction de la documentation.

Monographs on French and foreign affairs, with selected national and international texts and diplomatic documents. Supplemented by fortnightly Chronologie internationale (no. 1880). For index, see nos. 1913, 1914.

2017　Notes rapides sur la situation économique en France et à l'étranger. 1960 - 1967+. Paris. Institut nationale de la statistique et des études économiques. Monthly.

Published by France. Direction de la documentation.

2018　Notre république; organe de l'Union démocratique du travail. [S 1959 - 1967+]. Paris. Fortnightly.

Continued as separate organ even after U. N. R. -U. D. T. merger in 1963.

2019　Le Nouveau Candide. My 1961 - 1967+. Paris. Weekly.

Pro-Gaullist general information magazine.

2020　Nouveaux cahiers. Revue d'études et de libres débats publiée sous les auspices de l'Alliance Israélite universelle. S/N 1965. Paris.

2021　Le Nouvel observateur. N 1964 - 1967+. Paris. Weekly. Supersedes France-observateur (no. 1974).

General information magazine often close to P. S. U.

2022　La Nouvelle critique; revue du marxisme militant. D 1950 - 1967+. Index 1958. Paris. Monthly.

Closely tied to Parti communiste français and concerned with Marxist theory.

138

2023 Nouvelle frontière. My 1963 - 1967+. Paris. Quarterly.

Gaullist views on national and international affairs, though not directly tied to U.N.R.

2024 La Nouvelle revue française d'outre-mer. 1952 - Ag/O 1958. Paris. Monthly. Comité central français pour l'outre-mer. Superseded by Communautés et continents (no. 1894).

2025 Nouvelles européennes et mondiales. Ed. A F, Mr 1958; Jl - S 1959; Ed. B [Je 1959 - Mr 1960]. Paris. Fortnightly.

Newsletter on international affairs.

2026 L'Observation économique. 1954 - D 1960// Paris. Monthly. Institut d'observation économique. Absorbed 1961 by L'Observation économique-financière (no. 2027).

2027 L'Observation économique-financière. 1961 - D 1965. Paris. Monthly. Institut d'observation économique.

2028 L'Observation financière. D 1953 - D 1960// Paris. Monthly. Institut d'observation économique. Superseded by L'Observation économique-financière (no. 2027).

2029 L'ordre français. 1956 - Jl/Ag 1963. Paris. Monthly.

Traditional nationalist orientation.

2030* ORGANISATION COMMUNE DES REGIONS SAHARIENNES. SERVICE DES RELATIONS PUBLIQUES ET DE L'INFORMATION. Bulletin. S 1961 - F 1962. Paris. Monthly.

Semi-official organization concerned with Saharan development.

2031* ORGANISATION COMMUNE DES REGIONS SAHARIENNES. SERVICE STATISTIQUE. Statistiques. [1961 - 1962]. Paris. Monthly.

2032 L'Outre-mer africain. Ap 1958 - F 1959; My 1960 - F 1961// Paris. Irregular. Supplement to Economie (no. 1920).

2033 L'Ouvrier algérien; organe central de l'Union générale des travailleurs algériens. N 1958 - F 1962. Tunis. Monthly.

Began publ. in Algiers, following repression there publ. in France, then Tunisia.

2034 L'Ouvrier libre; cahiers mensuels d'information et d'étude. Je 1957 - S/D 1958. Paris. Bi-monthly.

Not affiliated with any trade union organization.

2035* PARTI SOCIALISTE (S.F.I.O). Arguments et ripostes; fiches socialistes. 1958 - F 1959. Paris. Monthly.

Issued in connection with party's election activities.

2036* PARTI SOCIALISTE (S.F.I.O.). Bulletin intérieur. 1947 - Ag 1958; 1959 - 1967+. Paris. Irregular.

Contains party's "rapports" to national congress. See nos. 1411, 1412.

2037* PARTI SOCIALISTE (S.F.I.O.). La documentation socialiste; bulletin hebdomadaire de la S.F.I.O. 1955 - D 1958; N 1959 - 1967+. Paris.

2038* PARTI SOCIALISTE UNIFIE. Le Courrier du PSU. S/O 1960 - 1967+. Paris. Monthly.

Contains texts of party congresses.

2039 Partisans. 1961 - 1967+. Paris. Bi-monthly. ML

Extreme leftist journal with special issues on such topics as education in France. Edited by François Maspero.

2040 Patrie et progrès. O 1962 - 1963. Paris. Irregular. Superseded by monthly page in Combat (no. 1885).

Organ of leftist Gaullist group by this name and edited by Jacques Gagliardi. For earlier issues, see no. 1442.

2041 Patronat français. N 1959 - 1967+. Paris. Monthly. Conseil national du patronat français.

2042 Penant. Revue de droit des pays d'Afrique. [1946 - D 1961]; Ja 1966 - 1967+. Boulogne-sur-Seine. Monthly.

2043 La Pensée; revue du rationalisme moderne. Mr/Ap 1950 - 1967+. Paris. Quarterly.

Closely tied to Communist Party and forum for Communist intellectuals and adademicians. Many articles on Marxism.

2044 Permanences. Organe de formation civique et d'action doctrinale selon le droit naturel et chrétien. Jl 1963 - 1967+. Paris. Monthly. Supersedes Verbe (no. 2125).

Organ of Cité catholique, a lay integrist Catholic group with highly conservative interpretation of Catholic dogma on social economic, and political issues. See also no. 1644.

2045 Perspective africaine; synthèses politiques et économiques. My 1959 - N 1963. Paris. Bi-monthly supplement to Bulletin de l'Afrique noire (no. 1854).

2046 Perspectives sahariennes; revue d'étude et de confrontation des problèmes africains. Je 1958 - Jl 1959// Rabat. Monthly.

Economic and political evolution in North Africa.

2047 Perspectives socialistes. Revue bimensuelle de l'Union de la gauche socialiste. Ja 1958 - 1967+. Paris.

Publ. continued independently after absorption of Union de la gauche socialiste into Parti socialiste unifié in 1960.

2048 Perspectives syndicalistes. Mensuel intersyndical édité par le G.E.D. interprofessionnel parisien groupant des militants de la C.G.T., de la C.F.T.C., de F.O., des Autonomes, et de la F.E.N. Je 1964, My 1965 - 1967+. Paris.

New approaches to socialism. Edited by Maurice Laudrain. (See also no. 1083.)

2049 Peuple européen. Le premier journal européen. S 1957 - Ag 1963. Lyons. Monthly. In French, Dutch, and Italian.

2050 Le Pied noir. Journal officiel d'information des rapatriés d'Afrique du Nord, d'outre-mer et leurs amis. F 1963 - 1967+. Paris. Monthly.

2051 Politique; revue internationale des doctrines et des institutions 1958 - 1967+. Paris. Annual. Académie internationale de science politique et d'histoire constitutionnelle. ML

Edited by Marcel Prélot. Mainly historical. Decennial table of contents in 1967 vol.

2052 Politique étrangère. D 1945 - 1967+. Paris. Bi-monthly. Centre d'études de politique étrangère.

2052a Le Populaire de Paris. Organe central du Parti socialiste. Ap 1966 - 1967+. Paris. Two issues a week, plus one monthly issue of Démocratie 66, 67, etc. (see no. 1910).

FOR LE POPULAIRE DE PARIS, PARIS, SEE ALSO NEWSPAPERS ON MICROFILM LIST

2053 Population. 1946 - 1967+. Paris. Quarterly. Institut national d'études démographiques. ML

2054 Positions. Etudes et documents pour l'action civique, familiale et sociale. [Ja 1960 - D 1962]; Je 1963 - 1967+. Moulins. Monthly.

Publication of political club by that name.

2055 Pourquoi? 1964 - 1967+. Paris. Monthly. Ligue de l'enseignement. Supersedes Action laïque (no. 1813).

Addressed to a wider audience than Action laïque.

2056 Présence africaine; revue culturelle du monde noir. Ap/Jl 1955 - 1967+. Paris. Bi-monthly.

In French and English. Index for 1947 - 1964.

2057 Preuves. Mr 1951 - 1967+. Paris. Monthly. Congress for cultural freedom.

2058 Les problèmes de l'Europe. [1958, 1960]. Paris-Rome.

1958 issues have texts of first and second meetings on "Problèmes de l'Europe." 1960 has text of 4th meeting, all dealing with European integration.

2059 Problèmes économiques. 1948 - 1967+. Paris. Weekly. France. Direction de la documentation.

Monographs on economic problems from French and foreign press.

2060 Programme communiste. Revue théorique du Parti communiste internationaliste. O 1957 - 1967+. Marseille-Paris. Quarterly. Monthly supplement entitled Le Prolétaire (no. 2062).

FOR LE PROGRES, LYON, SEE NEWSPAPERS ON MICROFILM LIST

2061 Projet. Civilisation, travail, économie. Ja 1966 - 1967+. Paris. Monthly. Supersedes Revue de l'action populaire (no. 2077).

2062 Le Prolétaire. Bulletin mensuel du Parti communiste internationaliste. Jl 1963 - 1967+. Paris. Comes as supplement to Programme communiste (no. 2060).

2063 Prospective. Publication du Centre d'études prospectives. Ap 1959, O 1961 - 1967+. Paris. 2 issues annually.

Center is directed by Bertrand de Jouvenel. See also no. 1227.

2064 Le Provençal. Journal des patriotes socialistes et républicains. Mr 1964 - O 1965. Marseille. Daily.

Publ. by Gaston Defferre. For evening ed. see Le Soir (no. 2102).

2065 Réalités, fémina-illustration. 1951 - 1967+. Paris. Monthly. ML

General information magazine.

2066 Réalités algériennes. Informationsdienst zum Algerienproblem. Ag 1960. Munich. In German.

Information about Mouvement national algérien, with July 1960 interview with Messali Hadj.

2067* Résistance algérienne; organe du Front de libération nationale algérienne, pour la défense de l'Afrique du Nord. Ed. B, [F - Jl 1957]; C, [D 1956 - Je 1957]. Clandestine. Monthly. Dist. in N.Y. In French and Arabic. Superseded by El-Moudjahid, August 1957 (no. 2005).

2068 Révolution africaine. 1963 - 1967+. Algiers. Weekly.

Organ of F. L. N. after independence.

2069 La Révolution prolétarienne; revue syndicale révolutionnaire. 1947 - Ja/F 1966. Paris. Fortnightly or monthly.

Not affiliated with major trade union organization, but representing anarcho-syndicalist tendencies.

2070 Revue; littérature, histoire, arts et sciences des deux mondes. 1948 - 1967+. Paris. Fortnightly. ML

2071 Revue africaine. Journal des travaux. 1856-1957, 1959 - 1962. Algiers. Quarterly. Société historique algérienne.

Algerian archeology, history and current social structure.

2072 Revue d'économie politique. 1887 - 1967+. Paris. Bi-monthly. ML

Includes descriptive articles on French economy.

2073 Revue d'histoire de la deuxième guerre mondiale. N 1950 - 1967+. Paris. Quarterly. Comité d'histoire de la deuxième guerre mondiale, Société de l'histoire de la guerre, Centre national de la recherche scientifique.

2074 Revue d'histoire économique et sociale. 1908 - 1967+. Paris. Quarterly. ML

Little current material.

2075 Revue d'histoire moderne et contemporaine. Jl/S 1957, Ap/Je 1959; Je/Mr 1960 - Jl/S 1961; 1954 - 1967+ in ML. Quarterly. Société d'histoire moderne.

2076 Revue de défense nationale. 1945 - 1967+. Paris. Monthly. Comité d'études de défense nationale.

Many high-ranking military figures are among contributors.

2077 Revue de l'action populaire. 1945 - D 1965// Paris. Monthly. Superseded by Project (no. 2061).

Political, social and economic questions from Catholic point of view. See also no. 522.

2078 Revue de la Méditerranée. Revue de pensée et d'information françaises. 1946 - 1961. Paris-Algiers. Quarterly.

Articles on French historical and literary subjects.

2079 Revue de Paris. 1901 - 1967+. Paris. Monthly. ML

General information magazine.

2080 Revue de science et de législation financière. 1953 - 1967+. Paris. Quarterly. ML

Includes survey of current economic legislation.

2081 Revue du droit public et de la science politique en France et à l'étranger. 1894 - 1967+. Paris. Bi-monthly. ML

Includes topical analysis of all current legislation and problems of administrative and constitutional law.

2082 Revue économique. 1957 - 1967+. Paris. Bi-monthly. ML

Published by VIe section de l'École Pratique des Hautes Etudes and Centre National de la Recherche Scientifique. Includes discussions on current economic issues and conditions.

2083 Revue française d'histoire d'outre-mer. 1913 - 1967+. Paris. Quarterly. Société française d'histoire d'outre-mer. 1932-1958 entitled Revue de l'histoire des colonies but not filed separately under that title.

2084 Revue française de science politique. 1952 - 1967+. Paris. Quarterly. ML

Published jointly by Fondation nationale des sciences politiques and Association française de science politique. Each year one issue has bibliography of unpublished theses on political science. (See no. 648) and all issues have excellent bibliographies on French politics. Special issue on Fifth Republic June 1963.

2085 Revue française de sociologie. 1960 - 1967+. Paris. Quarterly. Centre d'études sociologiques, Centre National de la Recherche Scientifique. ML

Important source of studies on French society.

2086 Revue historique. 1876 - 1967+. Paris. Quarterly. ML

Only material on historiography is contemporary.

2087 Revue historique de l'armée. S 1960 - 1967+. Paris. Quarterly. France. Ministère de la guerre.

2088 Revue juridique et politique de l'Union française. 1951 - D 1958. Paris. Quarterly. Superseded by Revue juridique et politique d'Outre-mer (not at Hoover) and in turn by Revue juridique et politique -- indépendance et coopération (no. 2088a).

2088a Revue juridique et politique -- indépendance et coopération. 1966 - 1967+. Paris. Quarterly.

2089 La Revue libérale. 1954 - D 1962. Paris. Quarterly.

Articles on non-political topics.

2090 Revue politique et parlementaire. 1894 - 1967+. Paris. Bi-monthly. ML

Important source for articles on current political issues by centrist parliamentarians. Lists all parliamentary documents.

2091 La Revue socialiste. 1946 - 1967+. Paris. Monthly.

Parti socialiste's forum for economic and political discussion.

2092 Rivarol; hebdomadaire de l'opposition nationale. D 1954 - 1967+. Paris. Weekly.

Nationalist orientation.

2093 Saturne. Ap/My 1958, Ja/Mr 1959. Brussels. Commission internationale contre le régime concentrationnaire.

Issues protesting Algerian war atrocities.

2094* SECRETARIAT SOCIAL D'ALGER. Information rapide. 1958 - Ap/Je 1959. Algiers. Irregular.

Looseleaf folders on social services and social policy in Algeria.

2095 Seine-Visconti. Journal de la cellule Visconti (Paris VIe) du Parti communiste français. [My 1965 - 1967+]. Paris. Weekly.

2096 SOCIETE D'ETUDES ET DE DOCUMENTATION ECONOMIQUES, INDUSTRIELLES ET SOCIALES. Bulletin SEDEIS. N - D 1964. Paris.

Edited by Bertrand de Jouvenel.

2097 SOCIETE D'HISTOIRE MODERNE. Bulletin. [1959 - 1960]. Paris.

2098 SOCIETE D'HISTOIRE NATURELLE DE L'AFRIQUE DU NORD. Bulletin. 1909 - D 1960. Algiers. Bi-monthly.

Society's main concern is Algerian agriculture.

2099 SOCIETE D'HISTOIRE NATURELLE DE L'AFRIQUE DU NORD. Mémoires. 1956 - 1961. Algiers. Annual.

Studies on Algerian plant life.

2100 SOCIETE DES AGRICULTEURS D'ALGERIE. Bulletin 1927 - Ap 1959/Je 1961. Algiers.

2101 Sociologie du travail. 1959 - 1967+. Paris. Quarterly. ML

Questions of industrial relations and trade unionism.

2102 Le Soir (evening ed.). Organe républicain quotidien. Mr 1964 - Ja 1967. Marseille. Evening ed. of Le Provençal (no. 2064).

2103 Sondages. Revue française de l'opinion publique. Mr 1951 - 1967+. Paris. Quarterly. Institut français d'opinion publique.

Each issue reports results of a public opinion poll by the I. F. O. P., many of them on political attitudes.

2104 Stratégie. Ag 1964 - 1967+. Paris. Quarterly. Centre d'études de politique étrangère. Institut français d'études stratégiques.

Discussions on military and foreign policy representative of official views. Edited by General André Beaufre.

2105 Syndicalisme. 1950 - 1967+. Paris. Weekly.

Organ of Confédération française des travailleurs chrétiens. Monthly "Magazine."

2106 Table ronde. 1948 - 1967+. Paris. Monthly. ML
General information magazine.

2107 Tam. Bimensuel des forces armées. Ag 1962 - Mr 1964. Paris. Weekly. Supersedes Bled; hebdomadaire militaire d'information (no. 1848).

2108 Tam-Tam. Revue des étudiants catholiques africains. D 1963-1967+. Paris. Quarterly.

2109 Le Télégramme de Paris. D 1955 - My/Je 1962. (On microfilm.) Paris. Monthly.

Published by Gaullist youth group active in bringing de Gaulle back to power. Editor Jacques Dauer headed Front du progrès and Mouvement pour la coopération en Algérie, Gaullist groups outside U. N. R. strongly favorable to de Gaulle's action in Algeria. See also nos. 434, 435.

2110 Témoignages et documents. Le journal qui publie les textes saisis et interdits. 1958 - Ap 1963// Paris. Irregular. Centre d'information et de coordination pour la défense des libertés et de la paix.

Important documentary source on Algerian war and opposition to war.

2111 Temps modernes. 1945 - 1967+. Paris. Monthly. ML

Leftist orientation. Edited by J.-P. Sartre. See also no. 260a.

2112 La Terre; hebdomadaire paysan du Parti communiste français. Jl 1961 - 1967+. Paris. Weekly.

2113 Terres australes et antarctiques françaises. 1959 - 1967+. Paris. Quarterly. France. Direction de la documentation.

2113a Tiers-monde; problèmes des pays sous-développés. 1960 - 1967+. Paris. Quarterly.

Edited by François Perroux.

2114   Today in France. 1963 - 1967+. New York. Monthly.

       Continues France Today (no. 1975). Edited by B. Protter. Organ of Society for French-American Affairs.

2115   Le travailleur européen; organe mensuel des Travailleurs européens pour les Etats-unis d'Europe. N 1956 - Jl 1958, 4th quarter 1962, 1st quarter 1963. Paris. Monthly, quarterly.

2116   Tribune des nations. 1956 - 1967+. Paris. Weekly. ML General information newspaper.

2117   Tribune du peuple. D 1957 - Ap 1960// Paris. Weekly. Parti d'union de la gauche socialiste. Supersedes Monde ouvrier (no. 2004). Superseded by Tribune socialiste (no. 2118).

2118   Tribune socialiste; hebdomadaire du Parti socialiste unifié. Ap 1960 - 1967+. Paris. Weekly. Supersedes Tribune du peuple (no. 2117) and merged with two other papers, Tribune du communisme and Tribune du socialisme, not at Hoover.

2119   U. S. /France report. Mr 1962 - Ag 1964// New York. Monthly. American Committee for France and Algeria. Anti-Gaullist publication with special emphasis on Algeria. Edited by Samuel Blumenfeld. See also nos. 1975, 2114.

2120* UNION DEMOCRATIQUE ET SOCIALISTE DE LA RESISTANCE. Bulletin hebdomadaire d'information et de liaison. D 1957, Ap - S 1958. Paris.

2121* UNION NATIONALE DES ETUDIANTS DE FRANCE. UNEF informations. [1961 - 1963]. Paris.

       Individual issues on current events, cultural questions, youth, internal organization, etc.

2122   UNION POUR LA NOUVELLE REPUBLIQUE. DELEGATION NATIONALE AUX RELATIONS PUBLIQUES. Bulletin de presse. Ap - N 1959// Paris. Continued as Courrier de la nouvelle république (no. 1901).

2123   Unir-débat. Pour le socialisme. 1967+. Paris. monthly. Supersedes Débat communiste (no. 1906).

2124   Union et défense. N 1956 - O 1957. Capdenac (Aveyron). Irregular. Union de défense des commerçants et artisans.

2125   Verbe. Revue mensuelle. [1950 - 1960]; Mr 1961-My 1963// Paris. Centre international de formation civique et d'action doctrinale selon le droit naturel et chrétien.

       Organ of Cité catholique, a lay (integrist) Catholic group defending extremely conservative interpretation of dogma in political, social, and economic issues. Superseded by Permanences (no. 2044). See also no. 1644.

2126   Vérité-Liberté. Cahiers d'information sur la guerre d'Algérie. My 1960 - F/Mr 1962// Paris. Irregular.

       Important documentary source on Algerian war and opposition to war. See also no. 381a.

2127   Vérités sur l'Algérie et le Sahara. Je - S, N 1960. Paris. Monthly. Centre d'information pour les problèmes de l'Algérie et du Sahara.

       Edited by Jacques Soustelle and organ for opposition to Gaullist Algerian policy.

2128   Le XXe siècle fédéraliste. 1952 - D 1962. Paris. Fortnightly.

       Articles on European integration as well as French and international political affairs.

2129   Vive la France. Organe de combat de l'armée nationale secrète. [S 1961 - S 1962]. Clandestine.

       O. A. S. publication.

2130   Vive le Léninisme. no. 1-3 1962. Paris. Albanian Embassy, Paris. See also no. 1931a.

2131   Voici pourquoi; bi-mensuel d'actualité nationale. D 1957 - Ap 1961// Paris.

       Edited by Jacques Soustelle and organ for defenders of French Algeria, first Gaullist, later strongly anti-Gaullist.

2132   La voie communiste. Organe mensuel de l'opposition communiste. S 1960 - D 1964// Paris.

       Includes Bulletin de liaison for Oct. 1963.

2133   La Voix de l'espérance. Jl 1959 - Mr 1962. Paris.

       Fundamentalist Protestant organ reproducing texts of radio broadcasts.

2134   La Voix de l'Occident. Je 1962 - 1963. Lisbon, Portugal. Monthly.

       French nationalists in exile, notably Ploncard d'Assac. See also nos. 89, 90. Texts were originally broadcast on Lisbon radio, of which Assac is editorialist.

                  Newspapers on microfilm, 1956 -

These newspapers are available through Interlibrary Loan from the Center of Research Libraries, Chicago.

       Combat. Paris.

       La Croix. Paris.

       Dépêche du Midi. Toulouse.

       Le Figaro. Paris.

       Force ouvrière. Paris.

       France-Soir. Paris.

       L'Humanité. Paris.

       Le Monde. Paris.

       New York Herald-Tribune. Paris.

       Le Populaire de Paris. Paris.

       Le Progrès. Lyon.

FOR NEWSPAPERS ON MICROFILM, SEE ALSO FRENCH FIFTH REPUBLIC COLLECTION, NO. 811(e) - (g).

Subject Index

See Introduction for discussion of most important subject headings. Unless specified, all headings refer to France under the Fifth Republic.

ADMINISTRATION, GOVERNMENTAL, 163, 425, 757, 1066, 1070, 1534; accounting methods, 1744; administrative law, 329, 739a, 739b, 1082, 2081; bibliographies, 645, 648, 1066; civil service, 163, 905, 1166, 1534; constitutional provisions, 163, 1082; directory, 763; education, 423; elections (see Préfecture de la Seine; Préfectures of other departments); executive responsibilities, 1352; fiscal affairs, 66, 948; foreign affairs, 16, 128, 216, 227a; information services, 227a, 313, 748, 901; military establishment, 207; ministries and other divisions, 763; planning, 907; police and secret services, 295, 384, 841, 1179, 1298, 1319, 1525, 1576; public opinion of, 313; recruitment, 1166; regional and departmental units, 746, 756, 907; reorganization, 907, 1070; repatriation aid, 342; research on, 1066; social services, 758, 760, 1076

ADVERTISING MEDIA, 1618

AFRICA, FRENCH. See Africa: serials; Assistance, technical and economic: Africa; Decolonization; French Community; French Union; individual states

AFRICA: serials, 1810, 1817, 1818, 1819, 1842, 1843, 1854, 1860, 1861, 1881, 1894, 1897, 1942, 1959-1961, 1969a, 1982, 1985, 1988, 1989, 2002, 2032, 2042, 2045, 2056, 2069, 2088

AFRICA, NORTH: agricultural and economic conditions, 516, 836; education, 370, 892; French cultural impact, 892, 1461; political developments, 815, 835, 908, 938, 1128, 1989; serials, 1820, 1933, 1989, 2000, 2046; trade unions, 1472. See also Algeria; Decolonization: Morocco; Decolonization: Tunisia

AFRICAN NATIONALISM, 603, 816, 819, 821, 956, 1098, 1487; and French counterterrorism, 956, 1013

AFRICAN PRESS: French language, 787

AFRICANS IN FRANCE, 578, 1197. See also Students, African

AFRICANS, NORTH IN FRANCE. See Algerians in France; Immigrants, North African

AGRICULTURE, 442, 444, 527, 642, 660, 686, 871, 1162, 1226, 1355, 1540, 1771, 1800; Gaullist policy, 300, 442, 686, 749, 871, 1042, 1226, 1771; and repatriates from Algeria, 1001, 2001; serials, 1986, 2001, 2112. See also Organizations, agricultural; Political parties: peasant; Rural life; Social groups: farmers

ALGERIA, 36, 60, 69, 743a, 1303; administration, 29, 36, 391, 891a; administration, judicial, 391, 1754a; Arab glossary, 231, 231a, 1036; bibliographies, 60, 580, 934, 1128; budget, 24; civilization, 231, 231a, 234, 497, 975, 1046, 1423, 1588, 1609, 1610, 2071 (see also Algeria: sociological studies); constitutional law, 1336, 1763; culture (French), 892; description, 31, 516, 673, 795, 796, 1037, 1048, 1278, 1549, 1676, 1699; economic policy (see Algeria: Gaullist policy; Fourth Republic: Algerian policy); education (see Algeria: social conditions, education); elections (see Algeria: political developments, elections); government propaganda, 23, 25-27, 31, 32, 34, 673, 674, 743a, 743b, 781, 795, 796, 811(a), 1699, 1822; government publications, 743a, 743b, 781, 794, 795 (see also ALGERIA in Part I and II; Algerian war: peace agreement, documents); industrialization (see Algeria: economic development); laws and statutes, 28, 30, 68, 1729, 1823, 1830 (see also Algeria: independence, laws and statutes; Algeria, post-independence: laws and statutes); literature, 540, 626, 892, 1471; maps, 30, 231; organizations, 1604-1610, 1676, 2071, 2098-2100 (see also Algeria: political parties); pictorial works, 23, 27, 32, 288, 795, 796, 1280, 1699; political institutions, 891a, 1763; political parties, 1345, 1486, 1493 (see also Parti communiste algérien in Author Index); population, 1549, 1605; press, 811(d), 811(f), 1434, 1822, 1924, 1926 (see also Algeria, post-independence: press; Algerian revolution: press); radio-television, 65, 1122, 1461, 1828; resettlement centers (see Algerian war: pacification program, resettlement centers); Sahara (see Sahara); social reforms, 26, 28; sociological studies, 231, 231a, 234, 495-497, 602, 603, 1274, 1327, 1520, 1562, 1609, 1610, 1629, 1700-1701, 1713, 2071; statistics, 23, 35, 36, 1549; trade unions, 1472, 1730, 2033; transportation and communications, 1424; workers, 1713; youth, 1604

-- agriculture: 231a, 516, 1001, 1084, 1676, 1699, 2098-2100; bibliography, 966; reform of, 966, 1061

-- economic conditions: 25, 618, 619, 674, 836, 863, 1358, 1424, 1588, 1604, 1606, 1740, 1759, 1822, 1826, 1831; bibliography, 1472; employment, 1713; investments, 259, 1424 (see also Algeria: economic development; Constantine Plan); Kabylia, 1274; statistics, 23, 24, 36, 720

-- economic development: 25, 29, 30, 259, 539, 579, 584, 678, 863, 926, 928, 966, 1061, 1358, 1606, 1608-1610, 1629, 1751, 1822; bibliography, 1061; micro-industry, 1606

-- European settlers: 125, 252, 499, 566, 1016, 1327, 1470, 1523, 1555, 1702, 1740; and Catholic Church, 547, 1470, 1924; contributions to economy, 535, 1001, 1140, 1280, 1483, 1523, 1676; employment, 353; exodus (see Algeria: independence, exodus); legal status, 45, 305, 468, 474 (see also Algerian question: minority problem); and Moslem Community, 1607; personal narratives and fiction, 499, 566, 1217; political attitudes, 456, 1120, 1318, 1327, 1474; population composition, 1268, 1523; press (see Algeria: press); pro-independence, 602, 1529, 1926; social conditions, 1822

-- Gaullist policy: 68, 116, 117, 120, 242, 353, 937, 942, 966, 1026, 1119, 1183, 1211, 1303, 1336, 1454, 1493, 1529, 1568, 1587, 1595, 1668, 1822, 2109; documents, 24, 29, 30, 428, 793; opposition to (pre-1962), 331, 365, 631, 984, 1015, 1568, 1648, 1650, 1652, 1716, 1863, 2127, 2131; opposition to (1962-), 52, 166, 224, 239, 312a, 332, 596, 879, 1304, 1306, 1325, 1651, 1655, 1657 (see also Algerian war: opposition to); personal narratives, 261, 1681. See also Fifth Republic: Algerian policy; Gaulle, Charles de: political philosophy, Algeria

-- history: 160, 562, 618, 661, 835, 881, 893, 1022, 1037, 1046, 1170, 1181, 1325, 1336; colonial and pre-colonial period, 2, 65, 224, 231, 234, 975, 1048, 1280, 1330, 1523, 1562, 1563, 2071; documents, 618; Kabylia, 1274

-- independence: 50, 51, 440, 510, 988, 989, 995; cooperation with France, 1438; economic prospects, 1438; exodus of European settlers and pro-French Moslems, 143, 222a, 223, 224, 498, 499, 637, 1217, 1325, 1440, 1458 (see also Algerian war: final months of violence; Repatriation); laws and statutes, 1824; social reforms, 1438. See also Algeria, post-independence; Algerian war: final months of violence

--political developments: 69, 160, 176a, 240, 242, 337, 434, 606, 908, 928, 995, 1119, 1120, 1128, 1170, 1181, 1229, 1230, 1233, 1305, 1345, 1349, 1351, 1554, 1710, 2046; chronology, 335, 870, 1229, 1230; elections and referenda, 46, 337, 476, 478, 783, 1120, 1345, 1493, 1763; Fourth Republic, 330, 1086, 1122, 1647. See also Algeria: Gaullist policy; Fourth Republic: Algerian policy

-- political developments 1958, May/June: 242, 337, 443, 456, 523, 542, 628-630, 811(a), 811(d), 870, 1016, 1079, 1113, 1119, 1348, 1351, 1486, 1568, 1710; bibliography, 443; documents, 870, 1113, 1348, 1486, 1508, 1707, 1710; personal narratives, 1054, 1345, 1626, 1716; in press (Algerian), 811(f), 1434. See also Fifth

Republic: inception, Algerian crisis; Fifth Republic: inception, personal narratives

-- political developments 1960, January (Barricades): 242, 245, 312a, 585, 607, 995, 1233, 1345, 1533, 1625, 1681, 1703; in Algerian press, 1434. See also Trials, political: Barricades

-- political developments 1961, April (Generals' Putsch): 121, 198, 199, 240, 261, 401, 566, 614, 995, 1026, 1233, 1488, 1568, 1581, 1681; in Algerian press, 1434. See also Trials, political: Generals' Putsch

-- political figures: European settlers, 111, 245, 330, 585, 607, 1054, 1091, 1112, 1345, 1493, 1554, 1625, 1626, 1711 (see also Algerian question: pro-French-Algerian polemics); non-European, 222a-224, 1493 (see also Algerian nationalism: leadership; Algerian revolution: leadership)

-- political reforms: Fifth Republic, 1763; Fourth Republic, 26, 330, 674

-- social conditions: 288, 1604-1608, 1740, 1829, 2094; Centres Sociaux, 627, 1700; education, 29, 36, 370, 626, 888, 1604, 1609; housing, 35, 1468; new settlements, 231a, 1468

ALGERIA, POST-INDEPENDENCE, 60, 264, 576, 661, 835, 893, 968, 1012, 1205, 1543; agreements with France, 745; agriculture, 231a, 1440, 1543, 1677; bibliography, 893; chronology, 440; Communist influence and support, 264, 1205; documents, 1156, 1543, 2000; economic conditions, 1831; economic development, 1005, 1440; economic reforms, 73, 307, 311, 1005, 1156, 1677; education and culture, 892, 893, 1440, 1543; European minority, 893, 1306, 1742, 1981; expropriation of French property, 520, 917; foreign relations, 264, 658, 835; and French public opinion, 50, 893, 1075, 1318; laws and statutes, 520, 1824, 1825; opposition to government, 14a, 225; political developments, 14a, 50, 51, 222a, 234a, 264, 311, 440, 603, 920, 921, 968, 995, 1012, 1046, 1219, 1233, 1306, 1475, 1543, 1989; political institutions, 51, 264, 1012; press, 893, 968, 1821, 1981, 2069; social conditions, 1278. See also Algeria: independence

-- French aid and cooperation: 214, 307, 349, 745, 893, 952, 1440, 1751, 1969; failure of, 214, 222a, 264, 1655, 1657

ALGERIAN COMMUNIST PARTY. See Parti communiste algérien in Author Index

ALGERIAN NATIONALISM, 4, 6, 7, 9, 14a, 44, 227, 437, 467, 817, 819, 820, 823, 1347, 1489, 1588; bibliography, 1068; Communist influence, 59, 224, 456, 1112, 1347 (see also Algerian revolution: Communist support); history, 2, 160, 311, 873, 937, 1048, 1068, 1128, 1181, 1205, 1219, 1330, 1347, 1475 (see also Algerian revolution: history); Kabylia's rôle, 1274; leadership, 2, 51, 225, 874, 1050, 1219, 1309, 1347, 1933; literary works, 874 (see also Algeria: literature); organizations, 865, 974, 1289, 1472, 1934, 2007, 2066 (see also Algerian revolution: political institutions); resistance to French civilization, 1562. See also Political trials: Algerian nationalists

ALGERIAN QUESTION, 160, 206, 272, 515, 627, 644, 671, 881, 1249, 1268, 1336, 1452, 1587, 1700-1703; and Arab states, 72; bibliographies, 266, 471, 580, 583; constitutional aspects, 1336; economic aspects, 39, 83, 152, 320, 504, 658, 726a, 1155, 1268, 1429, 1582, 1759; and French political life, 68, 76, 79, 261, 337, 438, 606,811(a), 879, 1041, 1239, 1273, 1295, 1454, 1637 (see also Fifth Republic: Algerianconflict; Fourth Republic: Algerian policy); and French political parties, 68, 428, 434, 529, 809, 1295 (see also Parti communiste français: Algerian policy; Parti socialiste: Algerian policy; Union pour la nouvelle république: Algerian policy); and French public opinion, 68, 900, 1238, 1295; integration, 337, 504, 542, 582, 631, 1091, 1092, 1099, 1548, 1562, 1587, 1647, 1649, 1716; minority problem, 45, 305, 305a, 353, 468, 474, 825, 1607; pro-French-Algerian polemics, 111, 152, 153, 177, 206, 224, 274, 365, 414, 451, 452, 456, 529, 535, 631, 1092, 1099, 1122, 1191, 1216, 1270, 1273, 1427, 1483, 1759, 2131 (see also Algeria: Gaullist policy, opposition to); pro-independence polemics, 83, 1273, 1577, 1587, 1753, 1933 (see also Algerian nationalism); sociological aspects, 231, 1562; and United Nations, 42, 43, 57, 72, 382, 466, 865, 990, 1229, 1230, 1249, 1463, 1464, 1579

-- political solutions: 111, 175, 472, 543, 594, 884, 910, 938, 951, 1091, 1236, 1249, 1529, 1719; communal reform, 1759; electoral reform, 542, 1652; federalism, 197, 1093, 1158; partition, 52, 482, 486, 1098, 1121, 1445

ALGERIAN REFUGEES. See Algerian war: refugees

ALGERIAN REVOLUTION, abbreviations, 1333; and African nationalism, 816, 819, 821, 1989; bibliographies, 266, 580; British support, 658, 659; causes, 61, 658, 1327, 1629; chronology, 618; Communist support and influence, 59, 224, 456, 604, 658, 659, 964, 1347, 1364, 1589; counterterrorism by Europeans, 1013; cultural impact, 602, 603 (see also Algerian war: cultural impact); documents, 266, 391, 618, 619, 818, 822, 988, 989, 992, 1035; French support, 213, 241, 260a, 266, 437, 602, 603, 876, 940, 1003, 1185 (see also Algerian war: opposition to; Trials, political: opponents of Algerian war); history, 9, 51, 242, 248, 337, 562, 604, 618, 619, 873, 874, 968, 1035, 1037, 1333, 1349 (see also Algerian nationalism: history); international aspects, 14a, 826, 1336, 1753, 1832 (see also Algerian question and United Nations; Algerian war: international aspects); Kabylia's rôle, 1274; leadership, 14a, 61, 248, 285, 401, 510, 528, 604, 874, 877, 990, 1194, 1219, 1349, 1702, 1803; military aspects, 37, 40, 41, 61, 248, 430, 528, 827, 1489, 1521, 1722; military organization (see Armée de la libération nationale in Author Index); pan-Arab support, 659, 964, 1654; pictorial works, 40, 41, 430, 903, 1521; political aims, 159, 808, 988, 989, 992, 1702; political institutions, 14a, 51, 159, 818, 822, 1037, 1832; press, 1832, 1889, 1979, 1989, 2025, 2009, 2033, 2067 (see also "El Moudjahid" in Title Index); tactics, 61, 424, 1718; U.S. support, 658, 659, 937; and youth, 1589. See also Algerian Front of National Liberation Delegation; Conseil national de la révolution algérienne; Delegation of the Provisional Government of the Algerian Republic, N.Y.; Front de libération nationale; Front de libération nationale. Fédération de France; Gouvernement provisoire de la république algérienne; Jabhat al-Tahrir al-Qawmi, in Author Index

ALGERIAN WAR, 176a, 337, 537, 543, 1041, 1196, 1230, 1318, 1333, 1349, 1366, 1702; abbreviations, 1333; bibliographies, 266, 471, 580, 1130; and Catholic Church (see Catholic Church and Algerian war); chronology, 52, 68, 1280; cultural impact, 231, 231a, 370, 602, 603, 1077b; documents, 85, 492, 1035, 1349, 1766, 2110, 2126; fiction, 252, 257, 343, 487, 566, 606, 970, 1003, 1020, 1077a, 1079, 1195, 1217, 1639; final months of violence, 143, 222a, 285, 484, 498, 499, 566, 627, 709, 1217, 1233, 1254, 1278, 1312, 1434, 1705, 1832 (see also Algeria: independence, exodus of European settlers; Organisation de l'armée secrète); and French political life (see Algerian question and French political life; Algerian war: opposition to; Fifth Republic: Algerian conflict); and French political parties (see Algerian question and French political parties); international aspects, 159, 164, 369, 382, 466, 590, 993, 1101, 1122, 1506, 1754a, 2093 (see also Algerian question and United Nations; Algerian revolution: international aspects); military and administrative directives, 381, 492, 1328, 1754a, 1766; military operations, 198, 199, 223, 252, 257, 343, 500, 1328, 1727, 1803, 1805 (see also Algerian revolution: military aspects; Algerian war: pacification program; Algerian war: personal narrative, French military); military strategy, 58, 61, 132, 215, 312a, 1627, 1718; origins, 85, 310 (see also Algerian revolution: causes); peace negotiations, 4, 5, 14a, 42, 51, 159, 261, 285, 305, 305a, 310, 466, 473, 905, 1120, 1128, 1219, 1233, 1249, 1318, 1445, 1681, 1708, 2007; pictorial works, 40, 41, 642a, 781, 1077b; prisoners of war, 1506, 1754a (see also Algerian war: atrocities, prisons and camps); refugees, 241, 369, 430, 437, 1101, 1489, 1498, 1506, 1555, 1679; support for, 56, 309, 492, 955, 1187, 1273, 1427 (see also Algeria: Gaullist policy, opposition to; Algerian question: pro-French Algerian polemics; Nationalist opposition to de Gaulle)

-- atrocities: 164, 385, 603, 626, 1034, 1296, 1499, 1528, 1537, 1663, 1730, 1766, 2093; bibliography, 1766; documents, 1035, 1754, 1766; prisons and camps, 54, 55, 64, 169, 470, 479, 485, 993, 1035, 1680, 1754, 1754a, 1765; terrorism by F.L.N., 48, 236, 489, 518, 781, 877, 1680, 1702, 1803; torture, 55, 158, 381, 385, 477, 559, 1129, 1183. See also Algerian war: final months of violence

-- opposition to: 236, 266, 363, 376, 380-382, 475, 626, 876, 940, 1004, 1029, 1186, 1318, 1555, 1638, 1719; documents, 266, 391, 1187, 2110, 2126; French intellectuals, 158a, 260a, 391, 626, 846, 1130; French Left, 438, 575, 846, 1273, 1380, 1417; military, 385, 559, 1499, 1663; personal narratives and fiction, 1186, 1195. See also Algerian question: pro-independence polemics; Algerian revolution: French support; Algerian war: atrocities; Parti communiste français: Algerian policy

-- pacification program: 26, 28, 56, 132, 309, 385, 431, 492, 626, 1435, 1528, 1627; chronology, 1766; psychological action, 226, 1353, 1435; resettlement centers, 231, 231a, 1435, 1468. See also Algerian war: personal narratives, French military

-- peace agreement: 49, 52, 166, 167, 222a, 510, 520, 793, 1306, 1438, 1728, 1804; documents, 52, 285, 520, 672, 708, 745, 780, 799, 800; opposition to, 52, 879, 1306, 1728; provisional government, 510

-- personal narratives: Algerian, 54, 55, 64, 169, 626, 1803; Algerian children, 1498; Algerian prisoners, 1035; Algerians in France, 1281; American and English, 241, 903, 1278; French civilian, 1120, 1186, 1555

-- personal narratives, French military: 132, 226, 309, 343, 385, 431, 432, 900, 955, 1167, 1195, 1254, 1296, 1435, 1528, 1627, 1638, 1704; Algerian officers, 1499; deserters, 213, 487, 617, 970; Foreign Legion, 1537, 1805; parachute troops, 56, 205, 465, 617, 1129, 1147, 1301, 1805

ALGERIANS IN BELGIUM, 590

ALGERIANS IN FRANCE, 1123, 1235, 1423, 1499; and F.L.N., 1003, 1428; persecution, 92, 374, 375, 381a, 470, 841, 1034, 1197, 1428; political attitudes, 1281, 1329; publications for, 1833; statistics, 581; working conditions, 1713. See also Harkis; Prisoners, political: Algerian nationalist; Trials, political - Algerian nationalists

ALGIERS, 1822

ANTARCTICA, FRENCH, 693, 2113

ANTI-AMERICANISM, 289, 832

ANTICLERICALISM, 929, 1207

ANTI-COMMUNISM, 11, 59, 93, 94, 209, 228, 297, 298, 397, 525, 633, 1085, 1112, 1410, 1569, 1580, 1768, 1871. See also Organizations, anti-communist

ANTI-SEMITISM, 1197, 1447. See also Jews in France

ARMY, 317, 689, 1146, 1467; bibliographies, 58, 625; demoralization of, 239, 240, 287, 551, 878, 1033, 1077a, 1255, 1466; Foreign Legion, 198, 199, 500, 616, 1334, 1581; Moslem auxiliary troops (see Army in Algeria: harkis; Harkis); parachute troops, 1126, 1436, 1727 (see also Army in Algeria: parachute troops); and politics (see Army: history, political; Civilian-military relations); serials, 1838, 1848, 1945, 2107; training program, 315, 1467, 1526. See also Algeria: political developments, 1961, April; Civilian-military relations; Fifth Republic: inception, military intervention; Military...; Organisation de l'armée secrète

-- history: 240, 625, 856, 1269, 1787, 2087; political, 58, 830, 878, 961, 1026, 1033, 1044, 1057, 1206

-- officers: legal provisions, 416; political attitudes, 1524, 1639; political rights, 1619; recruitment and pay, 878, 1524; reserve, 1838, 1945

ARMY IN ALGERIA, 245, 309, 312, 401, 431, 536, 585, 607, 614, 638, 642a, 830, 955, 1020, 1077a, 1079, 1120, 1206, 1254, 1269, 1275, 1328, 1349, 1435, 1554, 1627, 1716, 1848; chaplains, 287, 465; documents, 1349, 1493; draftees, 186, 849, 900; Foreign Legion, 47, 198, 199, 500, 1334, 1537, 1805; Harkis, 222a, 223, 1312; infantery - 9th regiment, 1328; parachute troops, 56, 205, 287, 465, 1077a, 1079, 1147, 1436, 1727, 1805; sections administratives spécialisées (S.A.S.), 1353. See also Algeria: political developments, 1961, April; Algerian war: military operations; Algerian war: pacification program; Algerian war: personal narratives, French military; Organisation de l'armée secrète: operations in Algeria

ARTS. See Cultural life

ASSISTANCE, TECHNICAL AND ECONOMIC, 19, 346, 439, 519, 545, 546, 661, 898, 952, 1005, 1142, 1142a, 1346; African states, 505, 744a, 787-789, 918, 928, 996, 1133, 1490, 1556, 1565, 1752, 1764; African students in France, 773, 1781; bibliography, 1346; Gaullist policy, 289, 683, 694, 727, 728, 794, 1346, 1490; history, 214, 952; organizations, 519; personal narratives, 404, 898; serials, 1810, 1819, 1894, 1900, 1911, 1942, 1961, 1985, 2088, 2113a. See also Fourth Republic: colonial policy

ATHEISM, 358

ATHLETICS, 732, 1228

ATLANTIC ALLIANCE, 133, 156, 355, 488, 654, 837, 1628; and European integration, 355, 1448; Gaullist policy, 441, 587, 654, 977, 1018, 1210, 1294, 1449, 1566, 1782; Gaullist views, 21, 180, 196, 1178; and public opinion, 502a, 803. See also Military strategy: Atlantic Alliance; North Atlantic Treaty Organization

ATLANTIC PARTNERSHIP, 53, 1263, 1264, 1266, 1267, 1462

ATOMIC ENERGY AND RESEARCH. See Nuclear technology

ATOMIC WEAPONS. See Nuclear weapons

AUTOMATION. See Technology, industrial

BARRICADES IN ALGIERS (Jan. 1960). See Algeria: political developments, 1960, Jan. (barricades)

BIBLIOGRAPHIES: acquisitions lists of libraries, 1302, 1947, 1953; Algeria, 471, 580; Catholic Church, 417; current French publications, 176b, 1131a, 1131b, 1846, 1846a; government publications, 438a, 1847; historical studies, 379; dissertations, 427, 648, 773, 2084; Documentation française publications, 748, 755; economic and social questions, 934, 1138a, 1276; Fifth Republic, 1138a, 1252, 2084; Indochina, 112; methodology for, 299; political science, 648, 652, 934, 1138a, 1227, 2084; public administration, 645; publishers' lists (see Catalogues); reference works, 652, 1430; Sahara, 188, serials, 1846, 1846a, 1847, 1850, 1850a, 1912-1914, 1947, 1953, 1959, 1961. See also under individual subjects, e.g., Algerian revolution: bibliographies

BIOGRAPHICAL DICTIONARIES, 405-407, 1109, 1789

BIOGRAPHIES: journalists, 1138; political figures, 609, 710, 840, 899, 924, 1615, 1760

BUDGET, 66, 1744; Algeria (see Algeria: budget)

BUREAUCRACY, 260, 313, 425

CARTOONS, POLITICAL, 11, 126, 273, 421, 560, 812-814, 1018, 1074, 1075, 1271, 1421, 1712

CATALOGUES, 934, 1131a, 1131b, 1138a

CATHOLIC CHURCH, 222, 364, 417, 490, 508, 1030, 1300, 1480;

and atheism, 358; in Algeria, 547, 1470, 1924; and Algerian war, 269, 287, 291, 326, 333, 465, 477, 547, 644, 965, 1218, 1318, 1666, 1849; and Army, 1524; bibliographies, 222, 364, 417; and colonial questions, 291, 508, 976, 1218, 1272, 1615, 1645, 1998; and communism, 334, 1253, 1580, 1612; and decolonization (see Catholic Church and colonial questions); economic doctrine, 1030; educational doctrine, 490, 1666 (see also Education: church and state); and European unification, 90; and Gaullist regime, 982; integrist groups, 269, 1113, 1474, 1524, 1644, 1871, 2044, 2125; and Jews, 1447; and left-wing groups, 290, 326, 986, 1666, 1849, 1998; and military service, 389, 965; press and publishing houses, 222, 269, 364, 417, 883, 1666, 1917, 1924, 1987, 2044, 2125; and rural communities, 1561, 1666; social action groups, 67, 222, 508, 519, 1634, 1666 (see also Catholic Church: integrist groups); social doctrine, 10, 67, 291, 356, 358, 508, 862, 923, 1030, 1480, 1571, 1644, 2044, 2125; and workers, 862, 1209, 1480, 1634

CATHOLIC INTELLECTUALS, 139, 268, 508, 1615, 1849, 1998

CATHOLIC ORGANIZATIONS. See Organizations, Catholic

CATHOLIC PHILOSOPHY, 845

CATHOLICS IN FRANCE, 364, 1666

CENSORED PUBLICATIONS: reprints, 2110

CENSORSHIP, 164, 381a, 559, 593, 635, 848, 901. See also Trials, political: censorship

CENSUS. See Population: census

CENTRAL AFRICAN REPUBLIC, 676

CHAD, 699

CHRONOLOGY, 69, 335, 1011, 1880, 1881

CHURCHES. See Catholic Church; Protestant Churches

CIVICS MANUALS, 187, 207, 218, 426, 1136, 1515

CIVIL LIBERTIES, 363, 1698, 1735, 1754a

CIVIL SERVANTS. See Social groups: civil servants

CIVIL SERVICE. See Administration, governmental: civil service

CIVILIAN - MILITARY RELATIONS, 17, 75, 121, 129, 131, 245, 317, 389, 455, 536, 551, 568, 614, 849, 927, 1020, 1044, 1073, 1255, 1301, 1349, 1353, 1436, 1466, 1524, 1526, 1619, 1790 (see also Army: history, political; Fifth Republic: inception, military intervention); bibliographies, 129, 317, 1033; Generals' putsch, 739, 1284, 1386, 1419, 1554, 1726, 1733, 1746 (see also Algeria: political developments, 1961, April; Trials, political: Generals' putsch)

CIVILIZATION, FRENCH, 202, 268, 507, 642, 753, 754, 801, 973, 1175, 1517, 1597, 1637; bibliographies, 801, 1430

CIVILIZATION, FUTURE, 669, 1227

CIVILIZATION, MODERN, 425, 665-667, 669, 833, 895, 946, 1363, 1495, 1641, 1678

CLUBS, POLITICAL, 15, 147, 372, 609, 1509-1510, 1667; biographies of leading personalities, 609; and Defferre candidacy, 22, 461, 1883, 1983; documents, 91; individual clubs, 135, 344-356, 513, 577, 915, 958, 1137; serials, 1867, 1876, 1882-1884, 1983, 2054

COLLOQUE DE GRENOBLE, 305a, 472

COMMON MARKET, 53, 524, 1106, 1117; and African states (former French Community), 996, 1477, 1556, 1752, 1942; British membership, 162, 1042, 1060, 1310, 1462, 1477, 1567, 1636, 1795; and European Free Trade Association, 589, 1265; and French agriculture, 642, 1042, 1795; and French business organizations, 591, 1673, 1758; and French economy, 280, 282, 283, 298a, 329, 373, 567, 592, 688, 922, 932, 1173, 1287, 1673, 1758, 1772; and French law, 329; and French planning, 298a, 960; and French private investment, 1148; and French social policy, 1731; history, 524, 1795; and intra-European trade, 1758; opposition to, 922; and trade unions, 298a, 522. See also European integration, economic

COMMUNISM, 362, 1580; and freemasonry, 1768. See also Anti-Communism; International communism; Marxism; Parti communiste français

COMMUNIST FRONT ORGANIZATIONS, 11, 290, 986

COMMUNIST INTELLECTUALS, 294, 1044a, 2043. See also Intellectuals and communism; Parti communiste français and intellectuals

COMMUNIST OPPOSITION GROUPS, 62, 304, 525, 1132, 1307, 1322, 1405, 1509-1510; serials, 615, 1852, 1855, 1865, 1896, 1906, 1930, 2014, 2060, 2062, 2123, 2130, 1232

COMMUNIST VOTERS, 275, 664

COMORO ISLANDS, 677

CONFERENCES, CONGRESSES, COLLOQUIA, MEETINGS, ETC., academic, 103, 254, 364, 367, 368, 512, 572, 642, 647, 916, 943, 1148, 1313, 1355, 1356, 1363, 1477, 1612-1613, 1615-1618, 1641; professional, 1731, 1769

-- political, 91, 298a, 354, 366, 371, 372, 557, 1000, 1509-1511, 1614, 2058; Algerian question, 305a, 363, 365, 369, 370, 472, 1719, 1735, 1753. See also individual political parties, e.g., Parti communiste français: congresses

CONGO (BRAZZAVILLE), 390, 700

CONSCIENTIOUS OBJECTORS. See Military service: conscientious objectors

CONSTANTINE PLAN, 30, 678, 926, 966, 1751. See also Algeria: economic development; Algeria: Gaullist policy

CONSTITUTION, 1946, 517, 757

CONSTITUTION, 1958: 258a, 327, 412, 548, 549, 741-743, 811(b), 838, 868, 891, 933, 950, 1010, 1153, 1484, 1494, 1515, 1539, 1658, 1774, 1808, 1809; administrative authority, 1082; Algeria, 1763; amendments, 742; bibliography, 1809; budgetary procedure, 66; economic policy organs, 1222; electoral system, 411 (see also Electoral law); French Community, 563, 891, 1425, 1444; genesis, 120, 246, 517, 552, 1326, 1465, 1531, 1809; implementation of, 116, 117, 1809; National Assembly, 185, 711, 838, 1362; overseas departments and territories, 1425; preliminary versions, 681, 740, 1484; presidency, 1773, 1806; propaganda for, 452, 811(b) (see also Referendums: 1958, Sept.); proposed reforms, 99 (see also Constitutional reform; Political institutions: presidential elections; Political institutions: presidential regime); referenda on (see Referendums: 1958, Sept.; Referendums: 1962, Oct.)

CONSTITUTIONAL COUNCIL. See France. Conseil Constitutionnel in Author Index

CONSTITUTIONAL HISTORY, 1773, 1806

CONSTITUTIONAL LAW, 553a, 739, 741, 838, 950, 1658, 2081. See also France. Conseil Constitutionnel in Author Index

CONSTITUTIONAL REFORM, 868, 872, 945, 1320, 1326. See also Political institutions: proposed reforms

CORPORATISM, 1112, 1113

COUNCIL OF STATE. See Political institutions: Council of State

COUNTER-INSURGENCY. See Military doctrine: counter-insurgency; Revolutionary warfare

COUNTER-REVOLUTION, 397, 551, 630, 1062, 1206, 1474, 1524, 1580, 1644, 1708, 1710

CULTURAL LIFE, 202, 211, 294, 643, 801, 842, 927, 967, 1102, 1163, 1517, 1802; pen names of writers and artists, 406; political literature, 1586, 1624; reading interests, 392, 1028; theater, 403; serials, 1927, 1937, 1946, 1995, 2056, 2057, 2070, 2078

DAHOMEY, 701

DECOLONIZATION, 439, 546, 602, 603, 658, 816, 821, 826, 884, 898, 1050, 1247, 1380, 1487, 1550, 1577, 1628, 1753; and Catholic Church (see Catholic Church and colonial questions); and French political life, 78, 120 (see also Fourth Republic: Colonial policies; Organizations, political pro-French North Africa; Parti communiste français: anti-colonial policy); Gaullist policy, 120, 546, 1133, 1142a, 1565; history, 19, 120, 178, 310, 661, 908, 928, 1764; Guinea, 563, 1050; Indochina, 112, 1050; Morocco, 182, 835, 836, 937, 1025, 1050, 1128, 1205, 1298, 1493; and neo-colonialism, 19, 571; and repatriation of French settlers, 1742; serials, 1810, 1989, 2088; sociology of, 88, 173, 439; Tunisia, 119, 125, 835, 836, 910, 937, 1025, 1050, 1128, 1205

DEMOCRACY, 77, 204, 258, 325, 366, 371, 655, 1522, 1553, 1614. See also Depolitization

DEMOCRACY, ECONOMIC, 10, 161, 191, 915, 1277, 1522

DEMOGRAPHY, 769, 1582, 2053. See also Population

DEPOLITIZATION, 96, 366, 663, 943, 1553

DESERTION AND INSUBORDINATION, 213, 559, 617, 970, 1185, 1186. See also Algerian revolution: French support; Military service: conscientious objectors

DIALECTICS, 890, 930, 931, 1578

DICTATORSHIP, 551, 896. See also Political institutions; Personalization of power

DICTIONARIES: biographical, (see Biographical dictionaries); encyclopedic, 502b, 1077

DIPLOMACY, 16, 128, 216

DIRECTORIES: libraries, (see Libraries: directories); Ministries and civil service (see Administration, governmental: directories); press (see Press: directories); telephone (see Paris: telephone directory)

DISARMAMENT, 502a, 803, 939, 1220a, 1248, 1283, 1736

DOCUMENTATION: governmental institutions, 748, 1356, 1847; indexing, 798; libraries, 765

ECONOMETRICS, 179, 1180, 1441

ECONOMIC AND SOCIAL COUNCIL. See France. Conseil économique et social in Author Index

ECONOMIC ASSISTANCE. See Assistance, technical and economic

ECONOMIC CONDITIONS, 20, 149, 189, 263, 296, 321, 378, 393, 408, 513, 752, 754, 770, 772, 802, 932, 941, 1081, 1107, 1363, 1426, 1642, 1684; agriculture (see Agriculture); Algeria (see Algeria: economic conditions); balance of payments, 1080, 1560; bibliographies, 253, 948, 1276, 1631; business cycles, 1476; Common Market (see Common Market and French economy); consumption, 368, 1769; employment structure, 114, 734, 767, 949, 1363, 1994; foreign trade, 408, 691 (see also Economic conditions: balance of payments; International economic relations); housing, 733, 1377; income distribution, 208, 1363, 1545; industrial output, 394, 444, 1549; industries (see Industries); investment institutions, 189; investments, 367, 954, 1148; investments in Franc Zone, 720; investments, foreign, 174, 263, 378, 408, 832, 1014, 1171, 1559, 1593; monopolistic concentration, 340, 408, 527, 1469; Paris, 71, 867; price level, 179, 1684; productivity, 179, 666, 735, 1631; projections, 669, 680, 725, 747; by regions, 1243, 1549; serials, 1845, 1874, 1920, 1921, 1925, 1966, 2002, 2017, 2026-2028, 2032, 2059, 2082, 2096; standard of living, 208, 211, 244, 249, 666, 1104, 1363, 1583, 1769, 1802; statistics, 71, 244, 249, 263, 513, 666, 720, 752, 770, 772, 802, 1180, 1744, 1966; strikes, 544, 885; U.S. investment in France (see Economic conditions: investments, foreign); wages, 179, 208, 1189, 1545, 1769

ECONOMIC DOCTRINE: free enterprise, 53, 356, 1058, 1096; full employment, 949; gold standard, 1559, 1560; planned economy, 954

ECONOMIC GROWTH, 244, 570, 666, 669, 722, 932, 1107, 1441; managerial factors, 735; and reduction of working hours, 669, 779; and social change, 1363, 1641; technological factors, 179, 941; in underdeveloped countries (see Assistance, technical and economic). See also Planning: Fourth, Fifth plan; Planning: long-range.

ECONOMIC POLICY, 145, 146, 150, 263, 300, 447, 448, 513, 612, 1081, 1317, 1426, 1631; bibliographies, 253, 948, 1276, 1631; chronology, 69, 145; constitutional aspects, 1222; credit, 731; employment, 949; Economic and Social Council, 953; fiscal and monetary measures, 66, 253, 378, 526, 721, 723, 731, 880, 932, 948, 1080, 1559, 1560, 1684, 2080; foreign aid (see Assistance, technical and economic); history, 18, 145, 1081, 1107; housing, 733, 758, 1377, 1665; income distribution, 179, 208, 762, 1189, 1769; investment, 731 (see also Planning: Third, Fourth, Fifth Plan); investment, foreign, 1014, 1171, 1593; legislation, 513, 1670, 2080; monetary measures (see Economic policy: fiscal and monetary measures); oil exploitation, 657; planning (see Planning); proposed reforms, 191, 192, 260, 372, 915, 1058, 1214, 1509-1511, 1585, 1684, 1720, 1777; repatriates' integration in French economy, 349; serials, 1840, 1866, 2059, 2081; structural reform of economy, 722; taxation (see Economic policy: fiscal and monetary measures); transportation, 316. See also Fourth Republic: economic policy; State and economy

ECONOMIC REFORM. See Economic policy: proposed reforms

ECONOMICS: bibliography, 1276; in France, 1476; serials, 1921, 1922, 2072, 2074, 2080, 2082; textbooks, 20, 189, 444, 503, 1348a

EDUCATION, 423, 714, 808a, 1139, 1157, 1526, 1678; administration, 423; bibliography, 808a, 1157; democratization, 916, 1614; enrollment of students, current and projected, 732, 767; foreign students, 578, 744a, 773, 1735, 1781, 1935; for handicapped children, 1141; personal narratives, 339, 1141; proposed reforms, 233, 267, 372, 808a, 916, 1734; serials, 1813, 1844, 1919, 2055; social factors, 233, 1363; statistics, 732, 767, 1157, 1844; teachers, 423; teachers' organizations, 339, 916, 1139

-- church and state, 222, 359, 360, 364, 573, 808a, 1204, 1207, 1433, 1813; legislation, 808a, 1204

-- Gaullist policy, 276, 423, 573, 732, 750, 767, 808a, 1157, 1204, 1228; opposition to, 359-361, 916, 1139, 1813

EDUCATION, ADULT, 265, 503, 758

EDUCATION, HIGHER: foreign students (see Education: foreign students); Grandes écoles, 767, 875, 1446; Ecole nationale de l'administration (E.N.A.), 1166; Ecole normale supérieure, 1446; historical studies, 379; political science, 648; sociology, 88, statistics on, 233, 707, student attitudes, 232, 233; teaching methods, 1734; technical fields, 767

EDUCATION, SECONDARY, 339, 426, 1139, 1678

EDUCATION, VOCATIONAL, 718, 734, 737, 750, 767, 971, 1141, 1994

ELECTIONS, 317a, 569, 886; Algeria (see Algeria: political developments, elections); bibliographies, 325, 411, 648, 1503; judicial procedure, 324; regulations, 325, 569, 1951 (see also Electoral law); research on, 1503; results, 69, 109, 411, 549, 782-786, 1951; sources, 1503; voter participation, 96, 1225. See also Parti communiste français: elections; Parti socialiste: elections; Referendums; Union pour la nouvelle république: elections

ELECTIONS, LEGISLATIVE (NATIONAL ASSEMBLY), 1956 (Jan.), 97, 411, 782

-- 1958 (Nov.), 98, 411; campaign, 93, 297, 712, 811(c), 811(g), 811(h), 1739; regulations, 697; results, 549, 783, 811(g), 811(i)

1808. See also Algeria: elections

-- 1962 (Nov.): campaign, 649, 712, 811(j), 811(k), 887, 1385; results, 306, 395, 784, 887, 1398

-- 1967 (March), 511, 620; campaign, 811(m), 811(n), 811(o), 1653

ELECTIONS, LEGISLATIVE (SENATE) 1959 (April), 785; 1965 (Sept.), 786

ELECTIONS, MUNICIPAL, 284, 298; 1959 (March), 811(c), 811(i)

ELECTIONS, PRESIDENTIAL: FOURTH REPUBLIC, 1208

ELECTIONS, PRESIDENTIAL: (FIFTH REPUBLIC, 1965), 419, 494, 1564, 1599, 1601, 1667; candidacies, 422, 1111, 1165, 1359, 1564; issues, 63, 180, 238, 448, 1317, 1601; public opinion, 63, 1111, 1664; regulations, 325, 739, 1893; results, 63, 109, 419, 494, 502, 811(l), 1111, 1664

-- campaign, 811(l); Gaullist, 448, 811(l), 1163, 1165; left-wing opposition to de Gaulle, 448, 521, 811(l), 1518; nationalist opposition to de Gaulle, 238, 811(l), 1655, 1715, 1938; radio-television, 448, 494, 811(l), 851, 1165, 1564

-- candidates: Defferre, 22, 127, 461, 929, 1292, 1450, 1495, 1667, 1721, 1883, 1983; de Gaulle, 851; Le canuet, 137, 303, 811(l), 1903; Marcilhacy, 118, 1175; Mitterrand, 399, 811(l), 1165, 1409, 1542, 1887; Tixier-Vignancour, 811(l), 1150

ELECTIONS, SOCIAL SECURITY SYSTEM, 12, 994

ELECTORAL LAW, 220, 411, 569, 775-777, 782-786, 994, 1496

ELECTORAL SOCIOLOGY, 555, 1131, 1664

ELECTORAL SYSTEMS, 271, 325, 411, 450, 555, 782, 950, 1131, 1136

ENCYCLOPEDIAS, 1077

EUROPEAN INTEGRATION, 586, 588, 1106, 1172, 1193, 1448, 1594, 1600, 1616, 1795, 2058; bibliographies, 1018, 1106, 1795; documents, 1018; Fourth Republic (see Fourth Republic: European policy); Gaullist views (see Gaullism: European doctrine); organizations supporting (see Organizations, political: pro-European unification); political institutions, 1019, 1448, 1547; political parties' views on, 157, 184 (see also European integration: Socialist views; Gaullism: European policy; Nationalism, European; Parti communiste français: European integration); public opinion, 63, 184, 502a, 803, 1114, 1124, 1220a, 1616; serials, 1836, 1890, 2049, 2058, 2115, 2128 (see also Organizations, political: pro-European unification); Socialist views, 250, 298a, 355, 372, 895, 1173, 1450, 1509, 1510, 1628, 1980

-- Gaullist policy, 415, 512, 671, 1018, 1106, 1172, 1193, 1317, 1330a, 1567, 1782, 1795, 1890; opposition to, 1060, 1317, 1448, 1462. See also European integration, economic: Gaullist policy; Gaulle, Charles de: political philosophy, European integration

EUROPEAN INTEGRATION, ECONOMIC, 53, 316, 1262, 1310, 1673, 1795 (see also Common Market); chronology, 335; Gaullist policy, 53, 162, 316, 612, 688, 1117, 1135, 1449; movement of capital and persons, 329, 1080, 1616.

EUROPEAN INTEGRATION, MILITARY, 156, 1021, 1124

EUROPEAN INTEGRATION, NUCLEAR, 1513

EUROPEAN NATIONALISM. See Nationalism, European

EUROPEAN UNIFICATION. See European integration; Organizations, political: pro-European unification

EVIAN AGREEMENT. See Algerian war: peace agreement

EXISTENTIALISM, 260a, 845, 1052, 1473, 1497, 1578

FASCISM, 133, 1206, 1436, 1474, 1624, 1708

FEDERALISM, 197, 1621

FICTIONAL WORKS: Algerian war (see Algerian war: fiction); Jews, 1447; O.A.S., 919

FIFTH REPUBLIC (GENERAL), 69, 116, 117, 163, 268, 317a, 413, 558, 661, 753, 754, 801, 882, 886, 977, 1071, 1252, 1449, 1456, 1546, 1549, 1760, 2084, 2090; appraisal, 77, 195, 448, 512, 596, 620, 832, 847, 864, 897, 911, 912, 977, 1060, 1160, 1535, 1546, 1761; first year of existence, 78, 183, 512, 1637, 831, 1455, 1549; appraisal, 183, 556, 665, 1190, 1451

FIFTH REPUBLIC: Algerian conflict (major works), 68, 76, 116 176a, 428, 1233, 1349, 1454, 1568, 1668, 1681 (see also Algeria: Gaullist policy; Algerian question and French political life); bibliographies, 116, 117, 163, 268, 558, 855, 886, 977, 1043, 1252, 1808, 1913, 2084; chronology, 69, 335, 1761; economic developments, 145, 448, 513, 514, 2059, 2080 (see also Economic conditions; Economic policy); foreign affairs (major works), 803, 911, 912, 1043, 1152, 1457, 1566 (see also Foreign policy; Foreign relations; International relations); political chronicles and diaries, 273, 544, 560, 605, 608, 643, 806, 812-814, 1074, 1075, 1102, 1176, 1199, 1257, 1421, 1517, 1599, 1603, 1802, 1851, 1943, 1951, 2003; political history, 18, 1055, 1206, 1557, 1592, 1662, 1668, 1711, 1721, 1761, 1783; political parties, 317a, 664, 811(c), 1071 (see also Political parties); social problems, 946; serials, 1840, 1866

-- Gaullist policies, 445, 448, 449, 512, 610, 675, 682, 764, 793, 831, 853-855, 859, 911, 912, 1055, 1738, 1745; documents, 1839, 2016; serials, 1841, 1866, 1872, 1873. See also Algeria: Gaullist policy; Assistance, technical and economic: Gaullist policy; Decolonization: Gaullist policy; Economic policy; Education: Gaullist policy; European integration: Gaullist policy; Foreign policy; Judicial reform: Gaullist; Laws and statutes; Military policy; North Atlantic Treaty Organization: Gaullist policy; Population: Gaullist policy; Social policy

-- inception, 317a, 552, 628, 629, 639, 811(a)-811(f), 868, 1010, 1153, 1220, 1232a, 1252, 1279, 1320, 1546, 1635, 1707, 1784, 1792; Algerian crisis, 76, 78, 197, 247, 331, 397, 443, 811(a), 811(d), 811(f), 1348, 1486, 1710, 1716 (see also Algeria: political developments, 1958, May/June); bibliographies, 256, 443, 628; Gaullists' rôle, 194, 435, 523, 628, 639, 1716, 2109; military intervention, 58, 247, 256, 1206; opposition to de Gaulle's return, 811(a), 958, 1110, 1244, 1324, 1373, 1375, 1405; personal narratives, 86, 194, 256, 435, 523, 1651; and political parties and politicians, 138, 219, 529, 532, 811(c), 978, 1053, 1116, 1127, 1212, 1257, 1453; in press, 443, 811(e), 811(f); and trade unions, 1103, 1640

-- political institutions, 116, 117, 120, 163, 258a, 553a, 553b, 664, 933, 950, 1071, 1362, 1456, 1522, 1534, 1601, 1675, 1760, 1809; bibliographies, 868, 950, 1675, 2084; first year of existence, 327, 512, 548, 550, 868, 957, 1010, 1153, 1182, 1455, 1515, 1779, 1792, 1808; polemics on, 340, 341, 396, 458, 530, 531, 663, 896, 1202, 1244, 1319, 1518, 1544, 1551 (see also Political institutions: proposed reforms). See also Constitution, 1958; Political institutions

FORCE DE FRAPPE. See Military policy: nuclear weapons

FORECASTING: astrological, 1602, 1671; economic, 669, 725, 768, 1720, 1744; political, 1019, 1227, 1536; serials, 2063

FOREIGN LEGION. See Army: Foreign Legion; Army in Algeria: Foreign Legion

FOREIGN POLICY, 128, 227a, 289, 415, 429, 612, 653, 832, 837, 853, 911, 912, 969, 973, 977, 1043, 1059, 1254a, 1457, 1566, 1599; constitutional provisions, 1125; documents, 759, 1018, 1152, 1294, 1636, 1711; evaluation, 355, 587, 620, 656, 832, 987, 1045, 1094, 1317, 1532; serials, 2052, 2104; socialist views, 372. See also Diplomacy; Foreign relations; Fourth Republic: foreign policy; International relations

FOREIGN RELATIONS: African states (ex-French), 390, 1133, 1894, 1969a (see also Assistance, technical and economic: African states; Decolonization); Algeria (post-independence), 745, 1599, 1969 (see also Algeria, post-independence: French aid and cooperation); Belgium, 382; Brazil, 653; Canada, 1711; China, communist, 227a; chronology, 69, 335, 441, 759; documents, 759; Germany, East, 107, 557, 1469; Germany, West, 74, 107, 217, 357, 413, 415, 429, 557, 587, 803, 806, 1090, 1144, 1210, 1254a, 1294, 1469, 1566, 1591, 1594, 1632, 1694, 1758, 1780, 1795, 1801, 1879; Germany, West, bibliography, 1795; Great Britain, 1457, 1879 (see also Common Market: British membership); Haiti, 289; international organizations, 19, 218; Italy, 1879; Latin America, 847, 1796; Morocco, 1179, 1576; Poland, 107, 290; Rumania, 656;

148

Soviet Union, 642, 1031, 1038-1040, 1254a, 1566, 1767, 1797, 1879, 1976; Spain, 982, 1659, 1879; survey, 1767; Tunisia, 1231; United Arab Republic, 1741; United Nations (see Algerian question and United Nations; Foreign relations: international organizations); United States, 355, 378, 671, 707, 832, 837, 847, 911, 969, 1210, 1449, 1566, 1636, 1770, 1796, 1874-1875, 1879, 1968, 1975, 2114; Vatican, 982; Vietnam, 1078

FOREIGN TRADE. See International economic relations

FOURTH REPUBLIC, 18, 78, 79, 194, 317a, 613, 1597, 1635, 1662; administrative institutions, 757; colonial policy, 19, 564, 726a, 751, 910, 928, 962, 1143, 1247, 1282, 1565, 1729 (see also French Union); constitutional reform, 945, 1320, 1326, 1531; economic policy, 151, 253, 564, 565, 770, 932, 941, 962, 1080, 1081, 1212, 1222, 1429, 1631, 1744; elections, 97; electoral reform, 782, 1131; European policy, 16, 157, 184, 194, 316, 1097, 1594; foreign policy, 16, 178, 194, 196, 277, 911-913, 1124, 1178; judicial institutions, 757; military policy, 131, 132, 155, 194, 196, 240, 317, 961, 969, 1124; political chronicles and diaries, 140, 176, 178, 194, 219, 261, 273, 544, 605, 643, 661, 806, 839, 958, 978, 1053, 1603, 1633, 1635, 1802, 1951; political parties, 101, 138, 157, 317a, 1151, 1208, 1793; social policy, 1076, 1365, 1611

-- Algerian policy, 23, 26, 28, 38, 42, 68, 83, 131, 176a, 177, 310, 674, 679, 966, 1047, 1212, 1295, 1305, 1413, 1429, 1454, 1595, 1647, 1652, 1729, 1822; opposition to official, 132, 414, 451, 1239, 1785, 2131

-- collapse, 78, 79, 82, 131, 176, 197, 811(e), 1232a, 1239, 1286, 1640, 1687; bibliography, 1808; causes, 131, 275, 331, 436, 541, 550, 613, 870, 897, 1085, 1190, 1206, 1466, 1674, 1714; constitutional aspects, 517, 945; in French press, 811(e), 1640, 1710; plots, 628, 639, 1465. See also Fourth Republic: political chronicle; Fourth Republic: political institutions

-- political institutions, 78, 120, 131, 757, 868, 945, 1115, 1116, 1151, 1192, 1208, 1551, 1793; bibliography, 1151

FRANC ZONE, 720, 1565

FRANCE: GENERAL. See Civilization, French

FREEMASONRY, 1447, 1768

FRENCH CIVILIZATION. See Civilization, French

FRENCH COMMUNIST PARTY. See Parti communiste français in Author Index and Subject Index

FRENCH COMMUNITY, 120, 122, 203, 452, 512, 538, 563, 891a, 918, 976, 1142a, 1321, 1425, 1494, 1774, 1808; chronicle, 1878; constitutions of member states, 891; economic conditions, 720, 928, 996, 1549, 1556, 1565, 1858; Executive Council, 538, 1444; Senate of, 711; serials, 1810, 1820, 1842, 1843, 1858, 1878, 1893, 1942, 1950, 1985, 2032, 2045, 2056 (see also Africa: serials)

-- dissolution, 19, 218, 310, 505, 816, 908, 928, 1133, 1620, 1764; successor states, 170, 171, 676, 699-705, 797 (see also Common Market and African states; Assistance, technical and economic: African states)

FRENCH OUTSIDE FRANCE, 507

FRENCH SOCIETY. See Civilization, French; Social classes

FRENCH UNION, 122, 203, 751, 811a, 884, 1142a, 1444, 1537a, 1729; bibliography, 1444, 1537a; chronicle, 1877, dissolution, 720, 891a, 908, 1764; documents, 811a, 811b; economic conditions, 726a, 1858; economic development, 962, 1282, 1942, 1985; "loi-cadre," 1143, 1247; proposed reforms, 906, 1158, 1247; serials, 1729, 1810, 1820, 1842, 1843, 1858, 1877, 1893, 1942, 1985, 2024, 2056, 2088

FRONT DE LIBERATION NATIONALE, 51, 159, 248, 437, 528, 604; activities in France, 469, 940, 1003, 1004; documents, 51, 391, 528, 618, 619, 672, 708, 808, 818, 822, 992, 989; negotiations with O.A.S., 285, 310; publications, 1889, 1979, 2005, 2009, 2067, 2068

GAULLE, CHARLES DE, anecdotes about, 84, 854, 1241, 1711; anthology on, 1794; and Army, 830, 1435; assassination attempts on, 141-143, 981, 999, 1233, 1705; autobiographical writings, 852, 860; bibliographies, 889, 1018, 1552; and Cagoule, 1708; choice of successor, 229, 395; and Communist Party, 1715; emergency powers, 739, 1362; and Great Britain, 829, 1788; indictment of, 596, 927, 1060, 1118, 1179, 1244, 1535, 1646 (see also Trials, political: censorship, offense to the Chief of State); interviews and conversations, 1711, 1768; language and style, 855, 864, 889, 1519; and Mauriac, 927, 1088, 1089, 1198; memoirs, 597, 852, 860; military conceptions, 856, 944, 1018, 1481, 1790; and Napoleon III, 531; and Pétain, 985, 1501, 1602, 1709; pictorial works on, 126, 1661; political methods, 136, 663, 864, 897, 911, 912, 1055, 1088, 1089, 1169, 1241, 1344, 1661, 1760, 1762, 1778, 1780; and Pompidou, 246; and public opinion, 1421, 1794; in Resistance and Liberation, 229, 235, 593, 829, 852, 860, 1087, 1088, 1089, 1118, 1198, 1215, 1237, 1535, 1682, 1770, 1778, 1788; return to power, 595, 628, 639, 1127; and Roosevelt, 1770; satire, cartoons etc., 126, 420, 464, 560, 632, 812-814, 1018, 1271, 1304, 1421, 1712; and U.N.R., 1707; and United States, 829, 1598, 1770, 1778, 1788; visits of state (see Visits of State (de Gaulle); and Weygand, 927; writings, 852, 856, 857, 860, 889, 1018, 1064, 1538, 1552, 1709

-- biographies, 84, 108, 126, 136, 293, 421, 593, 1051, 1055, 1297, 1421, 1598, 1661, 1711, 1783, 1794; pre-1958, 110, 210, 292, 338, 463, 597, 829, 843, 909, 1660, 1709

-- personality, 136, 593, 596, 864, 1055, 1088, 1089, 1118, 1169, 1215, 1344, 1519, 1660, 1709, 1711, 1775, 1780; graphology, 1602; horoscope, 1602, 1671

-- political philosophy, 293, 531, 572, 593, 595, 596, 853-855, 857, 1055, 1064, 1152, 1198, 1504, 1538, 1552, 1711, 1775; Algeria, 261, 428, 523, 854, 1454, 1668, 1681, 1707, 1711 (see also Algeria: Gaullist policy); democracy, 1010, 1105, 1779; European integration, 162, 415, 1018, 1060, 1152, 1168, 1172, 1193, 1299, 1330a, 1335, 1462, 1782 (see also European integration: Gaullist policy); Franco-German relations, 1632, 1711, 1782; international relations, 415, 911, 912, 977, 1018, 1043, 1045, 1152, 1299, 1457, 1532, 1711, 1782

-- speeches and press conferences, 21, 203, 415, 428, 429, 740, 811(l), 851, 858-860, 1018, 1481, 1620, 1839, 1954; excerpts from, 853-855, 857, 1152, 1169, 1330a, 1782; listing of, 748, 854, 855, 857, 859, 1018, 1913

GAULLISM, 84, 136, 180, 193, 414, 435, 454, 664, 1018, 1240, 1251, 1465, 1492, 1508, 1682, 1745, 2023; Algerian question, 414, 451, 1239; bibliographies, 323, 1552; economic doctrine, 145, 834; European doctrine, 21, 446, 832, 1018, 1114, 1168, 1513, 1566; France's international rôle, 21, 196, 832, 944, 1178, 1566; political reforms, 120, 446, 450, 453, 533, 1326, 1710, 1779, 1790, 1808; and Poujadist movement, 963, 1286; public support of, 194, 306, 864. See also Gaulle, Charles de: political philosophy; Press, political: Gaullist; Rassemblement du peuple français; Républicains sociaux; Union démocratique du travail; Union pour la nouvelle république in Author Index

GAULLISM AFTER DE GAULLE, 193, 195, 229

GAULLIST ORGANIZATIONS. See Organizations, political: Gaullist

GAULLIST REGIME. See Fifth Republic

GAULLISTS: biographies, 340, 408, 1760; outside U.N.R., 434, 833, 834, 1422, 1566, 1885, 2040, 2109 (see also Union démocratique du travail for 1959-1962, prior to U.N.R.-U.D.T. fusion); pre-1958, 194, 435, 523, 639, 834, 1239, 1240, 1326, 1491, 1507, 1651, 1682, 1714, 2109, 2131; satire and cartoons, 812-814

GENERALS' PUTSCH. See Civilian-military relations: generals' putsch

GEOGRAPHY MANUALS, 1549

GOVERNMENT DOCUMENTS. See ALGERIA; FRANCE; FRENCH UNION in Parts I and II

GOVERNMENT PUBLICATIONS: bibliographies, 748, 1847

GOVERNMENT: EXECUTIVE BRANCHES. See Administration, governmental

GUADELOUPE, 1931

GUIDED MISSILES, 196, 684

HARKIS, 223, 637, 1002, 1312, 1428

HEALTH SERVICES, 758

HISTORIOGRAPHY, 379, 719, 1356, 1816, 1957, 2008, 2097

HISTORY: serials, 379, 1816, 2073, 2074, 2075, 2083, 2086, 2087

HISTORY TEACHING, 339; manuals, 1154, 1799

HOUSING AND URBANISM, 733, 758, 1377

IDEOLOGIES, 89, 133, 664, 997, 1149, 1227, 1238, 1251, 1361, 1473, 1508, 1622-1624. See also Communism; Corporatism; Fascism; Federalism; Freemasonry; Marxism; Nationalism; Nationalism, European; Socialism; Technocracy

IMMIGRANTS, African, 578; Italian, 1259; North African, 581, 1123, 1235; Portuguese, 1260; Spanish, 1258

IMMIGRATION, 581, 734

INDOCHINA: bibliography, 112

INDUSTRIAL MANAGEMENT, 735, 1148

INDUSTRIAL RELATIONS, 10, 191, 356, 735, 885, 1058, 1277, 1316, 1571, 1611, 2101

INDUSTRIAL RESEARCH, 744

INDUSTRIAL TECHNOLOGY, 179, 1161, 1316

INDUSTRIES, 161, 189, 321, 394, 408, 514, 726, 1631, 1673; automobiles, 1277; aviation, 684; foreign participation in, 174, 408; mining, 1360; petroleum, 690; railroad, 1643; shipbuilding, 691. See also Nationalized industries

INFLATION. See Economic conditions: price level; Economic policy: fiscal and monetary measures

INFORMATION RETRIEVAL, 798, 1356

INFORMATION SERVICES, PUBLIC, 313. See also Libraries; Documentation; France: Direction de la documentation

INTELLECTUAL LIFE, 967, 1837, 1927, 2057

INTELLECTUALS, (see Social groups: intellectuals); and Algerian war, 158a, 1130, 1187; and Communism, 260a, 967, 1232, 1315, 1807; and neutralism, 1178; in politics, 260a, 1232, 1624

INTERNATIONAL COMMUNISM, 304, 334, 362, 456, 894, 1112, 1174, 1391, 1410, 1432, 1899, 2060, 2062; and Algeria, post-independence, 164, 1205; and Algerian war, 59, 456; Gaullist views on, 612. See also International relations

INTERNATIONAL ECONOMIC RELATIONS: Foreign investments in France (see Economic conditions: investments, foreign); French investments in Franc zone (see Assistance, technical and economic); taxation, 948; trade with Latin America, 847; shipping, 691. See also Atlantic partnership; Assistance, technical and economic; Common Market; Economic conditions: foreign trade; European integration, economic; European Free Trade Association in Author index

-- monetary aspects: 721, 723, 1080, 1559, 1560; Franc zone, 720, 726a, 996, 1565; gold standard, 1559, 1684

INTERNATIONAL RELATIONS, 16, 81, 289, 312a, 355, 546, 568, 654, 661, 806, 898, 1094, 1097, 1264, 1266, 1267, 1569, 1596, 1628, 1686; chronology, 335, 1011; Gaullist views, 21, 196, 612, 832, 837, 902, 944, 1566 (see also Gaulle, Charles de: political philosophy, international relations); Latin Union, 1796; military aspects, 154, 155, 196, 944, 1021, 1746, 1747; public opinion, 502a, 803, 912, 913, 946, 1043, 1220a, 1457; serials, 1839, 1874, 1875, 1879, 1880, 1909, 1916, 1929, 1942, 1987, 2025, 2052. See also Atlantic Alliance; Atlantic partnership; International communism

INVESTMENTS. See Economic conditions: investments

INVESTMENTS, FOREIGN, IN FRANCE. See Economic conditions: investments, foreign

INVESTMENTS IN FRANC ZONE. See Economic conditions: investments in Franc zone

IVORY COAST, 702, 797

JEANNENEY REPORT, 727, 728

JEWS (IN FRANCE), 364, 1197, 1447. See also Anti-semitism

JOURNALISM, 70, 243, 422, 653, 839, 876, 1138, 1491

JUDICIAL INSTITUTIONS, 757, 1136, 1244; and Algerian war, 1698, 1754a

JUDICIAL REFORM, 610, 1082, 1698, 1754a

JURISPRUDENCE, 502b, 739a, 739b, 1670, 2081

JUSTICE. See Trials, political; Trials, political: special tribunals

LABOR. See Economic conditions: employment structure; Immigrants; Labor movement; Social groups: workers; Trade unions

LABOR MOVEMENT, 228, 298a, 306, 894, 895, 972, 1083, 1103, 1104, 1314, 1791, 2069. See also Political organizations: Socialist; Political parties: left; Socialism; Trade unions

LABOR RELATIONS. See Industrial relations

LABOR UNIONS. See Trade unions

LAWS AND STATUTES, 779a, 1857a, 1955, 2081; agriculture, 749; Algeria (see Algeria: laws and statutes); budget, 66; Common Market applications, 329; economic measures, 300, 301, 513; education, vocational, 750; elections, 220, 325, 569, 775-777, 782-786, 994, 1496; French Union, 1729; judicial procedure, 610; labor relations, 758, 1258-1260, 1611; military organization, 778; military personnel, 207, 416, 1619; overseas departments and territories, 1963-1965; parliament, 711, 741; political agencies, 741; political parties, 1036; regional planning, 746, 907; repatriation aid and compensation, 342, 520, 917, 1742; Sahara, 1962, 1963, 1965; social security, 301; social welfare, 610, 758

LIBRARIES: classification system, 299; directory, 765; newspaper holdings, 1354

LITERATURE. See Cultural life

LOCAL GOVERNMENT, 284, 298, 533, 1516, 1534, 1815

MADAGASCAR, 1537a. See also Malagasy Republic

MALAGASY REPUBLIC, 170

MALI FEDERATION, 171

MAPS, 1077

MARSEILLE, 348

MARTINIQUE, 1997

MARXISM, 56a, 124, 327a, 845, 890, 894, 930, 931, 972, 1044a, 1052, 1132, 1315, 1614; bibliography, 1132; and Christianity, 845, 1030, 1612; critique of, 130, 260a, 665, 846, 959, 1184, 1314, 1322, 1497, 1541, 1578, 1807; exhibit on, 1401; publications on, 844; serials, 1837, 1922, 2022, 2043, 2060. See also International communism; Parti communiste français: ideology; Socialism

MIGRATION IN COMMON MARKET, 329, 1616

MILITARY DOCTRINE: counter-insurgency, 17, 58, 75, 121, 215, 287, 489, 492, 568, 625, 849, 878, 1033, 1206, 1353, 1474, 1527, 1718; history of, 286. See also Military strategy

MILITARY LEADERS, 154, 317, 568, 837, 961, 1021, 1023, 1024, 1026, 1467, 1716, 1746-1747, 1787, 2076. See also Army: officers; Trials, political: Generals' putsch; Trials, political: O.A.S.; Trials, political: Salan

MILITARY POLICY, 317, 689, 830, 837, 969, 1146, 1299, 1467, 1573, 1574, 1790; bibliography, 317; criticism of, 239, 830, 987, 1736 (see also Military policy: nuclear weapons, criticism of); disarmament, 803; serials, 2076, 2104 (see also Army: serials)

-- nuclear weapons: 17, 80, 154, 344, 612, 832, 837, 944, 1049, 1294, 1481, 1573, 1590, 1790; criticism of, 351, 506, 939, 1049, 1248, 1283, 1294, 1481, 1736; documents, 1294; and public opinion, 1481; Soviet views on, 1797

MILITARY ORGANIZATION, 207, 317, 849, 1146; bibliography, 317;

laws and statutes, 207, 416, 778, 849, 1619; officer recruitment and pay, 878; proposed reforms, 849, 1095, 1746. See also Army

MILITARY SERVICE: conscientious objectors, 389, 1186 (see also Desertion and insubordination); conscription, 849

MILITARY STRATEGY, 81, 155, 196, 811b, 944, 1021, 1294, 1596, 1747; Atlantic Alliance, 113, 154, 156, 351, 568, 1569

MILITARY TECHNOLOGY, 455, 684, 689, 1146. See also Guided missiles; Nuclear weapons

MINORITIES IN FRANCE, 1621. See also Africans in France; Algerians in France; Immigrants; Jews in France; Social groups: workers, immigrant

MINORITY PROBLEM. See Algerian question: minority problem; Anti-semitism; Race prejudice

MOROCCO. See Decolonization: Morocco; Foreign relations: Morocco

MOSELLE RIVER NAVIGATION, 316

N. A. T. O. See North Atlantic Treaty Organization

NATIONAL ASSEMBLY, Algerian deputies, 966, 1054, 1092; Algerian legislation, 68, 1092; budget approval, 66; biographies of deputies, 710, 1109; constitutional provisions, 185, 838, 1200, 1362; documents, 779a, 1955, 1956, 2090; elections (see Elections, legislative (National Assembly); eligibility for office, 325; Fourth Republic, 131, 782; history, 172, 412, 433; membership, (1958-1962), 710, 712, 783, 784, 1109; operation, 262, 314, 412, 711, 779a, 925, 1362 (see also Political institutions: executive-legislative balance; Political institutions: parliamentary function); parliamentary groups, 712, 811(k), 1408; presiding officer, 433; Senate (see Senate). See also France, Assemblée nationale in Author Index

NATIONALISM, 89, 90, 397, 1149, 1178, 1238, 1311, 1637, 1907, 1908, 2013, 2029, 2092

NATIONALISM, AFRICAN. See African nationalism

NATIONALISM, ALGERIAN. See Algerian nationalism

NATIONALISM, EUROPEAN, 90, 1021, 1149, 1478, 1685, 1686, 1940, 1990, 2011, 2012

NATIONALIST OPPOSITION TO DE GAULLE (1958-1961), 11, 106, 153, 230, 1112, 1270, 1648; (1962-), 142, 238-240, 279, 332, 596, 608, 632-635, 869, 927, 984, 1074, 1075, 1150, 1252, 1304, 1312, 1507, 1535, 1717; American sympathizers, 1975, 2114, 2119; in exile, 178, 905, 982, 1345, 1653, 1655, 1657; publications, 1851, 1928, 1938, 1939, 2131. See also Elections, presidential: (Fifth Republic, 1965): campaign, nationalist opposition to de Gaulle; Organisation de l'armée secrète

NATIONALIZED INDUSTRIES, 150, 151, 425, 1189, 1277, 1643

NEUTRALISM, 1178

NEWSPAPERS. See Press; Press: directories; Press, general information, daily and bi-daily

NORTH ATLANTIC TREATY ORGANIZATION, 156, 281, 1596, 1746, 1747, 1786; and Algerian war, 3; Gaullist policy, 281, 671, 759, 790, 969, 1024, 1210, 1599, 1636, 1786; military personnel in France, 1100. See also Atlantic Alliance; Military strategy: Atlantic Alliance

NUCLEAR TECHNOLOGY, 724, 1201, 1513, 1590, 1656; bibliography, 1590

NUCLEAR WEAPONS, 196, 1201, 1285, 1382, 1596, 1636, 1746; tests, 1579. See also Military policy: nuclear weapons

O. A. S. See Organisation de l'armée secrète in Author and Subject Index

OIL, 34, 39, 657, 690, 1155

ORGANISATION DE L'ARMEE SECRETE, 255, 1067, 1206, 1233, 1275, 1318, 1331, 1332, 1669, 1749; chronology, 1067; documents, 1067, 1275, 1332, 1342, 1669, 1749; government counter-measures, 1067; government sympathizers, 981, 1072; leadership, 285, 1073, 1332, 1342, 1568, 1749; operations in Algeria, 1323, 1342, 1568, 1749 (see also Algerian war: final months of violence); operations in France, 919, 1074, 1331, 1507, 1749; opposition to and victims of, 622, 805, 901, 1067, 1672; origins, 121, 905, 1013, 1269, 1708; personal narratives, 11, 1072, 1270, 1323, 1507, 1669; political aims, 869, 896, 1206, 1270, 1343, 1474, 1685, 1708; prisoners and their families, 670, 1485, 1748, 1749; public support in France, 866, 901, 980, 983, 1072, 1648, 1938; role in Algerian peace negotiation, 52, 285, 310, 1233. See also Algeria: political developments; Algerian war: final months of violence; Nationalist opposition to de Gaulle; Trials, political: O. A. S.; Conseil National de la Résistance and Organisation de l'armée secrète in Author Index

ORGANIZATIONS (GENERAL). See Pressure groups

ORGANIZATIONS, ACADEMIC AND RESEARCH: colonial and overseas problems, 1810, 1842, 1843, 1894, 1900, 1911, 2024, 2083 (see also Organizations, political: pro-French North Africa); economic questions, 765, 1769, 2026-2028; historical studies, 379, 719, 1816, 2008, 2073, 2097; military affairs, 2076, 2104; politics, internal, 95-102, 765, 2051, 1570 (see also Fondation nationale des sciences politiques in Author Index); politics, international, 335, 765, 1874, 1875, 1929, 2052, 2104; science and technology, 715, 724; social sciences, 88, 102, 716, 765, 844, 1302, 1847, 2063, 2085, 2096, 2103

ORGANIZATIONS, AGRICULTURAL, 102, 442, 660, 872, 953, 1162, 1771, 1800, 1986, 2001; in Algeria, 1676, 2098-2100

ORGANIZATIONS, ALGERIAN. See Algeria: organizations

ORGANIZATIONS, ALGERIAN NATIONALIST. See Algerian nationalism: organizations

ORGANIZATIONS, ANTI-COMMUNIST, 59, 93, 94, 1580, 1871

ORGANIZATIONS, ANTI-RACIST, 521, 1197

ORGANIZATIONS, ATHLETIC, 1228

ORGANIZATIONS, BUSINESS AND PROFESSIONAL, 200, 263, 283, 356, 378, 393, 565, 953, 1673, 1731, 1840, 1845, 2041

ORGANIZATIONS, CATHOLIC, 417; in Algeria, 1604-1610, 2094; businessmen, 1731; integrist groups, 1524, 1644, 1871, 2044, 2125; intellectuals, 75, 1615; social action, 67, 1580; students, 92, 386; youth, 971, 1209

ORGANIZATIONS, CIVIL LIBERTIES, 1029, 1698

ORGANIZATIONS, EDUCATIONAL, 267, 916, 1813, 1844, 2055

ORGANIZATIONS, EUROPEAN UNIFICATION. See Organizations, political: pro-European unification

ORGANIZATIONS, FRANCO-GERMAN, 107, 1144, 1469, 1591

ORGANIZATIONS, FRANCO-SOVIET, 1976

ORGANIZATIONS, FRANCO-U. S., 59, 378, 1874, 1875, 1968, 1975, 2114, 2119

ORGANIZATIONS, JEWISH, 2020

ORGANIZATIONS, LABOR. See Trade unions

ORGANIZATIONS, MILITARY, 1126, 1838, 1945. See also Organizations, veterans'

ORGANIZATIONS, MUNICIPAL, 621, 1815, 1894

ORGANIZATIONS, OFFICIAL OR SEMI-OFFICIAL, 259, 1337-1340, 1872, 1873, 1891, 1892, 1969, 1994, 2030, 2031. See also FRANCE; ALGERIA in Parts I and II

ORGANIZATIONS, PACIFIST, 290, 811a, 939, 1248, 1283, 1285

ORGANIZATIONS, POLITICAL, 405, 407; anti-Algerian war, 380, 381, 385, 1754, 2110; Centrist, 302, 303; Communist (see Parti communiste français; Communist opposition groups; Communist front organizations); counter-revolutionary, 630; federalist, 1093, 1621; Gaullist, 104, 105, 133, 434, 811(b), 834, 1841, 1885 (see also Rassemblement du peuple français; Républicains sociaux; Union démocratique du travail; Union pour la nouvelle république in Author Index); Leftist (see Organizations, political: socialist); Monarchist, 1859; Nationalist, 106, 457, 1006, 1311, 1717, 1868, 1930; pro-Castro, 1905; pro-European unification,

1008, 1172, 1287, 1811, 1812, 1856, 1890, 1895, 1904, 1941, 1944, 1980, 2006; pro-French North Africa, 365, 924, 951, 964, 1345, 1486, 1507, 1651, 1820, 1863, 1975, 2114, 2119, 2127; Socialist, 298a, 418, 1083, 1307, 1406, 1992, 2004. See also list of individual parties under Political parties

ORGANIZATIONS, PROFESSIONAL. See Organizations, business and professional

ORGANIZATIONS, REPATRIATES' FROM NORTH AFRICA, 917, 1971, 2001

ORGANIZATIONS, RESEARCH. See Organizations, academic and research

ORGANIZATIONS, SECRET, 956, 1708. See also Organisation de l'armée secrète; Conseil national de la Résistance in Author Index

ORGANIZATIONS, STUDENT, 92, 370, 374-376, 386, 622, 828, 914, 1007, 1009, 1395, 1697, 1726, 1733-1736, 1868, 1936; Africans in France, 1935; North African, 865, 1303, 1934; register, 773

ORGANIZATIONS, TERRORIST, 956, 1013

ORGANIZATIONS, VETERANS', 598, 922, 1328, 1732

ORGANIZATIONS, WOMEN'S, 1755-1757

ORGANIZATIONS, YOUTH, 971, 1008, 1017, 1697, 1814

OVERSEAS DEPARTMENTS AND TERRITORIES, 677, 693, 706, 1142a, 1425, 1537a, 1549, 1729; laws and statutes, 976, 1963-1965; serials, 1931, 1963-1965, 1997, 2113

PARIS, 71, 717, 867; master plan for, 685, 786a; telephone directory, 791. See also Préfecture de la Seine

PARLIAMENT. See National Assembly; Political institutions: executive-legislative balance; Political institutions: parliamentary function; Senate

PARTI COMMUNISTE FRANCAIS, 197, 525, 553, 624, 1132, 1232, 1392, 1393, 1691; agricultural program, 1540, 2112; and Algerian war, 534, 562, 600, 601, 804, 846, 1242, 1273, 1347, 1366, 1379, 1380, 1387, 1397, 1405, 1630, 1663, 1692, 1695, 1726, 1755, 1833; anti-colonialism, 308, 1380; athletics program, 1228; bibliography, 1437; and Catholic Church, 1207, 1253, 1300, 1480, 1612; conferences, congresses, etc., 1369, 1391-1398, 1402, 1403, 1541, 1687, 1689; cultural and scientific questions, 640; de-Stalinization, 56a, 1108, 1315; economic and social questions, 1368, 1370, 1377, 1613, 1690, 1757, 1922; education program, 359-361, 916, 1139, 1433, 1919; elections and referenda, 93, 297, 298, 811(c), 811(j), 811(n), 1371, 1378, 1381, 1383, 1385, 1390, 1394, 1397, 1398, 1404, 1542; European and foreign policy, 1369, 1505, 1542; exhibits, 1401; and Gaullist regime, 340, 341, 532, 544, 1279, 1284, 1322, 1373, 1375, 1386, 1405, 1693, 1715; German question, 217, 1367, 1384, 1694; history, 62, 420, 615, 624, 1374, 1400, 1437, 1791; ideology, 56a, 237, 362, 844, 1044a, 1132, 1174, 1389, 1541, 1688; and intellectuals, 294, 640, 1315, 1541; internal opposition, 123, 308, 624, 959, 1108, 1315, 1392, 1395, 1396, 1906 (see also Communist opposition groups); and international communism, 624, 1380, 1391, 1399, 1432; and local government, 298, 533; membership, 525, 1402; and non-communist Left, 228, 340, 422, 525, 624, 1083, 1372, 1373, 1376, 1389, 1394, 1398, 1437, 1541, 1542, 1687, 1695; nuclear weapons, 1382; and O.A.S., 805; organization and finances, 1393, 1402; Paris local organization, 2095; parliamentary activity, 1365, 1393; and political institutions, 530, 533, 1174, 1369, 1381, 1437, 1541, 1614; publications, 322, 599, 615, 1393, 1833, 1864, 1919, 1973, 1984, 2095, 2112; publishing houses, 11; research and documentation centers, 844, 1401; statutes, 549, 615; student organizations, 1395, 1697, 1726; teacher organizations, 339; training of party cadres, 1393; voters' (Communist) attitudes, 275, 664; women's organizations, 1390, 1755-1757; youth organizations, 641, 1284, 1697. See also Anti-Communism; Communist opposition groups; International Communism; Marxism; Parti communiste français in Author Index

PARTI SOCIALISTE (S.F.I.O.), 366, 372, 872, 1134, 1232, 1250, 1255-1257, 1450-1453, 1502, 1572, 1791; and Algerian question, 1255, 1413, 1452; bibliography, 1572; conferences, congresses, 1411-1413, 2036; and Defferre candidacy, 22; elections, 811(c), 811(j), 811(l), 1414, 2035; publications, 1910, 1999, 2035-2037,

2052a, 2091; statutes, 549; and unification of Left, 352, 1372, 1373, 1376, 1572; youth organizations, 1999. See also Parti socialiste (S.F.I.O.) in Author Index

PARTIES, POLITICAL. See Political parties

PEASANTRY. See Social groups: farmers; Agriculture

PETIT-CLAMART. See Trials, political: Petit Clamart

PHILOSOPHY, 130, 139, 327a, 845, 890, 930, 967, 1052, 1220, 1497, 1612; serials, 1837, 2043. See also Dialectics; Existentialism; Marxism

PIEDS-NOIRS. See Algeria: European settlers

PLANNING, 146, 148, 149, 190, 212, 254, 296, 647, 668, 687, 935, 947, 954, 1145, 1188, 1313, 1422; administration of, 163; bibliographies, 149, 935; and Common Market, 53, 960, 1042, 1616; Fifth Plan, 212, 680, 731-734, 736-738, 747, 768, 774, 779; Fifth Plan, counterproposals, 570, 1104; and fiscal policy, 66; and foreign trade, 936; Fourth Plan, 296, 361, 668, 687, 850, 1439, 1460; long-range projections, 669, 685, 725, 738, 768, 1063, 1536, 1585, 2063; methodology, 367, 368, 1313; objectives, 354, 960, 1188; political control on, 204, 953; theory, 936, 954, 1441, 2063; Third Plan, 726; and trade unions, 298a, 522, 1370; in Western Europe, 936, 954

PLANNING, REGIONAL, 685, 738, 746, 756, 786a, 867, 907, 1063, 1188, 1243, 1511, 1558, 1891; administration of, 163, 907; bibliography, 907; of educational facilities, 767; Southwest of France, 1561

POLICE, 295, 384, 1319, 1428, 1525, 1576. See also Administration, public: police and secret service

POLITICAL ATTITUDES, 572, 613, 664, 1000, 1178, 1220a, 1518, 1536, 1584; Communist voters, 275; elite, 502a, 803; officers, 1524; religious groups, 364; students, 232, 1238, 1361; theories on, 1221; voters, 221, 502, 887, 1151, 1225; workers, 943, 972, 1104, 1160, 1161, 1314. See also Ideologies; Public opinion

POLITICAL INSTITUTIONS, 77, 82, 187, 218, 258, 502b, 553, 554, 556, 572, 757, 882, 886, 897, 950, 1136, 1182, 1224, 1547 (see also Fifth Republic: political institutions; Fourth Republic: political institutions); administrative organs, 163 (see also Administration, governmental); Assembly of the presidents of the General Councils (Assemblée des présidents des Conseils généraux) 1516; bi-party system, 63, 95, 502, 553; bibliographies, 116, 117, 645, 648, 950, 1806; Cabinet, 262; centralism vs. regionalism, 1621; constitutional aspects, 116, 117, 741, 950, 1773, 1806, 1809; Constitutional Council (see France. Conseil Constitutionnel in Author Index); Council of State (Conseil d'Etat), 739a, 739b, 810; decentralization, 1511; democratization, 350, 366, 371, 530, 553, 662, 973, 1105, 1451, 1509, 1510, 1553, 1617; Economic and social council (see France. Conseil économique et social in Author Index); electoral systems (see Electoral systems; Political institutions: presidential election); executive-legislative balance, 412, 739, 838, 1362, 1551, 1773, 1806; military dictatorship, 551, 896; National Assembly (see National Assembly; Senate); national defense, 317; parliamentary function, 100, 131, 172, 204, 412, 433, 1115, 1116, 1151; personalization of power, 572, 663, 896, 1244, 1369, 1482; presidency, 1773, 1806; presidential election, 99, 115, 350, 530, 555, 1482, 1531, 1601, 1650, 1667, 1738 (see also Referendum: October 1962; Elections, presidential); presidential regime, 99, 115, 117, 127, 395, 868, 1675, 1809; pressure groups, 1224 (see also Pressure groups); proposed reforms, 135, 197, 238, 350, 366, 395, 446, 450, 453, 533, 552, 636, 649, 868, 872, 1213, 1311, 1422, 1531, 1570, 1717, 1721 (see also Constitutional reform; Fifth Republic: political institutions, polemics); referendum, 221; Senate (see Senate); suffrage, 325

POLITICAL PARTIES, 95, 101, 138, 317a, 322, 366, 405-407, 553, 556, 886, 1109, 1164; and Algerian question (see Algerian question and political parties); bibliography, 648; congresses, 69 (for major sets of stenographic records see Mouvement républicain populaire; Parti communiste français; Parti républicain radical et radical socialiste in Part I); constitutional provisions, 838, 1036; and depolitization of voters, 96, 135, 345, 366, 502, 1225, 1617; economic doctrines, 1583; election campaigns (see Elections and under individual parties); electoral reform, 411; Gaullist (see

Rassemblement du peuple français; Républicains sociaux; Union démocratique du travail; Union pour la nouvelle république); Left, communist (see Parti communiste français; Communist opposition groups); Left, non-communist, 15, 418, 1160, 1184, 1232, 1314, 1350, 1406, 1450, 1495, 1518, 1622, 1628 (see also Parti communiste français and non-Communist Left; Political parties : Unification of Left; Socialism and political parties listed individually in Author Index (see below); peasants' and farmers', 102, 1800 (see also Organizations, agricultural); programs, 157, 511; publications by, 1177; and referenda, 221; regrouping of, 63, 95, 345, 352, 395, 553, 1601 (see also Political institutions : bi-party system); research on, 322; Right, 1251, 1361, 1508, 1623 (see also Nationalism; Nationalist opposition to de Gaulle; and political parties listed individually in Author Index, see below); sources, 322, 1177; unification of the Center, 929; and unification of the Left, 15, 228, 306, 345, 352, 372, 418, 525, 553, 896, 958, 1394, 1411, 1427, 1509, 1510, 1542, 1572, 1614, 1628, 1667 (see also Parti communiste français and unification of Left); unification of Right, 553, 1715. See also Elections: results; Organizations, political; Sociology, political; political parties listed individually under Author Index: Centre démocrate; Centre national des indépendants et paysans; Centre républicain; Convention gauche de la Cinquième République; Convention républicaine; Fédération de la gauche démocrate et socialiste; Mouvement Poujade; Mouvement républicain populaire; Parti communiste français; Parti d'union de la gauche socialiste; Parti républicain radical et radical-socialiste; Parti socialiste (SFIO); Parti socialiste autonome; Parti socialiste unifié; Poujadist movement; Rassemblement du peuple français; Républicains indépendants; Républicains sociaux; Union démocratique du travail; Union démocratique et socialiste de la résistance; Union pour la nouvelle république; Union progressiste

POLITICAL SCIENCE, bibliographies, 645, 648, 1227; dissertations, 648, 2084; serials, 2051, 2081, 2084, 2090; in France, 911, 1459. See also Electoral sociology; Sociology, political

POLITICS : practical aspects, 262, 314

POPULATION, census (1962),771; French Community, 1549; Gaullist policy, 769, 1582; Paris, 71, 867; serials, 2053; statistics, 244, 758, 770, 772, 1549

POPULATION GROWTH AND FRENCH ECONOMY, 1582, 1583

POUJADIST MOVEMENT. See Mouvement Poujade in Author Index

POVERTY, 1056

PREFECTURE DE LA SEINE, 71, 811(h), 811(i), 811(k), 811(m); directory, 763. For other Prefectures see 811(h), 811(i), 811(m)

PRESS, 405, 407, 409, 807, 1138, 1491, 1618, 1776; and Algerian question, 50, 443, 580, 1458; bibliographies, 648, 1750, 1776; circulation, 270, 1032, 1776; and current issues, 144, 227a, 653, 1111 (see also Press, excerpts from); directories, 70, 405, 407, 409, 575, 1354, 1512; excerpts from, 50, 443, 587, 864, 866, 899, 1027, 1031, 1331, 1458, 1482, 1485, 1489a, 1839; financial control over, 611; freedom of, 876; government regulation and subsidies, 611, 1575; history of, 1138, 1750; magazines, 1138 (see also Press, general information : weekly and monthly), newsletters (see Press, confidential); and public opinion, 227a, 1491, 1618; technical aspects, 611, 1138, 1776. See also Journalism

PRESS, AGRICULTURAL, 1800, 1986, 2001, 2112

PRESS, ALGERIAN. See Algeria: press; Algeria, post-independence: press; Algerian revolution: press

PRESS, BUSINESS, 144, 1925, 2041

PRESS, CATHOLIC, 222, 364, 417,811(d),883, 986, 1849, 1917, 1924, 1932, 1987, 1998, 2044, 2077, 2125

PRESS, CONFIDENTIAL, 1138, 1486, 1851, 1874, 1875, 1916, 2025

PRESS, GENERAL INFORMATION, daily or bi-daily, 811(d)-811(g), 811(l),1032,1434, 1821, 1918, 2010, 1052a, 2064, 2102 (see also "La Croix," "Le Monde," "Libération," in Title Index); weekly and monthly, 811(d),1869, 1927, 1932, 1943, 1968, 1970, 1974, 1984, 1989, 2003, 2013, 2015, 2019, 2021, 2057, 2061, 2065, 2077, 2079, 2089, 2092, 2106, 2111, 2116, 2128, 2131 (see also "Canard enchaîné," "Témoignage chrétien," in Title Index)

PRESS, MILITARY, 811(d), 1838, 1848, 2107

PRESS, POLITICAL, Centrist, 1903, 1908a, 1948; Communist, 322, 599, 615, 1833, 1864, 1919, 1973, 1984, 2095, 2112; communist-oriented, 1909, 1922, 2022, 2043; communist-opposition, 615, 1896, 1906, 2014, 2060, 2132; Gaullist, 414, 435, 811(d), 1841, 1885, 2010, 2013, 2018, 2019, 2023, 2040, 2109; Leftist, 260a, 575, 811(d),1862,1902, 1905, 1910, 1943, 1974, 1992, 2004, 2021, 2039, 2047-2052a, 2111, 2117, 2118; nationalist, 243, 521, 811(d), 1907, 1908, 1923, 2013, 2029, 2092, 2134; nationalist European, 1940, 1990, 2011, 2012; nationalist opposition to de Gaulle, 1851, 1928, 1938, 1939, 1975, 2114, 2119, 2131

PRESS, REPATRIATES' FROM ALGERIA, 1971, 2001, 2050

PRESS AGENCIES, 1486, 1776, 1832, 1836, 1916

PRESS SERVICES. See Press agencies

PRESSURE GROUPS, 554, 953, 1223, 1224, 1673; bibliographies, 1065, 1224; business, 565, 1673; international finance, 153, 408, 531, 608, 1916; research on, 1065; technocrats, 147, 181, 514; trade unions, 1065; veterans, 598; and women, 1234. See also Organizations, agricultural; Organizations, business and professional; Social groups

PRISONERS, POLITICAL, Algerian nationalist, 54, 55, 64, 158, 169, 319, 470, 518, 1035, 1329, 1499, 1754, 1754a, 1765; O.A.S., 279, 670, 1074, 1507; right of asylum, 357, 369. See also Trials, political

PRISONERS OF WAR, ALGERIAN. See Algerian war: atrocities, prisons and camps

PRODUCTIVITY. See Economic conditions: productivity

PROPAGANDA, 227a, 509. See also Psychological warfare; Administration, governmental : information services

PROTESTANT CHURCHES, and Algerian war, 365, 537, 561, 1218; and communism, 1612

PROTESTANTS IN FRANCE, 364

PSYCHOLOGICAL WARFARE, 561, 1203, 1527. See also Military doctrine: counter-insurgency; Algerian war: pacification program, psychological action

PUBLIC OPINION, 326a, 526, 1491, 1583, 1584, 1641, 2103; bibliography, 648. See also Political attitudes

PUBLIC OPINION POLLS, 1220a, 1618, 1664, 2103

PUBLISHING HOUSES, 176b

RACE PREJUDICE, 521, 1197

RADICAL PARTY. See Parti Républicain radical et radical socialiste in Author Index

RADIO AND TELEVISION, 1776; Algeria (see Algeria: radio-television); bibliographies, 1618, 1776; broadcasts, 422, 448, 494, 649, 811(l), 811(o), 851, 1245; censorship, 901; laws and statutes, 1618; news programs, 227a, 901, 1488

REFERENCE WORKS, 69, 335, 379, 405-407, 502b, 661, 840, 1077, 1131a, 1430, 1846; administration, governmental, 763; Algeria, 60, 69; biographies, 405-407, 840, 1109, 1760; chronologies, 69, 335, 1729; economic conditions, 772; elections, 325; Fifth Republic, 855, 1252, 1951, 1952; French Union, 1729; government documents, 748; libraries, 765; organizations, 1224; Paris, 71, 791; political science, 648, 652; press, 70, 1354, 1512, 1523a. See also Bibliographies: serials; France. Direction de la documentation : serials in Author Index

REFERENDUMS, 221, 325; 1961 (Jan.), 71, 153, 650, 811(i), 1127, 1397, 1577; 1962 (April), 332, 651, 1692; 1962 (Oct.), 109, 246, 347, 784,811(j), 887, 1381, 1398, 1482, 1531 (see also Political institutions: presidential election

-- referendums, 1958 (Sept.), 98, 105, 452, 595, 811(b), 811(d), 1484, 1577; in Algeria, 46, 1763; in French Community, 203

REFUGEES, ALGERIAN. See Algerian war: refugees

REGIONAL PLANNING AND DEVELOPMENT. See planning, regional

REGIONALISM, 1511, 1561, 1621. See also Planning, regional

REPATRIATION OF FRENCH ALGERIANS AND COLONIAL SETTLERS, 637, 730, 1621, 1742, 1971, 2001, 2050; compensation for lost property, 520, 917; government aid, 342, 349, 729; laws and statutes, 342, 520, 917, 1742; personal narratives, 223, 224, 498, 637, 1002, 1140; proposals for, 349, 353; relocation centers, 637, 1002; statistics, 730. See also Algeria: independence, exodus

RESEARCH: historical studies, 379, 1356; industrial technology, 744; military technology, 684, 689, 798; social sciences, 88, 716, 930, 1641, 1769. See also Organization, academic and research

RESEARCH, SCIENTIFIC, 717, 1460, 1503a; atomic energy, 724; Gaullist policy, 318, 361, 1460

RESEAU JEANSON. See Trials, political: opponents of Algerian war; Jeanson, Francis in Author Index

RESETTLEMENT. See Repatriation of French Algerians and colonial settlers

REUNION ISLAND, 706

REVOLUTIONARY WARFARE, 61, 215, 397, 424, 456, 489, 1333, 1353, 1527, 1718. See also Military doctrine: counter-insurgency

RUEFF REPORT, 721, 723

RURAL LIFE, 1558, 1561, 1800. See also Agriculture

RUSSIAN AND POLISH WORKS, 18, 19, 571, 881, 928, 1044a, 1068, 1476, 1557, 1572, 1631, 1758, 1767, 1790

SAHARA, 692, 792, 888, 891a; bibliography, 188; economic conditions, 34, 39, 259, 1338, 2030, 2031; exploration of, 715; government propaganda, 33, 34, 692, 792; housing, 1337, 1339; laws and statutes, 1962, 1963, 1965; nomadic tribes, 377; nuclear tests, 1579; oil exploitation, 39, 657, 1155, 1656; political problems, 815, 2046, 2127

SATIRE, POLITICAL, 273, 812-814, 1304, 1802. See also Cartoons, political; Gaulle, Charles de: Satire, cartoons, etc.

SCHOOLS. See Education

SCIENCE. See Research, scientific

SEINE, DEPARTMENT OF. See Préfecture de la Seine; Paris

SENATE, 100, 238, 433, 533, 711, 925, 1261; documents, 1967; membership of, 713, 785, 786

SENATE OF FRENCH COMMUNITY, 711

SENEGAL, 704

SOCIAL CLASSES, 103, 237, 328, 717, 875, 1545. See also Social groups

SOCIAL CONDITIONS, 717, 753, 754, 758, 946, 1056, 1363, 1495, 1641; women, 717, 1234, 1613, 1756; youth, 402, 714, 971, 1017, 1678

SOCIAL GROUPS: business men, 200, 408, 1925, 2041; civil servants, 163, 425, 514; elite, 803, 875; farmers, 102, 103, 660, 871, 1540, 1800; intellectuals, 201, 260, 194, 1473 (see also Intellectuals and...); politicians, 262; religious, 364 (see also Catholics in France; Jews in France; Protestants in France); students, 232, 233 (see also Education: social factors; Education, higher; Organizations, student; Youth); technical experts and managers, 181, 260, 514, 1360. See also Social classes

-- army: 58, 207, 1524; draftees, 186, 315; officers, 416, 455, 878, 1044; reserve officers, 1838, 1945

-- workers: 103, 161, 734, 943, 972, 1028, 1277, 1316, 1360, 1500, 2034; Catholic, 862, 971; immigrant, 581, 734, 1235, 1616; skilled, 1161; women, 1756, 1757

SOCIAL HISTORY. See Historiography

SOCIAL MOBILITY, 237, 875, 1363

SOCIAL POLICY, 447, 718, 736, 758, 760, 1076; athletics, 1228; bibliography, 1076; chronology, 69; education (see Education: Gaullist policy); evaluation of, 1317; family allowances, 1769; family planning, 1234, 1613; housing, 733; immigrant workers, 1123, 1258-1260; legislation, 1076; proposed reforms, 192; repatriation aid (see Repatriation of French Algerians and colonial settlers: government aid); youth, 402, 946, 1017

SOCIAL SECURITY SYSTEM, 12, 301, 718, 736, 766, 1769

SOCIALISM, 553, 668, 1132, 1250, 1453, 1502, 2091; history, 1134, 1453; renovation of, 250, 306, 372, 418, 493, 894, 895, 1083, 1160, 1184, 1314, 1450-1453, 1509-1510, 1870, 2048. See also Labor movement; Marxism; Political parties: Left, non-Communist; Parti socialiste

SOCIALISM, COOPERATIVE, 1096

SOCIALIST PARTY. See Parti socialiste in Author and Subject Index

SOCIOLOGY, CASE STUDIES: Algerians in France, 1123, 1235, 1713; Algerian workers in France and Algeria, 1713; bureaucratic organizations, 425; Communist voters, 275; industrial relations, 1161, 1277, 1316, 1360; political attitudes of elite, 502a, 803; race prejudice, 1197; reading interests, 392, 1028; social mobility, 875, 971; students, 232, 233; students' political attitudes, 1238; tax payers, 526; women's professional rôle, 717; workers and culture, 1028, 1500; youth, 1357, 1678

SOCIOLOGY: methodology, 930, 931; research areas, 88, 1641; serials, 1862a, 1866a, 2085, 2101, 2103

SOCIOLOGY, INDUSTRIAL, 1161, 1277, 1316, 2101

SOCIOLOGY, POLITICAL, 77, 82, 88, 95, 96, 101-103, 221, 275, 364, 502, 550, 553-556, 664, 1232. See also Electoral sociology

SPECIAL COLLECTIONS AT HOOVER INSTITUTION, 401, 811, 1342, 1343, 1486, 1798

SPORTS. See Athletics

STANDARD OF LIVING. See Economic conditions: standard of living

STATE AND ECONOMY, 150, 151, 190, 191, 253, 340, 514, 735, 1058, 1081, 1222, 1611, 1631, 1670, 1777. See also Planning; Nationalized industries; Economic policy; Technocracy

STRIKES. See Economic conditions: strikes

STUDENTS: and Algerian war, 92, 1238, 1735; serials, 1936, 2108. See also Education, higher: student; Organizations, student; Political attitudes: students; Social groups: students

STUDENTS, AFRICAN, 578, 773, 1781, 1935, 2108

STUDENTS, ALGERIAN, 1735, 1934

TAXATION, 526, 948. See also Economic policy: fiscal and monetary measures

TECHNOCRACY, 135, 147, 181, 189, 204, 230, 340, 341, 356, 408, 458, 514, 931, 1166, 1431, 1465, 1536, 1547, 1571, 1583

TECHNOLOGY. See Civilization, modern

TECHNOLOGY, INDUSTRIAL, 507, 666, 667, 669, 1161, 1316, 1503a

TECHNOLOGY, MILITARY, 684

TELEPHONE DIRECTORY, PARIS AREA, 791

TELEVISION. See Radio-television

TORTURE, 55, 158, 236, 381, 382, 559, 841, 877, 1183, 1638. See also Algerian war: atrocities

TRADE UNIONS, 161, 278, 372, 491, 522, 544, 915, 953, 1065, 1103, 1104, 1360, 1530, 1611; in Algeria (see Algeria: trade unions); and communism, 94; and economic democracy, 915, 1370; participation in management, 10, 161, 1161; political activity, 12, 278, 306, 387, 943, 1104, 1232, 1672; serials, 1888, 2048, 2069, 2101, 2105; teachers' (see Education: teachers' organizations); and workers, 1277. See also Confédération française démocratique du travail; Confédération française des travailleurs chrétiens; Confédération générale du travail; Confédération nationale du travail; Force ouvrière; Union générale des travailleurs algériens in Author Index

TRANSPORTATION, MARITIME, 316

TRANSPORTATION, URBAN, 348

TREATIES AND AGREEMENTS, 745, 1133, 1142a. See also Algerian war: peace agreement

TRIALS, POLITICAL, 596, 739b, 984, 998, 1683, 1706; Algerian nationalists, 54, 158, 369, 460, 591, 877, 1754a; Barricades, 381, 905, 984, 1054, 1625, 1683; Ben Barka affair, 295, 383, 384, 1179, 1298, 1576; censorship, 164, 559, 635, 841, 876, 1312; censorship: offense against Chief of State, 980, 983, 1089, 1535, 1646; complot de Paris (April 1961), 410, 1074; Generals' Putsch, 74, 312, 312a, 410, 830, 905, 984, 1016, 1554, 1568; lawyers' rôle in, 979, 1150, 1705, 1706; O.A.S., 74, 279, 357, 830, 983, 1016, 1027, 1073, 1254, 1535, 1568, 1683, 1706, 1749 (see also Trials, political: Petit-Clamart); opponents of Algerian war, 158a, 475, 940, 984, 1130, 1187, 1683; Petain, 985; Petit-Clamart (de Gaulle assassination attempt), 141-143, 981, 999, 1485, 1705, 1706; and public opinion, 1027, 1074, 1075, 1485, 1489a; Réseau Jeanson (see Trials, political: opponents of Algerian war); Salan, 638, 1073, 1489a, 1568, 1683, 1706; special tribunals, 739, 980, 998, 1244, 1706

TUNISIA. See Decolonization: Tunisia; Foreign relations: Tunisia

U.N.R. See Union pour la nouvelle république in Author and Subject Index

UNION POUR LA NOUVELLE REPUBLIQUE, 116, 117, 323, 462, 549, 633, 636, 924, 1546, 1651, 1655; Algerian policy, 434, 1651, 1681; congresses, 284, 318, 1059, 1567, 1574, 1738; elections, 411, 811(c), 811(l), 811(n), 1739; foreign policy, 557, 1018, 1059, 1294; publications, 1901, 2010, 2122; statutes, 549, 1737

UNITED NATIONS, (see Foreign relations: international organizations); and Algerian question (see Algerian question and United Nations)

UPPER VOLTA, 705

URBAN PROBLEMS. See Housing and urbanism

VETERANS. See Organizations, veterans'; Pressure groups: veterans

VISITS OF STATE (de Gaulle), 203, 429, 653, 707, 847, 855, 1297, 1599, 1620, 1780

VISITS OF STATE (other government officials), 1659, 1741

VISITS OF STATE TO FRANCE, 390, 1006, 1031, 1038-1040

WAGES. See Economic conditions: wages

WOMEN, 717, 1234, 1613, 1755-1757

WORKER PRIESTS, 1634

WORKERS. See Social groups: workers

YEARBOOKS, 69-71, 335, 802, 1729

YOUTH, 402, 457, 714, 866, 971, 1017, 1357, 1442, 1678, 1995; in agriculture, 442; and Algerian war, 900, 1436, 1473; and communist organizations, 641, 1697; and O.A.S., 866; reading interests, 392; vocational training, 114, 1994. See also Social groups: students; Education

Author Index

Indexed names include:

1) All authors, editors, and compilers not listed in the alphabetical position in Part I.

2) All co-authors, co-editors, participants in colloquia, etc., and other important contributors mentioned either bibliographically or in the annotations.

3) Pen names when work is listed under author's real name.

4) Persons or organizations (political parties, clubs, academic institutions, etc.) responsible for or connected with issuing a work but not listed as authors in Part I. These have been indexed only when relevant to the Fifth Republic.

For 1-4, entry numbers are underlined. For example: Mendès-France, Pierre: 448 indicates that the name is that of the author.

5) Persons or organizations mentioned either bibliographically or in the annotations, when substantial information about them is provided. (However, the following names will also be found in the Subject Index: Gaulle, Charles de, Front de libération nationale, Organisation de l'armée secrète, Parti communiste français, Parti socialiste, and Union pour la nouvelle république.) In this case entry numbers are not underlined, as in Mendès-France, Pierre: 336.

A.E.R.S.E. See Association pour l'étude de la réforme des structures de l'état

A.L.N. See Armée de la libération nationale

Abbas, Ferhat 1-9, 401, 483, 808, 1050, 1309, 1562, 1933

Abelin, Pierre 1292

Académie des sciences coloniales 1810

Académie des sciences d'outre-mer 1810

Académie internationale de science politique et d'histoire constitutionnelle 2051

Acadi. See Association des cadres dirigeants de l'industrie . . .

Accords, Michel des 963

Action nationale contre-révolutionnaire 630

Action socialiste 1406

Algerian Communist Party. See Parti communiste algérien

Adam, Gérard 12-14, 1065

Ahmed, Hussein Ait 14a, 990

Ailleret, Charles (General) 944, 1294, 1568

Alazard, J. 975

Albertini, Georges 1929

Albord, Tony (General) 17

Algeria. Délégation générale du gouvernement 29, 30, 743a, 743b, 1830. See also France. Présidence du Conseil.Délégation générale en Algérie

Algeria. Gouvernement général 23, 25, 26, 28, 34, 1826-1829

Algeria. Office algérien d'action commerciale 1831

Algeria. Ministère du commerce 1831

Algerian Front of National Liberation Delegation 37-48, 865, 1047. See also Delegation of the Provisional Government of the Algerian Republic, New York

Algerian Office. See Delegation of the Provisional Government of the Algerian Republic, New York

Algiers. Université 2078

Allais, Maurice 52, 53, 368

Allary, Georges 840

Alleg, Henri 54, 55, 1765, 1821

Alliance israëlite universelle 2020

Alliance française 801

Alquier, Jean-Yves 309

Alvergnat, Louis 418

American Committee for France and Algeria 59, 1975, 2119

Amicale des anciens members du Parti communiste français 62, 1906

Amrouche, Jean 1471

Ancel 363

Andreu, Pierre 67, 1311, 1361

Anthérieu, Etienne 1481

Antoine, Jacques 1618

Antoine, Pierre 1522

Aragon, Louis 640, 1165, 1395, 1586

Arboussier, Gabriel d' 413

Ardant, Gabriel 439

Argoud, Antoine (Col.) 74, 178, 357, 381, 1233, 1749

Armand, Louis 514, 722

Arnaud, Georges [pseud.] See Girard, Henri Georges Charles Achille

Armée de la libération nationale 37, 40, 41, 159, 827, 991, 1521, 1722

Aron, Raymond 76-83, 88, 152, 371, 413, 583, 594, 1107, 1124, 1459, 1649

Assac, Jacques Ploncard d' 89, 90, 2134

Association d'études et d'informations politiques internationales 93, 94, 1929

Association de Sauve-Garde; Accords d'Evian 1981

Association des anciens du Centre des hautes études d'administration musulmane 1819

Association des anciens du 9. régiment d'infanterie 1328

Association des anciens élèves de l'Institut agricole d'Algérie 1676

Association des cadres dirigeants de l'industrie pour le progrès social et économique (ACADI) 1840

Association des étudiants musulmans nord-africains 370

Association française de science politique 95-102, 572, 2084

Association France-Algérie 1969

Association France-Cuba 1905

Association Horizon 80. See Horizon 80

Association internationale des juristes démocrates 159

Association nationales des Français d'Afrique du Nord et d'Outre-mer et leurs amis 1971

Association nationale pour le soutien de l'action du générale de Gaulle 104-105, 811(b), 1841

Association populaire franco-chinoise. See Comités pour la formation d'une Association. . . .

Association pour l'étude de la réforme des structures de l'état (A. E. R. S. E.) 106, 1717, 1930

Association pour la saufgarde des institutions judiciaires 1698

Astier de la Vigerie, Emmanuel d' 108, 422, 1165, 1317

Audin, Madame (Maurice) 158

Audin, Maurice 54, 380, 1765

Audin: Comité. See Comité Maurice Audin

Austruy, Jacques 1148

Axelos, Kostas 439

Barangé, 1275

Barberot, Roger 132, 309, 1627

Bardèche, Maurice 133, 457

Barrère, Alain 1618

Barrès, Claude 1147, 1328

Basdevant, Jules 16

Bastien-Thiry, Jean-Marie 141, 142, 143, 1485, 1705, 1711. See also Trials, political: Petit-Clamart

Battaglia, Adolfo 1060

Bauchet, Pierre 148-150, 1616

Beau de Loménie, Emmanuel 83, 152, 153, 583, 1361

Beaufré, André (General) 154-156, 2104

Beauvoir, Simon de 158, 158a, 479, 1473

Benabdallah, Abdessamad 164, 460

Ben Barka, al-Mahdi. See Bin Barakah, al-Mahdi

Ben Bella, Ahmed 1219

Bencheneb, S. 975

Ben Khedda, Ben Youssef 166-168, 1194

Benoist, Paul 1164

Bergheaud, Edmond 1232a, 1233

Berl, Emmanuel 1361

Bernard, J. 768

Berque, Jacques 88, 173, 439

Besse, Guy 1395

Bettelheim, Charles 367, 439

Beuve-Méry, Hubert 176

Bevan, Aneurin 1628

Biaggi, Jean Baptiste 456

Bibliothèque nationale. See Paris. Bibliothèque nationale

Bidault, Georges 177, 178, 194, 365, 1240

Bigeard, Marcel (Col.) 642a

Bigot, (General) 410

Billotte, Pierre 180, 1724, 1725

Billoux, François 1400

Bin Barakah, al-Mahdi   165, 182, 295, 383, 384, 1159, 1179, 1298, 1576

Bissardon, Henri   1268

Blardone, Gilbert   976

Blignière, Colonel de   1749

Blin, Maurice   1291

Bloch-Lainé, François   10, 190, 191, 356, 1058, 1189, 1522, 1571

Blondel, Jean   1534

Blumenfeld, Samuel   2119

Bollardière, Paris de (General)   132, 158, 1627

Bolle, Pierre   1011

Bondy, François   413, 586

Bonnard, Abel   1624

Bordeaux. Institut de géographie. Faculté des lettres   1861

Borne, Etienne   75

Boualam, Bachaga. See Boualam, Said Benissa

Boualam, Said Benissa   222a-224, 1003

Bouhired, Djamila   877

Bouju, Paul M.   878

Boumendjet, Ahmed   64, 1309

Boupacha, Djamila   158, 479

Bourdet, Claude   228, 418

Bourdieu, Pierre   231-234, 370, 1363, 1438, 1610, 1713

Bourges-Maunoury, Maurice   365, 489

Bourguiba, Habib   1050

Boutang, Pierre   236, 1311, 1361, 2013

Brace, Joan   241, 242

Brasillach, Robert   1624

Bridier, Manuel   924

Bromberger, Serge   245, 247, 248

Brown, Bernard E.   1153

Brune, Jean   74, 252, 1311

Bureau européen de la jeunesse et de l'enfance   1357

Bureau politique de Mgr le Comte de Paris   1859

Bureau universitaire de statistique et de documentation scolaires et professionnelles (B.U.S.)   1844

Burnham, James   59

Buron, Robert   261, 262, 1655

Business International Corporation   263

Bye, Maurice   579

C.F.D.T.   See Confédération française démocratique du travail

C.F.T.C.   See Confédération française des travailleurs chrétiens

C.G.T.   See Confédération générale du travail

C.G.T. - F.O.   See Force ouvrière

C.N.R.A.   See Conseil national de la révolution algérienne

Cachin, Marcel   1689

Calan, Pierre de. See La Lande de Calan, Pierre de

Calvez, Jean-Yves   96, 1617

Camus, Albert   271, 358, 626, 627, 1459

Camus, Madame Albert   1016

Capitant, René   99, 100, 649, 1725

Carpentier, Marcel (General)   113

Cardonnel,   1612

Casanova, Antoine   1612

Castellan, Georges   557

Cathala, Joseph   256

Cazes, Bernard   254, 296

Céline, Louis-Ferdinand   1624

Centre africain des sciences humaines appliquées   496, 497, 1520

Centre Catholique des intellectuels français   75, 1615

Centre chrétien des patrons et dirigeants d'entreprise français   1731

Centre d'action européenne fédéraliste   1811

Centre d'études de la consommativité   1769

Centre d'études de politique étrangère   335, 2052, 2104

Centre d'études et de recherches marxistes   844, 1612-1614

Centre d'études politiques et civiques   320, 1094, 1570

Centre d'études prospectives   2063

Centre d'études socialistes: Cahiers   298a, 1437, 1870

Centre d'études sociologiques   2085

Centre d'études supérieures de psychologie sociale   1580, 1871

Centre d'information civique   1872, 1873, 1891, 1892

Centre d'information pour la défense des libertés et de la paix   1754, 2110

Centre d'information pour les problèmes de l'Algérie et du Sahara   504, 1651, 2127

Centre démocrate   302, 303, 811(l), 1903, 1908a

Centre des hautes études américaines   1874, 1875

Centre international de formation européenne   1941

Centre international de recherche et de formation en vue du développement harmonieux   1911

Centre national d'information d'études et d'action sociale pour les jeunes travailleurs   1994

Centre national de la recherche scientifique. See France. Centre national de la recherche scientifique

Centre national des indépendants et paysans   137, 529, 811(c), 1009, 1972, 1996

Centre national des jeunes agriculteurs   442, 871, 1162

Centre national des jeunes patrons   356

Centre national des Républicains sociaux. See Républicains sociaux

Centre républicain   811(n), 1053

Cercle Tocqueville   1876

Chaban-Delmas, Jacques   433, 636, 649, 1465

Chaigneau, Yves   1440

Chambaz, Jacques   1174

Charlot, Monica   649

Charnay, Jean-Paul   324, 325, 439

Chassin, Lionel (General)   811(d), 1486

Chatagner, Jacques   326, 1849

Chateaubriant, Alphonse de   1624

Chauvel, Jean-François   245

Chenu, Marcel (Révérend Père)   158

Chevallier, Jacques   285, 330

Cheverny, Jules [pseud.]. See Gourdon, Alain

Chombart de Lauwe, Marie-José 717

Chombart de Lauwe, Paul-Henry 88, 717

Cincinnatus [pseud.]. See Greindl, E.

Cité catholique 1524, 1571, 1644, 2044, 2125

Citoyens 60 915, 1882

Claude, Henri 340, 341, 1174

Claudius-Petit, Eugène 768

Club démocratie nouvelle 345-348, 1883

Club des Jacobins 958

Club Jean Moulin 147, 191, 250, 307, 349-355, 356, 811(l), 872, 912, 915, 1137, 1161, 1665, 1667, 1675, 1884. See also Collection Jean Moulin in Title Index

Cogniot, Georges 359-362, 640, 1174, 1389

Collège coopératif. See Paris. Collège coopératif

Colloque de Grenoble 305a, 472

Colloque de la Brévière 1769

Colloque de Vincennes 365, 1651, 1863

Colloque international sur l'Algérie 369, 1753

Colloques socialistes 372, 1667

Colombel, Jeannette 1612

Comité central français pour l'outre-mer 1894, 2024

Comité d'action commune pour le référendum 811(b)

Comité d'action de défense démocratique 951, 964

Comité d'action pour une république fédérale française 1093

Comité d'entente des anciens combattants pour la défense de la France, de l'Union française et de son armée 922

Comité d'études de défense nationale 2076

Comité d'études et de liaison des démocrates français. See Centre démocrate

Comité d'études pour la République 506

Comité d'histoire de la deuxième guerre mondiale. See France. Comité d'histoire. . .

Comité de coordination pour la documentation des sciences sociales 1847

Comité de l'Afrique française 1820

Comité de la défense pour l'unité française 922

Comité de Vincennes 365, 1651, 1863

Comité des démocrates. See Centre démocrate

Comité des intellectuels 385

Comité du Maroc 1820

Comité du salut public (Algeria) 811(a), 870, 1054, 1113, 1486, 1508, 1626, 1716

Comité français pour l'union pan-européenne 1890

Comité France actuelle 1968

Comité Maurice Audin 380-381a, 1754, 1766

Comité national pour l'aménagement du territoire 1891

Comité national pour la préparation à l'élection présidentielle 1892

Comité universitaire d'information pédagogique 267

Comités pour la formation d'une Association populaire Franco-chinoise 1855

Commin, Pierre 1413

Commission internationale contre le régime concentrationnaire 2093

Comte de Paris. See Paris, Henri Robert, etc.

Confédération française démocratique du travail (C.F.D.T.) 522

Confédération française des travailleurs chrétiens 12, 13, 491, 522, 1370, 2105

After 1964 name changed to Confédération française démocratique du travail

Confédération générale du travail 12, 251, 387, 388, 491, 1277

Confédération générale du travail: Force Ouvrière. See Force Ouvrière

Confédération nationale des réserves 1838

Confédération nationale du travail 1888

Congress for cultural freedom 371, 2057

Conseil national de la résistance 142, 143, 178, 1275, 1342, 1507, 1835, 1898, 1993

Conseil national de la révolution algérienne 51, 480, 481, 988

Conseil national du patronat français 393, 394, 565, 591, 1673, 2041

Convention des institutions républicaines 398-400, 574, 609

Convention des institutions républicaines. Cahiers 398-400, 574, 577, 1245, 1246

Convention gauche de la Ve République 811(n)

Convention républicaine 811(c), 1739

Cooley, John K. 401

Coral [pseud.]. See Larocque-Latour, Jacques

Coston, Henri 405-408, 1109, 1443

Cotta, Michèle 409, 419, 649

Coty, René 698, 1568

Courrégé, Maurice 460, 1754, 1754a

Courthéoux, Jean-Paul 668

Couve de Murville, Maurice 790, 899, 1144, 1294, 1659, 1954

Cultiaux, Didier 1359

Dalloz 502b, 1857a

Dantsig, Boris Mozeivich 19

Darbel, Alain 1363, 1713

Darras 1363

Dauer, Jacques 434, 435, 2109

David, Marcel 96

Debré, Michel 146, 197, 414, 428, 445-454, 649, 695, 793, 1240, 1317, 1779, 1954

Debu-Bridel, Jacques 1724

Debzi, Laïd 497

Defferre, Gaston 22, 461, 2064, 2102. See also Elections, presidential (Fifth Republic, 1965): candidates, Defferre in Subject Index

Delbecque, Léon 462, 1016

Delegation of the Provisional Government of the Algerian Republic, New York 466-486, 993. See also Algerian Front of National Liberation Delegation, New York

Delmas, Claude 113, 488, 489

Démocratie chrétienne 811(c)

Demonque, 768

Denis, Jacques 1174

Depreux, Edouard 493, 649, 872, 1416, 1420

Descloîtres, Claudine 495, 496

Desmottes, Georges 1616

Desroche, Henri 1355

Deutsch, Karl W. 502a, 803

Deutsch-französisches Institut, Ludwigsburg. See Ludwigsburg. Deutsch-französisches. ...

Dib, Mohammed 1471

Dijon. Université. Centre d'études des relations politiques 572, 943

Direction de la Documentation. See France. Direction de la documentation

Djebar, Assid 1471

Documentation africaine 1982

Documentation française. See France. Direction de la documentation

Drancourt, Michel 513, 514, 1536

Drieu La Rochelle, Pierre 1624

Droit, Michel 851

Dronne, Raymond 523, 1016

Duboin, Jacques 1083

Duclos, Jacques 530-534, 640, 1369, 1400, 1614

Duhamel, Alain 615

Duhamel, Jacques 1317

Dumont, René 1440

Dumontier, Jacques 752

Dupeux, Georges 96

Dupuy, Richard 1705

Duroselle, Jean-Baptiste 973

Dutaret, Alain 1725

Duval, Léon Etienne (Archbishop) 547, 1924

Duverger, Maurice 95, 97-99, 101, 548-556, 572, 1131, 1152, 1675

Duvignaud, Jean 413

Editions de Minuit 559, 841

Elgey, Georgette 245

Eliard, Michel 232

Emanuel, Pierre 413

Emeri, Claude 411

Erdmer, Marcel 1101

Erhard, Ludwig 1171, 1426

Estier, Claude 574-577, 924

Estrangin, L. 768

Etudes sociales nord-africaines 578-584, 1123

European Free Trade Association 53, 589, 1265

European Movement. See Organisation française du Mouvement européen

European Union of Federalists. See Mouvement fédéraliste européen

F. L. N. See Front de libération nationale

Farine, Philippe 1616

Farran, Jean 1280

Faure, Edgar 194, 612, 649, 840, 1317

Faure, Jacques (General) 410

Faure, Maurice 113, 1317

Fauvet, Jacques 95, 98, 102, 366, 613-615, 1124, 1245

Fauvet, Jean-Christian 1618

Fédéralistes européens. See Mouvement fédéraliste européen

Fédération de la gauche démocrate et socialiste 15, 400, 609, 811(l), 1245, 1246, 1409, 1887

Fédération des étudiants d'Afrique noire en France 1935

Fédération des officiers de réserve républicaine 1838, 1945

Fédération des sous-officiers de réserve républicaine 1838, 1945

Fédération internationale des jeunesses libertaires, section française 1814

Fédération nationale des syndicats d'exploitants agricoles (F. N. S. E. A.) 1986

Fédération nationale des parachutistes français 1126

Fédération française contre l'armement atomique 939

Feraoun, Mouloud 626, 627, 1471

Flanner, Janet 643

Foccart, Jacques 1133

Folliet, Joseph 389

Fondation nationale des sciences politiques 645-648, 1850, 2084

Fondation nationale des sciences politiques. Bibliothèque 299, 322, 652, 1947

Fondation nationale des sciences politiques: Cahiers 12, 13, 96-98, 101, 102, 323, 324, 364, 411, 546, 647, 650, 651, 863, 878, 887, 907, 963, 1032, 1218, 1224, 1238, 1282, 1673

Fondation nationale des sciences politiques. Centre d'étude de la vie politique française 14, 109, 649-651, 887, 1067, 1290, 1362, 1407, 1516

Fondation nationale des sciences politiques. Centre d'études des relations internationales 510, 913, 1125, 1461, 1881, 2000

Fondation nationale des sciences politiques: Guides de recherches 322, 409, 417, 652, 1065, 1066, 1503

Fontaine, François 655, 1536

Fontaine, Pierre 458, 657-661

Fontanet, Joseph 662, 1291, 1292

Force ouvrière 12, 14, 1949

Forster, Clifford 59

Fourastié, Jean 666-669, 768

Fourgeaud, 368

Foyer, Jean 899

France. Ambassade. U. S. Service de presse et d'information 673-708, 858, 859, 1950-1954

France. Assemblée nationale (1958-) 710-712, 1955, 1956. See also National Assembly in Subject Index

France. Assemblée nationale: Sénat 713, 1967. See also Senate in Subject Index

France. Bibliothèque nationale. See Paris. Bibliothèque nationale

France. Centre de recherches sahariennes 715

France. Centre national de la recherche scientifique 88, 715-717

France. Comité d'histoire de la deuxième guerre mondiale 719, 1957, 2073

France. Commissariat général du plan d'équipement et de la productivité 726, 731-734, 736-738, 747, 774

France. Conseil constitutionnel 739, 1362

France. Conseil économique et social 522, 953, 1104, 1958

France. Direction de la documentation 335, 714, 718, 729, 731, 745-764, 771, 782, 783, 785, 797, 799, 811(l), 1133

France. Direction de la documentation: publications catalogue 748, 755

France. Direction de la documentation: Recueils et monographies 718, 745, 746, 749, 750, 756, 762, 767, 799, 1189

France. Direction de la documentation: serials 1818, 1839, 1847, 1866, 1877-1880, 1912-1915, 1966, 2000, 2016, 2017, 2059, 2113

France. Direction de la documentation: serials, indexes to 1912-1914

France. Groupe 1985   768

France. Institut national d'études démographiques (I. N. E. D.) 875, 2053

France. Institut national de la statistiques et des études économiques (I. N. S. E. E.) 770-772, 1858, 1959, 1960, 1966, 2017

France. Ministère d'état chargé des affaires algériennes 780, 799

France. Ministère de la coopération 505, 787-789, 1959, 1961

France. Ministère des finances et des affaires économiques 1858, 1959

France. Ministère du Sahara 1962

France. Ministère du Sahara, des départements d'outre-mer et des territoires d'outre-mer 1963, 1965

France. Ministre d'état chargé des départements et des territoires d'outre-mer 1963, 1964

France. Ministre délégué auprès du Premier Ministre 1962, 1963, 1965

France. Présidence du conseil. Délégation générale en Algérie 795, 796

France. Présidence du conseil. Secrétariat général du gouvernement 797, 1966

France. Sénat. See France. Assemblée nationale: Sénat

France—U.R.S.S. 1976

Francis, Ahmed 1309

Fréderic-Dupont, Edouard 456

Frenay, Henri 586

French Embassy. See France. Ambassade

Fressoz, Roger 812-814

Frey, Roger 649, 899

Freyssinet, Jacques 949

Front de libération nationale 815-823, 1889, 1979, 2005, 2009, 2067, 2068. See also Algerian Front of National Liberation Delegation, N. Y.; Delegation of the Provisional Government of the Algerian Republic, N. Y.; Gouvernement provisoire de la République algérienne; Jabhat al-Tahrir al-Qawmi;and Algerian revolution; Front de libération nationale in Subject Index

Front de libération nationale, Cairo 1, 5, 824

Front du progrès 2109

Front national français (Algeria) 1345

Front of National Liberation. See Front de libération nationale

Gagliardi, Jacques 832-834, 1422, 1885, 2040

Gallois, Pierre (General) 113, 512, 586, 837, 1481, 1536

Garaudy, Roger 640, 844-846, 1395, 1612

Gary, Romain 413

Gaulle, Charles de 21, 203, 415, 428, 429, 740, 851-861, 1018, 1152, 1169, 1330a, 1481, 1620, 1782, 1839, 1954. See also Gaulle, Charles de in Subject Index

Gauvin, Jean 1749

Gendarme, René 584, 863, 926

General Electric 183

Genêt [pseud.]. See Flanner, Janet

Gingembre, Maurice 1749

Girard, Henri Georges Charles Achilles 876, 877

Giraud, Emile 99

Giraud, Henri Honoré 235

Giscard d'Estaing, Valéry 880, 899, 981

Godard, Yves (Col.) 492

Godelier, Maurice 367

Godfrin, Philippe 883

Goguel, François 95, 97-99, 572, 650, 651, 886, 887, 973

Goldstein, Reine 971

Gorce, Paul Marie de la. See La Gorce, Paul Marie de

Gorz, André 260a, 894, 895

Gouin, Felix 1711

Gouraud, Michel (General) 410

Gourdon, Alain 896-898

Gournay, Bernard 645

Gouvernement provisoire de la République algérienne 1, 3-5, 8, 159, 166-168, 369, 401, 466, 483, 824, 991, 1336, 1521, 1804, 1832

Grandval, Gilbert 902, 1724

Grangé, Jean 925

Gravier, Jean-François 413

Grégoire, Roger 904, 1617

Greindl, E. 905

Grenoble. Université. Institut d'études politiques 647, 907, 1011

Grevisse, Suzanne 1076

Grosser, Alfred 572, 886, 911-913, 1124, 1294

Groupe d'Arras 1363

Groupe 1985. See France. Groupe 1985

Groupe Rencontres 513

Gruson, Charles 367, 768

Guillaumat, 768

Haddad, Malek 1471

Hadj, Messali 1289, 2066

Hagnauer, Roger 420

Halimi, Gisèle 158

Hamon, Léo 95, 96, 99, 572, 942-944, 1724

Hauriou, André 557, 950

Héduy, Philippe 90, 955

Held, Jean-François 956, 1197

Hentgen, Pierre 1040

Hernu, Charles 372, 958, 1165

Hersch, Jeanne 586

Hervé, Pierre 959, 1315

Heynaud, Maurice 431

Ho-Chi-Minh 1050

Hoffmann, Stanley 911, 963, 973, 1124

Horizon 80 461, 1495, 1983

Hunebelle, Danielle 1536

Hurst, Jean-Louis 559, 970

Hurtig, Serge 963

Indépendants et paysans. See Centre national des Indépendants...

Institut catholique de Paris 519

Institut d'étude du développement économique et social 1900

Institut d'études politiques. See Paris. Université. Institut d'études politiques

Institut d'observation économique   2026-2028

Institut de science économique appliquée: Cahiers   1180, 1477

Institut français d'histoire sociale   1816, 2008

Institut français d'opinion publique. See Paris. Institut français d'opinion publique

Institut Maurice Thorez   1174

Institut national d'études démographiques. See France. Institut national d'études démographiques

Institut national de la statistique et des études économiques (I. N. S. E. E.). See France. Institut national de la statistique. . .

Institute for International Social Research   275

Institute of Current World Affairs   1194

International Association of Democratic Lawyers   159

International Review Service   1229, 1230, 1231

Isorni, Jacques   143, 649, 979-985, 1179, 1443

Izard, Georges   593, 987

Jabhat al-Tahrir al-Qawmi   988-993

Jabin, André   777, 994, 1496

Jacquinot, Louis   899

Jaffré, Yves-Frédéric   998, 999, 1646

Jeanneney, Jean-Marcel   727, 728

Jeanson, André   1617

Jeanson, Francis   213, 260a, 307, 876, 940, 1003, 1004, 1005, 1185

Jeantet, Gabriel   1087

Jeune république   1406, 1992

Jeune Résistance   1185

Jeunes de la gauche européenne   1008, 1991

Jeunesse ouvrière catholique   971, 1209

Joannes, Victor   1174

Joly, Pierre   397, 1486

Jouvenel, Bertrand de   768, 1019, 1227, 1459, 2063, 2096

Joxe, Louis   899

Jureidini, Paul A.   61

Julien, Charles-André   515

Kahn, Jean-François   494

Kennedy, John   937

Kéréver, A.   20

Kerlan, Pierre   948

Kindleberger, Charles P.   973

Kessel, Joseph   1165

Khrushchev, Nikita S.   94, 1031, 1038-1040

Kirsanov, A. V.   18

Klein, Dieter   1469

Kock, Marc de   590

Koehler, Ulrich   1346

Kriegel, Annie   1437

Krieger, Annie   73

Krier, Mme.   768

Krim, Belkacem   401, 808

Lacheroy, Charles (Col.)   17, 1527, 1637

Lacoste, Robert   194, 365, 492, 1047, 1413

Laffont, Pierre   1711

Lafitte, J.   1789

Lafon, Monique   1380

Lagaillarde, Pierre   585, 607, 1054, 1270, 1625

La Gorce, Paul Marie de   593, 1055-1057, 1317

Lakhdar,   1562

La Lande de Calan, Pierre de   1058

Lalumière, Pierre   411

La Malène, Christian de   1059, 1568

La Morandière, F. Porteu de   1062

Lamour, Philippe   768, 1063

Lancelot, Alain   109, 1065, 1221, 1225

Langevin, Paul   916

Laroche, Fabrice   1072, 1073, 1875, 1938, 1939

Larocque-Latour, Jacques   1074, 1075

Laroque, Pierre   758, 1076

Lasierra, Raymond   1473, 1474

Lassus, Jean   1280

Laudrain, Maurice   1083, 2048

Laugier, Henri   875

Laurat, Lucien   1085, 1572

Laurent, Jacques   1086-1089, 1198, 1361

Lauriol, Marc   365, 1091-1094

Lavagne, François   85

Lavau, Georges   96, 1438

League of Red Cross Societies   1101

Leblanc-Penaud, Pierre   660

Le Bras, Gabriel   88

Le Brun, Pierre   372, 1104, 1585

Lecanuet, Jean   511, 662, 1291, 1292, 1317. See also Elections, presidential (Fifth Republic, 1965): candidates, Lecanuet in Subject Index

Leclerc, Albert A.-J.   1328

Lecoeur, Auguste   1108, 2014

Le Corroller,   1705

Leenhardt, Francis   872

Lefèvre, Bernard   585, 1112, 1113, 1625

Leglise,   1843

Legrand-Lane, Raymond   1448

Leites, Nathan   114-116, 1208

Lerouge, F.   20

Levard, G.   10, 768

Lévi-Strauss, Claude   967

Liberovici, Sergio   874

Ligue de l'enseignement   1813, 2055

Ligue des droits de l'homme   1029

Ligue nationale contre la force de frappe   1248

Lindon, Denis   502

Lindon, Jerome   559, 841

Lipkowski, Jean de   1567

Louis, Roger   1488

Ludwigsburg, Ger. Deutsch-Französisches Institut 1144, 1591

M. N. A. See Mouvement national algérien

M. R. P. See Mouvement républicain populaire

Mabileau, Albert 572

Machu, Jean 1011

Macridis, Roy C. 803, 1152, 1153

Maillot, Henri 224

Main rouge 956, 1013

Maison des agriculteurs français d'Algérie 2001

Malène, Christian de la. See La Malène, Christian de

Mallet, Serge 372, 943, 1160-1162

Malraux, André 639, 1069, 1163, 1586, 1741

Malterre, André 365

Mammeri, Mouloud 1471

Mandel, Ernest 298a

Mandouze, André 391, 992

Mannoni, Eugène 593, 1169

Marçais, Georges 1280

Marçais, Philippe 1092

Marchais, Georges 1402

Marchand, Jean José 1124

Marcel, Gabriel 236

Marcilhacy, Christiane 1724, 1725

Marcilhacy, Pierre 118, 1089, 1175, 1176, 1317

Marill, Alain 73

Maritain, Jacques 139

Marrou, Henri 515

Martel, Jacques 431

Martel, Robert 607

Martin, Marcel 757, 1182

Martinet, Gilles 372, 418, 872, 1184, 1420

Martinez, 1275

Martino, Gaetano 588

Maspero, François 1130, 1187, 2039

Massé, Pierre 762, 1188, 1189, 1313

Masselin, 1189

Massenet, Michel 309, 583, 1190, 1191, 1438

Massis, Henri 1021

Massu, Pierre (General) 1716

Mastias, Jean 1291

Maulnier, Thierry 309

Maunz, Theodor 1809

Mauriac, François 593, 927, 1088, 1089, 1198, 1199, 1655

Maurienne [pseud.]. See Hurst, Jean Louis

Max, Alfred 1536

May, Sherif Mahmud 808

Mayer, Daniel 158

Mégret, Maurice 75, 1203

Melnik, Constantin 1208, 1319

Memmi, Albert 1197

Mendès-France, Pierre 194, 336, 448, 501, 511, 811(o), 840, 872, 897, 910, 1085, 1211-1213, 1308, 1324, 1447, 1509, 1550, 1585, 1622, 1628, 1785, 1862, 1902

Mendras, Henri 96, 102

Mennevée, Roger 1916

Menzhinskii, E. A. 18

Merle, Marcel 96, 1218

Merleau-Ponty, Maurice 130, 260a, 967, 1220, 1497

Meynaud, Jean 1221-1228, 1673

Meyriat, Jean 546

Michel, Henri 719, 1237

Millet, Didier 63

Miquel, Roger (General) 256

Mitterrand, François 372, 649, 1085, 1110, 1165, 1244-1247, 1317, 1319, 1542, 1568, 1614, 1886, 1887. See also Elections, presidential (Fifth Republic, 1965): candidates, Mitterrand in Subject Index

Moch, Jules 1248-1250, 1572

Mollet, Guy 649, 840, 872, 1255-1257, 1317, 1413, 1453

Monnerot, Jules 456, 1311

Monnerville, Gaston 433, 1261

Monnet, Jean 194, 668, 1262-1267, 1335, 1462

Monteil (Captain) 207

Monteil, André 1291

Montvallon, Pierre 1271

Montvalon, Robert de 508, 1272

Morel, S. C. 773

Morice, André 365, 1273

Morin, Jean 29, 1568

Moulinier, Antoine 585

Mounier, Emanuel 1459

Moumié, Felix 956

Moureaux, Serge 590

Mouvement communiste démocratique et national 2014

Mouvement contre le racisme, l'anti-sémitisme et pour la paix 521, 1197

Mouvement d'action civique non-violente 811(a)

Mouvement de libération du peuple 1406, 2004

Mouvement de St. Cére. See Mouvement Poujade

Mouvement européen 282, 283

Mouvement fédéraliste européen 1812, 1944, 2006

Mouvement fédéraliste français 1287, 2128

Mouvement français pour l'abondance 1083

Mouvement national algérien (M.N.A.) 974, 2007, 2066

Mouvement populaire du 13 mai (M. P. 13) 811(d), 1486

Mouvement Poujade 459, 809, 963, 1286, 1288, 1478, 1728, 1857, 1977, 1978, 2124

Mouvement pour la communaute 434

Mouvement pour la coopération en Algérie 2109

Mouvement pour une société libre 53

Mouvement républicain populaire 222, 261, 262, 277, 366, 549, 662, 811(c), 811(j), 1290-1293, 1948, 1970. See also Centre démocrate

Mouvement socialiste pour les états-unis d'Europe 1980, 1991

Muhammad V, King of Morocco 1050

Mury, Gilbert 237, 1300, 1612

Mus, Paul 1301

Naroun, Amar 1022, 1309

National Council of the Algerian Revolution. See Conseil national de la révolution algérienne

Naville, Pierre 298a, 943, 1314-1316

Nenni, Pietro 1628

Neuwirth, Lucien 512

Noël, André 1138, 1851

Norr, Martin 948

Nouschi, André 1048, 1330

Nouvelle entreprise agricole 871

Nouvelle gauche 418, 1406

O.A.S. See Organisation de l'armée secrète

Ohio State University. Graduate Institute for World Affairs 642

Office des étudiants d'outre-mer 773

Orcival, François d' 1072

Organisation commune des régions sahariennes 188, 1337-1340, 1962, 2030, 2031

Organisation de l'armée secrète 1067, 1254, 1341-1343, 1834, 1835, 1898, 1993, 2011, 2129. See also Organisation de l'armée secrète in Subject Index

Organisation française du mouvement européen 1904

Ortiz, Joseph 585, 607, 1345

Ostertag, A. 392

Oudard, Georges 1729

Oussedik, Mourad 164, 460, 590

Ouzegane, Amar 1347, 1364

Paris, Henri Robert Ferdinand Marie Louis Philippe de Bourbon-Orléans, Comte de 229, 1859

Paris. Bibliothèque nationale 443, 765, 811(e)-811(g), 1354, 1512

Paris. Collège coopératif 1355

Paris. Institut français d'opinion publique 1220a, 1357, 2103

Paris. Université. Ecole pratique des hautes études. VIe section: sciences économiques et sociales 1860

Paris. Université. Faculté de droit et des sciences économiques: Travaux et recherches. Série "Science politique" 144, 227a, 872, 883, 925, 1137, 1493, 1601

Paris. Université. Institut d'études politiques 63, 317a, 1166, 1359

Parti communiste algérien 55, 169, 224, 227, 1347, 1364, 1630, 1765, 1821

Parti communiste français 1365-1404. See also Parti communiste français in Subject Index

Parti communiste guadeloupéen 1931

Parti communiste internationaliste 1405, 2060

Parti communiste martiniquais 1997

Parti communiste révolutionnaire de France 1865

Parti d'Union de la gauche socialiste 418, 811(c), 1173, 1307, 1314, 1406, 1798, 2004, 2047, 2117

Parti national syndicaliste français 457

Parti républicain radical et radical socialiste 134, 336, 549, 609, 646, 811(c), 958, 1324, 1407-1409, 1853

Parti socialiste (S.F.I.O.) 1410-1414, 1910, 1999, 2035-2037, 2052a, 2091. See also Parti socialiste in Subject Index

Parti socialiste autonome 1307, 1415, 1416, 1420

Parti socialiste unifié 228, 372, 493, 525, 549, 811(l), 872, 1134, 1160, 1184, 1232, 1307, 1314, 1417-1420, 1509, 1510, 2038, 2118

Pascal, Jean 832

Passeron, André 854, 855

Passeron, Jean-Claude 232, 233

"Pax" (Catholic Organization) 290, 986

Péju, Marcel 940

Pelletier, Pierre 128

Perillier, Louis 256

Perraux, François 1438-1441, 1900, 1911, 2113a

Pétain, Henri Philippe Bénoni Omer 985, 1443, 1501, 1602, 1660, 1709

Petit, André (General) 410

Pflimlin, Pierre 696, 840, 1292, 1448

Philip, André 413, 512, 586, 872, 943, 1416, 1449-1453, 1572

Philippe, J. 1602

Picht, Georg 1294

Piem [pseud.]. See Montvallon, Pierre de

Pinay, Antoine 840

Pineau, Christian 372, 1463, 1464

Piolot, Marc 251

Pirelli, Giovanni 1035

Pitts, Jesse R. 973

Planchais, Jean 75, 614, 961, 1466, 1467

Ploncard d'Assac. See Assac, Jacques Ploncard d'

Pokrovskii, A. I. 18, 1476

Poli, Joseph 1564

Pompidou, Georges 146, 246, 794, 811(o), 899, 1954

Poperen, Jean 1420

Porteu de la Morandière, F. See La Morandière, Porteu de

Potier, Michel 1276

Poujade, Pierre 194, 809, 1478. See also Mouvement Poujade

Pouteau, Micheline 266

Pré, Roland 1724

Prélot, Marcel 100, 572, 1484, 1492, 2051

Prenant, André 1048

Prévost, Jean-Pierre 75

Prinet, Jean 443

Protter, Benjamin 1975, 2114

Provisional Government of the Algerian Republic. See Gouvernement provisoire de la République algérienne

Puchala, Donald J. 1220a

Quermonne, Jean-Louis 1522

Quilliot, Roger 372, 1495, 1572

R.P.F. See Rassemblement du peuple français

Rabany, Charles 777, 1496

Racine, Nicole 649

Radoux, L. 1786

Rand Corporation, Reports 151, 1114, 1115, 1208, 1210, 1797

Randet, Pierre 867

Rassemblement démocratique 1408

Rassemblement du peuple français 857, 924, 1168, 1178, 1326, 1492, 1507. See also Gaullists, pre-1958 in Subject Index

Raux, Henri F. 1512

Rebatet, Lucien 1624

Red Cross. International Committee 485, 1506, 1679, 1680

Red Cross. League of national societies. See League of Red Cross Societies

Rémond, René 75, 96, 98, 364, 366, 1508, 1617

Républicains Indépendants 204, 811(n). See also Giscard d'Estaing, Valéry

Républicains sociaux 209, 811(c), 924, 1479, 1513, 1514

Rettenbach, Bernard 1137

Revel, Jean François 158, 419, 1517-1519

Reverdy, Jean-Claude 495, 496, 1520

Rey, 1843

Reynaud, Jean-Paul 1641

Reynaud, Paul 1294, 1531, 1532

Ribaud, André [pseud.] See Fressoz, Roger

Rieben, Henri 586

Rieunier, René 1535, 1646

Robert, Philippe 717

Roche, Emile 413

Rochet, Waldeck 640, 649, 1317, 1369, 1392, 1394, 1396-1398, 1402, 1540-1542, 1614

Rodet, Michel 434, 435

Roig, Charles 925

Rossillon, Philippe 834

Rolland, 363

Roque, Claude 849

Rosenfeld, Oreste 1416

Rostand, Jean 1165

Rottier, Georges 368

Roy, Jules 158, 536, 1554, 1555, 1933

Rueff, Jacques 301, 512, 721-723, 1426, 1559, 1560, 1684

Ruf, Werner 1346

S. F. I. O. See Parti socialiste (S. F. I. O.)

Sagan, Françoise 158

Saint-Laurent, Cécil [pseud.] See Laurent, Jacques

Saint-Marc, Denoux de (Commander) 410

Saint-Paulien, J. [pseud.]. See Sicard Maurice

Salan, Raoul 638, 1073, 1489a, 1568, 1669, 1716. See also Trials, political: O. A. S. in Subject Index

Sarrailh, J. 1526

Sartre, Jean-Paul 260a, 294, 358, 603, 845, 846, 894, 967, 1187, 1315, 1459, 1497, 1577, 1578, 1586, 1622, 1807, 2111

Sauge, George 1474, 1580, 1871

Sauvy, Alfred 515, 875, 1582-1585

Savary, Alain 372, 872, 1587

Sayad, Abdelmalek 231a

Schifres, Alain 144

Schuman, Robert 16, 588, 1600

Schumann, Maurice 16

Secrétariat social d'Alger 579, 584, 1604-1610, 1740, 2094

Ségnaire, Julien 1361

Sérant, Paul 1361, 1621-1624

Sérigny, Alain de 1016, 1625, 1626, 1918. See also Trials, political: barricades in Subject Index

Servan-Schreiber, Jacques 132, 1627, 1628

Service de documentation électorale 569

Servolin, Claude 871

Sfez, Lucien 872

Sicard, Maurice 1632

Simon, Pierre-Henri 75, 413, 583, 1324, 1638, 1639

Sirius [pseud.] See Beuve-Méry, Hubert

Société d'études et de documentation économiques, industrielles et sociales 2096

Société d'histoire moderne 2075, 2097

Société d'histoire naturelle de l'Afrique du Nord 2098, 2099

Société des agriculteurs d'Algérie 2100

Société française d'histoire d'outre-mer 2083

Société française de pédagogie 916

Société historique algérienne 2071

Society for French-American Affairs 2114

Solé, Jacques 1011

Soustelle, Jacques 83, 365, 391, 504, 512, 583, 636, 951, 1240, 1270, 1647-1657, 1975, 2127, 2131

Soyer, R. A. 1981

Stercken, Hans 853

Stibbe, Pierre 515

Stoetzel, Jean 1124, 1664

Strauss, Franz Joseph 1171

Sudreau, Pierre 899

Suffert, Georges 372, 1666, 1667

Susini, 254

Susini, Jean Jacques 285, 607, 1625, 1669

Tannery, Claude 144

Tautil, Christian 136

Taylor, S. 1789

Technique et Démocratie 135

Teissedre, Jean 752

Terrenoine, Louis 593, 1655, 1681

Texier, Geneviève 1234

Théry, Henri 1617

Thireau, Yann 1678

Thiriart, Jean 90, 1685, 1686, 1940, 1990, 2011, 2012

Thomas, Jean-Pierre 878, 1238

Thorez, Maurice 237, 640, 1374, 1391, 1395-1398, 1687-1697

Thorp, René 305a, 1698

Tillion, Germaine 583, 1700-1703

Tixier, Jean-Louis 143, 295, 521, 1089, 1150, 1568, 1705, 1706. See also Elections, presidential (Fifth Republic, 1965): candidates, Tixier-Vignancour in Subject Index

Tixier-Vignancour. See Tixier, Jean-Louis

Touchard, Jean 96, 97

Touré, Sékou 1050

Triboulet, Raymond 789, 1490, 1714

Travailleurs européens pour les Etats-unis d'Europe 2115

Trinquier, Roger (Col.) 106, 1715-1718, 1930

Turin, L. 20

U.D.C.A. See Union de défense des commerçants et artisans

U.D.S.R. See Union démocratique et socialiste de la Résistance

U.D.T. See Union démocratique du travail

U.N.E.F. See Union nationale des étudiants de France

U.N.R. See Union pour la nouvelle république

Union de défense des commerçants et artisans 1857, 1977, 2124. See also Mouvement Poujade

Union de la gauche socialiste. See Parti d'Union de la gauche socialiste

Union démocratique du travail (U.D.T.) 180, 902, 942, 1007, 1723-1725, 1743, 2018

After Nov. 1962, see Union pour la nouvelle république—Union démocratique du travail

Union démocratique et socialiste de la Résistance 811(c), 1886, 2120

Union des étudiants communistes de France 1395, 1697, 1726

Union des femmes françaises 1756

Union des forces démocratiques 1307

Union des jeunes filles de France 1755

Union générale des étudiants musulmans algériens 865, 1934

Union générale des travailleurs algériens 1472, 1730, 2033

Union nationale des étudiants de France (U.N.E.F.) 370, 622, 1733-1936, 2121

Union nationale des étudiants de France: dissident groups 623, 828, 914

Union nationale des étudiants de Tunisie 370

Union nationale des étudiants du Maroc 370

Union nationale des paysans de France 660

Union pour l'Algérie française 1507

Union pour la nouvelle république (U.N.R.) 811(c), 1737-1739, 1901, 2010, 2122. See also Union pour la nouvelle république in Subject Index

Union pour la nouvelle république—Union démocratique du travail (U.N.R.-U.D.T.) 284, 318, 811(l), 811(n), 1059, 1567, 1574, 2010, 2018

Union pour la présence française 1507

Union pour le salut et le renouveau de l'Algérie 924

Union progressiste 422

"Unir" 62

Unité socialiste 1406

United Nations High Commissioner for Refugees 1101

University of California, Berkeley 512

Vacherand, Janine 777, 994

Valentin, François 365

Valentino, André 1493

Vallon, Louis 649, 1240, 1724, 1725, 1743-1745

Vanuxem, Paul (General) 279, 1748, 1749

Varaut, Jean-Marc 1576, 1706

Vedel, Georges 96, 99, 366, 413, 520, 1317, 1675, 1809

Verdier, Robert 372

Vergès, Jacques 164, 460, 877, 1753-1754a

Vibert, Paul 1618

Vidal-Nacquet, Pierre 1754, 1765, 1766

Vigneau, Philippe 430

Villecourt, Louis 1460

Villiers de l'Isle Adam, G. (Col.) 75

Voisin, André 503

Wallon, Henri 916

Weil, Jean 871

Weil, Simone 1459

Weill, Pierre 502

Weizsaecker, Carl Friedrich von 1294

Wertheimer, Marcel 1061

Weygard, Maxime 129, 927, 1787

Wylie, Laurence 973

Ximenès, 1527

Yacef, Saadi 877, 1702, 1803

Yacine, Kateb 1471

Yazid, Mohamed 1196, 1804

Youlou, Fulbert 390

Zavrian, Michel 460, 1754, 1754a

Zeller, André 312

Title Index

Indexed titles include:

1) Book titles for works with complicated or ambiguous author entries, such as publications listed under compilers or organizations. Normally book titles have not been indexed.
2) Serial titles listed under the publishing agency (e.g., "French affairs" which is listed under France. Ambassade. U.S.).
3) Serial titles where title changes have occurred, or where supplements are listed under different titles.
4) Selected serial titles for which special issues are listed under other headings.
5) Serial titles about which substantial information is given elsewhere than under the serial heading in Part II.
6) Selected series or collection titles of special significance for the Fifth Republic (e.g., Cahiers libres, Tribune libre).

"Les accords d'Evian" 799
"Action fédéraliste européenne" 1812, 1944
"Action laïque" 1813, 2055
"Actualité de l'histoire" 1816, 2008
"L'administration française" 645
"L'Affaire Pax en France" 986
"Les affaires étrangères" 16
"Africain" 111
"Afrique—action" 1989
"Arguments et ripostes; fiches socialistes" 2035
"Alerte atomique" 1283
"Alger 26 mars" 709
"Algeria anno sette" 874
"L'Algeria e il socialismo" 1156
"Algerian developments, 1959" 1229
"The Algerian-French Conflict" 1230
"Algérie; accord de cessez-le-feu" 800
"Algérie; quelques aspects des problèmes économiques et sociaux" 23
"L'Algérie à l'heure de la paix" 780
"L'Algérie de demain" 1438
"Les Algériens et le droit des gens" 369
"Analyses de presse" 144
"Annuaire de la presse et de la publicité" 70
"Annuaire de la presse française et étrangère et du monde politique" See Annuaire de la presse et de la publicité
"Après de Gaulle?" 1405
"L'Armée française" 455
"Aspects et réalités de l'Algérie agricole" 1676
"Aspects of European Integration" 1477
"Aspects of the Algerian revolution" 40
"Aspects véritables de la rébellion algérienne" 781
"Les aspirations des jeunes français de 16 à 24 ans" 1357
"L'Assemblée introuvable; le trombinoscope de la Vème bis" 1109
"Aucune bête au monde" 642a

"Aurore" 811(e)
"Aux écoutes" 811(l)
"Avant le troisième tour" 63
"Barodet" 712
"Belgique-Afrique" 2011
"La Belgique devant le problème algérien" 382
"Le bi-partisme est-il possible en France?" 95
"Le Bled" 811(d), 1848, 2107
"Bottin" 791
"Le Bulletin. Douments et recherches" 326, 1849, 1998
"Bulletin d'information radical-socialiste" 1408, 1409, 1853
"Bulletin de conjoncture d'outre-mer" 1960
"Bulletin hebdomadaire de statistique" 1966
"Bulletin officiel de l'Organisation commune des régions sahariennes" 1962
"Bulletin SEDEIS" 2096
"Cahiers de l'Institut de science économique appliquée" See Institut de science. Cahiers in Author Index
"Cahiers de la Convention des institutions républicaines" See Convention des institutions républicaines. Cahiers in Author Index
"Cahiers de la Fondation nationale des sciences politiques" See Fondation nationale ... Cahiers in Author Index
"Cahiers de la République" 1862, 1902
"Cahiers du Centre d'études socialistes" See Centre d'Etudes socialistes. Cahiers in Author Index
"Cahiers du communisme" 1394, 1402, 1403, 1864
"Cahiers du Témoignage chrétien" 291, 383, 384, 1296, 1679, 1680
"Cahiers économiques" 1545
"Cahiers internationaux de sociologie" 103
"Cahiers libres" 123, 124, 182, 228, 307, 311, 402, 403, 431, 460, 576, 602, 603, 940, 992, 1035, 1046, 1185-1187, 1195, 1428, 1563, 1666
"Cahiers nord-africains" 578-584
"Canard enchainé" 144, 273, 812-814, 1102
"Carrefour" 177, 1869
"The Catholic avant-garde" 508
"Choix et efficience des investissements" 367

"Chronique sociale de France" 333, 334, 976, 1616-1618

"Chroniques d'outre-mer" 1877, 1878

"Chroniques de la Communauté" 1877, 1878

"Chronologie internationale" 335, 1880, 2016

"Vᵉ Plan de développement économique et social, 1966-1970" 731-734, 736, 737, 774

"Les classes sociales dans le monde d'aujourd'hue" 103

"Collection Jean Moulin" 115, 250, 355, 912, 915

"Collection U; Série Société politique" 163, 886, 1530

"Combat" 63, 811(e), 811(l), 1885

"Combat républicain" 398-400, 574, 577, 1245, 1246, 1886, 1887

"Le Combattant" 1889, 2005

"Communauté France-Eurafrique" 1893, 1969a

"Communautés et continents" 1894, 2024

"Les conditions de développement, de recrutement, de fonctionnement et de localisation des grandes écoles en France" 767

"La conduite des affaires étrangères en France" 1125

"La conscience chrétienne et les nationalismes" 1615

"Contrat social" 1899, 1929

"Coopération" 1981

"Coopération-hebdo" 1981

"Courrier de la colère" 414

"Courrier de la nouvelle république" 1901, 2010

"Courrier de la république" 1862, 1902

"Courrier des démocrates" 1903, 1908a

"Le Courrier du P.S.U." 2038

"Crapouillot" 419, 420, 839, 840

"La crise militaire française 1945-1962" 878

"La Croix" 811(e), 883

"De Gaulle: implacable ally" 1152

"De Gaulle, anachronism, realist, or prophet?" 1794

"De Gaulle, die Deutschen, Europa" 429

"De Gaulle et les patries" 21

"De Gaulle hat gesagt" 853

"De Gaulle parle des institutions, etc." 854

"De Gaulle parle, 1962-1966" 855

"Débat communiste" 62, 1906, 2123

"Débat sur la France de demain" 1536

"Défense de l'Occident" 133, 455-459, 660, 1908

"La défense nationale" 17

"La démocratie à l'épreuve du XXᵉ siècle" 371

"La démocratie à refaire" 366

"Démocratie aujourd'hui" 1522

"Démocratie et liberté" 1614

"Démocratie moderne" 1903, 1908a, 1948

"Démocratie 65" 1910, 2052a

"Dépêche de Constantine et de l'Est algérien" 811(f)

"Dépêche de l'Est" (Algeria) 811(e)

"Dépêche du Midi" 256

"La Dépêche quotidienne d'Algérie" 811(f), 1434

"La dépolitisation, mythe ou réalite" 96

"Dernière heure" (Algeria) 811(f)

"Le déserteur" 559

"La désignation des candidats à l'élection du président de la République 1359

"Deutschland-Frankreich" 1144

"Dictionnaire de la politique française" 405

"Dimanche matin" (Algeria) 811(d)

"Les disparus" 1754

"La documentation socialiste" 2037

"Documents" 54, 55, 64, 319, 381, 418, 437, 515, 617, 841, 876, 877, 1004, 1528, 1700-1702, 1754a, 1765, 1766

"Documents algériens" 391

"Documents algériens" 795, 796

"Documents algériens. Série economique" 1826

"Documents algériens. Série monographies" 1827

"Documents algériens. Série politique" 1828

"Documents algériens. Série sociale" 1829

"Documents et commentaires" 1731

"Documents sur la Constitution de la Vᵉ République" 1658

"12 hommes politiques répondent à 12 questions" 1317

"Le drame algérien commence maintenant" 456

"Le droit à l'insoumission" 1187

"Le droit et la colère" 1754a

"Echo d'Alger" 811(f), 1434, 1625, 1918

"Echo d'Oran" 811(f)

"Echo soir" (Algeria) 811(f)

"Les Echos" 811(e)

"L'Ecole et la nation" 1433, 1919

"Economic planning in France" 1313

"Economie" 1920, 2032

"L'économie française" 752

"Ecrits pour une renaissance" 1311

"L'éducation nationale" 423

"Les églises chrétiennes et la décolonisation" 1218

"Les élections du 2 janvier 1956" 97

"Les élections en France" 569

"L'Enseignement français" 1526

"Entreprise" 811(d), 1925

"Esprit public" 811(l), 1140, 1312, 1928

"Essais sur l'économie de l'Algérie nouvelle" 73

"Essential notions about Algeria" 26

"Est et Ouest" 93, 94, 1929

"L'établissement de la Cinquième République" 98

"Etudes politiques impartiales" 589

"Etudes tiers monde" 1061

"Les étudiants et leurs études" 232

"L'Europe" 1505

"Europe-Afrique" 2011

"Europe combattante" 1940, 1990

"L'Europe des personnes et des peuples" 1616

"Express" 438, 1273, 1628, 1943

"L'évaluation et le rôle des besoins de consommation" 368

"L'Evénement" 422

"Les fantômes accusent" 905

"Fédéralisme européen" 1812, 1944

"Femmes du XXe siècle" 1613

"Fidel Castro ou Tshombé?" 307

"Le Figaro" 811(e), 811(l)

"Le financement des entreprises et le Marché commun" 1148

"Die Force de frappe" 1294

"Forces nouvelles" 1908a, 1948

"Forces religieuses et attitudes politiques dans la France contemporaine" 364

"Les Français et le racisme" 1197

"France: a youthful nation rebuilds its future" 1503a

"France; its industries" 394

"France and NATO" 1786

"France and the European community" 642

"France defeats the E.D.C." 1124

"France-Eurafrique" 1893, 1969a

"France-Forum" 366, 1970

"France in crisis" 436

"France indépendante" 529, 1972, 1996

"La France sera la France" 857

"France-Observateur" 1273, 1473, 1974, 2021

"France Outre-mer" 1942

"France today" 1975, 2114

"France under de Gaulle" 977

"France-Soir" 811(e)

"François Mitterrand; on cet homme est dangereux" 1110

"French affairs" 1951

"Gauche européenne" 1980, 1991

"French aid; the Jeanneney report" 727

"French Fifth Republic" 512

"Futuribles" 1019, 1227, 1641

"Le grand débat" 448

"Les grandes énigmes de la IVe République" 1232a

"Les grandes énigmes de la Ve République" 1233

"Guerre, armée, société" 1524

"La guerre révolutionnaire; données et aspects . . ." 1527

"Les harkis à Paris" 1428

"L'Histoire au jour le jour" 50, 587, 864, 866, 899, 1027, 1331, 1458, 1482, 1489a

"Histoire de l'Algérie" 1280

"Histoire de la guerre d'Algérie" 1318

"Histoire du Parti communiste" 420

"Histoire du Parti communiste français" 62

"Histoire du Parti communiste français" 1400

"Histoire mondiale de l'après guerre" 661

"Hommage à Robert Schuman" 588

"Humanité" 599, 811(e), 811(l), 1369, 1802

"L'Homme chrétien et l'homme marxiste" 1612

"If God lets me live . . ." 1504

"L'indemnisation des spoliations d'outre-mer" 917

"Industrie algérienne" 25

"L'Information" 811(e)

"Informations catholiques internationales" 986, 1987

"Informations françaises" 811(d)

"Informations politiques et sociales" 297

"Les institutions politiques de la France" 757

"Les institutions politiques de la France; débat . . ." 99

"Les institutions sociales de la France" 758

"Les Jacobins" 958

"Jeune Europe" 1940, 1990, 2011

"La jeunesse" 457

"La jeunesse et le communisme" 641

"Jours de France" 144, 811(d)

"Journal d'Alger" 811(f), 1434

"Journal des indépendants" 1972, 1996

"Journal officiel" (Algeria) 811(f), 1823, 1830

"Journal officiel" (France) 1955, 1956, 1958, 1967

"Journal officiel de l'Etat algérien" 1824, 1825, 1830

"Journal officiel de la République algérienne démocratique et populaire" 1824, 1825

"Lectures françaises" 406, 407, 1109-1111, 1443

"La Lettre" 1849, 1998

"Lettre d'André Noël" 1851

"Lettres d'information politique" 1851

"Lettres d'ouvriers aux évêques" 862

"Lettres de rappelés" 309

"Lexique de mots-clés de l'armement" 798

"Libération" 422, 811(e)

"Livre blanc de notre honte" 1312

"Le Manifeste de la contre-révolution française" 630

"Manifeste des 14 membres du Salut Public d'Alger" 1113, 1508

"Manifeste pour l'éducation nationale" 267

"Manifeste des 121" 475, 1130, 1187

"Manuel général des élections" 777

"Le massacre d'Alger" 709

"Le Monde" 176, 326a, 811(e), 811(l), 1575, 2003

"Monde ouvrier" 2004, 2117

"Monsieur Mendès-France et les communistes" 336

"El Moudjahid" 1046, 1889, 2005, 2009, 2067

"Mouvement social" 1816, 2008

"al-Mujahid" 2005, 2009

"Nation-Belgique" 2011

"Nation-Europe" 1686, 1834, 2011

"Nation française" 236, 1311, 1312, 2013

"Nation socialiste" 1108, 2014

"La Nef" 1317-1319, 2015

"New York Herald Tribune" (Paris edit.) 811(e)

"Notes d'actualités" 811(d)

"Notes et études documentaires" 1880, 2016

"Notions essentielles sur l'Algérie" 26

"Notre république" 1723, 2018

"Nouveau dictionnaire des contemporains" 840

"Les nouveaux messieurs" 1111

"Nouveaux comportements politiques de la classe ouvrière" 943

"Nouvel observateur" 1974, 2021

"Nouvelle revue française d'outre-mer" 1894, 2024

"Nouvelle revue politique" 1359

"Nuremberg pour l'Algérie" 164

"Observateur municipal" 298

"October in Paris" 381a

"L'Officier et le sous-officier de réserve" 1945

"L'Opinion publique" 1618

"Oran républicain" 811(f)

"Organisation des services de police" 1525

"Organisation générale de la défense" 778

"Où va l'économie algérienne?" 504

"Outre-mer africain" 1920, 2032

"Paris Journal" 811(e)

"Paris-Match" 144, 811(d)

"Paris—Presse—L'Intransigeant" 811(e)

"Parisien libéré" 811(e)

"Paroles de chefs" 428

"Le Parti communiste français dans la lutte contre le colonialisme" 1380

"Le Parti communiste français, la culture et les intellectuels" 640

"Partis, journaux et hommes politiques d'hier et d'aujourd'hui" 407

"Partis politiques et classes sociales en France" 101

"Patrie et progrès" 133, 834, 1422, 1885, 2040

"Les paysans et la politique dans la France contemporaine" 102

"La pensée socialiste contemporaine" 372

"Permanences" 2044, 2125

"La personnalisation du pouvoir" 572

"Les pieds-noirs; la question du jour" 1523

"Le Plan Langevin-Wallon de réforme de l'enseignement" 916

"Le Plan Sauvy" 1585

"Planification et volontariat" 1355

"La police en France" 1319

"La politique de coopération avec les pays en voie de développement" 728

"Politiques nationales envers les jeunes états" 546

"Populaire de Paris" 811(e), 1910, 2052a

"Population de la France" 771

"Pour un front des travailleurs" 306

"Pour une démocratie économique" 915

"Pourquoi" 1813, 2055

"Préparation du Cinquième Plan" 779

"Le Prince qui nous gouverne" 1271

"Le problème de Berlin" 557

"Problèmes de l'Algérie indépendante" 1440

"Les problèmes de la planification" 254

"Le procès de l'attentat du Petit-Clamart" 143

"Le procès de Raoul Salan" 1568

"Le procès du déserteur" 559, 970

"Le procès du Petit-Clamart" 999

"Le procès du Réseau Jeanson" 940

"Le procès Vanuxem" 1749

"Programme communiste" 2060, 2062

"Programme et action du gouvernement en Algérie" 28

"Projet" 2061, 2077

"Le Prolétaire" 2060, 2062

"Prospective" 1227, 2063

"Le Provençal" 2064, 2102

"Provocation à la désobéissance" 559

"Les racistes contre la république" 521

"Radar" 811(d)

"La raison d'état" 1766

"Des rappelés, témoignent" 385

"Rapport sur l'activité de l'administration en Algérie au cours de l'année 1960" 29

"Rapport sur la situation financière" 721

"Rapport sur les obstacles à l'expansion économiques" 722

"Recensement de 1962" 771

"Recherches et débats" 75

"Recueil des actes administratifs de la Délégation générale" 1823, 1824, 1830

"Recueil des journaux d'Algérie" 1434

"Recueil des textes authentiques des programmes et engagements des députés proclamés élus à la suite des élections générales" 711

"Le référendum d'octobre et les élections de novembre 1962" 887

"Réflexions pour 1985" 768

"Les réformes de la Ve République" 610

"Rencontres: Nenni, Bevan, Mendès-France" 1628

"Le rendez-vous manqué" 1000

"Répertoire des bibliothèques d'étude et organismes de documentation" 765

"Répertoire permanent de l'administration française" 763

"Report on the financial situation of France" 723

"La République de Côte d'Ivoire" 797

"La République du Centre" 1603

"La réussite sociale en France" 875

"La révolution algérienne par les textes" 992

"Revue d'économie politique" 802, 2072

"Revue de l'action populaire" 1522, 2061, 2077

"Revue de l'histoire des colonies" 2083

"Revue de la Communauté France-Eurafrique" 1893

"Revue française de sciences politiques" 648, 2084

"La rivoluzione algerina" 808

"S. E. D. E. I. S." 2096

"Sans commentaire" 381

"Social Security in France" 766

"La société démocratique" 1617

"Le Soir" 2064, 2102

"Succès et faiblesses de l'effort social français" 1076

"Le suicide de la IVe République" 176

"Tableaux de l'économie algérienne" 36

"Tableaux de l'économie française" 772

"Tam" 1848, 2107

"Taxation in France" 948

"Télégramme de Paris" 435, 1566, 2109

"Témoignage chrétien" 269, 811(e), 1271, 1666, 1679, 1680

"Témoignage chrétien" See also Cahiers du Témoignage chrétien

"Temps modernes" 260a, 1473, 2111

"Tendances et volontés de la société française" 1641

"Tiers monde" 1438, 1440, 2113a

"Today in France" 1975, 2114

"Tribune du communisme" 1307, 1420, 2118

"Tribune du peuple" 2004, 2117, 2118

"Tribune du socialisme" 1415, 1416, 2118

"Tribune libre" 76, 83, 132, 196, 197, 309, 373, 446, 452, 454, 492, 529, 586, 589, 594, 619, 833, 834, 910, 941, 1021, 1053, 1190, 1192, 1239, 1247, 1256, 1311, 1445, 1451, 1452, 1466, 1587, 1623, 1649, 1747, 1762

"Tribune socialiste" 2117, 2118

"Trois documents sur la défense de l'école et de la laïcité" 1433

"Tunisian-French dispute" 1231

"Union française et parlement" 1893

"Unir-débat" 1906, 2123

"Le Verbe" 1524, 1644, 2044, 2125

"Verité des travailleurs" 1405

"Vérité-Liberté" 381a, 2126

"21/27" 1936

"Voix de l'Occident" 89, 90, 2134

"Western European attitudes on arms control, defense, and European unity, 1952-1963" 1220a

"White paper on the application of the Geneva convention of 1949 to the French-Algerian conflict" 993